Lecture Notes in Computer Science

Commenced Publication in 1973
Founding and Former Series Editors:
Gerhard Goos, Juris Hartmanis, and Jan v

Sihan Qing   Willy Susilo   Guilin Wang
Dongmei Liu (Eds.)

Information and Communications Security

13th International Conference, ICICS 2011
Beijing, China, November 23-26, 2011
Proceedings

 Springer

Volume Editors

Sihan Qing
Chinese Academy of Sciences
Institute of Software
Beijing 100190, China
E-mail: qsihan@mail.ss.pku.edu.cn

Willy Susilo
University of Wollongong
School of Computer Science & Software Engineering
Northfields Avenue, Wollongong NSW 2522, Australia
E-mail: wsusilo@uow.edu.au

Guilin Wang
University of Wollongong
School of Computer Science & Software Engineering
Northfields Avenue, Wollongong NSW 2522, Australia
E-mail: guilin@uow.edu.au

Dongmei Liu
Chinese Academy of Sciences
Institute of Software
Beijing 100190, China
E-mail: dongmeiliu77@gmail.com

ISSN 0302-9743   e-ISSN 1611-3349
ISBN 978-3-642-25242-6   e-ISBN 978-3-642-25243-3
DOI 10.1007/978-3-642-25243-3
Springer Heidelberg Dordrecht London New York

Library of Congress Control Number: 2011940847

CR Subject Classification (1998): E.3, D.4.6, K.6.5, K.4.4, C.2, F.2.1

LNCS Sublibrary: SL 4 – Security and Cryptology

Typesetting: Camera-ready by author, data conversion by Scientific Publishing Services, Chennai, India

Printed on acid-free paper

Springer is part of Springer Science+Business Media (www.springer.com)

Preface

The 13th International Conference on Information and Communications Security (ICICS 2011) was held in Beijing, China, during November 23–26, 2011. The ICICS conference series is an established forum that brings together people from universities, research institutes, industry and government institutions, who work in a range of fields within information and communications security. The ICICS conferences give attendees the opportunity to exchange new ideas and investigate developments in the state of the art. In previous years, ICICS has taken place in Spain (2010, 2004), UK (2008), China (2009, 2007, 2005, 2003, 2001 and 1997), USA (2006), Singapore (2002), and Australia (1999). On each occasion, as on this one, the proceedings have been published in the Springer LNCS series.

In total, 141 manuscripts from 16 countries and districts were submitted to ICICS 2011, and a total of 33 from 12 countries and districts were accepted (an acceptance rate of 23%). The accepted papers cover a wide range of disciplines within information security and applied cryptography. Each submission to ICICS 2011 was anonymously reviewed by three or four reviewers. We are very grateful to members of the Program Committee, which was composed of 70 members from 20 countries; we would like to thank them, as well as all the external referees, for their time and their valuable contributions to the tough and time-consuming reviewing process.

ICICS 2011 was organized and hosted by the Institute of Software, Chinese Academy of Sciences (CAS), and the Institute of Software and Microelectronics, Peking University, in co-operation with the International Communications and Information Security Association (ICISA). The conference was sponsored by the National Natural Science Foundation of China under Grant No. 60573042 and No. 60970135, the Microsoft Corporation, Beijing Tip Technology Corporation, and the Trusted Computing Group (TCG).

We would like to thank Dongmei Liu for the great work in arranging the publishing of the proceedings, and Mian Wan for his great contribution to the pre-conference arrangements and helping with many local details. Finally, we would like to thank the authors who submitted their papers to ICICS 2011, and the attendees from all around the world.

November 2011

Sihan Qing
Willy Susilo
Guilin Wang

ICICS 2011

13th International Conference on Information and Communications Security

Beijing, China
November 23–26, 2011

Organized by

Institute of Software, Chinese Academy of Sciences (CAS)
Institute of Software and Microelectronics, Peking University, China

Sponsored by

National Natural Science Foundation of China (NNSFC)
The Microsoft Corporation
Beijing Tip Technology Corporation, China
Trusted Computing Group (TCG)

In co-operation with

International Communications and Information Security Association (ICISA)

Program Chairs

Sihan Qing	Chinese Academy of Sciences and Peking University, China
Willy Susilo	University of Wollongong, Australia
Guilin Wang	University of Wollongong, Australia

Program Committee

Mikhail J. Atallah	Purdue University, USA
Man Ho Au	University of Wollongong, Australia
Tuomas Aura	Aalto University, Finland
Joonsang Baek	Khalifa University of Science Technology and Research, United Arab Emirates
Feng Bao	Institute for Infocomm Research, Singapore
Tom Berson	Anagram Laboratories, USA
Alex Biryukov	University of Luxembourg, Luxembourg

Publication Chair

External Reviewers

Table of Contents

Multimedia Security

Algorithms and Evaluation

Cryptanalysis

Security Applications

Wireless Network Security

System Security

Network Security

Forward Secure Ring Signature
without Random Oracles*

Joseph K. Liu[1], Tsz Hon Yuen[2], and Jianying Zhou[1]

[1] Institute for Infocomm Research, Singapore
{ksliu,jyzhou}@i2r.a-star.edu.sg
[2] University of Hong Kong, Hong Kong
thyuen@cs.hku.hk

Abstract. In this paper, we propose a forward secure ring signature scheme without random oracles. With forward security, if a secret key of a corresponding ring member is exposed, all previously signed signatures containing this member remain valid. Yet the one who has stolen the secret key cannot produce any valid signature belonged to the past time period. This is especially useful in the case of ring signature, as the exposure of a single secret key may result in the invalidity of thousands or even millions ring signatures which contain that particular user. However, most of the ring signature schemes in the literature do not provide forward security. The only one with this feature [15] relies on random oracles to prove the security. We are the *first* to construct a forward secure ring signature scheme that can be proven secure without random oracles. Our scheme can be deployed in many applications, such as wireless sensor networks and smart grid system.

1   Introduction

Ring signatures [20,24,14] allow a member of a group to sign a message on behalf of the whole group. The verifier does not know who is the real signer in the group. The group can be set dynamically by the signer and no collaboration is needed between the members of the group.

In traditional public key cryptography, the security of a cryptosystem is guaranteed under some intractability assumptions if the secret key is kept away from the adversary. However, there are many ways that a secret key may be comprised in the real world. Hackers may steal your secret key if your computer is infected with trojans, or when you use the secret key in a phishing website. Therefore, it is important to minimize the damage even if the entire secret key is lost. When the attacker has full access to your secret key, he can sign or decrypt on behalf of the victim. The situation is even worse for ring signatures, since the attacker can forge a message on behalf of the whole group. Moreover, the other members of the group may be completely unaware of such forgery, since they are unaware of being conscripted into the group.

---

* The first and third authors are supported by the EMA project SecSG-EPD090005RFP(D).

S. Qing et al. (Eds.): ICICS 2011, LNCS 7043, pp. 1–14, 2011.

Forward security for signatures [3] was designed to the key exposure problem. A forward secure signature in the past remains secure even if the current secret key is lost. The first solution was designed by Bellare and Miner [5]. The main idea is to divide the lifetime of the public key into T intervals, and in each time interval the same public key corresponds to different secret keys. A current secret key can be used to derive the secret key in the future, but not the past. Therefore, even a compromise of the current secret key does not enable the adversary to forge signatures pertaining to the past.

Forward secure ring signatures were proposed by Liu and Wong [15] to resolve the key exposure problem in ring signatures. The motivation is to reduce the damage of exposure of any secret key of users in ring signature. Even if a secret key is compromised, previously generated ring signatures remain valid and do not need to be re-generated. They proposed the security model and gave a concrete construction in the random oracle model. Here we first review some practical applications of forward secure ring signatures.

1.1 Applications

AD-HOC NETWORKS: The steadily growing importance of portable devices and mobile applications has spawned new types of groups of interacting parties: ad-hoc groups. The highly dynamic nature of such groups raises new challenges for networking. Ad-hoc networks may be described as networks with minimal infrastructure, lacking fixed routers or stable links. Wireless sensor network is a kind of ad-hoc network. Such networks inherently deal with spontaneous ad-hoc groups: a group of users who spontaneously wish to communicate sensitive data need a suite of protocols which do not involve any trusted third party or certification of any new public keys. Security goals have to be considered in this new context. Ring signatures are perfectly suited to such a setting, since no setup protocol is required. Without forward security, the compromise of a user secret key in the group may result in the invalidity of all previous ring signatures involved with this user (including this user in the ring). The consequence is very serious. The whole authentication system may be suspended if only one user secret key has been compromised. Thus forward security is an important addition to ring signature, especially in the application of ad-hoc group.

SMART GRID: Smart Grid [19] is a form of electricity network utilizing modern digital technology. The most distinctive feature in smart grid is its two-way capabilities for data communication: Not only the grid controller can issue commands to intelligent devices, consumers and devices can also send data to grid controllers. The ability to access, analyze, and respond to much more precise and detailed data from all levels of the electric grid is critical to the major benefits of the Smart Grid. As an example, Microsoft Hohm [18] provides a platform for consumers to upload energy usage data, based on which a statistical report is created. The purpose is to encourage consumers to compare their energy consumption with others (e.g., on the same street) and thus use electricity more efficiently. Data integrity is a necessary requirement in those applications since the comparison would be meaningless if the data is maliciously modified or faked. Privacy, on the other hand, is also a significant concern: Consumers may not want to give their identity information to any third-party service providers. Ring signature is a promising solution on applications (e.g., Microsoft Hohm) requiring both integrity and privacy. In ring signature, a valid signature will convince the service provider that the data is uploaded by a consumer on a certain street, without telling who exactly the consumer is. Forward-security is certainly desirable in this situation since a compromised private key within a time period will not have any negative impact on statistical reports generated previously. In other words, old statistical reports would remain valid if forward-security is satisfied.

1.2 Related Works

There are some ring signature schemes that do not rely on the random oracles. Xu et al. [25] described a ring signature scheme in the standard model, but the proof is not rigorous and is apparently flawed [7]. Chow et al. [11] proposed a ring signature scheme in the standard model, though it is based on a strong new assumption. Bender et al. [7] gave a ring signature secure in the standard model assuming trapdoor permutations exists. Their scheme uses generic ZAPs for NP as a building block, which may not be practical. Shacham and Waters [22] presented an efficient ring signature scheme without random oracles, based on standard assumption. They rely on composite order pairing that requires a trusted setup procedure. Schäge and Schwenk [21] gave another ring signature scheme in the standard model using basic assumption. In contrast to [22], they used prime order pairing instead. However, their security model does not allow the adversary to query any private key. All the above schemes do not provide forward security.

On the other side, the concept of forward secure signatures was first proposed by Anderson [3] for traditional signatures. It was formalized by Bellare and Miner [5]. The basic idea is to extend a standard digital signature algorithm with a key update algorithm, so that the secret key can be changed frequently while the public key stays the same. The resulting scheme is forward secure if the knowledge of the secret key at some point in time does not help forge signatures relative to some previous time period. The challenge is to design an efficient scheme of this concept. In particular the size of the secret key, public key and signature should not be dependent on the number of time period during the lifetime of the public key. Several schemes [2,13,1,12,17] have been proposed by traditional signatures and threshold signatures that satisfy this efficiency property. In addition, a forward secure group signature scheme and a forward secure identity-based signature scheme are proposed in [23] and [26] respectively.

Our Contributions. The security proofs for various cryptosystems used the random oracle model [6]. Several papers [9,4] showed that it is possible to prove a cryptosystem secure in the random oracle while the actual construction is insecure when the random oracle is instantiated by any real-world hash function.

Thus, it is desirable to design cryptosystems provably secure without requiring random oracles.

In this paper, we propose the *first* forward-secure ring signatures without random oracles. The forward secure ring signatures proposed by Liu and Wong [15] is only secure in the random oracle model. We prove the security under the CDH and subgroup decision problem.

2 Preliminaries

2.1 Pairings

We make use of bilinear groups of composite order. Let N be a composite number with factorization $N = pq$. We have: (1) $\mathbb{G}$ is a multiplicative cyclic group of order N. (2) $\mathbb{G}_p$ is its cyclic order-p subgroup, and $\mathbb{G}_q$ is its cyclic order-q subgroup. (3) g is a generator of $\mathbb{G}$, while h is a generator of $\mathbb{G}_q$. (4) $\mathbb{G}_T$ is a multiplicative group of order N. (5) e is a bilinear map such that $e : \mathbb{G} \times \mathbb{G} \to \mathbb{G}_T$ with the following properties: (i) *Bilinearity*: For all $u, v \in \mathbb{G}$, and $a, b \in \mathbb{Z}$, $e(u^a, v^b) = e(u, v)^{ab}$; (ii) *Non-degeneracy*: $\langle e(g, g) \rangle = \mathbb{G}_T$ whenever $\langle g \rangle = \mathbb{G}$; and (iii) *Computability*: It is efficient to compute $e(u, v)$ for all $u, v \in \mathbb{G}$. (6) $\mathbb{G}_{T,p}$ and $\mathbb{G}_{T,q}$ are the $\mathbb{G}_T$-subgroups of order p and q, respectively. (7) The group operations on $\mathbb{G}$ and $\mathbb{G}_T$ can be performed efficiently. (8) Bit strings corresponding to elements of $\mathbb{G}$ and of $\mathbb{G}_T$ can be recognized efficiently.

2.2 Mathematical Assumptions

Definition 1. *Computational Diffie-Hellman (CDH) in* $\mathbb{G}_p$. *Given the tuple (r, r^a, r^b), where $r \in_R \mathbb{G}_p$, and $a, b \in_R \mathbb{Z}_p$, compute and output r^{ab}. In the composite setting one is additionally given the description of the larger group $\mathbb{G}$, including the factorization (p, q) of its order N.*

The CDH assumption is formalized by measuring an adversary's success probability for computational Diffie-Hellman, that is,

$$Adv_{CDH} = \Pr[\text{ Adversary outputs } r^{ab}].$$

Definition 2. *Subgroup Decision*. *Given w selected at random either from $\mathbb{G}$ (with probability $1/2$) or from $\mathbb{G}_q$ (with probability $1/2$), decide whether w is in $\mathbb{G}_q$. For this problem one is given the description of $\mathbb{G}$, but not given the factorization of N.*

The assumption is formalized by measuring an adversary's guessing advantage for the subgroup decision problem. That is,

$$Adv_{SD} = \left| \Pr[\text{ Adversary guesses correctly }] - \frac{1}{2} \right|.$$

Note that if CDH in $\mathbb{G}_p$ is hard then so is CDH in $\mathbb{G}$. The assumption that the subgroup decision problem is hard is called Subgroup Hiding (SGH) assumption, and was introduced by Boneh et al [8].

3 Security Model

3.1 Syntax of Forward Secure Ring Signatures

A *forward secure ring signature* (FSRS) scheme, is a tuple of four algorithms (KeyGen, Sign, Verify and Update).

- $(sk_{i,0}, pk_i) \leftarrow$ KeyGen(1^λ) is a PPT algorithm which, on input a security parameter $\lambda \in \mathbb{N}$, outputs a private/public key pair $(sk_{i,0}, pk_i)$ such that the private key is valid for time $t = 0$.[1] We denote by $\mathcal{SK}$ and $\mathcal{PK}$ the domains of possible secret keys and public keys, respectively.
- $sk_{i,t+1} \leftarrow$ Update$(sk_{i,t}, t)$ is a PPT algorithm which, on input a private key for a certain time period t, outputs a new private key for the time period $t + 1$.
- $\sigma_t' = (n, \mathcal{Y}, \sigma) \leftarrow$ Sign$(t, n, \mathcal{Y}, sk_{i,t}, M)$ is a PPT algorithm which, on input a certain time period t, group size n, a set $\mathcal{Y}$ of n public keys in $\mathcal{PK}$, a secret key $sk_{i,t}$ whose corresponding public key $pk_i \in \mathcal{Y}$, and a message M, produces a signature σ_t'.
- $1/0 \leftarrow$ Verify(M, σ_t', t) is a deterministic algorithm which, on input a message-signature pair (M, σ_t') and a time t returns 1 or 0 for accept or reject, resp. If accept, the message-signature pair is *valid*.

In some cases, we also need to define some system parameters which might be shared by all users, like the group $\mathbb{G}$, the hash function, etc. Some parameters may be generated by a trusted authority, like the group order $N = pq$ whose factorization should not be known by any user. Therefore, we also define this (optional) algorithm:

- param $\leftarrow$ Global Setup(1^λ) is a PPT algorithm which, on input a security parameter $\lambda \in \mathbb{N}$, outputs a system parameter param.

If the algorithm Global Setup exists, then the other algorithms (KeyGen, Sign, Verify and Update) will take param as an additional input. In the following discussion on the security model, we omit Global Setup and param for simplicity. We note that the security model in [15] includes Global Setup (which was named as Init in [15]). We believe that this algorithm is optional and may not be included. We also observed that the Update algorithm in [15] is a deterministic algorithm. We think that the Update algorithm can be probabilistic and it is reflected in our model.

Correctness. We require that $1 \leftarrow$ Verify$(M, $Sign$(t, n, \mathcal{Y}, sk_{i,t}, M), t)$, where $(sk_{i,0}, pk_i) \leftarrow$ KeyGen(1^λ), $pk_i \in \mathcal{Y}$ and

$$sk_{i,t} \leftarrow \underbrace{\text{Update}(\text{Update}(\cdots(\text{Update}(sk_{i,0}, 0)\cdots), t-2), t-1)}_{t \text{ Update}}.$$

---

[1] We denote $sk_{i,t}$ to be the secret key of user i at time t.

3.2   Forward-Security

The notion of forward security is similar to the unforgeability of standard ring signatures. An adversary should not be able to output a signature $\sigma^*_{t^*} = (n^*, \mathcal{Y}^*, \sigma^*)$ for a time t^* and a message M^* such that $\mathsf{Verify}(M^*, \sigma^*_{t^*}, t^*) = 1$ unless either (1) one of the public keys in $\mathcal{Y}^*$ was generated by the adversary, or (2) a user whose public key is in $\mathcal{Y}^*$ explicitly signed M^* previously (with respect to the same ring $\mathcal{Y}^*$ and time t^*). Our model is similar to the *unforgeability w.r.t. insider corruption* in [7], which is the strongest security model for unforgeability in [7]. Our model adds the security related to forward security.

Forward-security for FSRS schemes is defined in the following game between a challenger and an adversary $\mathcal{A}$:

1. <u>Setup</u>. The challenger runs KeyGen for l times to obtain keypairs $(sk_{1,0}, pk_1), \ldots, (sk_{n',0}, pk_{n'})$. The challenger gives $\mathcal{A}$ the set of public keys $\mathcal{S} = (pk_1, \ldots, pk_{n'})$.
2. <u>Query</u>. $\mathcal{A}$ may adaptively query the following oracles.
   - $sk_{i,t} \leftarrow \mathcal{CO}(pk_i, t)$. The *Corruption Oracle*, on input a public key $pk_i \in \mathcal{S}$ and a time t, returns the corresponding secret key $sk_{i,t}$.
   - $\sigma'_t \leftarrow \mathcal{SO}(t, n, \mathcal{Y}, pk_i, M)$. The *Signing Oracle*, on input a time t, a group size n, a set $\mathcal{Y}$ of n public keys, a public key $pk_i \in \mathcal{Y}$ and a message M, returns a valid signature σ'_t for time t.
3. <u>Output</u>. $\mathcal{A}$ outputs a signature $\sigma^*_{t^*} = (n^*, \mathcal{Y}^*, \sigma^*)$, a time t^* and a message M^*.

$\mathcal{A}$ wins the game if: (1) $\mathsf{Verify}(M^*, \sigma^*_{t^*}, t^*) = 1$, (2) $\mathcal{Y}^* \subseteq \mathcal{S}$, (3) for all $pk_i^* \in \mathcal{Y}^*$, there is no $\mathcal{CO}(pk_i^*, t')$ query with time $t' \le t^*$ and (4) there is no $\mathcal{SO}(t^*, n^*, \mathcal{Y}^*, \cdot, M^*)$ query. We denote by $\mathbf{Adv}^{fs}_{\mathcal{A}}(\lambda)$ the probability of $\mathcal{A}$ winning the game.

Definition 3 (forward-secure). *An FSRS scheme is forward-secure if for all PPT adversary $\mathcal{A}$, $\mathbf{Adv}^{fs}_{\mathcal{A}}(\lambda)$ is negligible.*

3.3   Anonymity

The notion of anonymity is similar to that of standard ring signatures. Simply speaking, an adversary should not be able to tell which member of a ring generated a particular ring signature. (We note that anonymity can be defined in either a computational or an unconditional sense where, informally, anonymity holds for polynomial-time adversaries in the former case, and it holds for all-powerful adversaries in the latter case. For simplicity, we only present the computational version.) In our model, the adversary is also the given the secret keys of all users at time 0, which implies the secret keys of all users in the all time intervals. Our model is similar to the *anonymity against full key exposure* in [7], which is the strongest security model for anonymity in [7].

Anonymity for FSRS schemes is defined in the following game between a challenger and an adversary $\mathcal{A}$:

1. Setup. The challenger runs KeyGen for n' times to obtain keypairs $(sk_{1,0}, pk_1)$, ..., $(sk_{n',0}, pk_{n'})$. The challenger gives $\mathcal{A}$ the set of public keys $\mathcal{S} = (pk_1, \ldots, pk_{n'})$ and the set of secret keys $(sk_{1,0}, \ldots, sk_{n',0})$.
2. Query 1. $\mathcal{A}$ may query the signing oracle adaptively.
3. Challenge. $\mathcal{A}$ gives the challenger a time t^*, a group size n^*, a message M, a set $\mathcal{Y}^*$ of n^* public keys, such that two public keys $pk_{i_0}, pk_{i_1} \in \mathcal{S}$ are included in $\mathcal{Y}^*$. The challenger randomly picks a bit $b \in \{0, 1\}$ and runs $\sigma_{t^*}^* \leftarrow \mathsf{Sign}(t^*, n^*, \mathcal{Y}^*, sk_{i_b, t^*}, M^*)$. The challenger gives the signature $\sigma_{t^*}^*$ to $\mathcal{A}$.
4. Query 2. $\mathcal{A}$ may query the signing oracle adaptively.
5. Output. $\mathcal{A}$ returns his guess b'.

$\mathcal{A}$ wins the game if $b' = b$. Define the *advantage* as $\mathbf{Adv}_{\mathcal{A}}^{FS-Anon}(\lambda) = |\Pr[\mathcal{A} \text{ wins}] - 1/2|$ for security parameter λ.

Definition 4 (FS-Anonymity). *A FSRS scheme is anonymous if for any PPT adversary $\mathcal{A}$, $\mathbf{Adv}_{\mathcal{A}}^{FS-Anon}(\lambda)$ is negligible.*

4   Our Proposed Forward Secure Ring Signature Scheme

4.1   Intuition

Our construction is motivated from [22]. We add a binary tree key structure [10] to provide forward security. We first explain the intuition of our binary tree key structure here.

We use binary tree to evolve the secret key. In order to represent $T = 2^{\ell}$ time periods, we use a full binary tree with depth ℓ. We associate each time period with each leaf of tree from left to right. The leftmost leaf node denotes time period 0 and the rightmost leaf node denotes time period $T - 1$.

At the beginning, it stores the leftmost leaf node, and the right-child nodes ("1" node) starting from its parent node. That is, assume $\ell = 4$, the secret key for $T = 0$ contains the nodes $0000, 0001, 001, 01, 1$. (We put the current node as the first position.)

When it performs the first update, as the current node is a left-child ("0" node), we just delete the current node and move forward to its right-child ("1" node) under the same parent. In the above example, the secret key for $T = 1$ contains the nodes $0001, 001, 01, 1$.

When it performs the next update, as the current node is a right-child ("1" node), it first finds the last "0" node along the path. Extract the corresponding right-child ("1" node), generate the nodes under this node as in the beginning and delete the current node and its parent node. In the above example, the current node is 0001. The last "0" node is 000. Its corresponding right-child is 001. Thus we generate the nodes under the node 001. In this case, we just need to generate the node 0010 and 0011. Finally, the secret key for $T = 2$ contains the nodes $0010, 0011, 01, 1$.

Similarly, the next update is simple, by just deleting 0010 and replaced by 0011. The secret key for $T = 3$ contains the nodes $0011, 01, 1$.

For the next update, find the last "0" node, which is 00 in this case. Extract the corresponding right-child node, which is 01. Perform another node generation process under this node 01 and delete the current node and this node. The new nodes generated are $0100, 0101, 011$. Thus the secret key for $T = 4$ contains the nodes $0100, 0101, 011, 1$.

After a few updates, assume the current time period is $T = 7$. That is, the current node is 0111. For this update, first find the last "0" node, which is 0. Extract the corresponding right-child node, which is 1. Perform a node generation process under this node 1. Thus the secret key for $T = 8$ contains the nodes $1000, 1001, 101, 11$.

We hope by presenting this example, readers may now know the intuition and concept of our binary key structure for secret key and key update process.

4.2   Construction

In our ring signature all the users keys must be defined in a group $\mathbb{G}$ of composite order. That group must be set up by a trusted authority, since the factorization of its order N must be kept secret. In addition to setting up the group $\mathbb{G}$, the setup authority must also set up some additional parameters, using a global setup algorithm we now describe.

Global Setup. Let λ, κ be a security parameter and the total number of time periods $T = 2^\ell$. The setup algorithm runs the bilinear group generator $(N = pq, \mathbb{G}, \mathbb{G}_T, e) \leftarrow \mathcal{G}(1^\lambda)$. Let $H : \{0,1\}^* \rightarrow \{0,1\}^\kappa$ be a collision resistant hash function. Suppose the group generator $\mathcal{G}$ also gives the generators $g_1, B_0, u, u_1, \ldots, u_\kappa, v, v_1, \ldots, v_\ell \in \mathbb{G}$, $h_1 \in \mathbb{G}_q$ and $\alpha \in \mathbb{Z}_N$. Set $g_2 = g_1^\alpha$ and $h_2 = h_1^\alpha$. The public parameters are $(N, \mathbb{G}, \mathbb{G}_T, e, g_1, g_2, B_0, h_1, h_2, u, u_1, \ldots, u_\kappa, v, v_1, \ldots, v_\ell, H)$. Everyone can check the validity of g_1, g_2, h_1, h_2 using pairings.

KeyGen. Choose a random $s, r_{u_0}, r_{u_1} \in \mathbb{Z}_N$. First compute

$$SK_0 = \left(g_2^s v^{r_{u_0}}, g_1^{r_{u_0}}, v_2^{r_{u_0}}, \ldots, v_\ell^{r_{u_0}} \right),$$
$$SK_1 = \left(g_2^s (vv_1)^{r_{u_1}}, g_1^{r_{u_1}}, v_2^{r_{u_1}}, \ldots, v_\ell^{r_{u_1}} \right).$$

Then for $k = 2$ to ℓ do
BEGIN

   Parse
$$\left(a_0, a_1, b_k, \ldots, b_\ell \right) = \left(g_2^s v^{r'}, g_1^{r'}, v_k^{r'}, \ldots, v_\ell^{r'} \right) \leftarrow SK_{0^{k-1}},$$

   for some $r' \in \mathbb{Z}_N$, where $0^{k-1} = \underbrace{0 \ldots 0}_{k-1}$.

Select $t_0, t_1 \in_R \in \mathbb{Z}_N$ and compute

$$SK_{0^k} = \left(a_0 v^{t_0}, a_1 g_1^{t_0}, b_{k+1} v_{k+1}^{t_0}, \ldots, b_\ell v_\ell^{t_0} \right)$$

$$= \left(g_2^s v^{r_0}, g_1^{r_0}, v_{k+1}^{r_0}, \ldots, v_\ell^{r_0} \right),$$

where $r_0 = r' + t_0$, and

$$SK_{0^{k-1}1} = \left(a_0 v^{t_1} v_k^{t_1} v_k^{r'}, a_1 g_1^{t_1}, b_{k+1} v_{k+1}^{t_1}, \ldots, b_\ell v_\ell^{t_1} \right)$$

$$= \left(g_2^s v^{r_1} v_k^{r_1}, g_1^{r_1}, v_{k+1}^{r_1}, \ldots, v_\ell^{r_1} \right),$$

where $r_1 = r' + t_1$.

END

Set $pk_i = g_1^s$ be the public key of user i and $sk_{i,0} = \left\{ SK_{0^\ell}, (SK_1, SK_{01}, \ldots, SK_{0^{\ell-1}1}) \right\}$ be the secret key of user i in time period 0.

Update. On input a secret key $sk_{i,j}$ for user i and current time period j, if $j < T$ the user updates the secret key as follow:

1. Let $\langle j \rangle = j_1 \ldots j_\ell$ be the binary representation of j and let $b_l \in \{0,1\}$ be a bit, for $l = 1, \ldots, \ell$. We also define $j_0 = \epsilon$ and $b_0 = \epsilon$ to be empty strings.
   Parse $\left\{ SK_{\langle j \rangle}, \left(\{SK_{b_0 \ldots b_{k-1}1}\}_{k=1}^\ell : j_k = 0 \right) \right\} \leftarrow sk_{i,j}$.

2. If $j_\ell = 0$, the new secret key is

$$sk_{i,j+1} = \left\{ SK_{j_0 \ldots j_{\ell-1}1}, \left(\{SK_{b_0 \ldots b_{k-1}1}\}_{k=1}^{\ell-1} : j_k = 0 \right) \right\}.$$

3. If $j_\ell = 1$, find the largest integer ϕ such that $j_\phi = 0$. Let $c_l \in \{0,1\}$ be a bit, for $l = 1, \ldots, \phi$. We define $c_0 = j_0 = \epsilon$ to be an empty string and also define $c_0 = j_0 = \epsilon$, $c_1 = j_1, \ldots, c_{\phi-1} = j_{\phi-1}, c_\phi = 1$. Then for $k = \phi + 1$ to ℓ do
   BEGIN
   Parse

$$\left(a_0, a_1, b_k, \ldots, b_\ell \right) = \left(g_2^s \left(v \prod_{\delta=1}^{k-1} v_\delta^{c_\delta} \right)^{r'}, g_1^{r'}, v_k^{r'}, \ldots, v_\ell^{r'} \right) \leftarrow SK_{c_1 \ldots c_{k-1}}, \tag{1}$$

   for some $r' \in \mathbb{Z}_N$.
   Select $t_0, t_1 \in_R \in \mathbb{Z}_N$ and compute

$$SK_{c_1 \ldots c_{k-1}0} = \left(a_0 \left(v \prod_{\delta=1}^{k-1} v_\delta^{c_\delta} \right)^{t_0}, a_1 g_1^{t_0}, b_{k+1} v_{k+1}^{t_0}, \ldots, b_\ell v_\ell^{t_0} \right)$$

$$= \left(g_2^s \left(v \prod_{\delta=1}^{k-1} v_\delta^{c_\delta} \right)^{r_0}, g_1^{r_0}, v_{k+1}^{r_0}, \ldots, v_\ell^{r_0} \right),$$

where $r_0 = r' + t_0$, and

$$SK_{c_1 \ldots c_{k-1} 1} = \left(a_0 \left(v \prod_{\delta=1}^{k} v_\delta^{c_\delta} \right)^{t_1} v_k^{r'}, a_1 g_1^{t_1}, b_{k+1} v_{k+1}^{t_1}, \ldots, b_\ell v_\ell^{t_1} \right)$$

$$= \left(g_2^s \left(v \prod_{\delta=1}^{k} v_\delta^{c_\delta} \right)^{r_1}, g_1^{r_1}, v_{k+1}^{r_1}, \ldots, v_\ell^{r_1} \right),$$

where $r_1 = r' + t_1$.

We define a new bit c_k and set $c_k = 0$ at this stage. (Note that currently only $c_0, \ldots, c_{k-1}$ are well defined, but not c_k. We define c_k in this stage, as in the next loop, k will be increment by 1, this bit will be used as the last bit of the subscript notation in SK in equation(1).)

END

Return

$$sk_{i,j+1} = \left\{ SK_{j_0 \ldots j_{\phi-1} 10^{\ell-\phi}}, \left(\{ SK_{j_0 \ldots j_{\phi-1} 10^k 1} \}_{k=0}^{\ell-\phi-1} \right), \right.$$

$$\left. \left(\forall \, \{SK_b\} \in sk_{i,j} \; : \; |b| \leq \phi - 1 \right) \right\}.$$

where b is a binary string.
4. Erase $sk_{i,j}$.

Sign. To sign a message $M \in \{0,1\}^*$ in time period j, where $0 \leq j < T$, let $\langle j \rangle = j_1 \ldots j_\ell$ be the binary representation of j. On behalf of a list of distinct public keys $\mathcal{Y} = \{pk_1, \ldots, pk_n\} = \{g_1^{s_1}, \ldots, g_1^{s_n}\}$, a user with secret key $sk_{\tau,j}$, where $\tau \in \{1, \ldots, n\}$ computes the follow:

1. Compute $(m_1, \ldots, m_\kappa) = H(\mathcal{Y}, M, j)$.
2. Without loss of generality, suppose that τ is the index of the actual signer. Define f_i such that $f_i = 1$ if $i = \tau$. Otherwise $f_i = 0$.
3. For $i = 1, \ldots, n$, choose $x_i \in_R \mathbb{Z}_N$ and set $C_i = \left(\frac{g_1^{x_i}}{B_0} \right)^{f_i} h_1^{x_i}$ and $\pi_i = \left(\left(\frac{g_1^{x_i}}{B_0} \right)^{2f_i - 1} h_1^{x_i} \right)^{x_i}$. Here the value π_i acts as a proof that C_i is well-formed.
   Let $C = \prod_{i=1}^{n} C_i$ and $x = \sum_{i=1}^{n} x_i$. Then we have $B_0 C = h_1^x g_1^{s_\tau}$.
4. Extract $SK_{\langle j \rangle} \leftarrow sk_{\tau,j}$ and parse

$$(a_0, a_1) \leftarrow \left(g_2^{s_\tau} \left(v \prod_{\delta=1}^{\ell} v_\delta^{j_\delta} \right)^{r'}, g_1^{r'} \right) \qquad \text{for some} \qquad r' \in \mathbb{Z}_N.$$

5. Choose $r_\ell, r_\kappa \in_R \mathbb{Z}_N$ and compute

$$S_1 = a_0 \cdot \left(v \prod_{\delta=1}^{\ell} v_\delta^{j_\delta}\right)^{r_\ell} \cdot \left(u \prod_{\delta=1}^{\kappa} u_\delta^{m_\delta}\right)^{r_\kappa} \cdot h_2^x, \qquad S_2 = g_1^{r_\kappa} \qquad S_3 = a_1 \cdot g_1^{r_\ell}.$$

The signature σ is $\left(S_1, S_2, S_3, \{C_i, \pi_i\}_{i=1}^n\right)$.

Verify. To verify a signature σ for a message M, a list of public keys $\mathcal{Y}$ where $|\mathcal{Y}| = n$ and the time period j, first let $\langle j \rangle = j_1 \ldots j_\ell$ be the binary representation of j. Then:

1. Verify that no element is repeated in $\mathcal{Y}$ and output invalid otherwise.
2. Compute $(m_1, \ldots, m_\kappa) = H(\mathcal{Y}, M, j)$.
3. For $i = 1, \ldots, n$, check if

$$e\left(C_i, \frac{C_i}{\left(\frac{g_1^{s_i}}{B_0}\right)}\right) = e(h_1, \pi_i).$$

4. Compute $C = \prod_{i=1}^n C_i$ and check if:

$$e(S_1, g_1) = e\left(S_2, u \prod_{\delta=1}^{\kappa} u_\delta^{m_\delta}\right) \cdot e\left(g_2, B_0 C\right) \cdot e\left(S_3, v \prod_{\delta=1}^{\ell} v_\delta^{j_\delta}\right).$$

Output valid if all equalities hold. Otherwise output invalid.

Correctness:

$$e\left(S_2, u \prod_{\delta=1}^{\kappa} u_\delta^{m_\delta}\right) \cdot e\left(g_2, B_0 C\right) \cdot e\left(S_3, v \prod_{\delta=1}^{\ell} v_\delta^{j_\delta}\right)$$

$$= e\left(S_2, u \prod_{\delta=1}^{\kappa} u_\delta^{m_\delta}\right) \cdot e\left(g_2, h_1^x g_1^{s_\tau}\right) \cdot e\left(S_3, v \prod_{\delta=1}^{\ell} v_\delta^{j_\delta}\right)$$

$$= e\left(g_1^{r_\kappa}, u \prod_{\delta=1}^{\kappa} u_\delta^{m_\delta}\right) \cdot e(g_2, g_1^{s_\tau}) \cdot e(g_2, h_1^x) \cdot e\left(g_1^{r'+r_\ell}, v \prod_{\delta=1}^{\ell} v_\delta^{j_\delta}\right)$$

$$= e\left(g_1, g_2^{s_\tau} \cdot \left(u \prod_{\delta=1}^{\kappa} u_\delta^{m_\delta}\right)^{r_\kappa} \cdot \left(v \prod_{\delta=1}^{\ell} v_\delta^{j_\delta}\right)^{r'+r_\ell}\right) \cdot e(g_1, h_2^x)$$

$$= e(g_1, S_1).$$

Theorem 1. *Our scheme is forward-secure against insider corruption if the CDH assumption holds in $\mathbb{G}_p$.*

Theorem 2. *Our scheme is anonymous if the Subgroup Decision assumption holds in $\mathbb{G}$.*

Details of the security analysis of our scheme can be found in the full version of this paper [16].

4.3 Comparison

We compare our scheme with some ring signature schemes in the literature in Table 1. Denote the number of users in the group as n and the number of bits of the message as κ. The time of an exponentiation in a group $\mathbb{G}$ is $\exp_{\mathbb{G}}$, and the time of a multiplication in a group $\mathbb{G}$ is $\mathrm{mul}_{\mathbb{G}}$. The time of a pairing operation is pair.

Table 1. Comparison

Scheme	Signature Size	Sign Time	Verify Time	Model	Assumption	FS
Shacham - Waters [22]	$(2n+2)\mathbb{G}$	$3n+2 \exp_{\mathbb{G}}$, $2n+\kappa+2 \mathrm{mul}_{\mathbb{G}}$	$2n+3$ pair, $2n+\kappa+1 \mathrm{mul}_{\mathbb{G}}$ $1 \mathrm{mul}_{\mathbb{G}_T}$.	Full	CDH, Subgp	×
Schäge - Schwenk [21]	$(n+1)\mathbb{G}$	$n+2 \exp_{\mathbb{G}}$, $n+\kappa \mathrm{mul}_{\mathbb{G}}$.	$n+2$ pair, $\kappa \mathrm{mul}_{\mathbb{G}}$ $n \mathrm{mul}_{\mathbb{G}_T}$.	Chosen Subring	CDH	×
Liu - Wong [15]	$(2n+1)\mathbb{Z}_N$	$3n \exp_{\mathbb{Z}_N}$, $n \mathrm{mul}_{\mathbb{Z}_N}$	$3n \exp_{\mathbb{Z}_N}$, $n \mathrm{mul}_{\mathbb{Z}_N}$	ROM	Factorization	$\checkmark$
Our scheme	$(2n+3)\mathbb{G}$	$3n+4 \exp_{\mathbb{G}}$, $4n+\kappa+3 \mathrm{mul}_{\mathbb{G}}$.	$2n+5$ pair, $3n+\kappa+1 \mathrm{mul}_{\mathbb{G}}$ $3 \mathrm{mul}_{\mathbb{G}_T}$.	Full	CDH, Subgp	$\checkmark$

Note that the Schäge-Schwenk scheme [21] is the most efficient ring signature scheme in the standard model. However, it is only secure in the weaker chosen subring model for unforgeability. The first forward secure ring signatures by Liu-Wong [15] is only secure in random oracle model (ROM). Our scheme has a small overhead comparing with the Shacham-Waters scheme [22], while providing the extra forward security (FS) property in the standard model.

5   Conclusion

In this paper, we presented a forward secure ring signature scheme. Our construction is the first in the literature that can be proven secure without random oracles. The security relies on the CDH and subgroup decision problem. We believe there are a number of useful applications of forward secure ring signature scheme, such as wireless sensor networks and smart grid system.

References

1. Abdalla, M., Miner, S., Namprempre, C.: Forward-secure Threshold Signature Schemes. In: Naccache, D. (ed.) CT-RSA 2001. LNCS, vol. 2020, pp. 441–456. Springer, Heidelberg (2001)
2. Abdalla, M., Reyzin, L.: A New Forward-secure Digital Signature Scheme. In: Okamoto, T. (ed.) ASIACRYPT 2000. LNCS, vol. 1976, pp. 116–129. Springer, Heidelberg (2000)

3. Anderson, R.: Two remarks on public key cryptology. Technical Report UCAM-CL-TR-549, University of Cambridge, Computer Laboratory (December 2002); Relevant material presented by the author in an invited lecture at CCS 1997
4. Bellare, M., Boldyreva, A., Palacio, A.: An Uninstantiable Random-oracle-model Scheme for a Hybrid-Encryption Problem. In: Cachin, C., Camenisch, J.L. (eds.) EUROCRYPT 2004. LNCS, vol. 3027, pp. 171–188. Springer, Heidelberg (2004)
5. Bellare, M., Miner, S.: A Forward-secure Digital Signature Scheme. In: Wiener, M. (ed.) CRYPTO 1999. LNCS, vol. 1666, pp. 431–448. Springer, Heidelberg (1999)
6. Bellare, M., Rogaway, P.: Random oracles are practical: A paradigm for designing efficient protocols. In: ACM Conference on Computer and Communications Security, pp. 62–73. ACM Press (1993)
7. Bender, A., Katz, J., Morselli, R.: Ring Signatures: Stronger Definitions, and Constructions without Random Oracles. In: Halevi, S., Rabin, T. (eds.) TCC 2006. LNCS, vol. 3876, pp. 60–79. Springer, Heidelberg (2006)
8. Boneh, D., Goh, E.-J., Nissim, K.: Evaluating 2-dnf Formulas on Ciphertexts. In: Kilian, J. (ed.) TCC 2005. LNCS, vol. 3378, pp. 325–341. Springer, Heidelberg (2005)
9. Canetti, R., Goldreich, O., Halevi, S.: The Random Oracle Methodology, Revisited. In: STOC, pp. 209–218 (1998)
10. Canetti, R., Halevi, S., Katz, J.: A Forward-secure Public-key Encryption Scheme. In: Biham, E. (ed.) EUROCRYPT 2003. LNCS, vol. 2656, pp. 255–271. Springer, Heidelberg (2003)
11. Chow, S.S., Liu, J.K., Wei, V.K., Yuen, T.H.: Ring signatures without random oracles. In: ASIACCS 2006, pp. 297–302. ACM Press (2006)
12. Itkis, G., Reyzin, L.: Forward-secure Signatures with Optimal Signing and Verifying. In: Kilian, J. (ed.) CRYPTO 2001. LNCS, vol. 2139, pp. 332–354. Springer, Heidelberg (2001)
13. Krawczyk, H.: Simple forward-secure signatures from any signature scheme. In: The 7th ACM Conference on Computer and Communications Security, pp. 108–115. ACM Press (2000)
14. Liu, J.K., Wei, V.K., Wong, D.S.: A Separable Threshold Ring Signature Scheme. In: Lim, J.-I., Lee, D.-H. (eds.) ICISC 2003. LNCS, vol. 2971, pp. 352–369. Springer, Heidelberg (2004)
15. Liu, J.K., Wong, D.S.: Solutions to key exposure problem in ring signature. I. J. Network Security 6(2), 170–180 (2008)
16. Liu, J.K., Yuen, T.H., Zhou, J.: Forward secure ring signature without random oracles (full version). Cryptology ePrint Archive, Report 2011/472 (2011), http://eprint.iacr.org/
17. Malkin, T., Micciancio, D., Miner, S.: Efficient Generic Forward-secure Signatures with an Unbounded Number of Time Periods. In: Knudsen, L.R. (ed.) EUROCRYPT 2002. LNCS, vol. 2332, pp. 400–417. Springer, Heidelberg (2002)
18. Microsoft. Conserve Energy, Save Money - Microsoft Hohm (2009), http://www.microsoft-hohm.com/
19. N. I. of Standards and Technology. Nist ir 7628: Guidelines for smart grid cyber security. Technical report, http://csrc.nist.gov/publications/PubsNISTIRs.html
20. Rivest, R.L., Shamir, A., Tauman, Y.: How to Leak a Secret. In: Boyd, C. (ed.) ASIACRYPT 2001. LNCS, vol. 2248, pp. 552–565. Springer, Heidelberg (2001)
21. Schäge, S., Schwenk, J.: A Cdh-based Ring Signature Scheme with Short Signatures and Public Keys. In: Sion, R. (ed.) FC 2010. LNCS, vol. 6052, pp. 129–142. Springer, Heidelberg (2010)

22. Shacham, H., Waters, B.: Efficient Ring Signatures without Random Oracles. In: Okamoto, T., Wang, X. (eds.) PKC 2007. LNCS, vol. 4450, pp. 166–180. Springer, Heidelberg (2007)
23. Song, D.X.: Practical forward secure group signature schemes. In: The 8th ACM Conference on Computer and Communications Security, pp. 225–234. ACM Press (2001)
24. Wong, D.S., Fung, K., Liu, J.K., Wei, V.K.: On the RS-Code Construction of Ring Signature Schemes and a Threshold Setting of RST. In: Qing, S., Gollmann, D., Zhou, J. (eds.) ICICS 2003. LNCS, vol. 2836, pp. 34–46. Springer, Heidelberg (2003)
25. Xu, J., Zhang, Z., Feng, D.: A Ring Signature Scheme using Bilinear Pairings. In: Lim, C.H., Yung, M. (eds.) WISA 2004. LNCS, vol. 3325, pp. 160–170. Springer, Heidelberg (2005)
26. Yu, J., Hao, R., Kong, F., Cheng, X., Fan, J., Chen, Y.: Forward-secure identity-based signature: Security notions and construction. Information Sciences 181(3), 648–660 (2011)

Ring Signature Schemes from Lattice Basis Delegation

Jin Wang[1,2,*] and Bo Sun[1]

[1] National Computer Network Emergency Response Technical Team/Coordination Center of China, Beijing 100029, China
[2] Institute for Advanced Study , Tsinghua University, Beijing 100084, China
jimiwang@mail.tsinghua.edu.cn, {wj,sb}@cert.org.cn

Abstract. In this paper, we propose a set of ring signature (RS) schemes using the lattice basis delegation technique due to [6,7,12]. Our proposed schemes fit with ring trapdoor functions introduced by Brakerski and Kalai [18], and we obtain the first lattice-based ring signature scheme in the random oracle model. Moreover, motivated by Boyen's work [16], our second construction in the standard model achieves in stronger security definitions and shorter signatures than Brakeski-Kalai scheme.

Keywords: Ring signature, lattices, lattice basis delegation.

1 Introduction

Ring Signature. Ring signature [13] is a type of group-oriented signatures which provides anonymity in some scenarios. In a ring signature scheme, a message signer forms a ring of any set of possible signers including him/herself. The message signer can then generate a ring signature using his/her secret key and public keys of other ring members. The generated ring signature can convince an arbitrary verifier that the message was signed by one of the ring members without revealing exactly the singer's identity. Ring signature schemes could be used for many applications such as anonymous membership authentication, whistle blowing etc.

Motivations. Nowadays , most of the existing ring signature constructions are based on hard number theory assumes ranging from the large integer factorization [5,13] and the discrete logarithm problem [1,10] to the diffie-hellman problem of bilinear pairings [15]. However, above number theory problems will be solvable if practical quantum computers become reality, so it implies a potential security threat to these schemes. Thus, a natural question is how to design ring signature systems that are secure in the quantum environment. In recent years, lattices have emerged as a possible alternative to number theory. Lattice-based cryptography began with the seminal work of Ajtai[3], who showed

* Supported by 973 Project (No.2007CB807902), National Natural Science Foundation of China (NSFC Grant No.60910118).

that it is possible to construct cryptographic functions in which average-case security provably related to the worst-case complexity of hard lattice problems. Lattice-based constructions also enjoy great simplicity and is believed to be secure against quantum computers.

Our Contribution. Following above discussion, in this paper, we focus on constructing ring signature schemes from lattices. The idea behind our constructions is based on the lattice delegation method due to [6,7,12]. In our ring signature scheme, the public/secret key pair of each user is simply a matrix $\mathbf{A} \in \mathbb{Z}_q^{n \times m}$ and a corresponding short basis $\mathbf{B} \in \mathbb{Z}^{m \times m}$ for the lattice $\Lambda^\perp(\mathbf{A})$. For the ring set R of size l, the singer constructs a public matrix corresponding to the ring set as $\mathbf{A}_R = [\mathbf{A}_1\|...\|\mathbf{A}_l]$(for $i \in R, 1 \leq i \leq l$). Following the "hash-and-sign" paradigm as in [9], a message $M \in \{0,1\}^*$ is hashed to some point $\mathbf{y} = H(M)$. Using the basis delegation technique, each member in R should be able to deduce a signature (short vector $\mathbf{e} \in \mathbb{Z}^{lm}$) on M that satisfies $\mathbf{A}_R\mathbf{e} = \mathbf{y} \bmod q$. Since short basis for lattices essentially functions like cryptographic trapdoors [4,9], only the ring members in R can generate the signature successfully. Our ring signature scheme holds anonymity against full key exposure and unforgeability against insider corruption in the random oracle model. Moreover, using the similar technique in [16,17] , we can modify our basic construction to obtain a ring signature scheme in the standard model. To the best of author's knowledge, our constructions consist of the first lattice-based ring signature scheme in the random oracle model and achieve in stronger security definitions and shorter signatures than Brakeski and Kalai's work [18] in the standard model.

1.1   Related Work

Comparing with Brakerski and Kalai's Work. Brakerski and Kalai [18] recently presented a generic framework for constructing ring signature schemes in the standard model, and obtained a corresponding scheme based on SIS assumption. Our proposed ring signature schemes fit with ring trapdoor functions in [18] at a technical level. However, their work does not include ring signature in the random oracle model. For the lattice-based ring signature in the standard model, our construction is motivated by Boyen's work [16] and results in shorter signature than Brakeski-Kalai scheme. Moreover Brakeski-Kalai scheme is proved unforgeable under chosen subring attacks, and our standard model scheme is provable secure under a stronger model (unforgeability with insider corruption).

Lattice-based Signature. Our cryptographic constructions are based on the hardness assumption of the Small Integer Solution Problem (SIS)[11]. For reasonable choices of parameters, SIS is as hard as the shortest vector problem (SVP) in lattices. Gentry, Peikert, and Vaikuntanathan [9] constructed a kind of trapdoor primitive called Pre-image Sampling functions that, given a basis of a hard integer lattice, samples lattice points from a *Discrete Gaussian* probability distribution whose standard deviation is essentially the length of the longest

Gram-Schmidt vector of the basis. As the application of above trapdoors, Gentry et al. [9] constructed "hash and sign" digital signature schemes based on SIS. Another notable recent work is due to Cash et al.[6,7,12] who constructed a basis delegation technique that allows one to derive a short basis of a given lattice using a short basis of a related lattice. Using this basis delegation technique, Cash et al.[6] also constructed a stateless signature of lattice-based constructions.

2 Preliminaries

2.1 Notation

For a positive integer d, $[d]$ denotes the set $\{1, ..., d\}$. For an $n \times m$ matrix $\mathbf{A}$, let $\mathbf{A} = [\mathbf{a}_1, ..., \mathbf{a}_m]$, where $\mathbf{a}_i$ denotes the i-th column vector of $\mathbf{A}$. We define $\|\mathbf{a}\|$ for the Euclidean norm of $\mathbf{a}$, and $\|\mathbf{A}\| = \max_{i \in [m]} \|\mathbf{a}_i\|$.

2.2 Lattices

Lattices. Let $\mathbf{B} = \{\mathbf{b}_1, ..., \mathbf{b}_n\} \in \mathbb{R}^n$ consist of n linearly independent vectors. A n-dimensional lattice Λ generated by $\mathbf{B}$ is defined as

$$\Lambda = \mathcal{L}(\mathbf{B}) = \{\mathbf{Bc} : \mathbf{c} \in \mathbb{Z}^n\}$$

Here $\mathbf{B}$ is called a *basis* of the lattice $\Lambda = \mathcal{L}(\mathbf{B})$. For a basis $\mathbf{B} = \{\mathbf{b}_1, ..., \mathbf{b}_n\}$, let $\widetilde{\mathbf{B}}$ denote its *Gram-Schmidt orthogonalization*, defined iteratively as follows: $\tilde{b}_1 = b_1$, and for $i = 2, ..., n$, $\tilde{b}_i$ is the component of b_i orthogonal to $\mathrm{span}(b_1, ..., b_{i-1})$.

Hard Random Lattices. In this paper our cryptographic constructions will build on a certain family of m-dimensional integer lattices defined by Ajtai [4].

Definition 1. *Given a matrix* $\mathbf{A} \in \mathbb{Z}_q^{n \times m}$ *for some integers* q, m, n, *define:*

1 . $\Lambda^\perp(\mathbf{A}) = \{\mathbf{e} \in \mathbb{Z}^m : \mathbf{Ae} = 0 \bmod q\}$
2 . $\Lambda_\mathbf{y}^\perp(\mathbf{A}) = \{\mathbf{e} \in \mathbb{Z}^m : \mathbf{Ae} = \mathbf{y} \bmod q\}$

Observe that $\Lambda_\mathbf{y}^\perp(\mathbf{A}) = \mathbf{t} + \Lambda^\perp(\mathbf{A}) \bmod q$ where $\mathbf{t}$ is an arbitrary solution (over $\mathbb{Z}^m$) of the equation $\mathbf{At} = \mathbf{y} \bmod q$. Thus $\Lambda_\mathbf{y}^\perp(\mathbf{A})$ is the coset of $\Lambda^\perp(\mathbf{A})$.

Discrete Gaussians on Lattices. Here we review Gaussian functions used in lattice based cryptographic constructions. For any $r > 0$ the Gaussian function on $\mathbb{R}^n$ centered at $\mathbf{c}$ with deviation parameter r is defined as

$$\forall \mathbf{x} \in \mathbb{R}^n, \rho_{r,\mathbf{c}}(x) = \exp(-\pi \|\mathbf{x} - \mathbf{c}\|^2 / r^2)$$

For any $\mathbf{c} \in \mathbb{R}^n$, $r > 0$ and m-dimensional lattice Λ, the discrete gaussian distribution over Λ is defined as

$$\forall \mathbf{x} \in \Lambda, D_{\Lambda_{r,\mathbf{c}}}(x) = \frac{\rho_{r,\mathbf{c}}(\mathbf{x})}{\rho_{r,\mathbf{c}}(\Lambda)}$$

Small Integer Solution Problem. The most well known computational problem on lattices is the *shortest vector problem* (SVP), in which given a basis of a lattice Λ and the goal is to find the shortest vector $\mathbf{v} \in \Lambda \backslash \{0\}$. There is a special version of the SVP for the integer lattices, named *small integer solution* problem (SIS).

Definition 2. *The small integer solution problem* SIS *(in the Euclidean norm l_2) is as follows: given an integer q, a matrix $\mathbf{A} \in \mathbb{Z}_q^{n \times m}$ and a real β, find a nonzero integer vector $\mathbf{e} \in \mathbb{Z}^m$ such that $\mathbf{A}\mathbf{e} = 0 \bmod q$ and $\|\mathbf{e}\|_2 \leq \beta$.*

For functions $q(n)$, $m(n)$, and $\beta(n)$, $\mathsf{SIS}_{q,m,\beta}$ is the ensemble over instances $(q(n), \mathbf{A}, \beta(n))$, where $\mathbf{A} \in \mathbb{Z}_q^{n \times m}$ is uniformly random. In the following of the paper, a variant problem, the *inhomogeneous* small integer solution problem ISIS is also used. The ISIS problem is as follows: given an integer q, a matrix $\mathbf{A} \in \mathbb{Z}_q^{n \times m}$, $y \in \mathbb{Z}_q^n$, and a real β, find an integer vector $e \in \mathbb{Z}^m$ such that $\mathbf{A}e = y \bmod q$ and $\|\mathbf{e}\|_2 \leq \beta$. Using Gaussian techniques, Micciancio and Regev[11] showed that for any poly-bounded m, $\beta = poly(n)$ and for any prime $q \geq \beta \cdot \omega(\sqrt{n \log n})$, the average-case problem $\mathsf{SIS}_{q,m,\beta}$ and $\mathsf{ISIS}_{q,m,\beta}$ are as hard as approximating the SIVP problem (a variant of SVP) in the worst case within a factor $\tilde{O}(\beta \cdot \sqrt{n})$.

2.3   Trapdoors and Basis Delegation Functions

It was shown in [17] that if $\mathsf{SIS}_{q,m,2r\sqrt{m}}$ is hard, $\mathbf{A} \in \mathbb{Z}_q^{n \times m}$ defines a one-way function $f_{\mathbf{A}} : D_n \rightarrow R_n$ with $f_{\mathbf{A}}(\mathbf{e}) = \mathbf{A}\mathbf{e} \bmod q$, where $D_n = \{\mathbf{e} \in \mathbb{Z}^m : \|\mathbf{e}\| \leq r\sqrt{m}\}$ and $R_n = \mathbb{Z}_q^n$. The input distribution is $D_{\mathbb{Z}^m, r}$. A short basis $\mathbf{B} \in \mathbb{Z}^{m \times m}$ for $\Lambda^{\perp}(\mathbf{A})$ can be used as a trapdoor to sample from $f_{\mathbf{A}}^{-1}(\mathbf{y})$ for any $\mathbf{y} \in \mathbb{Z}_q^n$. Knowledge of such a trapdoor makes it easy to solve some hard problems relative to the lattice, such as SIS. Here we briefly introduce such a set of one-way preimage sampleble functions (defined in [9]), denoted as TrapGen, SampleD, SampleDom, SamplePre, which will be used as building blocks in our cryptographic constructions (we refer interested readers to [9] for more details). The following functions take the Gaussian smoothing parameter $r \geq \|\tilde{\mathbf{B}}\| \cdot \omega(\sqrt{\log m})$ as a parameter:

- TrapGen(1^{λ}): Let n, q, m be integers with $q \geq 2$, $m \geq 5n \log q$. TrapGen(1^{λ}) outputs a pair $(\mathbf{A}, \mathbf{B})$ such that $\mathbf{A}$ is statistically close to uniform on $\mathbb{Z}_q^{n \times m}$ and $\mathbf{B} \in \mathbb{Z}^{m \times m}$ is a good basis of $\Lambda^{\perp}(\mathbf{A})$ such that $\|\tilde{\mathbf{B}}\| \leq O(\sqrt{n \log q})$ and $\|\mathbf{B}\| \leq O(n \log q)$ with all but $n^{\omega(1)}$ probability. (Ajtai [4] showed how to sample a pair $(\mathbf{A}, \mathbf{B})$ with low Gram-Schmidt norm. Here we use an improved sampling algorithm from Alwen and Peikert[2]).
- SampleD$(\mathbf{B}, r, \mathbf{c})$: On input of a m-dimensional basis $\mathbf{B}$ of a lattice Λ, a parameter r, and a center vector $\mathbf{c} \in \mathbb{R}^m$, the algorithm SampleD samples from a discrete Gaussian distribution over the lattice Λ around the center $\mathbf{c}$ with the standard deviation r.
- SampleDom$(\mathbf{A}, r)$: Sample an $\mathbf{x}$ from distribution $D_{\mathbb{Z}^m, r}$ for which the distribution of $f_{\mathbf{A}}(\mathbf{x})$ is uniform over R_n.

- SamplePre($\mathbf{A}, \mathbf{B}, \mathbf{y}, r$): On input of $\mathbf{A} \in \mathbb{Z}_q^{n \times m}$, a good basis $\mathbf{B} \in \mathbb{Z}^{m \times m}$ for $\Lambda^{\perp}(\mathbf{A})$ as above, a vector $\mathbf{y} \in \mathbb{Z}_q^n$ and r; the conditional distribution of the output $\mathbf{e}$ is within negligible statistical distance of $D_{\Lambda_y^{\perp}(\mathbf{A}), r}$. The algorithm works as follows. First, choose via linear algebra an arbitrary $\mathbf{t} \in \mathbb{Z}^m$ such that $\mathbf{At} = \mathbf{y} \bmod q$. Then sample $\mathbf{v}$ from the Gaussian distribution $D_{\Lambda^{\perp}(\mathbf{A}), r, -\mathbf{t}}$ using SampleD($\mathbf{B}, r, -\mathbf{t}$), and output $\mathbf{e} = \mathbf{t} + \mathbf{v}$.

2.4   Ring Signature

Ring Signature. A ring signature scheme is a tuple of algorithms RS = (KeyGen, Ring-Sign, Ring-Verify) described as follows:

- KeyGen(λ): A probabilistic algorithm takes as input a security parameter λ and outputs a public key pk and a secret key sk.
- Ring-Sign(pk, sk, R, M): A probabilistic algorithm takes as input an user's key pair (pk, sk); a set of public keys R of the ring and a message M to be signed (Here $pk \in R$). It returns a ring signature σ of M under sk.
- Ring-Verify(R, M, σ): A deterministic algorithm takes as input a set of public keys R that constitutes the ring and a ring signature σ on a message M. It outputs "accept" if the ring signature is valid, or "reject" otherwise.

For consistency purposes, we require that for $l \in \mathbb{N}$, all $\{(pk_i, sk_i)_1^l\} \in [\text{KeyGen}(\lambda)]$, all $i \in [l]$ and all $M \in \{0, 1\}^*$: Ring-Verify(M, Ring-Sign(pk_i, sk_i, R, M)) $= 1$ where $R = (pk_1, ..., pk_l)$.

The security of a ring signature scheme consists of two requirements, namely *Anonymity* and *Unforgeability*. Here we follow the strongest security definitions for ring signatures: anonymity against full key exposure and unforgeability with insider corruption, presented by Bender, Katz, and Morselli[5].

Anonymity: Anonymity against full key exposure for a ring signature scheme RS is defined using the following game between a challenger $\mathcal{B}_1$ and an adversary $\mathcal{A}_1$: $\mathcal{B}_1$ firstly runs algorithm KeyGen l times to obtain public/private key pairs $(pk_1, sk_1), ..., (pk_l, sk_l)$. Here l is a game parameter. $\mathcal{A}_1$ is given the public keys $\{pk_i\}_1^l$ and allowed to make ring signing queries and corruption queries. A ring signing query is of the form (i, R, M) where M is the message to be signed, R is a set of public keys, and i is an user index with $pk_i \in R$. The challenger responds with $\sigma = $ Ring-Sign(sk_i, R, M). A corruption query is an index i. The challenger provides sk_i to $\mathcal{A}_1$. Finally, $\mathcal{A}_1$ requests a challenge by sending (i_0, i_1, R^*, M^*) to $\mathcal{B}_1$ such that M^* is a message to be signed with the ring R^*, and i_0 and i_1 are indices with $pk_{i_0}, pk_{i_1} \in R^*$. $\mathcal{B}_1$ chooses a bit $b \leftarrow \{0, 1\}$, computes the challenge signature $\sigma^* \leftarrow$ Ring-Sig($pk_{i_b}, sk_{i_b}, R^*, M^*$), and provides $\mathcal{A}_1$ with σ^*. The adversary $\mathcal{A}_1$ outputs a guess $b' \in \{0, 1\}$ and wins the game if $b' = b$.

Denote $\text{Adv}_{RS,l}^{anon}(\mathcal{A}_1)$ to be the advantage over $1/2$ of $\mathcal{A}_1$ in the above game. A ring signature scheme RS is anonymous, if for every probabilistic polynomial-time adversary $\mathcal{A}_1$ the advantage $\text{Adv}_{RS,l}^{anon}(\mathcal{A}_1)$ is negligible.

Unforgeability: For a ring signature scheme RS with l public keys, the existential unforgeability (with insider corruption) is defined as the following game between a challenger $\mathcal{B}_2$ and an adversary $\mathcal{A}_2$. $\mathcal{B}_2$ firstly runs the algorithm KeyGen to obtain public/private key pairs $(pk_1, sk_1), ..., (pk_l, sk_l)$. $\mathcal{A}_2$ is given the public keys $L = \{pk_i\}_1^l$ and is allowed to make ring signing queries and corruption queries as in the anonymity game. Finally $\mathcal{A}_2$ outputs a tuple (R^*, M^*, σ^*). $\mathcal{A}_2$ wins the game if all of following conditions satisfied: (1) $R^* \subseteq L \backslash C$, where C is the set of all the corrupted users; (2) (R^*, M^*) has not been submitted to the ring signing oracle; (3) Ring-Verify$(R^*, M^*, \sigma^*) =$ Accept.

$\mathcal{A}_2$'s advantage in above game is denoted to be $\mathrm{Adv}_{RS,l,\mathcal{A}_2}^{unfor} = \Pr[\mathcal{A}_2 \text{ wins}]$. A ring signature scheme RS is unforgeable if for every probabilistic polynomial-time adversary $\mathcal{A}_2$ the advantage $\mathrm{Adv}_{RS,l}^{unfor}(\mathcal{A}_2)$ is negligible.

3   Lattice Based Ring Signature in the Random Oracle Model

Our first construction is a lattice based ring signature scheme in the random oracle model. We start with a slight variant of the generalized sampling algorithm GenSamplePre which was first proposed in [7], with different choice of parameters and the structure of the extended lattice. The original algorithm enables the growth of extended matrices in a tree form. In our approach, we will handle with another extension policy better suited for our RS schemes given later.

3.1   Sampling Preimage for Extended Lattice

Let k, k_1, k_2, k_3, k_4 be positive integers and $k = k_1 + k_2 + k_3 + k_4$. Assume without loss of generality that $S = [k]$. We write $\mathbf{A}_S = [\mathbf{A}_{S_1} \| \mathbf{A}_{S_2} \| \mathbf{A}_{S_3} \| \mathbf{A}_{S_4}] \in \mathbb{Z}_q^{n \times km}$, where $\mathbf{A}_{S_1} \in \mathbb{Z}_q^{n \times k_1 m}$, $\mathbf{A}_{S_2} \in \mathbb{Z}_q^{n \times k_2 m}$, $\mathbf{A}_{S_3} \in \mathbb{Z}_q^{n \times k_3 m}$, $\mathbf{A}_{S_4} \in \mathbb{Z}_q^{n \times k_4 m}$. Let $\mathbf{A}_R = [\mathbf{A}_{S_1} \| \mathbf{A}_{S_3}] \in \mathbb{Z}_q^{n \times (k_1 + k_3)m}$. Given a short basis $\mathbf{B}_R$ for $\Lambda^{\perp}(\mathbf{A}_R)$ and an integer $r \geq \|\widetilde{\mathbf{B}}_R\| \cdot \omega(\sqrt{\log n})$, the algorithm GenSamplePre allows to sample a preimage of the function $f_{\mathbf{A}_S}(\mathbf{e}) = \mathbf{A}_S \mathbf{e} \bmod q$. GenSamplePre$(\mathbf{A}_S, \mathbf{A}_R, \mathbf{B}_R, \mathbf{y}, r)$ proceeds as follows:

1. Sample $\mathbf{e}_{S_2} \in \mathbb{Z}^{k_2 m}$ from the distribution $D_{\mathbb{Z}^{k_2 m}, r}$ and sample $\mathbf{e}_{S_4} \in \mathbb{Z}^{k_4 m}$ from the distribution $D_{\mathbb{Z}^{k_4 m}, r}$. Parse $\mathbf{e}_{S_2} = [\mathbf{e}_{k_1+1}, ..., \mathbf{e}_{k_1+k_2}] \in (\mathbb{Z}^m)^{k_2}$ and $\mathbf{e}_{S_4} = [\mathbf{e}_{k-k_4+1}, ..., \mathbf{e}_k] \in (\mathbb{Z}^m)^{k_4}$.
2. Let $\mathbf{z} = \mathbf{y} - \mathbf{A}_{S_2} \mathbf{e}_{S_2} - \mathbf{A}_{S_4} \mathbf{e}_{S_4} \bmod q$. Run SamplePre$(\mathbf{A}_R, \mathbf{B}_R, \mathbf{z}, r)$ to sample a vector $\mathbf{e}_R \in \mathbb{Z}^{(k_1+k_3)m}$ from the distribution $D_{\Lambda_{\mathbf{y}}^{\perp}(\mathbf{A}_S), r}$. Parse $\mathbf{e}_R = [\mathbf{e}_1, ..., \mathbf{e}_{k_1}, \mathbf{e}_{k_1+k_2+1}, ..., \mathbf{e}_{k-k_4}] \in (\mathbb{Z}^m)^{k_1+k_3}$ and let $\mathbf{e}_{S_1} = [\mathbf{e}_1, ..., \mathbf{e}_{k_1}] \in (\mathbb{Z}^m)^{k_1}$, $\mathbf{e}_{S_3} = [\mathbf{e}_{k_1+k_2+1}, ..., \mathbf{e}_{k-k_4}] \in (\mathbb{Z}^m)^{k_3}$.
3. Output $\mathbf{e} \in \mathbb{Z}^{km}$, as $\mathbf{e} = [\mathbf{e}_1, ..., \mathbf{e}_k]$.

Note that by construction, we have $\mathbf{A}_{S_1} \mathbf{e}_{S_1} + \mathbf{A}_{S_3} \mathbf{e}_{S_3} = \mathbf{A}_R \mathbf{e}_R = \mathbf{z} \bmod q$. Thus $\mathbf{A}_S \mathbf{e} = \sum_{i=1}^4 \mathbf{A}_{S_i} \mathbf{e}_{S_i} = \mathbf{y} \bmod q$, and the output vector $\mathbf{e}$ of GenSamplePre is contained in $\Lambda_{\mathbf{y}}^{\perp}(\mathbf{A}_S)$. For the analysis of the output distribution, Theorem 3.4 in [7] showed that $\mathbf{e}$ is within negligible statical distance of $D_{\Lambda_{\mathbf{y}}^{\perp}(\mathbf{A}_S), r}$.

3.2 Basic Construction

Let l, m, n, q, t be positive integers with $q \geq 2$ and $m \geq 5n\log q$. The ring signature scheme shares parameter functions L, r defined in [6] as follows:

- $\tilde{L} \geq O(\sqrt{n \log q})$: an upper bound on the Gram-Schmidt size of an user's secret basis;
- $r \geq \tilde{L} \cdot \omega(\sqrt{\log n})$: a Gaussian parameter used to generate the secret basis and short vectors.

The scheme employs a hash function $H_1 : \{0,1\}^* \rightarrow \mathbb{Z}_q^n$. The security analysis will view H_1 as a random oracle.

KeyGen(λ): On input a security parameter λ, an user with index i runs the trapdoor generation algorithm $\mathsf{TrapGen}(1^\lambda)$ (described in section 2.4) to generate $\mathbf{A}_i \in \mathbb{Z}_q^{n \times m}$ with a basis $\mathbf{B}_i \in \mathbb{Z}^{m \times m}$ for $\Lambda^\perp(\mathbf{A}_i)$. Note that by Theorem 3.2 in [2] we have $\|\tilde{\mathbf{B}}_i\| \leq \tilde{L}$. The public/private key pair for the user i is $\langle pk_i = \mathbf{A}_i, sk_i = \mathbf{B}_i \rangle$.

Ring-Sign(R, sk_i, M): Given a ring of l individuals with public keys R, assume for notational simplicity that $R = \{\mathbf{A}_1, ..., \mathbf{A}_l\} \in \mathbb{Z}_q^{n \times m}$, an user i's ($i \in [l]$) private key $sk_i = \mathbf{B}_i$ and a message $M \in \{0,1\}^*$, the user i does the following:
  - Set $\mathbf{A}_R = [\mathbf{A}_1\|...\|\mathbf{A}_l] \in \mathbb{Z}_q^{n \times lm}$ and $\mathbf{y} = H_1(M) \in \mathbb{Z}_q^n$. Define a label lab_R that contains information about how $\mathbf{A}_R$ is associated with the sequence of the ring members $\{1, ..., l\}$.
  - Generate $\mathbf{e} \leftarrow \mathsf{GenSamplePre}(\mathbf{A}_R, \mathbf{A}_i, \mathbf{B}_i, \mathbf{y}, r) \in \mathbb{Z}^{lm}$. Note that $\mathbf{e}$ is distributed according to $D_{\Lambda_{\mathbf{y}}^\perp \mathbf{A}_R, r}$.
  - Output the ring signature $\sigma = < \mathbf{e}, lab_R >$.

Ring-Verify(R, M, σ): Given a ring of public keys $R = \{\mathbf{A}_1, ..., \mathbf{A}_l\} \in \mathbb{Z}_q^{n \times m}$, a message M, and a ring signature $\sigma = < \mathbf{e}, lab_R >$, the verifier accepts the signature only if both the following conditions satisfied:
  - $0 \leq \|\mathbf{e}\| \leq r\sqrt{lm}$
  - $\mathbf{A}_R\mathbf{e} \bmod q = H_1(M)$.

Otherwise, the verifier rejects.

3.3 Correctness

The scheme's correctness is inherited by the properties of the trapdoor functions [9]. In the signing process, the ring members in R construct an one-way function $f_{\mathbf{A}_R} : D_R \rightarrow \mathbb{Z}_q^n$ as $f_{\mathbf{A}_R}(\mathbf{e}) = \mathbf{A}_R\mathbf{e} \bmod q$, where $D_R = \{\mathbf{e} \in \mathbb{Z}^{lm} : \|\mathbf{e}\| \leq r\sqrt{lm}\}$ with the following properties:

Correct Distributions: By Lemma 5.1 in [6], the distribution of the syndrome $\mathbf{y} = \mathbf{A}_R\mathbf{e} \bmod q$ is within statistical distance 2ϵ of uniform over $\mathbb{Z}_q^n$. By Theorem 3.4 in [7], algorithm $\mathsf{GenSamplePre}(\mathbf{A}_R, \mathbf{A}_i, \mathbf{B}_i, \mathbf{y}, r)$ samples an element $\mathbf{e}$ from the distribution within negligible statistical distance of $D_{\Lambda_{\mathbf{y}(\mathbf{A}_R), r}^\perp}$.

One-Wayness without Trapdoors: By Theorem 5.9 in [6], inverting a random function $f_{\mathbf{A}_R}$ on an uniform output $\mathbf{y} \in \mathbb{Z}_q^n$ is equivalent to solve the *inhomogeneous small integer solution* problem $\mathsf{ISIS}_{q,lm,r}$.

3.4   Security Analysis

We now prove that our ring signature scheme is anonymous against the full key exposure and unforgeable against the insider corruption following the definitions in section 2.4.

Full Anonymity: Before proving the fully anonymity, we prepare the following lemma on our ring signature scheme.

Lemma 1. *Let (i_0, i_1, R, M) be a tuple such that $M \in \{0, 1\}^*$ is a message to be signed with the ring $R = \{\mathbf{A}_1, ..., \mathbf{A}_l\} \in \mathbb{Z}_q^{n \times m}$, i_0 and i_1 are indices with $\mathbf{A}_{i_0}, \mathbf{A}_{i_1} \in R$. If $\mathsf{ISIS}_{q,lm,r}$ is hard, $\sigma_{i_0} \leftarrow \mathsf{Ring\text{-}Sign}(sk_{i_0}, R, M)$ and $\sigma_{i_1} \leftarrow \mathsf{Ring\text{-}}$ $\mathsf{Sign}(sk_{i_1}, R, M)$ are computationally indistinguishable.*

Proof: The proof is straightforward from the algorithm Ring-Sign. Recall that in the signing process, the ring signature σ_{i_0} and σ_{i_1} are only vectors in $\mathbb{Z}^{lm}$, they have the same distribution of the domain in $f_{\mathbf{A}_R}$ within negligible statistical distance of $D_{\Lambda_{H_1(M)}^{\perp}(\mathbf{A}_R), r}$ and it implies that σ_{i_0} and σ_{i_1} are computationally indistinguishable.

Theorem 1. *Let $q \geq 2$ and $m \geq 5n \log q$. If H_1 is modeled as a random oracle, the ring signature scheme above is fully-anonymous assuming that $\mathsf{ISIS}_{q,lm,r}$ is hard.*

Proof. Assume that there exists an adaptive adversary $\mathcal{A}_1$ attacking our ring signature scheme following the definition of anonymity against full key exposure. We construct a poly-time algorithm $\mathcal{B}_1$ to simulate the attacking environment for $\mathcal{A}_1$. Both $\mathcal{A}_1$ and $\mathcal{B}_1$ are given as input q_E, the total number of extraction queries that can be issued by $\mathcal{A}_1$. To respond to $\mathcal{A}_1$'s queries in the random oracle, $\mathcal{B}_1$ will maintain two lists H_1 and $\mathcal{G}$, which are initialized to be empty and will store tuples of values.

In the Setup phase, $\mathcal{B}_1$ runs the algorithm TrapGen q_E times to generate $\mathbf{A}_i \in \mathbb{Z}_q^{n \times m}$ with the corresponding short basis $\mathbf{B}_i \in \mathbb{Z}^{m \times m}$ $(1 \leq i \leq q_E)$. $\mathcal{B}$ stores the tuple $\langle i, \mathbf{A}_i, \mathbf{B}_i \rangle (1 \leq i \leq q_E)$ in list $\mathcal{G}$ and the system parameters $< \mathbf{A}_1 \| ... \| \mathbf{A}_{q_E} >$ are given to $\mathcal{A}_1$. In the query phase, $\mathcal{B}_1$ answers the hash queries, corruption queries and signing queries of $\mathcal{A}_1$ as follows:

- *Hash Query to $H_1(M_j)$* : $\mathcal{B}_1$ returns a random $\mathbf{y}_j \in \mathbb{Z}_q^n$ to $\mathcal{A}_1$ and stores $\langle M_j, \mathbf{y}_j \rangle$ in list-H_1.
- *Corruption Query (i)*: $\mathcal{B}_1$ looks for the tuple $\langle i, \mathbf{A}_i, \mathbf{B}_i \rangle$ in list $\mathcal{G}$ and returns $\mathbf{B}_i$ to $\mathcal{A}_1$.
- *Signing Query(i, M_j, R_j)*: It can be assumed, without loss of generality, that $\mathcal{A}_1$ has made a H_1 query on M_j. $\mathcal{B}_1$ searches the tuple $\langle M_j, \mathbf{y}_j \rangle$ in list-H_1 and returns $\mathbf{e}_j \leftarrow \mathsf{GenSamplePre}(\mathbf{A}_{R_j}, \mathbf{A}_i, \mathbf{B}_i, \mathbf{y}_j, r)$ to $\mathcal{A}_1$.

At some point, $\mathcal{A}_1$ provides $< i_0, i_1, R^*, M^* >$ such that M^* is a message to be signed with the ring R^*, and i_0 and i_1 are indices with $pk_{i_0}, pk_{i_1} \in R^*$. $\mathcal{B}_1$ chooses a bit $b^* \leftarrow \{0, 1\}$, and retrieves the tuple $\langle M^*, \mathbf{y}^* \rangle$ in list-H_1. Then $\mathcal{B}_1$ computes the challenge signature $\mathbf{e}^* \leftarrow \mathsf{GenSamplePre}(\mathbf{A}_{R^*}, \mathbf{A}_{i_{b^*}}, \mathbf{B}_{i_{b^*}}, \mathbf{y}^*, r)$, and provides $\mathcal{A}_1$ with $\mathbf{e}^*$. Finally, the adversary $\mathcal{A}_1$ outputs a guess $b' \in \{0, 1\}$. In the view of $\mathcal{A}_1$, the behavior of $\mathcal{B}_1$ is statistically close to the one provided by the real anonymity security experiment. Observe that the ring members in R^* construct a one-way function $f_{\mathbf{A}_{R^*}}(\mathbf{e}) = \mathbf{A}_{R^*}\mathbf{e}$ mod q: with the domain $D_{R^*} = \{\mathbf{e} \in \mathbb{Z}^{lm} : \|\mathbf{e}\| \leq r\sqrt{lm}\}$ and $\mathbb{Z}_q^n$. If $\mathcal{A}_1$ exhibits a different success probability in distinguishing between i_0 and i_1 with non-negligible probability, it will contradict with the lemma 1. Hence, we claim that the adversary $\mathcal{A}_1$ in the anonymity game under the simulated environment has negligible advantage to guess the correct identity.

Unforgeability: The unforgeability proof closely follows the proof for the original lattice signature scheme given by Gentry, Peikert, and Vaikuntanathan [9].

Theorem 2. *Our ring signature scheme is unforgeable with regard to the insider corruption assuming that H_1 is collision resistant and $\mathsf{SIS}_{q,lm,2r}$ is hard (l is a guess for the size of the challenge ring).*

Proof: Let $\mathcal{A}_2$ be an adversary that attacks the unforgeability of the ring signature scheme. We construct a poly-time adversary $\mathcal{B}_2$ that solves $\mathsf{SIS}_{q,lm,2r}$ with probability

$$\mathsf{Adv}_{q,lm,2r}^{\mathsf{SIS}}(\mathcal{B}_2) \geq \frac{\mathsf{Adv}_{RS,l}^{unfor}(\mathcal{A}_2)}{q_E \mathsf{C}_{q_E}^{q_E/2}} - \text{negl}$$

Both the adversary $\mathcal{A}_2$ and the challenger $\mathcal{B}_2$ are given as input q_E, the total number of extraction queries that can be issued by $\mathcal{A}_2$. $\mathcal{B}_2$ interacts with $\mathcal{A}_2$ as follows:

Setup: $\mathcal{B}_2$ chooses $l \in [q_E]$, a guess for the size of the challenge ring. Next $\mathcal{B}_2$ obtains an instance $\mathbf{A}_{R_t} \in \mathbb{Z}_q^{n \times lm}$ from the SIS oracle and parses it as $\mathbf{A}_{i^*} \in \mathbb{Z}_q^{n \times m}$ $(1 \leq i^* \leq l)$. $\mathcal{B}_2$ then picks a vector $\mathbf{t} = (t_1, ..., t_l) \in [q_E]$ and sets $R_t = \{t_1, ..., t_l\}$. To respond to $\mathcal{A}_2$'s hash queries and corruption queries in the random oracle, $\mathcal{B}_2$ will maintain two lists H_1 and $\mathcal{G}$, which are initialized to be empty and will store tuples of values. For $1 \leq i \leq q_E$ and $i \notin \mathbf{t}$, $\mathcal{B}_2$ runs the algorithm $\mathsf{TrapGen}$ to generate $\mathbf{A}_i \in \mathbb{Z}_q^{n \times m}$ with the corresponding short basis $\mathbf{B}_i \in \mathbb{Z}^{m \times m}$ and stores the tuple $\langle i, \mathbf{A}_i, \mathbf{B}_i \rangle$ in list $\mathcal{G}$. For $1 \leq i \leq q_E$ and $i = t_{i^*} \in \mathbf{t}$, $\mathcal{B}_2$ sets $\mathbf{A}_i = \mathbf{A}_{i^*} \in \mathbb{Z}_q^{n \times m}$. The system parameters $< \mathbf{A}_1 \| ... \| \mathbf{A}_{q_E} >$ are given to $\mathcal{A}_2$.

Query Phase: $\mathcal{B}_2$ answers the hash queries, corruption queries and signing queries of $\mathcal{A}_2$ as follows:

- *Hash Query to $H_1(M_j)$.* $\mathcal{B}_2$ chooses a random $\mathbf{e}_j \leftarrow D_{lm,r}$ by running the algorithm $\mathsf{SampleDom}(\mathbf{A}_{R_t}, r)$, returns $\mathbf{y}_j \leftarrow \mathbf{A}_{R_t}\mathbf{e}_j$ mod $q \in \mathbb{Z}_q^n$ to $\mathcal{A}_2$ and stores $\langle M_j, \mathbf{e}_j, \mathbf{y}_j \rangle$ in list-H_1.
- *Corruption Query (i).* If $i \notin \mathbf{t}$, $\mathcal{B}_2$ looks for the tuple $\langle i, \mathbf{A}_i, \mathbf{B}_i \rangle$ in list $\mathcal{G}$ and returns $\mathbf{B}_i$ to $\mathcal{A}_2$. Otherwise, $\mathcal{B}_2$ aborts.
- *Signing Query(i, M_j, R_j).* It can be assumed, without loss of generality, that $\mathcal{A}_2$ has made a H_1 query on M_j. If $R_j = R_t$, $\mathcal{B}_2$ searches the tuple $\langle M_j, \mathbf{e}_j \rangle$ in list-H_1 and returns $\mathbf{e}_j$ to $\mathcal{A}_2$. Otherwise if the tuple $\langle i, \mathbf{A}_i, \mathbf{B}_i \rangle$

contains in list $\mathcal{G}$, $\mathcal{B}_2$ retrieves the tuple $\langle M_j, \mathbf{e}_j, \mathbf{y}_j \rangle$ in list-H_1 and then returns $\sigma_j \leftarrow$ GenSamplePre$(\mathbf{A}_{R_j}, \mathbf{A}_i, \mathbf{B}_i, \mathbf{y}_j, r)$ to $\mathcal{A}_2$. Otherwise, $\mathcal{B}_2$ looks for a $k \in R_j$ such that $\langle k, \mathbf{A}_k, \mathbf{B}_k \rangle$ contains in list $\mathcal{G}$. $\mathcal{B}_2$ then computes $\sigma_j \leftarrow$ GenSamplePre$(\mathbf{A}_{R_j}, \mathbf{A}_k, \mathbf{B}_k, \mathbf{y}_j, r)$ and returns σ_j to $\mathcal{A}_2$.

Challenge: Finally, $\mathcal{A}_2$ outputs a forgery $\langle i^*, M^*, \sigma^*, R^* \rangle$. If $R^* \neq R_t$, $\mathcal{B}_2$ aborts. Otherwise, $\mathcal{B}_2$ looks up the tuple $\langle M^*, \mathbf{e}^*, \mathbf{y}^* \rangle$ in list-H_1 and outputs $\mathbf{e}_0 = \sigma^* - \mathbf{e}^*$ as a solution to the SIS instance $f_{\mathbf{A}_{R_t}}$.

Analysis. In above process, the probability of an abort is at most $1 - \frac{1}{q_E C_{q_E}^{q_E/2}}$. We claim that the view of $\mathcal{A}_2$ in the unforgeability attack is identical to its view as provided by $\mathcal{B}_2$. For each distinct query M_j to H_1, the value returned by $\mathcal{B}_2$ is $f_{\mathbf{A}_{R_t}}(\mathbf{e}_j) \in \mathbb{Z}_q^n$ where $\mathbf{e}_j \leftarrow$ SampleDom$(\mathbf{A}_{R_t}, r)$; by the uniform output property of the constructed function, this is identical to the uniformly random value of $H_1(M_j) \in \mathbb{Z}_q^n$ in the real environment. Therefore $\mathcal{A}_2$ outputs a valid forgery $\langle M^*, \sigma^* \rangle$ with probability (negligibly close to) ϵ. Since σ^* is a valid signature of the ring on M^*, we have $\sigma^* < r\sqrt{lm}$ and $f_{\mathbf{A}_{R_t}}(\sigma^*) = H_1(M^*) = f_{\mathbf{A}_{R_t}}(\mathbf{e}^*)$, and they form a collision in $f_{\mathbf{A}_{R_t}}$. Let $\mathbf{e}_0 = \sigma^* - \mathbf{e}^*$, we have $\|\mathbf{e}_0\| \leq 2r\sqrt{lm}$. The probability that $\mathbf{e}_0 = 0$ is at most $n^{-\omega(1)}$. Thus, $\mathcal{B}_2$ solves the SIS instance $\text{SIS}_{q, lm, 2r}$.

4   Ring Signature in the Standard Model

Recently, Boyen et al.[16] proposed a framework for fully secure lattice-based signatures in the standard model. Let $\mathbf{A}$ and $\mathbf{S}$ be matrices in $\mathbb{Z}_q^{n \times m}$ and let $\mathbf{R} \in \mathbb{Z}^{m \times m}$ have some distribution with $\|\tilde{\mathbf{R}}\| \leq \omega(\sqrt{\log m})\sqrt{m}$. The key construction in their work is the matrices of the form $\mathbf{F} = [\mathbf{A}|\mathbf{AR} + \mathbf{S}] \in \mathbb{Z}_q^{n \times 2m}$. Given a short basis for either $\Lambda^\perp(\mathbf{A})$ or $\Lambda^\perp(\mathbf{S})$, they showed that $\mathbf{F}$ is a two-sided preimage samplable function. Using the similar method as in [16,17], we can extend our basic construction in section 3.2 to a ring signature scheme in the standard model. Our construction involves a variant of $\mathbf{F}$ as follows.

Lemma 2. *Fix a matrix $\mathbf{S} \in \mathbb{Z}_q^{n \times m}$ with a short basis $\mathbf{T} \in \mathbb{Z}^{m \times m}$ for $\Lambda^\perp(\mathbf{S})$ and $\|\tilde{\mathbf{T}}\| \leq O(\sqrt{n \log q})$. For $(\mathbf{A}, \mathbf{F})$ such that $\mathbf{A}$ is statistically close to uniform on $\mathbb{Z}_q^{n \times lm}$, $\mathbf{R} \in \mathbb{Z}^{lm \times m}$ with $\|\tilde{\mathbf{R}}\| \leq \omega(\sqrt{\log m})\sqrt{lm}$; $\mathbf{F} = [\mathbf{A}|\mathbf{AR} + \mathbf{S}] \in \mathbb{Z}_q^{n \times (l+1)m}$ is a preimage-samplable function in the sense of section 2.3.*

Proof: The lemma differs from the lemma 23 in [16] in the choice of parameters of the matrices $(\mathbf{A}, \mathbf{R}, \mathbf{F})$, the proof can be deduced using the similar method as in the original one [16] and is omitted here.

4.1   Our Construction in the Standard Model

The scheme involves parameter functions $\tilde{L}, r$ as in section 3.2. For some integers l and d, the following construction assumes that messages are arbitrary $d+1$-bit strings in $\{0\} \times \{0, 1\}^d$. The public parameters also include $d+1$ independent matrices $\mathbf{C}_0, ..., \mathbf{C}_d \in \mathbb{Z}_q^{n \times m}$.

KeyGen(λ): As in the basic construction in section 3.2.

Ring-Sign(R, sk_i, M): Given a ring with public keys $R = \{\mathbf{A}_1, ..., \mathbf{A}_l\} \in \mathbb{Z}_q^{n \times m}$,
an user i's$(i \in [l])$ private key $sk_i = \mathbf{B}_i \in \mathbb{Z}^{m \times m}$ $(\|\widetilde{\mathbf{B}}_i\| \leq \widetilde{L})$, and a message
$M \in \{0\} \times \{0,1\}^d$, the user i does the following:

- Set $\mathbf{C}_M = \sum_{i=0}^{d}(-1)^{M[i]}\mathbf{C}_i \in \mathbb{Z}_q^{n \times m}$.
- Set $\mathbf{A}_R=[\mathbf{A}_1\|...\|\mathbf{A}_l\|\mathbf{C}_M] \in \mathbb{Z}_q^{n \times (l+1)m}$. Define a label lab_R that contains information about how $\mathbf{A}_R$ is associated with the sequence of the ring numbers $\{1, ..., l\}$.
- Generate $\mathbf{e} \leftarrow \mathsf{GenSamplePre}(\mathbf{A}_R, \mathbf{A}_i, \mathbf{B}_i, 0, r) \in \mathbb{Z}^{(l+1)m}$. Note that $\mathbf{e}$ is distributed according to $D_{\Lambda^{\perp}\mathbf{A}_R, r}$.
- Output the ring signature $\sigma =<\mathbf{e}, lab_R>$.

Ring-Verify(R, M, σ): Given a ring of public keys $R = \{\mathbf{A}_1, ..., \mathbf{A}_l\} \in \mathbb{Z}_q^{n \times m}$, a
message $M \in \{0\} \times \{0,1\}^d$ and a ring signature $\sigma =<\mathbf{e}, lab_R>$, the verifier
accepts the signature only if both the following conditions satisfied:

- $0 \leq \|\mathbf{e}\| \leq r\sqrt{(l+1)m}$
- $[\mathbf{A}_1\|...\|\mathbf{A}_l\| \sum_{i=0}^{d}(-1)^{M[i]}\mathbf{C}_i]\mathbf{e} =0 \bmod q$.

Otherwise, the verifier rejects.

Above ring signature scheme fits with ring trapdoor functions in the standard
model proposed by Brakerski and Kalai in [18]. Moreover, our construction is
motivated by Boyen's work [16] and results in shorter signatures than Brakeski-
Kalai scheme. The anonymity of the scheme can be proved using the similar
method as in Theorem 1. Since the concurrent ring signature scheme is based on
the signature scheme proposed by Boyen [16] which is existentially unforgeable
under a chosen message attacks, it can also be proved unforgeable using the
similar way as in [16].

Theorem 3. *Our ring signature scheme is unforgeable with regard to the insider corruption assuming that* $\mathsf{SIS}_{q,lm,r}$ *is hard (l is a guess for the size of the
challenge ring).*

The unforgeability proof closely follows the combination of the methods in the
proof of Theorem 2 and the proof of Theorem 23 in [16]. The proof sketch is
given in Appendix A.

5   Conclusion

In this paper, we propose a set of ring signature schemes using the lattice basis delegation technique. To the best of author's knowledge, our constructions
consist of the first lattice-based ring signature in the random oracle model and
achieve in stronger security models and shorter signatures than Brakeski and
Kalai's work in the standard model.

References

1. Abe, M., Ohkubo, M., Suzuki, K.: 1-out-of-n Signatures from a Variety of Keys. In: Zheng, Y. (ed.) ASIACRYPT 2002. LNCS, vol. 2501, pp. 415–432. Springer, Heidelberg (2002)
2. Alwen, J., Peikert, C.: Generating shorter bases for hard random lattices. In: Proc. of STACS 2009, pp. 75–86 (2009)
3. Ajtai, M., Dwork, C.: A public-key cryptosystem with worst-case/average-case equivalence. In: STOC, pp. 284–293 (1997)
4. Ajtai, M.: Generating Hard Instances of the Short Basis Problem. In: Wiedermann, J., Van Emde Boas, P., Nielsen, M. (eds.) ICALP 1999. LNCS, vol. 1644, pp. 1–9. Springer, Heidelberg (1999)
5. Bender, A., Katz, J., Morselli, R.: Ring Signatures: Stronger Definitions, and Constructions without Random Oracles. In: Halevi, S., Rabin, T. (eds.) TCC 2006. LNCS, vol. 3876, pp. 60–79. Springer, Heidelberg (2006)
6. Cash, D., Hofheinz, D., Kiltz, E., Peikert, C.: Bonsai Trees, or How to Delegate a Lattice Basis. In: Gilbert, H. (ed.) EUROCRYPT 2010. LNCS, vol. 6110, pp. 523–552. Springer, Heidelberg (2010)
7. Cash, D., Hofheinz, D., Kiltz, E.: How to delegate a lattice basis. In: Halevi, S. (ed.) CRYPTO rumption (2009). Cryptology ePrint Archive, Report 2009/351 (2009), http://eprint.iacr.org/2009/351
8. Chow, S.S.M., Wei, V.K., Liu, J.K., Yuen, T.H.: Ring Signatures without Random Oracles. In: ASIACCS 2006: Proceedings of the 2006 ACM Symposium on Information, Taipei, Taiwan. Computer and Communications Security, pp. 297–302. ACM Press, New York (2006)
9. Gentry, C., Peikert, C., Vaikuntanathan, V.: Trapdoors for hard lattices and new cryptographic constructions. In: STOC, pp. 197–206 (2008)
10. Herranz, J., Sáez, G.: Forking Lemmas for Ring Signature Schemes. In: Johansson, T., Maitra, S. (eds.) INDOCRYPT 2003. LNCS, vol. 2904, pp. 266–279. Springer, Heidelberg (2003)
11. Micciancio, D., Regev, O.: Worst-case to average-case reductions based on Gaussian measures. SIAM J. Comput. 37(1), 267–302 (2007); Preliminary version in FOCS 2004
12. Peikert, C.: Bonsai Trees: Arboriculture in Lattice-Based Cryptography (2009) (in manuscript)
13. Rivest, R.L., Shamir, A., Tauman, Y.: How to Leak a Secret. In: Boyd, C. (ed.) ASIACRYPT 2001. LNCS, vol. 2248, pp. 552–565. Springer, Heidelberg (2001)
14. Regev, O.: On lattices, learning with errors, random linear codes, and cryptography. In: STOC, pp. 84–93 (2005)
15. Shacham, H., Waters, B.: Efficient Ring Signatures without Random Oracles. In: Okamoto, T., Wang, X. (eds.) PKC 2007. LNCS, vol. 4450, pp. 166–180. Springer, Heidelberg (2007)
16. Boyen, X.: Lattice Mixing and Vanishing Trapdoors: A Framework for Fully Secure Short Signatures and More. In: Nguyen, P.Q., Pointcheval, D. (eds.) PKC 2010. LNCS, vol. 6056, pp. 499–517. Springer, Heidelberg (2010)
17. Agrawal, S., Boneh, D., Boyen, X.: Efficient Lattice (H)IBE in the Standard Model. In: Gilbert, H. (ed.) EUROCRYPT 2010. LNCS, vol. 6110, pp. 553–572. Springer, Heidelberg (2010)
18. Brakerski, Z., Kalai, Y.T.: A framework for efficient signatures, ring signatures and identity based encryption in the standard model. Cryptology ePrint Archive, Report 2010/086 (2010)

A   Proof of Theorem 3

Proof (Sketch): Let $\mathcal{A}_3$ be an adversary that attacks the unforgeability of the ring signature scheme. We construct a poly-time adversary $\mathcal{B}_3$ that solves $\text{SIS}_{q,lm,\beta}$ with probability

$$\mathsf{Adv}_{q,lm,\beta}^{\text{SIS}}(\mathcal{B}_3) \geq \frac{\mathsf{Adv}_{RS,l}^{unfor}(\mathcal{A}_3)}{qq_E \mathrm{C}_{q_E}^{q_E/2}} - \text{negl}$$

The proof takes $\beta = (1+\sqrt{d+1}\sqrt{lm}\omega\sqrt{\log lm})\sqrt{(l+1)mr}$ as a parameter. Both the adversary $\mathcal{A}_3$ and the challenger $\mathcal{B}_3$ are given as input q_E, the total number of extraction queries that can be issued by $\mathcal{A}_3$. $\mathcal{B}_3$ interacts with $\mathcal{A}_3$ as follows:

Setup: $\mathcal{B}_3$ constructs the system's public parameters:

1. Choose $l \in [q_E]$, a guess for the size of the challenge ring.

2. Obtain an instance $\mathbf{A}_{R_t} \in \mathbb{Z}_q^{n \times lm}$ from the SIS oracle and parses it as $\mathbf{A}_{i^*} \in \mathbb{Z}_q^{n \times m}$ $(1 \leq i^* \leq l)$. Then pick a vector $\mathbf{t} = (t_1, ..., t_l) \in [q_E]$ and set $R_t = \{t_1, ..., t_l\}$.

3. Run the algorithm $\mathsf{TrapGen}(1^\lambda)$ to generate $\mathbf{S}_0 \in \mathbb{Z}_q^{n \times m}$ with the corresponding short basis $\mathbf{T}_0 \in \mathbb{Z}^{m \times m}$ for $\Lambda^\perp(\mathbf{S}_0)$.

4. Construct a list $\mathcal{G}$ which is initialized to be empty. For $1 \leq i \leq q_E$ and $i \notin \mathbf{t}$, run the algorithm $\mathsf{TrapGen}(1^\lambda)$ to generate $\mathbf{A}_i \in \mathbb{Z}_q^{n \times m}$ with the corresponding short basis $\mathbf{B}_i \in \mathbb{Z}^{m \times m}$ and store the tuple $\langle i, \mathbf{A}_i, \mathbf{B}_i\rangle$ in list $\mathcal{G}$. For $1 \leq i \leq q_E$ and $i = t_{i^*} \in \mathbf{t}$, set $\mathbf{A}_i = \mathbf{A}_{i^*} \in \mathbb{Z}_q^{n \times m}$.

5. Pick $l+1$ short random matrices $\mathbf{R}_0, ..., \mathbf{R}_l \in \mathbb{Z}^{lm \times m}$. Fix $\mathbf{h}_0 = 1 \in \mathbb{Z}_q$ and pick uniformly random scalars $\mathbf{h}_1, ..., \mathbf{h}_l \in \mathbb{Z}_q$.

6. The system parameters $< \mathbf{A}_1, ..., \mathbf{A}_{q_E}, \mathbf{C}_0 = \mathbf{A}_{R_t}\mathbf{R}_0 + \mathbf{h}_0\mathbf{S}_0 \mod q, \mathbf{C}_1 = \mathbf{A}_{R_t}\mathbf{R}_1 + \mathbf{h}_1\mathbf{S}_0 \mod q, ..., \mathbf{C}_l = \mathbf{A}_{R_t}\mathbf{R}_l + \mathbf{h}_l\mathbf{S}_0 \mod q >$ are given to $\mathcal{A}_3$.

Query Phase: $\mathcal{B}_3$ answers the corruption queries and signing queries of $\mathcal{A}_3$ as follows:

- *Corruption Query* (i). If $i \notin \mathbf{t}$, $\mathcal{B}_3$ looks for the tuple $\langle i, \mathbf{A}_i, \mathbf{B}_i\rangle$ in list $\mathcal{G}$ and returns $\mathbf{B}_i$ to $\mathcal{A}_3$. Otherwise, $\mathcal{B}_3$ aborts.

- *Signing Query*(i, M_j, R_j). If $R_j = R_t$, $\mathcal{B}_3$ computes the matrix $\mathbf{R}_{M_j} = \sum_{k=0}^d (-1)^{M_j[k]}\mathbf{R}_k \in \mathbb{Z}^{(l+1)m}$ and $\mathbf{h}_{M_j} = \sum_{k=0}^d (-1)^{M_j[k]}\mathbf{h}_k \in \mathbb{Z}_q$. If $\mathbf{h}_{M_j} \neq 0$, $\mathcal{B}_3$ then constructs the matrix $\mathbf{F}_i = [\mathbf{A}_{R_t}\|\mathbf{A}_{R_t}\mathbf{R}_{M_j} + \mathbf{h}_{M_j}\mathbf{S}_0] \in \mathbb{Z}_q^{n \times (l+1)m}$ and finds a short random $\mathbf{e} \in \Lambda^\perp(\mathbf{F}_i) \subset \mathbb{Z}^{(l+1)m}$ using the trapdoor $\mathbf{T}_0$. Otherwise if the tuple $\langle i, \mathbf{A}_i, \mathbf{B}_i\rangle$ contains in list $\mathcal{G}$, $\mathcal{B}_3$ constructs $\mathbf{F}_j = [\mathbf{A}_{R_j}\|\sum_{i=0}^d(-1)^{M_j[i]}\mathbf{C}_i]$ and then returns $\sigma_j \leftarrow \mathsf{GenSamplePre}\,(\mathbf{F}_j, \mathbf{A}_i, \mathbf{B}_i, 0, r)$ to $\mathcal{A}_3$. Otherwise, $\mathcal{B}_3$ looks for a $k \in R_j$ such that $\langle k, \mathbf{A}_k, \mathbf{B}_k\rangle$ contains in list $\mathcal{G}$. $\mathcal{B}_3$ returns $\sigma_j \leftarrow \mathsf{GenSamplePre}\,(\mathbf{F}_j, \mathbf{A}_k, \mathbf{B}_k, 0, r)$ to $\mathcal{A}_3$.

Challenge: Finally, $\mathcal{A}_3$ outputs a forgery $\langle i^*, M^*, \sigma^*, R^*\rangle$. If $R^* \neq R_t$, $\mathcal{B}_3$ aborts. Otherwise, $\mathcal{B}_3$ does the following:

1. Compute $\mathbf{R}_{M^*} = \sum_{k=0}^d (-1)^{M^*[k]}\mathbf{R}_k$ and $\mathbf{h}_{M^*} = \sum_{k=0}^d (-1)^{M^*[k]}\mathbf{h}_k$.

2. If $\mathbf{h}_{M^*} \neq 0 \mod q$, abort the simulation.

3. Separate $\sigma^* \in \mathbb{Z}^{(l+1)m}$ into $\sigma_1^* \in \mathbb{Z}^{lm}$ and $\sigma_2^* \in \mathbb{Z}^m$ such that $\sigma^* = \begin{pmatrix} \sigma_1^* \\ \sigma_2^* \end{pmatrix}$

4. Return $\mathbf{e}^* = \sigma_1^* + \mathbf{R}_{M^*}\sigma_2^* \in \mathbb{Z}^{lm}$.

Analysis. Let $\mathbf{C}_{M^*} = \sum_{k=0}^{d}(-1)^{M^*[k]}\mathbf{C}_i = \sum_{k=0}^{d}(-1)^{M^*[k]}(\mathbf{A}_{\mathbf{R}^*}\mathbf{R}_k + \mathbf{h}_k\mathbf{S}_0)$. If $\mathbf{h}_{M^*} = 0 \mod q$, we have $\mathbf{C}_{M^*} = \mathbf{A}_{\mathbf{R}^*}\mathbf{R}_{M^*} \mod q$ and then $\mathbf{A}_{\mathbf{R}^*}\mathbf{e}^* = \mathbf{A}_{\mathbf{R}^*}(\sigma_1^*+\mathbf{R}_{M^*}\sigma_2^*)= [\mathbf{A}_{\mathbf{R}^*}|\mathbf{A}_{\mathbf{R}^*}\mathbf{R}_{M^*}]\begin{pmatrix} \sigma_1^* \\ \sigma_2^* \end{pmatrix} = [\mathbf{A}_{\mathbf{R}^*}|\mathbf{C}_{M^*}]\mathbf{e}^* = [\mathbf{A}_{\mathbf{R}_t}|\mathbf{C}_{M^*}]\mathbf{e}^* = 0 \mod q$. Using the similar method as in lemma 26 in [16], we can prove that $\mathbf{e}^*$ is a short non-zero vector with high probability as a solution to the given SIS instance. The probability of an abort in above simulation process is at most $1-\frac{1}{qq_E C_{q_E}^{q_E/2}}$. We claim that the view of $\mathcal{A}_3$ in the unforgeability attack is identical to its view as provided by $\mathcal{B}_3$. We also choose parameter β similar as in lemma 26,27 in [16] and the complete proof will be given in the full version of the paper.

Computational Soundness about Formal Encryption in the Presence of Secret Shares and Key Cycles*

Xinfeng Lei[1], Rui Xue[1], and Ting Yu[2]

[1] State Key Laboratory of Information Security
Institute of Software, Chinese Academy of Sciences, Beijing, China
leixinfeng@gmail.com, rxue@is.iscas.ac.cn
[2] Department of Computer Science, North Carolina State University, USA
yu@csc.ncsu.edu

Abstract. The computational soundness of formal encryption is studied extensively following the work of Abadi and Rogaway[1]. Recent work considers the scenario in which secret sharing is needed, and separately, the scenario when key cycles are present. The novel technique is the use of a co-induction definition of the adversarial knowledge. In this paper, we prove a computational soundness theorem of formal encryption in the presence of both key cycles and secret shares at the same time, which is a non-trivial extension of former approaches.

1 Introduction

There are mainly two approaches to security protocols analysis. One is based on formal models and the other is based on computational models. In the approach of formal models [2][3][4][5],

- messages are considered as formal expressions;
- the encryption operation is only an abstract function;
- security is modeled by formal formulas;
- and analysis of security is done by formal reasoning.

In the approach of computational models[6][7][8],

- messages are considered as bit-strings;
- the encryption operation of message is a concrete arithmetic;
- security is defined in terms of that a computationally bounded adversary can only attack successfully with negligible probability;
- and analysis of security is done by reduction.

Each of the approaches has its advantages and disadvantages. In general, the former is succinct but generally does not guarantee computational soundness. The

---

* This work is partially supported by NSFC grants (No. 60873260 and No. 60903210), the 863 Program (No. 2009AA01Z414), and the 973 Program (No. 2007CB311202).

S. Qing et al. (Eds.): ICICS 2011, LNCS 7043, pp. 29–41, 2011.

latter does exactly the opposite. From 1980"s, these two approaches developed along with their own directions independently. Till the beginning of this century, in their seminal work[1], Abadi and Rogaway started to bridge the gap between the two approaches, and established computational soundness for formal security analysis. Intuitively, in security analysis, computational soundness means that if two formal expressions are equivalent in formal model, their computational interpretations are indistinguishable in computational model. During the last decade, computational soundness has gained a lot of attention[1,9,10,11,12,13,14,15,16,17], and works in this area are still in full swing.

Our analysis is aimed at ensuring the computational soundness about formal encryption with the presence of secret shares and key cycles.

Secret Share. In a secret sharing scheme, a key may be separated into several secret shares, and only those who can get sufficient shares can reveal the key. Otherwise, nothing can be learned about this key. The concept of secret sharing was proposed in[18], and since then, it is used extensively in cryptography. Moreover, it can be used in other security applications. In [19], Miklau and Suciu implement access control policies in data publishing by using of cryptography(specifically, symmetric encryption and secret sharing). Using of secret sharing makes it more flexible to deploy the access control policy. What we concern about is whether a formal treatment of secret sharing keeps its computational soundness.

Key cycle. The concept of key cycles is first stated in [6], and then be noted since the work by Abadi and Rogway [1]. Informally, key cycle means that a key is encrypted by itself directly or indirectly. At the first glance, key cycles may not deserve so much attention due to few occurrences of them in a well-defined protocol. However, key cycles often happen in real world applications. For example, a backup system may store the key on disk and then encrypt the entire disk with the same key. Another example comes from the situation where a key cycle is needed 'by design"[20] in a system for non-transferable anonymous credentials. Moreover, key cycles paly an important role in solving the problem of computational soundness. In general, in a formal model, key cycles are allowed according to the definition of expressions[1] if there is no further restriction. While in a computational model, the occurrence of key cycles is often eliminated according to the standard notion of security for encryption [6]. This is the reason why key cycles gain so much attention in the research of computational soundness.

Related Work. In [1], Abadi and Rogaway give the definition of key cycles and then prove the computational soundness of security under formal setting in absence of key cycles. A natural problem is whether a formal encryption with key cycles is computationally sound. In recent years, this problem has been studied in many works[1,21,13,22,17]. In [21], Laud addresses the problem of reconciling symbolic and computational analysis in presence of key cycles by strengthening the symbolic adversary[21], i.e., weakening the symbolic encryption. Specifically, Laud uses an approach similar to that in [1] except giving adversaries the power to break the encryption with key cycles by adding some additional rules. In

[13,22], instead of using restricted or revised formal models, Adão et al. deal with key cycles by strengthening the computational notion. Specifically, Adão et al. adopt another security notion, i.e., Key-Dependent Message(KDM) security [23] in which the messages are chosen depending on the keys of the encryption scheme itself. Intuitively, different from the standard security notions(CPA or CCA), KDM security implies the security of key cycles and thus is closer to the concept of security in formal models. More and more works are focusing on constructing the KDM secure scheme[23,24,25], but most of them are given in the random-oracle model[23], or by a relaxed notion of KDM security[24], or under restricted adversaries[25]. Therefore, constructing such schemes is not an easy work. [26] shows that it is impossible to prove KDM security if the reductions in the proof of security treat both the adversary and the query function as black boxes. In this paper, we do not consider KDM security. Rather, our work is under CPA security.

In all the approaches mentioned above, when modeling the power of adversaries to obtain keys, an inductive method is used. Very recently, different from the inductive method, Micciancio [17] gives a general approach to dealing with the key cycles in which the power of the adversary to get keys is modeled by co-induction. The generalization of this approach makes it possible to deal with a larger class of cryptographic expressions, e.g., the expressions with pseudo-random keys [27]. Alternatively, in this paper, we will extend this approach to cryptographic expressions that use secret sharing schemes. Abadi and Warinschi [16] have given an approach to bridging the gap between formal and computational views in the presence of secret shares, but their approach does not consider key cycles.

Our contribution. The primary contribution of this paper is to show a stronger result over that in [16] and [17]. In particular, we define the equivalence between formal messages in the presence of both key cycles and secret shares, and then prove the computational soundness about formal encryption in this setting.

Organization. The rest of the paper is organized as follows. Section 2 presents the syntax of formal messages, patterns, and the notion of equivalence between messages. In section 3, the computational model is defined, and computational semantics of formal messages is given. Then, in section 4, the main result of this paper, theorem of computational soundness is provided and further discussion is given in section 5. Finally, we conclude in Section 6 and give the further works.

2   Formal Model

In this section we provide the basic notions for our work in a formal setting. We do this by summarizing the main definitions and results in previous papers [1,21,16,22,17] with some changes. Such changes are necessary because we take both key shares and key cycles into consideration.

2.1 Messages

In formal messages, anything is modeled by symbols. We use **Data** and **Keys** to denote the symbol sets of data, and keys respectively. Often, $d, d_1, d_2, \cdots$ range over **Data**, and $k, k_1, k_2, \cdots$ range over **Keys**. Assume a key can be divided in to several different secret shares, denoted by distinct symbols, we then define a set **Shares** as follows:

Assume a key can be divided into n secret shares, and k^j denotes the jth secret share of key k. Given $k \in$ **Keys** and $\mathbf{K} \subseteq$ **Keys**, we can define[1],

- $\mathbf{s}(k) = \{k^j \mid j \in [1, n]\}$;
- $\mathbf{s}(\mathbf{K}) = \bigcup_{k \in \mathbf{K}} \mathbf{s}(k)$;
- **Shares** $= \mathbf{s}(\mathbf{Keys})$.

For example, if **Keys** $= \{k_1, k_2, k_3\}$ and $n = 2$, by dividing each key into two secret shares, we have **Shares** $= \{k_1^1, k_1^2, k_2^1, k_2^2, k_3^1, k_3^2\}$.

The number of shares for every key n is the same. When a key is divided into n shares, we assume that, only when obtaining all the n shares will one be able to recover the key. One can learn nothing about the key with p shares where $p < n$.

Based on **Data**, **Keys** and **Shares**, we can define the set of messages **Msg** and the set of extended messages **MSG**.

$$\mathbf{Msg} ::= \mathbf{Data} \mid \mathbf{Keys} \mid \mathbf{Shares} \mid (\mathbf{Msg}, \mathbf{Msg}) \mid \{\!|\mathbf{Msg}|\!\}_{\mathbf{Keys}}$$
$$\mathbf{MSG} ::= \mathbf{Data} \cup \{\square\} \mid \mathbf{Keys} \cup \{\Diamond\} \mid \mathbf{Shares} \cup \{\Diamond^j\}$$
$$\mid (\mathbf{MSG}, \mathbf{MSG}) \mid \{\!|\mathbf{MSG}|\!\}_{\mathbf{Keys} \cup \{\Diamond\}}$$

Informally, (m_1, m_2) represents the concatenation of m_1 and m_2, and $\{\!|m|\!\}_k$ represents the encryption of m under k. $\square, \Diamond$ and $\Diamond^j$ denote the unknown data, keys and secret shares respectively.

To simplify our presentation, we will use some symbols of the first order logic in the following definition, and accept the following conventions of notations:

- $(m_1, m_2, \cdots, m_n) \triangleq (m_1, (m_2, \cdots, m_n))$;
- $\{\!|(m_1, m_2)|\!\}_k \triangleq \{\!|m_1, m_2|\!\}_k$;
- $\{\!|m|\!\}_\Diamond \triangleq \{\!|m|\!\}$.

Definition 1 (Sub-message). *Let* $m, m' \in$ **MSG**. *We say message* m' *is a sub-message of* m, *written as* $m' \preccurlyeq m$, *if one of the following holds:*

1. $m' = m$;
2. $m = (m_1, m_2) \wedge (m' \preccurlyeq m_1 \vee m' \preccurlyeq m_2)$;
3. $m = \{\!|m''|\!\}_k \wedge m' \preccurlyeq m''$.

Definition 2 (Occurrence). *Let* $x \in$ **Keys**$\cup$**Shares** *and* $m \in$ **MSG**. x *occurs in* m, *written as* $x \lessdot m$, *if one of the following holds:*

---

[1] By using $j \in [1, n]$, we mean $1 \leq j \leq n$.

1. $x = m$;
2. $m = (m_1, m_2) \wedge (x \lessdot m_1 \vee x \lessdot m_2)$;
3. $m = \{\!|m'|\!\}_k \wedge (x = k \vee x \lessdot m')$.

With Definition 2, we can define a function $\mathbf{keys} : \mathbf{MSG} \rightarrow \mathbf{Keys}$. Intuitively, $\mathbf{keys}(m)$ returns the set of keys that occur in a message or whose shares occur in this message. More formally, given $m \in \mathbf{MSG}$, we have

$$\mathbf{keys}(m) = \{k | (k \in \mathbf{Keys}) \wedge ((k \lessdot m) \vee \exists j \in [1, n].(k^j \lessdot m))\}.$$

Definition 3 (Encryption relation). *Let* $m \in \mathbf{MSG}, k_1, k_2 \in \mathbf{keys}(m)$. *We say* k_1 *encrypts* k_2 *in* m, *written as* $k_1 \sqsubset_m k_2$, *if there exists a message* m' *such that* $(\{\!|m'|\!\}_{k_1} \preccurlyeq m) \wedge (k_2 \in \mathbf{keys}(m'))$.

Definition 4 (Key cycle)

1. *The key graph of a message* m *is a directed graph* $G = (V, E)$, *in which* $V = \{k | k \in \mathbf{keys}(m)\}$ *is the set of the vertexes, and* $E = \{(k_1 k_2) | k_1 \in V \wedge k_2 \in V \wedge k_1 \sqsubset_m k_2\}$ *is the set of the edges.*
2. *We say there exists a key cycle in the message* m, *if and only if there exists a cycle in the key graph of* m.

From the definitions above, we can see that secret shares are considered in messages. Moreover, the rest of our work does not eliminate key cycles from messages. Both of them make our work different from previous ones.

2.2 Patterns

Owing to the presence of secret shares, the keys related to a message become more complicated. So, before formally defining the pattern, we need to give several functions from $\mathbf{MSG}$ to $\mathbf{Keys}$:

$$\mathbf{sbk}(m) = \{k | (k \in \mathbf{Keys}) \wedge ((k \preccurlyeq m) \vee \exists j \in [1, n].(k^j \preccurlyeq m))\}$$
$$\mathbf{rck}(m) = \{k | (k \in \mathbf{Keys}) \wedge ((k \preccurlyeq m) \vee \forall j \in [1, n].(k^j \preccurlyeq m))\}$$
$$\mathbf{psk}(m) = \mathbf{sbk}(m) \setminus \mathbf{rck}(m)$$
$$\mathbf{eok}(m) = \mathbf{keys}(m) \setminus \mathbf{sbk}(m).$$

Intuitively, "sbk" is an abbreviation for "sub-message keys", "rck" for "recoverable keys", "psk" for "partially shared keys" and "eok" for "encryption-only keys". By the definition above, we have more intuitive properties as follows:

$$(\mathbf{sbk}(m) \cup \mathbf{eok}(m) = \mathbf{keys}(m)) \wedge (\mathbf{sbk}(m) \cap \mathbf{eok}(m) = \emptyset); \tag{1}$$
$$(\mathbf{rck}(m) \cup \mathbf{psk}(m) = \mathbf{sbk}(m)) \wedge (\mathbf{rck}(m) \cap \mathbf{psk}(m) = \emptyset). \tag{2}$$

To define the pattern of a message, we need the functions of $\mathbf{p}$ and an auxiliary function $\mathbf{struct}$, which are defined in Fig. 1.

$\mathbf{struct}(d) = \square;$	$\mathbf{p}(d, \mathbf{K}) = d;$
$\mathbf{struct}(k) = \Diamond;$	$\mathbf{p}(k, \mathbf{K}) = k;$
$\mathbf{struct}(k^j) = \Diamond^j;$	$\mathbf{p}(k^j, \mathbf{K}) = k^j,$ (for $j \in \{1..n\}$);
$\mathbf{struct}((m_1, m_2)) =$	$\mathbf{p}((m_1, m_2), \mathbf{K}) = (\mathbf{p}(m_1, \mathbf{K}), \mathbf{p}(m_2, \mathbf{K}));$
$(\mathbf{struct}(m_1), \mathbf{struct}(m_2));$	$\mathbf{p}(\{\!\|m\|\!\}_k, \mathbf{K}) = \begin{cases} \{\!\|\mathbf{p}(m)\|\!\}_k & (\text{ if } k \in \mathbf{K}); \\ \{\!\|\mathbf{struct}(m)\|\!\}_k & (\text{otherwise.}). \end{cases}$
$\mathbf{struct}(\{\!\|m\|\!\}_k) = \{\!\|\mathbf{struct}(m)\|\!\}.$	

Fig. 1. Rules defining the function **p**, and auxiliary function **struct**

The function **p** and **rck** satisfy the following fundamental properties:

$$\mathbf{p}(m, \mathbf{keys}(m)) = m \tag{3}$$

$$\mathbf{p}(\mathbf{p}(m, \mathbf{K}), \mathbf{K}') = \mathbf{p}(m, \mathbf{K} \cap \mathbf{K}') \tag{4}$$

$$\mathbf{rck}(\mathbf{p}(m, \mathbf{K})) \subseteq \mathbf{rck}(m) \tag{5}$$

These three properties are similar to the properties of **p** and **r** in [17]. Moreover, about **p**, we have the following proposition:

Proposition 1. *If* $\mathbf{K}' \cap \mathbf{keys}(m) = \emptyset$, *then* $\mathbf{p}(m, \mathbf{K} \cup \mathbf{K}') = \mathbf{p}(m, \mathbf{K})$.

Intuitively, this proposition means that, given a message m and a key set $\mathbf{K}$, additional keys which are unrelated to m cannot provide additional information about m.

Definition 5 (Function $\mathcal{F}_m$). *Given a message m, a function $\mathcal{F}_m : \wp(\mathbf{Keys}) \to \wp(\mathbf{Keys})$ can be defined[2]. Precisely, given a set $\mathbf{K} \subseteq \mathbf{Keys}$, we have*

$$\mathcal{F}_m(\mathbf{K}) = \mathbf{rck}(\mathbf{p}(m, \mathbf{K})) \tag{6}$$

Intuitively, given message m and a key set $\mathbf{K}$, $\mathcal{F}_m(\mathbf{K})$ computes the set of keys which occur as the sub-message of $\mathbf{p}(m, \mathbf{K})$, or whose secret shares fully occur in $\mathbf{p}(m, \mathbf{K})$.

Proposition 2. *The function $\mathcal{F}_m : \wp(\mathbf{Keys}) \to \wp(\mathbf{Keys})$ is monotone.*

The monotonicity of the function $\mathcal{F}_m$ makes it possible to define the greatest fixpoint of $\mathcal{F}_m$: $\mathbf{FIX}(\mathcal{F}_m) = \bigcap_{i=0}^{\ell} \mathcal{F}_m^i(\mathbf{keys}(m))$, where $\ell = |\mathbf{keys}(m)|$. Obviously, by the the monotonicity of $\mathcal{F}_m$, we have $\mathbf{FIX}(\mathcal{F}_m) = \mathcal{F}_m^{\ell}(\mathbf{keys}(m))$.

Definition 6 (Patterns of messages). *The pattern of the message m, written as* $\mathbf{pattern}(m)$, *is define as:*

$$\mathbf{pattern}(m) = \mathbf{p}(m, \mathbf{FIX}(\mathcal{F}_m)) \tag{7}$$

---

[2] By using $\wp(\mathbf{Keys})$, we mean the power set of **Keys**.

2.3   Equivalence

As usual, the keys in a formal message are considered as bound names(like in spi calculus[5]). Thus, they can be renamed without effecting the essential meaning of the formal message. However, since the secret shares of keys are considered in the formal model, we must redefine the renaming.

Definition 7 (Renaming). *There are three types of renaming: K-renaming (Keys renaming), KS-renaming(Keys and shares renaming) and S-renaming (Shares only renaming). KS-renaming and S-renaming are all defined based on K-renaming.*

1. *Let $\mathbf{K} \subseteq \mathbf{Keys}$. A K-renaming on $\mathbf{K}$ is a bijection on $\mathbf{K}$, often written as $\sigma[\mathbf{K}]$ or $\theta[\mathbf{K}]$.*

2. *KS-renaming is defined by extending K-renaming. Let $\mathbf{K}, \mathbf{K}' \subseteq \mathbf{Keys}$, $\mathbf{K} \subseteq \mathbf{K}'$, and $\sigma[\mathbf{K}']$ be a K-renaming. A KS-renaming on $\mathbf{K} \cup \mathbf{s}(\mathbf{K})$, written as $\bar{\sigma}[\mathbf{K} \cup \mathbf{s}(\mathbf{K})]$, is defined as follows:*

$$\bar{\sigma}(k) = \sigma(k) \qquad (k \in \mathbf{K})$$
$$\bar{\sigma}(k^j) = \sigma(k)^j \qquad (k^j \in \mathbf{s}(\mathbf{K}))$$

3. *S-renaming is also defined based on K-renaming. Let $\mathbf{K}, \mathbf{K}' \subseteq \mathbf{Keys}$, $\mathbf{K} \subseteq \mathbf{K}'$, and $\sigma[\mathbf{K}']$ be a K-renaming. An S-renaming on $\mathbf{s}(\mathbf{K})$, written as $\hat{\sigma}[\mathbf{s}(\mathbf{K})]$, is defined as follows:*

$$\hat{\sigma}(k^j) = \sigma(k)^j \qquad (k^j \in \mathbf{s}(\mathbf{K}))$$

Recall that the secret shares of a key are different from each other. From definition 7, KS-renaming and S-renaming are also bijections.

As a conventional notation, we have

$$\sigma(\mathbf{K}) \triangleq \{k' | k \in \mathbf{K} \wedge \sigma(k) = k'\}.$$

Similar notations can be used on $\bar{\sigma}$ and $\hat{\sigma}$. When there is no confusion according to the context, we often write $\sigma[\mathbf{K}], \bar{\sigma}[\mathbf{K} \cup \mathbf{s}(\mathbf{K})]$ and $\hat{\sigma}[\mathbf{s}(\mathbf{K})]$ as σ, $\bar{\sigma}$ and $\hat{\sigma}$ respectively for short. Also, we use $m\sigma, m\bar{\sigma}$ and $m\hat{\sigma}$ to denote the applying of $\sigma, \bar{\sigma}$ and $\hat{\sigma}$ respectively to message m.

Here, KS-renaming is consistent renaming[16]. Informally speaking, consistent renaming means that, when k_i occurring in m is renamed to $k_{i'}$, the share of k_i, say k_i^j, is renamed to $k_{i'}^j$ accordingly. Obviously, S-renaming is not a consistent renaming, because the links between a key and its secret shares may be broken after applying S-renaming.

Definition 8 (Equivalence of messages). *Given $m, m' \in \mathbf{MSG}$, Message m' is said to be equivalent to m, written as $m' \cong m$, if and only if, there exists a KS-renaming $\bar{\sigma}$ based on K-renaming $\sigma[\mathbf{keys}(\mathbf{pattern}(m))]$, or, additionally an S-renaming $\hat{\theta}$ based on K-renaming $\theta[\mathbf{psk}(\mathbf{pattern}(m)\bar{\sigma})]$, such that one of the following holds:*

1. $\mathbf{pattern}(m') = \mathbf{pattern}(m)\bar{\sigma}$
2. $\mathbf{pattern}(m') = (\mathbf{pattern}(m)\bar{\sigma})\hat{\theta}$

This definition of equivalence differs from the equivalence in [16] in that the S-renaming is considered. So, for example, $(\{|k_2|\}_{k_1}, k_1^1)$ and $(\{|k_2|\}_{k_1}, k_3^1)$ are equivalent according to Definition 8, but not equivalent in [16].

3   Computational Model

In computational model, a message is just a bit-string which belongs to $\{0,1\}^*$.

Definition 9 (Computational model). *A computational model is a 4-tuple* $\mathbf{M} = (\mathbf{\Pi}, \mathbf{\Lambda}, \omega, \gamma)$, *in which*

- $\mathbf{\Pi}$ *is an encryption scheme which is composed of a tuple of algorithms* (**Gen, Enc, Dec**), *namely, the key-generation algorithms* **Gen**, *the encryption algorithm* **Enc**, *and the decryption algorithm* **Dec**. *It is required that* $\mathbf{Dec}_k(\mathbf{Enc}_k(m)) = m$.
- $\mathbf{\Lambda}$ *is a secret sharing scheme which is composed of a tuple of algorithms* (**Com, Crt**), *namely, the share creation algorithm* **Crt** *and the share combination algorithm* **Com**. *It is required that* $\mathbf{Com}(\mathbf{Crt}(k, 1^n)) = k$.
- $\omega : \mathbf{Data} \rightarrow \{0,1\}^*$ *is an interpretation function to evaluate each symbol in* **Data** *to a bit-string.*
- $\gamma : \{0,1\}^* \times \{0,1\}^* \rightarrow \{0,1\}^*$ *is a function to connect two bit-strings to a single bit-string. It can be viewed as the computational counterpart of message concatenation in formal model.*

Some strict definitions about the schemes in model $\mathbf{M}$ can be found in Appendix.

Definition 10 (Computational interpretation of messages). *Given a computational model* $\mathbf{M} = (\mathbf{\Pi}, \mathbf{\Lambda}, \omega, \gamma)$ *and a formal message* m, *we can get the computational interpretation of* m, *that is, associate a collection of distributions (i.e., ensemble) over a bit-string* $[\![m]\!]_{\mathbf{M}} = \{[\![m]\!]_{\mathbf{M}(\eta)}\}_{\eta \in \mathbb{N}}$ *to the formal message* m. *Assume* $\ell = |\mathbf{keys}(m)|$ *and the number of shares for each key is* n, *we can get* $[\![m]\!]_{\mathbf{M}}$ *by the following steps:*

1. *Initialization. Construct an* ℓ *vector* κ *to save the interpretation of keys, and an* $\ell \times n$ *array* ς *to save the interpretation of shares. Then, evaluate* $\kappa[i](1 \leq i \leq \ell)$ *and* $\varsigma[i,j](1 \leq i \leq \ell, 1 \leq j \leq n)$ *by the following procedure:*

$$for\ i\ =\ 1\ to\ \ell\ do\ \left\{ \begin{array}{l} \kappa[i] \leftarrow \mathbf{Gen}(1^n); \\ \{\varsigma[i,1], \varsigma[i,2], \cdots, \varsigma[i,n]\} \leftarrow \mathbf{Crt}(\kappa[i], 1^n). \end{array} \right\}$$

2. *Interpretation. Interpretation of the message* m *can be done recursively as follows:*
   - $[\![d]\!]_{\mathbf{M}} = \omega(d)$, *for* $d \in \mathbf{Data}$.
   - $[\![k_i]\!]_{\mathbf{M}} = \kappa[i]$, *for* $k_i \in \mathbf{Keys}$ *and* $1 \leq i \leq \ell$.
   - $[\![k_i^j]\!]_{\mathbf{M}} = \varsigma[i,j]$, *for* $k_i^j \in \mathbf{Shares}$ *and* $1 \leq j \leq n$.
   - $[\![(m_1, m_2)]\!]_{\mathbf{M}} = \gamma([\![m_1]\!]_{\mathbf{M}}, [\![m_2]\!]_{\mathbf{M}})$.
   - $[\![\{|m|\}_{k_i}]\!]_{\mathbf{M}} = \mathbf{Enc}_{[\![k_i]\!]_{\mathbf{M}}}[\![m]\!]_{\mathbf{M}}$.
   - $[\![\mathbf{struct}(m)]\!]_{\mathbf{M}} = 0^{|[\![m]\!]_{\mathbf{M}}|}$, *where* $|[\![m]\!]_{\mathbf{M}}|$ *denotes the length of* $[\![m]\!]_{\mathbf{M}}$.

4   Computational Soundness

Intuitively, Computational soundness means that, if two messages are equivalent in the formal model, their interpretation in computational model will be indistinguishable. To prove the computational soundness in this paper, we need some lemmas.

Lemma 1. *Let* $m \in \mathbf{MSG}$, $\bar{\sigma}$ *be a KS-renaming based on K-renaming* $\sigma[keys(m)]$. *Given a computational model* $\mathbf{M}$, *it holds that* $[\![m]\!]_{\mathbf{M}} \approx [\![m\bar{\sigma}]\!]_{\mathbf{M}}$.

Lemma 2. *Let* $m \in \mathbf{MSG}$, $\hat{\theta}$ *be an S-renaming based on K-renaming* $\theta[\mathbf{psk}(m)]$. *Given a computational model* $\mathbf{M} = (\mathbf{\Pi}, \mathbf{\Lambda}, \omega, \gamma)$, *if* $\mathbf{\Pi}$ *is a* $\mathbf{CPA}$ *secure encryption scheme and* $\mathbf{\Lambda}$ *is a secure secret sharing scheme, then, it holds that* $[\![m]\!]_{\mathbf{M}} \approx [\![m\hat{\theta}]\!]_{\mathbf{M}}$.

Lemma 3. *Let* $m \in \mathbf{MSG}$. *Given a K-renaming* $\theta[\mathbf{psk}(m)]$, *and thus an S-renaming* $\hat{\theta}[\mathbf{s}(\mathbf{psk}(m))]$, *if* $\theta(\mathbf{psk}(m)) \cap \mathbf{keys}(m) = \emptyset$, *then*

$$[\![\mathbf{p}(m\hat{\theta}, \mathbf{sbk}(m\hat{\theta}))]\!]_{\mathbf{M}} \approx [\![\mathbf{p}(m, \mathbf{rck}(m))]\!]_{\mathbf{M}}$$

Lemma 4. *Given a formal message* m, *and a computational model* $\mathbf{M} = (\mathbf{\Pi}, \mathbf{\Lambda}, \omega, \gamma)$, *if* $\mathbf{\Pi}$ *is a* $\mathbf{CPA}$ *secure encryption scheme and* $\mathbf{\Lambda}$ *is a secure secret sharing scheme, it holds that* $[\![m]\!]_{\mathbf{M}} \approx [\![\mathbf{p}(m, \mathbf{rck}(m))]\!]_{\mathbf{M}}$.

Lemma 5. *Given a formal message* m, *and a computational model* $\mathbf{M} = (\mathbf{\Pi}, \mathbf{\Lambda}, \omega, \gamma)$, *if* $\mathbf{\Pi}$ *is a* $\mathbf{CPA}$ *secure encryption scheme and* $\mathbf{\Lambda}$ *is a secure secret sharing scheme, then it holds that* $[\![m]\!]_{\mathbf{M}} \approx [\![\mathbf{pattern}(m)]\!]_{\mathbf{M}}$.

Lemma 1 holds because the distribution associated with a message is decided only by their meaning, not by the symbols used in the message. Lemma 2 can be proved by reduction based on the security of $\mathbf{\Lambda}$. Lemma 3 can be got by Proposition 1 and Lemma 2. It plays an important role in reconciling the gap between Lemma 2 and Lemma 4. Then, with the help of Lemma 3, Lemma 4 can be proved by reduction based on the $\mathbf{CPA}$ security of $\mathbf{\Pi}$. Lemma 5 can be easily got by Proposition 2 and Lemma 4 according to hybrid argument. Due to space limitation, we omit the detailed proofs of the lemmas which can be found in the full version of this paper[28].

Theorem 1. *Given two formal messages* m, m', *from which key cycles are not eliminated, and a computational model* $\mathbf{M} = (\mathbf{\Pi}, \mathbf{\Lambda}, \omega, \gamma)$, *in which* $\mathbf{\Pi}$ *is an* $\mathbf{CPA}$ *secure encryption scheme and* $\mathbf{\Lambda}$ *is a secure secret sharing scheme, if* $m \cong m'$, *then,* $[\![m]\!]_{\mathbf{M}} \approx [\![m']\!]_{\mathbf{M}}$.

Proof. Since $m \cong m'$, from Definition 8, we know that there exists a KS-renaming $\bar{\sigma}$ based on K-renaming $\sigma[\mathbf{keys}(m)]$, or, additionally an S-renaming $\hat{\theta}$ based on K-renaming $\theta[\mathbf{psk}(m\bar{\sigma})]$, such that $\mathbf{pattern}(m) = \mathbf{pattern}(m')\bar{\sigma}$ or $\mathbf{pattern}(m) = (\mathbf{pattern}(m')\bar{\sigma})\hat{\theta}$, both of which imply $[\![\mathbf{pattern}(m)]\!]_{\mathbf{M}} \approx [\![\mathbf{pattern}(m')]\!]_{\mathbf{M}}$ by using Lemma 1 and Lemma 2. Moreover, from Lemma 5, we have $[\![m]\!]_{\mathbf{M}} \approx [\![\mathbf{pattern}(m)]\!]_{\mathbf{M}}$ and $[\![m']\!]_{\mathbf{M}} \approx [\![\mathbf{pattern}(m')]\!]_{\mathbf{M}}$. Therefore, by the transitivity of indistinguishability, we get $[\![m]\!]_{\mathbf{M}} \approx [\![m']\!]_{\mathbf{M}}$.

This completes our proof.

5   Further Discussion

Since the detailed proofs of the lemmas are omitted, we will scratch the main idea in our proofs, and show that the extension in this paper is non-trivial.

Informally speaking, to prove the indistinguishability of two messages in the computational model, we can firstly assume they can be distinguished by a distinguisher, and then construct an adversary based on this distinguisher to break the security of the encryption scheme or secret sharing scheme. In such construction, the adversary is often required to evaluate a message with the help of encryption oracles. When considering key cycles and secret shares, it is infeasible for the adversary to evaluate a message by querying encryption oracle like in [16], because the adversary cannot invent a key and submit it to the oracle for encryption under itself. Still, the approach in [17] can only solve part of the problem. That is, the adversary is given the power to get the cycled keys and then completes the encryption without querying the encryption oracle. Both of them say nothing about how to evaluate secret shares in the presence of key cycle. In our setting, the encryption under a key to itself and the encryption under a key to parts of its secret shares are both defined as key cycles. The former is considered insecure, while the latter is considered secure, which means that the adversary cannot get the encryption key. Then, to evaluate the message in the latter case, the adversary can neither query the encryption oracle, nor complete such encryption by himself. This problem is solved in this paper with the help of S-renaming. That is, the shares of a partially shared key can be renamed to the shares of a newly generated key without changing their meaning in sense of indistinguishability.

6   Conclusion

We show the computational soundness of formal encryption in the presence of both secret shares and key cycles. Our work is an extension to that in [16] and [17], but the result is non-trivial. For example, when both keys and shares occur in a key cycle, we must reconsider what keys can be recovered from it and what cannot. Moreover, by using CPA secure encryption scheme in a computational model, we must deal with the conflict between the definition of CPA and key cycles, especially when secret shares are involved.

For future researches, one can extend this work to the setting of asymmetric cryptography. Another direction is to prove the computational soundness in the presence of active adversaries.

References

1. Abadi, M., Rogaway, P.: Reconciling Two Views of Cryptography (the Computational Soundness of Formal Encryption). In: Watanabe, O., Hagiya, M., Ito, T., van Leeuwen, J., Mosses, P.D. (eds.) TCS 2000. LNCS, vol. 1872, pp. 3–22. Springer, Heidelberg (2000)

2. Dolev, D., Yao, A.C.: On the security of public-key protocols. IEEE Transactions on Information Theory 30(2), 198–208 (1983)
3. Burrows, M., Abadi, M., Needham, R.: A logic of authentication. ACM Transactions on Computer Systems 8(1), 18–36 (1990)
4. Paulson, L.C.: The inductive approach to verifying cryptographic protocols. Journal of Computer Security 6, 85–128 (1998)
5. Abadi, M., Gordon, A.D.: A calculus for cryptographic protocols: The spi calculus. Information and Computation 148(1), 1–70 (1999)
6. Goldwasser, S., Micali, S.: Probabilistic encryption. JCSS 28(2), 270–299 (1984)
7. Yao, A.C.: Theory and application of trapdoor functions. In: Proc. 23rd IEEE Symp. on Foundations of Comp. Science, Chicago, pp. 80–91 (1982)
8. Bellare, M., Rogaway, P.: Entity Authentication and Key Distribution. In: Stinson, D.R. (ed.) CRYPTO 1993. LNCS, vol. 773, pp. 232–249. Springer, Heidelberg (1994)
9. Canetti, R.: Universally composable security: A new paradigm for cryptographic protocols. In: 42th IEEE Symposium on Foundations of Computers Science, pp. 136–145 (2001)
10. Backes, M., Pfitzmann, B., Waidner, M.: A universally composable cryptographic library. Report 2003/015, Cryptology ePrint Archive (January 2003)
11. Herzog, J.: Computational soundness for standard assumptions of formal cryptography. PhD thesis, Massachusetts Institute of Technology (2004)
12. Micciancio, D., Warinschi, B.: Soundness of Formal Encryption in the Presence of Active Adversaries. In: Naor, M. (ed.) TCC 2004. LNCS, vol. 2951, pp. 133–151. Springer, Heidelberg (2004)
13. Adão, P., Bana, G., Herzog, J., Scedrov, A.: Soundness of Formal Encryption in the Presence of Key-cycles. In: di Vimercati, S.D.C., Syverson, P.F., Gollmann, D. (eds.) ESORICS 2005. LNCS, vol. 3679, pp. 374–396. Springer, Heidelberg (2005)
14. Laud, P.: Symmetric encryption in automatic analyses for confidentiality against active adversaries. In: IEEE Symposium on Security and Privacy, pp. 71–85. IEEE Computer Society (2004)
15. Blanchet, B., Pointcheval, D.: Automated Security Proofs with Sequences of Games. In: Dwork, C. (ed.) CRYPTO 2006. LNCS, vol. 4117, pp. 537–554. Springer, Heidelberg (2006)
16. Abadi, M., Warinschi, B.: Security analysis of cryptographically controlled access to XML documents. Journal of the ACM 55(2), 6:1–6:29 (2008)
17. Micciancio, D.: Computational Soundness, Co-induction, and Encryption Cycles. In: Gilbert, H. (ed.) EUROCRYPT 2010. LNCS, vol. 6110, pp. 362–380. Springer, Heidelberg (2010)
18. Shamir, A.: How to share a secret. Communications of the ACM 22, 612–613 (1979)
19. Miklau, G., Suciu, D.: Controlling access to published data using cryptography. In: Freytag, J.C., Lockemann, P.C., Abiteboul, S., Carey, M.J., Selinger, P.G., Heuer, A. (eds.) VLDB 2003: Proceedings of 29th International Conference on Very Large Data Bases, Berlin, Germany, Los Altos, CA 94022, USA, September 9–12, pp. 898–909. Morgan Kaufmann Publishers (2003)
20. Camenisch, J., Lysyanskaya, A.: An Efficient System for Non-transferable Anonymous Credentials with Optional Anonymity Revocation. In: Pfitzmann, B. (ed.) EUROCRYPT 2001. LNCS, vol. 2045, pp. 93–117. Springer, Heidelberg (2001)
21. Laud, P.: Encryption cycles and two views of cryptography. In: Proceedings of the 7th Nordic Workshop on Secure IT Systems – NORDSEC 2002, Karlstad, Sweden, pp. 85–100 (2002)

22. Adão, P., Bana, G., Herzog, J., Scedrov, A.: Soundness and completeness of formal encryption: The cases of key cycles and partial information leakage. Journal of Computer Security 17(5), 737–797 (2009)

23. Black, J., Rogaway, P., Shrimpton, T.: Encryption-scheme Security in the Presence of Key-dependent Messages. In: Nyberg, K., Heys, H.M. (eds.) SAC 2002. LNCS, vol. 2595, pp. 62–75. Springer, Heidelberg (2003)

24. Hofheinz, D., Unruh, D.: Towards Key-dependent Message Security in the Standard Model. In: Smart, N.P. (ed.) EUROCRYPT 2008. LNCS, vol. 4965, pp. 108–126. Springer, Heidelberg (2008)

25. Boneh, D., Halevi, S., Hamburg, M., Ostrovsky, R.: Circular-secure Encryption from Decision Diffie-hellman. In: Wagner, D. (ed.) CRYPTO 2008. LNCS, vol. 5157, pp. 108–125. Springer, Heidelberg (2008)

26. Haitner, I., Holenstein, T.: On the (Im)possibility of Key Dependent Encryption. In: Reingold, O. (ed.) TCC 2009. LNCS, vol. 5444, pp. 202–219. Springer, Heidelberg (2009)

27. Micciancio, D.: Pseudo-randomness and partial information in symbolic security analysis. Cryptology ePrint Archive, Report 2009/249 (2009),
http://eprint.iacr.org/

28. Lei, X., Xue, R., Yu, T.: Computational soundness about formal encryption in the presence of secret shares and key cycles. Cryptology ePrint Archive, Report 2010/467 (2010), http://eprint.iacr.org

A Some Definitions

We briefly recall some definitions used in this paper. The detailed definitions can be found in many literatures about modern cryptography.

Definition 11 (Indistinguishability). *Let $D = \{D_\eta\}_{\eta\in\mathbb{N}}$ be an ensemble, i.e., a collection of distributions over strings. We say two ensembles D and D' are indistinguishable, written as $D \approx D'$, if for every probabilistic polynomial-time adversary $\mathcal{A}$, there exists a negligible function* **negl***, such that*

$$\mathbf{Pr}[x \leftarrow D_\eta : \mathcal{A}(1^\eta, x) = 1] - \mathbf{Pr}[x \leftarrow D'_\eta : \mathcal{A}(1^\eta, x) = 1] = \mathbf{negl}(\eta)$$

where $x \leftarrow D_\eta$ means that x is sampled from the distribution D_η.

A typical property of indistinguishability is that it is transitive [21], i.e.,

$$\text{if } D \approx D' \text{ and } D' \approx D'', \text{ then } D \approx D''$$

Definition 12 (Private-key encryption scheme). *A private-key encryption scheme is a tuple of algorithms* $\Pi = (\mathbf{Gen}, \mathbf{Enc}, \mathbf{Dec})$ *such that:*

1. *The key-generation algorithm* **Gen** *takes as input the security parameter 1^η and outputs a key k. This process can be written as $k \leftarrow \mathbf{Gen}(1^\eta)$.*

2. *The encryption algorithm* **Enc** *takes as input a key k and a message $m \in \{0,1\}^*$, and outputs a ciphertext c. This process can be written as $c \leftarrow \mathbf{Enc}_k(m)$.*

3. *The decryption algorithm* **Dec** *takes as input a key k and a ciphertext c, and outputs a message m. This process is often written as $m := \mathbf{Dec}_k(c)$.*

It is required that $\mathbf{Dec}_k(\mathbf{Enc}_k(m)) = m$.

We will use a standard notion of security for encryption scheme: indistinguishability against chosen plaintext attacks(CPA).

Definition 13 (CPA security). *For any probabilistic polynomial time adversaries* $\mathcal{A}$ *and polynomial* **poly***, let* $\Pi = (\mathbf{Gen}, \mathbf{Enc}, \mathbf{Dec})$ *be an encryption scheme,* $n = \mathbf{poly}(\eta)$, $k_1, \cdots, k_n$ *be the keys generated by* **Gen***,* $O_b(i, m)$ *be an encryption oracle that outputs* $\mathbf{Enc}_{k_i}(m)$ *if* $b = 1$, *or* $\mathbf{Enc}_{k_i}(0^{|m|})$ *if* $b = 0$. *The encryption scheme* Π *is indistinguishable under chosen plaintext attack(or is* **CPA***-secure) if there exists a negligible function* **negl** *such that*

$$\mathbf{Pr}[\mathcal{A}^{O_1}(1^\eta) = 1] - \mathbf{Pr}[\mathcal{A}^{O_0}(1^\eta) = 1] = \mathbf{negl}(\eta)$$

This definition is equivalent to the definition of **IND-CPA** in which only one encryption oracle is given[17].

Definition 14 (Secret sharing scheme). *An n-out-of-n secret sharing scheme for sharing keys of an encryption scheme* Π *is a tuple of algorithms* $\Lambda = (\mathbf{Crt}, \mathbf{Com})$ *such that:*

1. *The share creation algorithm* **Crt** *takes as input a key* k *and the security parameter* 1^η *and outputs* n *shares of* $k : k^1, k^2, \cdots, k^n$. *This process can be written as* $\{k^1, k^2, \cdots, k^n\} \leftarrow \mathbf{Crt}(k, 1^\eta)$.
2. *The share combination algorithm* **Com** *takes as input* n *shares* $k^1, k^2, \cdots, k^n$ *and outputs a key* k. *This process can be written as* $k := \mathbf{Com}(k^1, k^2, \cdots, k^n)$.

It is required that $\mathbf{Com}(\mathbf{Crt}(k, 1^\eta)) = k$.

Definition 15 (Security of secret sharing). *For any probabilistic polynomial time adversaries* $\mathcal{A}$ *and polynomial* **poly***, let* $\Pi = (\mathbf{Gen}, \mathbf{Enc}, \mathbf{Dec})$ *be an encryption scheme,* $\Lambda = (\mathbf{Crt}, \mathbf{Com})$ *be a secret sharing scheme,* $n = \mathbf{poly}(\eta)$, $\mathbf{sh}(k)$ *be the set of* n *secret shares of key* k *generated by* **Crt***, and* $\mathbf{sh}(k)|_S$ *be the restriction of* $\mathbf{sh}(k)$ *to the secret shares whose indexes are in* $S \subseteq \{1, \cdots, n\}$. *The secret sharing scheme* Λ *is secure if for any* $S \subset \{1, \cdots, n\}$(this implies *that* $S \neq \{1, \cdots, n\}$), *there exists a negligible function* **negl** *such that*

$$\mathbf{Pr}\left[k_0, k_1 \leftarrow \mathbf{Gen}(1^\eta), \mathbf{sh}(k_0) \leftarrow \mathbf{Crt}(k_0, 1^\eta) : \mathcal{A}(k_0, k_1, \mathbf{sh}(k_0)|_S) = 1\right] -$$
$$\mathbf{Pr}\left[k_0, k_1 \leftarrow \mathbf{Gen}(1^\eta), \mathbf{sh}(k_1) \leftarrow \mathbf{Crt}(k_1, 1^\eta) : \mathcal{A}(k_0, k_1, \mathbf{sh}(k_1)|_S) = 1\right]$$
$$= \mathbf{negl}(\eta)$$

A Variant of Boyen-Waters Anonymous IBE Scheme*

Song Luo[1,3,4], Qingni Shen[2,**], Yongming Jin[3,4],
Yu Chen[5], Zhong Chen[2,3,4], and Sihan Qing[2,6]

[1] College of Computer Science and Engineering,
Chongqing University of Technology, China
[2] School of Software and Microelectronics & MoE Key Lab of Network and Software
Assurance, Peking University, Beijing, China
[3] Institute of Software, School of Electronics Engineering and Computer Science,
Peking University
[4] Key Laboratory of High Confidence Software Technologies (Peking University),
Ministry of Education
[5] Institute of Information Engineering, Chinese Academy of Sciences, Beijing, China
[6] Institute of Software, Chinese Academy of Sciences, Beijing, China
{luosong,shenqn,jinym,chenyu,chen}@infosec.pku.edu.cn,
qsihan@ercist.iscas.ac.cn

Abstract. An identity-based encryption (IBE) scheme is called anonymous if the ciphertext leaks no information about the recipient's identity. In this paper, we present a novel anonymous identity-based encryption scheme. Our scheme comes from the analysis of Boyen-Waters anonymous IBE Scheme in which we find a method to construct anonymous IBE schemes. We show that Boyen-Waters anonymous IBE scheme can be transformed from BB_1-IBE scheme. Our scheme is also transformed from BB_1-IBE scheme and can be seemed as a variant of Boyen-Waters anonymous IBE scheme. The security proof shows the transformed scheme has the same semantic security as the original scheme and has anonymous security. We prove anonymity under the Decision Linear assumption.

Keywords: Identity-Based Encryption, Anonymity, Transformation.

1   Introduction

The notion of Identity-Based encryption (IBE) was first introduced by Shamir [25] to simplify the public-key infrastructure in public key encryption. Users can use arbitrary strings such as e-mail addresses, IP addresses or phone numbers to form public keys directly. All private keys are generated by private key generator (PKG). Anyone can encrypt messages using the identity, and only the owner of the corresponding secret key can decrypt the messages. But a concrete construction of IBE was not given by Shamir until Boneh and Franklin [8] presented

---

* Supported by National Natural Science Foundation of China (No.60873238, 61073156, 60970135, 60821003).
** Corresponding author.

S. Qing et al. (Eds.): ICICS 2011, LNCS 7043, pp. 42–56, 2011.

the first practical IBE scheme using efficiently computable bilinear maps. At the same year, Cocks proposed another but less efficient IBE scheme using quadratic residues [16].

Hierarchical identity-based encryption (HIBE) [21] is a generalization of IBE that mirrors an organizational hierarchy. In HIBE systems, a parent identity of the hierarchy tree can issue secret keys to its child identities, but cannot decrypt messages intended for other identities. The first HIBE scheme was proposed by Gentry and Silverberg [20] which can be seemed as an extension of Boneh-Franklin IBE scheme. Their scheme was proved to be secure in the random oracle model. Up to now, many new secure IBE or HIBE schemes are proposed without random oracles [12, 3, 4, 5, 10, 18, 15, 14, 28, 24, 19, 22, 13].

Recently, people found the anonymity of IBE and HIBE can help to construct Public Key Encryption with Keyword Search (PEKS) schemes [7,2,9,26]. Roughly speaking, an IBE or HIBE is said to be *recipient anonymous* or simply *anonymous* if the ciphertext leaks no information about the recipient's identity. Generally speaking, for pairing-based IBE schemes, we can use some equation to check whether one identity is the target identity. For example, let us see an instantiation of BB_1-IBE scheme. Let $C = M \cdot e(g_1, g_2)^s, C_1 = g^s, C_2 = (g_1^{ID} h)^s$ where s is the random integer chosen by the encryptor and g, g_1, h come from the public parameter. For such an instantiation C, C_1, C_2, we can easily construct $h_1 = g_1^{ID'} h$ and $h_2 = g^{-1}$ and check whether $e(C_1, h_1)e(C_2, h_2) = 1$, where $e : \mathbb{G} \times \hat{\mathbb{G}} \to \mathbb{G}_T$ denotes the bilinear map (or called "pairing") used in the scheme. If yes, then the target identity is ID'.

Generally but roughly speaking, if an IBE or HIBE scheme is *not* anonymous, supposing that $C_1, \cdots, C_k$ be components of a ciphertext of such a scheme, we can construct elements $h_1, \cdots, h_k$ from the public parameters and some identity ID to check whether $e(C_1, h_1) \cdots e(C_k, h_k) = 1$. If the equation is true, the target identity is ID. It is hard to construct anonymous IBE schemes, even more difficult for anonymous HIBE schemes. The difficulty or the feasibility of equation check roots in the bilinearity of bilinear maps, i.e., $\forall u \in \mathbb{G}, v \in \mathbb{G}_T$ and $\forall a, b \in \mathbb{Z}$, we have $e(u^a, v^b) = e(u^b, v^a)$. This is the key point why we can test whether some previous IBE or HIBE schemes are anonymous.

1.1 Our Contribution

We present a novel anonymous IBE scheme from the analysis of Boyen-Waters anonymous IBE Scheme. We find that in an IBE scheme, if the target identity in the original IBE scheme is *only* judged by the equation $e(C_1, h_1) \cdots e(C_k, h_k) = 1$ where $C_1, \cdots, C_k$ come from ciphertext and $h_1, \cdots, h_k$ are constructed from the public parameters and some identity. Then we can use the linear splitting technique in [10, 26] to make it hard to distinguish the identity from the ciphertext. Simply speaking, we divide nearly every component of the ciphertext C_i into four blind pieces $C_{i,1}, C_{i,2}, C_{i,3}, C_{i,4}$ which makes it hard to construct corresponding elements for equation test.

Using the proposed method, we show that Boyen-Waters anonymous IBE scheme [10] can be transformed from BB_1-IBE scheme. Our scheme is also transformed from BB_1-IBE scheme and can be considered as a variant of Boyen-Waters anonymous IBE scheme. The security proof shows the transformed scheme has the same semantic security as the original scheme and has anonymous security. And we prove anonymity under the Decision Linear assumption.

1.2   Related Works

Anonymous IBE was first noticed by Boneh et al. [7] and later formalized by Abdalla et al. [2, 1]. While there are several approaches to constructing an IBE scheme using bilinear maps, most constructions in the standard model are not recipient anonymous [12, 3, 4, 27]. BF-IBE [8] is intrinsically anonymous, but its HIBE version [20] is not anonymous. Gentry [18] proposed a concrete construction of anonymous IBE in the standard model and Boyen and Waters (BW-HIBE) [10] also proposed another anonymous IBE scheme and an anonymous HIBE scheme. Gentry's version is fully secure under a complicated and dynamic assumption and Boyen-Waters' constructions are selectively secure under the Decision BDH and the Decision Linear assumptions.

Seo et al. [24] proposed the first constant size ciphertext anonymous HIBE scheme in composite order groups. An extension of anonymous IBE, named committed blind anonymous IBE, was proposed by Camenisch et al. [11] in which a user can request the decryption key for a given identity without the key generation entity learning the identity. Recently, Caro et al. [13], Seo and Cheon [23] independently presented a new fully secure anonymous HIBE scheme with short ciphertexts in composite order groups. All of these schemes were proposed in the standard model without random oracles. Ducas [17] shows that if asymmetric bilinear maps are used in previous IBE and HIBE schemes with minor modification, anonymity can also be achieved.

1.3   Organization

The paper is organized as follows. We give necessary background information and definitions of security in Section 2. We first review Boyen-Waters anonymous IBE scheme and give an analysis in Section 3. Next we get a variant of Boyen-Waters anonymous IBE scheme in Section 4 and discuss some extensions in Section 5. Finally, we conclude the paper with Section 6.

2   Preliminaries

In this section, we briefly summarize the bilinear maps, and review the Decision Linear (D-Linear) assumption. Then we describe the concepts of IBE and its security models.

2.1   Bilinear Maps

Definition 1. *Let* $\mathbb{G}$, $\mathbb{G}_1$ *be two cyclic multiplicative groups with prime order* p. *Let* g *be be a generator of* $\mathbb{G}$ *and* $e : \mathbb{G} \times \mathbb{G} \to \mathbb{G}_1$ *be a bilinear map with the following properties:*

1. *Bilinearity: $\forall u, v \in \mathbb{G}$ and $\forall a, b \in \mathbb{Z}$, we have $e(u^a, v^b) = e(u, v)^{ab}$.*

2. *Non-degeneracy: The map does not send all pairs in $\mathbb{G} \times \mathbb{G}$ to the identity in $\mathbb{G}_1$. Observe that since $\mathbb{G}, \mathbb{G}_1$ are groups of prime order this implies that if g is a generator of $\mathbb{G}$ then $e(g, g)$ is a generator of $\mathbb{G}_1$.*

We say that $\mathbb{G}$ is a bilinear group if the group operation in $\mathbb{G}$ and the bilinear map $e : \mathbb{G} \times \mathbb{G} \to \mathbb{G}_1$ are both efficiently computable.

We assume that there is an efficient algorithm $\mathcal{G}$ for generating bilinear groups. The algorithm $\mathcal{G}$, on input a security parameter λ, outputs a tuple $G = [p, \mathbb{G}, \mathbb{G}_1, g \in \mathbb{G}, e]$ where g is a generator and $\log(p) = \Theta(\lambda)$.

2.2   Complexity Assumption

The Decision Linear (D-Linear) assumption was first proposed in [6] by Boneh, Boyen, and Shacham for group signatures. In anonymous IBE schemes, the D-Linear assumption is always used to prove anonymity.

Definition 2. *Let $c_1, c_2 \in \mathbb{Z}_p^*$ be chosen at random and $g, f, \nu \in \mathbb{G}$ be random generators. Let Z be a random element in $\mathbb{G}$. We define the advantage of an algorithm $\mathcal{A}$ in breaking the D-Linear assumption to be*

$$\left| \Pr[\mathcal{A}(g, f, \nu, g^{c_1}, f^{c_2}, \nu^{c_1+c_2}) = 1] - \Pr[\mathcal{A}(g, f, \nu, g^{c_1}, f^{c_2}, Z) = 1] \right|.$$

We say that the D-Linear assumption holds if no probabilistic polynomial-time algorithm has a non-negligible advantage in breaking the D-Linear assumption.

2.3   Algorithms

An IBE scheme consists of the following five algorithms: **Setup, KeyGen, Encrypt**, and **Decrypt**.

Setup(1^λ). This algorithm takes as input the security parameter λ, outputs a public key PK and a master secret key MK. The public key implies also a key space $\mathcal{K}(\text{PK})$ and an identity space $\mathcal{ID}(\text{PK})$.

KeyGen(MK, ID). This algorithm takes as input the master secret key MK and an identity $\text{ID} \in \mathcal{ID}(\text{PK})^{\le \ell}$ and outputs a secret key SK_{ID} associated with ID.

Encrypt$(\text{PK}, M, \text{ID})$. This algorithm takes as input the public key PK, a message M, and an identity ID, and outputs a ciphertext CT.

Decrypt$(\text{CT}, \text{SK}_{\text{ID}})$. This algorithm takes as input the ciphertext CT and a secret key SK_{ID}. If the ciphertext is an encryption to ID, then the algorithm outputs the encrypted message M.

2.4   Security Models

The chosen-plaintext security (semantic security) and anonymity of an IBE scheme are defined according to the following IND-ID-CPA game and ANON-ID-CPA game, respectively.

IND-ID-CPA Game

Setup. The challenger $\mathcal{C}$ runs the **Setup** algorithm and gives PK to the adversary $\mathcal{A}$.

Phase 1. The adversary $\mathcal{A}$ submits an identity ID. The challenger creates a secret key $\mathrm{SK_{ID}}$ for that identity and gives it to the adversary.

Challenge. $\mathcal{A}$ submits a challenge identity ID^* and two equal length messages M_0, M_1 to $\mathcal{B}$ with the restriction that each identity ID given out in the key phase must not be ID^*. Then $\mathcal{C}$ flips a random coin μ and passes the ciphertext $\mathrm{CT}^* = \textbf{Encrypt}(\mathrm{PK}, M_\mu, \mathrm{ID}^*)$ to $\mathcal{A}$.

Phase 2. Phase 1 is repeated with the restriction that any queried identity vector ID is not ID^*.

Guess. $\mathcal{A}$ outputs its guess μ' of μ.

The advantage of $\mathcal{A}$ in this game is defined as $Adv_\mathcal{A} = |\Pr[\mu' = \mu] - \frac{1}{2}|$.

Definition 3. *We say that an IBE scheme is* IND-ID-CPA *secure, if no probabilistic polynomial time adversary $\mathcal{A}$ has a non-negligible advantage in winning the* IND-ID-CPA *game.*

ANON-ID-CPA Game

Setup. The challenger $\mathcal{C}$ runs the **Setup** algorithm and gives PK to the adversary $\mathcal{A}$.

Phase 1. The adversary $\mathcal{A}$ submits an identity ID. The challenger creates a secret key $\mathrm{SK_{ID}}$ for that identity and gives it to the adversary.

Challenge. $\mathcal{A}$ submits two challenge identity vectors $\mathrm{ID}_0^*, \mathrm{ID}_1^*$ and a message M to $\mathcal{B}$ with the restriction that each identity ID given out in the key phase must not be ID_0^* or ID_1^*. Then $\mathcal{C}$ flips a random coin μ and passes the ciphertext $\mathrm{CT}^* = \textbf{Encrypt}(\mathrm{PK}, M, \mathrm{ID}_\mu^*)$ to $\mathcal{A}$.

Phase 2. Phase 1 is repeated with the restriction that any queried identity ID is not ID_0^* or ID_1^*.

Guess. $\mathcal{A}$ outputs its guess μ' of μ.

The advantage of $\mathcal{A}$ in this game is defined as $Adv_\mathcal{A} = |\Pr[\mu' = \mu] - \frac{1}{2}|$.

Definition 4. *We say that an IBE scheme is* ANON-ID-CPA *secure, if no probabilistic polynomial time adversary $\mathcal{A}$ has a non-negligible advantage in winning the* ANON-ID-CPA *game.*

Some schemes such as [10, 24] use weaker notions called IND-sID-CPA secure and ANON-sID-CPA secure, which are against selective identity. In the selective identity models, the adversary submits the target identity ID^* before public parameters are generated.

3 BW-AIBE Review and Analysis

3.1 Scheme Description

Setup(1^λ). Given the security parameter λ, the setup algorithm first gets $(p, \mathbb{G}, \mathbb{G}_T, g, e) \leftarrow \mathcal{G}(\lambda)$. Next it chooses another two random group elements $g_0, g_1 \in \mathbb{G}$ and five random integers $\omega, t_1, t_2, t_3, t_4 \in \mathbb{Z}_p$. Then the setup algorithm sets $\Omega = e(g, g)^{t_1 t_2 \omega}, v_1 = g^{t_1}, v_2 = g^{t_2}, v_3 = g^{t_3}, v_4 = g^{t_4}$. The public key PK is published as

$$\text{PK} = (\Omega, g, g_0, g_1, v_1, v_2, v_3, v_4),$$

and the master key MK is

$$\text{MK} = (\omega, t_1, t_2, t_3, t_4).$$

KeyGen(MK, ID). To generate the secret key SK_{ID} for an identity $\text{ID} \in \mathbb{Z}_p$, the key extract algorithm chooses random $r_1, r_2 \in \mathbb{Z}_p$ and outputs SK_{ID} as

$$\text{SK}_{\text{ID}} = \left(\begin{matrix} g^{r_1 t_1 t_2 + r_2 t_3 t_4}, g^{-\omega t_2}(g_0 g_1^{\text{ID}})^{-r_1 t_2}, g^{-\omega t_1}(g_0 g_1^{\text{ID}})^{-r_1 t_1}, \\ (g_0 g_1^{\text{ID}})^{-r_2 t_4}, (g_0 g_1^{\text{ID}})^{-r_2 t_3} \end{matrix} \right).$$

Encrypt(PK, ID, M). To encrypt a message $M \in \mathbb{G}_T$ for an identity ID, the algorithm chooses random integers $s, s_1, s_2 \in \mathbb{Z}_p$ and outputs the ciphertext CT as

$$\text{CT} = (M\Omega^s, (g_0 g_1^{\text{ID}})^s, v_1^{s-s_1}, v_2^{s_1}, v_3^{s-s_2}, v_4^{s_2}).$$

Decrypt(SK_{ID}, CT). To decrypt a ciphertext $\text{CT} = (C, C_1, C_2, C_3, C_4, C_5)$ for an identity ID, using the corresponding secret key $\text{SK}_{\text{ID}} = (d_1, d_2, d_3, d_4, d_5)$, outputs

$$M = C \cdot e(d_1, C_1) \cdot e(d_2, C_2) \cdot e(d_3, C_3) \cdot e(d_4, C_4) \cdot e(d_5, C_5).$$

3.2 Analysis

As the analysis of BB_1 scheme, for a ciphertext instance $C = M\Omega^s, C_1 = (g_0 g_1^{\text{ID}})^s$, $C_2 = v_1^{s-s_1}, C_3 = v_2^{s_1}, C_4 = v_3^{s-s_2}, C_5 = v_4^{s_2}$, we need to find h_1, h_2, h_3, h_4, h_5 such that $e(C_1, h_1)\, e(C_2, h_2)\, e(C_3, h_3)\, e(C_4, h_4)\, e(C_5, h_5) = 1$ where h_1, h_2, h_3, h_4, h_5 are constructed from public parameters and the target identity ID.

However, it is not easy to find such elements. As shown in the secret key, a direct construction is that $h_1 = g^{-t_1 t_2}$, $h_2 = (g_0 g_1^{\text{ID}})^{t_2}, h_3 = (g_0 g_1^{\text{ID}})^{t_1}$, ,$h_4 = (g_0 g_1^{\text{ID}})^{t_4}, h_5 = (g_0 g_1^{\text{ID}})^{t_3}$. Unfortunately, these elements cannot be provided due to the loss of $g_0^{t_1}, g_1^{t_1}, \cdots, g_1^{t_4}, g_1^{t_4}$.

This technique is called "linear splitting", because an important element g^s (corresponding to BB_1) is split into four parts: $v_1^{s-s_1}, v_2^{s_1}, v_3^{s-s_2}, v_4^{s_2}$. To make things appear clearer, we can rewrite these four elements as $g^{t_1 s} v_1^{-s_1}, v_2^{s_1}$, $g^{t_3 s} v_3^{-s_2}, v_4^{s_2}$. We can find that g^s is blinded by two elements $v_1^{-s_1}$ and $v_3^{-s_2}$. To remove the blindness factor in decryption, two extra elements $v_2^{s_1}, v_4^{s_2}$ are provided. In the security proof of BW-AIBE, we can see that all these elements are proved "random" at the view of adversary. So if we want hide the identity in ciphertext, we can blind the related elements to be "random". In BW-AIBE, g^s is blinded. In fact, we can change the target of blinded target, for example, blinding $(g_0 g_1^{\text{ID}})^s$. These analyses result in our generic construction in the next section.

3.3   Generic Construction

Let $\mathcal{E}$ be an IBE scheme and $e : \mathbb{G} \times \mathbb{G} \to \mathbb{G}_T$ is the bilinear map used in $\mathcal{E}$. Suppose a message $M \in \mathbb{G}_T$ is randomized as MY^s in the encryption process, where $Y \in \mathbb{G}_T$ comes from public key and $s \in \mathbb{Z}_p^*$ is randomly chosen by the encryptor. Then $\mathcal{E}$ is constructed as follows:

Setup. It outputs public key PK and master secret key MK.
KeyGen. For an identity ID, it outputs the corresponding secret key $\text{SK}_{\text{ID}} = (d_1, \cdots, d_n)$ where $d_1, \cdots, d_n \in \mathbb{G}$.
Encrypt. For a message $M \in \mathbb{G}_T$ and an identity ID, it outputs ciphertext $\text{CT} = (C = MY^s, C_1, \cdots, C_n)$ where $C \in \mathbb{G}_T$ and $C_1, \cdots, C_n \in \mathbb{G}$.
Decrypt. $M = C \cdot e(d_1, C_1) \cdots e(d_n, C_n)$.

As stated before, we require that the target identity in the IBE scheme can be *only* judged by the equation $e(C_1, h_1) \cdots e(C_n, h_n) = 1$ where $C_1, \cdots, C_n$ come from ciphertext and $h_1, \cdots, h_n$ are constructed from the public parameters and some identity. And we also require that every $h_i \neq 1, i = 1, \cdots, n$.

Let A be a non-empty set, $t \in \mathbb{Z}_p^*$, we define $A^t := \{x^t | x \in A\}$. This notation is the same as the definition of product of sets, but can be easily distinguished from its context. Let $A \backslash B$ be the difference of A and B, i.e., $A \backslash B = \{x | x \in A \wedge x \notin B\}$. Let g be a generator of $\mathbb{G}$. We transform the above scheme to an anonymous IBE scheme as follows:

Setup. This algorithm chooses two random integers $t_1, t_2, t_3, t_4 \in \mathbb{Z}_p^*$, computes $v_1 = g^{t_1}, v_2 = g^{t_2}, v_3 = g^{t_3}, v_4 = g^{t_4}$ and outputs the public key $\{Y^{t_1 t_2}, v_1, v_2, v_3, v_4\} \cup \text{PK}^{t_1} \cup \text{PK}^{t_3} \backslash \{Y^{t_1}, Y^{t_3}\}$ and the master secret key $\text{MK} \cup \{t_1, t_2, t_3, t_4\}$.
KeyGen. Let $h_1, \cdots, h_n$ be the elements constructed to judge the identity in the ciphertext, i.e., $e(h_1, C_1) \cdots e(h_n, C_n) = 1$ where $C_1, \cdots, C_n$ are the elements of ciphertext. Then we split the transformation into two parts. For $i = 1, \cdots, n-1$, the algorithm chooses random integer $r \in \mathbb{Z}_p^*$ and computes $d_{i,1} = d_i^{t_1}, d_{i,2} = d_i^{t_2}, d_{i,3} = h_i^{t_3 \cdot r}, d_{i,4} = h_i^{t_4 \cdot r}$. For $i = n$, it computes $d_n' = d_n^{t_1 t_2} \cdot h_n^{t_3 t_4 r}$. Then the secret key is

$$(\langle d_{i,1}, d_{i,2}, d_{i,3}, d_{i,4} \rangle_{i=1,\cdots,n-1}, d_n').$$

Encrypt. Like **KeyGen**, we also split the transformation into two parts. For $i = 1, \cdots, n-1$, this algorithm chooses $2(n-1)$ random integers $s_{1,1}, s_{1,2},$ $\cdots, s_{n-1,1}, s_{n-1,2} \in \mathbb{Z}_p^*$, computes $C_{i,1} = v_2^{s_{i,1}}, C_{i,2} = v_1^{-s_{i,1}} C_i^{t_1}, C_{i,3} =$

$v_4^{s_{i,2}}, C_{i,2} = v_3^{-s_{i,2}} C_i^{t_3}$. For $i = n$, it sets $C_n' = C_n$, leaving this element unchanged. Then the ciphertext is

$$(C' = MY^{t_1 t_2 s}, \langle C_{i,1}, C_{i,2}, C_{i,3}, C_{i,4} \rangle_{i=1, \cdots, n-1}, C_n').$$

Decrypt. This algorithm outputs

$$M = C' \cdot \left(\prod_{i=1}^{n-1} e(d_{i,1}, C_{i,1}) \cdot e(d_{i,2}, C_{i,2}) \cdot e(d_{i,3}, C_{i,3}) \cdot e(d_{i,4}, C_{i,4}) \right) \cdot e(d_n', C_n').$$

Correctness: The correctness of new decryption can be easily seen as follows. Note that in the original decryption process, we have $M = C \cdot e(d_1, C_1) \cdots e(d_n, C_n)$ which implies $Y^s \cdot e(d_1, C_1) \cdots e(d_n, C_n) = 1$. For $i = 1, \cdots, n-1$, we have

$$e(d_{i,1}, C_{i,1}) \cdot e(d_{i,2}, C_{i,2}) \cdot e(d_{i,3}, C_{i,3}) \cdot e(d_{i,4}, C_{i,4})$$
$$= e(d_i^{t_1}, v_2^{s_{i,1}}) e(d_i^{t_2}, v_1^{-s_{i,1}} C_i^{t_1}) e(h_i^{t_3 \cdot r}, v_4^{s_{i,2}}) e(h_i^{t_4 \cdot r}, v_3^{-s_{i,2}} C_i^{t_3})$$
$$= e(d_i, C_i)^{t_1 t_2} e(h_i, C_i)^{t_3 t_4 r}$$

For $i = n$, we have $e(d_n', C_n') = e(d_n^{t_1 t_2} \cdot h_n^{t_3 t_4 r}, C_n) = e(d_n, C_n)^{t_1 t_2} \cdot e(h_n, C_n)^{t_3 t_4 r}$. Note that $\prod_{i=1}^{n} e(h_i, C_i)^{t_3 t_4 r} = (\prod_{i=1}^{n} e(h_i, C_i))^{t_3 t_4 r} = 1$. So

$$C' \cdot \left(\prod_{i=1}^{n-1} e(d_{i,1}, C_{i,1}) \cdot e(d_{i,2}, C_{i,2}) \cdot e(d_{i,3}, C_{i,3}) \cdot e(d_{i,4}, C_{i,4}) \right) \cdot e(d_n', C_n')$$
$$= MY^{t_1 t_2 s} \cdot \prod_{i=1}^{n} e(d_i, C_i)^{t_1 t_2} \cdot \prod_{i=1}^{n} e(h_i, C_i)^{t_3 t_4 r}$$
$$= MY^{t_1 t_2 s} \cdot e(d_1, C_1)^{t_1 t_2} \cdots e(d_n, C_n)^{t_1 t_2}$$
$$= M(Y^s \cdot e(d_1, C_1) \cdots e(d_n, C_n))^{t_1 t_2}$$
$$= M$$

Observe that if the **Decrypt** algorithm is $M = C \cdot e(a_1, C_1) \cdots \frac{1}{e(a_k, C_k)} \cdots e(a_n, C_n)$, we don't need to modify the **Encrypt** and **Decrypt** algorithms. The **Encrypt** algorithm remains the same and the **Decrypt** algorithm is

$$M = C \cdot e(a_{1,1}, C_{1,1}) \cdot e(a_{1,2}, C_{1,2}) \cdot e(a_{1,3}, C_{1,3}) \cdot e(a_{1,4}, C_{1,4}) \cdots$$
$$\cdot \frac{1}{e(a_{k,1}, C_{k,1}) \cdot e(a_{k,2}, C_{k,2}) \cdot e(a_{k,3}, C_{k,3}) \cdot e(a_{k,4}, C_{k,4})} \cdot$$
$$\cdots e(a_{n,1}, C_{n,1}) \cdot e(a_{n,2}, C_{n,2}) \cdot e(a_{n,3}, C_{n,3}) \cdot e(a_{n,4}, C_{n,4}).$$

4   A Variant of BW-AIBE

We now transform the first Boneh-Boyen scheme (BB$_1$) [3] to an anonymous scheme. Note that BB$_1$ was proposed as an HIBE scheme but can be regarded as an IBE scheme with the hierarchy depth $= 1$. For ease of presentation, we denote the IBE and HIBE version by BB$_1$-IBE, BB$_1$-HIBE. Given an instance of BB$_1$-IBE ciphertext $M \cdot e(g_1, g_2)^s, g^s, (g_1^{\text{ID}} h)^s$, if we leave $(g_1^{\text{ID}} h)^s$ unchanged, then we can get Boyen-Waters anonymous IBE scheme (BW-AIBE). If we leave g^s unchanged, we can get a variant of BW-AIBE scheme. We denote this transformed scheme by BB$_1$-AIBE.

4.1   Construction

For an instance of ciphertext $C = M \cdot e(g_1, g_2)^s, C_1 = g^s, C_2 = (g_1^{ID} h)^s$, we choose $h_1 = (g_1^{ID} h)^{-1}$ and $h_2 = g$. It is easy to see that $e(C_1, h_1) e(C_2, h_2) = 1$. Then scheme BB_1-AIBE is constructed as follows.

Setup(1^λ). Given the security parameter λ, the setup algorithm first gets $(p, \mathbb{G}, \mathbb{G}_T, g, e) \leftarrow \mathcal{G}(\lambda)$. Next it chooses another two random generator $g_2, h \in \mathbb{G}$ and five random integers $\alpha, t_1, t_2, t_3, t_4 \in \mathbb{Z}_p^*$. Then the setup algorithm sets $g_1 = g^\alpha, Y = e(g_1, g_2)^{t_1 t_2}, v_1 = g^{t_1}, v_2 = g^{t_2}, v_3 = g^{t_3}, v_4 = g^{t_4}$. The public key PK is published as

$$PK = (Y, g, v_1, v_2, v_3, v_4, g_1^{t_1}, h^{t_1}, g_1^{t_3}, h^{t_3}),$$

and the master key MK is

$$MK = (g_2^\alpha, t_1, t_2, t_3, t_4).$$

KeyGen(MK, ID). To generate the secret key SK_{ID} for an identity $ID \in \mathbb{Z}_p$, the key extract algorithm chooses random $r_1, r_2 \in \mathbb{Z}_p$ and outputs SK_{ID} as

$$SK_{ID} = (g_2^{-\alpha t_1 t_2} (g_1^{ID} h)^{-r_1 t_1 t_2 - r_2 t_3 t_4}, v_1^{r_1}, v_2^{r_1}, v_3^{r_2}, v_4^{r_2}).$$

Encrypt(PK, ID, M). To encrypt a message $M \in \mathbb{G}_T$ for an identity ID, the algorithm chooses random integers $s, s_1, s_2 \in \mathbb{Z}_p$ and outputs the ciphertext CT as

$$CT = (MY^s, g^s, v_2^{s_1}, (g_1^{t_1 ID} h^{t_1})^s v_1^{-s_1}, v_4^{s_2}, (g_1^{t_3 ID} h^{t_3})^s v_3^{-s_2}).$$

Decrypt(SK_{ID}, CT). To decrypt a ciphertext $CT = (C, C_1, C_2, C_3, C_4, C_5)$ for an identity ID, using the corresponding secret key $SK_{ID} = (d_1, d_2, d_3, d_4, d_5)$, outputs

$$M = C \cdot e(d_1, C_1) \cdot e(d_2, C_2) \cdot e(d_3, C_3) \cdot e(d_4, C_4) \cdot e(d_5, C_5).$$

4.2   Security

We have the following result for the transformed scheme.

Theorem 1. *If the Decision BDH and D-Linear assumptions hold, scheme BB_1-AIBE is IND-sID-CPA secure and ANON-sID-CPA secure.*

The security (semantic security and anonymity) of the transformed scheme can be proved by hybrid experiments similar to that of [10]. We define the following hybrid games which differ on what challenge ciphertext is given by the simulator to the adversary:

- Game$_1$: $CT_1 = (C, C_1, C_2, C_3, C_4, C_5)$
- Game$_2$: $CT_2 = (R, C_1, C_2, C_3, C_4, C_5)$

- Game$_3$: CT$_3 = (R, C_1, C_2, R_1, C_4, C_5)$
- Game$_4$: CT$_4 = (R, C_1, C_2, R_1, C_4, R_2)$

Here $(C, C_1, C_2, C_3, C_4, C_5)$ denotes the challenge ciphertext given to the adversary during a real attack, R is a randomly chosen element from $\mathbb{G}_1$ and R_1, R_2 are randomly chosen elements from $\mathbb{G}$. Since every element of the challenge ciphertext in Game$_4$ is random group element, so it does not leak any information about the message or the identity. Therefore indistinguishability between games proves semantic security and anonymity.

Indistinguishability between Game$_1$ **and** Game$_2$

To prove the indistinguishability between Game$_1$ and Game$_2$, we can directly prove the transformed scheme is IND-sID-CPA secure. Here we prove this by an indirect way which is based on the semantic security of the original scheme, that is, if one can break the transformed scheme, the original scheme can also be broken.

Lemma 1 (Semantic Security). *If there is an adversary who can distinguish between* Game$_1$ *and* Game$_2$ *with advantage ϵ, a simulator can take the adversary as oracle and break* BB$_1$-IBE *in the* IND-sID-CPA *game with advantage ϵ.*

Proof. We show how to construct a simulator $\mathcal{B}$ which can take the adversary $\mathcal{A}$ as oracle to play the IND-sID-CPA game with the challenger $\mathcal{C}$ to break BB$_1$-IBE.

Init. The simulator $\mathcal{B}$ runs $\mathcal{A}$. $\mathcal{A}$ gives $\mathcal{B}$ a challenge identity ID*. Then $\mathcal{B}$ submits the challenge identity ID* to $\mathcal{C}$.

Setup. The challenger $\mathcal{C}$ generates the master public parameters PK$' = \{Y, g, g_1, h\}$ and gives them to $\mathcal{B}$. $\mathcal{B}$ chooses random integers $t_1, t_2, t_3, t_4 \in \mathbb{Z}_p^*$, computes $v_1 = g^{t_1}, v_2 = g^{t_2}, v_3 = g^{t_3}, v_4 = g^{t_4}$ and outputs the new public key PK $= \{Y^{t_1 t_2}, g, v_1, v_2, v_3, v_4, g_1^{t_1}, h^{t_1}, g_1^{t_3}, h^{t_3}\}$ and keeps $\{t_1, t_2, t_3, t_4\}$ secret. Then $\mathcal{B}$ gives PK to the adversary $\mathcal{A}$.

Phase 1. $\mathcal{A}$ submits ID to $\mathcal{B}$ with the restriction that $\mathcal{A}$ cannot request the secret key for ID*. Then $\mathcal{B}$ sends the same ID to $\mathcal{C}$. $\mathcal{C}$ gives $\mathcal{B}$ the secret key SK$'_{\text{ID}} = (d'_1, d'_2)$. Then $\mathcal{B}$ chooses a random integer $r \in \mathbb{Z}_p^*$, computes $d_1 = d_1'^{t_1 t_2} (g_1^{\text{ID}} h)^{-r t_3 t_4}, d_2 = d_2'^{t_1}, d_3 = d_2'^{t_2}, d_4 = v_3^r, d_5 = v_4^r$ and sets SK$_{\text{ID}} = (d_1, d_2, d_3, d_4, d_5)$. Finally $\mathcal{B}$ gives the new secret key to $\mathcal{A}$.

Challenge. $\mathcal{A}$ submits a message M to $\mathcal{B}$. $\mathcal{B}$ chooses a random element $R_0 \in \mathbb{G}_T$, sets $M_0 = R_0^{t_1^{-1} t_2^{-1}}, M_1 = M^{t_1^{-1} t_2^{-1}}$ and submits ID$^*, M_0, M_1$ to $\mathcal{C}$. Here we suppose that M_0 has the same length as M_1. $\mathcal{C}$ flips a random coin b and passes the ciphertext CT$'^* = \textbf{Encrypt}(\text{PK}, M_b, \text{ID}^*) = (C', C_1', C_2')$ to $\mathcal{B}$. Then $\mathcal{B}$ chooses random integers $s_1, s_2 \in \mathbb{Z}_p^*$, sets $C = C'^{t_1 t_2}, C_1 = C_1'$, computes $C_2 = v_2^{s_1}, C_3 = C_2'^{t_1} v_1^{-s_1}, C_4 = v_4^{s_2}, C_5 = C_2'^{t_3} v_3^{-s_2}$, and gives the new ciphertext CT$^* = (C, C_1, C_2, C_3, C_4, C_5)$ to $\mathcal{A}$.

Phase 2. Phase 1 is repeated.

Guess. $\mathcal{B}$ outputs its guess b' of b as follows: if $\mathcal{A}$ outputs 1 (Game$_1$), then $\mathcal{B}$ outputs its guess $b' = 1$; if $\mathcal{A}$ outputs 2 (Game$_2$), then $\mathcal{B}$ outputs its guess $b' = 0$. Note that $M = M_1^{t_1 t_2}$ and $MY^{t_1 t_2 s} = (M_1^{t_1^{-1} t_2^{-1}} Y^s)^{t_1 t_2}$, so if $b = 1$, CT* is the right ciphertext for message M. If $b = 0$, $C = R_0 Y^{t_1 t_2 s} = (R_0^{t_1^{-1} t_2^{-1}} Y^s)^{t_1 t_2}$ is a random element in $\mathbb{G}_1$.

Since the simulator plays Game$_1$ if and only if the given ciphertext CT* is encrypted for message M_1, the simulator's advantage in the IND-sID-CPA game is exactly ϵ.   □

According to [3, Theorem 1], we have the following result for BB$_1$-AIBE's semantic security:

Corollary 1. *If the Decision BDH assumption holds, scheme* BB$_1$-AIBE *is* IND-sID-CPA *secure.*

Indistinguishability between Game$_2$ **and** Game$_3$

Lemma 2 (Anonymity, Part 1). *If there is an adversary who can distinguish between* Game$_2$ *and* Game$_3$ *with advantage ϵ, a simulator can take the adversary as oracle and win the D-Linear game with advantage ϵ.*

Proof. We assume that there exists an adversary $\mathcal{A}$ who can distinguish between Game$_2$ and Game$_3$ with advantage ϵ. We show that the simulator $\mathcal{B}$ can win the D-Linear game with advantage ϵ by taking $\mathcal{A}$ as oracle.

Given a D-Linear instance $[g, f, \nu, g^{c_1}, f^{c_2}, Z]$ where Z is either $\nu^{c_1 + c_2}$ or random in $\mathbb{G}$ with equal probability. The simulator plays the game in the following stages.

Init. The simulator $\mathcal{B}$ runs $\mathcal{A}$. $\mathcal{A}$ gives $\mathcal{B}$ a challenge identity ID*.

Setup. $\mathcal{B}$ first chooses random exponents $\alpha, \omega, y, t_3, t_4 \in \mathbb{Z}_p$. It lets g in the simulation be as in the instance and sets $v_1 = \nu, v_2 = f$ which implies t_1, t_2 are unknown to the simulator. Next it sets $g_1 = g^{\alpha}, g_2 = g^{\omega}, h = g^y, v_3 = g^{t_3}, v_4 = g^{t_4}$. Then $Y = e(g_1, g_2)^{t_1 t_2} = e(f, \nu)^{\alpha \omega}$. The public key is published as:
$$\text{PK} = (Y, g, v_1, v_2, v_3, v_4, g_1^{t_1} = \nu^{\alpha}, h^{t_1} = \nu^y, g_1^{t_3}, h^{t_3}).$$

Phase 1. $\mathcal{A}$ submits ID to $\mathcal{B}$ with the restriction that $\mathcal{A}$ cannot request the secret key for ID*. Then $\mathcal{B}$ chooses random $r \in \mathbb{Z}_p$, computes $d_1 = g^{-r(\alpha \text{ID} + y)t_3 t_4}$, $d_2 = \nu^{-\frac{\alpha \omega}{\alpha \text{ID} + y}}, d_3 = f^{-\frac{\alpha \omega}{\alpha \text{ID} + y}}, d_4 = v_3^r, d_5 = v_4^r$ and sets SK$_{\text{ID}} = (d_1, d_2, d_3, d_4, d_5)$. We say this is a well formed secret key if we set $r_1 = -\frac{\alpha \omega}{\alpha \text{ID} + y}, r_2 = r$, then $d_1 = g_2^{-\alpha t_1 t_2}(g_1^{\text{ID}} h)^{-r_1 t_1 t_2 - r_2 t_3 t_4}, d_2 = v_1^{r_1}, d_3 = v_2^{r_1}, d_4 = v_3^{r_2}$ and $d_5 = v_4^{r_2}$. Finally $\mathcal{B}$ gives the secret key to $\mathcal{A}$.

Challenge. $\mathcal{A}$ submits a message M to $\mathcal{B}$ and $\mathcal{B}$ discard this message. $\mathcal{B}$ picks a random element $R \in \mathbb{G}_1$, a random integer $s_2 \in \mathbb{Z}_p$ and outputs the ciphertext as:
$$\text{CT}^* = (R, g^{c_1}, (f^{c_2})^{-(\alpha \text{ID}^* + y)}, Z^{\alpha \text{ID}^* + y}, v_4^{s_2}, (g^{c_1})^{(\alpha \text{ID}^* + y)t_3} v_3^{-s_2}).$$

If $Z = \nu^{c_1+c_2}$, then $C_1 = g^{c_1}$, $C_2 = (f^{c_2})^{-(\alpha\text{ID}^*+y)} = v_2^{s_1}$, $C_3 = \nu^{(c_1+c_2)(\alpha\text{ID}^*+y)}$
$= (g_1^{t_1\text{ID}^*} h^{t_1})^s v_1^{-s_1}$, $C_4 = v_4^{s_2}$, $C_5 = (g_1^{t_3\text{ID}^*} h^{t_3})^s v_3^{-k_2}$ where $s = c_1, s_1 = -(\alpha\text{ID}^* + y)c_2$; all parts of the challenge but C are thus well formed, and the simulator behaved as in Game$_2$. If instead, when Z is random, then C_3 are random elements from the adversarial viewpoint, i.e., the simulator responded as in Game$_3$.

Phase 2. Phase 1 is repeated.

Guess. $\mathcal{B}$ outputs its guess as follows: if $\mathcal{A}$ outputs 2 (Game$_2$), then $\mathcal{B}$ outputs its guess 1 ($Z = \nu^{c_1+c_2}$); if $\mathcal{A}$ outputs 3 (Game$_3$), then $\mathcal{B}$ outputs its guess 0 ($Z \neq \nu^{c_1+c_2}$).

By the simulation setup, the simulator's advantage in the D-Linear game is exactly ϵ. $\qquad\square$

Indistinguishability between Game$_3$ **and** Game$_4$

Lemma 3 (Anonymity, Part 2). *If there is an adversary who can distinguish between* Game$_3$ *and* Game$_4$ *with advantage ϵ, a simulator can take the adversary as oracle and win the D-Linear game with advantage ϵ.*

Proof. We assume that there exists an adversary $\mathcal{A}$ who can distinguish between Game$_3$ and Game$_4$ with advantage ϵ. We show that the simulator $\mathcal{B}$ can win the D-Linear game with advantage ϵ by taking $\mathcal{A}$ as oracle.

Given a D-Linear instance $[g, f, \nu, g^{c_1}, f^{c_2}, Z]$ where Z is either $\nu^{c_1+c_2}$ or random in $\mathbb{G}$ with equal probability. The simulator plays the game in the following stages.

Init. The simulator $\mathcal{B}$ runs $\mathcal{A}$. $\mathcal{A}$ gives $\mathcal{B}$ a challenge identity ID*.

Setup. $\mathcal{B}$ first chooses random exponents $\alpha, \omega, y, t_1, t_2 \in \mathbb{Z}_p$. It lets g in the simulation be as in the instance and sets $v_3 = \nu, v_4 = f$ which implies t_3, t_4 are unknown to the simulator. Next it sets $g_1 = g^\alpha$, $h = g^y$, $v_1 = g^{t_1}$, $v_2 = g^{t_2}$. Finally it sets $Y = e(f, \nu)^{\alpha\omega t_1 t_2}$. Note that it means $g_2 = g^{\omega t_3 t_4}$. The public key is published as:

$$\text{PK} = (Y, g, v_1, v_2, v_3, v_4, g_1^{t_1}, h^{t_1}, g_1^{t_3} = \nu^\alpha, h^{t_3} = \nu^y).$$

Phase 1. $\mathcal{A}$ submits ID to $\mathcal{B}$ with the restriction that $\mathcal{A}$ cannot request the secret key for ID*. Then $\mathcal{B}$ chooses random $r \in \mathbb{Z}_p$, computes $d_1 = g^{-r(\alpha\text{ID}+y)t_1 t_2}$, $d_2 = v_1^r, d_3 = v_2^r, d_4 = \nu^{-\frac{\alpha\omega t_1 t_2}{\alpha\text{ID}+y}}, d_5 = f^{-\frac{\alpha\omega t_1 t_2}{\alpha\text{ID}+y}}$ and sets SK$_\text{ID} = (d_1, d_2, d_3, d_4, d_5)$. We say this is a well formed secret key if we set $r_1 = r, r_2 = -\frac{\alpha\omega t_1 t_2}{\alpha\text{ID}+y}$, then $d_1 = g_2^{-\alpha t_1 t_2}(g_1^\text{ID} h)^{-r_1 t_1 t_2 - r_2 t_3 t_4}, d_2 = v_1^{r_1}, d_3 = v_2^{r_1}, d_4 = v_3^{r_2}$ and $d_5 = v_4^{r_2}$. Finally $\mathcal{B}$ gives the secret key to $\mathcal{A}$.

Challenge. $\mathcal{A}$ submits a message M to $\mathcal{B}$ and $\mathcal{B}$ discard this message. $\mathcal{B}$ picks a random element $R \in \mathbb{G}_1$, a random element $R_1 \in \mathbb{G}$, a random integer $s_1 \in \mathbb{Z}_p$ and outputs the ciphertext as:

$$\text{CT}^* = (R, g^{c_1}, v_2^{s_1}, R_1, (f^{c_2})^{-(\alpha\text{ID}+y)}, Z^{\alpha\text{ID}+y}).$$

If $Z = \nu^{c_1+c_2}$, then $C_1 = g^{c_1}$, $C_4 = (f^{c_2})^{-(\alpha \text{ID}+y)} = v_4^{s_2}$, $C_5 = \nu^{(c_1+c_2)(\alpha \text{ID}+y)}$ $= (g_1^{t_3 \text{ID}} h^{t_3})^s v_3^{-s_2}$, where $s = c_1$, $s_2 = -(\alpha \text{ID}+y)c_2$; all parts of the challenge but C are thus well formed, and the simulator behaved as in Game$_2$. If instead, when Z is random, then C_3 are random elements from the adversarial viewpoint, i.e., the simulator responded as in Game$_3$.

Phase 2. Phase 1 is repeated.

Guess. $\mathcal{B}$ outputs its guess as follows: if $\mathcal{A}$ outputs 3 (Game$_3$), then $\mathcal{B}$ outputs its guess 1 ($Z = \nu^{c_1+c_2}$); if $\mathcal{A}$ outputs 4 (Game$_4$), then $\mathcal{B}$ outputs its guess 0 ($Z \neq \nu^{c_1+c_2}$).

By the simulation setup, the simulator's advantage in the D-Linear game is exactly ϵ. ☐

Proof of Theorem 1. It is obvious from Corollary 1, Lemma 2 and Lemma 3. ☐

5   Discussion

5.1   Other Transformation

Note that the transformed scheme BB$_1$-AIBE is IND-sID-CPA secure and ANON-sID-CPA secure. To get fully secure anonymous schemes, we can transform fully secure schemes by using our method, such as another Boneh-Boyen IBE scheme [4], or Waters IBE scheme [27], or Waters dual system encryption IBE scheme [28], and these transformed schemes will be IND-ID-CPA secure and ANON-ID-CPA secure.

5.2   Anonymous HIBE

Another natural extension for our method is that whether our method can be used to transform an HIBE scheme to an anonymous HIBE scheme. There are two problems. One is that our framework is present for IBE not HIBE, so we should prove security under the security model of HIBE. Another obstacle is that we should consider the key derivation, i.e., an identity ID's secret key can be derived from another identity ID*'s secret key if ID* is a prefix of ID. Unfortunately, our method cannot be applied in previous HIBE schemes, such as BB$_1$-HIBE, BBG-HIBE, due to the key delegation of hierarchical identities. A possible approach would be to use the parallel technique introduced in [10] which re-randomizes the keys between all siblings and all children. We leave it an open problem to construct secure anonymous HIBE schemes by extending our method.

6   Conclusion

We analyse the construction of Boyen-Waters anonymous IBE Scheme and find a method to construct anonymous IBE schemes. We show that Boyen-Waters anonymous IBE scheme can be transformed from BB$_1$-IBE scheme. We give a new anonymous IBE scheme which is also transformed from BB_1-IBE scheme and can be seemed as a variant of Boyen-Waters anonymous IBE scheme. The security proof shows the transformed scheme has the same semantic security as the original BB_1-IBE scheme and has anonymous security. And we prove anonymity under the Decision Linear assumption.

References

1. Abdalla, M., Bellare, M., Catalano, D., Kiltz, E., Kohno, T., Lange, T., Malone-Lee, J., Neven, G., Paillier, P., Shi, H.: Searchable encryption revisited: Consistency properties, relation to anonymous IBE, and extensions. Journal of Cryptology 21(3), 350–391 (2008)
2. Abdalla, M., Bellare, M., Catalano, D., Kiltz, E., Kohno, T., Lange, T., Malone-Lee, J., Neven, G., Paillier, P., Shi, H.: Searchable Encryption Revisited: Consistency Properties, Relation to Anonymous IBE, and Extensions. In: Shoup, V. (ed.) CRYPTO 2005. LNCS, vol. 3621, pp. 205–222. Springer, Heidelberg (2005)
3. Boneh, D., Boyen, X.: Efficient Selective-id Secure Identity-based Encryption without Random Oracles. In: Cachin, C., Camenisch, J. (eds.) EUROCRYPT 2004. LNCS, vol. 3027, pp. 223–238. Springer, Heidelberg (2004)
4. Boneh, D., Boyen, X.: Secure Identity Based Encryption without Random Oracles. In: Franklin, M. (ed.) CRYPTO 2004. LNCS, vol. 3152, pp. 443–459. Springer, Heidelberg (2004)
5. Boneh, D., Boyen, X., Goh, E.-J.: Hierarchical Identity Based Encryption with Constant Size Ciphertext. In: Cramer, R. (ed.) EUROCRYPT 2005. LNCS, vol. 3494, pp. 440–456. Springer, Heidelberg (2005)
6. Boneh, D., Boyen, X., Shacham, H.: Short Group Signatures. In: Franklin, M. (ed.) CRYPTO 2004. LNCS, vol. 3152, pp. 41–55. Springer, Heidelberg (2004)
7. Boneh, D., Di Crescenzo, G., Ostrovsky, R., Persiano, G.: Public Key Encryption with Keyword Search. In: Cachin, C., Camenisch, J. (eds.) EUROCRYPT 2004. LNCS, vol. 3027, pp. 506–522. Springer, Heidelberg (2004)
8. Boneh, D., Franklin, M.: Identity-based Encryption from the Weil Pairing. In: Kilian, J. (ed.) CRYPTO 2001. LNCS, vol. 2139, pp. 213–229. Springer, Heidelberg (2001)
9. Boneh, D., Waters, B.: Conjunctive, Subset, and Range Queries on Encrypted Data. In: Vadhan, S.P. (ed.) TCC 2007. LNCS, vol. 4392, pp. 535–554. Springer, Heidelberg (2007)
10. Boyen, X., Waters, B.: Anonymous Hierarchical Identity-based Encryption (without Random Oracles). In: Dwork, C. (ed.) CRYPTO 2006. LNCS, vol. 4117, pp. 290–307. Springer, Heidelberg (2006)
11. Camenisch, J., Kohlweiss, M., Rial, A., Sheedy, C.: Blind and Anonymous Identity-based Encryption and Authorised Private Searches on Public Key Encrypted Data. In: Jarecki, S., Tsudik, G. (eds.) PKC 2009. LNCS, vol. 5443, pp. 196–214. Springer, Heidelberg (2009)
12. Canetti, R., Halevi, S., Katz, J.: A Forward-secure Public-key Encryption Scheme. In: Biham, E. (ed.) EUROCRYPT 2003. LNCS, vol. 2656, pp. 255–271. Springer, Heidelberg (2003)
13. Caro, A.D., Iovino, V., Persiano, G.: Fully secure anonymous hibe and secret-key anonymous ibe with short ciphertexts. Cryptology ePrint Archive, Report 2010/197 (2010), http://eprint.iacr.org/

14. Chatterjee, S., Sarkar, P.: Hibe with Short Public Parameters without Random Oracle. In: Lai, X., Chen, K. (eds.) ASIACRYPT 2006. LNCS, vol. 4284, pp. 145–160. Springer, Heidelberg (2006)

15. Chatterjee, S., Sarkar, P.: New Constructions of Constant Size Ciphertext Hibe without Random Oracle. In: Rhee, M.S., Lee, B. (eds.) ICISC 2006. LNCS, vol. 4296, pp. 310–327. Springer, Heidelberg (2006)

16. Cocks, C.: An Identity Based Encryption Scheme Based on Quadratic Residues. In: Honary, B. (ed.) Cryptography and Coding 2001. LNCS, vol. 2260, pp. 360–363. Springer, Heidelberg (2001)

17. Ducas, L.: Anonymity from Asymmetry: New Constructions for Anonymous Hibe. In: Pieprzyk, J. (ed.) CT-RSA 2010. LNCS, vol. 5985, pp. 148–164. Springer, Heidelberg (2010)

18. Gentry, C.: Practical Identity-based Encryption without Random Oracles. In: Vaudenay, S. (ed.) EUROCRYPT 2006. LNCS, vol. 4004, pp. 445–464. Springer, Heidelberg (2006)

19. Gentry, C., Halevi, S.: Hierarchical Identity Based Encryption with Polynomially Many Levels. In: Reingold, O. (ed.) TCC 2009. LNCS, vol. 5444, pp. 437–456. Springer, Heidelberg (2009)

20. Gentry, C., Silverberg, A.: Hierarchical ID-based Cryptography. In: Zheng, Y. (ed.) ASIACRYPT 2002. LNCS, vol. 2501, pp. 548–566. Springer, Heidelberg (2002)

21. Horwitz, J., Lynn, B.: Toward Hierarchical Identity-based Encryption. In: Knudsen, L.R. (ed.) EUROCRYPT 2002. LNCS, vol. 2332, pp. 466–481. Springer, Heidelberg (2002)

22. Lewko, A., Waters, B.: New Techniques for Dual System Encryption and Fully Secure Hibe with Short Ciphertexts. In: Micciancio, D. (ed.) TCC 2010. LNCS, vol. 5978, pp. 455–479. Springer, Heidelberg (2010)

23. Seo, J.H., Cheon, J.H.: Fully secure anonymous hierarchical identity-based encryption with constant size ciphertexts. Cryptology ePrint Archive, Report 2011/021 (2011), http://eprint.iacr.org/

24. Seo, J.H., Kobayashi, T., Ohkubo, M., Suzuki, K.: Anonymous Hierarchical Identity-based Encryption with Constant Size Ciphertexts. In: Jarecki, S., Tsudik, G. (eds.) PKC 2009. LNCS, vol. 5443, pp. 215–234. Springer, Heidelberg (2009)

25. Shamir, A.: Identity-based Cryptosystems and Signature Schemes. In: Blakely, G.R., Chaum, D. (eds.) CRYPTO 1984. LNCS, vol. 196, pp. 47–53. Springer, Heidelberg (1985)

26. Shi, E., Bethencourt, J., Chan, T.H.H., Song, D., Perrig, A.: Multi-dimensional range query over encrypted data. In: SP 2007: IEEE Symposium on Security and Privacy, pp. 350–364 (2007)

27. Waters, B.: Efficient Identity-based Encryption without Random Oracles. In: Cramer, R. (ed.) EUROCRYPT 2005. LNCS, vol. 3494, pp. 114–127. Springer, Heidelberg (2005)

28. Waters, B.: Dual System Encryption: Realizing Fully Secure Ibe and Hibe under Simple Assumptions. In: Halevi, S. (ed.) CRYPTO 2009. LNCS, vol. 5677, pp. 619–636. Springer, Heidelberg (2009)

Non-interactive Opening for Ciphertexts Encrypted by Shared Keys

Jiageng Chen[1,*], Keita Emura[2,**], and Atsuko Miyaji[1,***]

[1] School of Information Science, Japan Advanced Institute of Science and
Technology, 1-1, Asahidai, Nomi, Ishikawa, 923-1292, Japan
[2] Center for Highly Dependable Embedded Systems Technology, JAIST, Japan
{jg-chen,k-emura,miyaji}@jaist.ac.jp

Abstract. Let a sender Alice computes a ciphertext C of a message M by using a receiver Bob's public key pk_B. Damgård, Hofheinz, Kiltz, and Thorbek (CT-RSA2008) has proposed the notion *public key encryption with non-interactive opening* (PKENO), where Bob can make an non-interactive proof π that proves the decryption result of C under sk_B is M, without revealing sk_B itself. When Bob would like to prove the correctness of (C, M) (e.g., the information M sent to Bob is not the expected one), PKENO turns out to be an effective cryptographic primitive. A PKENO scheme for the KEM/DEM framework has also been proposed by Galindo (CT-RSA2009). Bob can make a non-interactive proof π that proves the decapsulation result of C under sk_B is K without revealing sk_B itself, where K is an encapsulation key of the DEM part. That is, no verifier can verify π without knowing K. This setting is acceptable if K is an ephemeral value. However, PKENO is not applicable if an encryption key is shared among certain users beforehand, and is used for a relatively long period before re-running the key agreement protocol, such as symmetric cryptosystems. In this paper, we define the notion *secret key encryption with non-interactive opening* (SKENO), and give a generic construction of SKENO from verifiable random function (VRF) and the Berbain-Gilbert IV-dependent stream cipher construction (FSE2007). Bob can make a non-interactive proof π that proves the decryption result of C under K is M, without revealing K itself.

1 Introduction

1.1 PKENO: Public Key Encryption with Non-interactive Opening

Let's first consider the following scenario. Assuming that a sender Alice computes a ciphertext C of a message M by using a receiver Bob's public key pk_B. In order to solve the dispute in some circumstances, Bob would like to prove

---

* This author is supported by the Graduate Research Program.
** This author is supported by the Center for Highly Dependable Embedded Systems Technology as a Postdoc researcher.
*** This work is supported by Grant-in-Aid for Scientific Research (B), 20300003.

S. Qing et al. (Eds.): ICICS 2011, LNCS 7043, pp. 57–68, 2011.

the correctness of the corresponding plaintext-ciphertext pair (C, M) (e.g., the information M sent to Bob is not the expected one). The easiest way to prove it is that Bob opens his secret key sk_B, demonstrates the decryption algorithm, and shows the decryption result of C under sk_B is M. However, no other ciphertext encrypted pk_B remains secure. To capture this situation above, Damgård, Hofheinz, Kiltz, and Thorbek [13] has proposed the notion *public key encryption with non-interactive opening* (PKENO), where Bob can make an non-interactive proof π that proves the decryption result of C under sk_B is M, without revealing sk_B itself. They also show a generic construction of PKENO from identity-based encryption (IBE) [9] and strongly existentially unforgeable one-time signature (OTS) [5]. Other generic construction of PKENO from group signature secure in the BSZ model [4] has been proposed [17], and concrete constructions of PKENO also have been proposed [20,21,28].

The main idea of PKENO construction is to make a decryption key which works about the corresponding ciphertext only, and the decryption key is set as a proof. For the sake of readability, we introduce the generic construction of PKENO (based on IBE and OTS) proposed by Damgård, Hofheinz, Kiltz, and Thorbek [13] as follows: Bob runs $(pk_B, sk_B) \leftarrow$ IBE.KeyGen(1^k), i.e., sk_B is a master key of the underlying IBE scheme. Alice runs $(vk, sk) \leftarrow$ OTS.KeyGen(1^k), and computes $C \leftarrow$ IBE.Enc(pk_B, vk, M), i.e., a verification key vk is regarded as the identity of the underlying IBE scheme, and computes $\sigma \leftarrow$ OTS.Sign(sk, C). The PKENO ciphertext is (C, σ, vk). Bob can decrypt (C, σ, vk) such that Bob verifies $1 =$ OTS.Verify(vk, σ, C), and computes $usk[vk] \leftarrow$ IBE.Extract(sk_B, vk) and $M \leftarrow$ IBE.Dec$(usk[vk], C)$. Then, $usk[vk]$ can be set as π, since anyone can prove whether $M =$ IBE.Dec(π, C) or not. Other ciphertexts encrypted by pk_B remain secure assuming that different vk is chosen in each encryption (this is a reasonable assumption of OTS).

1.2   PKENO with the KEM/DEM Framework and Its Limitation

A PKENO scheme for the KEM/DEM (Key Encapsulation/Decapsulation Mechanism) framework also have been proposed by Galindo [20]. To encrypt M, Alice compute $(K, C_1) \leftarrow$ Encapsulation(pk_B) and $C_2 \leftarrow$ DEM(K, M), where DEM is a symmetric cipher, and sends $C = (C_1, C_2)$ to Bob. Bob can compute $K \leftarrow$ Decapsulation(sk_B, C_1) and $M \leftarrow$ DEM(K, C_2). In the Galindo's scheme, Bob can make a non-interactive proof π that proves the decupsulation result of C_1 under sk_B is K without revealing sk_B itself. The construction methodology of the Galindo PKENO scheme with the KEM/DEM framework is also same as that of the previous PKENO scheme, where for a proof π anyone can compute $K' \leftarrow$ Decapsulation(π, C_1) and check whether $K = K'$ or not. That is, no verifier can verify π without knowing K. This setting is acceptable if K is an ephemeral value that changes per session (e.g., in the KEM/DEM usage). However, in some other applications where the secret key K is negotiated beforehand among a group of people, and it is then used by symmetric cryptosystems to do encryption for relatively a period of time (especially this is the case for IV-dependent stream cipher where the K is remained unchanged for many sessions

while IV is changed for each session and sent in plaintext form for synchronization), then the Galindo scheme does not work since the opening of K will expose
the unrelated messages as well. Here, we make it clear that the situation where
a ciphertext is encrypted by a shared key as follows.

- Let K be a shared key of Alice and Bob, and Charlie does not have K.
- Alice sends C to Bob, where C is a ciphertext of a message M under the
  key K.
- For Charlie, Bob wants to prove that the decryption result of C is M *without*
  revealing K.

PKENO is not capable to handle the situation above even a PKENO scheme
with the KEM/DEM framework has been proposed. Note that the proof itself is
the decryption key in the previous PKENO schemes. Since opening the shared
key K is not an option anymore, K should not be recognized as a proof. Thus, we
need to investigate a new methodology to handle the situation that a ciphertext
is encrypted by a shared key which cannot be revealed.

1.3   Our Contribution

In this paper, we define the notion *secret key encryption with non-interactive*
opening (SKENO), where

- Bob can make an non-interactive proof π that proves the decryption result
  of C under K is M, without revealing K itself,

and give a generic construction of SKENO from verifiable random function
(VRF) [2,14,15,26,30,33] and the Berbain-Gilbert IV-dependent stream cipher
construction [6], where IV is an initial vector.

In the Berbain-Gilbert construction, pseudo-random function (PRF) [23] is
regarded as a key scheduling algorithm (KSA) and a pseudo-random number
generator (PRNG) [8,36] is regarded as a pseudo-random generation algorithm
(PRGA). From an n-bit initial vector IV and a k-bit secret key K, PRF (say
$F_K(IV)$) outputs an m-bit initial state (say y) which is used as an input of
PRNG. Finally, PRNG (say $G(y)$) outputs L-bit keystream Z_{IV}. A ciphertext
C is $Z_{IV} \oplus M$, where $\oplus$ is the exclusive-or operation. Berbain and Gilbert give
a composition theorem where the composition $G \circ F_K$ is also PRF such that
$G \circ F : \{0,1\}^n \to \{0,1\}^L$. Therefore, $G \circ F$ can be a secure stream cipher, where
no adversary $\mathcal{A}$ can distinguish whether $G(F_K(IV))$ is a truly random number
or not, even if $\mathcal{A}$ can select IV.

A VRF is a PRF that provides a non-interactively verifiable proof: given
an input value x and its output $y = F_{SK}(x)$, a proof $\pi(x)$ proves that y is
the output of the function F indexed by SK given input x, without revealing a
secret key SK itself. Several applications of VRF have been considered, e.g., non-
interactive lottery system used in micropayment schemes [35], resettable zero-
knowledge proofs [34], updatable zero knowledge databases [29], set intersection
protocols [25], compact e-cash [12,3], adaptive oblivious transfer protocols [27],

keyword search [19], and so on. We make it clear that the usage of VRF for the PKENO functionality has not been appeared to the best of our knowledge.

We set IV as an input of VRF (as in the Berbain-Gilbert construction) and set a shared key K as a secret key of VRF. VRF leads to an m-bit initial state which is the input to the PRNG for generating a L-bit keystream Z_{IV}. A ciphertext C is $Z_{IV} \oplus M$. We set $\pi := (\pi', y = F_K(IV))$ a proof of (IV, C, M), where $K := SK$. Due to the VRF functionality, one can prove that m-bit initial state is the result of the underlying VRF without revealing K.

Although we have to mention that the VRF primitive is a relatively expensive assumption, our construction can be considered to be efficient in the environments where the key and IV setup phase is not executed frequently, since the execution of PRNG will play a dominant role in the encryption and decryption process.

2   Preliminaries

In this section, we define PRNG and VRF. We denote *State* as the state information transmitted by the adversary to himself across stages of the attack in experiments.

2.1   PRNG: Pseudo-Random Number Generator

Pseudo-random number generator (PRNG) $G : \{0,1\}^m \to \{0,1\}^L$ is used to expand an m-bit secret seed into an L-bit sequence ($m < L$).

Definition 1 (Pseudorandomness of PRNG). *We say that an function* $G : \{0,1\}^m \to \{0,1\}^L$ *is PRNG if for all probabilistic polynomial-time (PPT) adversary $\mathcal{A}$, the following advantage is a negligible function of the security parameter λ.*

$$\mathsf{Adv}_{G,\mathcal{A}}^{Pseudo}(1^\lambda) := |\Pr[y^* \xleftarrow{\$} \{0,1\}^m; \ b \xleftarrow{\$} \{0,1\};$$
$$Z_0^* \leftarrow G(y^*); \ Z_1^* \xleftarrow{\$} \{0,1\}^L; \ b' \leftarrow \mathcal{A}(1^\lambda, Z_b^*); \ b = b'] - \frac{1}{2}|$$

As a well-known result, PRNGs exist if and only if one-way functions exist [24]. Or rather, from a 1-1 one-way function f (i.e., one-way permutations, OWPs), a PRNG G is easily constructed [22] such that $G(y) = b(y)b(f(y))b(f^2(y)) \cdots b(f^{L-1}(y))$, where b is a corresponding hard-core.

2.2   VRF: Verifiable Random Function

Verifiable random functions (VRFs) were proposed by Micali, Rabin, and Vadhan [33], and many VRF constructions have been proposed by applying the complexity assumptions used in public-key encryption constructions (e.g., the strong RSA assumption [33], the q-Diffie-Hellman inversion assumption and the q-decisional bilinear Diffie-Hellman inversion assumption [15], the generalized Diffie-Hellman assumption [14], the ℓ-Decisional Diffie-Hellman Exponent assumption [26] and so on). Some black-box separations/constructions also have been shown by Brakerski, Goldwasser, Rothblum, and Vaikuntanathan [11], where VRF (both weak one and standard one) cannot be constructed from OWPs in a black-box manner, and the existence of weak VRF is essentially equivalent to the existence of non-interactive zero-knowledge proofs for all NP languages in the common random string model. Since OWPs are sufficient for constructing most of basic symmetric-key primitives, which include, e.g., PRNG, PRF, symmetric-key encryption schemes, and message authentication codes (Matsuda et al. [32] provide a nice summary of OWPs), VRF is a strong tool for constructing a stream cipher (Fiore and Schröder explained feasibility of VRF [18] in details). However, for handling the PKENO functionality in the symmetric cryptosystems such strong cryptographic assumption is required. It is an interesting open problem to clarify whether a black-box separation (or construction) of SKENO based on a weaker primitive than VRF exists or not.

Next, we define VRF by referring the Hohenberger-Waters VRF definition [26] as follows. Let $F : \{0,1\}^k \times \{0,1\}^n \to \{0,1\}^m$, where $k = k(\lambda)$, $n = n(\lambda)$, and $m = m(\lambda)$ are polynomials in the security parameter 1^λ, be an efficient computable function. For all $SK \in \{0,1\}^k$, simply we denote $F_{SK} : \{0,1\}^n \to \{0,1\}^m$.

Definition 2 (VRF [26]). *We say that F is a VRF if there exist algorithms* (VRF.Setup, VRF.Prove, VRF.Verify) *such that*

VRF.Setup(1^λ) *outputs a pair of keys* (PK, SK);

VRF.Prove(SK, x) *outputs a pair* (y, π'), *where* $y = F_{SK}(x)$ *is the function value of $x \in \{0,1\}^n$ and π' is the proof of correctness; and*

VRF.Verify(PK, x, y, π') *outputs 1 if $y = F_{SK}(x)$, and 0 otherwise.*

In addition, three security notions are required:

Provability: *This guarantees that an honestly generated proof is always accepted by the* Verify *algorithm, i.e., for all $(PK, SK) \leftarrow$ VRF.Setup(1^λ) and $x \in \{0,1\}^n$, if $(y, \pi') \leftarrow$ VRF.Prove(SK, x), then VRF.Verify(PK, x, y, π') = 1.*

Uniqueness: *This guarantees that no proof is accepted for different values $y_1 \neq y_2$ and a common x, i.e., for all $(PK, SK) \leftarrow$ VRF.Setup(1^λ) and $x \in \{0,1\}^n$, there does not exist a tuple $(y_1, y_2, \pi'_1, \pi'_2)$ such that $y_1 \neq y_2$ and VRF.Verify(PK, x, y_1, π'_1) = VRF.Verify(PK, x, y_2, π'_2) = 1. Note that no adversary can break uniqueness even SK is opened since such tuple does not exist. This property is used for realizing the proof soundness property (which is defined in Section 3).*

Pseudorandomness: *This guarantees that no adversary can distinguish whether an output of F is truely random or not, i.e., for all PPT adversary $\mathcal{A}$, the following advantage is a negligible function of the security parameter λ.*

$$\mathsf{Adv}_{F,\mathcal{A}}^{Pseudo}(1^{\lambda}) :=$$

$$|\Pr[(PK, SK) \leftarrow \mathsf{VRF.Setup}(1^{\lambda}); \ (x^*, State) \leftarrow \mathcal{A}^{\mathsf{VRF.Prove}(SK,\cdot)}(1^{\lambda}, PK);$$

$$b \xleftarrow{\$} \{0,1\}; y_0^* \leftarrow F_{SK}(x^*); \ y_1^* \xleftarrow{\$} \{0,1\}^m; \ b' \leftarrow \mathcal{A}^{\mathsf{VRF.Prove}(SK,\cdot)}(y_b^*, State);$$

$$b = b'] - \frac{1}{2}|$$

where $\mathsf{VRF.Prove}(SK, \cdot)$ *the the prove oracle which takes as input* $x \in \{0,1\}^n$ *$(x \neq x^*)$, outputs* $(F_{SK}(x), \pi')$.

Remark: As a similar cryptographic primitive of VRF, verifiable pseudo-random bit generators (VPRGs) has been introduced by Dwork and Naor [16], where the holder of the seed can generate proofs of consistency for some parts of the sequence without hurting the unpredictability of the remaining bits. Note that in our SKENO construction we do not have to use VPRG (instead of PRNG) by assuming that the underlying PRNG satisfies the soundness property, where no adversary can find $(y_1, y_2) \in \{0,1\}^m \times \{0,1\}^m$ such that $G(y_1) = G(y_2)$ and $y_1 \neq y_2$. Note that this requirement is natural, e.g., Bertoni, Daemen, Peeters, and Assche [7] have mentioned that *"loading different seeds into the PRNG shall result in different output sequences. In this respect, a PRNG is similar to a cryptographic hash function that should be collision-resistant"*.

3   SKENO: Secret Key Encryption with Non-interactive Opening

In this section, we give the definition of (IV-dependent) SKENO. We assume that each IV is randomly chosen for each encryption. A SKENO consists of five algorithms, KeyGen, Enc, Dec, Prove, and Verify.

Definition 3 (System operation of SKENO)

KeyGen(1^{λ}): *This algorithm takes as inputs a security parameter* $\lambda \in \mathbb{N}$, *and returns a public verification key* VK *and a secret key* K.

Enc(K, IV, M): *This algorithm takes as inputs* K *and an initial vector* $IV \in \{0,1\}^n$ *and a message* $M \in \{0,1\}^L$, *and returns a ciphertext* C. *We assume that* IV *is also sent to a decryptor.*

Dec(K, IV, C): *This algorithm takes as inputs* K *and* C, *and returns* M *or* $\perp$.

Prove(K, IV, C): *This algorithm takes as inputs* K, IV, *and* C, *and returns a proof* π.

Verify(VK, IV, C, M, π): *This algorithm takes as inputs* VK, IV, C, M, *and* π, *and returns 1 if* C *is the ciphertext of* M *and* IV *under* K, *and 0, otherwise.*

We require correctness and completeness as follows.

Definition 4 (Correctness). *For all* $(VK, K) \leftarrow \mathsf{KeyGen}(1^{\lambda})$, $IV \in \{0,1\}^n$, *and* $M \in \{0,1\}^L$, $\mathsf{Dec}(K, IV, \mathsf{Enc}(K, IV, M)) = M$ *holds.*

Definition 5 (Completeness). *For all $(VK, K) \leftarrow \mathsf{KeyGen}(1^\lambda)$, $IV \in \{0,1\}^n$ and for any ciphertext C, we have that for $M \leftarrow \mathsf{Dec}(K, IV, C)$, $\mathsf{Verify}(VK, IV, C, M, \mathsf{Prove}(K, IV, C)) = 1$ holds with overwhelming probability (note that M may be $\perp$).*

Next, we define security notions of SKENO, called indistinguishability under chosen-ciphertext and prove attacks (IND-CCPA) and proof soundness.

Definition 6 (IND-CCPA). *We say that a SKENO scheme Π is IND-CCPA secure if for all PPT adversary $\mathcal{A}$ the following advantage is negligible in the security parameter.*

$$\mathsf{Adv}_{\Pi,\mathcal{A}}^{Ind\text{-}ccpa}(1^\lambda) := |\Pr[(VK, K) \leftarrow \mathsf{KeyGen}(1^\lambda);$$
$$(IV^*, M_0^*, M_1^*, State) \leftarrow \mathcal{A}^{\mathsf{Enc}(K,\cdot,\cdot),\mathsf{Dec}(K,\cdot,\cdot),\mathsf{Prove}(K,\cdot,\cdot)}(1^\lambda, VK);$$
$$b \xleftarrow{\$} \{0,1\}; C^* \leftarrow \mathsf{Enc}(K, IV^*, M_b^*);$$
$$b' \leftarrow \mathcal{A}^{\mathsf{Enc}(K,\cdot,\cdot),\mathsf{Dec}(K,\cdot,\cdot),\mathsf{Prove}(K,\cdot,\cdot)}(C^*, State);\ b = b'] - \frac{1}{2}|$$

$\mathsf{Enc}(K, \cdot, \cdot)$ *is the encryption oracle which takes as input $IV \in \{0,1\}^n$ and $M \in \{0,1\}^L$, where $IV \neq IV^*$, outputs $C \leftarrow \mathsf{Enc}(K, IV, M)$. $\mathsf{Dec}(K, \cdot, \cdot)$ is the decryption oracle which takes as input $IV \in \{0,1\}^n$ and $C \in \{0,1\}^L$, where $(IV, C) \neq (IV^*, C^*)$, outputs $M/\perp \leftarrow \mathsf{Dec}(K, IV, M)$. $\mathsf{Prove}(K, \cdot, \cdot)$ is the the prove oracle which takes as input $IV \in \{0,1\}^n$ and $C \in \{0,1\}^L$, where $IV \neq IV^*$, outputs $\pi \leftarrow \mathsf{Prove}(K, IV, C)$.*

Indistinguishability under chosen-plaintext and prove attacks (IND-CPPA) is simply defined by excluding the Dec oracle from the IND-CCPA definition.

Definition 7 (Proof Soundness). *We say that a SKENO scheme Π satisfies proof soundness if for all PPT adversary $\mathcal{A}$ the following advantage is negligible in the security parameter.*

$$\mathsf{Adv}_{\Pi,\mathcal{A}}^{sound}(1^\lambda) := \Pr[(VK, K) \leftarrow \mathsf{KeyGen}(1^\lambda);\ (IV, M, State) \leftarrow \mathcal{A}(1^\lambda, VK, K);$$
$$C \leftarrow \mathsf{Enc}(K, IV, M);\ (\tilde{M}, \tilde{\pi}) \leftarrow \mathcal{A}(C, State);$$
$$\mathsf{Verify}(VK, IV, C, \tilde{M}, \tilde{\pi}) = 1;\ M \neq \tilde{M}]$$

4   Our SKENO Construction

In this section, we give our IND-CPPA secure SKENO scheme. An IND-CCPA secure SKENO scheme will be covered in Section 6. Let $(\mathsf{VRF.Setup}, \mathsf{VRF.Prove}, \mathsf{VRF.Verify})$ be a VRF and G be a PRNG.

Protocol 1 (Proposed IND-CPPA secure SKENO)

KeyGen(1^λ): *Run* $(PK, SK) \leftarrow$ VRF.Setup(1^λ), *and output* $(VK, K) = (PK, SK)$.

Enc(K, IV, M): *Run* $(y, \pi') \leftarrow$ VRF.Prove(K, IV) *and* $Z_{IV} \leftarrow G(y)$, *compute* $C = M \oplus Z_{IV}$, *and output* C.

Dec(K, IV, C): *Run* $(y, \pi') \leftarrow$ VRF.Prove(K, IV) *and* $Z_{IV} \leftarrow G(y)$, *compute* $M = C \oplus Z_{IV}$, *and output* M.

Prove(K, IV, C): *Run* $(y, \pi') \leftarrow$ VRF.Prove(K, IV) *and return* $\pi = (y, \pi')$.

Verify(VK, IV, C, M, π): *Parse* $\pi = (y, \pi')$. *If* $\pi' \neq \bot$, VRF.Verify(VK, IV, y, π') $= 1$, *and* $C \oplus G(y) = M$, *then output 1. Otherwise, output 0.*

The correctness clearly holds. In addition, completeness also holds if the underlying VRF satisfies provability.

Note that in our IND-CPPA secure SKENO the Dec algorithm never outputs $\bot$ (i,e., even if C was not generated by the Enc algorithm, the Dec algorithm outputs the corresponding decryption result which belongs to the plaintext space $\{0, 1\}^L$). Therefore, the Prove algorithm does not have to prove that C is an invalid ciphertext in the IND-CPPA secure SKENO, whereas, in the IND-CCPA SKENO (presented in Section 6), since the Dec algorithm outputs $\bot$ for invalid ciphertexts, the Prove algorithm needs to accept the proof that the decryption result of C is $\bot$.

5 Security Analysis

In this section, we give the security proofs of our SKENO construction.

Theorem 1. *Our SKENO construction is IND-CPPA secure if the underlying VRF and PRNG satisfy pseudorandomness.*

Proof. Let $\mathcal{A}$ be an adversary who can break the IND-CPPA security of our SKENO construction. We construct an algorithm $\mathcal{B}$ that breaks the pseudorandomness of the underlying VRF. Let $\mathcal{C}_{\mathrm{VRF}}$ be the challenger of the underlying VRF. $\mathcal{C}_{\mathrm{VRF}}$ sends PK to $\mathcal{B}$. $\mathcal{B}$ sets $VK = PK$ and sends VK to $\mathcal{A}$. To answer queries issued by $\mathcal{A}$, $\mathcal{B}$ manages a table $\{(IV, y, \pi')\}$.

Phase 1 query

Enc: Let (IV, M) be an encryption query issued by $\mathcal{A}$. If there exists the entry (IV, y, π'), then $\mathcal{B}$ returns $C = M \oplus G(y)$. Otherwise, $\mathcal{B}$ sends IV to $\mathcal{C}_{\mathrm{VRF}}$ as a VRF.Prove query, obtains (y, π'), adds (IV, M, y, π') to the table, and returns $C = M \oplus G(y)$.

Prove: Let (IV, C) be a prove query issued by $\mathcal{A}$. If there exists the entry (IV, y, π'), then $\mathcal{B}$ returns $\pi = (y, \pi')$. Otherwise (this means that C is not generated via the Enc oracle), then $\mathcal{B}$ sends IV to $\mathcal{C}_{\mathrm{VRF}}$ as a VRF.Prove query, obtains (y, π'), adds (IV, y, π') to the table, where $M = C \oplus G(y)$, and returns $\pi = (y, \pi')$.

Challenge phase

In the challenge phase, $\mathcal{A}$ sends (IV^*, M_0^*, M_1^*) to $\mathcal{B}$, and $\mathcal{B}$ sends IV^* to $\mathcal{C}_{\text{VRF}}$. $\mathcal{C}_{\text{VRF}}$ selects $b \in \{0,1\}$ and computes y^* such that $y^* = F_K(IV^*)$ if $b = 0$, and $y^* \xleftarrow{\$} \{0,1\}^m$ if $b = 1$, and sends y^* to $\mathcal{B}$. $\mathcal{B}$ randomly choses $b'' \in \{0,1\}$, computes $C^* = M_{b''}^* \oplus G(y^*)$, and sends C^* to $\mathcal{A}$.

Phase 2 query

Enc: The same as the phase 1 query since $\mathcal{A}$ never issues IV^* as an encryption query.

Prove: Let (IV, C) be a prove query issued by $\mathcal{A}$, where $IV \neq IV^*$. If there exists the entry (IV, y, π'), then $\mathcal{B}$ returns $\pi = (y, \pi')$. Otherwise (this means that C is not generated via the Enc oracle), then $\mathcal{B}$ sends IV to $\mathcal{C}_{\text{VRF}}$ as a VRF.Prove query, obtains (y, π'), adds (IV, y, π') to the table, where $M = C \oplus G(y)$, and returns $\pi = (y, \pi')$.

Guessing phase

Finally, $\mathcal{A}$ outputs $b' \in \{0,1\}$. Note that if $b = 0$ (i.e., $y^* = F_K(IV^*)$), then C^* is a valid ciphertext of $M_{b''}^*$. So, $\mathcal{A}$ has an advantage. Otherwise, let $b = 1$ (i.e., y^* is a random value, and is independent of IV^*). Then if there exist an algorithm that can distinguish the probabilistic distribution of $M_0^* \oplus G(y^*)$ and the probabilistic distribution of $M_1^* \oplus G(y^*)$, then it contradicts the fact that G is a PRNG. So, these distributions are identical if G is a PRNG. So $\mathcal{A}$ has no advantage in the case of $b = 1$. Therefore, if $b' = b''$, then $\mathcal{B}$ outputs 0, and 1, otherwise.   □

Theorem 2. *Our SKENO construction satisfies proof soundness if the underlying VRF satisfy uniqueness.*

Proof. Let $(M, \tilde{M})$ is a message pair and $C \leftarrow \text{Enc}(K, IV, M)$ (these are appeared in the proof soundness definition). Since $M \neq \tilde{M}$, for $Z_{IV} := C \oplus M$ and $\tilde{Z}_{IV} := C \oplus \tilde{M}$, $Z_{IV} \neq \tilde{Z}_{IV}$ holds. In addition, there exist $y, \tilde{y} \in \{0,1\}^m$ such that $Z_{IV} = G(y)$ and $\tilde{Z}_{IV} = G(\tilde{y})$. Note that $y \neq \tilde{y}$ since $Z_{IV} \neq \tilde{Z}_{IV}$ and G is a deterministic function. This never happen if the underlying VRF satisfy uniqueness.   □

6   SKENO with Chosen-Ciphertext Security

As in the conversion from CPA-secure DEM to CCA-secure DEM using message authentication code (MAC) [1], we can construct a IND-CCPA secure SKENO scheme. We use strongly existentially unforgeable against a one-time chosen-message attack (one-time sEU-CMA) MAC [10,31]. A MAC consists of two algorithms, MAC and Vrfy. The MAC algorithm takes as inputs a secret key $Z \in \{0,1\}^{L_2}$ and a message $M \in \{0,1\}^{L_1}$ $(L_1, L_2 \in \mathbb{N})$, and outputs a tag $t \leftarrow \text{MAC}_Z(M)$. The Vrfy algorithm takes as inputs Z and t, and outputs 0 (reject) or 1 (accept). We requre that for all Z and M we have $\mathsf{Vrfy}_Z(M, \mathsf{MAC}_Z(M)) = 1$.

Briefly, $Z_{IV} = G(F_K(IV))$ is divided into two part, say $Z_1 \in \{0,1\}^{L_1}$ and $Z_2 \in \{0,1\}^{L_2}$, where $L_1 + L_2 = L$ and L_2 is the key length of the underlying MAC algorithm (MAC,Vrfy). Then, a plaintext $M \in \{0,1\}^{L_1}$ is encrypted by Z_1 such that $c = M \oplus Z_1$, and a tag t is computed under the key Z_2 such that $t = \mathsf{MAC}_{Z_2}(c)$. The actual ciphertext is $C = (c, t)$. In the Dec algorithm, run $(y, \pi') \leftarrow \mathsf{VRF.Prove}(K, IV)$ and $Z_{IV} \leftarrow G(y)$, divide $Z_{IV} = Z_1 \| Z_2$, compute $M = c \oplus Z_1$, and output M if $\mathsf{Vrfy}_{Z_2}(c) = 1$ holds, and $\bot$, otherwise. In the Prove algorithm, run $(y, \pi') \leftarrow \mathsf{VRF.Prove}(K, IV)$ and $Z_{IV} \leftarrow G(y)$, and divide $Z_{IV} = Z_1 \| Z_2$. If $\mathsf{Vrfy}_{Z_2}(c) = 1$ holds, then set $\pi = (y, \pi')$. If $\mathsf{Vrfy}_{Z_2}(c) = 0$ holds, then set $\pi = (y, \bot)$. In the Verify algorithm, if $\pi' = \bot$ and $\mathsf{Vrfy}_{Z_2}(c) = 0$, then output 1. If $\pi' \neq \bot$, $\mathsf{VRF.Verify}(VK, IV, y, \pi') = 1$, and $\mathsf{Vrfy}_{Z_2}(c) = 1$, then output 1. Otherwise, output 0.

7 Conclusion

The previous proposed Non-interactive opening ciphertexts techniques are for public key cryptosystem, which cannot bring the solutions for the situation where the symmetric key cryptosystem is being used, and the secret key is shared among a group of people, since the key itself is not appropriate for opening to behave as a proof. This paper fills in the above gaps by proposing the first stream cipher based SKENO scheme that can be proved to be IND-CPPA and IND-CCPA secure, which can provide Non-interactive opening services in the shared key environment.

Acknowledgements. The authors would like to thank the anonymous reviewers of ICICS 2011 for their invaluable comments, and also would like to thank Dr. Takahiro Matsuda (AIST, Japan) for his invaluable comments to help to improve this paper.

References

1. ISO CD 18033-2. Encryption algorithms part 2: asymmetric ciphers (2004)
2. Abdalla, M., Catalano, D., Fiore, D.: Verifiable Random Functions from Identity-based Key Encapsulation. In: Joux, A. (ed.) EUROCRYPT 2009. LNCS, vol. 5479, pp. 554–571. Springer, Heidelberg (2009)
3. Belenkiy, M., Chase, M., Kohlweiss, M., Lysyanskaya, A.: Compact E-cash and Simulatable VRFs Revisited. In: Shacham, H., Waters, B. (eds.) Pairing 2009. LNCS, vol. 5671, pp. 114–131. Springer, Heidelberg (2009)
4. Bellare, M., Shi, H., Zhang, C.: Foundations of Group Signatures: The Case of Dynamic Groups. In: Menezes, A. (ed.) CT-RSA 2005. LNCS, vol. 3376, pp. 136–153. Springer, Heidelberg (2005)
5. Bellare, M., Shoup, S.: Two-tier Signatures, Strongly Unforgeable Signatures, and Fiat-shamir without Random Oracles. In: Okamoto, T., Wang, X. (eds.) PKC 2007. LNCS, vol. 4450, pp. 201–216. Springer, Heidelberg (2007)

6. Berbain, C., Gilbert, H.: On the Security of IV Dependent Stream Ciphers. In: Biryukov, A. (ed.) FSE 2007. LNCS, vol. 4593, pp. 254–273. Springer, Heidelberg (2007)

7. Bertoni, G., Daemen, J., Peeters, M., Van Assche, G.: Sponge-based Pseudo-random Number Generators. In: Mangard, S., Standaert, F.-X. (eds.) CHES 2010. LNCS, vol. 6225, pp. 33–47. Springer, Heidelberg (2010)

8. Blum, M., Micali, S.: How to generate cryptographically strong sequences of pseudo-random bits. SIAM J. Comput. 13(4), 850–864 (1984)

9. Boneh, D., Franklin, M.K.: Identity-based Encryption from the Weil Pairing. In: Kilian, J. (ed.) CRYPTO 2001. LNCS, vol. 2139, pp. 213–229. Springer, Heidelberg (2001)

10. Boneh, D., Katz, J.: Improved Efficiency for CCA-secure Cryptosystems Built Using Identity-based Encryption. In: Menezes, A. (ed.) CT-RSA 2005. LNCS, vol. 3376, pp. 87–103. Springer, Heidelberg (2005)

11. Brakerski, Z., Goldwasser, S., Rothblum, G.N., Vaikuntanathan, V.: Weak Ver-ifiable Random Functions. In: Reingold, O. (ed.) TCC 2009. LNCS, vol. 5444, pp. 558–576. Springer, Heidelberg (2009)

12. Camenisch, J.L., Hohenberger, S., Lysyanskaya, A.: Compact E-cash. In: Cramer, R. (ed.) EUROCRYPT 2005. LNCS, vol. 3494, pp. 302–321. Springer, Heidelberg (2005)

13. Damgård, I., Hofheinz, D., Kiltz, E., Thorbek, R.: Public-Key Encryption with Non-interactive Opening. In: Malkin, T. (ed.) CT-RSA 2008. LNCS, vol. 4964, pp. 239–255. Springer, Heidelberg (2008)

14. Dodis, Y.: Efficient Construction of (Distributed) Verifiable Random Functions. In: Desmedt, Y.G. (ed.) PKC 2003. LNCS, vol. 2567, pp. 1–17. Springer, Heidelberg (2002)

15. Dodis, Y., Yampolskiy, A.: A Verifiable Random Function with Short Proofs and Keys. In: Vaudenay, S. (ed.) PKC 2005. LNCS, vol. 3386, pp. 416–431. Springer, Heidelberg (2005)

16. Dwork, C., Naor, M.: Zaps and their applications. SIAM J. Comput. 36(6), 1513–1543 (2007)

17. Emura, K., Hanaoka, G., Sakai, Y.: Group Signature Implies PKE with Non-interactive Opening and Threshold PKE. In: Echizen, I., Kunihiro, N., Sasaki, R. (eds.) IWSEC 2010. LNCS, vol. 6434, pp. 181–198. Springer, Heidelberg (2010)

18. Fiore, D., Schröder, D.: Uniqueness is a different story: Impossibility of verifiable random functions from trapdoor permutations. Cryptology ePrint Archive, Report 2010/648 (2010), http://eprint.iacr.org/

19. Freedman, M.J., Ishai, Y., Pinkas, B., Reingold, O.: Keyword Search and Oblivious Pseudorandom Functions. In: Kilian, J. (ed.) TCC 2005. LNCS, vol. 3378, pp. 303–324. Springer, Heidelberg (2005)

20. Galindo, D.: Breaking and Repairing Damgård et al. Public Key Encryption Scheme with Non-interactive Opening. In: Fischlin, M. (ed.) CT-RSA 2009. LNCS, vol. 5473, pp. 389–398. Springer, Heidelberg (2009)

21. Galindo, D., Libert, B., Fischlin, M., Fuchsbauer, G., Lehmann, A., Manulis, M., Schröder, D.: Public-Key Encryption with Non-Interactive Opening: New Constructions and Stronger Definitions. In: Bernstein, D.J., Lange, T. (eds.) AFRICACRYPT 2010. LNCS, vol. 6055, pp. 333–350. Springer, Heidelberg (2010)

22. Goldreich, O.: Foundations of Cryptography. Basic Tools, vol. 1. Cambridge University Press, New York (2001)

23. Goldreich, O., Goldwasser, S., Micali, S.: How to construct random functions. J. ACM 33(4), 792–807 (1986)

24. Håstad, J., Impagliazzo, R., Levin, L.A., Luby, M.: A pseudorandom generator from any one-way function. SIAM J. Comput. 28(4), 1364–1396 (1999)
25. Hazay, C., Lindell, Y.: Efficient Protocols for Set Intersection and Pattern Matching with Security Against Malicious and Covert Adversaries. In: Canetti, R. (ed.) TCC 2008. LNCS, vol. 4948, pp. 155–175. Springer, Heidelberg (2008)
26. Hohenberger, S., Waters, B.: Constructing Verifiable Random Functions with Large Input Spaces. In: Gilbert, H. (ed.) EUROCRYPT 2010. LNCS, vol. 6110, pp. 656–672. Springer, Heidelberg (2010)
27. Jarecki, S., Liu, X.: Efficient Oblivious Pseudorandom Function with Applications to Adaptive OT and Secure Computation of Set Intersection. In: Reingold, O. (ed.) TCC 2009. LNCS, vol. 5444, pp. 577–594. Springer, Heidelberg (2009)
28. Lai, J., Deng, R.H., Liu, S., Kou, W.: Efficient CCA-secure PKE from Identity-based Techniques. In: Pieprzyk, J. (ed.) CT-RSA 2010. LNCS, vol. 5985, pp. 132–147. Springer, Heidelberg (2010)
29. Liskov, M.: Updatable Zero-knowledge Databases. In: Roy, B. (ed.) ASIACRYPT 2005. LNCS, vol. 3788, pp. 174–198. Springer, Heidelberg (2005)
30. Lysyanskaya, A.: Unique Signatures and Verifiable Random Functions from the DH-DDH Separation. In: Yung, M. (ed.) CRYPTO 2002. LNCS, vol. 2442, pp. 597–612. Springer, Heidelberg (2002)
31. Matsuda, T., Hanaoka, G., Matsuura, K., Imai, H.: An Efficient Encapsulation Scheme from Near Collision Resistant Pseudorandom Generators and its Application to IBE-to-PKE Transformations. In: Fischlin, M. (ed.) CT-RSA 2009. LNCS, vol. 5473, pp. 16–31. Springer, Heidelberg (2009)
32. Matsuda, T., Matsuura, K.: On Black-box Separations among Injective One-way Functions. In: Ishai, Y. (ed.) TCC 2011. LNCS, vol. 6597, pp. 597–614. Springer, Heidelberg (2011)
33. Micali, S., Rabin, M.O., Vadhan, S.P.: Verifiable random functions. In: FOCS, pp. 120–130 (1999)
34. Micali, S., Reyzin, L.: Soundness in the Public-key Model. In: Kilian, J. (ed.) CRYPTO 2001. LNCS, vol. 2139, pp. 542–565. Springer, Heidelberg (2001)
35. Micali, S., Rivest, R.L.: Micropayments Revisited. In: Preneel, B. (ed.) CT-RSA 2002. LNCS, vol. 2271, pp. 149–163. Springer, Heidelberg (2002)
36. Yao, A.C.-C.: Theory and applications of trapdoor functions (extended abstract). In: FOCS, pp. 80–91 (1982)

Lightweight RFID Mutual Authentication Protocol against Feasible Problems

Yongming Jin[1,2], Huiping Sun[3], Wei Xin[1,2], Song Luo[1,2], and Zhong Chen[1,2]

[1] School of Electronics Engineering and Computer Science
Peking University, Beijing, China
[2] Key Laboratory of High Confidence Software Technologies
Ministry of Education, Beijing, China
[3] School of Software and Microelectronics
Peking University, Beijing, China
{jinym,xinwei,luosong,chen}@infosec.pku.edu.cn,
sunhp@ss.pku.edu.cn

Abstract. The wide deployment of RFID systems has raised many concerns about the security and privacy. Many RFID authentication protocols are proposed for these low-cost RFID tags. However, most of existing RFID authentication protocols suffer from some feasible problems. In this paper, we first discuss the feasible problems that exist in some RFID authentication protocols. Then we propose a lightweight RFID mutual authentication protocol against these feasible problems. To the best of our knowledge, it is the first scalable RFID authentication protocol that based on the SQUASH scheme. The new protocol is lightweight and can provide the forward security. In every authentication session, the tag produces the random number and the response is fresh. It also prevents the asynchronization between the reader and the tag. Additionally, the new protocol is secure against such attacks as replay attack, denial of service attack, man-in-the-middle attack and so on. We also show that it requires less cost of computation and storage than other similar protocols.

Keywords: Security, RFID, Protocol, Authentication, SQUASH.

1 Introduction

Radio Frequency Identification (RFID) is a wireless automatic identification and data capture technology that uses radio signals to identify a product, animal or person without the need for physical access or line of sight. The architecture of an RFID system basically consists of the tag, the reader and the database. The tag is an identification device attached to items. The reader can read and access the tag's data by broadcasting an RF signal. The database connects to the reader via a secure network. The main benefits of RFID systems are that they can provide automated and multiple identification capture and system analysis, can read several tags in the field at the same time automatically, and can help to track valuable objects. However, the wide deployment of RFID systems has raised many concerns about the security and privacy[1].

S. Qing et al. (Eds.): ICICS 2011, LNCS 7043, pp. 69–77, 2011.
© Springer-Verlag Berlin Heidelberg 2011

A counterfeit reader can be used for communication with a real tag. It implements the same protocol and sends the messages the tag expects to receive. The attacker can capture the transmitted signals using suitable radio frequency equipment. In some scenes, it is possible to relay messages from a legitimate tag to a legitimate reader using a man-in-the-middle device. For this purpose, tags must be authenticated. The low cost demanded for RFID tags forces them to be very resource limited. Typically, the tags only have hundreds of store bits and 5-10K logic gates that only between 250 to 3000 gates can be devoted to security functions[2]. Much research has focused on providing RFID tags with lightweight cryptographic protocols. A lot of efforts have already been put in developing efficient RFID identification or authentication protocols[3,4]. However, there are several common feasible problems that exist in the RFID authentication protocols.

In this paper, we discuss these feasible problems and present a lightweight RFID mutual authentication protocol against feasible problems. We determine the feasible requirements of RFID authentication protocols. It is shown that if a protocol satisfies these requirements, the protocol will be feasible and practical.

The remainder of the paper is organized as follows. In Section 2, related work is reviewed. We propose the feasible problems and lightweight RFID mutual authentication protocol in Section 3 and Section 4 respectively. In Section 5, the security and performance is analyzed. Finally, we conclude our paper in Section 6.

2   Related Work

Ohkubo et al. propose an RFID privacy protection scheme providing indistinguishability and forward security [5]. This protocol uses a low-cost hash chain mechanism to update tag secret information to provide these two security properties. However, it is subject to replay attacks, and it permits an adversary to impersonate a tag without knowing the tag secrets.

Molnar and Wagner propose a private authentication protocol for library RFID which uses a shared secret and a pseudorandom number function to protect the messages communicated between tag and reader[6]. This scheme cannot provide forward security. Once a tag is compromised, the attacker can trace past communications from this tag, because a tag's identifier and secret key are static.

Dimitriou proposes an RFID authentication protocol that enforces user privacy and protects against tag cloning[7]. The protocol is based on the use of a secret shared between tag and database that is refreshed to avoid tag tracing. However, the scheme is prone to the asynchronization attack.

Lopez et al. propose a lightweight mutual authentication protocol for low-cost RFID tags, called LMAP[8]. It offers an adequate security level and can be implemented in the most RFID systems that only need around 300 gates. In order to implement the new protocol, tags should be fitted with a small portion of rewritable memory and another read-only memory. Lopez et al. also proposed a M^2AP protocol that has the similar properties[2]. However, the attacker can break the synchronization between the RFID reader and the tag in a single protocol run so that they cannot authenticate each other in any following protocol runs[9].

Chien and Chen introduce a mutual authentication protocol for RFID conforming to the EPC C1G2 standards[10]. The server database maintains copies of both old and new tag keys to resist the asynchronization attack. In order to give forward security, the authentication key and the access key are updated after a successful session. However, a strong attacker that compromises a tag can identify a tag's past interactions from the previous communications.

Berbain et al. proposed a novel forward private authentication scheme build upon less computationally expensive cryptographic ingredients instead of one way hash functions[11]. The new protocol is based on less complex cryptographic building blocks. This yields efficient hardware implementations compared to previous RFID protocols.

Ma et al. refine the definition of unp-privacy and proven that ind-privacy is weaker than unp-privacy. In this sense, a pseudorandom function family is the minimal requirement on an RFID tag's computational power for enforcing strong RFID system privacy. They also propose a new RFID protocol that satisfy the minimal requirement[12].

3   Feasible Problems

In this section, we discuss some feasible problems existing in the known RFID authentication protocols. We only discuss the most important requirement that RFID authentication protocols should be satisfied. If a protocol has these problems, it may be a theoretical protocol, not a feasible protocol. For example, the low cost demanded for RFID tags forces them to be very resource limited. Therefore the protocol should be lightweight and constructed on the base of the minimalist cryptography[13]. If a protocol is vulnerable to the asynchronization attack, the tag will be disfunctional and the reliability of the RFID system will be reduced. The tracking and forward security are also important issues along with the large-scale deployment of the RFID tags. We don't discuss the replay attack, man-in-the-middle attack, etc. in this section, because they are very common problems and many literature have discussed these requirements.

3.1   Lightweight

RFID tags are highly resource constrained and cannot support strong cryptography. Even a standard cryptographic hash function, such as MD5 or SHA-1, is beyond the capabilities of the most tags. Therefore, there is a strong need for new, lightweight cryptographic primitives that can be supported by low-cost RFID tags. In this paper, we introduce the SQUASH scheme (which is a squashed form of SQUare-hASH), which is ideally suited to RFID-based challenge-response authentication [14]. The basic idea of SQUASH is to mimic the operation of the Rabin encryption scheme, in which a message m is encrypted under key n. n is the product of at least two unknown prime factors. The cipher text $c = m^2$ (mod n). The scheme describes how to simplify and speed up the Rabin encryption scheme without affecting its well studied one-wayness. The details can be found in the literature [14].

3.2 Asynchronization

An adversary disturbs the interactions between reader and tag by intercepting or blocking messages transmitted. Such an attack could cause a reader and a tag to lose synchronization. This can be viewed as a kind of denial of service (DoS) attack. For example, in the DPLK protocol[15], the server might update the shared data, while the tag does not. In such a case they would no longer be able to authenticate each other.

3.3 Tracking

In some cases, outsiders to the RFID system may also be interested in monitoring and profiling the users of the RFID system. If a person does not want others to know what items he carries, then the RFID tags attached to these items must not reveal this information to unauthorized RFID readers[16]. The tracking problem means an attacker can link two different authentication actions to the same RFID tag. That is to say, the tag is tracked. In order to prevent the tracking, the protocol should be designed to respond with a fresh randomly messages in every interactive session.

3.4 Forward Security

If given all the internal state of a target tag at time t, the attacker is able to identify target tag interactions that occurred at a time $t' < t$. That is, knowledge of a tag's current internal state could help identify the tag's past interactions, and the past transcripts of a tag may allow tracking of the tag owner's past behavior. This issue is related to the leakage of tag's secret key. When the tag's current secret key is exposed, the tag's past interaction should be protected. Therefore, the protocol that satisfies this requirement should update the tag's secret key with the one-way cryptographical function. There are many RFID authentication protocols don't satisfy the forward security[11].

4   Lightweight RFID Authentication Protocol against Feasible Problems

Based on the above feasible problems, we propose a lightweight RFID mutual authentication protocol that satisfies these requirements. The new protocol can be viewed as a research case of the RFID feasible protocol. It is lightweight and the SQUASH is simple enough to be implemented on low-cost RFID tags[17,18]. Meanwhile, the SQUASH is provably as secure as the Rabin cryptosystem.

The new protocol save the previous secret key and can prevent the asynchronization between the reader and the tag. In every authentication session, the tag produces a random number and refreshs the response. If the authentication succeeds, the tag's secret key will be updated by Rabin algorithm. Nobody can identify the tag's past interactions even if he has the current secret key of the tag.

4.1 Definitions

We use the following definitions.

T_i: A tag
R_i: An RFID Reader
D_i: The Database of the T_i
k: A security parameter, $1200<k<1300$
n: The product of unknown prime factors, $n=2^k-1$
t: The length of the exchange ciphertext
s_i: A string of l bits assigned to T_i
t_i: T_i's identifier of l bits, which equals $s_i^2 \bmod n$
u_i: The previous string of l bits assigned to T_i
v_i: T_i's previous identifier of l bits, which equals $u_i^2 \bmod n$
U_i: The detailed information associated with tag T_i
s_i' : A new string of l bits assigned to T_i
t_i' : T_i's new identifier of l bits, which equals $s_i'^2 \bmod n$
$\oplus$: XOR operator
$[x]_t$: The value x's t bits.
$\leftarrow$: Substitution operator
x>>a: Right circular shift operator, which rotates all bits of x to the right by the bits, as if the right and left ends of x were joined.

4.2 Protocol Description

1. $R_i \rightarrow T_i$: Query request.
2. $T_i \rightarrow R_i \rightarrow D_i$: M, N.
    The tag selects a random number r_T, computes $M=t_i \oplus r_T$, $N'=r_T^2 \bmod n$, $N=[N']_t$, and sends (Query, M, N) to the reader, where the reader will forward (M, N) to the backend database. If an adversary forges a new message f_M by M and f_N by N, he needs to compute r_T and solve $SQUASH$ scheme. It is provably at least as secure as Rabin's public key encryption scheme.
3. $D_i \rightarrow R_i$: s_i, r_T ,U_i
    For each tuple (s_i,t_i) in the backend database, D_i computes $N'=(M \oplus t_i)^2 \bmod n$ and verifies whether the equations $N=[N']_t$. If it can find a match, then the tag T_i is successfully identified and authenticated, and the D_i will forward the tag's token (s_i,r_T) and information U_i to the R_i via the secure channel. If it can't find a match, it has two chooses which depends on the tradeoff between security and efficiency. In order to obtain the better security, D_i stops the process with failure. Otherwise, the D_i computes $N' = (M \oplus v_i)^2 \bmod n$ and verifies

whether the equations $N = [N']_t$ hold for each tuple (u_i, v_i) in its database. If there is a match, D_i sends (u_i, r_T) which replaces (s_i, r_T), and U_i to R_i. If not, it stops the process with failure. Finally, D_i computes $s'_i = t_i$, and $t'_i = s'^2_i$ mod n, updates the old secret value(u_i, v_i) by (s_i, t_i), and saves the new secret(s'_i, t'_i).

4. $R_i \rightarrow T_i : P$

To authentication itself to the tag and update the identification T_i on the tag, R_i computes $P = s_i \oplus (r_T >> l/2)$, and sends P to T_i.

5. The Tag T_i

T_i computes $s_i = P \oplus (r_T >> l/2)$. If $t_i = s^2_i$ mod n, then update t_i by $t'_i = t^2_i$ mod n.

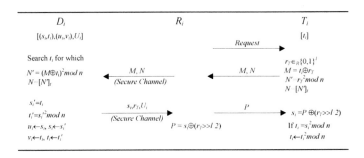

Fig. 1. Lightweight RFID Authentication Protocol Against Feasible Problems

5　Analysis

5.1　Security and Privacy

In this section, we give a security and privacy analysis of our proposed scheme.

Forward Security (FS): The new protocol can protect the privacy of the tag T_i. A strong attacker cannot identify the tag's past interactions, even if he knows the present internal state of T_i. Nobody is able to discover the previous identifiers of T_i because the reader and the tag produce new secrets $(s'_i, t'_i$) by Rabin algorithm. As a result, the attacker cannot find t_i to match $t'_i = t^2_i$ mod n.

Backward Security (BS): If the current tag secrets have been revealed, the only way of maintaining the backward security is to replace the exposed key to protect future transactions. This issue is related to tag ownership transfer. The new protocol can prevent the previous owners to read communications between the new owner and the tag. When the new owner updates secrets (s_i, t_i) for T_i using the Rabin Encryption Scheme in authentication process, the old owner cannot pry into the new owner's secrets using the knowledge of the exposed secrets.

Replay Attack (RA): The new protocol can protect against the replay attack. If an attacker uses the old message, for example, (M, N), the attacker cannot find a t_i to match $N' = (M \oplus t_i)^2$ mod n, $N = [N']_t$ because the tag's secret is changed and the old secret is no longer valid.

Denial of Service (DoS): To resist the DoS attack, we require the database to save the old values to recover synchronization with T_i. If an adversary prevents message P from reaching T_i, T_i will not update its identifier, but D_i will. In the following authentication process, T_i will use old secret value to compute M, N and D_i can recover the old secret value from (u_i, v_i).

Man-in-the-middle Attack (MITM): Any attacker can obtain the message (M, N) and P. He can prevent the correct message and send a different message. If he change the old message, he should find a t_i that exists in the database to satisfy the equation $N = (M \oplus t_i)^2 \bmod n$, $N = [N']_t$. Its security is based on the Rabin's public key encryption scheme. If an attacker changes the values P and try to let the tag update an error t_i, he needs know the r_T to find out t'_i, then computes the s'_i. However, the r_T is a random number produced by the tag T_i. It is very hard to find out.

The following table shows the comparison in the sense of security and privacy discussed in this Section.

Table 1. Security and Privacy Comparison

Schemes	FS	BS	RA	DoS	MITM
Ohkubo et al.[5]	√	√	×	√	√
Molnar et al.[6]	×	×	√	√	√
Dimitriou[7]	√	√	√	×	√
Lopez et al.[8]	√	√	√	×	√
Chien et al.[10]	*	√	√	√	√
Berbain et al.[11]	√	√	×	×	√
Ma et al.[12]	×	√	√	√	√
The new scheme	√	√	√	√	√

√: resist such an attack.
*: resist attack under some assumptions
×: can't protect against such an attack.

5.2 Efficiency Considerations

In the new protocol, the tag needs l bits of non-volatile memory to store its secret t_i. It is common condition that we can find out through the following table. Compare to other schemes, the new protocol has lower tag computation and tag communication cost.

Obviously, the new protocol needs the DB more storage cost to storage the old secret value (u_i, v_i) to prevent the asynchronization between the DB and the tag when the tag fails to receive the last message authentication code. In the practical application, it is a trade-in measure. Let l is the length of the random number and the secret value of T_i, k is the length of the tag's ID, q is the length of hash value. Let the number of total tags is n, p is the cost of PRNG operation, h is the cost of Hash function, r is the cost of Rabin encryption. In general, r is less than h. The cost of XOR, bit shift, etc. operation is negligible.

The table 2 shows the performance comparison between the existing scheme and the new scheme.

Table 2. Performance Comparison

Schemes	TC	TS	RC	RS	CC
Ohkubo et al.[5]	$2h$	l	$2h$	$l+k$	l
Molnar et al.[6]	$h+p$	$l+k$	$O(n)h+p$	$l+k$	$2l+2k$
Dimitriou[7]	$2h+p$	k	$2h+p$	k	$2l+3q$
Lopez et al.[8]	$O(1)$	$l+k$	$2p$	$l+k$	$5l$
Chien et al.[10]	p	$l+k$	p	$l+k$	$2l+2q$
Berbain et al.[11]	$3h$	l	$O(n)h+p$	$l+k$	$l+q$
Ma et al.[12]	$2h$	$l+q$	$2h+p$	$2q+l+k$	$l+2q$
The new scheme	$3r+p$	$l+q$	$O(n)h+h$	$2q+l+k$	$2l+t$

6   Conclusions

In this paper, we discuss the feasible problems that exist in the known RFID authentication protocols. Then a lightweight RFID mutual authentication protocol against these problems is proposed. It is based on the SQUASH, which is a new MAC scheme for highly constrained devices such as RFID Tags. It is exceptionally simple that can be efficiently implemented on processors and is provably at least as secure as Rabin's public key encryption scheme. The new protocol is lightweight and can provide the forward security. We also analyze the new scheme's security and efficiency and give the comparison with other schemes.

As a part of future work, a model of feasible RFID authentication protocol will be deeply researched. And by the formalized analyze, we try to prove that the new model has better architecture and arts.

Acknowledgments. Research works in this paper are partial supported by Natural Science Foundation of China (No.61170263).

References

1. Juels, A.: RFID security and privacy: A research survey. IEEE Journal on Selected Areas in Communications 24(2), 381–394 (2006)
2. Peris-Lopez, P., Hernandez-Castro, J.C., Estevez-Tapiador, J.M., Ribagorda, A.: M^{2}AP: A Minimalist Mutual-authentication Protocol for Low-cost RFID Tags. In: Ma, J., Jin, H., Yang, L.T., Tsai, J.J.-P. (eds.) UIC 2006. LNCS, vol. 4159, pp. 912–923. Springer, Heidelberg (2006)

3. Lehtonen, M., Staake, T., Michahelles, F.: From identification to authentication-a review of RFID product authentication techniques. In: Networked RFID Systems and Lightweight Cryptography, pp. 169–187 (2008)
4. Ohkubo, M., Suzuki, K., Kinoshita, S.: Cryptographic Approaches for Improving Security and Privacy Issues of RFID Systems. Wiley Online Library (2010)
5. Ohkubo, M., Suzuki, K., Kinoshita, S.: Cryptographic approach to "privacy-friendly" tags. In: RFID Privacy Workshop. MIT, MA (2003)
6. Molnar, D., Wagner, D.: Privacy and security in library RFID: Issues, practices, and architectures. In: Pfitzmann, B., Liu, P. (eds.) Conference on Computer and Communications Security – ACM CCS, pp. 210–219. ACM Press, Washington, DC (2004)
7. Dimitriou, T.: A lightweight RFID protocol to protect against traceability and cloning attacks. In: First International Conference on Security and Privacy for Emerging Areas in Communications Networks, pp. 59–66 (2005)
8. Peris-Lopez, P., Hernandez-Castro, J.C., Estevez-Tapiador, J.M., Ribagorda, A.: LMAP: A real lightweight mutual authentication protocol for low-cost RFID tags. In: Proceedings of 2nd Workshop on RFID Security (2006)
9. Li, T., Wang, G.: Security analysis of two ultra-lightweight RFID authentication protocols. In: New Approaches for Security, Privacy and Trust in Complex Environments, pp. 109–120 (2007)
10. Chien, H.-Y., Chen, C.-H.: Mutual authentication protocol for RFID conforming to EPC Class 1 Generation 2 standards. Computer Standards & Interfaces 29(2), 254–259 (2007)
11. Berbain, C., Billet, O., Etrog, J., Gilbert, H.: An efficient forward private RFID protocol. In: Proceedings of the 16th ACM Conference on Computer and Communications Security, pp. 43–53. ACM Press (2009)
12. Ma, C., Li, Y., Deng, R.H., Li, T.: RFID privacy: relation between two notions, minimal condition, and efficient construction. In: Proceedings of the 16th ACM Conference on Computer and Communications Security. ACM Press, New York (2009)
13. Juels, A.: Minimalist Cryptography for Low-Cost RFID Tags. In: Blundo, C., Cimato, S. (eds.) SCN 2004. LNCS, vol. 3352, pp. 149–164. Springer, Heidelberg (2005)
14. Shamir, A.: SQUASH – A New MAC with Provable Security Properties for Highly Constrained Devices such as RFID Tags. In: Nyberg, K. (ed.) FSE 2008. LNCS, vol. 5086, pp. 144–157. Springer, Heidelberg (2008)
15. Duc, D.N., Park, J., Lee, H., Kim, K.: Enhancing security of EPCglobal Gen-2 RFID tag against traceability and cloning. In: Symposium on Cryptography and Information Security, Hiroshima, Japan (2006)
16. Langheinrich, M.: A survey of RFID privacy approaches. Personal and Ubiquitous Computing 13(6), 413–421 (2009)
17. Koshy, P., Valentin, J., Zhang, X.: Implementation and performance testing of the SQUASH RFID authentication protocol. In: Applications and Technology Conference (LISAT), 2010 Long Island Systems. IEEE Press, New York (2010)
18. Gosset, F., Standaert, F.X., Quisquater, J.J.: FPGA implementation of SQUASH. In: Proceedings of the 29th Symposium on Information Theory in the Benelux (2008)

A Note on a Privacy-Preserving Distance-Bounding Protocol

Jean-Philippe Aumasson[1], Aikaterini Mitrokotsa[2],
and Pedro Peris-Lopez[3]

[1] Nagravision, Switzerland
jeanphilippe.aumasson@gmail.com
[2] EPFL, Switzerland
katerina.mitrokotsa@epfl.ch
[3] TU Delft, Netherlands
p.perislopez@tudelft.nl

Abstract. Distance bounding protocols enable a device to establish an upper bound on the physical distance to a communication partner so as to prevent location spoofing, as exploited by relay attacks. Recently, Rasmussen and Čapkun (ACM-CCS'08) observed that these protocols leak information on the location of the parties to external observers, which is undesirable in a number of applications—for example if the leaked information leads to the identification of the parties among a group of devices. To remedy this problem, these authors proposed a "privacy-preserving" distance bounding protocol, i.e. that leaks no information on the location of the parties. The present paper reports results from an in-depth security analysis of that new protocol, with as main result an attack that recovers the ephemeral secrets as well as the location information of the two parties for particular choices of parameters. Overall, our results do not contradict the preliminary security analysis by the designers, but rather extends it to other parts of the attack surface.

Keywords: wireless communication, distance bounding, privacy.

1 Introduction

Wireless communications often have security goals that include not only traditional cryptographic notions—confidentiality, integrity, authenticity, availability—but also guarantees about the geographical location of a communicating device. For example, secured location information is necessary in battlefield ad hoc networks [1], in access control systems [2], and even in certain satellite DTV conditional access systems [3]. A particular case is when a "verifier" device has to ensure that a "prover" legitimate device is in the vicinity of the former; a trivial countermeasure is to ensure that the signal is low enough to prevent reception from farther locations. But this can be easily bypassed using a "proxy" device that amplifies and forwards the signal to a remote attacker—such

S. Qing et al. (Eds.): ICICS 2011, LNCS 7043, pp. 78–92, 2011.

attacks are known as *relay attacks*[1]. A countermeasure against relay attacks is the use of *distance bounding protocols*.

As their name suggests, distance bounding protocols enable a *verifier* device (denoted V) to establish an upper bound on the physical distance to an untrusted *prover* device (P). These protocols were first introduced in 1994 by Brands and Chaum [5] to thwart distance fraud and the so-called mafia fraud attacks (two types of relay attacks) as applied against ATM's; the target application of [5] was thus to check the proximity between a legitimate ATM and a user's smartcard. Since this seminal work, a broad range of distance bounding protocols have been proposed for technologies as RFID [6, 7, 8, 9], ultra-wideband (UWB) devices [10,11,12], wireless ad hoc networks [13,14,15], or sensor networks [16]. Distance bounding can be extended to *location verification* (also called *secure positioning*) if multiple verifiers interact with the prover: the location returned is then in the intersection of the bounding spheres surrounding each verifier. Dedicated location verification protocols were proposed in [17, 14]. As an alternative to radio waves Sastry, Shankar, and Wagner [2] proposed to use ultrasound waves to obtain better spatial resolution, due to sound's much lower speed. However, this technology is susceptible to wormhole attacks [18] (e.g. if the signal is converted to a faster radio signal to deceive the verifier).

In 2008, Rasmussen and Čapkun noted [19] that known distance bounding protocols leak information to external observers on the distance and location of the prover and the verifier. In short, information leaks through the measure of messages' arrival times, which allows one to draw on the neighborhood map hyperboles representing physical bounds on the devices' location. Although locations and relatives distances are obvious in some cases—particularly with short-range signals, or with only two devices in the neighborhood—attackers are often not supposed to know them. For example, in a scenario with a large number of devices and vehicles (as a battlefield), it can be necessary to hide the identity of the communicating parties, who in turn need to ensure secure positioning; if an adversary can determine the relative position of the communicating parties, it then becomes much easier to identify them. Rasmussen and Čapkun thus investigated potential countermeasures against leakage of information and proposed a *privacy-preserving* distance bounding protocol [19].

Our contribution: The present work focuses on the Rasmussen-Čapkun (henceforth RČ) privacy-preserving distance bounding protocol, as specified in [19, 5.4]. We report results from our in-depth security analysis of the RČ protocol's, with as main result an attack against its privacy-preserving property. We argue that the properties of challenge numbers (called "nonces" in [19]) are of utmost importance for the security of the protocol, presenting attacks exploiting partial unpredictability as well as non-uniqueness. We provide a more complete specification of the protocol than in [19] in order to facilitate proof-of-concept implementations. Our results do not contradict the preliminary security analysis in [19], but rather extends it to other parts of the attack surface.

---

[1] An academic proof-of-concept relay attack against cars' remote locking has recently been realized by the team of Čapkun, as reported in [4].

2   Background

2.1   Distance Bounding Protocols

A distance bounding protocol enables a verifier V to calculate an upper-bound on his physical distance to a prover P. Distance bounding protocols are usually composed of two phases: the *initialization phase* and the *distance bounding phase* (see Fig. 1). The initialization phase is not time critical and usually involves P's commitment to some random number. The distance bounding phase is time critical and usually involves a *rapid bit exchange* (RBE), i.e. a sequence of challenge-responses performed at maximum bit rate. The number j of rounds of the RBE phase is a security parameter. The verifier selects j unpredictable challenges $c_1, \ldots, c_j$ and sends each of them to P. The prover generates the responses $r_1, \ldots, r_j$ using a function f that opens the commitment bit by bit, and that is parameterized by j and by the secret key; V then measures the response times $\Delta t_1, \ldots, \Delta t_j$ for each challenge.

By the end of the RBE, V verifies the correctness of the responses r_i, where $i = 1, 2, \ldots, j$ and calculates an upper bound on the distance of P based on the response time Δt_i of each challenge c_i, where $i = 1, 2, \ldots, j$. As information cannot travel faster than light, the distance between P and V is upper bounded by $c\Delta t_{\max}/2$, where $\Delta t_{\max}$ is the maximum delay time between sending out the bit c_i and receiving the bit r_i back.

Security thus relies on the unpredictability of the challenges and on the speed-of-light bound on the propagation of physical signals. For example with devices operating at a 1 Gbps bit rate (thus using 1 GHz carrier waves) one bit can be sent every nanosecond, resulting in a spatial resolution of approximately 30 cm; at 10 Mbps, the resolution is 30 meters, which is acceptable for large-scale use cases.

2.2   Information Leakage and Countermeasures

In previous distance bounding protocols, an attacker can compute the distance between P and V just by listening on the channel, as explained in [19, §3]. This can cause serious implications in applications where location and distance information is critical (as location-based access control). As noted earlier, relative distance information can assist a static observer in identifying the devices that are communicating among a larger population. To obtain information on the distance and or location of parties, the adversary only needs to measure the arrival time to his radio interface of two or three consecutive messages exchanged during the RBE [19, §3].

As a general countermeasure to preclude the distance and location leakage in distance bounding protocols, one should prevent the adversary from computing the "time-of-flight" of the signal between the verifier and the prover. Adding a random delay between messages transmitted during the RBE would reduce the adversary's knowledge but P could fool V into thinking that he waits longer than he actually does—making himself appear closer. Alternatively, V could

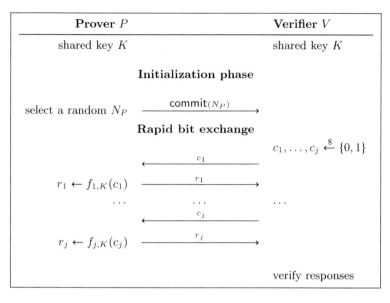

Fig. 1. A general view of distance bounding protocols ($\overset{\$}{\leftarrow}$ denotes sampling uniformly at random)

send multiple challenges to P before P responds. Nevertheless, the leakage of information is only alleviated if the adversary is unable to distinguish between the transmission originated from P and a transmission originated from V. As another countermeasure, P could send challenges at a fixed bit rate. By this mechanism, the adversary is not able to distinguish between receiving the responses from P and receiving the next challenge from V. Although this is an effective technique, in many scenarios the adversary can still compute the distance between V and P and his relative position to V or P. We refer to [19, §4] for a more detailed analysis of possible countermeasures.

Motivated by the fact that none of the above mentioned techniques provides effective protection against distance and location leakage, Rasmussen and Čapkun [19] proposed a new distance bounding protocol. The aim of the proposed protocol is to maintain the properties of existing distance bounding protocols while stoping the leakage of confidential information about distance and location.

3   The Rasmussen-Čapkun Protocol

The Rasmussen-Čapkun (RČ) protocol involves a prover P and a verifier V that communicate over an insecure channel. When the protocol succeeds V is able to calculate an upper bound on the physical distance to P, as in any distance bounding protocol. Fig. 2 gives a detailed description of the protocol, adding details that are only implicit in the original specification [19] (such as the authentication key K_2 used for computing and verifying the signatures).

Privacy preservation is ensured by hiding the actual RBE within a longer uninterrupted stream of bits.

3.1   Notations

The description of the RČ protocol in Fig. 2 assumes that P and V share the knowledge of:

- A k-bit encryption key K_1.
- A k-bit authentication key K_2.
- A symmetric encryption scheme (Enc, Dec).
- A symmetric authentication scheme (Sign, Verif) i.e. a MAC.
- A pseudorandom generator connected to a source of physical entropy.
- A timestamp counter of precision at least $1/r$ seconds, where r is the bit rate of the communication channel (for instance, with a 1 Gbps bit rate the precision should be up to a nanosecond).

In addition the RČ protocol is parameterized by the bit length n of N_P and N_V, the bit length m of M, and the (approximate) bit length of the bit streams of the distance bounding phase.

3.2   Detailed Description of the Protocol

The RČ protocol is composed of two main phases:

- **Initialization phase:** In this phase P selects a random N_P, which he encrypts-and-signs, before sending the resulting values to V. V decrypts and verifies the signatures and selects a random N_V and a random hidden marker M, which will be used in the distance bounding phase. V then encrypts-and-signs $M \| N_P$ and sends the results to P.
- **Distance bounding phase:** This phase involves the continuous exchange of bit streams between P and V. It can be separated into the following substeps:
  - a. Initially V sends to P random data $\mathsf{Rand}_V()$ (i.e. generated with its pseudorandom generator); P receives this random data, XORs it with his own random generated data ($\mathsf{Rand}_V() \oplus \mathsf{Rand}_P()$) and sends them back[2] to V.
  - b. At some randomly selected[3] point (within a setup window) V stops transmitting random data and starts transmitting the marker M. P keeps XORing the data received from V (at this time the M) with his own random data ($M \oplus \mathsf{Rand}_P()$) and sends them back to V.

---

[2] It would be equivalent, both functionally and in terms of security, to send back only $\mathsf{Rand}_P()$. The purpose of the XOR is rather to ensure a constant-time processing of the challenges, since XOR must be used later in a critical step of the distance bounding phase.

[3] The distribution considered is not specified in [19].

c. As soon as the hidden marker M has been transmitted V starts transmitting N_V and starts storing the response that he will receive. P continuously monitors the data received to detect M, and as soon as it detects M he XORs the subsequent bits received with N_P followed by random bits.

d. By the time V has sent the last bit of N_V, he starts again transmitting random data. Similarly, P starts XORing the received random data with his own random data ($\mathsf{Rand}_V() \oplus \mathsf{Rand}_P()$). After some short random delay V stops transmitting data and similarly after another random delay P ceases his transmission, to avoid leaking information on the synchronization of P and V.

By the end of the distance bounding phase, V counts the number of bits received between the time he transmitted the first bit of N_V and the time he received the first bit of $N_V \oplus N_P$. Given the bit rate and the processing delay, V can calculate the round trip time and thus an upper bound on the distance to P.

4 Attacks for the RČ Protocol with Predictable Nonces

This section presents attacks when nonces are predictable, as in stream ciphers or block ciphers in CTR mode. The attacks are simple and only aim to give evidence that unpredictability is necessary.

4.1 Are Nonces Nonces?

The values N_P and N_V are referred to as "nonces" in [19], but defined as random numbers that are not necessarily unique. In cryptography, however, nonces are often defined as "numbers used only once" and have as only requirement their uniqueness, as for stream ciphers or block ciphers in CTR mode; a (long enough) counter can there be used securely. In many applications nonces are public, and need not be unpredictable, as their sole purpose is to ensure the "freshness" of a protocol session.

In the context of distance bounding protocols, Hancke and Kuhn used "nonces" defined as "unpredictable bitstrings that will never again be used for the same purpose" [6, §3.1]. Ensuring both uniqueness and unpredictability can be achieved by several means:

1. The combination of a counter, ensuring uniqueness, and of a random generator, ensuring unpredictability (e.g. by concatenation of the two values).
2. The use of random numbers and the storage in memory of previously generated numbers to ensure uniqueness.
3. The use of random numbers and of a probabilistic data structure to reduce the memory requirement, compared to the previous solution. For instance, the use of a Bloom filter to encode the set of previously used seed would ensure uniqueness of nonces, with a false positive probability parametrized by the size of the register. Such a solution, however, requires the implementation of an additional—non cryptographic—hash function.

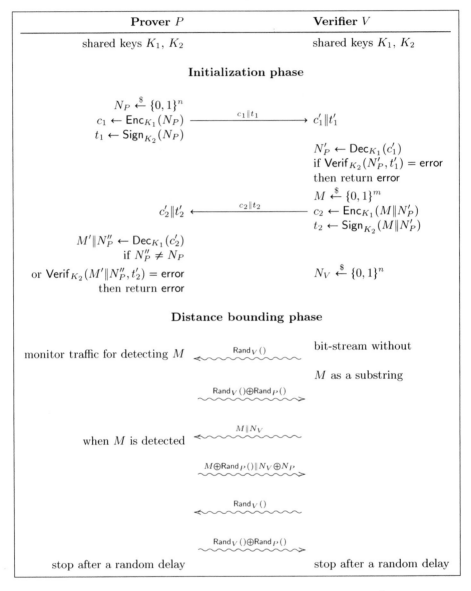

Fig. 2. Rasmussen and Čapkun's distance bounding protocol, where $\overset{\$}{\leftarrow}$ denotes sampling uniformly at random, $\leftarrow$ denotes a simple message transmission, and $\leftsquigarrow$ denotes a continuous stream transmission at maximal bit rate

To the best of our knowledge, it is not known how to design nonce generators of type 1 that are both cheap to implement and that do not leak the value of the counter, thus making nonces partially predictable. The other two solutions require non-negligible memory, and are thus inappropriate for the most lightweight devices.

In the following, we present attacks on variants of the RČ protocol that use unique and predictable, or partially predictable, nonces. We then present an attack on the original RČ protocol, exploiting the non-uniqueness of nonces, and propose efficient countermeasures.

For more about the problem of generating and resetting nonces, we refer the reader to the extensive study by Zenner [20]. We conclude this section with Anderson's definition of a nonce, which proves appropriate to the RČ protocol: "The term *nonce* can mean anything that guarantees the freshness of a message. A nonce may, according to the context, be a random number, a serial number, or a random challenge received from a third party. There are subtle differences between the three approaches, such as in the level of resistance they offer to various kinds of replay attacks. But in very low-cost systems, the first two predominate, as it tends to be cheaper to have a communication channel in one direction only." [21, p15].

4.2   Attack with a Predictable N_V

Suppose that given the value of N_V used at some distance bounding session, P can determine the N_V that V will use at the subsequent run of the protocol. It follows that in the distance bounding phase of the said subsequent session, P can start sending $N_V \oplus N_P$ before the complete M is received, thus deceiving V in concluding that P is closer than it actually is. Secure distance bounding is thus not ensured.

If N_V is only partially predictable (for example, a 64-bit N_V is formed of a 32-bit predictable counter followed by a 32-bit random string), then the above attack does not work.

4.3   Attack with a Predictable N_P

Suppose an attacker comes to know the N_P of a given session, and can predict the value of N_P that will be used at the subsequent session. The privacy-breaking attack then consists in identifying N_V by searching for a collision between contiguous n-bit windows from the V-to-P stream and the n-bit windows formed from XORing each contiguous n-bit window of the P-to-V stream with N_P, for the windows chronologically following those of the V-to-P stream. Efficient substring search methods as the Boyer-Moore algorithm [22] may be employed.

This attack requires the recording of the sessions, and allows the attacker to determine (a bound on) the distance of P to V, as computed by the latter.

If N_P is only partially predictable, the attack works with a slightly lower success probability, due to the increased chance of false positives. That probability depends on the parameters n and ℓ and on the amount of predictable information in N_P.

4.4 Discussion

The analysis in this section suggests that the best choice for P is to use totally unpredictable nonces N_P, and to choose them as random (thus potentially non-unique) numbers for the sake of efficiency. This is exactly how N_P is defined in [19]. The next section shows how to detect and exploit repetitions of nonces, and suggests a modification in the protocol to dissimulate nonces repetition, thus thwarting our attack.

5 Attack for the Original RČ Protocol

We present a passive attack that recovers N_P, N_V, and M for two sessions of the RČ protocol, which allows an attacker to deduce information on the relative distance of P and V during each of those sessions. The distance between P and V does not need to be the same at each session. More precisely, we show how one can exploit repeated occurrences of the same N_P in two distinct sessions to recover the ephemeral secrets of those sessions.

Below we first give a general description of our attack, then we provide a detailed complexity analysis for each part of the attack, with concrete performance figures for typical parameters of the RČ protocol.

5.1 Description of the Attack

The proposed attack observes many sessions of the RČ protocol between P and V, and goes as follows:

1. For each session observed, record synchronously the two data streams exchanged after c_2 is sent, and store the c_1's in a dynamically sorted table. When a value of c_1 has appeared twice—i.e., when an N_P has been repeated—stop recording sessions and delete all previous recordings but those of the two sessions where the repetition occurred.
2. For each of the two sessions with a same N_P, do the following:
   (a) divide the V-to-P stream into n-bit windows $VP_0, VP_1, \ldots$
   (b) divide the P-to-V stream into n-bit windows $PV_0, PV_1, \ldots$
   (c) construct and sort a table containing all $VP_i \oplus PV_j$ values, $0 < i < j$
   Since the two sessions used the same N_P, each of the two tables T_1 and T_2 will contain an element equal to this N_P. Indeed, the XOR between VP_i's and PV_i's will cancel the value of each N_V ($N_V \oplus (N_V \oplus N_P) = N_P$).
3. Search for a collision between an element of T_1 and an element of T_2. If a unique collision is found, then the value is N_P.
4. Given N_P, identify M and N_V in the bit-streams of each session. Count the number of bits between the reception of N_V from the verifier and the reception of P's response to deduce information on the relative positions of P and V.

5.2 Complexity Analysis

We analyse the generic time and space complexity of the proposed attack, assuming that ℓ is the least number of bits sent by either P or V during the distance bounding phase.

Memory required before detecting a collision. Since N_P is n-bit long, an N_P will be repeated after approximately $2^{n/2}$ sessions. One thus needs to record of the order of $2 \cdot \ell \cdot 2^{n/2}$ bits.

Memory to store the tables. There are $W = \ell - n + 1$ distinct windows of n bits in the V-to-P stream. The i-th window, starting from the first one when $i = 1$, is XORed with $W - i - 1$ n-bit windows of the P-to-V stream. Thus, there are in total:

$$N = \sum_{i=1}^{W}(W - 1 - i) = \frac{W^2 - 3W}{2}$$

entries in each table.

Computation to sort the tables. Sorting with comparison-based algorithm (as heap sort or quicksort) takes $O(N \log N)$ comparisons, where N is the number of n-bit words in the table (the above values). As the cost of comparing n-bit elements is arguably proportional to n, this gives a complexity $O(nN \log N)$. Using radix sort, one can achieve complexity $O(nN)$ complexity (see e.g. [23] for a similar analysis). However, note that this analysis ignores the extra cost caused by memory accesses to a large table, which arguably makes the above estimates misleading.

An alternative to classical sort algorithm, discussed in [23], is to use Schimmler's [24] or Schnorr-Shamir's [25] algorithms on a parallel machine. The later sorts N elements using a $\sqrt{N} \times \sqrt{N}$ mesh of N processors in approximately $3\sqrt{N}$ steps.

Number of false alarms. After sorting the two N-element tables, we search for an element common in the two tables. One collision is known to exist, as each table is known to contain N_P. Other collisions that may be found are thus "false positives". The expected number of false alarms is the expected number of collisions besides the known N_P collision, that is $(N^2 - 1)/2^n$.

Efficiency for typical parameters. In section [19, §5.4] is discussed an implementation of the protocol over a communication channel of bit rate 1 Gbps (i.e., one bit is transmitted each nanosecond) with hidden markers M of $m = 160$ bits, such that the distance bounding phase lasts (approximately) 500 milliseconds. In this case streams of 2^{30} bits are exchanged in each direction. As noted in [19, §5.4], however, an attacker has no way to verify a guess of M, but only a guess of N_P in time approximately N for each of the 2^n possible values.

No value is suggested for the length n of the random numbers N_P and N_V, nor for the length of K_1 or K_2. We shall thus study the efficiency of our attack for the typical values of n, as 32, 64, or 128. Note that the cost of an offline

Table 1. Evaluation of our attack for several typical parameters (length of RBE ℓ, in bits, and length of the nonces n). Time complexity of sorting the table is that of the Schnorr-Shamir parallel algorithm. The number of collisions is at least one, in which case the unique collision corresponds to the solution for N_P. If more than one collision are found, then the solution is known to lie in this set.

(n, ℓ)	sessions monitored	memory required	tables size (N)	sorting time	number of collisions
$(32, 2^{10})$	2^{16}	2^{27}	2^{19}	2^{11}	2^6
$(32, 2^{20})$	2^{16}	2^{37}	2^{39}	2^{21}	2^{45}
$(64, 2^{10})$	2^{32}	2^{43}	2^{19}	2^{10}	1
$(64, 2^{20})$	2^{32}	2^{53}	2^{39}	2^{21}	2^{14}
$(64, 2^{30})$	2^{32}	2^{63}	2^{59}	2^{31}	2^{53}
$(128, 2^{10})$	2^{64}	2^{75}	2^{19}	2^{11}	1
$(128, 2^{20})$	2^{64}	2^{85}	2^{39}	2^{21}	1
$(128, 2^{30})$	2^{64}	2^{95}	2^{59}	2^{31}	1

attack recovering N_P and N_V (and thus M) for a given session has complexity $N2^n$, as observed above.

Table 1 summarizes the complexity of our attack for various combinations of choices of n and ℓ. The theoretical complexity bottleneck (in time and space) is the recording of $2^{n/2}$ sessions of the protocol. The attack is clearly practical when using 32-bit nonces with a 2^{10}-bit long distance bounding phase; increasing the nonce to 64-bit still gives an attack arguably practical ("only" 1 Tb of memory is necessary). In any case, the attack is only applicable if a large number of protocol sessions can be initiated, and if the communication can be captured and recorded at an appropriate rate (which, admittedly, may be impossible for the highest frequencies).

6 Strengthening the RČ Protocol

We propose the following modifications to the RČ protocol to thwart our collision-based attack, and as countermeasures against future attacks on components or implementations of the attacks.

- **Probabilistic encryption**, so that repetitions of N_P cannot be detected (since two ciphertexts of the same N_P are then distinct). This modification alone is sufficient to thwart the attack in §5.
- **Better nonces**: as discussed in §4, unique N_P nonces should be used, if possible, for example by using Bloom filters to save memory at the price of a non-zero false positive probability.
- **Encrypt-then-sign** instead of encrypt-and-sign; the former being at least as secure as the latter, and benefiting of provable security properties (cf. [26]).

– **Distinct keys** for encryption and for authentication; this modification is included in our description of the protocol, but was not explicit in its original definition in [19].

7 Security against Relay Attacks

In this section we analyse the security of the RČ protocol against distance, mafia, and terrorist fraud attacks. For a detailed description of each of the attacks we urge the reader to consult [5].

7.1 Distance Fraud

A distance fraud attack is possible when there is no relationship between the challenge bits and the response bits exchanged during the distance verification. If a fraudulent prover $\overline{P}$ knows when the challenge bits will be sent, it can trick V by sending the response bits before receiving the challenge bits. Thus, V computes a wrong upper bound regarding its physical distance to $\overline{P}$.

In RČ, the response bit-streams are functions of the challenges. More precisely, the response bit-stream $N_v \oplus N_P$ is used for distance-checking. So, the probability that an attacker performs a successful distance fraud attack is upper bounded by $(1/2)^n$ [5], where n is the bit-length of N_V and N_P.

7.2 Mafia Fraud

The best known strategy to launch a successful mafia fraud attack consists in querying the prover P before receiving the challenge from the verifier V and obtaining the right response for this value. When the actual challenge bit is sent to P, in half of all cases, the adversary knows the response beforehand because this value coincides with the value that was previously queried. In the other half of cases, the attacker can answer a random challenge. If a protocol is vulnerable to the above attack, the success probability with which a mafia fraud attack can succeed is bounded by $(\frac{3}{4})^n$, which is higher than the optimal value $(\frac{1}{2})^n$, where n is the number of bits exchanged in the RBE.

In [27], Munilla and Peinado proposed a protocol inspired by [6] in which the success probability of an adversary to accomplish a mafia fraud attack is reduced. The proposal is based on *void* challenges in order to detect that P is not waiting to receive the challenge bits. A void challenge is a challenge which V intentionally leaves without sending. That is, the challenge bit sent by P can take three different values $\{0, 1, void\}$. If V detects that a response bit is received during the interval of a void challenge, the dishonest prover $\overline{P}$ is detected. Although, from a theoretical point of view the proposal is interesting, the feasibility of this scheme is questionable since it requires three physical states.

Alternatively, Rasmussen and Čapkun introduced the use of a hidden marker M which provides the advantage of detecting whether P is waiting to receive the challenge bit-streams. The position of the hidden marker M is randomly chosen in the setup window. The adversary may try to guess the start of hidden marker M and then may use the strategy of asking in advance to know the response of the bit-stream N_V. Let r be the bit rate of the channel and consider a setup window of ω_s seconds. The success probability with which a mafia attack can succeed is upper bounded by:

$$\left(\frac{1}{2}\right)^{r \cdot \omega_s} \cdot \left(\frac{3}{4}\right)^n$$

where n is the bit-length of N_V and N_P. Thus, the probability of running a successful mafia fraud attack is reduced. Nevertheless, there are some drawbacks that the reader should be aware. First of all, the number of bits (streams) exchanged during the RBE is significantly increased in comparison with when only the challenge bits (N_V bit-stream) are sent. Secondly, the time required to complete the distance checking is thus longer, which means a decrease in the efficiency of the protocol and an increase in the power consumption required by P.

7.3   Terrorist Fraud

This attack can be viewed as an extension of the mafia fraud. In this fraud, the dishonest prover collaborates with a terrorist prover $\overline{P}$: P uses $\overline{P}$ to convince V that he lies in close proximity, while he does not. Despite the cooperation between P and $\overline{P}$, it is assumed that the long-term secret key of P is not revealed to $\overline{P}$.

In the RČ protocol, a dishonest P can reveal N_P and M to a terrorist prover $\overline{P}$, without compromising the secret keys K_1 and K_2. Then, the distance-bounding phase is executed between V and $\overline{P}$, while the latter is nearer to V than P is. Thus, $\overline{P}$ misleads V into believing that P is located nearer. Thus, the probability that an attacker runs a successfully terrorist fraud attack is 1. This attack can be avoided by making interdependent the bit-streams $\{N_P, M\}$ and the secret keys, as in [28, 29].

8   Conclusions

We reported the first third-party cryptanalysis of the Rasmussen-Čapkun privacy-preserving distance bounding protocol: we identified strengths and weaknesses of that protocol, and presented a detailed attack exploiting nonce collisions. We proposed simple modifications to the protocol to thwart our attack and to enhance the overall security of the protocol. These modifications include the use of probabilistic encryption and the implementation of an encrypt-then-sign (rather than encrypt-and-sign) scheme. Furthermore, we investigated the security of the RČ protocol against distance, terrorist and mafia fraud attacks.

Our detailed definition of the protocol and the results of our in-depth security analysis are complementary to the preliminary security and implementation analysis in [19]. The natural next step is a proof-of-concept implementation of the Rasmussen-Čapkun protocol.

Acknowledgments. This work was partially supported by the Marie Curie IEF project "PPIDR: Privacy-Preserving Intrusion Detection and Response in Wireless Communications", grant number: 252323 and the ICT programme under contract ICT-2007-216676 ECRYPT II.

References

1. Papadimitratos, P., Poturalski, M., Schaller, P., Lafourcade, P., Basin, D., Čapkun, S., Hubaux, J.P.: Secure neighborhood discovery: a fundamental element for mobile ad hoc networking. IEEE Communications Magazine 46(2), 132–139 (2008)
2. Sastry, N., Shankar, U., Wagner, D.: Secure verification of location claims. In: Proceedings of the 2nd ACM Workshop on Wireless Security (WiSe 2003), pp. 1–10 (2003)
3. BroadcastEngineering: TV GLOBO TVDR, Article available online at http://broadcastengineering.com/excellence-awards/tv-globo-tdvr/ (accessed January 11, 2011)
4. Francillion, A., Danev, B., Čapkun, S.: Relay attacks on passive keyless entry and start systems in modern cars. In: Cryptology ePrint Archive: Report 2010/332 (2010) (to appear in proceedings of NDSS 2011)
5. Brands, S., Chaum, D.: Distance Bounding Protocols. In: Helleseth, T. (ed.) EUROCRYPT 1993. LNCS, vol. 765, pp. 344–359. Springer, Heidelberg (1994)
6. Hancke, G.P., Kuhn, M.G.: An RFID distance bounding protocol. In: Proceedings of the First International Conference on Security and Privacy for Emerging Areas in Communication Networks (SECURECOMM 2005), pp. 67–73 (2005)
7. Tu, Y.J., Piramuthu, S.: RFID Distance Bounding Protocols. In: Proceedings of the First International EURASIP Workshop on RFID Technology (2007)
8. Munilla, J., Peinado, A.: Distance bounding protocols for RFID enhanced by using void-challenges and analysis in noisy channels. Wireless Communications and Mobile Computing 8(9), 1227–1232 (2008)
9. Kim, C.H., Avoine, G., Koeune, F., Standaert, F.X., Pereira, O.: The Swiss-Knife RFID Distance Bounding Protocol. In: Lee, P.J., Cheon, J.H. (eds.) ICISC 2008. LNCS, vol. 5461, pp. 98–115. Springer, Heidelberg (2009)
10. Lee, J.Y., Scholtz, R.A.: Ranging in a dense multipath environment using an UWB radio link. IEEE Journal on Selected Areas in Communications 20(9) (2002)
11. Gezici, S., Tian, Z., Biannakis, G.B., Kobayashi, H., Molisch, A.F., Poor, V., Sahinoglu, Z.: Localization via ultra-wideband radius: a look at positioning aspects for future sensor networks. IEEE Signal Processing Magazine 22(4), 70–84 (2005)
12. Kuhn, M., Luecken, H., Tippenhauer, N.O.: UWB impulse radio based distance bounding. In: Proceedings of the 7th Workshop on Positioning, Navigation and Communication 2010, WPNC 2010 (2010)
13. Čapkun, S., Buttyán, L., Hubaux, J.P.: SECTOR: secure tracking of node encounters in multi-hop wireless networks. In: Proceedings of the 2003 ACM Workshop on Security of Ad Hoc and Sensor Networks (SASN 2003), pp. 21–32 (2003)
14. Singelee, D., Preneel, B.: Location verification using secure distance bounding protocols. In: Proceedings of the IEEE International Conference on Mobile Adhoc and Sensor Systems (MASS 2005), pp. 834–840 (2005)

15. Clulow, J., Hancke, G.P., Kuhn, M.G., Moore, T.: So near and yet so far: Distance-bounding attacks in wireless networks. In: Proceedings of the Third European Workshop on Security and Privacy in Ad hoc and Sensor Networks, pp. 83–97 (2006)
16. Meadows, C., Syverson, P., Chang, L.: Towards more efficient distance bounding protocols for use in sensor networks. In: Proceedings of the International Conference on Security and Privacy in Communication Networks (SECURECOMM 2006), pp. 1–5 (2006)
17. Čapkun, S., Hubaux, J.P.: Secure positioning of wireless devices with application to sensor networks. In: Proceedings of the 24th Annual Joint Conference of the IEEE Computer and Communications Societies (INFOCOM 2005), Miami, FL, USA, pp. 1917–1928 (2005)
18. Hu, Y.C., Perrig, A., Johnson, D.B.: Packet leashes: A defense against wormhole attacks in wireless networks. In: Proceedings of the 22nd Annual Joint Conference of the IEEE Computer and Communications (INFOCOM 2003), San Francisco, CA, USA, vol. 3, pp. 1976–1986 (2003)
19. Rasmussen, K.B., Čapkun, S.: Location privacy of distance bounding protocols. In: Proceedings of the 15th ACM Conference on Computer and Communications Security (ACM CCS 2008), pp. 149–160 (2008)
20. Zenner, E.: Nonce Generators and the Nonce Reset Problem. In: Samarati, P., Yung, M., Martinelli, F., Ardagna, C.A. (eds.) ISC 2009. LNCS, vol. 5735, pp. 411–426. Springer, Heidelberg (2009)
21. Anderson, R.J.: Security Engineering: A Guide to Building Dependable Distributed Systems, 2nd edn. Wiley (2008)
22. Boyer, R.S., Moore, J.S.: A fast string searching algorithm. Communications of the ACM 20(10), 762–772 (1977)
23. Bernstein, D.J.: Better price-performance rations for generalized birthday attacks. In: Proceedings of the International Conference on Special-purpose Hardware for Attacking Cryptographic Systems, SHARCS 2007 (2007)
24. Schimmler, M.: Fast sorting on the instruction systolic array. Technical Report 8709, Christian-Albrechts Universität Kiel (1987)
25. Schnorr, C.P., Shamir, A.: An optimal sorting algorithm for mesh connected computers. In: Proceedings of the 18th Annual ACM Symposium on Theory of Computing (STOC 1986), pp. 255–263 (1986)
26. Percival, C.: Encrypt-then-MAC. Blog entry on Daemonic Dispatches, http://www.daemonology.net/blog/2009-06-24-encrypt-then-mac.html (accessed January 11, 2011)
27. Munilla, J., Peinado, A.: Distance bounding protocols for RFID enhanced by using void-challenges and analysis in noisy channels. Wireless Communications and Mobile Computing 8(9), 1227–1232 (2008)
28. Bussard, L., Bagga, W.: Distance-bounding proof of knowledge to avoid real-time attacks. In: Security and Privacy in the Age of Ubiquitous Computing. IFIP AICT, pp. 223–238 (2005)
29. Reid, J., Gonzalez Nieto, J.M., Tang, T., Senadji, B.: Detecting relay attacks with timing-based protocols. In: Proceedings of the 2nd ACM Symposium on Information, Computer and Communications Security (ASIACCS 2007), pp. 204–213. ACM, Singapore (2007)

Delegable Provable Data Possession
for Remote Data in the Clouds

Shiuan-Tzuo Shen and Wen-Guey Tzeng*

Department of Computer Science,
National Chiao Tung University,
Hsinchu, Taiwan 30010
{vink,wgtzeng}@cs.nctu.edu.tw

Abstract. Many storage systems need to do authorized verification for data integrity. For example, a user stores his data into cloud storage servers and shares his data with his friends. They check data integrity periodically to ensure data intact. However, they don't want a stranger to check data integrity on their data. Therefore, public verification is undesired in this situation. The user can share his private key to his friends for private verification. However, his friends may reveal his private key to others. In this paper, we proposed the delegable provable data possession (delegable PDP) model to solve this problem. Delegable PDP allows a user to control who can check data integrity of his data, and guarantee that delegated verifiers cannot re-delegate this verification capability to others. Delegable PDP enjoys advantage of authorized verification and convenience of public verification.

We define a delegable PDP model and provide a construction for it. User $\mathcal{U}$ generates verifiable tags of his data and the delegation key $dk_{\mathcal{U} \to \mathcal{V}}$ for delegated verifier $\mathcal{V}$. $\mathcal{U}$ uploads his data, tags, and $dk_{\mathcal{U} \to \mathcal{V}}$ to storage servers. When integrity check, storage servers can use $dk_{\mathcal{U} \to \mathcal{V}}$ to transform $\mathcal{U}$'s tags into the form that $\mathcal{V}$ can verify with his private key $sk_{\mathcal{V}}$. Our model allows $\mathcal{U}$ to revoke $\mathcal{V}$'s verification capability by removing $dk_{\mathcal{U} \to \mathcal{V}}$ from storage servers directly. We prove our protocol secure in the random oracle model. Our protocol achieves proof unforgeability, proof indistinguishability, and delegation key unforgeability.

1 Introduction

Cloud computing provides computing services via networks such that a user can access these services anywhere at any time. For example, Amazon Elastic Compute Cloud (Amazon EC2) provides cloud computation and Amazon Simple Storage Service (Amazon S3) provides cloud storage. Storing data in a cloud storage system is quite convenient. One can share data to other users or synchronize copies in local devices. However, it brings security issues, privacy and integrity, on stored data. Users don't want their data leaked or modified without

---

* This research is supported by parts of NSC projects NSC100-2218-E-009-003-, NSC100-2218-E-009-006-, and NSC100-2219-E-009-005-, Taiwan.

their permission. In general, encryption can provide data privacy and signature can provide data integrity. Users can encrypt their data and sign ciphertexts before uploading them to cloud storage servers. One way to make sure that a ciphertext is stored intactly is to retrieve the ciphertext together with its signature and verify it. This approach needs large bandwidth since data are retrieved back through networks. Thus, many researchers proposed methods to reduce the bandwidth need.

Ateniese et al. proposed a provable data possession (PDP) model [1]. Their PDP model allows a storage server to generate a probabilistic proof of size $O(1)$ for data integrity check so that a verifier can validate the proof efficiently. Their PDP protocol is asymmetric-key based such that public verification is done by everyone using the public key of the owner. However, public verification is undesirable in many circumstances. In contrast, private verification allows only the owner who possesses the secret key to verify data integrity. The owner can share this secret key to another user for data integrity check. However, the other one may leak this secret key.

In this paper, we define a model for delegable provable data possession (delegable PDP) that allows delegable (authorized) verification. In delegable PDP, a user who owns data can authorize another user to verify data integrity of his data. The authorized user cannot re-delegate this verification capability to others unless the authorized user reveals his private key. The delegable PDP model provides a balance between totally public and totally private integrity checking. Delegable PDP has two goals:

- Proof of data possession. A storage server can generate a valid proof if and only if it really stores the data. This proof can be verified without retrieving back the data from the storage server.
- Delegation of verification capability. A user can delegate his verification capability on his data to another user. The delegated user cannot re-delegate this verification capability to others. The delegated user can verify data integrity with storage servers on behalf of the user. The user can revoke the right of integrity checking from the delegated user directly.

Our delegable PDP model is efficient. To delegate, data owner $\mathcal{U}$ doesn't need to re-tag his data for delegated verifier $\mathcal{V}$. Instead, $\mathcal{U}$ generates the delegation key $dk_{\mathcal{U} \to \mathcal{V}}$ and uploads it to storage servers. Thus, $\mathcal{V}$ doesn't store and doesn't know $dk_{\mathcal{U} \to \mathcal{V}}$. To revoke, $\mathcal{U}$ sends the revoking command of deleting $dk_{\mathcal{U} \to \mathcal{V}}$ to storage servers directly. The cost of delegation is lightweight.

1.1   Delegable Provable Data Possession

There are three roles, user (data owner) $\mathcal{U}$, delegated verifier $\mathcal{V}$, and storage server $\mathcal{S}$, in the delegable PDP model. The data are stored in $\mathcal{S}$ after tagged by $\mathcal{U}$'s private key $sk_{\mathcal{U}}$. For delegation, $\mathcal{U}$ computes the delegation key $dk_{\mathcal{U} \to \mathcal{V}}$ by using $sk_{\mathcal{U}}$ and $\mathcal{V}$'s public key $pk_{\mathcal{V}}$, and sends it to $\mathcal{S}$. $\mathcal{S}$ transforms the tags of the data by using $dk_{\mathcal{U} \to \mathcal{V}}$ such that $\mathcal{V}$ can use his private key $sk_{\mathcal{V}}$ to verify the data by the transformed tags.

A delegable PDP scheme has three phases: the setup phase, the delegation phase, and the integrity check phase. The setup phase consists of three algorithms, Setup, KeyGen, and TagGen, as follows:

- Setup(1^k) → π. It is a probabilistic polynomial time algorithm run by the system manager to set up a delegable PDP system. Setup takes as input the security parameter k and outputs the public parameter π.
- KeyGen(π) → (sk, pk). It is a probabilistic polynomial time algorithm run by a user to generate his key pair. KeyGen takes as input the public parameter π and outputs a private-public key pair (sk, pk) for the user.
- TagGen(π, sk, m) → (σ, t). It is a deterministic polynomial time algorithm run by a user to generate verifiable tags for his data. TagGen takes as input the public parameter π, the user's private key sk, and the user's data m, and outputs a tag σ for m and an identifier t for σ.

The delegation phase consists of two algorithms, GenDK and VrfyDK, as follows:

- GenDK($\pi, sk_\mathcal{U}, pk_\mathcal{V}$) → $dk_{\mathcal{U} \to \mathcal{V}}$. It is a deterministic polynomial time algorithm run by $\mathcal{U}$ to generate a delegation key for $\mathcal{V}$. GenDK takes as input the public parameter π, $\mathcal{U}$'s private key $sk_\mathcal{U}$, and $\mathcal{V}$'s public key $pk_\mathcal{V}$, and outputs the delegation key $dk_{\mathcal{U} \to \mathcal{V}}$.
- VrfyDK($\pi, dk_{\mathcal{U} \to \mathcal{V}}, pk_\mathcal{U}, pk_\mathcal{V}$) → $\{true, false\}$. It is a deterministic polynomial time algorithm run by $\mathcal{S}$ to verify delegation keys. VrfyDK takes as input the public parameter π, the delegation key $dk_{\mathcal{U} \to \mathcal{V}}$, $\mathcal{U}$'s public key $pk_\mathcal{U}$, and $\mathcal{V}$'s public key $pk_\mathcal{V}$, and outputs the verification result.

The integrity check phase consists of three algorithms, GenChal, GenProof, and VrfyProof, as follows:

- GenChal(π, t) → $chal$. It is a probabilistic polynomial time algorithm run by $\mathcal{V}$ to generate a challenge to $\mathcal{S}$ for $\mathcal{U}$'s stored data. GenChal takes as input the public parameter π and tag identifier t, and outputs the challenge $chal$.
- GenProof($\pi, m, \sigma, dk_{\mathcal{U} \to \mathcal{V}}, chal$) → $pf_{chal, \mathcal{V}}$. It is a probabilistic polynomial time algorithm run by $\mathcal{S}$ to generate a proof for integrity of the challenged data. GenProof takes as input the public parameter π, the stored data m, the tag σ for m, the delegation key $dk_{\mathcal{U} \to \mathcal{V}}$, and the challenge $chal$, and outputs the proof $pf_{chal, \mathcal{V}}$.
- VrfyProof($\pi, chal, pf_{chal, \mathcal{V}}, t, sk_\mathcal{V}$) → $\{true, false\}$. It is a deterministic polynomial time algorithm run by $\mathcal{V}$ to verify a proof from $\mathcal{S}$. VrfyProof takes as input the public parameter π, the challenge $chal$, the proof $pf_{chal, \mathcal{V}}$, the identifier t, and $\mathcal{V}$'s private key $sk_\mathcal{V}$, and outputs the verification result.

1.2   Related Work

Ateniese et al. [1] defined the PDP model. They proposed an asymmetric-key based PDP construction which uses homomorphic verifiable tags on stored data. Under the homomorphic property, storage servers can generate proofs for any linear combination of the stored data. Later on, Ateniese et al. [2] proposed a symmetric-key PDP construction which supports dynamic operations on stored data. Their construction is scalable and efficient. However, the number of data possession checkings is limited by the number of embedded tokens. Erway et al. [12] proposed dynamic provable data possession (DPDP) which uses rank-based skip list to support dynamic data operations. Ateniese et al. [3] proposed a framework for constructing public-key based PDP protocols. Their framework builds public-key homomorphic linear authenticators (HLAs) from public-key identification schemes, which satisfy certain homomorphic properties, and uses the HLA as a building block to construct PDP protocols.

Juels and Kaliski [14] proposed the proofs of retrievability (POR) model. POR ensures that stored data can be retrieved by users, while PDP ensures that data are stored in storage servers. Juels and Kaliski's construction embeds sentinels (verifying information of precomputed challenge-response pairs) into stored data, and the number of checkings is limited by the number of embedded sentinels. Later on, Shacham and Waters [15] proposed a compact POR which achieves an unlimited number of checkings. Bowers et al. [7] proposed a theoretical framework of designing POR protocols. This framework employs two layers of error correcting codes which recover user data from a series of responses. Their framework improves previous results of POR and has security proved in the fully Byzantine adversarial model. Wang et al. [17] proposed a POR scheme which supports dynamic operations and public verification on stored data. Their construction uses Merkle hash tree to support data dynamics.

To simultaneously achieve high availability and integrity checking for stored data, multiple replicas or the coding theory can be employed. Curtmola et al. [10] proposed MR-PDP that makes sure each unique replica exists in storage servers. Curtmola et al. [9] proposed a robust remote data integrity checking method that uses forward error correction codes. Later on, Bowers et al. [6] proposed HAIL which provides a high-availability and integrity layer for cloud storage. HAIL uses erasure codes on the single server layer and multiple sever layer respectively. It ensures data retrievability among distributed storage servers.

A cloud storage system may be viewed as a set of distributed storage servers. One can use the network coding technique to dispatch data to storage servers. For this model, Chen et al. [8] proposed a remote data integrity checking method for network coding-based distributed storage systems.

Wang et al. [16] proposed privacy-preserving public auditing for data storage security in cloud computing. Public data integrity checking may leak information about stored data by proofs to verifiers. Wang et al. use a blinding technique to hide information about stored data in proofs.

2   Preliminary

Our delegable PDP protocol uses the *bilinear map*. The security of our protocol is based on the *truncated (decision) bilinear Diffie-Hellman exponent assumption*, the *inverse computation Diffie-Hellman assumption*, and the *knowledge of exponent assumption* in the random oracle model.

Bilinear Map. Let q be a large prime, $G = \langle g \rangle$ and $G_T = \langle g_T \rangle$ be two multiplicative groups of prime order q. A bilinear map $\hat{e} : G \times G \to G_T$ should satisfy the following properties:

- Bilinearity. $\forall x, y \in \mathbb{Z}_q$, $\hat{e}(g^x, g^y) = \hat{e}(g, g)^{xy}$.
- Non-Degeneration. $\hat{e}(g, g) = g_T$.
- Computability. $\forall x, y \in \mathbb{Z}_q$, $\hat{e}(g^x, g^y)$ can be computed in polynomial time.

Truncated Bilinear Diffie-Hellman Exponent Assumption. Boneh et al. introduced the *bilinear Diffie-Hellman exponent* (BDHE) problem [4,5]. Later on, Gentry introduced two variants: the *augmented bilinear Diffie-Hellman exponent* (ABDHE) problem and the *truncated version* of the ABDHE problem [13].

The ℓ-BDHE problem is that: given a vector

$$\left(g', g, g^\alpha, g^{\alpha^2}, \ldots, g^{\alpha^\ell}, g^{\alpha^{\ell+2}}, g^{\alpha^{\ell+3}}, \ldots, g^{\alpha^{2\ell}}\right) \in G^{2\ell+1} \quad,$$

output $\hat{e}(g, g')^{\alpha^{\ell+1}} \in G_T$. The *truncated version* of the ℓ-BDHE problem, omitting $(g^{\alpha^{\ell+2}}, g^{\alpha^{\ell+3}}, \ldots, g^{\alpha^{2\ell}})$ from the input vector, is defined as that: given a vector

$$\left(g', g, g^\alpha, g^{\alpha^2}, \ldots, g^{\alpha^\ell}\right) \in G^{\ell+2} \quad,$$

output $\hat{e}(g, g')^{\alpha^{\ell+1}} \in G_T$. The advantage for an algorithm $\mathcal{A}$ that solves the *truncated* ℓ-BDHE problem is defined as:

$$\Pr\left[\mathcal{A}(g', g, g^\alpha, g^{\alpha^2}, \ldots, g^{\alpha^\ell}) = \hat{e}(g, g')^{\alpha^{\ell+1}} : g, g' \in_R G, \alpha \in_R \mathbb{Z}_q\right] \quad.$$

The advantage for an algorithm $\mathcal{A}$ that solves the *truncated decisional* ℓ-BDHE problem is defined as:

$$\left| \Pr[\mathcal{A}(g', g, g^\alpha, g^{\alpha^2}, \ldots, g^{\alpha^\ell}, \hat{e}(g, g')^{\alpha^{\ell+1}}) = 0 : g, g' \in_R G, \alpha \in_R \mathbb{Z}_q] \right. -$$
$$\left. \Pr[\mathcal{A}(g', g, g^\alpha, g^{\alpha^2}, \ldots, g^{\alpha^\ell}, Z) = 0 : g, g' \in_R G, \alpha \in_R \mathbb{Z}_q, Z \in_R G_T] \right| \quad.$$

Definition 1. *We say that the truncated (decisional) BDHE assumption is (t, ϵ, ℓ)-secure if no t-time algorithms have advantage over ϵ in solving the truncated (decisional) ℓ-BDHE problem.*

Inverse Computational Diffie-Hellman Assumption. The InvCDH problem is defined as that: given $(g, g^\alpha) \in G^2$ as input, output $g^{\frac{1}{\alpha}} \in G$. The advantage for a probabilistic algorithm $\mathcal{A}$ to solve the InvCDH problem is:

$$\Pr\left[\mathcal{A}(g, g^\alpha) = g^{\frac{1}{\alpha}} : \alpha \in_R \mathbb{Z}_q\right] \quad.$$

Definition 2. *We say that the InvCDH assumption is (t, ϵ)-secure if no t-time algorithms have advantage over ϵ in solving the InvCDH problem*

Knowledge of Exponent Assumption. Damgard introduced the *knowledge of exponent assumption* (KEA1) [11]. Consider the problem: given $(g, g^\alpha) \in G^2$, output $(C, Y) \in G^2$ such that $C^\alpha = Y$. One way to output the pair is to choose $c \in_R \mathbb{Z}_q$ and let $(C, Y) = (g^c, g^{\alpha c})$. The KEA1 says that this is the only way to output such a pair in polynomial time. That is, if an adversary $\mathcal{A}$ takes (g, g^α) as input and outputs (C, Y) such that $C^\alpha = Y$, he must know the exponent c of $g^c = C$. There exists an extractor $\overline{\mathcal{A}}$ who extracts the exponent c such that $g^c = C$ when he is given the same inputs as $\mathcal{A}$'s.

3   Construction

In this section, we provide a delegable PDP scheme. Let k be the security parameter, q be a large prime with $|q| = k$, and $G = \langle g \rangle$ and $G_T = \langle g_T \rangle$ be two order-q multiplicative groups with a bilinear map $\hat{e} : G \times G \to G_T$. The system manager chooses three cryptographic hash functions $H_1 : \{0, 1\}^* \to G$, $H_2 : G \to G$, and $H_3 : (\mathbb{Z}_q)^* \to G$. The public parameter is $\pi = (q, G, g, G_T, g_T, \hat{e}, H_1, H_2, H_3)$.

Key Generation. $\mathcal{U}$ chooses $x \in_R \mathbb{Z}_q$ as his private key $sk_\mathcal{U}$ and computes g^x as his public key $pk_\mathcal{U}$ and $H_2(g^x)^x$ as his key token $kt_\mathcal{U}$. $\mathcal{U}$'s key tuple is $(sk_\mathcal{U}, pk_\mathcal{U}, kt_\mathcal{U}) = (x, g^x, H_2(g^x)^x)$. $\mathcal{U}$ registers $pk_\mathcal{U}$ to the system manager.

Tag Computation. $\mathcal{U}$ has data $\mathcal{M} = (m_1, m_2, \ldots, m_n)$, each block k-bit long, and would like to store them in $\mathcal{S}$. $\mathcal{U}$ chooses data identifier $h_\mathcal{M} \in_R G$ and tag identifier seed $T_\mathcal{M} \in_R \{0, 1\}^*$ for $\mathcal{M}$. $\mathcal{U}$ may have many different data. Thus, he needs to choose a unique data identifier for each of his data. Each block m_i is tagged to a homomorphic verifiable tag σ_i which is identified by $h_\mathcal{M}$ and tag identifier $T_\mathcal{M}||i$. $\mathcal{U}$ computes these homomorphic verifiable tags $\Sigma = (\sigma_1, \sigma_2, \ldots, \sigma_n)$ for $\mathcal{M}$ as follows:

$$\sigma_i = [H_1(T_\mathcal{M}||i)h_\mathcal{M}^{m_i}]^{sk_\mathcal{U}} \quad , \text{ for } 1 \leq i \leq n .$$

$\mathcal{U}$ uploads $(\mathcal{M}, h_\mathcal{M}, \Sigma)$ to $\mathcal{S}$, and holds $(h_\mathcal{M}, T_\mathcal{M})$ for identifying and verifying Σ.

Delegation. $\mathcal{V}$ gives his key token $kt_\mathcal{V}$ to $\mathcal{U}$ over a secure channel, and obtains $h_\mathcal{M}$ and $T_\mathcal{M}$ from $\mathcal{U}$. $\mathcal{U}$ uses $\mathcal{V}$'s public key $pk_\mathcal{V}$ to verify validity of $kt_\mathcal{V}$ by checking whether $\hat{e}(g, kt_\mathcal{V}) = \hat{e}(pk_\mathcal{V}, H_2(pk_\mathcal{V}))$. Then, $\mathcal{U}$ computes the delegation key

$$dk_{\mathcal{U} \to \mathcal{V}} = kt_\mathcal{V}^{1/sk_\mathcal{U}}$$

and gives it to $\mathcal{S}$. $\mathcal{S}$ uses $pk_\mathcal{U}$ and $pk_\mathcal{V}$ to verify validity of $dk_{\mathcal{U} \to \mathcal{V}}$ by checking whether $\hat{e}(pk_\mathcal{U}, dk_{\mathcal{U} \to \mathcal{V}}) = \hat{e}(pk_\mathcal{V}, H_2(pk_\mathcal{V}))$. To revoke $\mathcal{V}$, $\mathcal{U}$ commands $\mathcal{S}$ to remove $dk_{\mathcal{U} \to \mathcal{V}}$ from its storage directly.

Integrity Check. To check integrity of $\mathcal{M}$, $\mathcal{V}$ chooses coefficients $C = (c_1, c_2, \ldots, c_n) \in_R \mathbb{Z}_q^n$ and gives $\mathcal{S}$ the challenge

$$chal = (C,\ C',\ C'') = (C,\ h_{\mathcal{M}}^s,\ H_3(C)^s),\quad \text{where } s \in_R \mathbb{Z}_q\ .$$

After receiving $chal$, $\mathcal{S}$ verifies it by checking whether $\hat{e}(C', H_3(C)) = \hat{e}(h_{\mathcal{M}}, C'')$. If so, $\mathcal{S}$ uses $(\mathcal{M}, \Sigma, dk_{\mathcal{U} \to \mathcal{V}}, chal)$ to generate a proof $pf_{chal,\mathcal{V}} = (\rho, V, V', V'', V''')$ and gives it to $\mathcal{V}$ as a response. $pf_{chal,\mathcal{V}}$ is computed as follows:

$$pf_{chal,\mathcal{V}} = \left(\hat{e}(\prod_{i=1}^{n} \sigma_i^{c_i},\ dk_{\mathcal{U} \to \mathcal{V}})^t,\ C'^{\sum_{i=1}^{n} c_i m_i},\ C''^{\sum_{i=1}^{n} c_i m_i}, H_2(pk_{\mathcal{V}})^t,\ g^t \right),\ \text{where } t \in_R \mathbb{Z}_q.$$

After receiving $pf_{chal,\mathcal{V}}$, $\mathcal{V}$ uses $(sk_{\mathcal{V}}, h_{\mathcal{M}}, T_{\mathcal{M}}, C, s)$ to verify $pf_{chal,\mathcal{V}}$ by checking whether

- $\rho^s = \hat{e}\,(\prod_{i=1}^{n} H_1(T_{\mathcal{M}}||i)^{sc_i} V,\ V'')^{sk_{\mathcal{V}}}$
- $\hat{e}\,(V,\ H_3(C)) = \hat{e}\,(h_{\mathcal{M}},\ V')$
- $\hat{e}\,(V'',\ g) = \hat{e}\,(H_2(pk_{\mathcal{V}}),\ V''')$

$\mathcal{V}$ can verify data integrity of $\mathcal{M}$ multiple times to achieve a desire security level.

Correctness. Although tag $\sigma = [H_1(T_{\mathcal{M}})h_{\mathcal{M}}^m]^{sk_{\mathcal{U}}}$ is called homomorphic verifiable in the literature, it is really not homomorphic. Instead, σ is combinably verifiable since we can combine multiple tags together and verify them at the same time. Nevertheless, we cannot obtain a tag for the combined data. For example, combing $\sigma_i = [H_1(T_{\mathcal{M}}||i)h_{\mathcal{M}}^{m_i}]^{sk_{\mathcal{U}}}$ and $\sigma_j = [H_1(T_{\mathcal{M}}||j)h_{\mathcal{M}}^{m_j}]^{sk_{\mathcal{U}}}$ together results in $\sigma' = [H_1(T_{\mathcal{M}}||i)H_1(T_{\mathcal{M}}||j)h_{\mathcal{M}}^{m_i+m_j}]^{sk_{\mathcal{U}}}$. Although we have $m_i + m_j$ in the exponent of $h_{\mathcal{M}}$, we don't have $H_1(T_{\mathcal{M}}||k)$ in the combined tag σ' for some k (treat $m_i + m_j = m_k$). The tag is unforgeable, proved in Sect. 4.1 (proof unforgeability implies tag unforgeability). It is hard to obtain $\sigma' = [H_1(T_{\mathcal{M}}||k)h_{\mathcal{M}}^{m_i+m_j}]^{sk_{\mathcal{U}}}$ without the knowledge of private key $sk_{\mathcal{U}}$.

In integrity check, $\mathcal{V}$ chooses coefficients $C = (c_1, c_2, \ldots, c_n)$ and then $\mathcal{S}$ combines stored tags $\Sigma = (\sigma_1, \sigma_2, \ldots, \sigma_n)$ as $\prod_{i=1}^{n} \sigma_i^{c_i} = [\prod_{i=1}^{n} H_1(T_{\mathcal{M}}||i)^{c_i} \times h_{\mathcal{M}}^{\sum_{i=1}^{n} c_i m_i}]^{sk_{\mathcal{U}}}$ by C. If $\mathcal{S}$ deviates, the combination will not be identical to $\prod_{i=1}^{n} H_1(T_{\mathcal{M}}||i)^{c_i}$. Once $\mathcal{S}$ combines these tags correctly, we have $\sum_{i=1}^{n} c_i m_i$ in the exponent of $h_{\mathcal{M}}$. On the other hand, $\mathcal{S}$ has to use stored data $\mathcal{M} = (m_1, m_2, \ldots, m_n)$ to compute $V = C'^{\sum_{i=1}^{n} c_i m_i} = (h_{\mathcal{M}}^s)^{\sum_{i=1}^{n} c_i m_i}$ and $V' = C''^{\sum_{i=1}^{n} c_i m_i} = [H_3(C)^s]^{\sum_{i=1}^{n} c_i m_i}$. Our verification, $\rho^s = \hat{e}\,(\prod_{i=1}^{n} H_1(T_{\mathcal{M}}||i)^{sc_i} V, V'')^{sk_{\mathcal{V}}}$, checks whether ρ contains the correct combination $\prod_{i=1}^{n} H_1(T_{\mathcal{M}}||i)^{c_i}$ and whether V contains the same exponent

$\sum_{i=1}^{n} c_i m_i$, with respect to $h_{\mathcal{M}}^s$, as that in ρ, with respect to $h_{\mathcal{M}}$. If $\mathcal{S}$ passes this verification, he possesses $\mathcal{M}$.

Let's examine the verification equations. Assume that $pf_{chal,\mathcal{V}}$ is well-formed and $chal = (C, C', C'') = (C, h_{\mathcal{M}}^s, H_3(C)^s)$, that is,

$$\rho = \hat{e}(\prod_{i=1}^{n} \sigma_i^{c_i}, dk_{\mathcal{U}\to\mathcal{V}})^t \tag{1}$$

$$V = C'^{\sum_{i=1}^{n} c_i m_i} = h_{\mathcal{M}}^{s\sum_{i=1}^{n} c_i m_i} \tag{2}$$

$$V' = C''^{\sum_{i=1}^{n} c_i m_i} = H_3(C)^{s\sum_{i=1}^{n} c_i m_i} \tag{3}$$

$$V'' = H_2(pk_{\mathcal{V}})^t \tag{4}$$

$$V''' = g^t \tag{5}$$

We have:

- $\rho^s = \hat{e}(\prod_{i=1}^{n} H_1(T_{\mathcal{M}}||i)^{sc_i} V, V'')^{sk_{\mathcal{V}}}$ by (1), (2), and (4)

$$\rho^s = \hat{e}(\prod_{i=1}^{n} \sigma_i^{c_i}, dk_{\mathcal{U}\to\mathcal{V}})^{ts}$$

$$= \hat{e}(\prod_{i=1}^{n} (H_1(T_{\mathcal{M}}||i)h_{\mathcal{M}}^{m_i})^{sk_{\mathcal{U}}c_i}, H_2(pk_{\mathcal{V}})^{sk_{\mathcal{V}}/sk_{\mathcal{U}}})^{ts}$$

$$= \hat{e}(\prod_{i=1}^{n} (H_1(T_{\mathcal{M}}||i)h_{\mathcal{M}}^{m_i})^{sc_i}, H_2(pk_{\mathcal{V}})^{sk_{\mathcal{V}}})^t$$

$$= \hat{e}(\prod_{i=1}^{n} H_1(T_{\mathcal{M}}||i)^{sc_i} h_{\mathcal{M}}^{s\sum_{i=1}^{n} c_i m_i}, H_2(pk_{\mathcal{V}})^t)^{sk_{\mathcal{V}}}$$

$$= \hat{e}(\prod_{i=1}^{n} H_1(T_{\mathcal{M}}||i)^{sc_i} V, V'')^{sk_{\mathcal{V}}}$$

- $\hat{e}(V, H_3(C)) = \hat{e}(h_{\mathcal{M}}, V')$ by (2) and (3)

$$\hat{e}(V, H_3(C)) = \hat{e}(h_{\mathcal{M}}^{s\sum_{i=1}^{n} c_i m_i}, H_3(C))$$

$$= \hat{e}(h_{\mathcal{M}}, H_3(C)^{s\sum_{i=1}^{n} c_i m_i})$$

$$= \hat{e}(h_{\mathcal{M}}, V')$$

- $\hat{e}(V'', g) = \hat{e}(H_2(pk_{\mathcal{V}}), V''')$ by (4) and (5)

$$\hat{e}(V'', g) = \hat{e}(H_2(pk_{\mathcal{V}})^t, g)$$

$$= \hat{e}(H_2(pk_{\mathcal{V}}), g^t)$$

$$= \hat{e}(H_2(pk_{\mathcal{V}}), V''')$$

3.1   Performance

We analyze performance of our construction in three aspects: the computation cost of each algorithm, the storage cost of each party, and the communication cost of each phase. Table 1 shows the computation cost of each algorithm.[1] We measure the numbers of additions in $\mathbb{Z}_q$, multiplications in G, scalar exponentiations in G, hashes, and pairings.

Table 1. Computation cost of each algorithm

Algorithm	Addition	Multiplication	Scalar Exponentiation	Hash	Pairing
Setup	0	0	0	0	0
KeyGen	0	0	2	1	0
TagGen	0	n	$2n$	n	0
GenDK	0	0	1	1	2
VrfyDK	0	0	0	1	2
GenChal	0	0	2	1	0
GenProof	$n-1$	$2n-1$	$n+5$	2	3
VrfyProof	0	n	$n+3$	$n+2$	5

n is the number of data blocks.

Table 2 shows the storage cost of each party. User $\mathcal{U}$ stores his key tuple $(sk_{\mathcal{U}}, pk_{\mathcal{U}}, kt_{\mathcal{U}})$, data identifier $h_{\mathcal{M}}$, and tag identifier seed $T_{\mathcal{M}}$. Delegated verifier $\mathcal{V}$ stores his key tuple $(sk_{\mathcal{V}}, pk_{\mathcal{V}}, kt_{\mathcal{V}})$, data identifier $h_{\mathcal{M}}$, and tag identifier seed $T_{\mathcal{M}}$. Storage server $\mathcal{S}$ stores $\mathcal{U}$'s data $\mathcal{M}$, data identifier $h_{\mathcal{M}}$, tags Σ, and the delegation keys. Table 3 shows the communication cost of each phase. In setup phase, $\mathcal{U}$ uploads $\mathcal{M}$, Σ, and $h_{\mathcal{M}}$ to $\mathcal{S}$. In delegation phase, $\mathcal{V}$ gives $\mathcal{U}$ his key token $kt_{\mathcal{V}}$. $\mathcal{U}$ gives $h_{\mathcal{M}}$ and $T_{\mathcal{M}}$ to $\mathcal{V}$, and gives the delegation key $dk_{\mathcal{U}\to\mathcal{V}}$ to $\mathcal{S}$. In integrity check phase, $\mathcal{V}$ gives $\mathcal{S}$ the challenge $chal$,[2] and $\mathcal{S}$ gives $\mathcal{V}$ the proof $pf_{chal,\mathcal{V}}$.

---

[1] To achieve better performance, one can choose binary coefficient $c_i \in \{0,1\}$, $1 \leq i \leq n$, to reduce computation on multiplications and scalar exponentiations. Thus, in algorithm GenProof, we don't need to do scalar exponentiations on σ_i to compute $\sigma_i^{c_i}$, and multiplications on m_i to compute $c_i m_i$. Thus, it reduces the computation cost from $2n-1$ multiplications in G and $n+5$ scalar exponentiations in G to $n-1$ multiplications in G and 5 scalar exponentiations in G for GenProof. And in algorithm VrfyProof, we don't really do scalar exponentiations on $H_1(T_{\mathcal{M}}||i)$ to compute $H_1(T_{\mathcal{M}}||i)^{c_i}$, either. Thus, it reduces the computation cost from $n+3$ scalar exponentiations in G to 3 scalar exponentiations in G for VrfyProof.

[2] To reduce the communication cost on transmitting $chal$, one can choose a random seed c of size ℓ' for computing coefficients $c_i = H(c,i)$, $1 \leq i \leq n$, and send c only. Thus, it reduces the communication cost from $nk + 6p + p_T$ bits to $\ell' + 6p + p_T$ bits in integrity check phase.

Table 2. Storage cost of each party

Party	Storage Cost (Bit)
User	$k + 3p + \ell$
Delegated Verifier	$k + 3p + \ell$
Storage Server	$nk + (1 + n + v)p$

- k is the security parameter
- p is the size of an element in G
- l is the length of tag identifier seed $T_{\mathcal{M}}$
- n is the number of data blocks
- v is the number of delegated verifiers

Table 3. Communication cost of each phase

Phase	Communication Cost (Bit)
Setup	$\mathcal{U} \to \mathcal{S} : nk + p + np$
Delegation	$\mathcal{V} \leftrightarrow \mathcal{U} : 2p + \ell$ $\mathcal{U} \to \mathcal{S} : p$
Integrity Check	$\mathcal{V} \leftrightarrow \mathcal{S} : nk + 6p + p_T$

- k is the security parameter
- p is the size of an element in G
- p_T is the size of an element in G_T
- l is the length of tag identifier $h_{\mathcal{M}}$
- n is the number of data blocks

4   Security Analysis

The security requirements of a delegable PDP model consists of **proof unforgeability**, **proof indistinguishability**, and **delegation key unforgeability**. We introduce the security games in the rest subsections and prove that our construction satisfies these security requirements in the random oracle model.

4.1   Proof Unforgeability

This game models the notion that a storage server cannot modify stored data without being detected by verifiers. In this game, the challenger $\mathcal{C}$ plays the role of the verifier and the adversary $\mathcal{A}$ plays the role of the storage server. $\mathcal{A}$ is given the access right to oracles $\mathcal{O}_{\mathsf{Tag}}$ and $\mathcal{O}_{\mathsf{DK}}$. $\mathcal{A}$ chooses data adaptively and obtains corresponding tags. Once $\mathcal{A}$ decides the target data $\mathcal{M}^*$, he modifies $\mathcal{M}^*$ to $\mathcal{M}'$ such that $\mathcal{M}' \neq \mathcal{M}^*$ and receives a challenge from $\mathcal{C}$. If $\mathcal{A}$ returns a proof that passes the verification algorithm, he wins this game.

The proof unforgeability game $\mathsf{Game}^{\mathsf{PF-UF}}$ is as follows:

Setup. $\mathcal{C}$ generates public parameter π, user $\mathcal{U}$'s key tuple $(sk_{\mathcal{U}}, pk_{\mathcal{U}}, kt_{\mathcal{U}})$, delegated verifier $\mathcal{V}$'s key tuple $(sk_{\mathcal{V}}, pk_{\mathcal{V}}, kt_{\mathcal{V}})$, and the delegation key $dk_{\mathcal{U} \to \mathcal{V}}$. $\mathcal{C}$ forwards $(\pi, pk_{\mathcal{U}}, pk_{\mathcal{V}}, dk_{\mathcal{U} \to \mathcal{V}})$ to $\mathcal{A}$.

Query. $\mathcal{A}$ queries oracle $\mathcal{O}_{\mathsf{Tag}}$ and oracle $\mathcal{O}_{\mathsf{DK}}$ to obtain tags and delegation keys.

- $\mathcal{O}_{\mathsf{Tag}}$: $\mathcal{A}$ chooses data $\mathcal{M}$ and obtains tags Σ, data identifier $h_{\mathcal{M}}$, and tag identifier seed $T_{\mathcal{M}}$ for $\mathcal{M}$.
- $\mathcal{O}_{\mathsf{DK}}$: $\mathcal{A}$ chooses a user $\mathcal{U}'$ and obtains the delegation key $dk_{\mathcal{U} \to \mathcal{U}'}$.

Challenge. After the query phase, $\mathcal{A}$ indicates which $\mathcal{O}_{\mathsf{Tag}}$-oracle query is the target, denoted as $(\mathcal{M}^*, \Sigma^*, h_{\mathcal{M}^*}, T_{\mathcal{M}^*})$, and modifies $\mathcal{M}^* = (m_1^*, m_2^*, \ldots, m_n^*)$ to $\mathcal{M}' = (m_1', m_2', \ldots, m_n')$ such that $\mathcal{M}' \neq \mathcal{M}^*$ ($\exists i, m_i' \neq m_i^*$). $\mathcal{C}$ gives challenge $chal = (C, h_{\mathcal{M}^*}^s, H_3(C)^s)$.

Answer. $\mathcal{A}$ returns proof $pf_{chal,\mathcal{V}}$ by using $\mathcal{M}'$. $\mathcal{A}$ wins $\mathsf{Game}^{\mathsf{PF-UF}}$ if $\mathsf{VrfyProof}(\pi, chal, pf_{chal,\mathcal{V}}, h_{\mathcal{M}^*}, T_{\mathcal{M}^*}, sk_{\mathcal{V}}) = true$ and $\mathcal{M}' \neq \mathcal{M}^*$ ($\exists i, m_i' \neq m_i^*$). The advantage $Adv_{\mathcal{A}}^{\mathsf{PF-UF}}$ is defined as $\Pr[\mathcal{A} \text{ wins } \mathsf{Game}^{\mathsf{PF-UF}}]$.

We show that our scheme is proof unforgeable under the *truncated* 1-BDHE assumption and the KEA1.

Theorem 1. *If the truncated BDHE problem is $(t, \epsilon, 1)$-secure, the above scheme is $(t - q_1 t_1 - q_2 t_2 - q_T t_T - q_K t_K - 2t_{\overline{A}}, \frac{2^\ell}{2^\ell - (q_1 + q_T) q_T} \frac{2^k}{2^k - 1} \epsilon)$ proof unforgeable in the random oracle model, where hash functions H_1 and H_2 are modeled as random oracles $\mathcal{O}_{H_1}$ and $\mathcal{O}_{H_2}$, (q_1, q_2, q_T, q_K) are the numbers of times that an adversary queries $(\mathcal{O}_{H_1}, \mathcal{O}_{H_2}, \mathcal{O}_{\mathsf{Tag}}, \mathcal{O}_{\mathsf{DK}})$-oracles, (t_1, t_2, t_T, t_K) are the time used by $(\mathcal{O}_{H_1}, \mathcal{O}_{H_2}, \mathcal{O}_{\mathsf{Tag}}, \mathcal{O}_{\mathsf{DK}})$-oracles to respond an oracle query, $t_{\overline{A}}$ is the time used by the KEA1 extractor $\overline{A}$ to extract an exponent, k is the security parameter, and ℓ is the bit-length of a tag identifier seed.*

Proof. Let $\mathcal{A}$ be a probabilistic black-box adversary who wins the proof unforgeability game $\mathsf{Game}^{\mathsf{PF-UF}}$ with advantage ϵ' in time t'. We construct an algorithm $\mathcal{B}$ that uses $\mathcal{A}$ to solve the *truncated* 1-BDHE problem as follows:

Setup. Given an instance (g, g^α, g') of the *truncated* 1-BDHE problem, $\mathcal{B}$ sets the public parameter $\pi = (q, G, g, G_T, g_T, \hat{e}, H_3)$, user $\mathcal{U}$'s key tuple $(sk_{\mathcal{U}}, pk_{\mathcal{U}}, kt_{\mathcal{U}}) = (\alpha u, g^{\alpha u}, H_2(g^{\alpha u})^{\alpha u})$, where $H_2(g^{\alpha u}) = g^{\alpha u'}$ and $u, u' \in_R \mathbb{Z}_q$, and delegated verifier $\mathcal{V}$'s key tuple $(sk_{\mathcal{V}}, pk_{\mathcal{V}}, kt_{\mathcal{V}}) = (\alpha v, g^{\alpha v}, H_2(g^{\alpha v})^{\alpha v})$, where $H_2(g^\alpha v) = g^{\alpha v'}$ and $v, v' \in_R \mathbb{Z}_q$. Then $\mathcal{B}$ computes the delegation key

$$dk_{\mathcal{U} \to \mathcal{V}} = H_2(pk_{\mathcal{V}})^{sk_{\mathcal{V}}/sk_{\mathcal{U}}} = (g^{\alpha v'})^{\alpha v / \alpha u} = g^{\alpha v v'/u}$$

and invokes $\mathcal{A}$ as a subroutine: $\mathcal{A}^{\mathcal{O}_{H_1}, \mathcal{O}_{H_2}, \mathcal{O}_{\mathsf{Tag}}, \mathcal{O}_{\mathsf{DK}}}(\pi, pk_{\mathcal{U}}, pk_{\mathcal{V}}, dk_{\mathcal{U} \to \mathcal{V}})$.

Query. $\mathcal{A}$ can query oracles $\mathcal{O}_{H_1}$, $\mathcal{O}_{H_2}$, $\mathcal{O}_{\mathsf{Tag}}$, and $\mathcal{O}_{\mathsf{DK}}$ during his execution. $\mathcal{B}$ handles these oracles as follows:

- $\mathcal{O}_{H_1}$. $\mathcal{B}$ maintains a table $\mathcal{T}_{H_1} = \{(x, H_1(x), r)\}$ to look up the $\mathcal{O}_{H_1}$-query records. $\mathcal{B}$ takes $x \in \{0, 1\}^*$ as input and outputs y if record $(x, y, *)$ exists in $\mathcal{T}_{H_1}$. Otherwise, $\mathcal{B}$ outputs $H_1(x) = g^r$ and inserts (x, g^r, r) into $\mathcal{T}_{H_1}$, where $r \in_R \mathbb{Z}_q$.

- $\mathcal{O}_{\mathsf{H}_2}$. $\mathcal{B}$ maintains a table $\mathcal{T}_{\mathsf{H}_2} = \{(g^x, \mathsf{H}_2(g^x), r)\}$ to look up the $\mathcal{O}_{\mathsf{H}_2}$-query records. $\mathcal{B}$ takes g^x as input and outputs y if record $(g^x, y, *)$ exists in $\mathcal{T}_{\mathsf{H}_2}$. Otherwise, $\mathcal{B}$ outputs $\mathsf{H}_2(g^x) = g^{\alpha r}$ and inserts $(g^x, g^{\alpha r}, r)$ into $\mathcal{T}_{\mathsf{H}_2}$, where $r \in_R \mathbb{Z}_q$.
- $\mathcal{O}_{\mathsf{Tag}}$. $\mathcal{B}$ maintains a table $\mathcal{T}_{\mathsf{Tag}} = \{(\mathcal{M}, h_{\mathcal{M}}, r, T_{\mathcal{M}}, \Sigma)\}$ to look up the $\mathcal{O}_{\mathsf{Tag}}$-query records. $\mathcal{B}$ takes $\mathcal{M} = (m_1, m_2, \dots, m_n)$ as input, sets data identifier $h_{\mathcal{M}} = g^{\prime r}$, where $r \in_R \mathbb{Z}_q$, and chooses tag identifier $T_{\mathcal{M}} \in_R \{0, 1\}^\ell$ randomly. For $1 \le i \le n$, if $T_{\mathcal{M}} \| i$ has been queried to oracle $\mathcal{O}_{\mathsf{H}_1}$, $\mathcal{B}$ aborts. Otherwise, $\mathcal{B}$ inserts each $(T_{\mathcal{M}} \| i, g^{r_i} / h_{\mathcal{M}}^{m_i}, r_i)$ into table $\mathcal{T}_{\mathsf{H}_1}$, where $r_i \in_R \mathbb{Z}_q$, outputs $(h_{\mathcal{M}}, T_{\mathcal{M}}, \Sigma = (\sigma_1, \sigma_2, \dots, \sigma_n))$, where

$$\sigma_i = (\mathsf{H}_1(T_{\mathcal{M}} \| i) h_{\mathcal{M}}^{m_i})^{sk_{\mathcal{U}}} = ((g^{r_i} / h_{\mathcal{M}}^{m_i}) h_{\mathcal{M}}^{m_i})^{\alpha u} = g^{\alpha u r_i} ,$$

and inserts $(\mathcal{M}, h_{\mathcal{M}}, r, T_{\mathcal{M}}, \Sigma)$ into $\mathcal{T}_{\mathsf{Tag}}$.
- $\mathcal{O}_{\mathsf{DK}}$. $\mathcal{B}$ takes user $\mathcal{U}$'s public key $pk_{\mathcal{U}} = g^x$ and key token $kt_{\mathcal{U}'}$ as input, looks up whether record $(g^x, *, *)$ exists in table $\mathcal{T}_{\mathsf{H}_2}$, and checks whether $\hat{e}(g, kt_{\mathcal{U}'}) = \hat{e}(g^x, \mathsf{H}_2(g^x))$. If not, $\mathcal{B}$ rejects. Otherwise, $\mathcal{B}$ outputs the delegation key

$$dk_{\mathcal{U} \to \mathcal{U}'} = \mathsf{H}_2(g^x)^{sk_{\mathcal{U}'} / sk_{\mathcal{U}}} = (g^{\alpha r})^{x / \alpha u} = g^{xr/u} .$$

Challenge. After the query phase, $\mathcal{A}$ indicates which $\mathcal{O}_{\mathsf{Tag}}$-query is the target and modifies data to $\mathcal{M}'$. $\mathcal{B}$ looks up the corresponding record in table $\mathcal{T}_{\mathsf{Tag}}$, denoted as $(\mathcal{M}^* = (m_1^*, m_2^*, \dots, m_n^*), h_{\mathcal{M}^*} = g^{\prime r^*}, r^*, T_{\mathcal{M}^*}, \Sigma^* = (\sigma_1^*, \sigma_2^*, \dots, \sigma_n^*))$, and returns challenge $chal = (C = (c_1, c_2, \dots, c_n), h_{\mathcal{M}^*}^s, \mathsf{H}_3(C)^s)$, where $c_i, s \in_R \mathbb{Z}_q$.

Answer. $\mathcal{A}$ returns integrity proof $pf_{chal, \mathcal{V}} = (\rho, V, V', V'', V''')$ using $\mathcal{M}'$. If $\mathcal{M}' \ne \mathcal{M}^*$, we have $V \ne h_{\mathcal{M}^*}^{s \sum_{i=1}^n c_i m_i^*}$ except for a negligible probability. That is, $\Pr[\mathcal{A}$ guesses $\sum_{i=1}^n c_i m_i^* : c_i \in_R \mathbb{Z}_q$ and $\mathcal{M}' \ne \mathcal{M}^*] = \frac{1}{q}$. Otherwise, $\mathcal{A}$ knows the knowledge of $\mathcal{M}^{*3}$. Thus, if $pf_{chal, \mathcal{V}}$ can pass the verification procedure and $\mathcal{M}' \ne \mathcal{M}^*$, we have:

$$\rho^s = \hat{e}(\prod_{i=1}^n \mathsf{H}_1(T_{\mathcal{M}^*} \| i)^{sc_i} V, V'')^{sk_{\mathcal{V}}} \tag{6}$$

$$\hat{e}(V, \mathsf{H}_3(C)) = \hat{e}(h_{\mathcal{M}^*}, V') \tag{7}$$

$$\hat{e}(V'', g) = \hat{e}(\mathsf{H}_2(pk_{\mathcal{V}}), V''') \tag{8}$$

$$V \ne h_{\mathcal{M}^*}^{s \sum_{i=1}^n c_i m_i^*} \tag{9}$$

---

[3] $\mathcal{B}$ can extract $\mathcal{M}^*$ by choosing a sequence of linearly independent coefficients adaptively until collecting n valid responses from $\mathcal{A}$. These n linearly independent vectors C_i, $1 \le i \le n$, form an $n \times n$ non-singular matrix $[C_1 \ C_2 \ \dots \ C_n]^{\mathsf{T}} = [c_{i,j}]_{1 \le i \le n, \ 1 \le j \le n}$. $\mathcal{B}$ uses the KEA1 extractor $\overline{\mathcal{A}}$ to extract the n constant terms $\sum_{j=1}^n c_{i,j} m_j^*$ from V_i and V_i', $1 \le i \le n$, and solves the system of linear equations to obtain $\mathcal{M}^*$.

$\mathcal{B}$ can compute $\hat{e}(g, g')^{\alpha^2}$ as follows:

1. Since (7) holds, we have $h_{\mathcal{M}^*}^{\Delta} = H_3(C)$ and $V^{\Delta} = V'$ for some $\Delta \in_R \mathbb{Z}_q$. Thus, $\mathcal{B}$ can use the KEA1 extractor $\overline{\mathcal{A}}$ to extract $m' = \overline{\mathcal{A}}(h_{\mathcal{M}^*}^s, H_3(C)^s, V, V')$ such that $V = (h_{\mathcal{M}^*}^s)^{m'}$. Since (9) holds, we have $m' \neq \sum_{i=1}^{n} c_i m_i^*$.
2. Similarly, since (8) holds, $\mathcal{B}$ can use the KEA1 extractor $\overline{\mathcal{A}}$ to extract $t = \overline{\mathcal{A}}(H_2(pk_{\mathcal{V}}), g, V'', V''')$ such that $V'' = H_2(pk_{\mathcal{V}})^t$.
3. After knowing m' and t, since (6) and $m' \neq \sum_{i=1}^{n} c_i m_i^*$ hold, $\mathcal{B}$ can compute $\hat{e}(g, g')^{\alpha^2}$ as follows:

$$\rho^s = \hat{e}(\prod_{i=1}^{n} H_1(T_{\mathcal{M}^*}||i)^{s c_i} V, V'')^{s k_{\mathcal{V}}}$$

$$\Rightarrow \rho^s = \hat{e}(\prod_{i=1}^{n} (g^{r_i^*}/h_{\mathcal{M}^*}^{m_i^*})^{s c_i} h_{\mathcal{M}^*}^{s m'}, H_2(pk_{\mathcal{V}})^t)^{\alpha v}$$

$$\Rightarrow \rho^s = \hat{e}(\prod_{i=1}^{n} (g^{r_i^*}/g'^{r^* m_i^*})^{s c_i} g'^{r^* s m'}, g^{\alpha v' t})^{\alpha v}$$

$$\Rightarrow \rho = \hat{e}(\prod_{i=1}^{n} (g^{c_i r_i^*}/g'^{r^* c_i m_i^*}) g'^{r^* m'}, g^{\alpha v' t})^{\alpha v}$$

$$\Rightarrow \rho = \hat{e}(g^{\sum_{i=1}^{n} c_i r_i^*} g'^{r^* (m' - \sum_{i=1}^{n} c_i m_i^*)}, g^{\alpha v' t})^{\alpha v}$$

$$\Rightarrow \hat{e}(g'^{r^* (m' - \sum_{i=1}^{n} c_i m_i^*)}, g^{\alpha v' t})^{\alpha v} = \frac{\rho}{\hat{e}(g^{\alpha \sum_{i=1}^{n} c_i r_i^*}, g^{\alpha v' t})^v}$$

$$\Rightarrow \hat{e}(g, g')^{\alpha^2} = \left(\frac{\rho}{\hat{e}(g^{\alpha \sum_{i=1}^{n} c_i r_i^*}, g^{\alpha v' t}) v}\right)^{1/v v' t r^* (m' - \sum_{i=1}^{n} c_i m_i^*)}$$

$\mathcal{B}$ aborts on handling oracle $\mathcal{O}_{\mathsf{Tag}}$ if tag identifier $T_{\mathcal{M}}$ has been queried to oracle $\mathcal{O}_{\mathsf{H}_1}$. That is, record $(T_{\mathcal{M}}, *, *)$ exists in table $\mathcal{T}_{\mathsf{H}_1}$. For each $\mathcal{O}_{\mathsf{Tag}}$-query, we have $\Pr[(T_{\mathcal{M}}, *, *) \in \mathcal{T}_{\mathsf{H}_1}] = |\mathcal{T}_{\mathsf{H}_1}|/2^{|T_{\mathcal{M}}|} \leq (q_1 + q_T)/2^{\ell}$. Take the union bound on the q_T $\mathcal{O}_{\mathsf{Tag}}$-queries, we have $\Pr[\mathcal{B} \text{ aborts}] \leq (q_1 + q_T) q_T/2^{\ell}$. Moreover, $\mathcal{B}$ loses a negligible portion $\frac{1}{q} = \frac{1}{2^k}$ that $\mathcal{M}' \neq \mathcal{M}^*$ but $V = h_{\mathcal{M}^*}^{s \sum_{i=1}^{n} c_i m_i^*}$. Therefore, the reduced advantage is $\epsilon = (1 - \frac{(q_1 + q_T) q_T}{2^{\ell}})(1 - \frac{1}{2^k})\epsilon'$. Besides of handling $(\mathcal{O}_{\mathsf{H}_1}, \mathcal{O}_{\mathsf{H}_2}, \mathcal{O}_{\mathsf{Tag}}, \mathcal{O}_{\mathsf{DK}})$-oracles, $\mathcal{B}$ uses the KEA1 extractor $\overline{\mathcal{A}}$ two times to extract two exponents. Therefore, the reduced time is $t = t' + q_1 t_1 + q_2 t_2 + q_T t_T + q_K t_K + 2 t_{\overline{\mathcal{A}}}$. By choosing appropriate $q_1, q_2, q_T, q_K, \ell \in \mathsf{Poly}(k)$, we have $((q_1 + q_T) q_T/2^{\ell}, 1/2^k) \in \mathsf{negl}(k)^2$ and $q_1 t_1 + q_2 t_2 + q_T t_T + q_K t_K \in \mathsf{Poly}(k)$. $\qquad \square$

In the proof unforgeability game $\mathsf{Game}^{\mathsf{PF-UF}}$, the challenge $chal$ is chosen by the challenger $\mathcal{C}$. $\mathsf{Game}^{\mathsf{PF-UF}}$ can be adapted for existential unforgeability by letting adversary $\mathcal{A}$ choose $chal$ by himself. In our security proof, this modification only needs one more execution of the KEA1 extractor to know $\mathcal{A}$'s choice for the randomness s of $chal$.

4.2   Proof Indistinguishability

This game models the notion that a third party without being authorized cannot verify validity of data integrity proofs even if he eavesdrops network communications after the setup phase. In this game, the challenger $\mathcal{C}$ plays the role of the storage server, and the adversary $\mathcal{A}$ plays the role of the third-party user. $\mathcal{A}$ is given access right to oracle $\mathcal{O}_{\mathsf{Proof}}$. $\mathcal{A}$ is trained with valid proofs and tries to verify validity of the target proof. If $\mathcal{A}$ answers validity correctly, he wins this game.

The proof indistinguishability game $\mathsf{Game}^{\mathsf{PF-IND}}$ is as follows:

Setup. $\mathcal{C}$ generates public parameter π, user $\mathcal{U}$'s key tuple $(sk_\mathcal{U}, pk_\mathcal{U}, kt_\mathcal{U})$, delegated verifier $\mathcal{V}$'s key tuple $(sk_\mathcal{V}, pk_\mathcal{V}, kt_\mathcal{V})$, delegation key $dk_{\mathcal{U}\to\mathcal{V}}$, data $\mathcal{M} = (m_1, m_2, \ldots, m_n)$, tags $\Sigma = (\sigma_1, \sigma_2, \ldots, \sigma_n)$, data identifier $h_\mathcal{M}$, and tag identifier seed $T_\mathcal{M}$ for $\mathcal{M}$. $\mathcal{C}$ forwards $(\pi, pk_\mathcal{U}, pk_\mathcal{V}, kt_\mathcal{V}, dk_{\mathcal{U}\to\mathcal{V}}, h_\mathcal{M}, T_\mathcal{M})$ to $\mathcal{A}$.

Query-1. $\mathcal{A}$ queries oracle $\mathcal{O}_{\mathsf{Proof}}$ to obtain samples of valid proofs.

 – $\mathcal{O}_{\mathsf{Proof}}$: $\mathcal{A}$ chooses challenge $chal$ and obtains a valid proof $pf_{chal,\mathcal{V}}$ for $(\mathcal{M}, chal)$.

Challenge. Same as the query-1 phase except that validity of the returned proof $pf^*_{chal,\mathcal{V}}$ depends on an uniform bit b. If $b = 1$, the $\mathcal{C}$ returns a valid proof. Otherwise, $\mathcal{C}$ returns an invalid proof.

Query-2. Same as the query-1 phase.

Answer. $\mathcal{A}$ answers b' for the challenged proof $pf^*_{chal,\mathcal{V}}$. $\mathcal{A}$ wins $\mathsf{Game}^{\mathsf{PF-IND}}$ if $b' = b$. The advantage $Adv_\mathcal{A}^{\mathsf{Prf-IND}}$ is defined as $\left| \Pr[\mathcal{A} \text{ wins } \mathsf{Game}^{\mathsf{PF-IND}}] - \frac{1}{2} \right|$.

We show that our scheme is proof indistinguishable under the *truncated decisional* 1-BDHE assumption.

Theorem 2. *If the truncated decisional BDHE problem is $(t, \epsilon, 1)$-secure, the above scheme is $(t - q_1 t_1 - q_2 t_2 - q_P t_P, 2\epsilon)$ proof indistinguishable in the random oracle model, where hash functions H_1 and H_2 are modeled as random oracles $\mathcal{O}_{H_1}$ and $\mathcal{O}_{H_2}$, (q_1, q_2, q_P) are the numbers of times that an adversary queries $(\mathcal{O}_{H_1}, \mathcal{O}_{H_2}, \mathcal{O}_{\mathsf{Proof}})$-oracles, and (t_1, t_2, t_P) are the time used by $(\mathcal{O}_{H_1}, \mathcal{O}_{H_2}, \mathcal{O}_{\mathsf{Proof}})$-oracles to respond an oracle query.*

Proof. Let $\mathcal{A}$ be a probabilistic black-box adversary who wins the proof indistinguishability game $\mathsf{Game}^{\mathsf{PF-IND}}$ with advantage ϵ' in time t'. We construct an algorithm $\mathcal{B}$ that uses $\mathcal{A}$ to solve the *truncated decisional* 1-BDHE problem as follows:

Setup. Given an instance (g, g^α, g', Z) of the *truncated decision* 1-BDHE problem, $\mathcal{B}$ sets the public parameter $\pi = (q, G, g, G_T, g_T, \hat{e}, H_3)$, user $\mathcal{U}$'s key tuple $(sk_\mathcal{U}, pk_\mathcal{U}, kt_\mathcal{U}) = (\alpha u, g^{\alpha u}, H_2(g^{\alpha u})^{\alpha u})$, where $H_2(g^{\alpha u}) = g^{u'}$ and $u, u' \in_R \mathbb{Z}_q$, delegated verifier $\mathcal{V}$'s key tuple $(sk_\mathcal{V}, pk_\mathcal{V}, kt_\mathcal{V}) = (\alpha v, g^{\alpha v}, H_2(g^{\alpha v})^{\alpha v})$, where $H_2(g^{\alpha v}) = g^{v'}$ and $v, v' \in_R \mathbb{Z}_q$, and the delegation key $dk_{\mathcal{U}\to\mathcal{V}} = kt_\mathcal{V}^{1/sk_\mathcal{U}} =$

$g^{vv'/u}$. Then $\mathcal{B}$ chooses data $\mathcal{M} = (m_1, m_2, \ldots, m_n)$, sets data identifier $h_{\mathcal{M}} = g^{'r}$, where $r \in_R \mathbb{Z}_q$, and chooses tag identifier seed $T_{\mathcal{M}}$. For $1 \leq i \leq n$, $\mathcal{B}$ sets $H_1(T_{\mathcal{M}}||i) = g^{r_i}$, where $r_i \in_R \mathbb{Z}_q$. Then $\mathcal{B}$ invokes $\mathcal{A}$ as a subroutine: $\mathcal{A}^{\mathcal{O}_{H_1}, \mathcal{O}_{H_2}, \mathcal{O}_{\mathsf{Proof}}}(\pi, pk_{\mathcal{U}}, pk_{\mathcal{V}}, kt_{\mathcal{V}}, dk_{\mathcal{U} \to \mathcal{V}}, h_{\mathcal{M}}, T_{\mathcal{M}})$.

Query-1. $\mathcal{A}$ can query oracles $\mathcal{O}_{H_1}$, $\mathcal{O}_{H_2}$, and $\mathcal{O}_{\mathsf{Proof}}$ during his execution. $\mathcal{B}$ handles these oracles as follows:

- $\mathcal{O}_{H_1}$. $\mathcal{B}$ maintains a table $\mathcal{T}_{H_1} = \{(x, H_1(x), r)\}$ to look up the $\mathcal{O}_{H_1}$-query records. $\mathcal{B}$ takes $x \in \{0, 1\}^*$ as input and outputs y if record $(x, y, *)$ exists in $\mathcal{T}_{H_1}$. Otherwise, $\mathcal{B}$ outputs $H_1(x) = g^r$ and inserts (x, g^r, r) into $\mathcal{T}_{H_1}$, where $r \in_R \mathbb{Z}_q$.
- $\mathcal{O}_{H_2}$. $\mathcal{B}$ maintains a table $\mathcal{T}_{H_2} = \{(g^x, H_2(g^x), r)\}$ to look up the $\mathcal{O}_{H_2}$-query records. $\mathcal{B}$ takes g^x as input and outputs y if record $(g^x, y, *)$ exists in $\mathcal{T}_{H_2}$. Otherwise, $\mathcal{B}$ outputs $H_2(g^x) = g^r$ and inserts (g^x, g^r, r) into $\mathcal{T}_{H_2}$, where $r \in_R \mathbb{Z}_q$.
- $\mathcal{O}_{\mathsf{Proof}}$. $\mathcal{B}$ takes challenge $chal = (C = (c_1, c_2, \ldots, c_n), C', C'')$ as input and checks whether $\hat{e}(C', H_3(C)) = \hat{e}(h_{\mathcal{M}}, C'')$. If not, $\mathcal{B}$ aborts. Otherwise, $\mathcal{B}$ outputs a valid proof $pf_{chal, \mathcal{V}} = (\rho, V, V', V'', V''')$ as below: Let $t \in_R \mathbb{Z}_q$.

$$\rho = \hat{e}(\prod_{i=1}^{n} \sigma_i^{c_i}, dk_{\mathcal{U} \to \mathcal{V}})^t$$

$$= \hat{e}(\prod_{i=1}^{n}(H_1(T_{\mathcal{M}}||i)h_{\mathcal{M}}^{m_i})^{sk_{\mathcal{U}} c_i}, H_2(pk_{\mathcal{V}})^{sk_{\mathcal{V}}/sk_{\mathcal{U}}})^t$$

$$= \hat{e}(\prod_{i=1}^{n}(g^{r_i}g^{'rm_i})^{c_i}, g^{v'\alpha v})^t$$

$$= \hat{e}(g^{\sum_{i=1}^{n} c_i r_i}g^{'r \sum_{i=1}^{n} c_i m_i}, g^{\alpha})^{vv't} \quad ,$$

$$V = C'^{\sum_{i=1}^{n} c_i m_i} \quad , \quad V' = C''^{\sum_{i=1}^{n} c_i m_i} \quad , \quad V'' = g^{v't} \quad , \text{ and } V''' = g^t \ .$$

Challenge. After the query-1 phase, $\mathcal{A}$ chooses challenge $chal = (C = (c_1, c_2, \ldots, c_n), C', C'')$, and $\mathcal{B}$ checks whether $\hat{e}(C', H_3(C)) = \hat{e}(h_{\mathcal{M}}, C'')$. If not, $\mathcal{B}$ aborts. Otherwise, $\mathcal{B}$ outputs a proof $pf_{\mathcal{V}}^* = (\rho^*, V, V', V'', V''')$ as follows, where $pf_{\mathcal{V}}^*$ is valid if $Z = \hat{e}(g, g')^{\alpha^2}$. Let $t = \alpha$.

$$\rho^* = \hat{e}(g^{\sum_{i=1}^{n} c_i r_i}g^{'r \sum_{i=1}^{n} c_i m_i}, g^{\alpha})^{vv't}$$

$$= \hat{e}(g^{\sum_{i=1}^{n} c_i r_i}, g^{\alpha})^{vv'\alpha} \times \hat{e}(g^{'r \sum_{i=1}^{n} c_i m_i}, g^{\alpha})^{vv'\alpha}$$

$$= \hat{e}(g^{\alpha \sum_{i=1}^{n} c_i r_i}, g^{\alpha})^{vv'} \times \hat{e}(g', g)^{\alpha^2 vv'r \sum_{i=1}^{n} c_i m_i}$$

$$= \hat{e}(g^{\alpha \sum_{i=1}^{n} c_i r_i}, g^{\alpha})^{vv'} \times Z^{vv'r \sum_{i=1}^{n} c_i m_i} \quad ,$$

$$V = C'^{\sum_{i=1}^{n} c_i m_i} \quad , \quad V' = C''^{\sum_{i=1}^{n} c_i m_i} \quad , \quad V'' = g^{\alpha v'} \quad , \text{ and } V''' = g^{\alpha} \ .$$

Query-2. Same as the query-1 phase.

Answer. $\mathcal{A}$ answers validity b of $pf_{\mathcal{V}}^{*}$, and $\mathcal{B}$ uses b to answer the *truncated decisional* 1-BDHE problem directly.

In the above reduction, $\mathcal{B}$ doesn't abort. When $Z = \hat{e}(g, g')^{\alpha^2}$, $\mathcal{A}$ has advantage ϵ' to break proof indistinguishability game. Therefore, the reduced advantage of $\mathcal{B}$ is $\epsilon = \epsilon'/2$ and the reduced time is $t = t' + q_1 t_1 + q_2 t_2 + q_P t_P$. By choosing appropriate $(q_1, q_2, q_P) \in \mathsf{Poly}(k)^3$, we have $q_1 t_1 + q_2 t_2 + q_P t_P \in \mathsf{Poly}(k)$.   □

4.3   Delegation Key Unforgeability

This game models the notion that a third party cannot generate a valid delegation key even if he eavesdrops network communications during the delegation phase and corrupts some delegated verifiers. In this game, the challenger $\mathcal{C}$ provides samples of public keys, key tokens, and delegation keys. The adversary $\mathcal{A}$ corrupts some of the samples to obtain the corresponding private keys and tries to generate a valid delegation key for a user $\mathcal{V}^*$.

The delegation key unforgeability game $\mathsf{Game}^{\mathsf{DK-UF}}$ is as follows:

Setup. $\mathcal{C}$ generates public parameter π and user $\mathcal{U}$'s key tuple $(sk_{\mathcal{U}}, pk_{\mathcal{U}}, kt_{\mathcal{U}})$. $\mathcal{C}$ forwards $(\pi, pk_{\mathcal{U}})$ to $\mathcal{A}$.

Query. $\mathcal{A}$ queries oracle $\mathcal{O}_{\mathsf{Dlg}}$ and oracle $\mathcal{O}_{\mathsf{Cor}}$ to obtain samples of public keys, key tokens, and delegation keys, and the corresponding private keys.

- $\mathcal{O}_{\mathsf{Dlg}}$: It samples a user $\mathcal{V}$ and returns $(pk_{\mathcal{V}}, kt_{\mathcal{V}}, dk_{\mathcal{U} \to \mathcal{V}})$.
- $\mathcal{O}_{\mathsf{Cor}}$: $\mathcal{A}$ chooses $(pk_{\mathcal{V}}, kt_{\mathcal{V}}, dk_{\mathcal{U} \to \mathcal{V}})$ from $\mathcal{O}_{\mathsf{Dlg}}$ and obtains $sk_{\mathcal{V}}$ from $\mathcal{O}_{\mathsf{Cor}}$.

Answer. $\mathcal{A}$ generates a valid delegation key $dk_{\mathcal{U} \to \mathcal{V}^*}$ for a user $\mathcal{V}^*$. $\mathcal{A}$ returns $(sk_{\mathcal{V}^*}, pk_{\mathcal{V}^*}, kt_{\mathcal{V}^*}, dk_{\mathcal{U} \to \mathcal{V}^*})$ to $\mathcal{C}$, where $(sk_{\mathcal{V}^*}, pk_{\mathcal{V}^*}, kt_{\mathcal{V}^*})$ is a valid key tuple for $\mathcal{V}^*$. $\mathcal{A}$ wins $\mathsf{Game}^{\mathsf{DK-UF}}$ if $\mathsf{VrfyDK}(\pi, dk_{\mathcal{U} \to \mathcal{V}^*}, pk_{\mathcal{U}}, pk_{\mathcal{V}^*}) = true$. The advantage $Adv_{\mathcal{A}}^{\mathsf{DK-UF}}$ is defined as $\Pr[\mathcal{A}$ wins $\mathsf{Game}^{\mathsf{DK-UF}}]$.

We show that our scheme is delegation key unforgeable under the InvCDH assumption.

Theorem 3. *If the InvCDH problem is (t, ϵ)-secure, the above scheme is $(t - q_2 t_2 - q_D t_D - q_C t_C, eq_C \epsilon)$ delegation key unforgeable in the random oracle model, where hash function H_2 is modeled as random oracle $\mathcal{O}_{H_2}$, e is the Euler's number, (q_2, q_D, q_C) are the numbers of times that an adversary queries $(\mathcal{O}_{H_2}, \mathcal{O}_{\mathsf{Dlg}}, \mathcal{O}_{\mathsf{Cor}})$-oracles, and (t_2, t_D, t_C) are the time used by $(\mathcal{O}_{H_2}, \mathcal{O}_{\mathsf{Dlg}}, \mathcal{O}_{\mathsf{Cor}})$-oracles to respond an oracle query.*

Proof. Let $\mathcal{A}$ be a probabilistic black-box adversary who wins the delegation key unforgeability game $\mathsf{Game}^{\mathsf{DK-UF}}$ with advantage ϵ' in time t'. We construct an algorithm $\mathcal{B}$ that uses $\mathcal{A}$ to solve the InvCDH problem as follows:

Setup. Given an instance (g, g^{α}) of the InvCDH problem, $\mathcal{B}$ sets the public parameter $\pi = (q, G, g, G_T, g_T, \hat{e}, H_1, H_3)$ and user $\mathcal{U}$'s key tuple $(sk_{\mathcal{U}}, pk_{\mathcal{U}}, kt_{\mathcal{U}}) = (\alpha, g^{\alpha}, H_2(g^{\alpha})^{\alpha})$, where $H_2(g^{\alpha}) = g^u$ and $u \in_R \mathbb{Z}_q$. $\mathcal{B}$ invokes $\mathcal{A}$ as a subroutine: $\mathcal{A}^{\mathcal{O}_{H_2}, \mathcal{O}_{\mathsf{Dlg}}, \mathcal{O}_{\mathsf{Cor}}}(\pi, pk_{\mathcal{U}})$.

Query. $\mathcal{A}$ can query oracles $\mathcal{O}_{H_2}$, $\mathcal{O}_{Dlg}$, and $\mathcal{O}_{Cor}$ during his execution. $\mathcal{B}$ handles these oracles as follows: $\mathcal{B}$ chooses probability $\delta = \frac{q_C}{q_C+1}$.

- $\mathcal{O}_{H_2}$. $\mathcal{B}$ maintains a table $\mathcal{T}_{H_2} = \{(g^x, H_2(g^x), r)\}$ to look up the $\mathcal{O}_{H_2}$-query records. $\mathcal{B}$ takes g^x as input and outputs y if record $(g^x, y, *)$ exists in $\mathcal{T}_{H_2}$. Otherwise, $\mathcal{B}$ outputs $H_2(g^x) = g^{\alpha r}$ with probability δ or outputs $H_2(g^x) = g^r$ with probability $1 - \delta$, and inserts $(g^x, H_2(g^x), r)$ into $\mathcal{T}_{H_2}$, where $r \in_R \mathbb{Z}_q$.

- $\mathcal{O}_{Dlg}$. $\mathcal{B}$ maintains a table $\mathcal{T}_{Dlg} = \{(v, pk_V)\}$ to look up the $\mathcal{O}_{Dlg}$-query records. $\mathcal{B}$ samples a fresh delegated verifier V, $(pk_V, *, *)$ doesn't exist in table $\mathcal{T}_{H_2}$, randomly and generates V's key tuple $(sk_V, pk_V, kt_V) = (v, g^v, H_2(g^v)^v = (g^{\alpha v'})^v)$ with probability δ or $(sk_V, pk_V, kt_V) = (\alpha v, g^{\alpha v}, H_2(g^{\alpha v})^{\alpha v} = (g^{v'})^{\alpha v})$ with probability $1 - \delta$, where $v, v' \in_R \mathbb{Z}_q$. $\mathcal{B}$ inserts $(pk_V, H_2(pk_V), v')$ into $\mathcal{T}_{H_2}$ and inserts (v, pk_V) into $\mathcal{T}_{Dlg}$. Then $\mathcal{B}$ outputs $(pk_V, kt_V, dk_{\mathcal{U} \to V})$, where

$$dk_{\mathcal{U} \to V} = kt_V^{1/sk_\mathcal{U}} = (g^{\alpha v v'})^{1/\alpha} = g^{v v'} .$$

- $\mathcal{O}_{Cor}$. $\mathcal{B}$ takes $(pk_V, kt_V, dk_{\mathcal{U} \to V})$ as input and rejects if either record $(pk_V, *, *)$ doesn't exist in table $\mathcal{T}_{H_2}$, record $(*, pk_V)$ doesn't exist in table $\mathcal{T}_{Dlg}$, or $(kt_V, dk_{\mathcal{U} \to V})$ isn't consistent with $\mathcal{T}_{H_2}$ and $\mathcal{T}_{Dlg}$. $\mathcal{B}$ outputs $sk_V = v$ if $pk_V = g^v$. Otherwise, $sk_V = \alpha v$, and $\mathcal{B}$ aborts.

Answer. $\mathcal{A}$ forges a delegation key $dk_{\mathcal{U} \to V^*}$ for a user V^* whose key tuple is $(sk_{V^*}, pk_{V^*}, kt_{V^*})$, and outputs $(sk_{V^*}, pk_{V^*}, kt_{V^*}, dk_{\mathcal{U} \to V^*})$. $\mathcal{B}$ rejects if either record $(pk_{V^*}, *, *)$ doesn't exist in table $\mathcal{T}_{H_2}$ or $\hat{e}(pk_\mathcal{U}, dk_{\mathcal{U} \to V^*}) \neq \hat{e}(pk_{V^*}, H_2(pk_{V^*}))$. If $H_2(pk_{V^*}) = g^{\alpha r^*}$, $\mathcal{B}$ aborts. Otherwise, $H_2(pk_{V^*}) = g^{r^*}$, and $\mathcal{B}$ computes $g^{\frac{1}{\alpha}}$ as follows:

$$\hat{e}(pk_\mathcal{U}, dk_{\mathcal{U} \to V^*}) = \hat{e}(pk_{V^*}, H_2(pk_{V^*}))$$
$$\Rightarrow \hat{e}(g^\alpha, dk_{\mathcal{U} \to V^*}) = \hat{e}(g^{sk_{V^*}}, g^{r^*})$$
$$\Rightarrow dk_{\mathcal{U} \to V^*} = g^{sk_{V^*} r^* / \alpha}$$
$$\Rightarrow g^{\frac{1}{\alpha}} = (dk_{\mathcal{U} \to V^*})^{1/sk_{V^*} r^*}$$

In the above reduction, $\mathcal{B}$ doesn't abort with probability $\delta^{q_C}(1-\delta)$. When choosing $\delta = \frac{q_C}{q_C+1}$, we have $\delta^{q_C}(1-\delta) = (1 - \frac{1}{q_C+1})^{q_C} \frac{1}{q_C+1} = (1 - \frac{1}{q_C+1})^{q_C+1} \frac{1}{q_C} \geq \frac{1}{e q_C}$. Therefore, the reduced advantage is $\epsilon = \frac{\epsilon'}{e q_C}$, and the reduced time is $t = t' + q_2 t_2 + q_D t_D + q_C t_C$. By choosing appropriate $(q_2, q_D, q_C) \in \mathsf{Poly}(k)^3$, we have $(e q_C, q_2 t_2 + q_D t_D + q_C t_C) \in \mathsf{Poly}(k)^2$. $\quad\square$

5   Conclusion

We proposed a delegable provable data possession model that provides delegable (authorized) verification on remote data. Delegable PDP allows a trusted third party to check data integrity under data owner's permission and prevents the trusted third party to re-delegate this verification capability to others. This feature is desired on private data in the public cloud. We provided a construction for the delegable PDP problem and proved its security in the random oracle model.

Due to using pairing operations on blocks directly, each block m_i is limited to k-bit long. We shall develop a new delegation method without using pairing in the future. Dynamic operations, such as insertion, deletion, modification, etc., on stored data is useful. Supporting efficient dynamic operations on stored data is another direction of our future works.

References

1. Ateniese, G., Burns, R., Curtmola, R., Herring, J., Kissner, L., Peterson, Z., Song, D.: Provable data possession at untrusted stores. In: Proceedings of the 14th ACM Conference on Computer and Communications Security, CCS 2007, pp. 598–609 (2007)
2. Ateniese, G., Di Pietro, R., Mancini, L.V., Tsudik, G.: Scalable and efficient provable data possession. In: Proceedings of the 4th International Conference on Security and Privacy in Communication Networks, SecureComm 2008, pp. 9:1–9:10 (2008)
3. Ateniese, G., Kamara, S., Katz, J.: Proofs of Storage from Homomorphic Identification Protocols. In: Matsui, M. (ed.) ASIACRYPT 2009. LNCS, vol. 5912, pp. 319–333. Springer, Heidelberg (2009)
4. Boneh, D., Boyen, X., Goh, E.-J.: Hierarchical Identity Based Encryption with Constant Size Ciphertext. In: Cramer, R. (ed.) EUROCRYPT 2005. LNCS, vol. 3494, pp. 440–456. Springer, Heidelberg (2005)
5. Boneh, D., Gentry, C., Waters, B.: Collusion Resistant Broadcast Encryption with Short Ciphertexts and Private Keys. In: Shoup, V. (ed.) CRYPTO 2005. LNCS, vol. 3621, pp. 258–275. Springer, Heidelberg (2005)
6. Bowers, K.D., Juels, A., Oprea, A.: Hail: a High-availability and Integrity Layer for Cloud Storage. In: Proceedings of the 16th ACM Conference on Computer and Communications Security, CCS 2009, pp. 187–198 (2009)
7. Bowers, K.D., Juels, A., Oprea, A.: Proofs of retrievability: theory and implementation. In: Proceedings of the 2009 ACM Workshop on Cloud Computing Security, CCSW 2009, pp. 43–54 (2009)
8. Chen, B., Curtmola, R., Ateniese, G., Burns, R.: Remote data checking for network coding-based distributed storage systems. In: Proceedings of the 2010 ACM Workshop on Cloud Computing Security Workshop, CCSW 2010, pp. 31–42 (2010)
9. Curtmola, R., Khan, O., Burns, R.: Robust remote data checking. In: Proceedings of the 4th ACM International Workshop on Storage Security and Survivability, StorageSS 2008, pp. 63–68 (2008)
10. Curtmola, R., Khan, O., Burns, R., Ateniese, G.: Mr-pdp: Multiple-replica provable data possession. In: Proceedings of the 2008 the 28th International Conference on Distributed Computing Systems, ICDCS 2008, pp. 411–420 (2008)
11. Damgård, I.B.: Towards Practical Public Key Systems Secure Against Chosen Ciphertext Attacks. In: Feigenbaum, J. (ed.) CRYPTO 1991. LNCS, vol. 576, pp. 445–456. Springer, Heidelberg (1992)
12. Erway, C., Küpçü, A., Papamanthou, C., Tamassia, R.: Dynamic provable data possession. In: Proceedings of the 16th ACM Conference on Computer and Communications Security, CCS 2009, pp. 213–222 (2009)

13. Gentry, C.: Practical Identity-based Encryption without Random Oracles. In: Vaudenay, S. (ed.) EUROCRYPT 2006. LNCS, vol. 4004, pp. 445–464. Springer, Heidelberg (2006)
14. Juels, A., Kaliski Jr., B.S.: Pors: proofs of retrievability for large files. In: Proceedings of the 14th ACM Conference on Computer and Communications Security, CCS 2007, pp. 584–597 (2007)
15. Shacham, H., Waters, B.: Compact Proofs of Retrievability. In: Pieprzyk, J. (ed.) ASIACRYPT 2008. LNCS, vol. 5350, pp. 90–107. Springer, Heidelberg (2008)
16. Wang, C., Wang, Q., Ren, K., Lou, W.: Privacy-preserving public auditing for data storage security in cloud computing. In: Proceedings of the 29th Conference on Information Communications, INFOCOM 2010, pp. 525–533 (2010)
17. Wang, Q., Wang, C., Li, J., Ren, K., Lou, W.: Enabling Public Verifiability and Data Dynamics for Storage Security in Cloud Computing. In: Backes, M., Ning, P. (eds.) ESORICS 2009. LNCS, vol. 5789, pp. 355–370. Springer, Heidelberg (2009)

Unconditionally Secure Oblivious Transfer Based on Channel Delays

Kai-Yuen Cheong and Atsuko Miyaji

Japan Advanced Institute of Science and Technology,
1-1 Asahidai, Nomi, Ishikawa, 923-1292 Japan
{kaiyuen,miyaji}@jaist.ac.jp

Abstract. Without the use of computational assumptions, unconditionally secure oblivious transfer (OT) is impossible in the standard model where the parties are using a clear channel. Such impossibilities can be overcome by using a noisy channel. Recently, Palmieri and Pereira proposed a protocol based on random channel delays only. Their scheme is secure in the semi-honest model, but not in the general malicious model. In this paper we study oblivious transfer in the same setting but we improve the result to obtain a fully secure protocol in the malicious model.

Keywords: Oblivious transfer, unconditional security, channel delay.

1 Introduction

Oblivious Transfer (OT) is a two-party cryptographic protocol with a simple function. However, it is an important primitive because any secure computation can be based on OT [7,11]. It is considered a universal primitive for cryptographic functionalities where the users do not fully trust each other.

In the first OT system introduced by Rabin [9], a message is received with probability $1/2$ and the sender does not know whether the message reaches the other side. Even et al. defined the 1-out-of-2 OT [6], where the sender has two secrets and the receiver can choose one of them in an oblivious manner. That is, the sender cannot know the receiver's choice and the receiver cannot know more than one of the sender's secrets. The 1-out-of-2 OT is equivalent to the Rabin OT [1]. Also, we may assume that the sender's secrets are one-bit messages in 1-out-of-2 OT, because the case with string messages is reducible to it efficiently [5].

By simple arguments, it can be shown that OT cannot achieve information theoretic security for both parties over a standard, noiseless communication channel. If a noisy channel of certain form is available between the sender and the receiver, OT can be constructed with unconditional security [2,4,10]. While OT based on noisy channels with transmission errors are relatively well-studied, in 2010 Palmieri and Pereira [8] proposed a new scheme using a completely different source of channel randomness. In their paper, the channel does not have any error on the content but a transmission delay. This seems to be a remarkably weaker assumption than the noisy channel, and random channel delays are abundant in media like the Internet.

S. Qing et al. (Eds.): ICICS 2011, LNCS 7043, pp. 112–120, 2011.

In [8], a semi-honest OT protocol is proposed, where the parties follow the protocol strictly, but may try to compute more information afterwards from the communication transcript. In this paper, we improve it by removing the semi-honest assumption. The final protocol is unconditionally secure. Some techniques we use are from the standard ones [3] for general OT enhancement.

Our paper is organized as follows: Section 2 describes the preliminaries including the assumptions about the channel used and the definition of OT. In Section 3 we describe a basic protocol which only works in the semi-honest model, similar to the protocol in [8]. The main contribution of this paper is shown in Section 4 where we provided the fully secure protocol, before the conclusion in Section 5.

2   Preliminaries

2.1   Delay Channel

Following the tracks of [8], we first define the properties of the channel called the binary discrete-time delaying channel (BDDC). In this model, the channel accepts binary strings called packets and delivers them with some delay. It is a memoryless channel such that delays happen to each packet independently according to certain known probabilistic distribution. The channel operates at discrete times, such that there is a fixed set of allowed time for transmitting and receiving the packets. A packet always arrives as a whole at the same time, without being broken into parts. The channel has no other forms of errors.

A delay probability is denoted by p with $p < 1/2$. We assume that p is publicly known, and set $q = 1 - p$. Neither the sender nor the receiver gets any feedback information about the delay that occurred. The BDDC has the following properties:

1. There is a discrete (either finite or infinite) set of allowed input times $T = \{t_0, t_1, ...\}$ and output times $U = \{u_0, u_1, ...\}$.
2. A packet sent at t_i will arrive at u_i if there is no delay. Otherwise it will arrive at u_j with probability p_{ij}. A packet may delay once with probability p, and is subject to further delays with the same probability. Therefore, for $j \geq i$ we have $p_{ij} = p^{j-i} - p^{j-i+1}$. For $j < i$, $p_{ij} = 0$.

It is clear that $p_{ii} = q$ denotes the probability that the packet arrives on time. The assumption that $p < 1/2$ can generally be justified. First, p should be low for an efficient channel. Also, in reality, time is an analog quantity, and the mean and variance of the actual delay can be used to derive the interval in which the packet is expected to arrive with high probability. In [8], it is also assumed that $p < 1/2$.

2.2   Oblivious Transfer

In this paper, the 1-out-of-2 bit OT with perfect security is defined as:

1. The sender Alice inputs a pair of secret bits (s_0, s_1) and the receiver Bob inputs a choice bit c.

2. **Correctness:** If both Alice and Bob are honest, Bob outputs s_c and Alice outputs nothing.
3. **Security for Alice:** Regardless of Bob's actions, if Alice is honest, there exists $c' \in \{0, 1\}$ such that Bob receives zero information of $s_{c'}$.
4. **Security for Bob:** If Bob is honest, Alice receives zero information on c regardless of her actions.

In the case where the properties above are not perfectly satisfied, if the failure probability for each of them is negligible, we say that the OT protocol is unconditionally secure. A protocol is said to be in the semi-honest model if all parties are assumed to follow the protocol. Otherwise it is in the malicious model, where the cheating party does not need to follow the protocol. Therefore, security in the malicious model is strictly stronger than security in semi-honest model.

3 A Building Block Protocol

3.1 Semi-honest OT

In this part we introduce a protocol similar to [8]. It is a semi-honest OT protocol. A small modification is made to reduce the communication cost. Impact to security is basically none but the analysis becomes easier in our version. The change is that we set the variables e_i to be one bit, rather than a general binary string. Our version of the protocol is:

1. For security parameter n, Alice prepares random bits $e_1, e_2, ...e_n$. For convenience n is an even number. For $1 \le i \le n$ she prepares $v_i = i||e_i$ which is the string created by the concatenation of index i and bit e_i. Next, she also creates $v_i' = i||(1 - e_i)$.
2. At time t_0, Alice sends all v_i to the BDDC. At time t_1, she sends all v_i'. Each of v_i and v_i' is treated as one packet in the BDDC channel.
3. At time u_0, Bob receives the packets coming from the BDDC. If fewer than $n/2$ packets are received, Bob aborts the protocol.
4. Otherwise Bob randomly selects a set of indices $I_c \subset \{1, 2, \ldots n\}$, where c is his OT choice bit, under the condition that $|I_c| = n/2$ and Bob has received a string in the form $i||*$ at u_0 for all $i \in I_c$. He sets I_{1-c} to be the set of all $i \in \{1, 2, \ldots n\}$ such that $i \notin I_c$.
5. Bob sends (I_0, I_1) over a clear channel to Alice. If there are no other channels the BDDC can also be used for this purpose. In either case we do not add extra assumptions about the properties of the channels used in the protocol.
6. Alice computes

$$\beta_0 = \bigoplus_{i \in I_0} e_i$$
$$\beta_1 = \bigoplus_{i \in I_1} e_i \tag{1}$$

and then sets $\sigma_0 = s_0 \oplus \beta_0$ and $\sigma_1 = s_1 \oplus \beta_1$.

7. Alice sends (σ_0, σ_1) to Bob.
8. Bob knows e_i whenever $i \in I_c$. He computes $\beta_c = \bigoplus_{i \in I_c} e_i$ and finally $s_c = \sigma_c \oplus \beta_c$.

In essence, in the protocol v_i is a random message Alice sends to Bob and v'_i is for confusion such that Bob will not be able to get Alice's message if he gets v_i and v'_i at the same time. Thus the setting has the feature of Rabin OT [1]. It is then used to construct the 1-out-of-2 OT in the standard way.

3.2 Security in the Semi-honest Model

Following the definition of OT, the proof of security properties and functionality is divided into three parts, correctness, security for Alice, and security for Bob.

Correctness: If both parties are honest, the packets sent at t_0 follows a binomial distribution regarding to whether they are delayed or not. Failure happens when there are not enough packets received at u_0. Same as [8] we use the Hoeffding's inequality to see that the upper bound of failure probability is $e^{-2n(\frac{1}{2}-p)^2}$. As it decreases exponentially with the increase of n, we can say that it is negligible.

Alice's security: We can show that the protocol is secure even against a malicious Bob, which is stronger than the semi-honest Bob. To simplify the analysis further, let us assume that the malicious Bob is equipped with a special power: whenever a packet is received at or after u_2, Bob can tell the time that the packet in question is sent. Therefore, the only uncertainty is on the packets received at u_1, which may be sent at t_0 or t_1. Note that the real Bob has no such power and is thus strictly weaker.

For any i, if both v_i and v'_i are received at u_1, they are indistinguishable to Bob, and he would have zero information on e_i. For one i, the probability for this to happen is pq^2. Therefore, the probability that it never happens for $1 \le i \le n$ is $(1 - pq^2)^n$. Note that this probability falls exponentially with n.

Otherwise, there exists at least one i such that Bob has zero information on e_i. Since either $i \in I_0$ or $i \in I_1$, it is ensured that there exists c' such that Bob cannot get $s_{c'}$.

Bob's security: If Alice follows the protocol, it is clear that she cannot get any information about c because all possible sets of (I_0, I_1) are equally likely. Therefore the protocol is perfectly secure against the semi-honest Alice.

4 Constructing the Full Protocol

4.1 Insecurity of the Basic Protocol

The problem with the semi-honest protocol is that when Alice is malicious, it is insecure. Note that Alice will not send the same packet twice or send something with incorrect format, because they are detectable with absolute certainty. On the other hand, the honest Bob does not need to look at packets arriving at u_1 or later in the protocol, so Alice also does not need to care about what she sends to the BDDC at time t_1 and after. Moreover, Alice cannot gain any information about c after the last message from Bob. Therefore it is clear that the malicious Alice will only focus on adding or deleting messages to be sent at t_0 in the following manner. For each i, essentially there are only three possible deviations from the protocol:

1. Alice sends v_i' instead of v_i at t_0.
2. Alice sends both v_i and v_i' at t_0.
3. Alice sends neither v_i nor v_i' at t_0.

The first case cannot cause any harm to Bob as it is equivalent to flipping the randomly chosen e_i before the protocol begins. For the second case, Bob can detect it with probability q^2 by seeing both v_i and v_i' at u_0. This is a weak attack, but not to be ignored. The third case is a strong attack which leaves the scheme completely broken. Bob will not detect anything wrong, and it becomes certain that $i \in I_{1-c}$. Therefore Alice can get Bob's choice c with absolute certainty at zero risk. These problems are to be solved in the full protocol.

4.2   The Enhancement Scheme

Using a method in [3], any OT scheme can be used k times as sub-protocols, to build a stronger OT for Bob's security against the malicious Alice. At the end, only the XOR value of all the Bob's choice bits is his real choice. For completeness, we describe the general method here:

1. At the beginning, Alice has OT input $\{s_0, s_1\}$, while Bob has a choice c.
2. Alice generates a list of $k-1$ random bits $(\phi_{0,1}, \phi_{0,2} \ldots \phi_{0,k-1})$.
3. Alice chooses $\phi_{0,k}$ such that $\bigoplus_{i=1}^{k} \phi_{0,i} = s_0$.
4. Alice sets the second list of bits as $\phi_{1,i} = \phi_{0,i} \oplus s_0 \oplus s_1$ for all i.
5. The two parties run k copies of the sub-protocol OT. For each i, they use it to transfer the pair $(\phi_{0,i}, \phi_{1,i})$.
6. Bob makes the choices randomly, except that the XOR of all choices represents the real choice c. That is, denoting the choices in the OT sub-protocols by c_i, we have

$$\bigoplus_{i=1}^{k} c_i = c. \tag{2}$$

7. The final output of the receiver is s_c, as it can be computed from

$$s_c = \bigoplus_{i=1}^{k} \phi_{c_i, i}. \tag{3}$$

In this enhancement scheme, if Alice wants to guess c, she has to guess each of the c_i correctly. Therefore it can enhance Bob's security such that only one of the sub-protocols needs to be secure for Bob.

But in our case, using this enhancement only does not give a secure protocol from the semi-honest protocol, because the semi-honest protocol is completely insecure for Bob. Some extras measures are required to build a full OT scheme.

4.3   The Complete Protocol

In our full protocol, we set $k = n^3$. Alice and Bob run k times the semi-honest OT, using it as a sub-protocol. The idea is that, for each sub-protocol, Bob records the number of packets received at u_0. If Alice cheats by sending neither v_i nor v'_i for at least one i, the expected number of packets received at u_0 drops to $q(n-1)$ or below from the value of nq in the honest case. To distinguish the two distributions, we use the mid-point $q(n - \frac{1}{2})$ of the two mean values. After seeing all k sub-protocols, Bob aborts the main protocol if there are more than $k/2$ sub-protocols where the number of packets received at u_0 is below $q(n-\frac{1}{2})$. The full protocol is:

1. The k sub-protocols to be run in parallel are indexed by j. Alice prepares a matrix of random bits e_{ij} for $1 \le i \le n$ and $1 \le j \le k$ and sets $v_{ij} = j||i||e_{ij}$. She also sets $v'_{ij} = j||i||(1 - e_{ij})$.
2. Alice sends all v_{ij} to the BDDC at t_0, and all v'_{ij} at t_1.
3. Bob waits to receive all packets and records their time of arrival. He checks for basic consistency, such that for every i and j he receives both $j||i||0$ and $j||i||1$ for exactly once each. He also checks that he does not receive both $j||i||0$ and $j||i||1$ at u_0. He aborts the protocol if any of these tests fail.
4. Otherwise Bob sets a counter $X = 0$ and enter the following procedure. For $1 \le j \le k$, he records the number of packets in format $j||*$ received in u_0. For any j, if this number is smaller than $n/2$, Bob aborts the protocol. If it is larger than $n/2$ but smaller than $q(n - \frac{1}{2})$, Bob adds one to the counter X.
5. Finishing the procedure above, Bob aborts the protocol if $X > \frac{k}{2}$.
6. If the protocol is not aborted, Bob selects c_j randomly for $1 \le j \le k$ except that

$$c = \bigoplus_{i=1}^{k} c_i. \tag{4}$$

7. For $1 \le j \le k$ Bob randomly selects a set of indices I_{j,c_j}, such that $|I_{j,c_j}| = n/2$ and for all $i \in I_{j,c_j}$ Bob has received some $j||i||*$ at time u_0. He sets $I_{j,1-c_j}$ to be the set of all $i \in \{1, 2, \ldots n\}$ such that $i \notin I_{j,c_j}$. Bob sends all $(I_{j,0}, I_{j,1})$ to Alice.
8. Alice generates a list of $k - 1$ random bits $(\phi_{0,1}, \phi_{0,2} \ldots \phi_{0,k-1})$.
9. Alice chooses $\phi_{0,k}$ such that $\bigoplus_{j=1}^{k} \phi_{0,j} = s_0$.
10. Alice sets the second list of bits as $\phi_{1,j} = \phi_{0,j} \oplus s_0 \oplus s_1$ for all j.
11. For each j, Alice computes

$$\beta_{j,0} = \bigoplus_{i \in I_{j,0}} e_{ij}$$

$$\beta_{j,1} = \bigoplus_{i \in I_{j,1}} e_{ij} \tag{5}$$

and then sets $\sigma_{j,0} = \phi_{0,j} \oplus \beta_{j,0}$ and $\sigma_{j,1} = \phi_{1,j} \oplus \beta_{j,1}$.
12. Alice sends all $(\sigma_{j,0}, \sigma_{j,1})$ to Bob.

13. Bob knows e_{ij} whenever $i \in I_{j,c_j}$. He computes $\phi_{c_j,j}$ for all j.
14. The final output of Bob is s_c, as it can be computed from

$$s_c = \bigoplus_{j=1}^{k} \phi_{c_j,j}. \tag{6}$$

4.4 Security Analysis

As usual, the proof of security is divided into correctness, Alice's security and Bob's security. Relying on the security of the sub-protocol, we show that the complete protocol has negligible failure probabilities in these three aspects.

Correctness: Observe that when both parties are honest, correctness is ensured if Bob does not abort the protocol. In this case, Bob may abort the protocol in two possible ways. The first possibility is at least one of the k sub-protocols has more than $n/2$ delayed packets. By the union bound, the probability for this is bounded by

$$n^3 e^{-2n(\frac{1}{2}-p)^2} \tag{7}$$

which is negligible in n. Next, the second possibility to abort is that $X > \frac{k}{2}$. For one sub-protocol, regarding to the probability of having the number of packets received at u_0 to be below $q(n - \frac{1}{2})$, the Hoeffding's inequality gives the upper bound as

$$\frac{1}{2} e^{\frac{-q^2}{2n}}. \tag{8}$$

Note that this quantity increases with n. This is because, when n is larger, the variance of the number of delayed packets is also larger. Next, we deal with the total number of such cases in the k runs of the sub-protocol. Setting

$$\delta = \frac{1}{2} - \frac{1}{2} e^{\frac{-q^2}{2n}}, \tag{9}$$

the probability of getting $X > \frac{k}{2}$ is bounded by

$$e^{-2k\delta^2} = e^{-2n^3\delta^2} \tag{10}$$

using the Chernoff bound. Observe that

$$n\delta = n\left(\frac{1}{2} - \frac{1}{2} e^{\frac{-q^2}{2n}}\right) \tag{11}$$

is a quantity that increases with n, but bounded such that

$$\lim_{n \to \infty} n\left(\frac{1}{2} - \frac{1}{2} e^{\frac{-q^2}{2n}}\right) = \frac{q^2}{4}. \tag{12}$$

Therefore the value of $e^{-2k\delta^2}$ falls exponentially in n. Thus the correctness of the final protocol is established.

Alice's security: By union bound, the probability of failure in Alice's security in the final protocol is no more than k times that of the sub-protocol. That is, it is upper bounded by $n^3(1 - pq^2)^n$. This quantity drops exponentially in n too.

Bob's security: The malicious Alice must be dishonest in every sub-protocol in order to have any hope to get information on c. Security is perfect for Bob otherwise. Recall that Alice can only do the following for cheating:

1. For some i, j Alice sends both v_{ij} and v'_{ij} at t_0.
2. For some i, j Alice sends neither v_{ij} nor v'_{ij} at t_0.

We argue that, for the first type of cheating, if Alice sends both v_{ij} and v'_{ij} at t_0, this behavior will be detected with probability q^2. Therefore Alice can only do this a few times. To be more precise, let us assume that Alice does this m_1 times. It is clear that $m_1 < n$, or the probability of detection will be overwhelming with the increase of n. On the other hand, for the second type of cheating, if Alice sends neither v_{ij} nor v'_{ij} at t_0, it will not be detected immediately. Let us assume that Alice is doing this m_2 times. In order to gain any real advantage, she has to do at least one of either types of cheating in every sub-protocol. Therefore $m_2 > k - n$, and there are at least $k - n$ sub-protocols where only the second type of cheating occurs.

Focusing on such cases, the chance for that sub-protocol to have more than $q(n - \frac{1}{2})$ packets received at u_0 is upper bounded by

$$\mu = \frac{1}{2}e^{\frac{-q^2}{2(n-1)}}. \tag{13}$$

In the protocol, to deter Alice from cheating, Bob aborts if $X > \frac{k}{2}$. We show that X can reach $\frac{k}{2}$ even if we only consider these $k - n$ sub-protocols and ignore the rest. With the Hoeffding's inequality, the probability that X fails to reach $\frac{k}{2}$ is upper bounded by

$$e^{\frac{-2}{k-n}(\frac{k}{2}-n-(k-n)\mu)^2} \tag{14}$$

where we see that

$$\frac{-2}{k-n}(\frac{k}{2} - n - (k-n)\mu)^2 = \frac{-2}{n^3-n}(\frac{n^3}{2} - n - \frac{1}{2}(n^3 - n)e^{\frac{-q^2}{2(n-1)}})^2$$

$$= \frac{-2}{n^3-n}(\frac{n^3}{2}(1 - e^{\frac{-q^2}{2(n-1)}}) - \frac{ne^{\frac{-q^2}{2(n-1)}}}{2} - n)^2. \tag{15}$$

Using the fact that $n(1 - e^{\frac{-q^2}{2(n-1)}})$ converges to $\frac{q^2}{2}$ asymptotically, it is clear that the probability of $X > \frac{k}{2}$ is overwhelming with the increase of n.

5   Conclusion

With failure probabilities on correctness, Alice's security and Bob's security being negligible in n, we obtain the unconditionally secure OT protocol. Our protocol is the first to give unconditionally security in OT using channel delays. The practical value of our protocol is still limited, because accurate knowledge of p is required for Bob's security. Relaxing of this non-trivial assumption would be interesting for future study. Also, this protocol relies on the BDDC model. We believe a scheme based on the real, analog time channel delay may be possible. The final communication overhead of our protocol is $O(n^4 \log n)$ for security parameter n. This is rather high and it would be better if it can be reduced.

References

1. Crépeau, C.: Equivalence Between Two Flavours of Oblivious Transfers. In: Pomerance, C. (ed.) CRYPTO 1987. LNCS, vol. 293, pp. 350–354. Springer, Heidelberg (1988)
2. Crépeau, C.: Efficient Cryptographic Protocols Based on Noisy Channels. In: Fumy, W. (ed.) EUROCRYPT 1997. LNCS, vol. 1233, pp. 306–317. Springer, Heidelberg (1997)
3. Crépeau, C., Kilian, J.: Achieving oblivious transfer using weakened security assumption. In: Proc. IEEE FOCS, pp. 42–52 (1988)
4. Crépeau, C., Morozov, K., Wolf, S.: Efficient Unconditional Oblivious Transfer from Almost Any Noisy Channel. In: Blundo, C., Cimato, S. (eds.) SCN 2004. LNCS, vol. 3352, pp. 47–59. Springer, Heidelberg (2005)
5. Crépeau, C., Savvides, G.: Optimal Reductions between Oblivious Transfers Using Interactive Hashing. In: Vaudenay, S. (ed.) EUROCRYPT 2006. LNCS, vol. 4004, pp. 201–221. Springer, Heidelberg (2006)
6. Even, S., Goldreich, O., Lempel, A.: A randomized protocol for signing contracts. Communications of the ACM 28(6), 637–647 (1985)
7. Kilian, J.: Founding cryptography on oblivious transfer. In: Proc. 20th ACM Symposium on Theory of Computing, pp. 20–31 (1988)
8. Palmieri, P., Pereira, O.: Building Oblivious Transfer on Channel Delays. In: Lai, X., Yung, M., Lin, D. (eds.) Inscrypt 2010. LNCS, vol. 6584, pp. 125–138. Springer, Heidelberg (2011)
9. Rabin, M.: How to exchange secrets by oblivious transfer, Technical Report TR-81, Aiken Computation Laboratory, Harvard University (1981)
10. Wullschleger, J.: Oblivious Transfer from Weak Noisy Channels. In: Reingold, O. (ed.) TCC 2009. LNCS, vol. 5444, pp. 332–349. Springer, Heidelberg (2009)
11. Yao, A.: Protocols for secure computations. In: Proc. 23rd IEEE Symposium on Foundations of Computer Science, pp. 160–164 (1982)

Preserving Security and Privacy in Large-Scale VANETs

Bo Qin[1,3], Qianhong Wu[1,2], Josep Domingo-Ferrer[1], and Lei Zhang[4]

[1] Universitat Rovira i Virgili, Department of Computer Engineering and
Mathematics UNESCO Chair in Data Privacy, Tarragona, Catalonia
{bo.qin,qianhong.wu,josep.domingo}@urv.cat
[2] Key Laboratory of Aerospace Information Security and Trusted Computing,
Ministry of Education, School of Computer, Wuhan University, China
[3] School of Science, Xi'an University of Technology, China
[4] Software Engineering Institute, East China Normal University, China
leizhang@sei.ecnu.edu.cn

Abstract. Upcoming vehicular *ad hoc* networks (VANETs) allowing
vehicles to talk to each other are expected to enhance safety and efficiency in transportation systems. This type of networks is especially
attractive in highly populated urban areas overwhelmed with traffic
congestions and accidents. Besides vulnerabilities versus attacks against
traffic safety and driver privacy, a large-scale VANET in a metropolitan
area raises scalability and management challenges. This paper employs
identity-based group signatures (IBGS) to divide a large-scale VANET
into easy-to-manage groups and establish liability in vehicular communications while preserving privacy. Each party's human-recognizable identity is used as its public key and no additional certificate is required.
This efficiently avoids the complicated certificate management of existing protocols. We further investigate selfish verification approach to accelerate message processing in VANETs. With this approach, a vehicle
selects only the messages affecting its driving decisions and validates the
selected messages as if they were a single one.

Keywords: Vehicular *ad hoc* networks, Mobile wireless communication,
Identity management, Security, Privacy.

1 Introduction

As information and communication technologies (ICT) become increasingly pervasive, vehicles are expected to be equipped in the near future [3] with intelligent devices and radio interfaces, known as On-Board Units (OBUs). OBUs
are allowed to talk to other OBUs and the road-side infrastructure formed by
Road-Side Units (RSUs). The OBUs and RSUs, equipped with on-board sensory,
processing, and wireless communication modules, form a self-organized vehicular
network, commonly referred to as VANET, a commercial instantiation of mobile
ad hoc networks with vehicles as the mobile nodes.

S. Qing et al. (Eds.): ICICS 2011, LNCS 7043, pp. 121–135, 2011.
© Springer-Verlag Berlin Heidelberg 2011

VANET systems aim at providing a platform for various applications that can improve traffic safety and efficiency, driver assistance, transportation regulation, infotainment, etc. There is substantial research and industrial effort to develop this market. Vehicular communications are supported by the Car2Car Communication Consortium [7] in Europe and the Dedicated Short Range Communications (DSRC) standard [1] in the USA. In Europe, several projects such as SEVECOM [28] and NOW [19] are under way. It is estimated that the market for vehicular communications will reach several billions of euros by 2012.

While the tremendous benefits expected from vehicular communications and the huge number of vehicles are strong points of VANETs, there are still challenges to deploy practical VANETs. A very important one is to guarantee the security of vehicle-generated reports. In what regards security, selfish vehicles may attempt to clear up the way ahead or mess up the way behind with false traffic reports; criminals being chased may disseminate bogus notifications to other vehicles in order to block police cars. Such attacks may result in serious harm, even loss of lives. Another challenge is to protect the privacy of vehicles. VANETs open a big window to observers. It is very easy to collect information about the speed, status, trajectories and whereabouts of the vehicles in a VANET. By mining this information, malicious observers can make inferences about a driver's personality (*e.g.* someone driving slowly is likely to be a calm person), living habits and social relationships (visited places tell a lot about people's lives). This private information may be traded in underground markets, exposing the observed vehicles and drivers to harass (*e.g.* junk advertisements), threats (*e.g.* blackmail if the driver often visits an embarrassing place, like a red-light district) and dangers (*e.g.* hijacks). Finally, VANETs are especially attractive in highly populated urban areas overwhelmed with traffic congestions and accidents. Besides vulnerabilities versus attacks against traffic safety and driver privacy, a large-scale VANET in a metropolitan area raises scalability and management challenges. Therefore, security, privacy and scalable management motivate the work described in this paper.

1.1   Related Work

For VANETs to be viable, the first requirement is to guard them against erroneous information. For example, an attacker may simply put a piece of ice on the vehicle temperature sensor and then a wrong temperature will be reported, even if the hardware sensor is tamper-proof. To counter fraudulent data, detection mechanisms are needed. A general scheme aiming at detection and correction of malicious data was given by Golle *et al.* in 2004 [14]. The authors assume that the simplest explanation of some inconsistency in the received information is most probably the correct one. A specific proposal was made by Leinmüller *et al.* in 2006 [17] and focuses on verifying the position data sent by vehicles. All position information received from a vehicle is stored for some time period; this is used to perform the checks, the results of which are weighted in order to form a metric on the neighbor's trust. Raya *et al.* [23] and Daza *et al.* [9] introduced a threshold mechanism to prevent the generation of fraudulent messages: a message is given credit only if it was endorsed by a threshold of vehicles in the vicinity.

In addition to guaranteeing correctness of vehicular reports, VANETs should also provide authentication to establish liability for the prevention, investigation, detection and prosecution of serious criminal offences. To meet this requirement, vehicular communications must be signed to provide authentication, integrity and non-repudiation so that they can be collected as judicial evidence. Several proposals (*e.g.*, [21, 24, 25, 32, 33]) suggest the use of a public key infrastructure (PKI) and digital signatures to secure VANETs. To evict misbehaving vehicles, Raya *et al.* further proposed protocols focusing on revoking certifications of malicious vehicles [26]. A big challenge arising from the PKI-based schemes in VANETs is the heavy burden of certificate generation, storage, delivery, verification, and revocation.

To guarantee vehicle privacy, some proposals suggest anonymous authentication in VANETs. Among them there are two research lines, *i.e.* pseudonym mechanisms and group signatures. The pseudonym of a node is a short-lived public key authenticated by a certificate authority (CA) in the vehicular PKI ([11, 13, 20]). The pseudonymity approach mainly focuses on how often a node should change a pseudonym and with whom it should communicate. Sampigethaya *et al.* [27] proposed to use a silent period in order to hamper linkability between pseudonyms, or alternatively to create groups of vehicles and restrict vehicles in one group from listening to messages of other groups. To avoid delivery and storage of a large number of pseudonyms, Calandriello *et al.* [5] proposed self-generating pseudonyms with the help of group signatures locally produced by the vehicles. Noting that group signatures can be directly used to anonymously authenticate vehicular communications without additionally generating a pseudonym, Guo *et al.* [15] proposed a group signature-based security framework which relies on tamper-resistant devices (requiring password access) for preventing adversarial attacks on vehicular networks. However, neither concrete instantiations nor simulation results are provided. Lin *et al.* [18] introduced a security and privacy-preserving protocol for VANETs by integrating the techniques of group signatures. With the help of group signatures, vehicle-to-vehicle (V2V) communications are authenticated while maintaining conditional privacy. Wu *et al.* [30] distinguished linkability and anonymity of group signatures to improve the trustworthiness of vehicle-generated messages.

Some recent proposals provide both authentication to establish liability and vehicle privacy in VANETs. When these schemes are implemented in large-scale VANETs in densely populated urban areas, unaddressed challenges remain. Pseudonym-based schemes face the challenge of generating, distributing, verifying and storing a huge number of certificates. Group signature-based schemes in the traditional PKI setting face problems such as how to manage numerous vehicles and especially compromised vehicles. A common concern of both classes of schemes is how to process the large volume of messages received every time unit. These observations call for novel mechanisms to address these challenges in an efficient way.

1.2 Contribution and Plan of This Paper

We propose a set of mechanisms to address the security, privacy, and management requirements in a large-scale VANET. These conflicting concerns are conciliated by exploiting identity-based group signatures (IBGS) and dividing a large-scale VANET into a number of easy-to-manage smaller groups. In the system, each party, including the group managers (*i.e.* the transportation offices) and the signers (*i.e.* the vehicles), has a unique, human-recognizable identity as its public key, and a corresponding secret key generated by some trusted authority. For instance, the public keys of the administration offices, road-side units [16] and vehicles can be, respectively, the administration name, the RSU geographical address and the traditional vehicle license plate. Certificates are no longer needed because the public key of each party is a human-recognizable identity. This feature greatly reduces the security-related management challenges.

After registering to transportation offices, any vehicle can anonymously authenticate any message. These vehicle-generated messages can be verified by the identities (*e.g.* the name) of the transportation offices and the public key of the escrow authority. If a message is later found to be false, the identity of the message generator can be traced by traffic police offices. Considering the redundancy in vehicular communications, we present a selfish verification mechanism to speed up message processing in VANETs. With this technique, although each vehicle may receive a large number of messages, the vehicle only selects for verification those messages affecting its traffic decisions. The selected messages can can be verified in a batch as if they were a single one. These mechanisms are crucial to deploy VANETs in densely populated urban areas.

The rest of this paper is organized as follows. Section 2 describes our design goals and the challenges to those goals. The proposal is specified in Section 3. Section 4 presents an extension to speed up vehicular message verification. The last section is a conclusion.

2 Design Goals and Challenges

2.1 Design Goals

In order to obtain an implementable system to enhance the trustworthiness of V2V communications in a large-scale VANET, we keep in mind the following main design goals:

- **Liability.** The fundamental security functions in vehicular communications consist of ensuring liability for the originator of a data packet. Liability implies that the message author is held responsible for the message generated. To establish liability without disputes, authentication, integrity and non-repudiation must be provided in vehicular protocols. Authentication allows verifying that the message was generated by the originator as claimed, rather than by an impersonator. Integrity guarantees that the message has not been tampered with after it was sent. Non-repudiation implies that the message generator cannot deny message authorship.

- **Anonymity.** There is anonymity if, by monitoring the communication in a VANET, message originators cannot be identified, except perhaps by designated parties. Since message authentication requires knowledge of a public identity such as a public key or a license plate, if no anonymity was provided, an attacker could easily trace any vehicle by monitoring the VANET communication. This would be surely undesirable for the drivers; hence, anonymity should be protect for vehicles.
- **Scalable Management.** For a VANET deployed in a highly populated metropolitan area, managing up to (tens of) millions of vehicles is a substantial concern. Specifically, in such a large VANET, every day some registered vehicles might be stolen or their secret keys might be occasionally leaked. This entails extra burden to manage the system while preserving the liability and the privacy of vehicles. Hence, it is essential to take the scalable management requirement into consideration when the system is designed.

2.2 Challenges to the Goals

It is challenging to simultaneously achieve the above design goals. The first challenge derives from the fact that liability and anonymity are conflicting in nature. The liability requirement implies that cheating vehicles distributing bogus messages should be caught. On the other hand, the anonymity requirement implies that attackers cannot trace the original vehicles who generated reports. Hence, there must be some tradeoff between liability and anonymity in a VANET. A well-designed scheme should protect privacy for honest vehicles while allowing to find the identities of dishonest vehicles.

Network volatility is another factor that increases the difficulty of securing VANETs. Connectivity among vehicles can often be highly transient due to their high speeds (*e.g.* think of two vehicles crossing each other in opposite directions in a highway). This implies that protocols requiring multiple rounds or strong cooperation such as voting mechanisms may be impractical. Due to their high mobility, vehicles may never again connect with each other after one occasional connection. This puts the public key infrastructure implemented for securing VANETs under strain: if public-key certificates are used, vehicles are confronted to a lot of certificates probably issued by several different CAs; due to the mobility, there is little hope that caching the verified certificates of vehicles and CAs will result in any significant speed-up of the next verifications.

The size of VANETs deployed in metropolitan areas with millions of vehicles is another challenge. Transportation systems are governed by a constellation of authorities with different interests, which complicates things. A technically, and perhaps politically, convincing solution is a prerequisite for any security architecture. Another challenge is the sheer scale of the network: the system has to manage (tens of) millions of nodes of which some may join or leave the VANET occasionally and some may be compromised. This rules out protocols requiring massive distribution of data to all mobile nodes. Furthermore, in case of high vehicular density in metropolitan areas, each node may be flooded with a large number of incoming messages requiring verification.

3 The Proposal

In this section, we propose an authentication protocol to enforce liability, privacy and scalable management in vehicle-generated messages. Underlying is an efficient IBGS scheme [29] to avoid the heavy burden of certificate generation, delivery and verification in a large-scale VANET. The protocol exploits the features of existing transportation systems to simplify the system administration overhead.

3.1 Underlying Technologies and High-level Description

A number of proposals have employed group signatures [8] to secure VANETs with conditional privacy. For a large VANET, it may be impractical to organize millions of vehicles into a single group. This implies that the group public parameters have to change whenever any vehicle is compromised, which may occur frequently in a large VANET. It is resource-consuming to distribute these frequent changes to all the nodes. Identity-based group signatures are an extension of standard group signatures. As depicted in Figure 1, in an IBGS scheme [29] there are four types of parties, *i.e.* the trusted escrow authority (TEA), the group registration manager (GRM), an identity-opening authority (IOA) and the group members. Each of them has a unique identity, *i.e.* its name. TEA has a public-private key pair and the public key can be accessed by any entity. By taking as input the identity of any entity in the system, TEA generates a private key for that entity. Any group member having obtained a private key from TEA can register to GRM to become a group member and then can anonymously sign any message on behalf of the group. The signature can be verified using TEA's public key and the identities of GRM and IOA. If necessary, IOA can open the identity of the signer of any doubtable signature.

We observe that IBGS can be exploited to simplify the system management while preserving liability and privacy in a large VANET. In most cities, the transportation administration authorities include the public security department, vehicle management bureaus and traffic police offices, who can serve as the TEA, GRMs and IOAs, respectively. The public security department's public key can be stored in each vehicle. The identities of GRMs and IOAs are their respective public keys. Each vehicle's unique identity is also its public key. GRMs and IOAs first need to contact TEA to generate their private keys and set up the corresponding administration units. This human-recognizable identity-based feature eliminates the certificate management requirement of other proposals.

The system management can be further reduced by dividing the huge number of vehicles into groups in light of their regulatory status, *e.g.* one can distinguish groups like police cars, ambulances, fire trucks, taxis, buses, commercial vehicles, personal vehicles, etc. Police cars, ambulances and fire trucks may have privilege on using road, and taxis, buses and commercial vehicles are also run and managed by some organizations (or companies). The personal cars may still be too numerous in densely populated areas and can be further properly divided into smaller groups, *e.g.*, according to the regions where they have registered. One

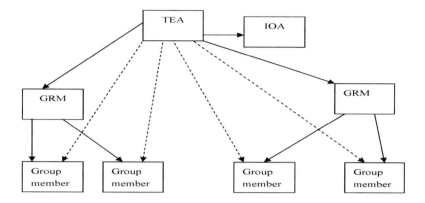

Fig. 1. Model of identity-based group signature

may note that splitting vehicles into smaller subgroups reduces the privacy of vehicles. However, this privacy loss could be minimized if the vehicles are properly
divided into subgroups so that the division does not leak more identity information than the one leaked by the vehicles' physical features. For instance, one can
easily distinguish police cars from other vehicles from their visible features and
organizing the police cars into one sub-group does not leak much information on
individual police vehicles. The gains of easy management outweigh a little loss
of privacy and the ensuing trade-off between management and privacy seems
reasonable in practice.

Employing IBGS can also simultaneously provide liability and privacy in
VANET. After registration, a vehicle can authenticate messages without dis-
closing its identity. When receiving an authenticated message, the receiver can
verify it with the stored system public key of TEA and the identity of the group
the vehicle belongs to. Note here that the signing vehicle's identity is not required for validation of the signed message due to anonymity. If the verification
procedure indicates that the message is authentic (but not necessarily correct),
then the receiving vehicle can use it as a proof. This proof can be submitted
to the traffic police office for investigation if the message is later found to be
incorrect and causes any harm. If necessary, the police can open the identity of
the message generator and perhaps punish him/her.

3.2 System Set-up

Our scheme is realized in bilinear groups ([4]). We use the notations of [31]. Let
PGen be an algorithm which, on input a security parameter 1^ℓ, outputs a pairing
$\Upsilon = (p, \mathbb{G}_1, \mathbb{G}_2, \mathbb{G}_3, g, h, e)$, where finite cyclic groups $\mathbb{G}_1 = \langle g \rangle$ and $\mathbb{G}_2 = \langle h \rangle$
have the same prime order p, and $e : \mathbb{G}_1 \times \mathbb{G}_2 \to \mathbb{G}_3$ is an efficient non-degenerate
bilinear map such that $\hat{e}(g, h) \neq 1$ and for any $a, b \in \mathbb{Z}$, $\hat{e}(g^a, h^b) = \hat{e}(g, h)^{ab}$.

The TEA, *e.g.* the public security department, runs `PGen` and obtains a pairing $\Upsilon = (p, \mathbb{G}_1, \mathbb{G}_2, \mathbb{G}_3, g, h, \hat{e})$ as above. Let g_1, g_2, g_3, g_4, g_5 be randomly selected generators of $\mathbb{G}_1$. Define cryptographic hash functions $H_V : \{0,1\} \rightarrow \mathbb{G}_1$, $H_O : \{0,1\} \rightarrow \mathbb{G}_1$, $H_R : \{0,1\} \rightarrow \mathbb{Z}_p^*$, $H : \{0,1\} \rightarrow \mathbb{Z}_p^*$. The TEA's private key is a randomly chosen value $x \in \mathbb{Z}_p^*$ and its public key is $K = h^x \in \mathbb{G}_2$. Then the public system parameters are $param = (\Upsilon, g_1, \cdots, g_5, H_R, H_V, H_O, H, K)$ which can be accessed by each party in the VANET.

3.3 Key Generation

With this procedure, the TEA generates private keys for the group registration managers (GRMs), the identity-opening authorities (IOAs) and the individual vehicles by taking as inputs their public identities.

- On input the identity ID_R of a GRM, TEA randomly generates $r \in \mathbb{Z}_p^*$ and computes $A = h^r$, $x_1 = r + H_R(A||ID_R)x \mod p$. Finally GRM gets (x_1, A), where A is an auxiliary string that can be known by the vehicles in the group, and x_1 is the private key of the GRM.
- On input the identity ID_O of an IOA, TEA generates the IOA's private key by computing $x_0 = H_O(ID_O)^x$.
- On input a vehicle's identity ID_V, TEA uses x to compute the vehicles's private key $X = H_V(ID_V)^x$.

3.4 Registration

With this procedure, a vehicle with identity ID_V can register to one of the groups ID_R in the VANET. Note that the vehicle does not need to contact the identity-opening authority and the registration procedure is simple.

- The vehicle firstly proves to the GRM that it knows the secret key $X = H_V(ID_V)^x$ corresponding to its identity ID_V without leaking any information on X. This can be done with the protocol due to Qin *et al.* [22] to guarantee that the vehicle has identity ID_V as claimed.
- GRM randomly selects $e \in \mathbb{Z}_p^*$, and computes $B = (g_5/H_V(ID_V))^{1/(e+x_1)}$. The GRM sends the secret group certificate (B, e, A) to the vehicle via a confidential channel.
- The vehicle accepts the certificate if and only if

$$\hat{e}(g_5, h) = \hat{e}(B, h)^e \hat{e}(B, S) \hat{e}(H_V(ID_V), h),$$

  where $S = AK^{H_R(A||ID_R)} = h^{x_1}$.
- GRM computes $W = \hat{e}(H_V(ID_V), h)$, and records (ID_V, B, e, W) in its local database.

3.5   Authentication of Vehicle-Generated Messages

A registered vehicle ID_V in group ID_R with secret key X and certificate (B, e, A) can anonymously sign message m while allowing the identity-opening authority IOA to open the signature. The detailed instantiation is as follows.

- The vehicle randomly selects $s_1 \in Z_p^*$, and computes
  $s_2 = es_1 \mod p$, $\sigma_0 = g^{s_1}$, $\sigma_1 = Xg_1^{s_1}$,
  $\sigma_2 = H_V(ID_V)g_2^{s_1}$, $\sigma_3 = Bg_3^{s_1}$, $\sigma_5 = \sigma_3^e g_4^{s_1}$.
- The vehicle randomly selects $d \in Z_p^*$ and computes
  $C_1 = \hat{e}(H_V(ID_V), h)\hat{e}(H_O(ID_O), K)^d$, $C_2 = h^d$.
- The vehicle randomly selects $r_1, r_2, r_3, r_4 \in \mathbb{Z}_p^*$, $R_1, R_2, R_3 \in \mathbb{G}_1$, and computes
  $\rho_0 = g^{r_1}$, $\rho_1 = R_1 g_1^{r_1}$, $\rho_2 = R_2 g_2^{r_1}$, $\rho_3 = R_3 g_3^{r_1}$,
  $\rho_4 = [\hat{e}(g_1, h)^{-1}\hat{e}(g_2, K)]^{r_1}$, $\rho_5 = \sigma_3^{r_3} g_4^{r_1}$, $\rho_6 = \hat{e}(g_3, h)^{r_2}[\hat{e}(g_3, S)\hat{e}(g_2 g_4, h)]^{r_1}$,
  $\rho_7 = h^{r_4}$, $\rho_8 = \hat{e}(H_O(ID_O), K)^{r_4}\hat{e}(g_2, h)^{-r_1}$.
- The vehicle computes the hash challenge
  $c = H((\sigma_0, \cdots, \sigma_3, \sigma_5)||(\rho_0, \cdots, \rho_8)||A||C_1||C_2||m)$.
- The vehicle computes the responses to the hash challenge
  $z_0 = r_1 - cs_1 \mod p$, $Z_1 = R_1 X^{-c}$, $Z_2 = R_2 H_V(ID_V)^{-c}$, $Z_3 = R_3 B^{-c}$,
  $z_4 = r_3 - ce \mod p$, $z_5 = r_2 - cs_2 \mod p$, $z_6 = r_4 - cd \mod p$.
- The resulting signature σ on message m is:
  $\sigma = (\sigma_0, \cdots, \sigma_3, \sigma_5)||(z_0, Z_1, Z_2, Z_3, z_4, z_5, z_6)||c||A||C_1||C_2$.

3.6   Message Verification

Upon receiving a signature σ on message m, the receiving vehicle computes

$$\sigma_4 = \hat{e}(\sigma_1, h)^{-1}\hat{e}(\sigma_2, K), \sigma_6 = \hat{e}(g_5, h)^{-1}\hat{e}(\sigma_2\sigma_5, h)\hat{e}(\sigma_3, S),$$
$$\sigma_8 = C_1 \cdot \hat{e}(\sigma_2, h)^{-1}, \rho_0 = g^{z_0}\sigma_0^c, \rho_1 = Z_1 g_1^{z_0}\sigma_1^c, \rho_2 = Z_2 g_2^{z_0}\sigma_2^c,$$
$$\rho_3 = Z_3 g_3^{z_0}\sigma_3^c, \rho_4 = [\hat{e}(g_1, h)^{-1}\hat{e}(g_2, K)]^{z_0}\sigma_4^c,$$
$$\rho_5 = \sigma_3^{z_4} g_4^{z_0}\sigma_5^c, \rho_6 = \hat{e}(g_3, h)^{z_5}[\hat{e}(g_3, S)\hat{e}(g_2 g_4, h)]^{z_0}\sigma_6^c, \quad (1)$$
$$\rho_7 = h^{z_6}C_2^c, \rho_8 = \hat{e}(H_O(ID_O), K)^{z_6}\hat{e}(g_2, h)^{-z_0}\sigma_8^c, S = AK^{H(A||ID_R)}$$

and checks that

$$c = H((\sigma_0, \cdots, \sigma_3, \sigma_5)||(\rho_0, \cdots, \rho_8)||A||C_1||C_2||m) \quad (2)$$

If Equation (2) holds, the message is accepted. Else, the message is rejected.

3.7   Revoking Doubtable Messages

If the verifying vehicle receives a message with a valid signature but the message is doubtable, e.g. a bogus message, the verifier can submit the message along with its signature to IOA. IOA can use its secret key x_0 to open the encryption in the signature σ. IOA computes $W = \hat{e}(H_V(ID_V), h) = C_1/\hat{e}(x_0, C_2)$ and looks up W in the registration table reg. If no entry W is found, IOA reports failure for the tracing procedure, else it outputs the vehicle identity ID_V.

Regarding revocation of malicious signers in group signature-based authentication in VANETs, another subtle issue is the case when some signer's secret key was compromised (*e.g.* stolen) for various reasons. It is a known open problem how to efficiently distinguish the compromised signers in group signatures. Some proposals suggest a public revocation list (by releasing the secret signing information of the compromised signer) and, whenever a verifier verifies a vehicular-generated message [18], the verifying vehicle first checks whether the signer is in the revocation list. If the signer is in the list, then the message will be discarded. Note that the revocation list grows linearly after the system is deployed. Hence, the performance of the system degrades as time passes. Another disadvantage is that one can also determine the authorship of the messages previously signed by the compromised vehicle. Hence, the vehicle's privacy cannot be guaranteed for messages signed before it was compromised.

We observe that the identity-based feature of IBGS-based privacy-preserving VANETs can be exploited to mitigate these disadvantages. When requesting the private key from TEA, each GRM's identity can be appended a tag specifying the lifetime (*e.g.* days or weeks) of the GRM's public key, *i.e.* {GRM's identity, lifetime}. Before the lifetime expires, each vehicle managed by this GRM contacts the GRM and updates its secret group signing key (see Section 3.4). For the verifying vehicles, they can just verify the received message as in Section 3.6 by additionally comparing their local time with the lifetime of the GRM's public key. This mechanism is very efficient because it only affects a subgroup of vehicles, *i.e.* the signing vehicles managed by the GRM, while the verifying vehicle (which can be any vehicle in the VANET) will not be affected. After employing this approach, an attacker can only sign messages on behalf of the compromised vehicles during a short time interval. If the signed message is false and is forwarded to IOA by the receiving vehicles, the misbehaving compromised vehicle can be located immediately and stopped by police cars.

3.8   Message Size

A vehicular report includes six fields: (`Message Type`; `Payload`; `Timestamp`; `TTL`; `Group ID`; `Signature`). Message ID defines the message type which is about 2 bytes, and the payload field may include information on the vehicle's position, direction, speed, traffic events, event time and so on. According to the DSRC standard [1], the payload of a message is 100 bytes. The timestamp is about 4 bytes and specifies the signature generation time, which is used to prevent replay attacks. It also ensures that an honest vehicle can report the same traffic situation at different times without being accused of multiple signatures on the same message. The TTL field is about 1 byte to specify Time To Live and determines how long the message is allowed to remain in the VANET. Group ID is about 2 bytes used to identify which group the vehicle belongs to. The signature field is the vehicle's signature on the first five fields. We denote the first five fields by m and the whole six fields by M. The length of vehicle-generated

Table 1. Format of vehicle-generated messages (suggested field lengths in bytes)

Mes. Type	Payload	Timestamp	TTL	Group ID	Sig.
2	100	4	1	2	460

messages can be expressed as $L_M = L_{\texttt{MessageType}} + L_{\texttt{Payload}} + L_{\texttt{Timestamp}} + L_{TTL} + L_{\texttt{GroupID}} + L_{\texttt{Signature}}$. To provide a typical security level of 2^{80}, we can set p a 170-bit long prime and then the element in $\mathbb{G}_1$ is 171 bits long [12], and $L_{sig} = 460$ bytes. Thus, $L_M = 2 + 100 + 4 + 1 + 2 + 460 = 569$ bytes. Table 1 summarizes the length of the report fields.

3.9 Security Analysis

We first analyze liability in our vehicular authentication protocol. The underlying IBGS scheme is proven non-frameable in the sense that no player except the trusted TEA can produce a signature that can be accepted by the verification procedure and for which the tracing procedure outputs the identity of a signer who did not generate the signature, even if the attacking players are allowed to collude [29]. This strong security property guarantees that, if a vehicle does not register to the VANET, it cannot generate messages accepted by other vehicles, and no vehicles, IOAs or GRMs can impersonate an innocent registered vehicle to authenticate vehicular communications. In other words, if a message is accepted as valid, it must have been generated by a single registered vehicle and not have been tampered with since it was sent. A message which passes the verification procedure can be used as a convincing argument in accident investigation if necessary. With this feature, the liability desirable in VANETs is properly guaranteed.

The underlying IBGS scheme is shown to be anonymous [29], even if there are only two signers in the group. This implies that no one except the designated IOA can distinguish messages from the various vehicles in a VANET. Thus an attacker cannot trace the vehicles by monitoring the communications in the VANET and the identity privacy of vehicles is well protected.

It is shown that the underlying IBGS is traceable and no group member or set of colluding members can generate a group signature accepted by the verification procedure which is not linkable to the actual signer [29]. In other words, if a vehicular message is accepted, the third-party IOA can always identify the actual message generator. This fact guarantees that cheating vehicles can always be caught by revoking their anonymity whenever fraudulent vehicular communications are detected.

4 Selfish Batch Verification

In a VANET, each vehicle periodically sends messages over a single hop every 300ms within a distance of 10s travel time [1], which means a distance range between 10m and 300m. This implies that a vehicle will receive a large number of messages to be verified in a given time interval. To see this point, assume that the vehicle is in a 40m wide road with a density of 80 vehicles/km^2; hence, there will be 192 vehicles within a 300m range (backward and forward). In one period of 300ms, the vehicle will receive 192 messages/signatures (excluding multi-hop messages forwarded by neighboring vehicles) to be verified. It requires several milliseconds to verify each group signature and more than 300ms to verify all the received messages if they are verified one by one. This verification delay is much larger than the allowed maximum end-to-end message processing delay, *i.e.* 100ms. Hence, we need additional mechanisms to speed up message verification in large-scale VANETs.

We observe that the great redundancy of vehicular communications can be exploited to alleviate the burden of message verification. Only a small fraction of relevant messages actually need verification. If the number of messages selected for verification is still large, additional ways to reduce the verification overhead need to be devised. In what follows, we employ the batch verification technique ([2, 6, 10, 30]) to enable time-saving message processing in VANETs. This technique exploits the fact that a multi-base exponentiation (pairing) takes a similar time as a single-base exponentiation (pairing).

Lemma 1 (Batch verification lemma). *To verify exponential equations*

$$g_i^{x_i} f_i^{y_i} = 1, \quad for \ i = 1, \cdots, n \tag{3}$$

where $x_i, y_i \in \mathbb{Z}_p^*$ are known, and g_i, f_i are two elements of a finite cyclic group $\mathbb{G}$ of prime order p, one can randomly pick a vector $\Delta = (\delta_1, \cdots, \delta_n)$ for $\delta_i \in \{0, 1\}^l$ and verify that

$$\prod_{i=1}^{n} g_i^{\delta_i x_i} f_i^{\delta_i y_i} = 1. \tag{4}$$

If Equations (3) are accepted whenever Equation (4) holds, a batch $\{(g_i, f_i)|i = 1, \cdots, n\}$ will be always accepted if it is valid, while an invalid batch will be accepted with probability at most 2^{-l}.

The above claim is ready to be extended to batch verification of bilinear equations since these are indeed exponentiation equations in $\mathbb{G}_3$. In this case, we only need to additionally note that $1 = \hat{e}(g_1, h)^a \hat{e}(g_2, h)^b$ can be equivalently rewritten as $1 = \hat{e}(g_1^a g_2^b, h)$ to save computations due to bilinearity and the fact that exponentiations in $\mathbb{G}_1$ are more efficient than those in $\mathbb{G}_3$.

To employ the above batch verification technique, the basic group signature needs to be extended. That is, the extended signature is now $\sigma' = \sigma||(\sigma_4, \sigma_6, \sigma_8)|| (\rho_0, \cdots, \rho_8)||S$. Clearly, this modification does not affect any security property of the group signature because $(\sigma_4, \sigma_6, \sigma_8)|| (\rho_0, \cdots, \rho_8)||S$ can be reconstructed from σ (see Section 3.6). The receiving vehicle needs to check Equations (1) and (2).

Let the vehicle select n message-signature pairs (m_i, σ_i') for batch verification, where $1 \leq i \leq n$ and $\sigma_i' = \sigma_i||(\sigma_{4,i}, \sigma_{6,i}, \sigma_{8,i})||(\rho_{0,i}, \cdots, \rho_{8,i})||S_i$. Then the vehicle needs to verify the equations:

$$\sigma_{4,i}\hat{e}(\sigma_{1,i},h)\hat{e}(\sigma_{2,i}^{-1},K)=1,\ \sigma_{6,i}^{-1}\hat{e}(g_5^{-1}\sigma_{2,i}\sigma_{5,i},h)\hat{e}(\sigma_{3,i},S_i)=1,$$
$$\rho_{4,i}^{-1}\hat{e}(g_1^{-z_{0,i}},h)\hat{e}(g_2^{z_{0,i}},K)\sigma_{4,i}^c=1,\ \rho_{6,i}^{-1}\hat{e}(g_3^{z_{5,i}}(g_2g_4)^{z_{0,i}},h)\hat{e}(g_3^{z_{0,i}},S_i)\sigma_{6,i}^{c_i}=1,$$
$$\rho_{8,i}^{-1}\hat{e}(H_O(ID_{O_i})^{z_{6,i}},K)\hat{e}(g_2^{-z_{0,i}},h)\sigma_{8,i}^{c_i}=1,\ \sigma_{8,i}^{-1}C_{1,i}\hat{e}(\sigma_{2,i}^{-1},h)=1,$$
$$\rho_{0,i}^{-1}g^{z_0}\sigma_{0,i}^{c_i}=1,\ \rho_{1,i}^{-1}Z_{1,i}g_1^{z_{0,i}}\sigma_{1,i}^{c_i}=1,\ \rho_{2,i}^{-1}Z_{2,i}g_2^{z_{0,i}}\sigma_{2,i}^{c_i}=1,$$
$$\rho_{3,i}^{-1}Z_{3,i}g_3^{z_{0,i}}\sigma_{3,i}^{c_i}=1,\ \rho_{5,i}^{-1}\sigma_{3,i}^{z_{4,i}}g_4^{z_{0,i}}\sigma_{5,i}^{c,i}=1,$$
$$\rho_{7,i}^{-1}h^{z_{6,i}}C_{2,i}^{c_i}=1,\ S_i^{-1}A_iK^{H(A_i\|ID_{R_i})}=1$$

and

$$c_i=H((\sigma_{0,i},\cdots,\sigma_{3,i},\sigma_{5,i})\|(\rho_{0,i},\cdots,\rho_{8,i})\|A_i\|C_{1,i}\|C_{2,i}\|m_i).$$

Note that the first six equations, the middle five equations and the last two equations excluding the hash computation c_i are in the same finite cyclic groups $\mathbb{G}_3$, $\mathbb{G}_1$ and $\mathbb{G}_2$, respectively. Then Lemma 1 can be applied to each of those three batches of equations. We roughly compare the overheads of individual message verification with those of batch verification. For n messages, without using the batch approach, we need $O(N)$ multi-base pairing computations and multi-base exponentiations, as well as n hashes. However, after the batch verification is applied, the verifying vehicle needs only $O(1)$ multi-base pairing computations and multi-base exponentiations, as well as n hashes. According to state-of-the-art experimental results [10], a typical pairing takes tens of times longer than one exponentiation in $\mathbb{G}_1$, and compared to an exponentiation, the overhead of a hash computation is negligible. Hence, the batch approach offers a significant cost reduction and is very useful to speed up message verifications when the vehicular density is high, as in metropolitan areas.

5   Conclusions

The first VANETs are likely to be deployed in urban areas which particularly suffer from traffic accidents and congestions. In addition to vulnerabilities to attacks against traffic safety and drivers' privacy, a large-scale VANET in a metropolitan area poses a management problem. This paper proposed a set of mechanisms which conciliate system management, security and privacy requirements very well. We exploited IBGS to divide a large-scale VANET into easy-to-manage groups and establish liability in vehicular communications while preserving privacy. We further presented a selfish batch verification approach to accelerate message processing in VANETs. These techniques make our protocol scalable for deployment in big metropolitan areas.

Acknowledgments. This paper are partly supported by the EU 7FP through project "DwB", the Spanish Government through projects CTV-09-634, PTA2009-2738-E, TSI-020302-2010-153, PT-430000- 2010-31, TIN2009-11689, CONSOLIDER INGENIO 2010 "ARES" CSD2007-0004 and TSI2007-65406-C03-01, by the Government of Catalonia under grant SGR2009-1135, and by the NSF of China under grants 60970116, 61173154, 61003214, 91018008, 61021004, 61100173 and 11061130539. The authors also acknowledge support by the Fundamental Research Funds for the Central Universities of China through Project

3103004, Beijing Municipal Natural Science Foundation through Project 4112052, and Shaanxi Provincial Education Department through Scientific Research Program 2010JK727. The fird author is partially supported as an ICREA-Acadèmia researcher by the Catalan Government. The authors are with the UNESCO Chair in Data Privacy, but this paper does not necessarily reflect the position of UNESCO nor does it commit that organization.

References

1. 5GHz Band Dedicated Short Range Communications (DSRC), ASTM E2213-03, http://www.iteris.com/itsarch/html/standard/dsrc5ghz.htm
2. Bellare, M., Garay, J.A., Rabin, T.: Fast Batch Verification for Modular Exponentiation and Digital Signatures. In: Nyberg, K. (ed.) EUROCRYPT 1998. LNCS, vol. 1403, pp. 236–250. Springer, Heidelberg (1998)
3. Blau, J.: Car talk. IEEE Spectrum 45(10), 16 (2008)
4. Boneh, D., Lynn, B., Shacham, H.: Short Signatures from the Weil Pairing. Journal of Cryptology 17(4), 297–319 (2004)
5. Calandriello, G., Papadimitratos, P., Lioy, A., Hubaux, J.-P.: Efficient and Robust Pseudonymous Authentication in VANET. In: ACM International Workshop on Vehicular Ad Hoc Networks-VANET, pp. 19–28. ACM Press (2007)
6. Camenisch, J., Hohenberger, S., Pedersen, M.Ø.: Batch Verification of Short Signatures. In: Naor, M. (ed.) EUROCRYPT 2007. LNCS, vol. 4515, pp. 246–263. Springer, Heidelberg (2007)
7. Car2Car Communication Consortium, http://www.car-2-car.org/
8. Chaum, D., van Heyst, E.: Group Signatures. In: Davies, D.W. (ed.) EUROCRYPT 1991. LNCS, vol. 547, pp. 257–265. Springer, Heidelberg (1991)
9. Daza, V., Domingo-Ferrer, J., Sebé, F., Viejo, A.: Trustworthy Privacy-Preserving Car-generated Announcements in Vehicular Ad-Hoc Networks. IEEE Transaction on Vehehicluar Technology 58(4), 1876–1886 (2009)
10. Ferrara, A.L., Green, M., Hohenberger, S., Pedersen, M.Ø.: On the Practicality of Short Signature Batch Verification, http://eprint.iacr.org/2008/015.pdf
11. Fonseca, E., Festag, A., Baldessari, R., Aguiar, R.L.: Support of Anonymity in VANETs - Putting Pseudonymity into Practice. In: IEEE Wireless Communications and Networking Conference-WCNC, pp. 3400–3405. IEEE Press (2007)
12. Galbraith, S.D., Paterson, K.G., Smart, N.P.: Pairings for Cryptographers, http://eprint.iacr.org/2006/165.pdf
13. Gerlach, M., Festag, A., Leinmüller, T., Goldacker, G., Harsch, C.: Security Architecture for Vehicular Communication. In: WIT 2005 (2005), http://www.network-on-wheels.de/downloads/wit07secarch.pdf
14. Golle, P., Greene, D., Staddon, J.: Detecting and Correcting Malicious Data in VANETs. In: ACM International Workshop on Vehicular Ad Hoc Networks-VANET, pp. 29–37. ACM Press (2004)
15. Guo, J., Baugh, J.P., Wang, S.: A Group Signature Based Secure and Privacy-preserving Vehicular Communication Framework. In: Mobile Networking for Vehicular Environments 2007, pp. 103–108 (2007)
16. Lee, J.-H., Lee-Kwang, H.: Distributed and Cooperative Fuzzy Controllers for Traffic Intersections Group. IEEE Transactions on Systems, Man & Cybernetics 29(2), 263–271 (1999)

17. Leinmüller, T., Maihöfer, C., Schoch, E., Kargl, F.: Improved Security in Geographic Ad-Hoc Routing through Autonomous Position Verification. In: ACM International Workshop on Vehicular Ad hoc Networks-VANET, pp. 57–66. ACM Press (2006)
18. Lin, X., Sun, X., Ho, P.-H., Shen, X.: GSIS: A Secure and Privacy Preserving Protocol for Vehicular Communications. IEEE Transaction on Vehehicluar Technology 56(6), 3442–3456 (2007)
19. Network on Wheels, http://www.network-on-wheels.de/
20. Papadimitratos, P., Buttyan, L., Hubaux, J.-P., Kargl, F., Kung, A., Raya, M.: Architecture for Secure and Private Vehicular Communications. In: International Conference on ITS Telecommunications, pp. 1–6 (2007)
21. Parno, B., Perrig, A.: Challenges in Securing Vehicular Networks. In: HOTNETS 2005, http://conferences.sigcomm.org/hotnets/2005/papers/parno.pdf
22. Qin, B., Wu, Q., Susilo, W., Mu, Y.: Publicly Verifiable Privacy-Preserving Group Decryption. In: Yung, M., Liu, P., Lin, D. (eds.) Inscrypt 2008. LNCS, vol. 5487, pp. 72–83. Springer, Heidelberg (2009)
23. Raya, M., Aziz, A., Hubaux, J.-P.: Efficient Secure Aggregation in VANETs. In: ACM International Workshop on Vehicular Ad hoc Networks-VANET, pp. 67–75. ACM Press (2006)
24. Raya, M., Hubaux, J.-P.: The Security of Vehicular Ad-Hoc Networks. In: ACM Workshop on Security of Ad hoc and Sensor Networks-SASN, pp. 11–21. ACM Press (2005)
25. Raya, M., Hubaux, J.-P.: Securing Vehicular Ad Hoc Networks. Journal of Computer Security 15(1), 39–68 (2007)
26. Raya, M., Papadimitratos, P., Aad, I., Jungels, D., Hubaux, J.-P.: Eviction of Misbehaving and Faulty Nodes in Vehicular Networks. IEEE Journal Selected Areas in Communication 25(8), 1557–1568 (2007)
27. Sampigethaya, K., Huang, L., Li, M., Poovendran, R., Matsuura, K., Sezaki, K.: CARAVAN: Providing Location Privacy for VANET. In: ESCAR 2005, http://www.ee.washington.edu/research/nsl/papers/ESCAR-05.pdf
28. Secure Vehicle Communication, http://www.sevecom.org/
29. Wei, V.K., Yuen, T.H., Zhang, F.: Group Signature Where Group Manager, Members and Open Authority Are Identity-based. In: Boyd, C., González Nieto, J.M. (eds.) ACISP 2005. LNCS, vol. 3574, pp. 468–480. Springer, Heidelberg (2005)
30. Wu, Q., Domingo-Ferrer, J., González-Nicolás, U.: Balanced Trustworthiness, Safety and Privacy in Vehicle-to-vehicle Communications. IEEE Transaction on Vehehicluar Technology 59(2), 559–573 (2010)
31. Wu, Q., Mu, Y., Susilo, W., Qin, B., Domingo-Ferrer, J.: Asymmetric Group Key Agreement. In: Joux, A. (ed.) EUROCRYPT 2009. LNCS, vol. 5479, pp. 153–170. Springer, Heidelberg (2009)
32. Zarki, M.E., Mehrotra, S., Tsudik, G., Venkatasubramanian, N.: Security Issues in a Future Vehicular Network. In: European Wireless (2002), http://www.ics.uci.edu/~dsm/papers/sec001.pdf
33. Zhang, L., Wu, Q., Solanas, A., Domingo-Ferrer, J.: A Scalable Robust Authentication Protocol for Secure Vehicular Communications. IEEE Transactions on Vehicular Technology 59(4), 1606–1617 (2010)

A Probabilistic Secret Sharing Scheme for a Compartmented Access Structure[*]

Yuyin Yu [1,2] and Mingsheng Wang [1,2]

[1,2] The State Key Laboratory of Information Security, Institute of Software Chinese
Academy of Sciences, Beijing 100190, China
[1,2] Graduate University of the Chinese Academy of Sciences, Beijing 100049, China
`yuyuyin@163.com, mswang@yahoo.cn`

Abstract. In a compartmented access structure, there are disjoint participants $C_1, \ldots, C_m$. The access structure consists of subsets of participants containing at least t_i from C_i for $i = 1, \ldots, m$, and a total of at least t_0 participants. Tassa [2] asked: whether there exists an efficient ideal secret sharing scheme for such an access structure? Tassa and Dyn [5] realized this access structure with the help of its dual access structure. Unlike the scheme constructed in [5], we propose a direct solution here, in the sense that it does not utilize the dual access structure. So our method is compact and simple.

Keywords: Secret sharing, Compartmented access structure, Ideality.

1 Introduction

Shamir [1] and Blake [6] proposed a (t, n) threshold secret sharing scheme, that is, sharing a secret among a given set of n participants, such that every $k(k \leq n)$ of those participants could recover the secret by pooling their shares together, while no subset of less than k participants can do so. Simmons [3] generalized this scheme, he described a new scheme: compartmented access structure. In this scheme, there are disjoint participants $C_1, \ldots, C_m$. The access structure consists of subsets of participants containing at least t_i from C_i for $i = 1, \ldots, m$, and a total of at least t_0 participants. We give a formal definition and some related concepts in the following.

Definition 1 (Ideality). *[3,5] A secret sharing scheme with domain of secrets $\mathcal{S}$ is ideal if the domain of shares of each user is $\mathcal{S}$. An access structure Γ is ideal if for some finite domain of secrets $\mathcal{S}$, there exists an ideal secret sharing scheme realizing it.*

Definition 2 (Compartmented Access Structure). *[3,5] Let $\mathcal{C}$ be a set of n participants and assume that $\mathcal{C}$ is composed of compartments, i.e., $\mathcal{C} = \bigcup_{i=1}^{m} \mathcal{C}_i$*

---

[*] This work was partially supported by Natural Science Foundation of China under
grant (60970134) and Innovation Foundation of Institute of Software under grant
(ISCAS2009-QY04).

S. Qing et al. (Eds.): ICICS 2011, LNCS 7043, pp. 136–142, 2011.

where $C_i \cap C_j = \emptyset$ for all $1 \leq i < j \leq m$. Let $\mathbf{t} = \{t_i\}_{i=0}^{m}$ be a sequence of integers such that $t_0 \geq \sum_{i=1}^{m} t_i$. Then the $(\mathbf{t}, n)$-compartmented access structure is

$$\Gamma = \{\mathcal{V} \subset \mathcal{C} : \mid \mathcal{V} \cap C_i \mid \geq t_i \text{ for all } i \in \{1, \ldots, m\} \text{ and } \mid \mathcal{V} \mid \geq t_0\}. \quad (1)$$

Brickell [4] studied this scheme later, he proved that this access structure is ideal, but the secret sharing scheme that he proposed suffered from the same problem of inefficiency as Simmons's schemes [3] did (namely, the dealer must perform possibly exponentially many checks when assigning identities and shares to the participants). So Tassa [2] asked: whether there exists an efficient ideal secret sharing scheme for such access structures? In [5], Tassa and Dyn gave a positive answer. Their idea results from the following conclusion [8,9]: If an access structure Λ is computed by a monotone span program $\mathcal{M}$, then the dual access structure Λ^* is computed by a monotone span program $\mathcal{M}^*$ of the same size, and $\mathcal{M}^*$ can be efficiently computed from $\mathcal{M}$. Tassa and Dyn gave a solution to the dual access structure of (1), so they can efficiently construct a solution for (1). This is a good idea, but still can be improved. As a matter of fact, we do not need to use the idea of dual span program, just make a little amendment of the idea from [5], then we can get an easier solution for the compartmented access structure (1). First, let us neglect the restriction of ideality, then there is nothing difficult, we describe a solution to realize the weaken version of the access structure (1) here:

- The dealer generates a random polynomial $R(y) = \sum_{i=1}^{t_0} a_i y^i$, and then the dealer generates other random polynomials $P_i(x) = \sum_{j=1}^{t_i} b_{ij} x^j$ $(1 \leq i \leq m)$.
- The secret is $S = a_1 + \sum_{i=1}^{m} b_{i1}$.
- Each participant c_{ij} from compartment C_i will be identified by a unique public point (x_{ij}, y_{ij}), where $x_{ij} \neq x_{il}$ for $j \neq l$ and $y_{ij} \neq y_{kl}$ for $(i,j) \neq (k,l)$. The participant c_{ij}'s private share will be $(P_i(x_{ij}), R(y_{ij}))$.

This idea can be explained as a compound version of shamir's (t,n) threshold, but it is not ideal. In this paper, we try to modify this idea and finally get an ideal solution. The solution uses similar idea as in [5], especially their proof techniques. The drawback of this solution is: although $\mathcal{V} \in \Gamma$, sometimes the participants in $\mathcal{V}$ cannot recover the secret either. To our exciting, it is only a small probability event, so this solution is useful. we will prove this result in the rest of this paper.

In the following context, we use $\mathbb{F}$ to denote the finite field of size q. We discuss problems in $\mathbb{F}$ throughout this paper. In this paper, the following lemma plays an important role:

Lemma 1 (Schwartz-Zippel Lemma). *[5] Let $G(z_1, z_2, \ldots, z_k)$ be a nonzero polynomial of k variables over a finite field $\mathbb{F}$ of size q. Assume that the highest degree of each of the variables z_j in G is no larger than d. Then the number of zeros of G in $\mathbb{F}^k$ is bounded from above by kdq^{k-1}.*

2   New Solution and Proofs

In this section we will describe a probabilistic scheme to realize the compartmented access structure Γ and give its proof.

2.1   New Solution

1. The dealer generates a random polynomial $R(y) = \sum_{i=1}^{l} a_i y^i$, where $l^1 = \deg(R(y)) = t_0 - \sum_{i=1}^{m} t_i$, and then the dealer generates other m random polynomials $P_i(x) = \sum_{j=1}^{t_i} b_{ij} x^j$, let $Q_i(x, y) = P_i(x) + R(y)$ $(1 \leq i \leq m)$.
2. The secret is $S = a_1 + \sum_{i=1}^{m} b_{i1}$.
3. Each participant c_{ij} from compartment C_i will be identified by a unique public point (x_{ij}, y_{ij}), where $x_{ij} \neq x_{il}$ for $j \neq l$ and $y_{ij} \neq y_{kl}$ for $(i, j) \neq (k, l)$. The participant c_{ij}'s private share will be $Q_i(x_{ij}, y_{ij})$.

Remark 1. It seems natural to start the indices with 0, but in that case, the scheme will fail all the times, so we do not use the constant terms in the above polynomials. The price is that we must select all the points to be nonzero. we will give a detailed explanation after Example 1.

The scheme is similar as "Secret Sharing Scheme 4" in [5], but we solve different problems here. In [5], Tassa and Dyn gave a solution for the dual access structure of (1) (See "Secret Sharing Scheme 2"). They stated that using the explicit construction described in [8], they can translate the dual access structure into (1). But they did not give the detailed process. We give a direct solution here, which means that we do not utilize the dual access structure. Note that there are m random polynomials here, but only one in [5]. So we can do more things here. Obviously, this is an ideal scheme since the private shares of all users are taken from the domain of secrets $\mathbb{F}$. The unknown variables are coefficients of all the polynomials $R(y)$ and $P_i(x)$ $(1 \leq i \leq m)$, the total number of these variables is t_0. In view of the above, if any participants want to recover the secret S, they must recover all the polynomials before-mentioned, so the total number of these participants is at least t_0, and the members from C_i is at least t_i. In brief, this scheme satisfies the constraints in Γ. Such a demonstration may not be convincing, we proceed to give a strict proof.

2.2   Proofs

Theorem 1. *If $V \in \Gamma$, it may recover the secret S with probability $1 - Cq^{-1}$, where the constant C depends on $t_0, t_1, \cdots t_m$.*

Proof. When the participants try to recover the secret from their shares, they have to solve the corresponding system of linear equations that is induced by the shares. Let V be a minimal set in Γ, then $|V| = t_0$. We assume that $|V \cap C_i| = k_i \geq$

---

[1] If l=0, then it it a trivial problem, we omit such situation.

$t_i, 1 \leq i \leq m$. If $\mathcal{V} \cap \mathcal{C}_i = \{c_{i1}, \cdots, c_{ik_i}\}$ and c_{ij} is identified by the point (x_{ij}, y_{ij}), then we can reduce the recover of the polynomials $R(y)$ and $P_i(x)$ $(1 \leq i \leq m)$ to the solution of the following linear equations:

$$M \cdot A = Q, \tag{2}$$

where

$$M = \begin{pmatrix} M_1 & & & & G_1 \\ & M_2 & & & G_2 \\ & & \ddots & & \vdots \\ & & & M_m & G_m \end{pmatrix}, \tag{3}$$

$$A = \begin{pmatrix} b_{11} \cdots b_{1t_1} \cdots b_{m1} \cdots b_{mt_m} \ a_1 \cdots a_l \end{pmatrix}^t,$$

and

$$Q = \begin{pmatrix} Q_1(x_{11}, y_{11}) \cdots Q_1(x_{1k_1}, y_{1k_1}) \cdots Q_m(x_{m1}, y_{m1}) \cdots Q_m(x_{mk_m}, y_{mk_m}) \end{pmatrix}^t.$$

The pairs of blocks M_i and G_i, $1 \leq i \leq m$, represents the equations that are contributed by the k_i participants from compartment $\mathcal{C}_i$. They have the following form:

$$(M_i \cdots G_i) = \begin{pmatrix} x_{i1} & x_{i1}^2 & \cdots & x_{i1}^{t_i} & \cdots & y_{i1} & y_{i1}^2 & \cdots & y_{i1}^l \\ x_{i2} & x_{i2}^2 & \cdots & x_{i2}^{t_i} & \cdots & y_{i2} & y_{i2}^2 & \cdots & y_{i2}^l \\ \vdots & \vdots & \vdots & \vdots & \cdots & \vdots & \vdots & \vdots & \vdots \\ x_{ik_i} & x_{ik_i}^2 & \cdots & x_{ik_i}^{t_i} & \cdots & y_{ik_i} & y_{ik_i}^2 & \cdots & y_{ik_i}^l \end{pmatrix}.$$

Here, M_i is a block of size $k_i \times t_i$, and G_i is a block of size $k_i \times l$ (We omit the trivial situation $l = 0$, so G always exists). Besides M_i and G_i, all the other places of M is 0. The size of M is $t_0 \times t_0$.

The unknown variables are the components of A. According to the knowledge of linear algebra, the equation (2) has only one solution only when $\det(M) \neq 0$, so the probability that we can solve A is equal to the probability that $\det(M) \neq 0$. Now we will consider the expansion of $\det(M)$. Clearly, it has the following properties:

(1) $\det(M)$ is a nonzero polynomial of $2t_0$ variables over the finite field $\mathbb{F}$.
(2) The highest degree of each of the variables in $\det(M)$ is no larger than $d = \max(t_1, \cdots, t_m, l)$.

According to Lemma 1, we may conclude that the number of zeros of $\det(M)$ in $\mathbb{F}^{2t_0}$ is bounded by $2t_0 d q^{2t_0 - 1}$. But in $\det(M)$, the $2t_0$ variables can have q^{2t_0} values. So the probability that $\det(M) = 0$ is bounded by $2t_0 d q^{2t_0 - 1} \cdot q^{-2t_0} = 2t_0 d q^{-1}$. $\qquad \square$

Example 1. We give an example here, suppose $m = 3, t_0 = 9, t_1 = 2, t_2 = 2, t_3 = 3, k_1 = 3, k_2 = 2, k_3 = 4$, then

$$M = \begin{pmatrix} x_{11} & x_{11}^2 & 0 & 0 & 0 & 0 & 0 & y_{11} & y_{11}^2 \\ x_{12} & x_{12}^2 & 0 & 0 & 0 & 0 & 0 & y_{12} & y_{12}^2 \\ x_{13} & x_{13}^2 & 0 & 0 & 0 & 0 & 0 & y_{13} & y_{13}^2 \\ 0 & 0 & x_{21} & x_{21}^2 & 0 & 0 & 0 & y_{21} & y_{21}^2 \\ 0 & 0 & x_{22} & x_{22}^2 & 0 & 0 & 0 & y_{22} & y_{22}^2 \\ 0 & 0 & 0 & 0 & x_{31} & x_{31}^2 & x_{31}^3 & y_{31} & y_{31}^2 \\ 0 & 0 & 0 & 0 & x_{32} & x_{32}^2 & x_{32}^3 & y_{32} & y_{32}^2 \\ 0 & 0 & 0 & 0 & x_{33} & x_{33}^2 & x_{33}^3 & y_{33} & y_{33}^2 \\ 0 & 0 & 0 & 0 & x_{34} & x_{34}^2 & x_{34}^3 & y_{31} & y_{34}^2 \end{pmatrix},$$

and $d = \max(2, 2, 3, 2) = 3$. We just give the form of M here, and it will be helpful to understand this theorem. In the next part of this section, we will use computer to illustrate the validity of the above theorem. We give the results in tables only, without any more details. In the following two tables, q is the size of the finite field $\mathbb{F}$, other parameters are as in the above. The column "Times" denotes how many experiments have we made, "Results" denotes the probability of $\det(M) = 0$ in the experiments, "Theoretical" denotes the lower bound probability of $\det(M) = 0$ under Theorem 1.

Table 1. $q = 4999$

Parameters	Times	Results	Theoretical
$t_1 = 2, t_2 = 3, m = 2$ $k_1 = 3, k_2 = 6, t_0 = 9$	10000	99.98%	$> 98.55\%$
$t_1 = 1, t_2 = 1, t_3 = 1, m = 3$ $k_1 = 1, k_2 = 1, k_3 = 2, t_0 = 4$	10000	99.96%	$> 99.83\%$
$t_1 = 2, t_2 = 2, t_3 = 3, m = 3$ $k_1 = 3, k_2 = 2, k_3 = 4, t_0 = 9$	10000	99.93%	$> 98.91\%$

Table 2. $q = 832809541$

Parameters	Times	Results	Theoretical
$t_1 = 2, t_2 = 3, m = 2$ $k_1 = 3, k_2 = 6, t_0 = 9$	10000	100%	$> 1 - 9 \times 10^{-8}$
$t_1 = 1, t_2 = 1, t_3 = 1, m = 3$ $k_1 = 1, k_2 = 1, k_3 = 2, t_0 = 4$	10000	100%	$> 1 - 1 \times 10^{-8}$
$t_1 = 2, t_2 = 2, t_3 = 3, m = 3$ $k_1 = 3, k_2 = 2, k_3 = 4, t_0 = 9$	10000	100%	$> 1 - 7 \times 10^{-8}$

From the tables above, it can be seen that if q is large enough, then we can recover the secret with probability very close to 1. That is, when q is larger, the probability will be closer to 1. The results is in accord with the theorem.

The results imply that if we want to put the above idea into practice, we must chose a large finite field $\mathbb{F}$.

We explain why we choose to start the indices with 0 in our new solution (See Setc. 2.1). For example, if we use constant terms in those polynomials, then the matrix M in Example 1 will be changed into:

$$
M = \begin{pmatrix}
1 & x_{11} & 0 & 0 & 0 & 0 & 0 & 1 & y_{11} \\
1 & x_{12} & 0 & 0 & 0 & 0 & 0 & 1 & y_{12} \\
1 & x_{13} & 0 & 0 & 0 & 0 & 0 & 1 & y_{13} \\
0 & 0 & 1 & x_{21} & 0 & 0 & 0 & 1 & y_{21} \\
0 & 0 & 1 & x_{22} & 0 & 0 & 0 & 1 & y_{22} \\
0 & 0 & 0 & 0 & 1 & x_{31} & x_{31}^2 & 1 & y_{31} \\
0 & 0 & 0 & 0 & 1 & x_{32} & x_{32}^2 & 1 & y_{32} \\
0 & 0 & 0 & 0 & 1 & x_{33} & x_{33}^2 & 1 & y_{33} \\
0 & 0 & 0 & 0 & 1 & x_{34} & x_{34}^2 & 1 & y_{34}
\end{pmatrix}.
$$

Note that the first three constant columns span the fourth, so $\det(M) = 0$, according to the proof of Theorem 1, we cannot recover the secret in this case, the scheme will fail under such condition. As a matter of fact, $\det(M) \equiv 0$ if we start the indices with 0, these situation should be avoided in our scheme, so we start the indices with 1.

In [5], Tassa and Dyn chose to start the indices with 0, but in practice, their scheme cannot handle the case when there needs only one partiticipant in some compartment $\mathcal{C}_i$, that is, when $\min(t_1, \cdots, t_m) = 1$, their scheme will fail. Moreover, according to our experiments, the probability that $\det(M) \neq 0$ will become a little higher when we start the indices with 1, so it is a better choice.

Theorem 2. *If $\mathcal{V} \notin \Gamma$, then with probability $1 - Cq^{-1}$ it may not learn any information about the secret $\mathcal{S}$, where the constant C depends on $t_0, t_1, \cdots, t_m$.*

Proof. Assume that $\mathcal{V} \notin \Gamma$, we choose $\mathcal{V}$ to be a maximal unauthorized subset, namely, a subset that lacks only one participant to becoming an authorized subset, then there are only two situations to be considered: $|\mathcal{V} \cap \mathcal{C}_i| = k_i < t_i$ for some $1 \leq i \leq m$ or $|\mathcal{V}| < t_0$ but $|\mathcal{V} \cap \mathcal{C}_i| \geq t_i$ for all $1 \leq i \leq m$. In the first case, let $k_i = t_i - 1$ for some i. If $\mathcal{V} \cap \mathcal{C}_i = \{c_{i1}, c_{i2}, \cdots, c_{i(t_i-1)}\}$ and c_{ij} is identified by the point (x_{ij}, y_{ij}), consider the matrix as follows:

$$
M_i' = \begin{pmatrix}
1 & 0 & 0 & 0 \\
x_{i1} & x_{i1}^2 & \cdots & x_{i1}^{t_i} \\
x_{i2} & x_{i2}^2 & \cdots & x_{i2}^{t_i} \\
\vdots & \vdots & \vdots & \vdots \\
x_{i(t_i-1)} & x_{i(t_i-1)}^2 & \cdots & x_{i(t_i-1)}^{t_i}
\end{pmatrix}.
$$

M_i' is a matrix of size $t_i \times t_i$. If we can recover the value of b_{i1}, then the first row must be spanned by the rest, which implies that $\det(M') = 0$. But according to the property of vandermonde determinant, it is easy to conclude that $\det(M') \neq 0$.

So we cannot get b_{i1}, nor can we recover the secret $\mathcal{S}$. In the second case, without lose of generality, suppose $|\mathcal{V}| = t_0 - 1$, define a t_0 dimension vector

$$e = \begin{pmatrix} 1 \cdots 0 \cdots 1 \cdots 0 \, 1 \cdots 0 \end{pmatrix}^t.$$

e can be seen as a vector transformed from A, if we replace b_{i1} ($1 \leq i \leq m$) and a_1 by 1, replace other components by 0, we will get e. Similar as the proof of Theorem 1, we can get a matrix M', the differences are: in equation (3) the size of M is $t_0 \times t_0$, but here the size of M' is $(t_0 - 1) \times t_0$. We need to show that the vector e is, most probably, not spanned by the rows of M'. In order to show this, we augment M' by adding to it the vector e as the first row and note the augmented matrix as M'', we need to show that the probability of $\det(M'') = 0$ is $1 - Cq^{-1}$. The proof goes along the same as in the proof of Theorem 1.   □

3   Conclusions

We give a probabilistic solution of the open problem proposed in [2], using the similar idea as in [5]. The solution result from Tassa's idea, but easier than his. In practical application, q, the size of the finite field $\mathbb{F}$, is large, so the value of $1 - Cq^{-1}$ is close to 1, which implies the practicability of this scheme. Moreover, ideality is a theoretic notation, in practical application, we need not restrict the scheme to be ideal. In such case, the scheme proposed in the introduction of this paper will be a good choice.

References

1. Shamir, A.: How to share a secret. Commun. ACM 22, 612–613 (1979)
2. Tassa, T.: Hierarchical threshold secret sharing. J. Cryptology 20, 237–264 (2007)
3. Simmons, G.J.: How to (Really) Share a Secret. In: Goldwasser, S. (ed.) CRYPTO 1988. LNCS, vol. 403, pp. 390–448. Springer, Heidelberg (1990)
4. Brickell, E.F.: Some ideal secret sharing schemes. Journal of Combinatorial Mathematics and Combinatorial Computing 6, 105–113 (1989)
5. Tassa, T., Dyn, N.: Multipartite secret sharing by bivarite interpolation. J. Cryptology 22, 227–258 (2009)
6. Blakley, G.R.: Safeguarding cryptographic keys. In: Proc. AFIPS 1979 NCC, Arlington, Va, vol. 48, pp. 313–317 (June 1979)
7. Herranz, J., Sáez, G.: New results on multipartite access structures. IEE Proc. Inf. Secur. 153, 153–162 (2006)
8. Fehr, S.: Efficient construction of the dual span program (May 1999) (manuscript)
9. Karchmer, M., Wigderson, A.: On Span Programs. In: The Eighth Annual Structure in Complexity Theory, pp. 102–111 (1993)

Ideal Secret Sharing Schemes
with Share Selectability

Keita Emura[1], Atsuko Miyaji[2], Akito Nomura[3],
Mohammad Shahriar Rahman[2], and Masakazu Soshi[4]

[1] Center for Highly Dependable Embedded Systems Technology, Japan Advanced
Institute of Science and Technology (JAIST), Japan
[2] School of Information Science, JAIST, Japan
[3] Institute of Science and Engineering, Kanazawa University, Japan
[4] Graduate School of Information Sciences, Hiroshima City University, Japan
{k-emura,miyaji,mohammad}@jaist.ac.jp, anomura@t.kanazawa-u.ac.jp,
soshi@hiroshima-cu.ac.jp

Abstract. In this paper, we investigate a new concept, called *share
selectable secret sharing*, where no unauthorized set can obtain information of the secret (in the information-theoretic sense) even if shares are
selectable as arbitrary values which are independent of the secret. We
propose two totally selectable (i.e., all users' shares are selectable) secret
sharing schemes with unanimous structure. We also propose a quasi-
selectable (i.e., a part of each user's share is selectable) secret sharing
scheme with certain hierarchical structures which contains special cases
of the hierarchical threshold structures introduced by Tamir Tassa in
TCC2004 (or its full version (J. Cryptology2007)). If all selectable shares
are randomly chosen, then our schemes are perfect. Finally, we discuss
the effect of the leakage information of the secret if a weak secret is
indicated as a selectable share.

1 Introduction

1.1 Cryptography with Information-Theoretic Security

In cryptography, security models are classified roughly according to computational security and unconditional security (or information-theoretic security).
An adversary is modeled as a probabilistic polynomial time algorithm in computational security, whereas it is defined as an infinitely powerful adversary in
unconditional security. Nowadays, unconditional secure protocols have become
more noticeable as one of the post-quantum cryptographic schemes. Many unconditional secure protocols have been proposed so far. Secret sharing is one
of the most popular schemes among such primitives. Briefly, the flow of secret
sharing is described as follows. Each user is given a piece of the secret called
share, and an authorized set of users can recover the secret value by using their
shares. On the contrary, unauthorized set can obtain information of the secret.
Until now, several kind of research issues of secret sharing have been proposed,

S. Qing et al. (Eds.): ICICS 2011, LNCS 7043, pp. 143–157, 2011.

e.g., realizing flexible access structures [9,24,25,41,42,44], multi secret sharing [6], dynamic secret sharing [5], information rate (which indicates the lower bound of the share size in the case of corresponding access structure[1]) [10,12,31], rational secret sharing [18,20,23,27,32] (i.e., with game-theoretic analyses), and so on. In addition, for the purpose of establishing secret sharing with shorter share size, computational secure secret sharing also have been proposed [3,28]. As one of such schemes, computational secure on-line secret sharing schemes have been proposed [11,22,35,40], where an auxiliary public value is opened to abridge the secret and the shares. Secret sharing is used in other cryptographic primitive as a building tool, e.g., attribute-based encryption [2,34,45], threshold encryption [7,14,36], and so on. In this paper, we attempt to revisit secret sharing from a perspective different from previous works above.

1.2   Research Background

Recently, construction of cryptographic protocols from weak secrets (e.g., a short human selected password with low Shannon's entropy) has been considered. Some examples are, password-based authenticated key exchange (where cryptographically strong key can be exchanged even user has a very weak secret) [16,17,26,30,38,46], distributed public-key cryptography (where even if each group member holds a small secret password only, they can associate to a public-key cryptosystem) [1,8], and symmetric-key cryptography from weak secrets (where two users share a secret key which might not be uniformly random) [15], and so on. However, to the best of our knowledge, there is no proposal of unconditional secret sharing with such attempt so far (here, we exclude computational secure secret sharing which can treat such weak secrets under the computational security). Moreover, no consideration has been made about the cases where a dealer can "select" shares independently with the secret. As a simple example, in the Shamir's secret sharing scheme [37], a share is a random value on a randomly-chosen polynomial (with the condition that the constant value equals the secret value). That is, it is impossible to select the values of shares as particular values (for certain purposes) in the Shamir's secret sharing scheme.

1.3   Our Contribution

In this paper, we innovate a new concept, called *share selectable secret sharing*, where

- Shares are selectable as arbitrary values.
    - The word "arbitrary" means that shares are independent of the secret.
- No unauthorized set can obtain information of the secret even if shares are selectable.

---

[1] Note that unconditionally secure secret sharing requires that every qualified user should have a share at least as large as the secret itself. Secret sharing is said to be *ideal* if and only if the size of share is the same as that of the secret (i.e., the corresponding information rate is 1).

Of course, it is impossible to reconstruct the secret only from shares which are independently selected of the secret. Therefore, we introduce an auxiliary public value which works as a bridge between the secret and the shares. That is, it is required that even if unauthorized set of users obtain the auxiliary public value, it is not possible to obtain any information on the secret.

Briefly, we investigate ρ_s-quasi selectable secret sharing, where ρ_s is the selectability ratio estimating the number of users' shares that are selectable (i.e., $\rho_s=(|\text{Share selectable users}|/|\text{All users}|)$, and selectable secret sharing is said to be totally selectable if and only if $\rho_s = 1$. In this paper, we propose two (n, n)-threshold totally selectable secret sharing schemes, where n is the total number of users. We also propose a $(1 - \frac{\ell}{n})$-quasi selectable secret sharing scheme with certain hierarchical structures, where ℓ ($0 \le \ell \le n - 2, \ell \ne 1$) is the number of users who have un-selectable shares. Briefly speaking, these hierarchical structures contain special cases of the hierarchical threshold structures of Tassa [41] (or its full version [42]). Note that Tassa [41,42] (and [43] also) applies polynomial derivatives and Birkhoff interpolation for achieving hierarchical structures, whereas we apply the classical Lagrange interpolation technique only. That is, our quasi scheme implements hierarchical threshold structures by different methodology from that of Tassa's constructions.

Remark1: Trivial Non-ideal Share Selectable Secret Sharing with Flexible Access Structures: Ito, Saito, and Nishizeki [24] proposed a secret sharing scheme with general access structure from any (n, n) secret sharing scheme. Since a (n, n)-threshold totally selectable secret sharing scheme can be constructed easily (e.g., protocol 1 in Section 2), we also realize a totally selectable secret sharing scheme with general access structure. However, this totally selectable scheme is not ideal (i.e., the size of share is larger than that of the secret). We make it clear that the main objective of this paper is to construct "ideal" secret sharing schemes (i.e., the size of share is the same as that of the secret) with share selectability, and we stick resolutely to such ideal schemes in this paper.

Remark2: The Csirmaz-Tardos On-line Secret Sharing: To the best of our knowledge, the case that shares are independently selected with the secret to be distributed has not been considered except in the following scheme proposed by Csirmaz and Tardos. Very recently, Csirmaz and Tardos proposed on-line secret sharing [13] for graph based access structures (which is totally different from the computational on-line ones [11,22,35,40]). In the Csirmaz-Tardos on-line secret sharing scheme, the dealer *assigns* shares in the order the participants show up knowing only those qualified subsets whose all members she have seen. Users form a queue in the on-line share distribution, and they receive their shares in the order they appear. The users receive their shares one by one and the assigned share cannot be changed later on. Csirmaz and Tardos insist that their on-line scheme is useful when the set of users is not fixed in advance. Since their purpose and construction method are totally different from ours, we do not discuss their on-line secret sharing anymore although there might be somewhat relationships between share selectable secret sharing and the Csirmaz-Tardos on-line secret sharing. There is space for argument on this point.

1.4   Requirement of Shannon's Entropy of Selected Shares

Here, we clarify the requirement of selectable shares, especially, the difference between selectable shares and weak secrets with low entropy. For achieving "perfect" secret sharing (i.e., no information can revealed from any unauthorized set of users), we cannot assume that a low entropy value (e.g., a human selected password) is indicated as a share. That is, we can say that:

- If selectable shares are randomly chosen, then our schemes are perfect.
    - I.e., we assume that the guessing probability of each share is smaller than that of the secret itself, namely $H(S) \leq H(W_i)$ holds, where $H(\cdot)$ is the Shannon's entropy, S and W_i are the random variables induced by the secret s and a share ω_i. We explain other notations in Section 2.
- If a weak secret is indicated as a selectable share, then users gain some information by guessing the share of uncorrupted users.
    - This setting is essentially the same as that of ramp secret sharing [4,29].

From the above considerations, first, we propose selectable secret sharing schemes. We also prove that these schemes are perfect if selectable shares are randomly chosen (Appendix). Finally, we discuss the effect of the leakage information of the secret if a weak secret is indicated as a selectable share (Section 4).

1.5   Another Significance of the Share Selectability

Although our research starts with mainly mathematical interests, cryptographic applications of share selectable secret sharing are also expected. For example, in cryptographic schemes, where secret sharing approach is used, secret keys are computed by using shares of the master key. That is, if a decryptor has legitimate secret keys, then she can decrypt the corresponding ciphertext by combining the secret keys in the secret sharing manner (e.g., applying Lagrange interpolations). In this case, each share is also changed if access structures are changed. Hence the secret keys of users need to be updated as well. For example, in access trees (e.g., [19]), first a secret value of the root node is chosen, and next a polynomial is defined with the condition that the constant value is equal to the root secret, and a secret value of a child node is set as a value on the polynomial. So, a secret value of the leaf node is computed at the end. Therefore, if the structure of the access tree is changed, these procedures must be executed again. On the contrary, each share can be independently selected under the share selectability. So, it is expected that access structures can be updated by applying share selectable secret sharing without changing secret keys of users. In an opposite manner, secret keys might be updated without changing access structures and the master key (which is the same motivation of proactive secret sharing [21,33,39]). Since we mainly focus on the share selectability, we do not argue on updating the access structures or shares anymore.

2   Preliminaries

Throughout this paper, we use the following notations. Let $n \in \mathbb{N}$ be the number of participants, p be a prime number of $p > n$ (and $ID \bmod p \neq 0$ for all public identity), $H(X)$ be Shannon's entropy of a random variable X, $H(X|Y)$ be conditional Shannon's entropy of random variables X and Y, $|\mathcal{X}|$ be the number of elements of a finite set $\mathcal{X}$, and $2^{\mathcal{X}}$ be the family of all subsets of $\mathcal{X}$. Operations are done over the field $\mathbb{F}_p$.

2.1   Share Selectable Secret Sharing

Here, we define share selectable secret sharing (notations are referred by [29]). Let $\mathcal{P} = \{P_1, P_2, \ldots, P_n\}$ be a set of participants, and $D \notin \mathcal{P}$ be a dealer who selects a secret $s \in \mathcal{S}$, computes the corresponding auxiliary public value $u \in \mathcal{U}$, and gives a share $w_i \in \mathcal{W}_i$ to $P_i \in \mathcal{P}$ for $i \in [1, n]$, where $\mathcal{S}$ denotes the set of secrets, $\mathcal{U}$ denotes the set of auxiliary public values, and $\mathcal{W}_i$ denotes the set of possible shares that P_i might receive. The access structure $\Gamma \subset 2^{\mathcal{P}}$ is a family of subsets of $\mathcal{P}$.

Definition 1 (Share selectable secret sharing). *Let S, U, and W_i be the random variables induced by s, u, and ω_i, respectively, and $\mathcal{V}_A = \{W_i | P_i \in A\}$ be the set of random variable of shares given to every participant $P_i \in A \subset \mathcal{P}$. Let SSGen be a selectable-share generation algorithm, which takes as an input the description of the underlying group $\mathbb{G}$ (in our schemes, $\mathbb{G} = \mathbb{Z}_p$), and returns a share $\omega \in \mathbb{G}$. A share selectable secret sharing scheme is said to be perfect if the following holds.*

$$H(S|\mathcal{V}_A, U) = \begin{cases} 0 & (A \in \Gamma) \\ H(S) & (A \notin \Gamma) \end{cases}$$

Our major argument is the secret s is not included in the input of the SSGen algorithm. That is, a share $\omega \leftarrow \mathsf{SSGen}(\mathbb{G})$ is totally independent with the secret s, and is called selectable. Therefore, for a selectable share ω,

$$H(S|\mathcal{V}) = H(S)$$

holds, where $\mathcal{V} \subset \mathcal{W} := \bigcup_{i=1}^n \mathcal{W}_i$ be a random variable of shares induced by ω.

As a remark, we definitely distinguish the equation $H(S|\mathcal{V}) = H(S)$ above and the case that $H(S|\mathcal{V}_A) = H(S)$ for $A \notin \Gamma$ in conventional perfect secret sharing manner. That is, in share selectable secret sharing, even if all selectable shares are collected (i.e., A might be in Γ), there is no way to recover the secret. Therefore, if all shares are selectable, then some auxiliary public value $u \in \mathcal{U}$ is indispensable for reconstructing the secret s. Note that if a part of shares are non-selectable, then there is room for reconstructing the secret s without using any auxiliary public value $u \in \mathcal{U}$.

Next, we define the selectability ratio which estimates the number of users' shares that are selectable.

Definition 2 (The Selectability Ratio). *Let* $0 \leq n_s \leq n$ *be the number of users who have a selectable share. The selectabilty ratio* ρ_s *is defined as* $\rho_s = n_s/n$.

Definition 3 (Quasi Selectability and Total Selectability). *A secret sharing is said to be* ρ_s-*quasi selectable secret sharing if its selectability ratio* ρ_s *is* $0 < \rho_s < 1$. *A secret sharing is said to be totally selectable if its selectability ratio* ρ_s *is* 1.

The case $\rho_s = 0$ represents the conventional secret sharing schemes. Note that there have been secret sharing schemes having $\rho_s > 0$. For example, for a secret $s \in \mathbb{Z}_p$, the dealer D selects $\omega_i \in \mathbb{Z}_p$ for all $i \in [1, n-1]$ (so, these shares are selectable, since these can be selected independently with s), sets $\omega_n := s - \sum_{i=1}^{n-1} \omega_i$ (so, ω_n is unselectable), and gives ω_i to P_i for all $i \in [1, n]$. s can be reconstructed by $\sum_{i=1}^{n} \omega_i$. Then, obviously this scheme is a $(1 - \frac{1}{n})$-quasi selectable (n, n)-threshold secret sharing scheme, and is perfect.

3   Proposed Schemes

In this section, we propose two totally selectable (n, n)-threshold secret sharing schemes, and a $(1 - \frac{\ell}{n})$-quasi selectable secret sharing scheme with certain hierarchical structures $(\ell \ (0 \leq \ell \leq n - 2, \ell \neq 1)$ is defined in the third scheme). The first construction (protocol 1) is somewhat trivial since it is a simple modification of the $(1 - \frac{1}{n})$-quasi selectable (n, n)-threshold secret sharing scheme introduced in the previous section. However, this scheme is easy-to-understand due to its simple structure. In our all schemes, the $\mathsf{SSGen}(\mathbb{Z}_p)$ algorithm simply returns $\omega \in \mathbb{Z}_p$.

Protocol 1 (The first scheme: A totally selectable (n,n)-threshold secret sharing scheme).

Distribution Phase:

1. *The dealer* D *selects the secret* $s \in \mathbb{Z}_p$
2. D *selects a share* $\omega_i \in \mathbb{Z}_p$ *for all* $i \in [1, n]$ *such that* $\omega_i \leftarrow \mathsf{SSGen}(\mathbb{Z}_p)$.
3. D *sets* $u := s - \sum_{i=1}^{n} \omega_i$.
4. D *gives* ω_i *to* P_i *for all* $i \in [1, n]$, *and opens* u *as the auxiliary public value.*

Reconstruction Phase: *Compute* $s = u + \sum_{i=1}^{n} \omega_i$.

Next, we propose a polynomial-based totally selectable (n, n)-threshold secret sharing scheme. This second scheme can be seen as a special case of our quasi one (protocol 3). Let ID_i be the (public) identity of $P_i \in \mathcal{P}$ and $\Gamma = \{P_1, P_2, \ldots, P_n\}$, namely, Γ is a (n, n)-threshold structure. We require $ID_i \neq ID_j$ $(i \neq j)$.

Protocol 2 (The second scheme: A polynomial-based totally selectable (n,n)-threshold secret sharing scheme).

Distribution Phase:

1. The dealer D selects the secret $s \in \mathbb{Z}_p$.
2. D selects a share $\omega_i \in \mathbb{Z}_p$ for all $i \in [1, n]$ such that $\omega_i \leftarrow \mathsf{SSGen}(\mathbb{Z}_p)$.
3. Let $f(x)$ be a polynomial of degree at most n such that $f(ID_i) = \omega_i$ $(P_i \in \Gamma)$ and $f_j(0) = s$. D chooses $ID_D \in \mathbb{Z}_p$ such that $ID_D \notin \{ID_i\}_{i=1}^n$, and computes $u = f(ID_D)$.
4. D gives ω_i to P_i for all $i \in [1, n]$, and opens u as the auxiliary public value.

Reconstruction Phase: By using Lagrange interpolation, $f(x)$ can be reconstructed from (ID_D, u) and all $\{(ID_i, \omega_i)\}_{i=1}^n$, and $s = f(0)$ can be computed.

Next, we propose a $(1 - \frac{\ell}{n})$-quasi selectable secret sharing scheme, which is the most interesting construction in this paper. First, we define the access structures of this quasi scheme.

Definition 4 (Hierarchical access structures realized in our quasi scheme). Let ℓ $(0 \leq \ell \leq n - 2, \ell \neq 1)$ be the number of users who have an unselectable share, and set $\mathcal{P}^\ell := \{U_{j_1}, U_{j_2}, \ldots, U_{j_\ell}\}$ as the set of such ℓ users. Let $n' := n - \ell$ be the number of user who have a selectable share, and set $\mathcal{P}' := \{U_{i_1}, U_{i_2}, \ldots, U_{i_{n'}}\}$ as the set of such n' users. We require $\mathcal{P} = \mathcal{P}^\ell \cup \mathcal{P}'$ and $\mathcal{P}^\ell \cap \mathcal{P}' = \emptyset$. Let $\Gamma' \subset 2^{\mathcal{P}'}$ is a family of subsets of $\mathcal{P}'$, and $m = |\Gamma'|$. For $A_j \in \Gamma'$ $(j \in [1, m])$, set $|A_j| = n_j$. Let $\Gamma^\ell := \{A \in 2^{\mathcal{P}^\ell} : |A| \geq k\}$, where $k \in \mathbb{N}$ be the threshold value and $2 \leq k \leq \ell$. The actual access structure Γ is defined as follows.

$$\Gamma := \{A : A = A^\ell \cup A' \text{ such that } A^\ell \in \Gamma^\ell \wedge A' \in \Gamma'\}$$

As one exception, if $\ell = 0$, then Γ' is restricted as the (n, n)-threshold structure only.

Note that the restriction case $(\ell = 0)$ is exactly the second construction, and therefore the second scheme is a special case of the third scheme. In addition, Γ contains special cases of the hierarchical threshold structures [41,42][2]. For example, let Γ' be (n', n')-threshold structure, then $\Gamma = \{A \subset \mathcal{P} : |A \cap \mathcal{P}'| = n' \wedge |A \cap |\mathcal{P}' \cup \mathcal{P}^\ell|| \geq n' + k\}$ holds. This is a special case of the hierarchical threshold structures with $k_0 = n'$, $k_1 = n'+k$, $\mathcal{P}_0 = \mathcal{P}'$, and $\mathcal{P}_1 = \mathcal{P}^\ell$. In addition to this hierarchical threshold structure, the above Γ can represent any kind of access structure for $\mathcal{P}'$ (not $\mathcal{P}$). More precisely, we can achieve general access structures [24,25,44] for $\mathcal{P}'$ although our scheme is ideal. Note that our result

---

[2] In the hierarchical threshold structures, a set of users $\mathcal{P}$ is divided as N hierarchy $\mathcal{P} := \cup_{i=1}^N \mathcal{P}_i$ such that $\mathcal{P}_i \cap \mathcal{P}_j = \emptyset$ for $0 \leq i < j \leq N$. Let $\mathbf{k} = (k_0, k_1, \ldots, k_N)$ be monotonically increasing sequence of integers $0 < k_0 < \cdots < k_N$. $(\mathbf{k}, n)$ hierarchical threshold structure is defined as $\Gamma = \{A \subset \mathcal{P} : |A \cap (\cup_{i=0}^N \mathcal{P}_i)| \geq k_i \ \forall i \in [0, N]\}$.

does not contradict with certain impossible results (e.g., there exist families of special access structures with n participants where the size of some shares increases unboundedly as $n \to \infty$, i.e., at least about $n/\log n$ times the secret size [12]), since access structures are restricted as threshold ones for $\mathcal{P}^\ell$ (that is, for $\mathcal{P} = \mathcal{P}^\ell \cup \mathcal{P}'$, our access structure is not general).

Here, we give our quasi scheme. We omit the case $\ell = 0$ in the following scheme, since it has already been shown as the second scheme.

Protocol 3 (The third scheme : A $(1\text{-}\frac{\ell}{n})$-quasi selectable secret sharing scheme).

Distribution Phase:

1. The dealer D selects the secret $s \in \mathbb{Z}_p$.
2. D selects a share $\omega_i \in \mathbb{Z}_p$ for all $P_i \in \mathcal{P}'$ such that $\omega_i \leftarrow \mathsf{SSGen}(\mathbb{Z}_p)$.
3. D chooses $ID_{\mathcal{A}_j} \in \mathbb{Z}_p$ for all $j \in [1, m]$ such that $ID_{\mathcal{A}_j} \notin \{ID_i\}_{i=1}^n$ and $ID_{\mathcal{A}_i} \neq ID_{\mathcal{A}_j}$ ($i \neq j$).
4. For each $A_j \in \Gamma'$ ($j \in [1, m]$), let $f_j(x)$ be a polynomial of degree at most n_j such that $f_j(ID_i) = \omega_i$ ($U_i \in A_j$) and $f_j(0) = s$. Set $D_j := (ID_{\mathcal{A}_j}, f_j(ID_{\mathcal{A}_j}))$.
5. Let $g(x)$ be a polynomial of degree at most $m - 1$ such that $g(ID_{\mathcal{A}_j}) = f_j(ID_{\mathcal{A}_j})$ for all $j \in [1, m]$.
6. For all $P_i \in \mathcal{P}^\ell$, D computes $\omega_i := g(ID_i)$ (we make it clear that this step is NOT for users $P_i \in \mathcal{P}'$, their shares $\{\omega_i\}_{P_i \in \mathcal{P}'}$ have been "selected" in Step 2).
7. D randomly chooses $(m - k)$ coordinates on the polynomial $g(x)$, excluding all D_j and $(ID_i, g(ID_i))$ for all $P_i \in \mathcal{P}^\ell$, and sets these $(m - k)$ coordinates as u. If $k \geq m$, then $u = \emptyset$.
8. D gives ω_i to P_i for all $i \in [1, n]$, and opens u as the auxiliary public value.

Reconstruction Phase:

1. As in the Shamir (k, ℓ)-threshold secret sharing, by using Lagrange interpolation, $g(x)$ is reconstructed from all ω_i of $P_i \in \mathcal{P}^\ell$ (and u if $k < m$).
2. By using Lagrange interpolation, $f_j(x)$ can be reconstructed from $(ID_{\mathcal{A}_j}, g(ID_{\mathcal{A}_j}))$ and (ID_i, ω_i) for all $P_i \in A_j \in \Gamma'$, and $s = f_j(0)$ can be computed.

The first and second schemes are totally selectable (n, n)-threshold secret sharing schemes, and the third scheme is a $(1 - \frac{\ell}{n})$-quasi selectable secret sharing scheme realizing Γ defined in Definition 4. Security proofs are given in the Appendix.

4   Share Selectable Secret Sharing with Weak Shares

In this Section, we discuss the effect of the leakage information of the secret when a weak secret (e.g., a short human selected password with low Shannon's entropy) is indicated as a selectable share. To give the maximum information to an unauthorized set of users A, we consider the situation where (1) A will be an authorized set if only one more user (who has a share ω) is added to A, (2) ω is a selectable share, and (3) ω is the weakest share in the underlying system (i.e., for the random variables W induced by ω, $H(W) = \min\{H(W_i) : H(W_i) < H(S)\}$ holds). Note that ω is a independent value of the secret s. Therefore, the mutual information between s and ω is 0 since $I(S; W) := H(S) + H(W) - H(S, W) = H(S) + H(W) - H(S) - H(W) = 0$. It is thus easy to conclude that $H(S|\mathcal{V}_A, U) = H(W) < H(S)$ holds.

5   Conclusion and Future Work

In this paper, we investigate the new concept *share selectable secret sharing*, where a dealer D can select shares independent of the secret. We propose two totally selectable (i.e., all users' share are selectable) secret sharing schemes with unanimous structure, and a quasi-selectable (i.e., a part of users' share are selectable) secret sharing scheme with certain hierarchical structures which contains special cases of the hierarchical threshold structures [41,42]. Our quasi scheme can be seen as an ideal secret sharing with flexible hierarchical structures which has not been done before to the best of our knowledge, and is of independent interest.

Although our research resorts mainly on the mathematical interest, applications of share selectable secret sharing are also realizable (as discussed in Section 1.5). As future work, it might be interesting to update access structures (resp. shares) without changing shares (resp. access structures).

References

1. Abdalla, M., Boyen, X., Chevalier, C., Pointcheval, D.: Distributed Public-key Cryptography from Weak Secrets. In: Jarecki, S., Tsudik, G. (eds.) PKC 2009. LNCS, vol. 5443, pp. 139–159. Springer, Heidelberg (2009)
2. Attrapadung, N., Libert, B., de Panafieu, E.: Expressive Key-policy Attribute-based Encryption with Constant-size Ciphertexts. In: Catalano, D., Fazio, N., Gennaro, R., Nicolosi, A. (eds.) PKC 2011. LNCS, vol. 6571, pp. 90–108. Springer, Heidelberg (2011)
3. Béguin, P., Cresti, A.: General Short Computational Secret Sharing Schemes. In: Guillou, L.C., Quisquater, J.-J. (eds.) EUROCRYPT 1995. LNCS, vol. 921, pp. 194–208. Springer, Heidelberg (1995)
4. Blakley, G.R., Meadows, C.: Security of Ramp Schemes. In: Blakely, G.R., Chaum, D. (eds.) CRYPTO 1984. LNCS, vol. 196, pp. 242–268. Springer, Heidelberg (1985)
5. Blundo, C., Cresti, A., De Santis, A., Vaccaro, U.: Fully dynamic secret sharing schemes. Theor. Comput. Sci. 165(2), 407–440 (1996)
6. Blundo, C., De Santis, A., Di Crescenzo, G., Gaggia, A.G., Vaccaro, U.: Multi-secret Sharing Schemes. In: Desmedt, Y.G. (ed.) CRYPTO 1994. LNCS, vol. 839, pp. 150–163. Springer, Heidelberg (1994)
7. Boneh, D., Boyen, X., Halevi, S.: Chosen Ciphertext Secure Public Key Threshold Encryption without Random Oracles. In: Pointcheval, D. (ed.) CT-RSA 2006. LNCS, vol. 3860, pp. 226–243. Springer, Heidelberg (2006)

8. Boyen, X., Chevalier, C., Fuchsbauer, G., Pointcheval, D.: Strong Cryptography from Weak Secrets. In: Bernstein, D.J., Lange, T. (eds.) AFRICACRYPT 2010. LNCS, vol. 6055, pp. 297–315. Springer, Heidelberg (2010)

9. Brickell, E.F.: Some Ideal Secret Sharing Schemes. In: Quisquater, J.-J., Vandewalle, J. (eds.) EUROCRYPT 1989. LNCS, vol. 434, pp. 468–475. Springer, Heidelberg (1990)

10. Brickell, E.F., Stinson, D.R.: Some improved bounds on the information rate of perfect secret sharing schemes. J. Cryptology 5(3), 153–166 (1992)

11. Cachin, C.: On-line secret sharing. In: IMA Conf., pp. 190–198 (1995)

12. Csirmaz, L.: The size of a share must be large. J. Cryptology 10(4), 223–231 (1997)

13. Csirmaz, L., Tardos, G.: On-line secret sharing. Cryptology ePrint Archive, Report 2011/174 (2011), http://eprint.iacr.org/

14. Desmedt, Y., Frankel, Y.: Threshold Cryptosystems. In: Brassard, G. (ed.) CRYPTO 1989. LNCS, vol. 435, pp. 307–315. Springer, Heidelberg (1990)

15. Dodis, Y., Wichs, D.: Non-malleable extractors and symmetric key cryptography from weak secrets. In: STOC, pp. 601–610 (2009)

16. Gennaro, R.: Faster and Shorter Password-authenticated Key Exchange. In: Canetti, R. (ed.) TCC 2008. LNCS, vol. 4948, pp. 589–606. Springer, Heidelberg (2008)

17. Gentry, C., MacKenzie, P.D., Ramzan, Z.: Password authenticated key exchange using hidden smooth subgroups. In: ACM Conference on Computer and Communications Security, pp. 299–309 (2005)

18. Gordon, S.D., Katz, J.: Rational Secret Sharing, Revisited. In: De Prisco, R., Yung, M. (eds.) SCN 2006. LNCS, vol. 4116, pp. 229–241. Springer, Heidelberg (2006)

19. Goyal, V., Pandey, O., Sahai, A., Waters, B.: Attribute-based encryption for fine-grained access control of encrypted data. In: ACM Conference on Computer and Communications Security, pp. 89–98 (2006)

20. Halpern, J.Y., Teague, V.: Rational secret sharing and multiparty computation: extended abstract. In: STOC, pp. 623–632 (2004)

21. Herzberg, A., Jarecki, S., Krawczyk, H., Yung, M.: Proactive Secret Sharing or: How to Cope with Perpetual Leakage. In: Coppersmith, D. (ed.) CRYPTO 1995. LNCS, vol. 963, pp. 339–352. Springer, Heidelberg (1995)

22. Hwang, R.-J., Chang, C.-C.: An on-line secret sharing scheme for multi-secrets. Computer Communications 21(13), 1170–1176 (1998)

23. Isshiki, T., Wada, K., Tanaka, K.: A rational secret-sharing scheme based on RSA-OAEP. IEICE Transactions 93-A(1), 42–49 (2010)

24. Ito, M., Saito, A., Nishizeki, T.: Secret sharing scheme realizing general access structure. In: Proceedings IEEE Globecom 1987, pp. 99–102 (1987)

25. Iwamoto, M., Yamamoto, H., Ogawa, H.: Optimal multiple assignments based on integer programming in secret sharing schemes with general access structures. IEICE Transactions 90-A(1), 101–112 (2007)

26. Katz, J., Ostrovsky, R., Yung, M.: Efficient Password-authenticated Key Exchange using Human-memorable Passwords. In: Pfitzmann, B. (ed.) EUROCRYPT 2001. LNCS, vol. 2045, pp. 475–494. Springer, Heidelberg (2001)

27. Kol, G., Naor, M.: Games for exchanging information. In: STOC, pp. 423–432 (2008)

28. Krawczyk, H.: Secret Sharing Made Short. In: Stinson, D.R. (ed.) CRYPTO 1993. LNCS, vol. 773, pp. 136–146. Springer, Heidelberg (1994)

29. Kurihara, J., Kiyomoto, S., Fukushima, K., Tanaka, T.: A fast (k, L, n)-threshold ramp secret sharing scheme. IEICE Transactions 92-A(8), 1808–1821 (2009)

30. MacKenzie, P.D., Shrimpton, T., Jakobsson, M.: Threshold password-authenticated key exchange. J. Cryptology 19(1), 27–66 (2006)

31. Martí-Farré, J., Padró, C.: Secret sharing schemes on access structures with intersection number equal to one. Discrete Applied Mathematics 154(3), 552–563 (2006)
32. Micali, S., Shelat, A.: Purely Rational Secret Sharing (Extended Abstract). In: Reingold, O. (ed.) TCC 2009. LNCS, vol. 5444, pp. 54–71. Springer, Heidelberg (2009)
33. Nikov, V., Nikova, S.: On Proactive Secret Sharing Schemes. In: Handschuh, H., Hasan, M.A. (eds.) SAC 2004. LNCS, vol. 3357, pp. 308–325. Springer, Heidelberg (2004)
34. Nishide, T., Yoneyama, K., Ohta, K.: Attribute-based encryption with partially hidden ciphertext policies. IEICE Transactions 92-A(1), 22–32 (2009)
35. Oba, T., Ogata, W.: Provably secure on-line secret sharing scheme. IEICE Transactions 94-A(1), 139–149 (2011)
36. Qin, B., Wu, Q., Zhang, L., Domingo-Ferrer, J.: Threshold Public-key Encryption with Adaptive Security and Short Ciphertexts. In: Soriano, M., Qing, S., López, J. (eds.) ICICS 2010. LNCS, vol. 6476, pp. 62–76. Springer, Heidelberg (2010)
37. Shamir, A.: How to share a secret. Commun. ACM 22(11), 612–613 (1979)
38. Shin, S., Kobara, K., Imai, H.: Security analysis of two augmented password-authenticated key exchange protocols. IEICE Transactions 93-A(11), 2092–2095 (2010)
39. Stinson, D.R., Wei, R.: Unconditionally Secure Proactive Secret Sharing Scheme with Combinatorial Structures. In: Heys, H.M., Adams, C.M. (eds.) SAC 1999. LNCS, vol. 1758, pp. 200–214. Springer, Heidelberg (2000)
40. Sun, H.-M.: On-line multiple secret sharing based on a one-way function. Computer Communications 22(8), 745–748 (1999)
41. Tassa, T.: Hierarchical Threshold Secret Sharing. In: Naor, M. (ed.) TCC 2004. LNCS, vol. 2951, pp. 473–490. Springer, Heidelberg (2004)
42. Tassa, T.: Hierarchical threshold secret sharing. J. Cryptology 20(2), 237–264 (2007)
43. Tassa, T., Dyn, N.: Multipartite secret sharing by bivariate interpolation. J. Cryptology 22(2), 227–258 (2009)
44. Tochikubo, K.: Efficient secret sharing schemes realizing general access structures. IEICE Transactions 87-A(7), 1788–1797 (2004)
45. Yamada, S., Attrapadung, N., Hanaoka, G., Kunihiro, N.: Generic Constructions for Chosen-ciphertext Secure Attribute Based Encryption. In: Catalano, D., Fazio, N., Gennaro, R., Nicolosi, A. (eds.) PKC 2011. LNCS, vol. 6571, pp. 71–89. Springer, Heidelberg (2011)
46. Yoneyama, K.: Does secure password-based authenticated key exchange against leakage of internal states exist? IEICE Transactions 92-A(1), 113–121 (2009)

Appendix: Security Proofs

Here, we give security proofs of our schemes. As a reminder, we do not assume that a weak share is indicated as a selectable share (such weak cases has been considered in Section 4).

Theorem 1. *The first scheme is a totally selectable (n, n)-threshold secret sharing scheme.*

Proof. The condition $H(S|\mathcal{V}_A, U) = 0$ is clear when $A = \mathcal{P}$, since s can be reconstructed by computing $s = u + \sum_{i=1}^{n} \omega_i$. In addition, the condition $H(S|\mathcal{V}) = H(S)$ holds since each ω_i is independently chosen with the secret s. W.l.o.g., we set $\mathcal{V}_A := (P_1, \ldots, P_{n-1})$ as the unqualified set of users. Then, since the secret s is independent from $(u, \omega_1, \ldots, \omega_{n-1})$, $H(S|\mathcal{V}_A, U) = H(S)$ holds.   □

Theorem 2. *The second scheme is a totally selectable (n, n)-threshold secret sharing scheme.*

Since the second scheme is a special case of the third scheme, we give the security proof of Theorem 2 with the proof of Theorem 3.

Theorem 3. *The third scheme is a $(1-\frac{\ell}{n})$-quasi selectable secret sharing scheme realizing Γ defined in Definition 4.*

As in Theorem 1, the condition $H(S|\mathcal{V}_A, U) = 0$ $(A \in \Gamma)$ and $H(S|\mathcal{V}) = H(S)$ hold, where $\mathcal{V} \subset \mathcal{W} := \bigcup_{i=1}^{n'} \mathcal{W}_i$ be a random variable of shares of users in $\mathcal{P}'$. So, the remaining part is $H(S|\mathcal{V}_A, U) = H(S)$ if $A \notin \Gamma$. Before giving the proof, we prove the following Proposition and Lemmas. Below in this proposition, the notation (M, N) represents the numbers of rows and columns, respectively.

Proposition 1. *Let A be an $M \times N$ matrix over a field, and the first column of A is $C = [c_1, c_2, \ldots, c_M]^T$, where $A = [\ C\ |\ B\ ]$. Then the first component of the solution for simultaneous equation $A\boldsymbol{x} = \boldsymbol{s}$ is not unique if and only if $rank(A) = rank(B)$.*

Proof. Let $W_A = \{\boldsymbol{x}|A\boldsymbol{x} = \boldsymbol{0}\}$. Then $\dim W_A = N - rank(A)$. We assume that $\boldsymbol{u}$ is a solution for $A\boldsymbol{x} = \boldsymbol{s}$. Then we can express the general solution for $A\boldsymbol{x} = \boldsymbol{s}$ as $\boldsymbol{x} = \boldsymbol{u} + \boldsymbol{x}'$, where $\boldsymbol{x}'$ satisfies $A\boldsymbol{x}' = \boldsymbol{0}$. We further assume that $\boldsymbol{x}''$ satisfies $B\boldsymbol{x}'' = \boldsymbol{0}$. Then,

The first component of $\boldsymbol{x}$, which is the solution for $A\boldsymbol{x} = \boldsymbol{s}$, is unique.

$\Longleftrightarrow$ $\boldsymbol{x}' = [0, \boldsymbol{x}'']^T$.

$\Longleftrightarrow$ $\dim W_A = \dim W_B$

$\Longleftrightarrow$ $N - rank(A) = N - 1 - rank(B)$

$\Longleftrightarrow$ $rank(A) = rank(B) + 1$

Since $rank(A)$ is equal to $rank(B)$ or $rank(B) + 1$, then the first component of the solution for simultaneous equation $A\boldsymbol{x} = \boldsymbol{s}$ is not unique if and only if $rank(A) = rank(B)$. $\qquad\square$

Next, we prove the following Lemma. For simplicity, we assume that $g(x)$ is a polynomial of degree at most $m - 1$ which passes through m coordinates $(ID_{A_j}, f_j(ID_{A_j}))$. Let P_s be an "imaginary" participant who has $g(x)$ as P_s's share, and $\mathcal{P}'$ be the set of users. Note that, here $\mathcal{P}^\ell$ is not considered, since P_s can be seen as $\mathcal{P}^\ell$ by using the Shamir (k, ℓ)-threshold scheme for the secret $g(x)$. Let $\mathcal{C}$ be the set of malicious participants such that they know the shares of one another.

Lemma 1. *We assume that the number of malicious participants be t $(n'+1 \geq t)$ in n' participants and one imaginary participant P_s. We calculate simultaneous equations for coefficient polynomial f_j $(j = 1, 2, \ldots, m)$ and shares of $n' + 1 - t$ honest participants. Let $V(n' + 1, m, t)$ be the number of unknown quantities and*

$R(n'+1, m, t)$ be the number of simultaneous equations for malicious participants. Then $V(n' + 1, m, t)$ and $R(n' + 1, m, t)$ satisfy the following:

$$V(n' + 1, m, t) = \begin{cases} R(n' + 1, m, t) + (n' - t + 1) & (P_s \notin \mathcal{C}) \\ R(n' + 1, m, t) + (n' - t - m + 2) & (P_s \in \mathcal{C}) \end{cases}$$

Proof.

The case of $P_s \notin \mathcal{C}$: W.l.o.g., we assume that P_i $(i = 1, 2, \ldots, t)$ are malicious participants. Let $\mathcal{C} = \{P_1, P_2, \ldots, P_t\} \notin \Gamma$ be the set of malicious participants. A polynomial of degree at most n_j is made for each qualified set A_j. So, the number of coefficients of the polynomial (except the secret value s) is n_j. We add the share of $n' - t$ honest participants, the share of a special participant P_s (i.e., a polynomial $g(x)$) and the secret value s to this, $V(n' + 1, m, t) = 1 + n' - t + m + \sum_{j=1}^{m} n_j$. Now we assume that $P_i \in A_{k_j}$ $(j = 1, 2, \ldots, r_i)$, i.e., r_i is the number of qualified sets P_i belongs to. Then we can obtain r_i simultaneous equations. More specifically, $\omega_i = f_{k_1}(ID_i) = f_{k_2}(ID_i) = \cdots = f_{k_{r_i}}(ID_i)$. Moreover, we add a condition such that each polynomial f_j passes through coordinate $(ID_{A_j}, f_j(ID_{A_j}))$, $R(n' + 1, m, t) = m + \sum_{i=1}^{n'} r_i$ holds. Then $\sum_{i=1}^{n'} r_i = \sum_{j=1}^{m} n_j$ holds, and therefore $\sum_{i=1}^{n'} r_i = \sum_{j=1}^{m} n_j = V(n' + 1, m, t) - (m + n' - t + 1) = R(n' + 1, m, t) - m$ holds.

The case of $P_s \in \mathcal{C}$: W.l.o.g., we assume that P_i $(i = 1, 2, \ldots, t - 1)$ are malicious participants. Let $\mathcal{C} = \{P_s, P_1, P_2, \ldots, P_{t-1}\} \notin \Gamma$ represents the set of malicious participants. Similar to the case of $P_s \notin \mathcal{C}$, the number of coefficients of the polynomial (except the secret value s) is n_j. We add the share of $n' - (t-1)$ honest participants and the secret value s to this, $V(n'+1, m, t) = 1 + n' - (t-1) + \sum_{j=1}^{m} n_j$ holds. Moreover, $R(n'+1, m, t) = m + \sum_{i=1}^{n'} r_i$ holds. So $\sum_{i=1}^{n'} r_i = \sum_{j=1}^{m} n_j = V(n' + 1, m, t) - (n' - t + 2) = R(n' + 1, m, t) - m$ holds. $\square$

Lemma 2. *We assume that $P_s \notin \mathcal{C}$. In this situation, the secret value s cannot be determined with $R(n' + 1, m, n')$ simultaneous equations.*

Proof. Let $\Gamma'' = \{A' = A \cup \{U_s\} : A \in \Gamma\}$. For any $B_j \in \Gamma''$, let $f_j(x) = s + a_{j_1}x + a_{j_2}x^2 + \cdots + a_{j_{n_j}}x^{n_j}$ be the polynomial associated with $B_j = \{P_s, P_{j_1}, P_{j_2}, \ldots, P_{j_{n_j}}\}$. Note that $f_j(ID_{A_j}) = g(ID_{A_j})$. So, simultaneous equations for s, a_{j_1}, $a_{j_2}, \ldots, a_{j_n}, g(ID_{A_j})$ are (1)

$$N_j = \begin{bmatrix} 1 & 0 & ID_{j_1} & ID_{j_1}^2 & \cdots & ID_{j_1}^{n_j} \\ 1 & 0 & ID_{j_2} & ID_{j_2}^2 & \cdots & ID_{j_2}^{n_j} \\ \vdots & \vdots & \vdots & & \ddots & \vdots \\ 1 & 0 & ID_{j_{n_j}} & ID_{j_{n_j}}^2 & \cdots & ID_{j_{n_j}}^{n_j} \\ 1 & -1 & x_{d,j} & x_{d,j}^2 & \cdots & x_{d,j}^{n_j} \end{bmatrix} \text{ and } N_j \begin{bmatrix} s \\ g(ID_{A_j}) \\ a_{j_1} \\ a_{j_2} \\ \vdots \\ a_{j_{n_j}} \end{bmatrix} = \begin{bmatrix} \omega_{j_1} \\ \omega_{j_2} \\ \vdots \\ \omega_{j_{n_j}} \\ 0 \end{bmatrix} \quad (1)$$

Moreover, we define that $C = [\ \overbrace{1, 1, \ldots, 1}^{1+m+\sum_{j=1}^{m} n_j}\ ]^T$,

$$
M_j = \begin{bmatrix} 0 & ID_{j_1} & ID_{j_1}^{2} & \cdots & ID_{j_1}^{n_j} \\ 0 & ID_{j_2} & ID_{j_2}^{2} & \cdots & ID_{j_2}^{n_j} \\ \vdots & \vdots & \vdots & \ddots & \vdots \\ 0 & ID_{j_{n_j}} & ID_{j_{n_j}}^{2} & \cdots & ID_{j_{n_j}}^{n_j} \\ -1 & ID_{A_j} & ID_{A_j}^{2} & \cdots & ID_{A_j}^{n_j} \end{bmatrix} \quad and\ M' = \begin{bmatrix} & & 0 \cdots 0 & 0 \cdots 0 \\ M_1 & \vdots \ddots \vdots & \vdots \ddots \vdots \\ & & 0 \cdots 0 & 0 \cdots 0 \\ 0 \cdots 0 & & 0 \cdots 0 \\ \vdots \ddots \vdots & \ddots & 0 \cdots 0 \\ 0 \cdots 0 & & 0 \cdots 0 \\ 0 \cdots 0 & 0 \cdots 0 & \\ \vdots \ddots \vdots & \vdots \ddots \vdots & M_m \\ 0 \cdots 0 & 0 \cdots 0 & \end{bmatrix}
$$

Then, all simultaneous equations are as follows:

$$
[C \mid M'] \begin{bmatrix} s \\ g(ID_{A_1}) \\ a_{1_1} \\ \vdots \\ a_{1_{n_1}} \\ g(ID_{A_2}) \\ a_{2_1} \\ \vdots \\ \vdots \\ g(ID_{A_m}) \\ a_{m_1} \\ \vdots \\ a_{m_{n_m}} \end{bmatrix} = \begin{bmatrix} * \\ * \\ * \\ \vdots \\ * \\ * \\ * \end{bmatrix}
$$

Here, we prove that matrices $M_1, M_2, \ldots, M_m$ are regular. Let a_h ($h = 1, 2, \ldots, n_j + 1$) be column vectors and $c_h \in \mathbb{F}_p$ be scalars on M_j. Then $c_1 a_1 + c_2 a_2 + \cdots + c_{n_j+1} a_{n_j+1} = 0$ holds. Let M_j' be the matrix which is M_j except the first column and the $(n_j + 1)$'th row. Then M_j' is regular, since it is a Vandermonde matrix. We can obtain that $c_2 = c_3 = \ldots = c_{n_j+1} = 0$ since $a_1 = [0, 0, \ldots, 0, -1]^T$. Therefore $-c_1 = 0$ holds (and so $c_1 = 0$). That is, M_j is regular.

Let $C_j = [1, 1, \ldots, 1]^T$ ($j = 1, \ldots, m$) which is the first column of N_j. Then, there exist $\alpha_i \in \mathbb{F}_p$ such that $C_j = \sum_{i=1}^{n_j+1} \alpha_i a_i$. Since this condition is satisfied for all j ($j = 1, 2, \ldots, m$), $rank([C \mid N]) = rank(N)$ holds. By Proposition 1, an unqualified set cannot compute any information about s. □

Similar to the above, we prove Corollary 1. The notion was defined in the proof of Lemma 2.

Corollary 1. *We assume that $P_s \notin C$. In this situation, $g(ID_{A_j})$ ($j = 1, 2, \ldots, m$) cannot be determined from $R(n' + 1, m, n')$ simultaneous equations.*

Proof. Similar to Lemma 2, let $C_j = [1, 1, \ldots, 1]^T$ which is the first column of N_j. Then, there exist $\alpha_i \in \mathbb{F}_p$ such that $C_j = \sum_{i=1}^{n_j+1} \alpha_i a_i$. Then also $[C_j \mid a_2\ a_3\ \cdots\ a_{n_j+1}]$ is a Vandermonde matrix. Then, there exist β_i ($i = 1, 2, \ldots, n_j + 1$) such that $a_1 = \beta_1 C_j + \sum_{i=2}^{n_j+1} \beta_i a_i$. By Proposition 1, an unqualified set cannot compute any information about $g(ID_{\mathcal{A}_j})$. We previously assumed that $ID_{\mathcal{A}_i} \neq ID_{\mathcal{A}_j}$. Therefore $g(ID_{\mathcal{A}_j})$ only appear on N_j, and an unqualified set cannot compute any information about $g(ID_{\mathcal{A}_j})$ ($j = 1, 2, \ldots, m$). □

By Lemma 2 and Corollary 3, Theorem 3 is proven by regarding as the share of P_s, $g(x)$, is distributed by using the Shamir (k, ℓ)-threshold secret sharing.

Next, we assume that $P_s \in \mathcal{C}$, i.e., malicious participants can obtain a polynomial $g(x)$. We can obtain the corollary as follows:

Corollary 2. *We assume that an access structure for n' participants and one special participant P_s is unanimous, i.e., $(n'+1, n'+1)$ threshold structure. Then $V(n'+1, m, t) > R(n'+1, m, t)$.*

Proof. The case $P_s \notin \mathcal{C}$, obviously hold. We assume that $P_s \in \mathcal{C}$. Then the number of participants that can collude is n' ($n'-1$ participants and P_s). Therefore $V(n'+1, m, t) = R(n'+1, m, t) + (n'-t-m+2) > R(n'+1, m, t) + (n'-n'-1+2) = R(n'+1, m, t) + 1$ holds. □

Lemma 3. *We assume that an access structure for n' participants and one special participant P_s is unanimous, i.e., $(n'+1, n'+1)$ threshold structure. Then the secret value s cannot be determined from $R(n'+1, m, n')$ simultaneous equations.*

Proof. Let $f(x) = s + a_1 x + a_2 x^2 + \cdots + a_{n'} x^{n'}$ be the polynomial associated with $B = \{P_s, P_1, P_2, \ldots, P_{n'}\}$. W.l.o.g., we assume P_1 to be the honest participant. So, malicious participants can obtain simultaneous equation as follows (2):

$$N' = \begin{bmatrix} 1 & -1 & ID_1 & ID_1^2 & \cdots & ID_1^{n'} \\ 1 & 0 & ID_2 & ID_2^2 & \cdots & ID_2^{n'} \\ \vdots & \vdots & \vdots & \vdots & \ddots & \vdots \\ 1 & 0 & ID_{n'} & ID_{n'}^2 & \cdots & ID_{n'}^{n'} \\ 1 & 0 & ID_D & ID_D^2 & \cdots & ID_D^{n'} \end{bmatrix} \text{ and } N' \begin{bmatrix} s \\ \omega_1 \\ a_1 \\ a_2 \\ \vdots \\ a_{n'} \end{bmatrix} = \begin{bmatrix} 0 \\ \omega_2 \\ \omega_3 \\ \vdots \\ \omega_{n'} \\ g(ID_D) \end{bmatrix} \quad (2)$$

Similar to Lemma 2, the $(n'+1) \times (n'+1)$ matrix which is N' except the first column is Vandermonde. Moreover, the $(n'+1) \times (n'+1)$ matrix which is N' except the second column is also Vandermonde. By Proposition 1, the set of malicious participants cannot determine the secret value s and the shares of honest participants. □

By Lemma 3, Theorem 2 is proven by regarding as the share of P_s, i.e., $g(ID_D) = f(ID_D)$, is publicly opened as u.

A Novel Pyramidal Dual-Tree Directional Filter Bank Domain Color Image Watermarking Algorithm*

Panpan Niu[1,**], Xiangyang Wang[2], and Mingyu Lu[1]

[1] School of Information Science & Technology, Dalian Maritime University,
Dalian, 116026, China
[2] School of Computer & Information Technology, Liaoning Normal University,
Dalian 116029, China
niupanpan3333@yahoo.com.cn, wxy37@126.com

Abstract. Geometric distortion is known as one of the most difficult attacks to resist, for it can desynchronize the location of the watermark and hence causes incorrect watermark detection. It is a challenging work to design a robust color image watermarking scheme against geometric distortions. Based on the Support Vector Regression (SVR) and Pyramidal Dual-Tree Directional Filter Bank (PDTDFB), a new color image watermarking algorithm against geometric distortion is proposed. Experimental results show that the proposed scheme is not only invisible and robust against common image processing operations such as median filtering, noise adding, and JPEG compression etc., but also robust against the geometrical distortions and combined attacks.

Keywords: Color image watermarking, geometric distortion, pyramidal dual-tree directional filter bank (PDTDFB), support vector regression (SVR).

1 Introduction

In recent years, there is an unprecedented development in the robust image watermarking field [1]. However, numerous watermarking schemes have been proposed and applied for gray images. Several existing watermarking schemes for color images are robust to common signal processing, but show severe problems to geometric distortion. Even a slight geometric distortion may significantly influence the extraction of watermark because the synchronization of the watermark is destroyed. Hence, it is a challenging work to design a robust color image watermarking scheme against geometrical distortions.

Nowadays, several approaches that counterattack geometric distortions for color images have been developed. These schemes can be roughly divided into invariant transform, template insertion and feature-based algorithms [2]-[3].

---

* This work was supported by the National Natural Science Foundation of China under Grant No. 60873222 & 61073133, and Liaoning Research Project for Institutions of Higher Education of China under Grant No. L2010230.
** Corresponding author.

S. Qing et al. (Eds.): ICICS 2011, LNCS 7043, pp. 158–172, 2011.

Invariant transform: The most obvious way to achieve resilience against geometric distortions for color images is to use an invariant transform. In[4]-[5], the watermark is embedded in an affine-invariant domain by using Multidimensional Fourier transform, generalized Radon transform, QSVD transform, and geometric moments respectively. Tsui *et al.* [6] encodes the $L^*a^*b^*$ components of color images and watermarks are embedded as vectors by modifying the Spatiochromatic Discrete Fourier Transform (SCDFT) coefficients and using the Quaternion Fourier Transform (QFT). Jiang et al. [7] transferred the color host image into hypercomplex frequency domain and selected some real parts of the hypercomplex frequency spectra of the color host image. Despite that they are robust against common signal processing, those techniques involving invariant domain suffer from implementation issues and are vulnerable to global affine transformations.

Template insertion: Another solution to cope with geometric distortions for color images is to identify the transformation by retrieving artificially embedded references. Fu *et al.* [8] presented a novel oblivious color image watermarking scheme based on Linear Discriminant Analysis (LDA). Jiang *et al.* [9] proposed a new watermarking scheme based on the multi-channel image watermarking framework, which generates a watermarking template from one of image channels data. However, this kind of approach can be tampered with by the malicious attack. As for random bending attacks, the template-based methods will be incompetent to estimate the attack parameters. Furthermore, the volume of watermark data is lesser.

Feature-based: The last category that counterattacks geometric distortions for color images is based on media features. Its basic idea is that, by binding the watermark with the geometrically invariant image features (Local Feature Region, LFR) [10], the watermark detection can be done without synchronization error. In [11], the steady color image feature points are extracted by using multi-scale Harris-Laplace detector, and the LFRs are ascertained adaptively according to the feature scale theory. However, some drawbacks indwelled in current feature-based schemes for color images restrict the performance of watermarking system. Firstly, the feature point extraction is sensitive to image modification. Secondly, the fixed value is used to determine the size of LFR so that the watermarking scheme is vulnerable to the scale change of the image. Thirdly, the current feature-based watermarking has not constructed the invariant region of LFR, which lower the robustness against local geometric attacks.

In order to effectively resolve the problem of resisting geometric distortions, the support vector machine (SVM) theory is introduced to the color image watermarking domain [12]-[13]. Wang et al. [14] propose a robust image watermarking algorithm against geometric distortions. In watermark detection, according to the high correlation among subimages, the digital watermark can be recovered by using SVR technique. Based on a large number of theory analyses and experimental results, we can easily come to the conclusion that it is possible to resist geometric distortions by utilizing the advanced SVM, but the current SVM based image watermarking have shortcomings as follows: (i) They are not very robust against some geometric distortions, such as cropping, mixed attacks etc; (ii) In watermark detection procedure, the original watermark signal is needed, so it is unfavorable to practical application.

In this paper, a new color image watermarking algorithm with good visual quality and reasonable resistance toward geometric distortions is proposed, in which the Support Vector Regression (SVR) and Pyramidal Dual-Tree Directional Filter Bank (PDTDFB) are utilized.

2   An Introduction to Pyramidal Dual-Tree Directional Filter Bank

The pyramidal dual-tree directional filter bank (PDTDFB) is a new image decomposition, which is recently proposed in [15]. The PDTDFB transform has the following advantages: multiscale and multidirectional transform, efficient implementation, high angular resolution, low redundant ratio, shiftable subbands, and provide local phase information. For the PDTDFB transform, the image decomposition implemented by a filter bank (FB) consists of a Laplacian pyramid and a pair of directional filter banks (DFBs), designated as primal and dual DFBs. Both DFBs are constructed by a binary-tree of two channel fan FBs. The filters of these FBs are designed to have special phase functions so that the overall directional filters of the dual DFB are the Hilbert transforms of the corresponding filters in the primal DFB. Therefore, the two DFBs can be viewed as a single FB with complex directional filters producing complex subband images, whose real and imaginary parts are the outputs of the primal and dual DFB, respectively. A multiresolution representation is obtained by reiterating the decomposition at the lowpass branch. It is shown in [15] that if the lowpass filters used in the Laplacian pyramid have bandpass regions restricted in $[-\pi/2, \pi/2]^2$, then the complex directional subbands at all scale are shiftable.

The object of combining the Laplacian pyramid and dual-tree DFB is to provide a FB that is multiresolution and multidirectional at the same time. However, the Laplacian pyramid structure is not essential to the shiftability of the overall FB. In fact, we can combine any shiftable two-channel 2-D multiresolution FB with the dualtree DFB to obtain an overall shiftable FB. Moreover, it can be shown that the synthesis side of the Laplacian pyramid structure is suboptimal. In this paper, we utilized the construction of a shiftable FB by combining the dual-tree DFBs with a multiresolution FB as in Fig. 1. The advantage of the shiftable FB is that it provides an approximately tight-frame decomposition, which is a desirable property in an overcomplete decomposition. However, the FB is no longer exactly perfect reconstruction and the pyramidal filters are nonseparable.

The new structure for the PDTDFB is illustrated in Fig. 1. The input image is first pass through a two-channel undecimated FB. The filters satisfy perfect reconstruction (PR) condition:

$$|R_0(\omega)|^2 + |L_0(\omega)|^2 = 1 \tag{1}$$

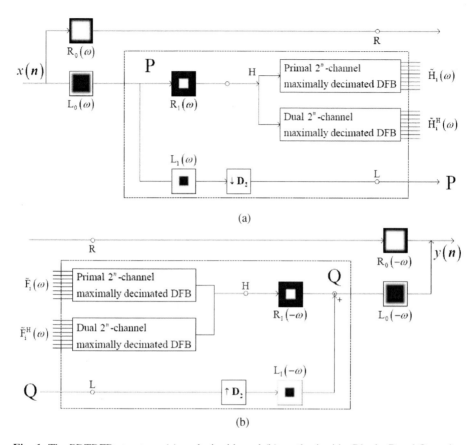

(a)

(b)

Fig. 1. The PDTDFB structure: (a) analysis side and (b) synthesis side. Blocks P and Q can be reiterated at lower scale for a multiscale representation.

The filter $L_0(\omega)$ is a wide-band lowpass filter while $R_0(\omega)$ is a highpass filter. A slice of the two-dimensional frequency responses of these two filters are in Fig. 2(a). After the undecimated FB, the PDTDFB consists of multiple levels of block P (or Q for the synthesis side) for each scale. This block consists of two filters $R_1(\omega)$ and $L_1(\omega)$ and the dual-tree DFBs. The low frequency component, after filtered by the low-pass filter $L_1(\omega)$ and decimated by $D_2 = 2I$, is fed into the second level decomposition for the second resolution of directional subbands. The filters in blocks P and Q are designed to satisfy the PR and non-aliasing condition (see Fig. 2(b)):

$$\left| R_1(\omega) \right|^2 + \frac{1}{4}\left| L_1(\omega) \right|^2 = 1 \tag{2}$$

This condition can be approximated by FIR filters. Similar to the Steerable pyramid, the synthesis filters are the time reverse versions of the analysis filters. The design of the PDTDFB can be divided into two parts as follows:

•   The design of two-channel FBs, which are used to create multiresolution decomposition. The first is the undecimated two-channel FB with two filters $R_0(\omega)$ and $L_0(\omega)$ (see Fig. 1). The second is the multirate FB with two filters $R_1(\omega)$ and $L_1(\omega)$.

•   The design of the fan FBs of the DFBs. Since the design of the conventional DFB has been discussed extensively, for this part we will only focus on the fan FB at the second level of the binary-tree of the dual DFB, which satisfies the phase constraints.

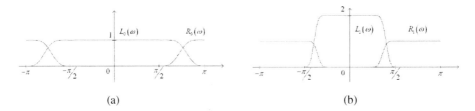

            (a)   (b)

Fig. 2. A slice of the 2-D frequency responses of (a) $R_0(\omega)$ and $L_0(\omega)$, and (b) $R_1(\omega)$ and $L_1(\omega)$

Each of the two filter design problems above has different design constraints. Since all of these constraints are on the frequency responses, all filters will be designed in frequency domain. In theory, these filters have infinite impulse responses. Sufficiently smooth transition band will be included in order to obtain reasonably short and effective impulse responses. Our approach is to define the ideal filters in frequency domain by using the Meyer function. Then the approximation FIR filters are obtained by truncation of the inverse discrete Fourier transform of the ideal filters. Fig.3. gives experimental results of applying the pyramidal dual-tree directional filter bank (PDTDFB) decomposition with 4 scale and 8 directions on Zoneplate image.

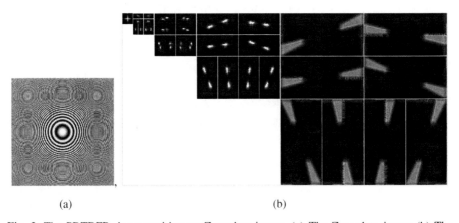

          (a)   (b)

Fig. 3. The PDTDFB decomposition on Zoneplate image. (a) The Zoneplate image (b) The PDTDFB decomposition result.

The PDTDFB transform has all the nice properties of the contourlet transform, such as multiresolution, multidirectional and low redundancy ratio. Moreover, its subbands are shiftable and provide local phase information. The nonsubsampled contourlet transform [14] also provides shiftable subbands but at the cost of much higher redundant ratio and computational complexity. Therefore, the PDTDFB has been proven to be more efficient in image processing compared to other directional multi-resolution transforms.

3   Watermark Embedding Scheme

Based on the above ideas, a new PDTDFB domain color image watermarking algorithm with good visual quality and reasonable resistance toward geometric distortions is proposed. Firstly, the geometrically invariant space is constructed by using color image normalization, and a significant region is obtained from it. Secondly, the PDTDFB transform is performed on the green channel of the significant region, and the digital watermark is embedded into host color image by modifying the low frequency PDTDFB coefficients, in which the HVS masking is used to control the watermark embedding strength.

Let $I = \{f^R(x, y), f^G(x, y), f^B(x, y)\}(0 \leq x < M, 0 \leq y < N)$ denote a host digital image (color image), and $f^R(x, y), f^G(x, y), f^B(x, y)$ are the color component values at position (x, y).

$W = \{w(i, j), 0 \leq i < P, 0 \leq j < Q\}$ is a binary image to be embedded within the host image, and $w(i, j) \in \{0,1\}$ is the pixel value at (i, j). The digital watermark embedding scheme can be summarized as follows.

3.1   Watermark Preprocessing

In order to dispel the pixel space relationship of the binary watermark image, and improve the robustness of the whole digital watermark system, the binary watermark image is scrambled from W to W_1 by using Arnold transform. Then, it is transformed into a one-dimensional sequence of ones and zeros as follows:

$$W_2 = \{w_2(k) = w_1(i, j), 0 \leq i < P, 0 \leq j < Q, k = i \times Q + j, w_2(k) \in \{0,1\}\} \quad (3)$$

3.2   Image Normalization and Significant Region Extraction

In order to improve the robustness against geometrical distortions, we apply the color image normalization on origin host image to produce the standard size normalized image, as shown in Fig. 4(b). The significant region is extracted from the normalized color image by using the invariant centroid, which is more suitable for embedding digital watermark, as shown in Fig.4(c).

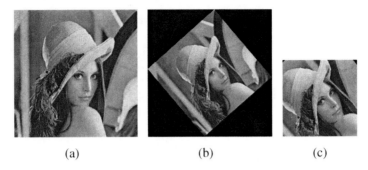

| (a) | (b) | (c) |

Fig. 4. The color image normalization and significant region extraction: (a) The color image, (b) The normalized version, (c) The significant region

3.3   The PDTDFB of the Significant Region

When the RGB components of the colored images are visualized separately, the green channel shows the best contrast, whereas the red and blue channels show low contrast and are very noisy. Therefore, the green component of significant region was selected to be embedded watermarking in this paper.

We perform one level PDTDFB decomposition on the green component of significant region, and then obtain the corresponding lowpass subband A.

3.4   Digital Watermark Embedding

Watermark embedding method

The lowpass subband A is divided into 3×3 PDTDFB coefficients blocks A_i $(i = 0,1,\cdots, S_1/3 \times S_2/3 - 1)$. By using secret key K_1, $P \times Q$ PDTDFB coefficients blocks are selected from the lowpass subband A. The digital watermark is embedded into the green component of significant region by modifying the selected $P \times Q$ PDTDFB coefficient blocks B_k.

$$b'_k(x+l, y+r) = \begin{cases} b_k(x+l, y+r) + C(x+l, y+r) \cdot S(h^2(B_k)), if \ w_2(k)=1 \\ b_k(x+l, y+r) - C(x+l, y+r) \cdot S(h^2(B_k)), if \ w_2(k)=0 \end{cases} \quad (4)$$

$$(k = 0,1,\cdots, P \times Q - 1) \quad (l = -1,0,1; r = -1,0,1; \mod(l+r,2)=0)$$

where $b'_k(x+l, y+r)$ is the modified PDTDFB coefficients in block B_k, $b_k(x+l, y+r)$ is the original PDTDFB coefficients in block B_k, and $C(x, y)$ is the watermark embedding strength according to the HVS masking of the color image, adaptively. $S(h^2(B_k))$ is the sum of the homogeneity features for all PDTDFB coefficients in block B_k:

$$S(h^2(B_k)) = \sum_{l=-1}^{1}\sum_{r=-1}^{1}(h^2(b_k(x+l, y+r)))$$ (5)

In this paper, we employ the concept of the homogeneity [16] to extract homogeneous regions in each PDTDFB coefficient in the lowpass subband A. Assume $b(x, y)$ is the PDTDFB coefficient at the location (x, y) in the lowpass subband A. The homogeneity is represented by:

$$h(b(x, y)) = 1 - E(b(x, y), w_m(x, y)) \times V(b(x, y), w_n(x, y))$$ (6)

$$V(b(x, y), w_n(x, y)) = \frac{v(x, y)}{\max\{v(x, y)\}}, \quad E(b(x, y), w_m(x, y)) = \frac{e(x, y)}{\max\{e(x, y)\}}$$ (7)

$e(x, y)$ and $v(x, y)$ are the discontinuity and the standard deviation of the coefficient $b(x, y)$ at the location (x, y).

Computing the quantization step

We determine the different mask properties of the human vision system about the luminance, texture and edge of the color host image, and then combine these three masking together to get a comprehensive final masking for the watermark embedding strength $C = M_T - M_E + M_L$. M_L is the luminance masking, M_T is the texture masking, and M_E is the edge masking. The calculations of these three maskings are as follows:

(1) Let $f_A(x, y)$ is the luminance value of the pixel at (x, y), and $\overline{f_A}$ denote the local average luminance value of the pixels within the sliding window of size 5×5:

$$f_A = \sqrt{f_R^2(x, y) + f_G^2(x, y) + f_B^2(x, y)}, P_L = (\overline{f_A} - \overline{f_{mid}})^2$$ (8)

where $\overline{f_{mid}}$ is the midst luminance value of the color host image [7]. The calculation of the luminance masking M_L is as follows:

$$M_L = round\left(\frac{8P_L}{\max(P_L)}\right)$$ (9)

(2) As for the texture masking, firstly, we use the absolute value of the distance between each pixel and local average value of the pixels within the sliding window as the masking. The size of the sliding window is still 3×3:

$$P_{TCo} = \left|Co(x, y) - \overline{Co}(x, y)\right|$$ (10)

$$\bar{Co}(x, y) = \frac{1}{(2L+1)^2} \sum_{k=-L}^{L} \sum_{l=-L}^{L} Co(x+k, y+l) \tag{11}$$

where, $Co(x, y)$ is the color component values at position (x, y), $Co = \{R, G, B\}$. P_{TCo} denote the texture masking of each color channel, and $(2L+1)^2$ represents the number of pixels in the image block[17].

Then, we calculate the average value of the texture masking of three color channels and the calculation of M_T is as follows:

$$P_T = \frac{1}{3}(P_{TR} + P_{TG} + P_{TB}), M_T = round\left(\frac{8P_T}{max(P_T)}\right) \tag{12}$$

(3) The way to create edge masking is using Canny's algorithm and the dilated edge detection. Canny's algorithm is good at detecting the weak edges. The dilated edge detection of the image can be used as a filter to wipe off the non-edge regions in the edge masking derived from the Laplacian filter and to only keep the edge areas. The calculation of the edge masking M_E is as follows:

$$P_E = E_{D2}(E_{D1}(I)), M_E = round\left(\frac{8P_E}{max(P_E)}\right) \tag{13}$$

where I is the original image, $E_{D1}(\cdot)$ is the edge detection operation, and $E_{D2}(\cdot)$ is the dilation operation.

3.5   Obtaining the Watermarked Color Image

Firstly, the watermarked green component of significant region can be obtained by performing the inverse PDTDFB transform with the modified lowpass PDTDFB coefficients. Secondly, the watermarked significant region of the normalized color image can be obtained by combining the watermarked green component, and original red component and blue component. Finally, we can obtain the watermarked color image by performing the inverse color image normalization with the watermarked significant region.

4   Watermark Detection Scheme

According to the high correlation among different channels of the color image, a robust color image watermarking detection algorithm based on support vector regression (SVR) [18] is proposed, which neither needs the original host color image nor any other side information. The main steps of the watermark detecting procedure developed can be described as follows.

4.1   Image Normalization and Significant Region Extraction

Color image normalization is applied on the watermarked color image I^* to produce the standard size normalized image. The significant region is extracted from the normalized watermarked color image by using the invariant centroid.

4.2   The PDTDFB of the Significant Region

After one level PDTDFB decomposition has been applied on red component and green component of significant region, the corresponding lowpass subbands RA^* and GA^* are obtained.

4.3   Selecting the Embedded Position

The lowpass subbands RA^* and GA^* are divided into 3×3 PDTDFB coefficients blocks RA_i^* and GA_i^* $(i=0,1,\cdots,\frac{S_1}{3}\times\frac{S_2}{3}-1)$. By using the same secret key K_1, $P\times Q$ PDTDFB coefficients blocks RB_k^* and GB_k^* $(k=0,1,\cdots,P\times Q-1)$ are selected from RA_i^* and GA_i^*, respectively. Here, the PDTDFB coefficients RB_{k1}^* and GB_{k1}^* are used for training the SVR model, and the other PDTDFB coefficients RB_{k2}^* and GB_{k2}^* are used for extracting digital watermark.

$$CB_{k1}^* = \{b_k^C(x+l, y), b_k^C(x, y+r), l=-1,1, r=-1,1, k=0,1,\cdots,P\times Q-1\}\ (C\in\{R,G\}) \quad (14)$$

$$CB_{k2}^* = \{b_k^C(x, y), b_k^C(x+l, y+r), l=-1,1, r=-1,1, k=0,1,\cdots,P\times Q-1\}\ (C\in\{R,G\}) \quad (15)$$

4.4   SVR Training

Let $S(h^2(B_{k1}))$ (see equation (5)) be the sum of the homogeneity features for all PDTDFB coefficients in block RB_{k1}^*, and RV_{k1}^* be the average value of a part of the coefficients in block RB_{k1}^*:

$$RV_{k1}^* = \frac{1}{4}\left(\sum_{l=-1}^{1} b_k^R(x+l, y) + \sum_{r=-1}^{1} b_k^R(x, y+r) - 2b_k^R(x, y)\right) \quad (16)$$

In the same way, GV_{k1}^* is the average value of a part of the coefficients in block GB_{k1}^*.

Then, let RV_{k1}^* and $S(h^2(B_{k1}))$ be the feature vectors for training, and GV_{k1}^* be the training objective. We can obtain the training samples as following:

$$\Omega_k^* = \left\{ GV_{k1}^*, RV_{k1}^*, S(h^2(RB_{k1})) \right\} (k = 0,1,\cdots,P\times Q-1)$$

So, the SVR model can be obtained by training.

4.5   Digital Watermark Extracting

Let $S(h^2(B_{k2}))$ (see equation (5)) be the sum of the homogeneity features for all PDTDFB coefficients in block RB_{k2}^*. RV_{k2}^* is the average value of a part of the coefficients in block RB_{k2}^*:

$$RV_{k2}^* = \frac{1}{5}\left(\sum_{l=-1}^{1} b_k^R(x+l, y+l) + \sum_{r=-1}^{1} b_k^R(x-r, y+r) - b_k^R(x, y) \right) \qquad (17)$$

Let RV_{k2}^* and $S(h^2(B_{k2}))$ be the input vector.

Then, the actual output vector $\overline{GV}_{k2}^*$ can be obtained by using the well trained SVR model. The digital watermark $w_2^*(k)$ can be extracted by comparing the actual output vector $\overline{GV}_{k2}^*$ with the GV_{k2}^* (GV_{k2}^* is the average value of a part of the coefficients in block GB_{k2}^*), and the rule of extracting digital watermark can be described

$$w_2^*(k) = \begin{cases} 1, & if \quad GV_{k2}^* > \overline{GV}_{k2}^* \\ 0, & else \end{cases}, (k = 0,1,\cdots,P\times Q-1) \qquad (18)$$

4.6   Watermark Postprocessing

All the detected watermark bits $w_2^*(k)$ are rearranged to form the binary watermark image W_1^*, and the watermark image $W^* = \{w^*(i,j), 0 \le i < P, 0 \le j < Q\}$ can be obtained by descrambling.

5   Simulation Results

We test the proposed watermarking scheme on the popular 24bit true color images 512×512 Lena, Mandrill, and Barbara, and a 32×32 binary image is used as the digital watermark, as shown in Fig.5. The size of the significant region is $S_1 = S_2 = 256$, the number of training sample is 3072, and the radius-based function (RBF) is selected as the SVR kernel function, and other parameters are set respectively to $\gamma = 0.125$, $C = 78$. Besides, the PSNR (Peak Signal-to-Noise Ratio) is used to measure the visual quality of the watermarked images. Finally, experimental results are compared with schemes in [14] [19] and [8].

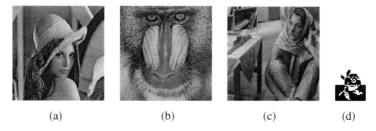

(a)   (b)   (c)   (d)

Fig. 5. The test images and digital watermark: (a) The test image Lena, (b) The test image Mandrill, (c) The test image Barbara, (d) The digital watermark

5.1   Performance Test

As shown in Fig.6, (a), (b) and (c) are the watermarked color images (Lena, Mandrill, and Barbara) and the extracted watermarks obtained by using the proposed scheme. The transparency comparison results in terms of PSNR listed in Table 1 clearly show that proposed method outperforms other three methods.

(a)   (b)   (c)

Fig. 6. The watermarked color images and the extracted watermarks obtained by the proposed scheme: (a) Lena (PSNR=40.32dB, BER=0.0078), (b) Mandrill (PSNR=40.01dB, BER=0), (c) Barbara (PSNR=40.34dB, BER=0.0088)

Table 1. The performance test for different color image watermarking scheme

Test image		Our me-thod	Scheme [14]	Scheme [19]	Scheme [8]
Lena	BER	0.0078	0.0166	0.0098	0.0186
	PSNR(dB)	40.32	41.93	39.43	38.11
Mandrill	BER	0	0.0020	0.0146	0.0889
	PSNR(dB)	40.01	41.67	38.54	38.91
Barbara	BER	0.0088	0.0176	0.0107	0.0430
	PSNR(dB)	40.34	40.71	38.53	39.72

5.2   Performance Test

In order to test the robustness of the proposed scheme, we have done extensive experiments. In this study, reliability was measured as the bit error rate (BER) of extracted watermark. Fig.7, Fig.8 and Fig.9 show the results of comparison with scheme [14] [19] and [8].

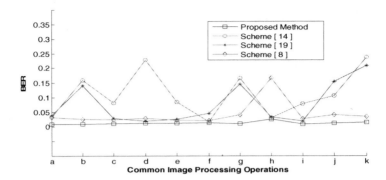

Fig. 7. The watermark detection results for common image processing operations(Lena): (a) Gaussian filtering (3×3), (b) Wiener filtering, (c) Salt and peppers noise (0.01), (d) Speckle noise （0.03, (e) Sharpening, (f) Histogram equalization, (g) Blurring, (h) Gamma correction, (i) JPEG90, (j) JPEG70, (k) JPEG50

Common image processing operations: Traditional signal processing attacks affect watermark detection by reducing the watermark energy. Fig.7 shows the quantitative results for the common image processing operations. It is evident that our scheme is more robust against wiener filtering, histogram equalization, blurring, gamma correction etc., compared with scheme [14] [19] and [8].

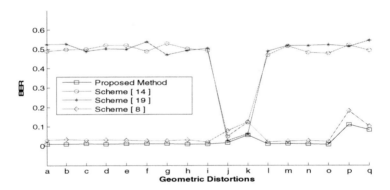

Fig. 8. The watermark detection results for geometric attacks(Lena): (a) Rotation 5°, (b) Rotation 45°, (c) Rotation 70°, (d) Scaling 1.2, (e) Scaling 1.5, (f) Scaling 2, (g) Translation(H 20,V 20), (h) Translation(H 15,V 5), (i) Translation(H 0,V 50), (j) Cropping 10%, (k) Cropping 30%, (l) Length- width ratio change(1.1,1.0), (m) Length-width ratio change(1.2,1.0), (n) Affine Transformation[5; 1.0, 1.0; 0.3, 0.1], (o) Affine Transformation[10; 1.0, 1.0; 0.5, 0.2], (p) Flip Horizontally, (q) Flip Vertically

Geometric distortions: Our scheme can resist RST attacks and it can extract the watermarks directly from the watermarked color images without any auxiliary operations. Fig.8 shows the quantitative results for the geometric distortions, respectively. From these quantity results, it is verified that our scheme yields better robustness than those in scheme [14] [19] and [8].

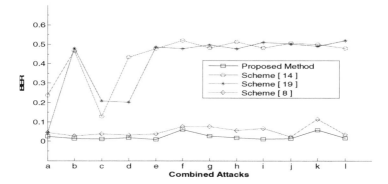

Fig. 9. The watermark detection results for combined attacks(Lena): (a) Gaussian Noise (0.05)+Sharpening, (b) Median Filtering (3×3) + JPEG70, (c) Sharpening+JPEG70, (d) Salt and Peppers Noise (0.01) + Gaussian Filtering (3×3)+JPEG70, (e) Rotation 15°+Scaling1.2, (f) Scaling1.2+Translation(H 5,V15), (g) Rotation 15° +Cropping10%, (h) Rotation 45° +Translation (H 20,V20)+Scaling1.2, (i) Rotation 5° + Median Filtering (3×3), (j) Scaling1.2+ Gaussian Noise(0.05), (k) Translation(H5,V15)+Salt and Peppers Noise(0.01), (l) Affine Transformation[-10; 1.0, 1.0; -0.5, -0.2]+JPEG50

Combined attacks: Except for individual attack, we also conduct some attacks that combine two or more kind of attacks. The combined attacks include median filtering plus Gaussian noise, rotation plus scaling plus translation, affine transformation plus JPEG compression etc. Fig.9 provides the quantitative results for the combined attacks, respectively. It is verified that our scheme yields better robustness than those in scheme [14] [19] and [8].

To sum up, the proposed scheme can efficiently resist common image processing operations, geometric distortions and combined attacks. Comparisons show that the overall performance of our scheme is superior to the existing schemes.

6   Conclusion

This paper presents a blind color image watermarking algorithm by using the Support Vector Regression (SVR) and Pyramidal Dual-Tree Directional Filter Bank (PDTDFB). The extensive experimental works have shown that the proposed color image watermarking has conquered those challenging geometric distortions, such as rotation, translation, scaling, and length-width ratio change etc. Also, the digital watermark can resist some common image processing operations, the geometric distortions and combined attacks.

References

1. Lian, S., Kanellopoulos, D., Ruffo, G.: Recent advances in multimedia information system security. Informatica 33, 3–24 (2009)
2. Zheng, D., Liu, Y., Zhao, J.Y., Saddik, A.E.: A survey of RST invariant image watermarking algorithms. ACM Computing Surveys 39, 1–91 (2007)

3. Zheng, D., Wang, S., Zhao, J.Y.: RST invariant image watermarking algorithm with mathematical modeling and analysis of the watermarking processes. IEEE Trans. on Image Processing 18, 1055–1068 (2009)
4. Lin, S.D., Shie, S.C., Guo, J.Y.: Improving the robustness of DCT-based image watermarking against JPEG compression. Computer Standards & Interfaces 32, 54–60 (2010)
5. Xing, Y., Tan, J.: A color image watermarking scheme resistant against geometrical attacks. Radio Engineering 19, 62–67 (2010)
6. Kin, T.T., Zhang, X.P., Androutsos, D.: Color Image Watermarking Using Multidimensional Fourier Transforms. IEEE Trans. on Information Forensics and Security 3, 16–28 (2008)
7. Jiang, S.H., Zhang, J.Q., Hu, B.: An adaptive watermarking algorithm in the hypercomplex space of a color image. Acta Electronica Sinica 37, 1773–1778 (2009)
8. Fu, Y.G., Shen, R.M.: Color image watermarking scheme based on linear discriminant analysis. Computer Standard & Interfaces 30, 115–120 (2008)
9. Zheng, J.B., Feng, S.: A Color Image Watermarking Scheme in the Associated Domain of DWT and DCT Domains Based on Multi-channel Watermarking Framework. In: Kim, H.-J., Katzenbeisser, S., Ho, A.T.S. (eds.) IWDW 2008. LNCS, vol. 5450, pp. 419–432. Springer, Heidelberg (2009)
10. Liu, K.C.: Wavelet-based watermarking for color images through visual masking. AEU - International Journal of Electronics and Communications 64, 112–124 (2010)
11. Wang, X.Y., Meng, L., Yang, H.Y.: Geometrically invariant color image watermarking scheme using feature points. Science in China Series F-Information Sciences 52, 1605–1616 (2009)
12. Wang, X.Y., Xu, Z.H., Yang, H.Y.: A robust image watermarking algorithm using SVR detection. Expert Systems with Applications 36, 9056–9064 (2009)
13. Tsai, H.H., Sun, D.W.: Color image watermark extraction based on support vector machines. Information Sciences 177, 550–569 (2007)
14. Niu, P.P., Wang, X.Y., Yang, Y.P., Lu, M.Y.: A novel color image watermarking scheme in nonsampled contourlet-domain. Expert Systems with Applications 38, 2081–2098 (2011)
15. Nguyen, T.T., Oraintara, S.: The shiftable complex directional pyramid-part I: theoretical aspects. IEEE Trans. on Signal Processing 56, 4651–4660 (2008)
16. Chaabane, S.B., Sayadi, M., Fnaiech, F.: Colour image segmentation using homogeneity method and data fusion techniques. EURASIP Journal on Advances in Signal Processing, 1–11 (2010)
17. Qi, H.Y., Zheng, D., Zhao, J.Y.: Human visual system based adaptive digital image watermarking. Signal Processing 88, 174–188 (2008)
18. Vapnik, V.: The nature of statistical learning theory. Springer, New York (1995)
19. Peng, H., Wang, J., Wang, W.X.: Image watermarking method in multiwavelet domain based on support vector machines. Journal of Systems and Software 83, 1470–1477 (2010)

Detection for Multiplicative Watermarking in DCT Domain by Cauchy Model

Xiang Yin, Shuoling Peng, and Xinshan Zhu

Department of Information Engineering, Yangzhou University,
Yangzhou, 225009, China
yinxiang@yzu.edu.cn
pengshuoling_02@163.com
ih_yh@yahoo.com.cn

Abstract. In the last decade, the requirement for copyright protection of digital multimedia has become more and more urgent. As an efficient method to address this issue, watermarking has gained a lot of attention. To watermarking system, detectors have an important influence on its performance. In this paper, we propose a new optimal detector to multiplicative watermarking in the discrete cosine transform (DCT) domain, which is based on Cauchy models. Furthermore, theoretical analysis is also presented. The performance of the new detector is confirmed by various experiments.

Keywords: Image watermarking, optimal detector, Cauchy distribution.

1 Introduction

Technology of watermarking has emerged as the digital data security and copyright protection issues has become increasingly important during last few years [1,2]. The basic principle of watermarking is to hide a specific information into a host data (e.g. image, audio, text, etc.) that it is intended to protect. The embedded information can be recovered or detected in the receiving end in order to verify ownership or intellectual property rights.

Up to now, most of published watermark approaches can be divided into two categories according to the different domains that watermark information is embedded: 1) spatial or time domain methods and 2) transform domain methods. Spatial domain methods are not popular for the reason that it can hardly maintain imperceptibility after information embedding, and it also relatively weak to intentional or unintentional attacks, such as filtering, compression, cropping and so on. On the contrary, transform domain methods could easily achieve good transparency of original works by exploiting characteristics of human visual system (HVS). Meanwhile it is robust to many digital data manipulations.

In order to verify the rightful ownership of a digital work, detection of the watermark is necessary. If the original image is available in receiving end, detection becomes simple. But in many real applications such as data monitoring

S. Qing et al. (Eds.): ICICS 2011, LNCS 7043, pp. 173–183, 2011.

or tracking, the original data is not always available, as a result, most of published literatures are concerned with design of blind detectors, which means the original host data is not required during the detection process. The most commonly used detector is the correlation detector, which is optimal only if the host data follows Gaussian distribution [3]. According to signal detection theory, the model of original data is very important and has a crucial influence on the performance of a detector. Since DCT domain coefficients are far from Gaussian distribution, correlation detector can hardly optimal nor robust. As a result, various literatures have considered DCT coefficients with more accurate models to improve the performance of watermark detectors. To additive watermarks, different probability density functions (PDF) have been used, such as generalized Gaussian(GG) and Laplacian [4] to DCT domain coefficients, Laplacian [5], student-t [6], modified Gauss-Hermite (MGD)[7] and NIG [8] to DWT domain coefficients. To multiplicative watermarks, a robust optimum detector in DCT, DWT and DFT domain is proposed by applying generalized Gaussian(GG) and Weibull distribution in [9]. In [10], the locally optimum detector for Barni's multiplicative watermarking scheme is proposed.

Since multiplicative watermarks are robust and suitable for copyright protection, this paper presents our investigation on robust optimum detection of multiplicative watermarks in DCT domain. The low- and mid-frequency DCT coefficients are modeled by Cauchy PDF, originally proposed in [11]. Furthermore, theoretical analysis of the detector is developed. Extensive experiments are carried out to demonstrate the performance of the proposed detector.

2   Multiplicative Watermarking Embedding Process

In this section, we briefly describe the multiplicative watermark embedding procedure in DCT domain [12]. Specifically, consider an image $\mathbf{f}$ in the spatial domain, whose pixels are denoted by $f(i, j)$. Let $\mathbf{x} = \{x_1, x_2, \ldots, x_N\}$ be a set of N host data, each element in$\mathbf{x}$, e.g. $x_i(i = 1, 2, \ldots, N)$, denotes the DCT transform coefficient of original image $\mathbf{f}$. We will apply the DCT transform in blocks of pixels, as in the JPEG standard. We represent watermark signal as $\mathbf{w} = \{w_1, w_2, \ldots, w_N\}$, then the commonly used multiplicative watermark embedding rule is:

$$y_i = x_i(1 + \alpha w_i) \qquad i = 1, 2, \ldots, N \qquad (1)$$

where y_i is the sequence of watermarked signal, and α is an amplitude parameter which corresponds to a watermark power. α can be decided in two ways, one is the deterministic method which means α is set to be a specific value that is usually much smaller than 1.0 in multiplicative watermarks to keep the watermark imperceptible. The other method is to select α adaptively according to each subband DCT coefficients. For simplicity, in this paper, we set α to a specific value.

3 Proposed Watermark Detector

In general, most copyright protection applications contain a known watermark that is available both to the sender and receiver. Hence, the verification of existence, i.e. the detection of the watermark, is sufficient. Similar to signal detection problem in communications, watermark signal is regarded as the desired signal and host image data play the role of unknown noise. Thus, the verification of the existence of watermark in DCT coefficients of an image can be formulated as a binary hypothesis test given by

$$H_0 : y_i = x_i$$
$$H_1 : y_i = x_i(1 + \alpha \cdot w_i)$$

(2)

where two hypotheses are established, i.e. the null and the alternative hypotheses, corresponding to the existence and non-existence of the watermark, respectively. Based on Neyman-Pearson criterion, the decision rule of watermark detection can be formulated as follows:

$$\Lambda(\mathbf{Y}) \underset{H_0}{\overset{H_1}{\gtrless}} \eta$$

(3)

where η is the decision threshold, it is selected by the rule that minimizes the probability of miss-detection for a bounded false alarm probability. $\Lambda(\mathbf{Y})$ is the likelihood ratio defined as

$$\Lambda(\mathbf{Y}) = \frac{p(\mathbf{Y}|H_1)}{p(\mathbf{Y}|H_0)}$$

(4)

This ratio is often simplified by taking natural logarithm, which leads to

$$l(\mathbf{Y}) = \ln\left(\frac{p(\mathbf{Y}|H_1)}{p(\mathbf{Y}|H_0)}\right) \underset{H_0}{\overset{H_1}{\gtrless}} \eta$$

(5)

In order to obtain an optimal detector, an accurate model to the statistical characteristics of the DCT coefficients is crucial, the more accuracy of the model, the higher performance of the detector. In previous literatures, Laplacian and generalized Gaussian distribution (GGD) have often been used to characterize the data. But as pointed out in [4], even the GGD, are not appropriate for DCT coefficients, as they exhibit heavier tails than GGD can describe. In this paper, we model original data by Cauchy distribution, as this PDF shows heavier tails than GGD, and meets with the feature of DCT subband coefficients [13]. The PDF of Cauchy distribution is as follows

$$p_{\mathbf{X}}(x) = \frac{1}{\pi} \frac{\gamma}{\gamma^2 + (x - \delta)^2}$$

(6)

where γ is the data dispersion and δ is the location parameter. In order to attain the statistical decision function in (5), the two PDFs under both hypotheses H_0

and H_1 are required. From above discussion, we know that the low- and mid-frequency DCT coefficients of original image follow Cauchy distribution, to get PDF of watermarked data y_i, two assumptions are provided.

Assumption 1: y_i are i.i.d random variables.

Assumption 2: y_i follows the same distribution as x_i, i.e. Cauchy distribution, but has different parameters.

The first assumption comes from the fact that DCT transform approximates Karhunen-Loeve transform, and the second assumption lies in that usually the embedding strength is much smaller than 1 to keep the imperceptibility requirement of watermarked image.

Combined with assumption 1,2 and (5)(6), we can attain the optimal decision rule

$$
\begin{aligned}
l(\mathbf{Y}) &= \ln\left(\frac{p(\mathbf{Y}|H_1)}{p(\mathbf{Y}|H_0)}\right) = \ln\left(\frac{\prod\limits_{i=1}^{N}\frac{1}{1+\alpha w_i}p_{\mathbf{x}}\left(\frac{y_i}{1+\alpha w_i}\right)}{\prod\limits_{i=1}^{N}p_{\mathbf{x}}(y_i)}\right) \\
&= \ln\left(\frac{\prod\limits_{i=1}^{N}\frac{1}{\pi}\frac{\gamma}{\gamma^2+(\frac{y_i}{1+\alpha w_i}-\delta)}\frac{1}{1+\alpha w_i}}{\prod\limits_{i=1}^{N}\frac{1}{\pi}\frac{\gamma}{\gamma^2+(y_i-\delta)^2}}\right) \\
&= \sum_{i=1}^{N}\ln\left(\frac{(1+\alpha w_i)(\gamma^2+(y_i-\delta)^2)}{\gamma^2(1+\alpha w_i)^2+(y_i-(1+\alpha w_i)\delta)^2}\right)
\end{aligned}
\tag{7}
$$

where N is the number of subband coefficients to be watermarked.

4   Performance Analysis

Based on Neyman-Pearson criterion, the performance of the detectors can be measured by the probability of detection (p_{det}) under a given probability of false alarm (p_{fa}). The probability of false alarm is

$$
\begin{aligned}
p_{fa} &= \Pr\left(l\left(\mathbf{Y}\right)|H_0 > \eta\right) \\
&= Q\left(\frac{\eta-m_0}{\sigma_0}\right)
\end{aligned}
\tag{8}
$$

where $Q(x) = \frac{1}{\sqrt{2\pi}}\int_x^{+\infty}e^{-t^2/2}dt$, m_0 is the mean and σ_0^2 is the variance of $l(\mathbf{Y})$ under hypothesis H_0, respectively.

The detection probability is

$$
\begin{aligned}
p_{\text{det}} &= \Pr\left(l\left(\mathbf{Y}\right)|H_1 > \eta\right) \\
&= Q\left(\frac{\eta-m_1}{\sigma_1}\right) \\
&= Q\left(\frac{m_0-m_1+\sigma_0 Q^{-1}(P_{fa})}{\sigma_1}\right)
\end{aligned}
\tag{9}
$$

where m_1 is the mean and σ_1^2 is the variance of $l(\mathbf{Y})$ under hypothesis H_1, respectively. Therefore, the theoretical performance to a detector can be determined by m_0, m_1, σ_0 and σ_1. To the proposed detector, these parameters are estimated as follows

$$
m_0 = \sum_{i=1}^{N}\ln\frac{(1-\alpha)^{1/2}(\gamma^2+(x_i-\delta)^2)}{x_1 x_2}
\tag{10}
$$

$$m_1 = \sum_{i=1}^{N} \ln \frac{(1-\alpha^2)^{1/2}}{x_3 x_4} \tag{11}$$

$$\sigma_0^2 = \sum_{i=1}^{N} \frac{1}{2} \left[\ln^2 \frac{(1+\alpha)x_2}{(1-\alpha^2)^{1/2}x_1} + \ln^2 \frac{(1-\alpha)x_1}{(1-\alpha^2)^{1/2}x_2} \right] \tag{12}$$

$$\sigma_1^2 = \sum_{i=1}^{N} \frac{1}{2} \left[\ln^2 \left(\frac{1+\alpha}{(1-\alpha^2)^{1/2}} \frac{x_4}{x_3} \right) + \ln^2 \left(\frac{1-\alpha}{(1-\alpha^2)^{1/2}} \frac{x_3}{x_4} \right) \right] \tag{13}$$

where

$$x_1 = \left[\gamma^2 (1+\alpha)^2 + (x_i - (1+\alpha)\delta)^2 \right]^{1/2} \tag{14}$$

$$x_2 = \left[\gamma^2 (1-\alpha)^2 + (x_i - (1-\alpha)\delta)^2 \right]^{1/2} \tag{15}$$

$$x_3 = \left\{ \frac{\gamma^2 (1+\alpha)^2 + \left[(x_i(1+\alpha) - (1+\alpha)\delta)^2 \right]^2}{\gamma^2 + [x_i(1+\alpha) - \delta]^2} \right\}^{1/2} \tag{16}$$

$$x_4 = \left\{ \frac{\gamma^2 (1-\alpha)^2 + \left[(x_i(1-\alpha) - (1-\alpha)\delta)^2 \right]^2}{\gamma^2 + [x_i(1-\alpha) - \delta]^2} \right\}^{1/2} \tag{17}$$

5 Experimental Results

In order to verify the superiority of the new detector proposed in this paper, we conduct several experiments with various actual images. Due to space limitation, here we only demonstrate the results for "Lena" and "Peppers" of size 512×512. The image is transformed by 8×8 block-wise DCT, and low- and mid-frequency coefficients are selected out to be embedded with watermark. Watermark signal $\mathbf{w}$ is generated by a pseudorandom sequence (PRS) generator, which takes the value of $+1$ and -1 with equal probability, that is $\sum_{i=1}^{N} w_i = 0$. To quantify the detection performance, the receiver operating characteristics (ROC) curves are plotted.

In our experiments, multiplicative watermark embedding rule of section 2 is used. Monte Carlo tests are conducted to experimentally validate the estimated ROC. Embedding strength α is fixed to a specific value much smaller than 1, for larger α, ROC curves are all straight lines with detection probabilities all equal to 1. The effectiveness of different detection schemes is compared with different "Watermark to Document Ratio" (WDR), which is defined as

$$WDR = 10 \log \left(\frac{\sigma_w^2}{\sigma_x^2} \right) \tag{18}$$

where σ_w^2 is the variance of watermark signal and σ_x^2 is the variance of original DCT coefficients, respectively.

5.1   Performance Comparison of Different Detectors

In this set of experiments, three different detectors, i.e. Cauchy, GG and Laplacian detector, are implemented to make a comparison of their effectiveness. Cauchy detector is derived by (7), GG and Laplacian detectors are from literature [9]. To get ROCs, the probability of false alarm is set from 10^{-4} to 1, to each p_{fa}, the threshold is computed by (8), then the likelihood ratio $l(\mathbf{Y})$ under hypothesis H_1 is empirically estimated and this value is compared to corresponding threshold. If it is above the threshold, the watermark is detected.

Fig. 1 shows the ROCs to image "Lena" and "Peppers". It is obvious that under the same p_{fa}, p_{det} of the proposed detector is much higher than that of the GG and Laplacian detectors, which meets with the fact that the Cauchy distribution is most appropriate for modeling the DCT data. Therefore the proposed detector is superior to the previous ones.

5.2   Empirical and Theoretical ROC

We also conduct experiments to verify the accuracy of theoretical analysis derived in section 4, with a specific embedding strength $\alpha = 0.08$. The analytical mean and variance of the detector can be directly computed from the data via (10)-(13), and by (9) we can get the theoretical ROC. The empirical ROC is plotted from the simulations mentioned above. Both ROCs are demonstrated in Fig. 2. From Fig. 2(a),(b), it can be seen that the empirical performance and theoretical one are in good agreement, therefore the correctness of our theoretical analysis can be confirmed.

5.3   Detection Performance of Different WDR

In order to compare the performance of the three detectors for different watermark strength, we carry out this set of experiments. The embedding strength is measured by WDR, as defined by (18). To our test images, WDR varies from -53dB to -42dB. Here, we consider the case that the probability of false alarm is fixed while measuring the corresponding probability of detection. In our tests, the probability of false alarm is set to 10^{-3}. The results are demonstrated by Fig. 3. It can be observed that the probability of detection increases with the strength of embedded watermark increases for all detectors. This is in line with intuitive sense, that the higher power of embedded signal, the easier to detect it. On the other side, we can find that the performance of Cauchy detector is better than that of the GG and Laplacian detector under any WDR.

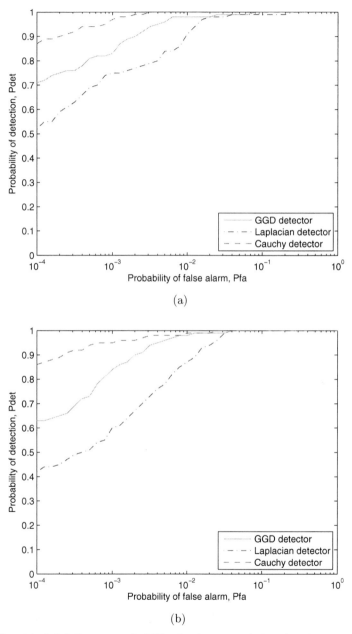

Fig. 1. Empirical ROC curves of GGD, Laplacian and Cauchy detectors. (a)Lena. (b)Peppers.

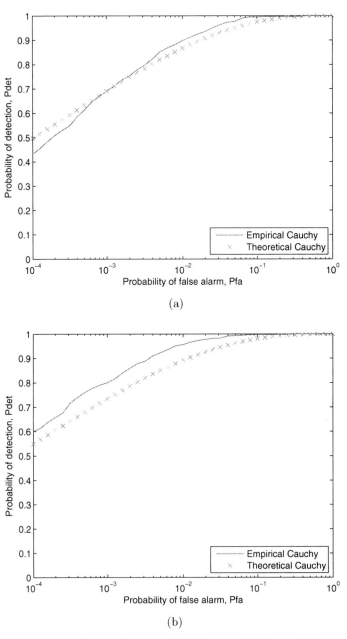

Fig. 2. Empirical and theoretical ROC curves. (a)Lena. (b)Peppers.

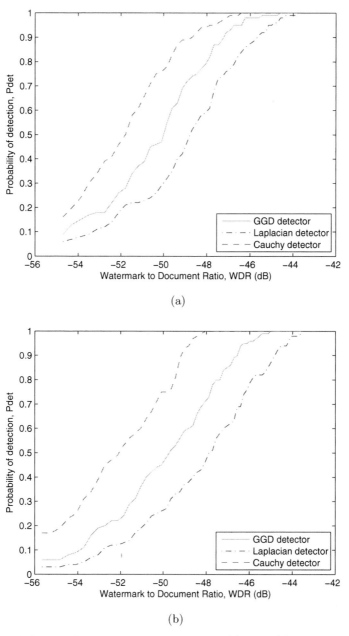

Fig. 3. ROC curves of different WDR. (a)Lena. (b)Peppers.

6   Conclusion

In this paper, a novel detector for the DCT-based multiplicative watermarking scheme is proposed by modeling the data with Cauchy distribution, which is more appropriate to describe the heavy-tailed characteristics of DCT coefficients. The theoretical performance of the detector has also been derived. The experimental results have validated the correctness of theoretical analysis and shown superior performance of the newly developed detector over that of conventional GG and Laplacian detector.

We note that in [14,15], a locally most powerful detector to multiplicative watermark in curvelet domain is developed, in which GGD, Laplacian distribution and Cauchy distribution are used to model the coefficients, respectively. They conclude that detector based on Cauchy distribution has superior performance, which is similar to our work. But we argue that compared with curvelet transform, DCT is easier to implement and more widely used in image processing, especially in image compression, therefore our method has more application in real practice.

In this paper, attacks to detectors are not considered, such as geometrical attacks, compression, coding and so on. As a important measure index to a detector, the robustness of our scheme will be the focus of research in the future.

Acknowledgments. This work is supported by the National Natural Science Foundation of China under Grant No.60803122 and the Collegiate Natural Science Foundation of Jiangsu Province under Grant No.11KJD520011.

References

1. Seitz, J.: Digital Watermarking for Digital Media. Information Science, Hershey (2005)
2. Comesaa, P., Merhav, N., Barni, M.: Asymptotically Optimum Universal Watermark Embedding and Detection in the High-SNR Regime. IEEE Trans. Information Theory 56, 2804–2815 (2010)
3. Zhong, J.D., Huang, S.T.: Double-Sided Watermark Embedding and Detection. IEEE Trans. Information Forensics and Security 2, 297–310 (2007)
4. Hernandez, J.R., Amado, M., Perez-Gonzalez, F.: DCT-domain watermarking techniques for still images: Detector performance analysis and a new structure. IEEE Trans. Image Process. 9, 55–68 (2000)
5. Ng, T.M., Garg, H.K.: Maximum-likelihood detection in DWT domain image using Laplacian modeling. IEEE Signal Process. Lett. 12(4), 285–288 (2005)
6. Mairgiotis, A.K., Chantas, G., Galatsanos, N.P., Blekas, K., Yang, Y.: New detectors for watermarks with unknown power based on Student-t image priors. In: Proc. IEEE Int. Workshop Multimedia Signal Processing, Crete, Greece, pp. 353–356 (2007)
7. Rahman, S.M.M., Ahmad, M.O., Swamy, M.N.S.: A New Statistical Detector for DWT-Based Additive Image Watermarking Using the Gauss-Hermite Expansion. IEEE Trans. Image Process. 18, 1782–1796 (2009)

8. Bhuiyan, M.I.H., Rahman, R.: DCT-domain watermark detector using a normal inverse Gaussian prior. In: Proc. 23rd Canadian Conf. Electrical and Computer Engineering, Canadian, pp. 1–4 (2010)
9. Cheng, Q., Huang, T.S.: Robust Optimum Detection of Transform Domain Multiplicative Watermarks. IEEE Trans. Signal Process. 51, 906–924 (2003)
10. Wang, J.W., Liu, G.J., Dai, Y.W., Sun, J.S., Wang, Z.Q., Lian, S.G.: Locally optimum detection for Barni's multiplicative watermarking in DWT domain. Signal Processing 88, 117–130 (2008)
11. Tsihrintzis, G.A., Nikias, C.L.: Performance of optimum and suboptimum receivers in the presence of impulsive noise modeled as an alpha-stable process. IEEE Trans. Commun. 43(3), 904–914 (1995)
12. Cox, J., Kilian, J., Leighton, F.T., Shamoon, T.: Secure spread spectrum watermarking for multimedia. IEEE Trans. Image Process. 6, 1673–1687 (1997)
13. Briassouli, A., Tsakalides, P., Stouraitis, A.: Hidden Messages in Heavy-Tails: DCT-Domain Watermark Detection Using Alpha-Stable Models. IEEE Trans. Multimedia 7, 700–715 (2005)
14. Deng, C.Z., Wang, S.Q., Sun, H., Cao, H.Q.: Multiplicative spread spectrum watermarks detection performance analysis in curvelet domain. In: Proc. IEEE Int. Conf. E-Business and Information System Security, Wuhan, China, pp. 1–4 (2009)
15. Deng, C.Z., Zhu, H.S., Wang, S.Q.: Curvelet domain watermark detection using alpha-stable models. In: Proc. Fifth Int. Conf. on Information Assurance and Security, Xi'an, China, pp. 313–316 (2009)

Extension of Barreto-Voloch Root Extraction Method

Zhengjun Cao and Xiao Fan

Department of Mathematics, Shanghai University, Shanghai, China
caozhj@yahoo.cn

Abstract. Root extraction is a classical problem in computers algebra. It plays an essential role in cryptosystems based on elliptic curves. In 2006, Barreto and Voloch proposed an algorithm to compute rth roots in $\mathbb{F}_{q^m}$ for certain choices of m and q. If $r \,||\, q-1$ and $(m,r) = 1$, they proved that the complexity of their method is $\widetilde{\mathcal{O}}(r(\log m + \log \log q)m \log q)$. In this paper, we extend the Barreto-Voloch algorithm to the general case that $r \,||\, q^m - 1$, without the restrictions $r \,||\, q - 1$ and $(m,r) = 1$. We also specify the conditions that the Barreto-Voloch algorithm can be preferably applied.

Keywords: Barreto-Voloch   algorithm,   Adleman-Manders-Miller algorithm.

1   Introduction

Consider the problem to find a solution to $X^r = \delta$ in $\mathbb{F}_{q^m}$, where $q = p^d$ for some prime p and some integer $d > 0$. Clearly, it suffices to consider the following two cases:

$$(1)\ (r, q^m - 1) = 1, \qquad (2)\ r|q^m - 1$$

Root extraction is a classical problem in computational algebra and number theory. It plays an essential role in cryptosystems based on elliptic curves. The typical applications of root extraction are point compression in elliptic curves and operation of hashing onto elliptic curves [3,4,9].

Adleman, Manders and Miller [1] proposed a method to solve the problem, which extends Tonelli-Shanks [7,10] square root algorithm. The basic idea of Adleman-Manders-Miller rth root extraction in $\mathbb{F}_q$ can be described as follows. If $r|q - 1$, we write $p - 1$ in the form $r^t \cdot s$, where $(s, r) = 1$. Given a rth residue δ, we have $(\delta^s)^{r^{t-1}} = 1$. Since $(s, r) = 1$, it is easy to find the least nonnegative integer α such that $s|r\alpha - 1$. Hence, $\left(\delta^{r\alpha-1}\right)^{r^{t-1}} = 1$. If $t - 1 = 0$, then δ^α is a rth root of δ. From now on, we assume that $t \geq 2$. Given a rth non-residue $\rho \in \mathbb{F}_q$, we have

$$\left(\rho^s\right)^{i \cdot r^{t-1}} \neq \left(\rho^s\right)^{j \cdot r^{t-1}} \quad \text{where } i \neq j,\ i, j \in \{0, 1, \cdots, r - 1\}$$

S. Qing et al. (Eds.): ICICS 2011, LNCS 7043, pp. 184–189, 2011.

Set $K_i = (\rho^s)^{i \cdot r^{t-1}}$ and $\mathbb{K} = \{K_0, K_1, \cdots, K_{r-1}\}$. It is easy to find that all K_i satisfy $X^r = 1$. Since $\left(\left(\delta^{r\alpha-1} \right)^{r^{t-2}} \right)^r = 1$, there is a unique $j_1 \in \{0, 1, \cdots, r-1\}$ such that $\left(\delta^{r\alpha-1} \right)^{r^{t-2}} = K_{r-j_1}$ (where $K_r = K_0$). Hence, $\left(\delta^{r\alpha-1} \right)^{r^{t-2}} K_{j_1} = 1$. That is

$$\left(\delta^{r\alpha-1} \right)^{r^{t-2}} (\rho^s)^{j_1 \cdot r^{t-1}} = 1$$

Likewise, there is a unique $j_2 \in \{0, 1, \cdots, r-1\}$ such that

$$\left(\delta^{r\alpha-1} \right)^{r^{t-3}} (\rho^s)^{j_1 \cdot r^{t-2}} (\rho^s)^{j_2 \cdot r^{t-1}} = 1$$

Consequently, we obtain $j_1, \cdots, j_{t-1}$ such that

$$\left(\delta^{r\alpha-1} \right) (\rho^s)^{j_1 \cdot r} (\rho^s)^{j_2 \cdot r^2} \cdots (\rho^s)^{j_{t-1} \cdot r^{t-1}} = 1$$

Thus, we have

$$\left(\delta^{\alpha} \right)^r \left((\rho^s)^{j_1 + j_2 \cdot r + \cdots j_{t-1} \cdot r^{t-2}} \right)^r = \delta$$

It means that $\delta^{\alpha} (\rho^s)^{j_1 + j_2 \cdot r + \cdots j_{t-1} \cdot r^{t-2}}$ is a rth root of δ. The complexity of Adleman-Manders-Miller rth root extraction algorithm is $\mathcal{O}(\log^4 q + r \log^3 q)$. Notice that the algorithm can not run in polynomial time if r is sufficiently large.

In 2006, Barreto and Voloch [2] proposed an algorithm to compute rth roots in $\mathbb{F}_{q^m}$ for certain choices of m and q. If $r \,||\, q - 1$ and $(m, r) = 1$, where the notation $a^b || c$ means that a^b is the highest power of a dividing c, they proved that the complexity of their method is $\widetilde{\mathcal{O}}(r(\log m + \log \log q)m \log q)$.

Our contributions. We extend the Barreto-Voloch root extraction method to the general case that $r \,||\, q^m - 1$, without the restrictions $r \,||\, q - 1$ and $(m, r) = 1$. We also specify the conditions that the Barreto-Voloch algorithm can be preferably applied.

2 Barreto-Voloch Method

Barreto-Voloch method takes advantage of the periodic structure of v written in base q to compute rth roots in $\mathbb{F}_{q^m}$, where $v = r^{-1} \pmod{q^m - 1}$ if $(r, q^m - 1) = 1$. This advantage is based on the following fact [2]:

Fact 1. *Let $\mathbb{F}_{q^m}$ be a finite field of characteristic p and let s be a power of p. Define the map*

$$\phi_n : \mathbb{F}_{q^m} \to \mathbb{F}_{q^m}, y \mapsto y^{1+s+\cdots+s^n} \text{ for } n \in \mathbb{N}^*$$

We can compute $\phi_n(y)$ with $\mathcal{O}(\log n)$ multiplications and raisings to powers of p.

Notice that raising to powers of p has negligible cost, if we use a normal basis for $\mathbb{F}_{q^m}/\mathbb{F}_q$. Since it only requires $\mathcal{O}(\log n)$ multiplications and raisings to powers of p to compute $y^{1+s+\cdots+s^n}$, where p is the characteristic of $\mathbb{F}_{q^m}$ and s is a power of p, their method becomes more efficient for certain choices of m and q. They obtained the following results [2].

Lemma 1. *Given q and r with $(q(q-1), r) = 1$, let $k > 1$ be the order of q modulo r. For any $m > 0$, $(m, k) = 1$, let $u, 1 \leq u < r$ satisfy $u(q^m - 1) \equiv -1 \pmod{r}$ and $v = \lfloor q^m u / r \rfloor$. Then $rv \equiv 1 \pmod{q^m - 1}$. In addition, $v = a + b \sum_{j=0}^{n-1} q^{jk}, a, b < q^{2k}, n = \lfloor m/k \rfloor$.*

Theorem 1. *Let q be a prime power, let $r > 1$ be such that $(q(q-1), r) = 1$ and let $k > 1$ be the order of q modulo r. For any $m > 0$, $(m, k) = 1$, the complexity of taking rth roots in $\mathbb{F}_{q^m}$ is $\widetilde{\mathcal{O}}((\log m + r \log q)m \log q)$.*

Lemma 2. *Given q and r with $r \mid (q - 1)$ and $((q - 1)/r, r) = 1$, for any $m > 0$, $(m, r) = 1$, let $u, 1 \leq u < r$ satisfy $u(q^m - 1)/r \equiv -1 \pmod{r}$ and $v = \lceil q^m u / r \rceil$. Then $rv \equiv 1 \pmod{(q^m - 1)/r^2}$. In addition, $v = a + b \sum_{j=0}^{n-1} q^{jr}, a, b < q^{2r}, n = \lfloor m/r \rfloor$.*

Theorem 2. *Let q be a prime power and let $r > 1$ be such that $r \mid (q - 1)$ and $((q - 1)/r, r) = 1$. For any $m > 0$, $(m, r) = 1$, given $x \in \mathbb{F}_{q^m}$ one can compute the rth root of x in $\mathbb{F}_{q^m}$, or show it does not exist, in $\widetilde{\mathcal{O}}(r(\log m + \log \log q)m \log q)$ steps.*

3   Analysis of Barreto-Voloch Method

3.1   On the Conditions of Barreto-Voloch Method

In Theorem 1, it requires that

$$(q(q-1), r) = 1 \text{ and } (m, k) = 1$$

where $k > 1$ is the order of q modulo r. These conditions imply $(q^m - 1, r) = 1$. But these are not necessary to the general case. Likewise, in Theorem 2, it requires that

$$r \mid\mid q - 1 \text{ and } (m, r) = 1$$

These imply $r \mid\mid q^m - 1$. But these are not necessary, too. We will remove the restrictions and investigate the following cases:

(1) $(r, p^m - 1) = 1$;   (2) $r \mid\mid p^m - 1$.

where p is a prime. As for the general case, $p^m - 1 = r^\alpha s, \alpha \geq 2, (r, s) = 1$, we refer to [1].

3.2   On the Technique of Periodic Structure

As we mentioned before, Barreto-Voloch method takes advantage of the periodic structure of v written in base q. Precisely, in Lemma 1

$$v = a + b \sum_{j=0}^{n-1} q^{jk}, a, b < q^{2k}, n = \lfloor m/k \rfloor \tag{1}$$

where $k > 1$ is the order of q modulo r. From the expression, we know it requires that $n = \lfloor m/k \rfloor \geq 1$. It is easy to find that *the advantage of Barreto-Voloch method* *due to the periodic expansion in base q requires that m is much greater than k.* That is, the length of such periodic expansion, n, should be as large as possible.

Since raising to a power of p is a linear bijection in characteristic p, the complexity of such operation is no larger than that of multiplication, namely, $\widetilde{\mathcal{O}}(m \log p)$ using FFT techniques [5,6,8]. In light of that $q = p^d$ for some prime p, it is better to write v as

$$v = a' + b' \sum_{j=0}^{n'-1} p^{jk'}, a', b' < p^{2k'}, n' = \lfloor md/k' \rfloor \tag{2}$$

where k' is the order of p modulo r. That is, the periodic expansion in base p could produce a large expansion length, instead of the original periodic expansion in base q. This claim is directly based on the following fact

$$n' = \lfloor md/k' \rfloor \geq \lfloor md/kd \rfloor = n \tag{3}$$

(This is because $k' \mid kd$. See the definitions of k, k'.)

4 Extension of Barreto-Voloch Method

4.1 Taking rth Roots When r is Invertible

We first discuss the problem to take rth roots over $\mathbb{F}_{p^m}$ if $(r, p^m - 1) = 1$, where p is a prime.

Lemma 3. *Suppose that $(p^m - 1, r) = 1$. Let k be the order of p modulo r. Let $u, 1 \leq u < r$ satisfy $u(p^m - 1) \equiv -1 \,(\mathrm{mod}\, r)$. Then $rv \equiv 1 \,(\mathrm{mod}\, p^m - 1)$, where $v = \lfloor p^m u/r \rfloor$. In addition, if $m > k$, then $v = a + b \sum_{j=0}^{n-1} p^{jk}, a, b < p^{2k}, n = \lfloor m/k \rfloor$.*

Proof. Since $u(p^m - 1) \equiv -1 \,(\mathrm{mod}\, r)$ and $1 \leq u < r$, we have $p^m u/r = \lfloor p^m u/r \rfloor + (u-1)/r$ and $r\lfloor p^m u/r \rfloor \equiv 1 \,(\mathrm{mod}\, p^m - 1)$. Let $z = u(p^k - 1)/r$. Then z is an integer and $z < p^k - 1$. Hence, $p^m u/r = p^m z/(p^k - 1)$. If $m > k$, then we have the following expansion

$$p^m z/(p^k - 1) = p^{m-k} z \sum_{j=0}^{\infty} p^{-jk} = p^{m-nk} z \sum_{j=0}^{n-1} p^{jk} + p^{m-k} z \sum_{n}^{\infty} p^{-jk}$$

Take $a = \lfloor p^{m-k} z \sum_{n}^{\infty} p^{-jk} \rfloor, b = p^{m-nk} z$. This completes the proof. □

Theorem 3. *Suppose that $(p^m - 1, r) = 1$. Let k be the order of p modulo r. If $m > k$, then the complexity of taking rth roots of δ in $\mathbb{F}_{p^m}$ is $\widetilde{\mathcal{O}}((\log m + k \log p) m \log p)$.*

Proof. Given $\delta \in \mathbb{F}_{p^m}$, clearly, $\delta^{r^{-1}}$ is a root of $X^r = \delta$ if $(p^m - 1, r) = 1$, where r^{-1} is the inverse of r modulo $p^m - 1$.

By Lemma 3, if $m > k$, then $r^{-1} = a + b \sum_{j=0}^{n-1} p^{jk} \,(\mathrm{mod}\, p^m - 1), a, b < p^{2k}, n = \lfloor m/k \rfloor$. Raising to the power $\sum_{j=0}^{n-1} p^{jk}$ takes $\mathcal{O}(\log n)$ multiplications and raisings to powers of p. The raising to the power a takes $\mathcal{O}(k \log p)$ multiplications due to the bound on the exponent. So does the raising to the power b. The total computation cost is therefore $\mathcal{O}(\log m + k \log p)$ operations of complexity $\widetilde{\mathcal{O}}(m \log p)$ (if directly using the form $r^{-1} = \frac{u(p^m-1)+1}{r}$, it takes time $\widetilde{\mathcal{O}}(m^2 \log^2 p)$). This completes the proof. □

4.2   Taking rth Roots When r is Not Invertible

We now discuss the problem to take rth roots over $\mathbb{F}_{p^m}$ if $r \,\|\, p^m - 1$, where p is a prime.

Lemma 4. *Suppose that $r \,\|\, p^m - 1$. Let k be the order of p modulo r. Let $u, 1 \le u < r$ satisfy $u(p^m - 1)/r \equiv -1 \pmod{r}$ and $v = \lceil p^m u/r^2 \rceil$. Then $rv \equiv 1 \pmod{(p^m - 1)/r}$. In addition, if $m > kr$, then $v = a + b \sum_{j=0}^{n-1} p^{jkr}, a, b < p^{2kr}, n = \lfloor m/kr \rfloor$.*

Proof. Since $u(p^m - 1)/r \equiv -1 \pmod{r}$ and $1 \le u < r$, we have $p^m u/r^2 = \lceil p^m u/r^2 \rceil + (u-r)/r^2$ and $r \lceil p^m u/r^2 \rceil \equiv 1 \pmod{(p^m-1)/r}$. Let $z = u(p^{kr}-1)/r^2$. Then z is an integer and $z < p^{kr} - 1$. Hence, $p^m u/r^2 = p^m z/(p^{kr} - 1)$. If $m > kr$, then we have the following expansion

$$p^m z/(p^{kr} - 1) = p^{m-kr} z \sum_{j=0}^{\infty} p^{-jkr} = p^{m-nkr} z \sum_{j=0}^{n-1} p^{jkr} + p^{m-kr} z \sum_{n}^{\infty} p^{-jkr}$$

Take $a = \lfloor p^{m-kr} z \sum_{n}^{\infty} p^{-jkr} \rfloor, b = p^{m-nkr} z$. This completes the proof. □

Theorem 4. *Suppose that $r \,\|\, p^m - 1$. Let k be the order of p modulo r. If $m > kr$, then one can compute the rth root of δ in $\mathbb{F}_{p^m}$, or show it does not exist, in $\widetilde{\mathcal{O}}((\log m + kr \log p) m \log p)$ steps.*

Proof. Given $\delta \in \mathbb{F}_{p^m}$, we have $\delta^{p^m - 1} = 1$. If $r \,\|\, p^m - 1$ and $\delta^{(p^m-1)/r} = 1$, then there exists an integer v such that $\frac{p^m-1}{r} \,|\, vr - 1$ and $(\delta^v)^r = \delta$. Hence, it suffices to compute the inverse of r modulo $\frac{p^m-1}{r}$.

By Lemma 4, if $m > kr$, $r^{-1} \equiv v = a + b \sum_{j=0}^{n-1} p^{jkr} \pmod{(p^m - 1)/r}, a, b < p^{2kr}, n = \lfloor m/kr \rfloor$, Since raising to the power $\sum_{j=0}^{n-1} p^{jkr}$ takes $\mathcal{O}(\log n)$ multiplications and raisings to powers of p. Raising to the power a takes $\mathcal{O}(kr \log p)$ multiplications due to the bound on the exponent. So does raising to the power b. The cost of raising to v is therefore $\mathcal{O}(\log m + kr \log p)$ operations of complexity $\widetilde{\mathcal{O}}(m \log p)$. To check that $\rho = \delta^v$ is a correct root, we compute ρ^r with cost $\widetilde{\mathcal{O}}(m \log r \log p)$. If δ is a rth power, then $\rho^r = \delta$, otherwise ρ^r is not equal to δ. The total computation cost is therefore $\widetilde{\mathcal{O}}((\log m + kr \log p) m \log p)$ (if directly using the form $r^{-1} = \frac{u(p^m-1)+r}{r^2}$, it takes time $\widetilde{\mathcal{O}}(m^2 \log^2 p)$). This completes the proof. □

5   Conclusion

In this paper, we analyze and extend the Barreto-Voloch method to compute rth roots over finite fields. We specify the conditions that the Barreto-Voloch algorithm can be preferably applied. We also give a formal complexity analysis of the method.

Acknowledgements. We thank the anonymous referees' for their detailed suggestions. This work is supported by the National Natural Science Foundation of China (Project 60873227), and the Key Disciplines of Shanghai Municipality (S30104).

References

1. Adleman, L., Manders, K., Miller, G.: On Taking Roots in Finite Fields. In: Proceedings of the 18th IEEE Symposium on Foundations of Computer Science, pp. 175–177. IEEE Press, New York (1977)
2. Barreto, P., Voloch, J.: Efficient Computation of Roots in Finite Fields. Designs, Codes and Cryptography 39, 275–280 (2006)
3. Boneh, D., Boyen, X., Shacham, H.: Short Group Signatures. In: Franklin, M. (ed.) CRYPTO 2004. LNCS, vol. 3152, pp. 41–55. Springer, Heidelberg (2004)
4. Boneh, D., Franklin, M.: Identity-based Encryption from the Weil Pairing. SIAM J. Computing 32(3), 586–615 (2003)
5. Gao, S., Gathen, J., Panario, D., Shoup, V.: Algorithms for Exponentiation in Finite Fields. J. Symbolic Computation 29, 879–889 (2000)
6. Gathen, J., Gerhard, J.: Modern Computer Algebra, 2nd edn. Cambridge University Press (2003)
7. Shanks, D.: Five Number-theoretic Algorithms. In: Proc. 2nd Manitoba Conf., pp. 51–70. Numer. Math. (1972)
8. Shoup, V.: A Computational Introduction to Number Theory and Algebra. Cambridge University Press (2005)
9. Smart, N.: An Identity Based Authenticated Key Agreement Protocol Based on the Weil Pairing. Electronics Letters 38, 630–632 (2002)
10. Tonelli, A.: Bemerkungüber die Auflösung quadratischer Congruenzen. Nachrichten der Akademie der Wissenschaften in Göttingen, 344–346 (1891)

Two Applications of an Incomplete Additive Character Sum to Estimating Nonlinearity of Boolean Functions[*]

Yusong Du[1,2] and Fangguo Zhang[1,3]

[1] School of Information Science and Technology
Sun Yat-sen University, Guangzhou 510006, P.R. China
[2] Key Lab of Network Security and Cryptology
Fujian Normal University, Fuzhou 350007, P.R.China
[3] State Key Laboratory of Information Security, Institute of Software
Chinese Academy of Sciences, Beijing, P.R. China
yusongdu@hotmail.com, isszhfg@mail.sysu.edu.cn

Abstract. In recent years, several classes of Boolean functions with good cryptographic properties have been constructed by using univariate (or bivariate) polynomial representation of Boolean functions over finite fields. The estimation of an incomplete additive character sum plays an important role in analyzing the nonlinearity of these functions. In this paper, we consider replacing this character sum with another incomplete additive character sum, whose estimation was firstly given by A.Winterhof in 1999. Based on Winterhof's estimation, we try to modify two of these functions and obtain better nonlinearity bound of them.

Keywords: Boolean function, incomplete additive character sum, nonlinearity, algebraic degree, algebraic immunity.

1 Introduction

In order to resist all kinds of cryptographic attacks, Boolean functions used in stream ciphers should have good cryptographic properties including balancedness, high algebraic degree, high nonlinearity, high resiliency and large algebraic immunity. Construction of Boolean functions with good cryptographic properties has been an important problem for many years.

In 2008, Carlet and Feng exploited the univariate polynomial representation of Boolean functions in finite fields and constructed successfully a class of balanced Boolean functions with optimal algebraic degree, optimal algebraic immunity and good nonlinearity [1]. Before this result, none of constructed Boolean functions with optimal algebraic immunity could be proven to have good nonlinearity. This class of functions was then called the Carlet-Feng function. From

[*] This work is supported by Funds of Key Lab of Fujian Province University Network Security and Cryptology (2011008) and National Natural Science Foundations of China (Grant No. 61070168, Grant No. 10971246).

S. Qing et al. (Eds.): ICICS 2011, LNCS 7043, pp. 190–201, 2011.

then on, Boolean functions with optimal algebraic immunity constructed by using univariate (or bivariate) polynomial representation received more attention [2,3,4,5,6,7,8].

P.Rizomiliotis discussed the resistance of Boolean functions against (fast) algebraic attacks and provided a sufficient and necessary condition of Boolean function having optimal algebraic immunity under univariate polynomial representation [7]. Before long, X.Zeng *et al.* exploited the sufficient and necessary condition and provided more constructions of Boolean functions with optimal algebraic immunity under univariate polynomial representation [8].

Tu and Deng firstly studied the algebraic immunity of a subclass of the so-called *Partial Spread* functions introduced by Dillon [9]. They obtained a class of bent functions with optimal algebraic immunity based on an unproven combinatoric conjecture and constructed a class of Boolean functions in even variables with optimal algebraic degree, better nonlinearity (than that of the Carlet-Feng function) and optimal algebraic immunity based on the conjecture [3]. This class of functions was then called the Tu-Deng function. They also proposed a class of 1-resilient functions in even variables with optimal algebraic degree, good nonlinearity and suboptimal algebraic immunity based on the conjecture [5].

Before long, X.Tang *et al.* generalized Tu-Deng's results. Based on Tu-Deng's conjecture, they further improved the nonlinearity of balanced Boolean functions with optimal algebraic immunity and also gave a class of 1-resilient functions in even variables with optimal algebraic degree, good nonlinearity and suboptimal algebraic immunity [6].

It is easy to see that the estimation of the incomplete additive character sum over $\mathbb{F}_{2^n}$,

$$\left| \sum_{i=2^{n-1}-1}^{2^n-2} (-1)^{tr(\lambda \alpha^i)} \right| \leq 2^{\frac{n}{2}} n \cdot \ln 2 + 1, \quad (\lambda \in \mathbb{F}_{2^n}^*)$$

plays an important role in analyzing the nonlinearity of the Carlet-Feng function, the Tu-Deng function and Tu-Deng's 1-resilient function, where α is a primitive element of $\mathbb{F}_{2^n}$ and $tr(\cdot) = tr_{\mathbb{F}_{2^n}/\mathbb{F}_2}(\cdot)$ is the absolute trace function.

In this paper, we would like to consider replacing this character sum with another incomplete additive character sum, whose estimation was firstly given by A.Winterhof in 1999 [10]. Based on the character sum considered by Winterhof, we try to modify the Tu-Deng function and Tu-Deng's 1-resilient function. Using Winterhof's estimation, we can obtain better nonlinearity bound of these two functions.

The nonlinearity bound of the modified functions will be better than that of the original functions, but unfortunately it is worse than that of the Boolean functions given by X.Tang *et al.* in [6]. Moreover, the algebraic degree of the modified Tu-Deng function will decrease compared with the original function. This means that the modified functions given by us may not be a good choice for stream ciphers. However, we believe that our work will help us understand the impact of incomplete additive character sums on the estimation of nonlinearity of Boolean functions.

The rest of the paper is organized as follows. Section 2 provides some preliminaries and recalls the character sum considered by Winterhof. Section 3 and Section 4 modify the Tu-Deng function and Tu-Deng's 1-resilient function respectively and discuss their cryptographic properties.

2   Preliminaries

Let n be a positive integer. We denote by $\mathbb{B}_n$ the set of all the n-variable Boolean functions. Any n-variable Boolean function has a unique representation as a multivariate polynomial over $\mathbb{F}_2$, called the *algebraic normal form*(ANF),

$$f(x_1, x_2, \cdots, x_n) = a_0 + \sum_{1 \leq i \leq n} a_i x_i + \sum_{1 \leq i < j \leq n} a_{ij} x_i x_j + \cdots + a_{12\ldots n} x_1 x_2 \cdots x_n,$$

where $a_0, a_i, a_{ij}, \ldots, a_{12\ldots n}$ belong to $\mathbb{F}_2$. The algebraic degree of Boolean function f, denoted by $\deg(f)$, is the degree of this polynomial, i.e., the number of variables in the highest order term with nonzero coefficient. A boolean function is *affine* if there exists no term of degree strictly greater than 1 in the ANF.

A Boolean function $g \in \mathbb{B}_n$ is called an *annihilator* of $f \in \mathbb{B}_n$ if $fg = 0$. The lowest algebraic degree of all the nonzero annihilators of f and $1 + f$ is called *algebraic immunity* of f, denoted by $\mathcal{AI}_n(f)$. It has been also proved that $\mathcal{AI}_n(f) \leq \lceil \frac{n}{2} \rceil$ for a given $f \in \mathbb{B}_n$ [11,12]. A Boolean function $f \in \mathbb{B}_n$ has *optimal (suboptimal) algebraic immunity* if $\mathcal{AI}_n(f) = \lceil \frac{n}{2} \rceil \, (= \lceil \frac{n}{2} \rceil - 1)$.

For $f \in \mathbb{B}_n$, the set of $x = (x_1, x_2, \cdots, x_n) \in \mathbb{F}_2^n$ for which $f(x) = 1$ (resp. $f(x) = 0$) is called the on-set (resp. off-set) of f, denoted by $\mathrm{supp}(f)$ (resp. $\mathrm{supp}(1 + f)$). The Hamming weight of f is the cardinality of $\mathrm{supp}(f)$, denoted by $\mathrm{wt}(f)$. f is called balanced if $\mathrm{wt}(f) = 2^{n-1}$.

The Hamming distance of $f \in \mathbb{B}_n$ from $g \in \mathbb{B}_n$ is the Hamming weight of $f + g$. The nonlinearity of an n-variable Boolean function f is its minimum Hamming distance from all the n-variable affine functions. The nonlinearity of $f \in \mathbb{B}_n$ can be described through its Walsh transform:

$$nl(f) = 2^{n-1} - \frac{1}{2} \max_{\omega \in \mathbb{F}_2^n} |W_f(\omega)|,$$

where $W_f(\omega) = \sum_{x \in \mathbb{F}_2^n} (-1)^{f(x) + \omega \cdot x}$ and $\omega \cdot x \in \mathbb{F}_2$ is the usual inner product over $\mathbb{F}_2^n$. Moreover, $W_f(\omega) = -2 \sum_{\mathrm{supp}(f)} (-1)^{\omega \cdot x}$ for $\omega \neq 0$.

By identifying the finite field $\mathbb{F}_{2^n}$ with the vector space $\mathbb{F}_2^n$, an n-variable Boolean function f can be written as a univariate polynomial over $\mathbb{F}_{2^n}$: $f(x) = \sum_{i=0}^{2^n-1} f_i x^i$, where $f_0, f_{2^n-1} \in \mathbb{F}_2$ and $f_{2i} = (f_i)^2 \in \mathbb{F}_{2^n}$, $1 \leq i \leq 2^n - 2$. The algebraic degree $\deg(f)$ (not the degree of the polynomial over $\mathbb{F}_{2^n}$) is given by the largest integer $s = \mathrm{wt}_2(i)$ such that $f_i \neq 0$, where $\mathrm{wt}_2(i)$ is the number of nonzero coefficients in the binary representation of i.

Let $n = 2k$ then $\mathbb{F}_{2^n} \cong \mathbb{F}_{2^k} \times \mathbb{F}_{2^k}$ and an n-variable Boolean function f can be written as a bivariate polynomial over $\mathbb{F}_{2^k}$: $f(x, y) = \sum_{i=0}^{2^k-1} \sum_{j=0}^{2^k-1} h_{i,j} x^i y^j$, where $h_{i,j} \in \mathbb{F}_{2^k}$. The algebraic degree of Boolean function f, $\deg(f)$ is given by the largest integer $s = \text{wt}_2(i) + \text{wt}_2(j)$ such that $h_{i,j} \neq 0$. Under bivariate polynomial representation over $\mathbb{F}_{2^k}$ the Walsh transform of Boolean function $f(x, y) \in \mathbb{B}_{2k}$ is given by $W_f(a, b) = \sum_{(x,y) \in \mathbb{F}_{2^k} \times \mathbb{F}_{2^k}} (-1)^{f(x,y) + tr(ax+by)}$ where $tr(\cdot)$ is the absolute trace function. Moreover, for $(a, b) \neq 0$, we have

$$W_f(a, b) = -2 \sum_{(x,y) \in \text{supp}(f)} (-1)^{tr(ax+by)}.$$

Let ψ be the additive canonical character of $\mathbb{F}_{2^n}$, i.e.,

$$\psi(c) = (-1)^{tr(c)} \quad \text{for all} \quad c \in \mathbb{F}_{2^n},$$

and $g(x) \in \mathbb{F}_{2^n}[x]$ be a univariate polynomial over $\mathbb{F}_{2^n}$. Winterhof gave the following results.

Lemma 1. *[10] If the degree of $g(x)$ as a polynomial over $\mathbb{F}_{2^n}$, denoted by $\deg(g)$, is more than 2 and $\gcd(\deg(g), 2) = 1$, then*

$$\left| \sum_{x \in V} \psi(g(x)) \right| \leq (\deg(g) - 1) \cdot 2^{\frac{n}{2}}$$

holds for any additive subgroup V of $\mathbb{F}_{2^n}$.

3   The Modified Tu-Deng Functions with a Better Nonlinearity Bound

In this section we modify the Tu-Deng function according to Lemma 1, i.e., the incomplete additive character sum considered by Winterhof. Before this we recall the Tu-Deng function, which can be considered as a bivariate polynomial over $\mathbb{F}_{2^k}$.

Definition 1. *$2k$-variable Boolean function $F : \mathbb{F}_{2^k} \times \mathbb{F}_{2^k} \to \mathbb{F}_2$ is called the Tu-Deng function if*

$$F(x, y) = \begin{cases} f(\frac{x}{y}) & \text{if} \quad x \cdot y \neq 0 \\ 1 & \text{if} \quad x = 0, y \in \Delta \ , \\ 0 & \text{otherwise} \end{cases}$$

where the k-variable Boolean function $f : \mathbb{F}_{2^k} \to \mathbb{F}_2$ is defined by

$$\text{supp}(f) = \{1, \alpha^1, \cdots, \alpha^{2^{k-1}-1}\},$$

α is a primitive element of $\mathbb{F}_{2^k}$ and $\Delta = \{\alpha^i : i = 2^{k-1} - 1, 2^{k-1}, \cdots, 2^k - 2\}$.

In the following content in this paper, the k-variable Boolean function $f : \mathbb{F}_{2^k} \to \mathbb{F}_2$ is always defined by $\text{supp}(f) = \{1, \alpha^1, \cdots, \alpha^{2^{k-1}-1}\}$ and α is a primitive element of $\mathbb{F}_{2^k}$.

It was proven that the Tu-Deng function has the optimal algebraic immunity if Tu-Deng's conjecture is true [3,4]. According to the fact that $2k$-variable Boolean function $H : \mathbb{F}_{2^k} \times \mathbb{F}_{2^k} \to \mathbb{F}_2$ defined by

$$H(x, y) = \begin{cases} f(\frac{x}{y}) & \text{if} \quad x \cdot y \neq 0 \\ 0 & \text{otherwise} \end{cases},$$

is a bent function and the estimation of the incomplete additive character sum over $\mathbb{F}_{2^k}$ given by Carlet and Feng,

$$\left| \sum_{i=2^{k-1}-1}^{2^k-2} (-1)^{tr(\lambda \alpha^i)} \right| \leq 2^{\frac{k}{2}} k \cdot \ln 2 + 1, \quad (\lambda \in \mathbb{F}_{2^k}^*)$$

it was shown also in [3,4] that the nonlinearity of the Tu-Deng function is greater and equal to

$$2^{2k-1} - 2^{k-1} - 2^{\frac{k}{2}} \cdot k \cdot \ln 2 - 1.$$

Now we give the modified Tu-Deng function. Let V be an additive subgroup (or considered as a vector subspace over $\mathbb{F}_2$) of dimension $k-1$ of $\mathbb{F}_{2^k}$, t be a positive integer and

$$V^t = \{\gamma^t \mid \gamma \in V\}.$$

It is not hard to see that $|V^t| \leq |V|$ and the equality holds if $\gcd(t, 2^k - 1) = 1$.

Definition 2. $2k$-variable Boolean function $G_t : \mathbb{F}_{2^k} \times \mathbb{F}_{2^k} \to \mathbb{F}_2$ is defined by

$$G_t(x, y) = \begin{cases} f(\frac{x}{y}) & \text{if} \quad x \cdot y \neq 0 \\ 1 & \text{if} \quad x = 0, y \in V^t \\ 0 & \text{otherwise} \end{cases},$$

where V is an additive subgroup of dimension $k - 1$ of $\mathbb{F}_{2^k}$ and t is a positive integer.

We discuss respectively the algebraic immunity, balanceness, nonlinearity and algebraic degree of $G_t(x, y) \in \mathbb{B}_{2k}$.

Recall the proof of the Tu-Deng function about optimal algebraic immunity in [3,4], we can see that replacing Δ in Definition 1 with V^t in Definition 2 does not essentially affect the procedures of the proof (Note that $h(x, 0) =$ for $\forall x \in \mathbb{F}_{2^k}^*$ can imply that $h_{i,0} = 0$ for $1 \leq i \leq 2^k - 2$ but for $0 \leq i \leq 2^k - 1$). Therefore, $G_t(x, y) \in \mathbb{B}_{2k}$ still has optimal algebraic immunity if Tu-Deng's conjecture is true.

Theorem 1. *Boolean function* $G_t(x, y) \in \mathbb{B}_{2k}$ *defined as in Definition 2 has optimal algebraic immunity if Tu-Deng's conjecture is true.*

It is clear that $\text{wt}(G_t(x, y)) = 2^{k-1}(2^k - 1) + |V^t|$. Since $|V^t| = |V| = 2^{k-1}$ if $\gcd(t, 2^k - 1) = 1$, about the balanceness of $G_t(x, y)$ we have the following result directly.

Theorem 2. *Boolean function $G_t(x, y) \in \mathbb{B}_{2k}$ defined as in Definition 2 is balanced if $\gcd(t, 2^k - 1) = 1$.*

Note that

$$2^k - 1 \equiv (-1)^k - 1 \equiv (-2) \bmod 3$$

if k is odd and

$$2^k - 1 \equiv (-1)^{\frac{k}{2}} - 1 \equiv (-2) \bmod 5$$

if $k \equiv 2 \bmod 4$. Then we have the following corollaries.

Corollary 1. *Boolean function $G_3(x, y) \in \mathbb{B}_{2k}$ defined as in Definition 2 is balanced if k is odd.*

Corollary 2. *Boolean function $G_5(x, y) \in \mathbb{B}_{2k}$ defined as in Definition 2 is balanced if $k \equiv 2 \bmod 4$.*

Theorem 3. *Let Boolean function $G_t(x, y) \in \mathbb{B}_{2k}$ be defined as in Definition 2. If $t > 2$ and $\gcd(t, 2^k - 1) = 1$ then its nonlinearity satisfies*

$$nl(G_t(x, y)) \geq 2^{2k-1} - 2^{k-1} - (t - 1) \cdot 2^{\frac{k}{2}}.$$

In particular,

$$nl(G_3(x, y)) \geq 2^{2k-1} - 2^{k-1} - 2^{\frac{k}{2}+1}$$

if k is odd, and

$$nl(G_5(x, y)) \geq 2^{2k-1} - 2^{k-1} - 2^{\frac{k}{2}+2}$$

if $k \equiv 2 \bmod 4$.

Proof. Since $\gcd(t, 2^k - 1) = 1$, G_t is balanced by Theorem 2 and $W_{G_t}(0, 0) = 0$. Let $0 \neq (a, b) \in \mathbb{F}_{2^k} \times \mathbb{F}_{2^k}$, then

$$|W_{G_t}(a, b)| = \left| -2 \sum_{(x,y) \in \mathrm{supp}(G_t)} (-1)^{tr(ax+by)} \right|$$

$$= \left| W_H(a, b) - 2 \sum_{x=0, y \in V^t} (-1)^{tr(ax+by)} \right|$$

$$\leq 2^k + 2 \left| \sum_{y \in V^t} (-1)^{tr(by)} \right|,$$

where the $2k$-variable Boolean function H as mentioned before is a bent function. From Lemma 1, if $t > 2$ and $\gcd(t, 2^k - 1) = 1$ then

$$\left| \sum_{y \in V^t} (-1)^{tr(by)} \right| = \left| \sum_{z \in V} (-1)^{tr(bz^t)} \right| \leq (t - 1) \cdot 2^{\frac{k}{2}},$$

which implies that

$$nl(G_t(x,y)) \geq 2^{2k-1} - 2^{k-1} - (t-1) \cdot 2^{\frac{k}{2}}.$$

It is trivial that the rest of the theorem holds.   □

It is not hard to see that the nonlinearity bound of $G_3(x,y) \in \mathbb{B}_{2k}$ for odd k and $G_5(x,y) \in \mathbb{B}_{2k}$ for k with $k \equiv 2 \bmod 4$ are better than the nonlinearity bound of the original Tu-Deng function except for some small k. In other words, with Winterhof's estimation, in most of cases (at least three-fourth of all) the Tu-Deng function can be simply modified to have better nonlinearity bound.

However, the nonlinearity bound of $G_3(x,y)$ and $G_5(x,y)$ are still worse than the nonlinearity bound of the Boolean function given by X.Tang *et al.* in [6]. This is because H.Dobbertin's balanced Boolean function with very high nonlinearity [13] was involved cleverly in [6].

Before we determine the algebraic degree of $G_t(x,y) \in \mathbb{B}_{2k}$, we need two lemmas.

Lemma 2. *Let $0 \leq i \leq 2^k - 1$. If V is an additive subgroup of dimension $k-1$ of $\mathbb{F}_{2^k}$, then*

$$\sum_{\gamma \in V} \gamma^{-i} \neq 0$$

if and only if i is a power of 2.

Proof. Let $l(x) \in \mathbb{B}_k$ such that its on-set is V, i.e., $\mathrm{supp}(l(x)) = V$. Then $l(x)$ can be written as a univariate polynomial over $\mathbb{F}_{2^k}$:

$$l(x) = \sum_{\gamma \in V} (x+\gamma)^{2^k-1} = \sum_{i=0}^{2^k-1} \left(\sum_{\gamma \in V} \gamma^{2^k-1-i} \right) x^i = \sum_{i=0}^{2^k-1} \left(\sum_{\gamma \in V} \gamma^{-i} \right) x^i.$$

Then $\sum_{\gamma \in V} \gamma^{-i}$ is the coefficient of term x^i. Since V is an additive subgroup of dimension $k-1$ of $\mathbb{F}_{2^k}$, it is not hard to see that $l(x)$ is affine. Therefore,

$$l(x) = \sum_{j=0}^{k-1} \left(\sum_{\gamma \in V} \gamma^{2^k-1-2^j} \right) x^{2^j} = \sum_{j=0}^{k-1} \left(\sum_{\gamma \in V} \gamma^{-2^j} \right) x^{2^j}.$$

Comparing the coefficients of two equations above, we get desire result.   □

Lemma 3. *Let k be a positive integer and j be a non-negative integer less than k. If k is odd then $\mathrm{wt}_2(\frac{2^k-1-2^j}{3}) = \frac{k-1}{2}$ where $j = 0, 2, 4, \cdots, k-1$. If $k \equiv 2 \bmod 4$ then $\mathrm{wt}_2(\frac{2^k-1-2^j}{5}) = \frac{k}{2}$ where $j = 3, 7, 11, \cdots, k-3$.*

Proof. If k is odd and $j = 0$, it is not hard to see that

$$2^k - 1 - 1 = 2(2^{k-1}-1) = 2 \sum_{i=0}^{(k-3)/2} (2^{2i} + 2^{2i+1}) = 3 \sum_{i=0}^{(k-3)/2} 2^{2i+1}.$$

Thus, $\text{wt}_2(\frac{2^k-2}{3}) = \frac{k-1}{2}$. Generally, for $j = 2, 4, 6, \cdots, k-1$, we have

$$2^k - 1 - 2^j = 2(2^{k-1}-1) - (2^j - 1) = 3 \sum_{i=0}^{(k-3)/2} 2^{2i+1} - 3 \cdot 2^{j-2},$$

which implies that

$$\text{wt}_2(\frac{2^k-1-2^j}{3}) = \text{wt}_2(\sum_{i=0}^{(k-3)/2} 2^{2i+1} - 2^{j-2}) = \frac{k-1}{2}.$$

Similarly, if $k \equiv 2 \bmod 4$ and $j = 3$ we have

$$2^k - 9 = 4(2^{k-2}-1) - 5 = 5 \sum_{i=0}^{(k-6)/4} (2^{4i+2} + 2^{4i+3}) - 5$$

Therefore $\text{wt}_2(\frac{2^k-9}{5}) = \frac{k-2}{2} + 1 = \frac{k}{2}$. Generally, for $j = 7, 11, \cdots, k-3$ we have

$$2^k - 1 - 2^j = 4(2^{k-2}-1) - (2^j - 3) = 4(2^{k-2}-1) - 3(2^{j-3}-1) - 5 \cdot 2^{j-3}$$

$$= 5 \sum_{i=0}^{(k-6)/4} (2^{4i+2} + 2^{4i+3}) - 5 \sum_{i=0}^{(j-7)/4} (2^{4i} + 2^{4i+3}) - 5 \cdot 2^{j-3}$$

$$= 5 \sum_{i=(j+1)/4}^{(k-6)/4} (2^{4i+2} + 2^{4i+3}) + 5 \sum_{i=0}^{(j-7)/4} (2^{4i} + 2^{4i+1}) + 5(2^{j-1} + 2^j) - 5 \cdot 2^{j-3}$$

$$= 5 \sum_{i=(j+1)/4}^{(k-6)/4} (2^{4i+2} + 2^{4i+3}) + 5 \sum_{i=0}^{(j-7)/4} (2^{4i} + 2^{4i+1}) + 5(2^{j-3} + 2^{j-2} + 2^j).$$

Therefore $\text{wt}_2(\frac{2^k-1-2^j}{5}) = \frac{k-2}{2} - 2 + 3 = \frac{k}{2}$. □

Theorem 4. *Let $G_t(x, y) \in \mathbb{B}_{2k}$ be defined as in Definition 2. If k is odd then $\deg(G_3(x, y)) = \frac{3k+1}{2}$. If $k \equiv 2 \bmod 4$ then $\deg(G_5(x, y)) = \frac{3k}{2}$.*

Proof. Function $G_t(x, y)$ can be written as a bivariate polynomial over $\mathbb{F}_{2^k}$.

$$G_t(x, y) = H(x, y) + \sum_{a=0, b \in V^t} (1 + (x+a)^{2^k-1})(1 + (y+b)^{2^k-1})$$

$$= H(x, y) + \sum_{b \in V^t} (1 + x^{2^k-1})(1 + (y+b)^{2^k-1}),$$

where the $2k$-variable Boolean function H as mentioned before is a bent function. Since $\deg(H) \leq k$, the algebraic degree of G_t is then determined by

$$\sum_{b \in V^t} (1 + x^{2^k-1})(1 + (y+b)^{2^k-1})$$

$$= (1 + x^{2^k-1})(1 + y^{2^k-1}) + \sum_{b \in (V^t)^*} (1 + x^{2^k-1})(1 + (y+b)^{2^k-1})$$

$$= x^{2^k-1} + y^{2^k-1} + \sum_{b \in (V^t)^*} \sum_{i=1}^{2^k-1} b^i y^{2^k-1-i} x^{2^k-1} + \sum_{b \in (V^t)^*} (y+b)^{2^k-1}$$

Thus, $\deg(G_t) = k + \mathrm{wt}_2(2^k - 1 - i)$ if and only if $\mathrm{wt}_2(2^k - 1 - i)$ is the largest integer such that

$$\sum_{b \in (V^t)^*} b^i \neq 0.$$

From Lemma 2, if k is odd, for $G_3(x, y)$,

$$\frac{2^k - 1 - 2^j}{3}, \quad j = 0, 2, 4, \cdots, k-1$$

are all the integers such that

$$\sum_{b \in (V^3)^*} b^{\frac{2^k-1-2^j}{3}} = \sum_{b \in V^3} b^{\frac{2^k-1-2^j}{3}} = \sum_{b \in V} b^{2^k-1-2^j} = \sum_{b \in V} b^{-2^j} \neq 0.$$

By Lemma 3, $\mathrm{wt}_2(2^k - 1 - \frac{2^k-1-2^j}{3}) = k - \mathrm{wt}_2(\frac{2^k-1-2^j}{3}) = \frac{k+1}{2}$, i.e., $\deg(G_3) = k + \frac{k+1}{2} = \frac{3k+1}{2}$.

Similarly, from Lemma 2, if $k \equiv 2 \bmod 4$, for $G_5(x, y)$,

$$\frac{2^k - 1 - 2^j}{5}, \quad j = 3, 7, 11, \cdots, k-3$$

are all the integers such that $\sum_{b \in (V^t)^*} b^{\frac{2^k-1-2^j}{5}} \neq 0$. By Lemma 3, $\mathrm{wt}_2(2^k - 1 - \frac{2^k-1-2^j}{5}) = k - \mathrm{wt}_2(\frac{2^k-1-2^j}{5}) = \frac{k}{2}$, i.e., $\deg(G_5) = k + \frac{k}{2} = \frac{3k}{2}$. The proof is completed. $\square$

4   The Modified Tu-Deng's 1-Resilient Functions with a Better Nonlinearity Bound

Being similar to Section 3, in this section, we modify the 1-resilient Boolean function given by Tu and Deng according to Lemma 1, then discuss its cryptographic properties respectively.

Lemma 4. [5] Let $F(x, y)$ be a $2k$-variable Boolean function, i.e., $F : \mathbb{F}_{2^k} \times \mathbb{F}_{2^k} \to \mathbb{F}_2$. If its on-set $\mathrm{supp}(F)$ is constituted by the following four disjoint parts:

1. $\{(x, y) : y = \alpha^i x, x \in \mathbb{F}_{2^k}^*, i = 1, 2, \cdots, 2^{k-1} - 1\}$
2. $\{(x, y) : y = x, x \in \mathcal{A}\}$
3. $\{(x, 0) : x \in \mathbb{F}_{2^k} \setminus \mathcal{A}\}$
4. $\{(0, y) : y \in \mathbb{F}_{2^k} \setminus \mathcal{A}\}$

where $\mathcal{A} = \{0, 1, \alpha, \alpha^2, \cdots, \alpha^{2^{k-1}-1}\}$. Then F is 1-resilient, $\deg(F) = 2k - 2$, $nl(F) \geq 2^{2k-1} - 2^{k-1} - 3 \cdot k \cdot 2^{\frac{k}{2}} \ln 2 - 7$ and $\mathcal{AI}_{2k}(F) \geq k - 1$ if Tu-Deng's conjecture is true.

The function $F(x, y)$ defined as in Lemma 4 is called Tu-Deng's 1-resilient function. Now we give the modified Tu-Deng's 1-resilient function.

Definition 3. Let V be an additive subgroup of dimension $k-1$ of $\mathbb{F}_{2^k}$ and $t \neq 2$ be a positive integer such that $\gcd(t, 2^k - 1) = 1$. We define $2k$-variable Boolean function $G_t(x, y) : \mathbb{F}_{2^k} \times \mathbb{F}_{2^k} \to \mathbb{F}_2$, whose on-set $\mathrm{supp}(G_t)$ is constituted by the following four disjoint parts:

1. $\{(x, y) : y = \alpha^i x, x \in \mathbb{F}_{2^k}^*, i = 1, 2, \cdots, 2^{k-1} - 1\}$
2. $\{(x, y) : y = x, x \in \mathcal{B}\}$
3. $\{(x, 0) : x \in \mathbb{F}_{2^k} \setminus \mathcal{B}\}$
4. $\{(0, y) : y \in \mathbb{F}_{2^k} \setminus \mathcal{B}\}$

where $\mathcal{B} = V^t \cup \{\beta\}$ and $\beta \in \mathbb{F}_{2^k} \setminus V^t$.

Recall the proofs of Tu-Deng's 1-resilient function about balanceness, 1-resiliency and optimal algebraic immunity respectively, we can see that replacing $\mathcal{A}$ in Lemma 4 with $\mathcal{B}$ in Definition 3 does not essentially affect the procedures of the proofs.

Theorem 5. Let Boolean function $G_t(x, y) \in \mathbb{B}_{2k}$ be defined as in Definition 3. Then it is balanced and 1-resilient, and $\mathcal{AI}_{2k}(G_t) \geq k - 1$ if Tu-Deng's conjecture is true.

Theorem 6. Let Boolean function $G_t(x, y) \in \mathbb{B}_{2k}$ be defined as in Definition 3. Its nonlinearity satisfies

$$nl(G_t(x, y)) \geq 2^{2k-1} - 2^{k-1} - 3(t-1) \cdot 2^{\frac{k}{2}} - 4.$$

In particular,

$$nl(G_3(x, y)) \geq 2^{2k-1} - 2^{k-1} - 3 \cdot 2^{\frac{k}{2}+1} - 4$$

if k is odd, and

$$nl(G_5(x, y)) \geq 2^{2k-1} - 2^{k-1} - 3 \cdot 2^{\frac{k}{2}+2} - 4$$

if $k \equiv 2 \bmod 4$.

Proof. Since G_t is balanced $W_{G_t}(0, 0) = 0$. Let $0 \neq (a, b) \in \mathbb{F}_{2^k} \times \mathbb{F}_{2^k}$, then

$$W_{G_t}(a, b) = -2 \sum_{(x,y) \in \mathrm{supp}(G_t)} (-1)^{tr(ax+by)}$$

$$= -2 \sum_{i=1}^{2^{k-1}-1} \sum_{x \in \mathbb{F}_{2^k}^*} (-1)^{tr((a+b\alpha^i)x)} - 2 \sum_{x \in \mathcal{B}} (-1)^{tr((a+b)x)}$$

$$-2 \sum_{x \in \mathbb{F}_{2^k} \setminus \mathcal{B}} (-1)^{tr(ax)} - 2 \sum_{y \in \mathbb{F}_{2^k} \setminus \mathcal{B}} (-1)^{tr(by)}$$

Since $t \neq 2$ and $\gcd(t, 2^k - 1) = 1$, from Lemma 1, we have

$$\left| \sum_{x \in \mathcal{B}} (-1)^{tr(ax)} \right| \leq \left| \sum_{x \in V^t} (-1)^{tr(ax)} \right| + 1 = \left| \sum_{z \in V} (-1)^{tr(az^t)} \right| + 1 \leq (t-1) \cdot 2^{\frac{k}{2}} + 1.$$

Similarly,

$$\left| \sum_{x \in \mathbb{F}_{2^k} \setminus \mathcal{B}} (-1)^{tr(ax)} \right| \leq (t-1) \cdot 2^{\frac{k}{2}} + 1.$$

Therefore, it can be verified that

$$\frac{1}{2} \left| \max_{(a,b) \in \mathbb{F}_{2^k} \times \mathbb{F}_{2^k}} W_{G_t}(a, b) \right| \leq 2^{k-1} + 1 + 3(t-1) \cdot 2^{\frac{k}{2}} + 3$$

which implies that

$$nl(G_t(x, y)) \geq 2^{2k-1} - 2^{k-1} - 3(t-1) \cdot 2^{\frac{k}{2}} - 4.$$

It is trivial that the rest of the theorem holds.   □

Theorem 7. *Let Boolean function $G_t(x, y) \in \mathbb{B}_{2k}$ be defined as in Definition 3. If $k \neq 3$ then $\deg(G_3(x, y)) = \deg(G_5(x, y)) = 2k - 2$.*

Proof. Let $F(x, y) \in \mathbb{B}_{2k}$ be defined as in Lemma 4. In [5] it was proved that $\deg(F) = 2k - 2$ if

$$\sum_{\gamma \notin \mathcal{A}} \gamma^2 \neq 0.$$

It can be also see that replacing $\mathcal{A}$ in Lemma 4 with $\mathcal{B}$ in Definition 3 does not affect this result holding, i.e., for Boolean function $G_t(x, y) \in \mathbb{B}_{2k}$ defined as in Definition 3, $\deg(G_t) = 2k - 2$ if

$$\sum_{\gamma \notin \mathcal{B}} \gamma^2 \neq 0.$$

Note that

$$\sum_{\gamma \notin \mathcal{B}} \gamma^2 + \sum_{\gamma \in \mathcal{B}} \gamma^2 = \sum_{\gamma \in \mathbb{F}_{2^k}} \gamma^2 = \left(\sum_{\gamma \in \mathbb{F}_{2^k}} \gamma \right)^2 = 0.$$

Then we have

$$\sum_{\gamma \notin \mathcal{B}} \gamma^2 = \sum_{\gamma \in \mathcal{B}} \gamma^2 = \sum_{\gamma \in V^t} \gamma^2 + \beta^2 = \left(\sum_{\gamma \in V^t} \gamma \right)^2 + \beta^2 = \left(\sum_{\gamma \in V} \gamma^t \right)^2 + \beta^2,$$

where $0 \neq \beta \in \mathbb{F}_{2^k} \setminus V^t$. According to Lemma 2, $\sum_{\gamma \in V} \gamma^3$ or $\sum_{\gamma \in V} \gamma^5$ can be nonzero only if $k = 3$. This means that

$$\sum_{\gamma \notin \mathcal{B}} \gamma^2 \neq 0$$

for $t = 3, 5$ when $k \neq 3$. Therefore $\deg(G_3(x, y)) = \deg(G_5(x, y)) = 2k - 2$ when $k \neq 3$.   □

5   Conclusion

In this paper, according to the incomplete additive character sum over finite filed $\mathbb{F}_{2^k}$ considered by Winterhof, we modify the Tu-Deng function and Tu-Deng's 1-resilient function respectively. Using Winterhof's estimation, we can obtain better nonlinearity bound of these two functions compared with the original functions. We also discuss other cryptographic properties of them.

References

1. Carlet, C., Feng, K.: An Infinite Class of Balanced Functions with Optimal Algebraic Immunity, Good Immunity to Fast Algebraic Attacks and Good Nonlinearity. In: Pieprzyk, J. (ed.) ASIACRYPT 2008. LNCS, vol. 5350, pp. 425–440. Springer, Heidelberg (2008)
2. Wang, Q., Peng, J., Kan, H., Xue, X.: Constructions of cryptographically significant Boolean functions using primitive polynomials. IEEE Trans. Inform. Theory 56(6), 3048–3053 (2010)
3. Tu, Z., Deng, Y.: A conjecture about binary strings and its applications on constructing Boolean functions with optimal algebraic immunity. Designs, Codes and Cryptography 60(1), 1–14 (2011)
4. Tu, Z., Deng, Y.: A Conjecture on Binary String and Its Applications on Constructing Boolean Functions of Optimal Algebraic Immunity. Cryptology ePrint Archive, http://eprint.iacr.org/2009/272.pdf
5. Tu, Z., Deng, Y.: Boolean functions with all main cryptographic properties. Cryptology ePrint Archive, http://eprint.iacr.org/2010/518.pdf
6. Tang, X., Tang, D., Zeng, X., Hu, L.: Balanced Boolean functions with (almost) optimal algebraic immunity and very high nonlinearity. Cryptology ePrint Archive, http://eprint.iacr.org/2010/443
7. Rizomiliotis, P.: On the Resistance of Boolean Functions Against Algebraic Attacks Using Univariate Polynomial Representation. IEEE Trans. Inform. Theory 56(8), 4014–4024 (2010)
8. Zeng, X., Carlet, C., Shan, J., Hu, L.: Balanced Boolean Functions with Optimum Algebraic Immunity and High Nonlinearity. Cryptology ePrint Archive, http://eprint.iacr.org/2010/606
9. Dillon, J.F.: Elementary Hadamard Difference Sets. PhD thesis, University of Maryland (1974)
10. Winterhof, A.: Incomplete Additive Character Sums and Applications. In: Jungnickel, D., Niederreiter, H. (eds.) The Fifth International Conference on Finite Fields and Applications Fq5 1999, pp. 462–474. Springer, Berlin (2001)
11. Courtois, N., Meier, W.: Algebraic Attacks on Stream Ciphers with Linear Feedback. In: Biham, E. (ed.) EUROCRYPT 2003. LNCS, vol. 2656, pp. 345–359. Springer, Heidelberg (2003)
12. Meier, W., Pasalic, E., Carlet, C.: Algebraic Attacks and Decomposition of Boolean Functions. In: Cachin, C., Camenisch, J.L. (eds.) EUROCRYPT 2004. LNCS, vol. 3027, pp. 474–491. Springer, Heidelberg (2004)
13. Dobbertin, H.: Construction of Bent Functions and Balanced Boolean Functions with High Nonlinearity. In: Preneel, B. (ed.) FSE 1994. LNCS, vol. 1008, pp. 61–74. Springer, Heidelberg (1995)

Evaluating Optimized Implementations
of Stream Cipher ZUC Algorithm on FPGA⋆

Lei Wang, Jiwu Jing, Zongbin Liu, Lingchen Zhang, and Wuqiong Pan

State Key Lab of Information Security, Graduate University of CAS, China
{lwang,jing,zbliu,lchzhang,wqpan}@is.ac.cn

Abstract. Compared with block ciphers, stream ciphers are more efficient when implemented in hardware environment, like Field Programma-ble Gate Array (FPGA). In this paper, we propose three optimized schemes in the FPGA implementation of a novel and recently proposed stream cipher, ZUC, which is a new cryptographic algorithm proposed for inclusion in the '4G' mobile standard called LTE (Long Term Evolution). These three schemes are based on reusing area of S-box, calculation of CSA tree and pipelined architecture to implement ZUC on FPGA respectively. We also evaluate each optimized scheme in terms of performance and consumed area in Xilinx FPGA device to compare their actual hardware efficiency. According to the evaluation results, the third scheme, namely pipelined architecture implementation, optimizes hardware implementation of ZUC for the best performance and achieves a throughput of 7.1 Gbps using only 575 slices by speeding up the keystream generating on FPGA. To our knowledge, it is an extremely efficient hardware implementation of ZUC at present. Moreover, it also shows that ZUC is quite flexible to balance different throughput with consumed area.

Keywords: FPGA, optimization, ZUC, hardware evaluation.

1 Introduction

Nowadays there are many stream cipher algorithms proposed in both academic and industrial research. Stream cipher is an important category of symmetric encryption algorithms [1], what's more, synchronous stream ciphers do not suffer from error propagation, because each bit is independently encrypted/decrypted from any other. Compared with block ciphers, most stream ciphers are generally much faster and have greater software efficiency. Due to these features, stream ciphers have been becoming the best choice for several communication protocols, especially that used in wireless field [2]. Block ciphers are memoryless algorithms that permute N-bit blocks of plain text data under the influence of the secret key

---

⋆ This work was supported by National Natural Science Foundation of China (Grant No. 70890084/G021102 and 61003274), Knowledge Innovation Program of Chinese Academy of Sciences (Grant No. YYYJ-1013), and National Science & Technology Pillar Program of China (Grant No. 2008BAH32B00 and 2008BAH32B04).

S. Qing et al. (Eds.): ICICS 2011, LNCS 7043, pp. 202–215, 2011.

and generate N-bit blocks of encrypted data, whereas stream ciphers contain internal states and typically operate serially by generating a stream of pseudo random key bits, namely the keystream (stream ciphers are also called keystream generators). The keystream is then bitwise XORed with the data to encrypt/decrypt.

ZUC [3,4,5,6] is a word-oriented stream cipher, which is proposed by Data Assurance and Communication Security Research Center (DACAS) of the Chinese Academy of Sciences. It takes a 128-bit initial key and a 128-bit initial vector as input, and outputs a keystream of 32-bit words (where each 32-bit word is henceforth called a key-word). This keystream is used to encrypt the plain text.

ZUC algorithm specification was firstly published on June 18, 2010. To ensure the security of ZUC algorithm, it is evaluated through public assessments worldwide and was modified once on January 4, 2011 in the initialization for some flaws [3]. The revision of ZUC has been open for public evaluation until June 2011.

Presently, the hardware implementation of cryptographic algorithms plays an important role in many application areas for its high throughput performance. Consequently, whether the cipher algorithms can be implemented in hardware and achieve greater efficiency is becoming a hot and important topic [7, 8, 9, 10]. At present, few results regarding hardware implementations of ZUC have been published. Original documentations provided by designers of the submitted algorithm contain only the software implementation of ZUC. Since the Linear Feedback Shift Registers (LFSRs) are pretty efficient in hardware and are the main building blocks of this cipher, it is possible to implement ZUC in hardware and achieve higher throughput.

In this paper, we take advantage of properties of LFSRs to implement the newly proposed stream cipher ZUC, which is in the newest revision, on Field Programmable Gate Array (FPGA) and attempt to optimize the implementation. We propose three optimized schemes which are based on reusing area of S-box, calculation of CSA tree and pipelined architecture implementation, and evaluate their performance respectively. We found that ZUC is quite appropriate to be implemented in hardware because it is flexible to balance different throughput with consumed area. Experimental results show that our Scheme 3, that is described in detail in Section 3.3, achieves maximum throughput of 7.1 Gbps and consumes only 575 slices, and it also achieves maximum value of throughput per area compared with the other two schemes. Besides, Scheme 1 consumes least area of them and achieves throughput of 2 Gbps. Our experiments are all executed on FPGA, which is a kind of programmable hardware devices and where the computation is performed by logical cells and connections among the cells are reconfigurable, and it is a highly promising alternative to ASIC in implementing cryptographic algorithms, because it is programmable at any time and the cost is pretty low [2] compared with ASIC.

The remainder of the paper is organized as follows. Section 2 gives a brief description of the ZUC algorithm. The three optimized schemes are described in detail in Section 3. Section 4 shows the evaluation results of the three kinds of optimized hardware implementations of ZUC. Finally, the last section concludes the whole paper.

2   Preliminaries: ZUC Algorithm

Cipher systems are usually subdivided into block ciphers and stream ciphers. Block ciphers tend to simultaneously encrypt groups of characters, whereas stream ciphers operate on individual characters of a plain text message one at a time [11]. The new stream cipher ZUC is a word-oriented stream cipher [3]. It takes a 128-bit initial key and a 128-bit initial vector as input, and outputs a keystream of 32-bit words, which is used to encrypt/decrypt the plain/encrypted data. There are two stages in the execution of ZUC: initialization stage and working stage. In the first stage of ZUC, it performs key/IV initialization procedure, i.e., the cipher is clocked without producing output. The second stage is a working stage and the algorithm produces a 32-bit word of output per loop of the working stage with every clock pulse.

According to the ZUC specification [3], ZUC is composed of three logical layers. The top layer is a linear feedback shift register (LFSR) of 16 stages; the middle layer is bit-reorganization (BR) procedure, and the bottom layer is a nonlinear function F procedure.

2.1   The Linear Feedback Shift Register (LFSR)

The linear feedback shift register (LFSR) has 16 of 31-bit registers $(S_0, S_1, \cdots, S_{15})$. Each register $S_i (0 \leqslant i \leqslant 15)$ is restricted to take values from the following set: $\{1, 2, 3, \ldots, 2^{31} - 1\}$. The LFSR has two modes of operations: the initialization mode and working mode. The initialization mode works as Algorithm 1 shown.

Algorithm 1. LFSRWithInitialisationMode

Input: u

1 **begin**
2 $\quad$ $v = \{2^{15}S_{15} + 2^{17}S_{13} + 2^{21}S_{10} + 2^{20}S_4 + (1 + 2^8)S_0\} \bmod (2^{31} - 1)$;
3 $\quad$ $S_{16} = (v + u) \bmod (2^{31} - 1)$;
4 $\quad$ **if** $S_{16} = 0$ **then**
5 $\quad\quad$ $\lfloor$ set $S_{16} = 2^{31} - 1$
6 $\quad$ $\lfloor$ $(S_1, S_2, \ldots, S_{15}, S_{16}) \to (S_0, S_1, \ldots, S_{14}, S_{15})$;

In the working mode, the LFSR does not receive any input, and it works as Algorithm 2 shown. It illustrates that the LFSR works independently with other parts of ZUC, which inspires us that if we acquire S_{16} per clock pulse, the shift registers perform shifts per clock cycle, meaning that we generate a 32-bit key every clock cycle. Therefore, we propose Scheme 2 and Scheme 3 of optimized implementations of ZUC in Section 3.

Algorithm 2. LFSRWithWorkMode

---

begin

    $S_{16} = \{2^{15}S_{15} + 2^{17}S_{13} + 2^{21}S_{10} + 2^{20}S_4 + (1 + 2^8)S_0\} \bmod (2^{31} - 1);$

    if $S_{16} = 0$ **then**

        $\lfloor$ set $S_{16} = 2^{31} - 1$

    $(S_1, S_2, \ldots, S_{15}, S_{16}) \rightarrow (S_0, S_1, \ldots, S_{14}, S_{15});$

2.2 The Bit-Reorganization (BR)

The middle layer of ZUC is the bit-reorganization (BR) procedure. Assuming that S_0, S_2, S_5, S_7, S_9, S_{11}, S_{14} and S_{15} are eight registers of LFSR. Then the BR forms four 32-bit words X_0, X_1, X_2 and X_3 in accordance with Algorithm 3, and the first three words are passed to the next bottom layer, nonlinear function F. More detailed description can be found in [3]. Compared with software implementations, to realize the concatenation of signals in hardware, we only need to change the wires order, and it hardly costs any time to complete this. Therefore, BR procedure should mix with the nonlinear function F operation together to save clock cycles.

Algorithm 3. Bitreorganization

---

begin

    $X_0 = S_{15H} \parallel S_{14L};$

    $X_1 = S_{11L} \parallel S_{9H};$

    $X_2 = S_{7L} \parallel S_{5H};$

    $X_3 = S_{2L} \parallel S_{0H};$

2.3 The Nonlinear Function F

There are two 32-bit memory cells, R_1 and R_2, in the nonlinear function F procedure. The input of F is X_0, X_1 and X_2, which are the first three words of output of BR procedure, and it outputs a 32-bit word W. The detailed process of the nonlinear function F is described in Algorithm 4.

In Algorithm 4, S is a 32×32 S-box; L_1 and L_2 are linear transformations, which are defined as Equation (1) and (2) respectively:

$$L_1(X) = X \oplus (X \lll_{32} 2) \oplus (X \lll_{32} 10) \oplus (X \lll_{32} 18) \oplus (X \lll_{32} 24) \quad (1)$$

$$L_2(X) = X \oplus (X \lll_{32} 8) \oplus (X \lll_{32} 14) \oplus (X \lll_{32} 22) \oplus (X \lll_{32} 30) \quad (2)$$

In the nonlinear function F stage, the critical path is the calculation of $W_1 = R_1 \boxplus X_1$, where $\boxplus$ denotes the modulo 2^{32} addition. Compared with the modulo addition, the other operations in nonlinear function F cost negligible time.

Algorithm 4. The Nonlinear Function F

   Input: X_0, X_1, X_2

1 **begin**

2     $W = (X_0 \oplus R_1) \boxplus R_2$;

3     $W_1 = R_1 \boxplus X_1$;

4     $W_2 = R_2 \oplus X_2$;

5     $R_1 = S(L_1(W_{1L} \parallel W_{2H}))$;

6     $R_2 = S(L_2(W_{2L} \parallel W_{1H}))$;

So we assume that the nonlinear function F and bit reorganization operation can be done in one clock cycle, that is to say, if LFSR complete the update every clock cycle, ZUC is able to generate a 32-bit key per clock cycle. We will focus on designing different optimized schemes to achieve different throughput and consumed area of FPGA implementation of ZUC in Section 3.

2.4 The Execution of ZUC

The execution of ZUC is composed of two stages: the initialization stage and working stage. During the initialization stage, the cipher algorithm runs the following operations 32 times to finish the initialization:

1. Bitreorganization();
2. $w = F(X_0, X_1, X_2)$;
3. $LFSRWithInitialisationMode(w >> 1)$;

After the initialization stage, the algorithm moves into the working stage. At the beginning of this stage, the algorithm executes the following operations once, and discards the output W of nonlinear function F:

1. Bitreorganization();
2. $F(X_0, X_1, X_2)$;
3. $LFSRWithWorkMode()$;

Then the algorithm goes into the stage of producing keystream, i.e., for each iteration, the following operations are executed once, and a 32-bit word Z is produced as an output:

1. Bitreorganization();
2. $Z = F(X_0, X_1, X_2) \oplus X_3$;
3. $LFSRWithWorkMode()$;

In the whole implementation of ZUC on FPGA, we found that LFSR procedure is far more wasteful and produces more costs than the BR procedure and nonlinear function F procedure before any optimization, and Equation (3) is the most time consuming component among LFSR procedure, hence calculation of Equation (3) is the critical path of LFSR procedure. The efficiency of ZUC implementation on FPGA is dependent on the costs of the critical path of the whole algorithm, namely maximum value of the critical path among that of LFSR procedure, BR procedure and nonlinear function F procedure. On the face of it, there are five modulo $(2^{31} - 1)$ additions when executing the update operation in LFSR procedure each time, according to Equation (3). The critical path is excessively long if we complete an update of LFSR during each clock cycle without any optimization on calculation of Equation (3). With regards to this, we propose three optimized schemes to implement LFSR procedure of ZUC, in order to best optimize and evaluate the hardware efficiency of ZUC implementation on FPGA.

$$\{2^{15}S_{15} + 2^{17}S_{13} + 2^{21}S_{10} + 2^{20}S_4 + (1 + 2^8)S_0\} \bmod (2^{31} - 1) \qquad (3)$$

3   Optimized FPGA Implementations of ZUC

In this section, we propose three optimized schemes to implement ZUC on FPGA and each scheme focuses on different optimizations of implementation.

3.1   Scheme 1: Reusing the Consumed Area of S-Box

At first appearance, we need five modulo $(2^{31} - 1)$ additions to complete each update in LFSR procedure. To achieve low overhead and high efficiency of FPGA implementation of ZUC, we strive to divide the calculation of Equation (3) into two parts and accomplish each part in one clock cycle, i.e., the whole calculation costs two clock cycles. We cut down the critical path of LFSR procedure into two modulo $(2^{31}-1)$ additions from originally five because of the reallocation. What's more, this scheme also reduces half of the consumed area of S-box implementation by means of reuse, due to the features of S-box, i.e., $S = (S_0, S_1, S_2, S_3)$, where $S_0 = S_2$ and $S_1 = S_3$. S_0 and S_1 are both 8×8 S-boxes.

In our FPGA implementation, we denote Equation (3) as Equation (4), where $A = 2^{15}S_{15}$, $B = 2^{17}S_{13}$, $C = 2^{21}S_{10}$, $D = 2^{20}S_4$, $E = S_0$, $F = 2^8S_0$. And we explain how this scheme works in just two clock cycles to accomplish the update of LFSR as follows.

$$\{A + B + C + D + E + F\} \bmod (2^{31} - 1) \qquad (4)$$

In the first clock cycle, we calculate Equation (5), (6) and (7) parallelly. Then we compute Equation (8) in the second clock cycle, as Fig. 1 shown. With this allocation of calculations, the critical path of LFSR is cut down to two modulo $(2^{31} - 1)$ additions. Therefore, the critical path of LFSR procedure becomes the calculation of Equation (8). We utilize Carry-Save Addition (CSA) to implement the addition in order to save time further. Taking advantage of CSA to calculate Equation (8), the modulo $(2^{31} - 1)$ addition of three numbers is cut down to only two.

$$T_1 = \{A + B\} \bmod (2^{31} - 1) \qquad (5)$$

$$T_2 = \{C + D\} \bmod (2^{31} - 1) \tag{6}$$

$$T_3 = \{E + F\} \bmod (2^{31} - 1) \tag{7}$$

Then the main difficulty of optimization is the implementation of modulo addition, i.e., Equation (9) and multiplication, i.e., $2^k x$ over $GF(p)$, however, since the modulus $p = 2^{31} - 1$ is a special prime [6], modulo addition and multiplication have faster implementations. Let $x, y \in GF(p)$ and write $x + y = z + c2^{31}$ for some integer $c \in \{0, 1\}$, where z is low-order of 31 bits of $x + y$, so it turns out to be $x + y = z + c$, which means that we do not have to do the modulo p addition directly, because when the sum of x and y is greater than p, Equation $(x + y) \bmod p = z + 1$, i.e., $c = 1$, is tenable. As to multiplication, for arbitrary integer $0 \leqslant k \leqslant 30$, we have $2^k x \bmod p = (x \lll_{31} k)$, which means we treat x as a 31-bit value and cyclically shift it towards the MSB by k-bit positions. Since the implementation of cyclic shift in hardware is quite fast that we only need to change the wires order. Fig. 2 depicts how to accomplish the calculation of Equation (9) faster. The time delayed by Equation (9) is equivalent to delay of two 32-bit additions and one multiplexer.

$$\{T_1 + T_2 + T_3\} \bmod (2^{31} - 1) \tag{8}$$

$$\{x + y\} \bmod (2^{31} - 1) \tag{9}$$

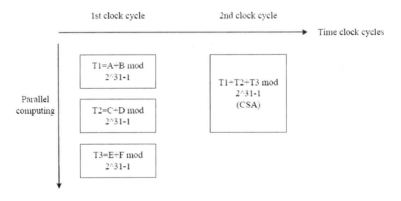

Fig. 1. The calculation flow of scheme 1

After the optimization of LFSR procedure, we consider the BR procedure and nonlinear function F procedure to implement them in two clock cycles. Based on the hardware implementation, BR procedure is accomplished only by adjusting the wire order, hence, it hardly generates additional delay to critical path of ZUC. Therefore, we focus on the nonlinear function F procedure where S-box lookup becomes the most time consuming calculation. To reuse the S-box, we need to

calculate equations of Algorithm 4 in two clock cycles to obtain integrated value
of R_1 and R_2. Noting that we only calculate part value of R_1 and R_2 in the
first clock cycle because of using half of original S-box. The rest part of them
is calculated in the second clock cycle in order to reduce the consumed area
on FPGA. So we save two 8×8 S-boxes areas altogether. The critical path
of nonlinear function F procedure is delay of two logical circuit cells and one
modulo 2^{32} addition, and apparently, it is shorter than the critical path of LFSR
procedure in this scheme. Therefore, the critical path of ZUC is the critical path
of LFSR procedure, namely calculation of Equation (8), which is the most time
consuming computation of the whole algorithm.

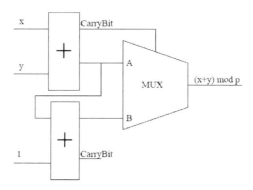

Fig. 2. The architecture of computing $(x + y) \bmod (2^{31} - 1)$

In this way, we reduce the computing number of modulo $(2^{31}-1)$ additions and
the consumed area to optimize the FGPA implementation of ZUC, and make
the critical path of ZUC shorter than the original one which is computation
of Equation (3), whereas it seems that we can optimize the implementation
further to achieve much higher throughput. Regarding Scheme 1, the 32-bit key
is produced in two clock cycles which costs a little more time than we expect,
hence, we are wondering if it can generate the 32-bit key in just one clock cycle,
that inspires us to propose Scheme 2 and Scheme 3.

3.2 Scheme 2: CSA Tree Implementation

In original ZUC algorithm, the most time consuming component is calculation
of Equation (3), which is also its critical path. With CSA method, we strive to
shorten the critical path and increase the working frequency. Due to Equation (3)
and the particular prime $(2^{31} - 1)$, we utilize a hierarchic CSA tree whose depth
is three to calculate Equation (3) as Fig. 3 shown. Because of the particular
prime $(2^{31} - 1)$, we utilize CSA method to calculate Equation (3) in the form
of Equation (10). We should notice that each value of carry in Fig. 3 should
shift 1-bit circularly to the left and $Adder(\bmod 2^{31} - 1)$ denotes two numbers

of modulo $(2^{31} - 1)$ addition. In this way, we simplify the modulo $(2^{31} - 1)$ addition of Equation (3) into the form of Equation (9), which is calculated in accordance with what Fig. 2 shows.

$$\{(A + B + C) + (D + E + F)\} \bmod (2^{31} - 1) \tag{10}$$

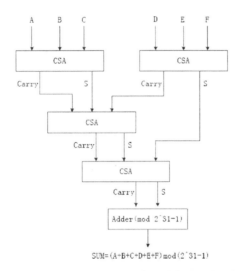

Fig. 3. The architecture of calculation in Scheme 2

Therefore, the critical path of ZUC implementation is shortened to three levels CSA circuits of calculating Equation (4) and it is computed in just one clock cycle. The BR procedure and nonlinear function F procedure are also implemented in one clock cycle, so four S-boxes are needed. Compared with Scheme 1, Scheme 2 needs three CSA circuits and two S-boxes more. The update period of LFSR is reduced to one clock cycle at the cost of more resources.

Regarding the BR procedure and nonlinear function F procedure, the critical path of LFSR is the delayed time of calculating Equation (4), whereas the critical path of nonlinear function F procedure is delay of two logical circuit cells and one modulo 2^{32} addition, which is equivalent to that of Scheme 1. Obviously, the critical path of ZUC of Scheme 2 is computation of Equation (4), which is longer than that of nonlinear function F procedure and that of Scheme 1. Now that the critical path of nonlinear function F procedure is quite short, we are able to achieve more efficient implementation of ZUC on FPGA if we make it become the critical path of the whole ZUC algorithm. Therefore, we propose Scheme 3, a pipelined architecture of ZUC implementation.

3.3   Scheme 3: Pipelined Architecture Implementation

As the specification of the working stage shown, the BR procedure and nonlinear function F procedure only rely on the registers of LFSR. If we design a pipelined architecture to realize Equation (3) in one clock cycle, the 32-bit key is generated per clock cycle. Therefore, we focus on implementation of Equation (3) and give a novel architecture to renew LFSR in just one clock cycle, because of the great impact of Equation (3) on working frequency of ZUC's hardware implementation.

In this section, we propose the pipelined architecture of ZUC implementation, which generates the 32-bit key per clock cycle and reduces the critical path of LFSR procedure to be one modulo $(2^{31} - 1)$ addition, like Equation (9). In order to construct a pipeline to implement Equation (3), first of all we should transform the computation of Equation (3) into the form of Equation (9). Afterwards, we should accomplish calculation of Equation (9) in just one clock cycle. To achieve the target, we add extra registers to store the sum of $(x + y)$, and use the carry bit of $(x + y)$ to select the result, as Fig. 2 shown.

Next we describe the novel pipelined architecture in detail. Table 1 depicts the pipelined work flow of Scheme 3, and the first four clock cycles are the initialization stage of the pipeline. The new architecture consists of five independent processes, which are named as A, B, C, D and E respectively. Equation in the form of $AddM(x, y)$ in the table denotes Equation (9). In order to build the pipeline, some pre-computations are needed to initialize the pipelined architecture, which constitute the pipeline initialization stage. During the pipeline initialization stage, the registers of LFSR don't shift. The pipeline initialization stage lasts four clock cycles. The registers of LFSR shift to the right per clock cycle and the 32-bit key is also outputted per clock cycle after the initialization stage.

In the first clock cycle, process A and B begin to parallelly calculate Equation (11) and (12) respectively at the same time. The rest of the processes don't work in this clock cycle and they all stay in the waiting state.

$$(S_0 + 2^8 S_0) \bmod (2^{31} - 1) \tag{11}$$

$$(2^{20} S_4 + 2^{21} S_{10}) \bmod (2^{31} - 1) \tag{12}$$

Originally, in the second clock cycle, process A calculates the new result of Equation (11) of the second round, however, in order to do the pre-computations, we calculate Equation (13) instead, because the registers of LFSR doesn't shift in this clock cycle. The calculation procedure of process B is similar to that of process A. Compared with the first clock cycle, process C begins to calculate the result of Equation (14) in the second clock cycle. The rest of the processes are still in the waiting state in this clock cycle.

$$(S_1 + 2^8 S_1) \bmod (2^{31} - 1) \tag{13}$$

$$(S_0 + 2^8 S_0 + 2^{20} S_4 + 2^{21} S_{10}) \bmod (2^{31} - 1). \tag{14}$$

In the third clock cycle, process A and B calculate the result of Equation (11) and (12) of the third round respectively. Process C calculates the result of Equation (14) of the second round and the result of Equation (15) of the first round is calculated by process D.

$$\{2^{17}S_{13} + 2^{21}S_{10} + 2^{20}S_4 + (1 + 2^8)S_0\} \bmod (2^{31} - 1) \tag{15}$$

$$\{2^{17}S_{13} + 2^{21}S_{10} + 2^{20}S_4 + 2^{15}S_{15} + (1 + 2^8)S_0\} \bmod (2^{31} - 1) \tag{16}$$

The execution of the fourth clock cycle is similar to that of the third one except that process A, B, C and D move into the next calculation round as shown in Table 1, and process E performs the first round calculation of Equation (16).

Process E gets the S_{16} in the fifth clock cycle, which is the S_{15} of the second round. Before this clock cycle, the registers of LFSR do not shift. After the fourth clock cycle, we need to shift the S_{16} into S_{15}, and also shift the other registers of LFSR to the right to renew them. Then the initialization of pipeline is completed and the pipeline enters into the working stage, where the registers of LFSR shift to the right every clock cycle.

Table 1. The pipeline flow

Clock	Process A	Process B	Process C	Process D	Process E
1	$AddM(S_0, 2^8 S_0)$	$AddM(2^{20}S_4, 2^{21}S_{10})$			
2	$AddM(S_1, 2^8 S_1)$	$AddM(2^{20}S_5, 2^{21}S_{11})$	$AddM(A_1, B_1)$		
3	$AddM(S_2, 2^8 S_2)$	$AddM(2^{20}S_6, 2^{21}S_{12})$	$AddM(A_2, B_2)$	$AddM(C_2, 2^{17}S_{13})$	
4	$AddM(S_3, 2^8 S_3)$	$AddM(2^{20}S_7, 2^{21}S_{13})$	$AddM(A_3, B_3)$	$AddM(C_3, 2^{17}S_{14})$	$AddM(D_3, 2^{15}S_{15})$
5	$AddM(S_3, 2^8 S_3)$	$AddM(2^{20}S_7, 2^{21}S_{13})$	$AddM(A_4, B_4)$	$AddM(C_4, 2^{17}S_{14})$	$AddM(D_4, 2^{15}S_{15})$
6	$AddM(S_3, 2^8 S_3)$	$AddM(2^{20}S_7, 2^{21}S_{13})$	$AddM(A_5, B_5)$	$AddM(C_5, 2^{17}S_{14})$	$AddM(D_5, 2^{15}S_{15})$

After the calculation of processes A, B, C, D and E of the first four clock cycles, the pipelined architecture implementation of ZUC completes the prerequisites and then we acquire a keystream of 32-bit words per clock cycle and cut down the critical path of LFSR into just one modulo $(2^{31} - 1)$ addition, which is the calculation of $AddM(x, y)$. In accordance with the calculation method of Equation (9) shown in Fig. 2, the critical path of LFSR becomes delay of two 32-bit additions and one multiplexer. The critical path of BR is still negligible and the critical path of nonlinear function F procedure stays the same as that of this procedure of Scheme 1 and Scheme 2, namely delay of two logical circuit cells and one modulo 2^{32} addition, which is larger than delay of two 32-bit additions and one multiplexer. Hence, the critical path of ZUC implementation of Scheme 3 on FPGA turns out to be the critical path of the nonlinear function F procedure, which is the shortest one of all implementations we expect.

4   Evaluation

In this section, we evaluated the three schemes of ZUC implementation aforementioned. All of them were implemented in Verilog Hardware Description Language

(Verilog HDL) and their results were verified by the C implementation. The results are represented as performance (in terms of throughout) and consumed area (in terms of Xilinx FPGA slices) and the experimental results are presented in Table 2. The design was synthesized in Virtex-5 XC5VLX110T FPGA that is the representative of modern FPGA.

Table 2. Hardware resource utilization and performance of ZUC

Optimized Schemes	Freq(MHz)	Area(slices)	Throughout(Mbps)	Throughout/Area
Scheme 1	126	311	2016	6.5
Scheme 2	108	356	3456	9.7
Scheme 3	222.4	575	7111	12.3

As Table 2 shown, the stream cipher algorithm, ZUC, is able to satisfy different requirements for adjustments of throughput and consumed area of hardware resources in the implementation on FPGA according to different scenarios, which meets the design requirements of modern cryptographic algorithms. On the basis of the numerical results listed in Table 2, the third scheme, pipelined architecture of ZUC implementation, achieves maximum speed by utilizing a little more consumed area, 575 slices and it also achieves the best optimization on average throughput per area, 12.3 comparing with 6.5 of Scheme 1 and 9.7 of Scheme 2. Besides, Scheme 1 consumes the least area of them, 311 slices and achieves throughput of 2 Gbps.

Experimental results show that the critical path of Scheme 3 is indeed the shortest, because of its largest working frequency, which is inversely proportional to the critical path. Although the critical path of the first and second scheme is that of LFSR procedure, their actual values are different due to different optimized measures, whereas the critical path of Scheme 3 is that of nonlinear function F procedure and shorter than that of both Scheme 1 and Scheme 2, therefore, the third scheme achieves maximum throughput, i.e., 7.1 Gbps with only 575 slices of consumed area, what's more, it also obtains the largest average throughput per area.

Table 3. Comparison of performance of ZUC and Snow

Algorithm	Freq(MHz)	Area(slices)	Throughout(Mbps)	Throughout/Area
ZUC	107	1723	3424	1.98
Snow 2.0	167	2420	5351	2.21

What's more, we compared the performance and area utilization of the pipelined architecture implementation of ZUC with another stream cipher Snow [12] as Table 3 depicted. Both of them were implemented on Xilinx Virtex-II device. The evaluation results listed in Table 3 show that the FPGA implementation of stream cipher Snow, whose evaluation result appeared in [1], is more efficient than that of ZUC, which was implemented by Scheme 3, because of different architecture of the algorithm itself.

5   Conclusion

In this paper, we proposed three optimized schemes to implement ZUC, which is a novel stream cipher and is proposed for inclusion in the '4G' mobile standard, on FPGA and compared them in terms of both performance and consumed area. The experimental results show that different optimized scheme incurs different throughput and consumed area. It is quite flexible and resilient to implement ZUC on FPGA, and people should adopt appropriate optimized scheme according to their own requirements, considering the throughput and consumed area. According to our experiments, the third scheme, namely pipelined architecture of ZUC, achieves the most efficient hardware implementation of ZUC, and it also obtains the best optimization on average throughput per area.

References

1. Leglise, P., Standaert, F., Rouvroy, G., Quisquater, J.: Efficient implementation of recent stream ciphers on reconfigurable hardware devices. In: 26th Symposium on Information Theory in the Benelux, pp. 261–268 (2005)
2. Galanis, M., Kitsos, P., Kostopoulos, G., Sklavos, N., Koufopavlou, O., Goutis, C.: Comparison of the hardware architectures and FPGA implementations of stream ciphers. In: Proceedings of the 2004 11th IEEE International Conference on Electronics, Circuits and Systems, ICECS 2004, pp. 571–574. IEEE (2005)
3. Specification of the 3GPP Confidentiality and Integrity Algorithms 128-EEA3 & 128-EIA3. Document 2: ZUC Specification, version 1.5, January 4 (2011)
4. Specification of the 3GPP Confidentiality and Integrity Algorithms 128-EEA3 & 128-EIA3.Document 1: 128-EEA3 and 128-EIA3 Specification, version 1.5, January 4 (2011)
5. Specification of the 3GPP Confidentiality and Integrity Algorithms 128-EEA3 & 128-EIA3.Document 3: Implementor's Test Data, version 1.1, January 4 (2011)
6. Specification of the 3GPP Confidentiality and Integrity Algorithms 128-EEA3 & 128-EIA3. Document 4: Design and Evaluation Report, version 1.3, January 4 (2011)
7. Batina, L., Lano, J., Mentens, N., Ors, S., Preneel, B., Verbauwhede, I.: Energy, performance, area versus security trade-offs for stream ciphers. In: The State of the Art of Stream Ciphers: Workshop Record, pp. 302–310. Citeseer (2004)
8. Elbirt, A., Yip, W., Chetwynd, B., Paar, C.: An FPGA implementation and performance evaluation of the AES block cipher candidate algorithm finalists. In: The Third AES Candidate Conference, Printed by the National Institute of Standards and Technology, Gaithersburg, MD, pp. 13–27. Citeseer (2000)
9. Gaj, K., Southern, G., Bachimanchi, R.: Comparison of hardware performance of selected Phase II eSTREAM candidates. In: State of the Art of Stream Ciphers Workshop (SASC 2007), eSTREAM, ECRYPT Stream Cipher Project, Report, vol. 26, p. 2007. Citeseer (2007)

10. Hwang, D., Chaney, M., Karanam, S., Ton, N., Gaj, K.: Comparison of FPGA-targeted hardware implementations of eSTREAM stream cipher candidates. The State of the Art of Stream Ciphers, 151–162 (2008)
11. Braeken, A., Lano, J., Mentens, N., Preneel, B., Verbauwhede, I.: SFINKS: A synchronous stream cipher for restricted hardware environments. In: SKEW-Symmetric Key Encryption Workshop, Citeseer (2005)
12. Ekdahl, P., Johansson, T.: SNOW-a new stream cipher. In: Proceedings of First Open NESSIE Workshop, KU-Leuven, Citeseer (2000)

First Differential Attack
on Full 32-Round GOST[*]

Nicolas T. Courtois[1] and Michał Misztal[2]

[1] University College London, Gower Street, London, UK
n.courtois@cs.ucl.ac.uk
[2] Military University of Technology, Kaliskiego 2, Warsaw, Poland
mmisztal@wat.edu.pl

Abstract. GOST 28147-89 is a well-known block cipher and the official encryption standard of the Russian Federation. A 256-bit block cipher considered as an alternative for AES-256 and triple DES, having an amazingly low implementation cost and thus increasingly popular and used [12,15,13,20]. Until 2010 researchers have written that: "despite considerable cryptanalytic efforts spent in the past 20 years, GOST is still not broken", see [15] and in 2010 it was submitted to ISO 18033 to become a worldwide industrial encryption standard. In 2011 it was suddenly discovered that GOST is insecure on more than one account. There is a variety of recent attacks on GOST [3,7]. We have reflection attacks [14,7], attacks with double reflection [7], and various attacks which do not use reflections [7,3]. The final key recovery step in these attacks is in most cases a software algebraic attack [7,3] and sometimes a Meet-In-The-Middle attack [14,7].

In this paper we show that GOST is NOT SECURE even against (advanced forms of) differential cryptanalysis (DC). Previously Russian researchers postulated that GOST will be secure against DC for as few as 7 rounds out of 32 [9,19] and Japanese researchers were already able to break about 13 rounds [18]. In this paper we show a first advanced differential attack faster than brute force on full 32-round GOST.

Keywords: Block ciphers, GOST, differential cryptanalysis, sets of differentials, aggregated differentials, iterative differentials.

1 Introduction on GOST

GOST 28147-89 was standardized in 1989 [10] and is an official standard for the protection of confidential information in Russia, and formerly in the Soviet Union. Several specifications in English are also is available [11,12]. Unlike DES which could only be used to protect unclassified information, and like AES, GOST allows to protect also classified and secret information apparently without

[*] This work was supported by Polish Ministry of Science and Higher Education under research project Nr O R00 0111 12 and by the European Commission under the FP7 project number 242497 Resilient Infrastructure and Building Security (RIBS).

S. Qing et al. (Eds.): ICICS 2011, LNCS 7043, pp. 216–227, 2011.

any limitations, which is explicitly stated by the Russian standard, see the first page of [11]. Therefore GOST is much more than a Russian equivalent of DES, and its large key size of 256 bits make GOST a plausible alternative for AES-256 and 3-key triple DES. The latter for the same block size of 64 bits offers keys of only 168 bits. Clearly GOST is a very serious military-grade cipher.

The GOST S-boxes can be secret and they can be used to constitute a secondary key which is common to a given application, further extending key size to a total of 610 bits. Two sets of GOST S-boxes have been explicitly identified as being used by the two of most prominent Russian banks and financial institutions cf. [19,13]). The Russian banks need to securely communicate with tens of thousands of branches to protect assets worth many hundreds of billions of dollars against fraud.

One set of S-boxes known as "GostR3411_94_TestParamSet" [13] was published in 1994 as a part of the Russian standard hash function specification and according to Schneier [19] this set is used by the Central Bank of the Russian Federation. This precise version of GOST 28147-89 block cipher is the most popular one, and it is commonly called just "the GOST cipher" in the cryptographic literature. In this paper we concentrate on this set of S-boxes. The most complete current reference implementation of GOST which is of genuine Russian origin and is a part of OpenSSL library, contains eight standard sets of S-boxes [13]. Other (secret) S-boxes could possibly be recovered from a chip or implementation, see [17,8].

1.1 GOST Is Very Competitive

In addition to the very long bit keys GOST has a much lower implementation cost than AES or any other comparable encryption algorithm. For example in hardware GOST 256 bits requires less than 800 GE, while AES-128 requires 3100 GE, see [15]. Accordingly in 2010 GOST was submitted to ISO to become a worldwide encryption standard. ISO is still in the process of standardizing GOST at the time of writing.

2   Security of GOST

GOST was widely studied in the literature and while it is widely understood that the structure of GOST is in itself quite weak, for example compared to DES, and in particular the diffusion is not quite as good, it was however always stipulated that this should be compensated by a large number of 32 rounds cf. [9,19,18] and also by the additional non-linearity and diffusion provided by modular additions [9,16]. As far as traditional encryption applications of GOST with random keys are concerned, until 2011, no cryptographically significant single-key attack on GOST was ever found, which was summarized in 2010 in these words: "despite considerable cryptanalytic efforts spent in the past 20 years, GOST is still not broken", see [15].

In the well known Schneier textbook written in the late 1990s we read: "Against differential and linear cryptanalysis, GOST is probably stronger than

DES", see [19]. Then in 2000 Russian researchers claimed that "breaking the GOST with five or more rounds is very hard". and explain that as few as 5 to 7 rounds are sufficient to protect GOST against linear and differential cryptanalysis. In the same year, Japanese researchers [18], explain that in addition, such straightforward classical differential attack with one single differential characteristic are unlikely to work **at all** for a larger number of rounds. This is due to the fact that they only work for a fraction of keys, likely to rapidly decrease with the number of rounds, see [18]).

Yet in the same paper [18], more advanced differential attacks on GOST are described. They show how to break about 13 rounds of GOST and until now it was not clear if these attacks can be extended in any way to a larger number of rounds such as full 32 rounds, because partial internal differences generated in such attack become very hard to distinguish from differences which occur naturally at random. These questions are the central topic in this paper.

2.1   Recent Attacks on GOST

A new attack which finally breaks GOST, was very recently presented at FSE 2011, see [14]. A related but different, simpler and faster attack, appears in [7]. Many other new attacks have been recently developed, see [3,7].

3   Linear and Differential Cryptanalysis of GOST

3.1   Previous Research and Application to GOST

A basic assessment of the security of GOST against linear cryptanalysis (LC) and differential cryptanalysis (DC) has been conducted in 2000 by Gabidulin *et al*, see [9]. The results are quite impressive: at the prescribed security of level of 2^{256}, 5 rounds are sufficient to protect GOST against LC. Moreover, even if the S-boxes are replaced by identity, and the only non-linear operation in the cipher is the addition modulo 2^{32}, the cipher is still secure against LC after 6 rounds out of 32. In [9] the authors also estimate that, but here only w.r.t. the security level of about 2^{128}, roughly about 7 rounds should be sufficient to protect GOST against DC.

3.2   Classical Biham-Shamir DC Attacks and GOST

The difficulty is explained by the Japanese researchers in 2000 [18]. If we consider the straightforward classical differential attack with one single differential characteristic it is in fact **unlikely to work at all** for a larger number of rounds.

This is due to the fact that when we study reasonably "good" iterative differential characteristics for a limited number of rounds (which already propagate with probabilities not better than $2^{-11.4}$ per round, cf. [18]), we realize that they only work for a fraction of keys smaller than half. For full 32-round GOST such an attack with a single characteristic would work only for a negligible fraction of keys of about 2^{-62} (and even for this tiny fraction it would propagate with a probability not better than 2^{-360}).

3.3   Advanced Differential Attacks on GOST

This however does not prevent more advanced differential attacks on GOST which are the central topic in this paper. They have been introduced in 2000 in the same already cited Japanese paper [18]. They can be seen in two different ways, either as attacks which use sets of differentials as they are formalized in [18], or more specifically, as it is the case for the most interesting attacks of this type known (from [18] and in this paper), as attacks in which differentials are truncated, so that the best sets of differentials actually follow certain patterns, for example certain bits or whole S-boxes have zero differentials, and only some bits are active and have non-zero differentials.

3.4   Previous Advanced DC Attack on GOST

The best key recovery attack proposed in [18] has the

1. An initial extension with a small number of active bits at the input.
2. An iterative set of differentials with 24 active bits which can propagate for an arbitrary number of rounds.
3. A final extension differential with again a much smaller number of active bits,
4. A method for key recovery with guessing some key bits.

Attacks with sets of differentials can be applied to other ciphers, for example Q [1] and more recently PP-1 [5]. Our final key recovery method uses the key scheduling of GOST and thus is different than in previously published works [18,1,5].

In [18] the main iterative set of differentials occur naturally with higher probability of 2^{-50}, which is not negligible anymore like in DES [2]. We are no longer dealing with exceptional events which never happen by accident, and which when they happen, happen for a specific reason and yield a lot of information when they happen, like in DES [2]. For GOST, when some differentials in a set are attained, there is a lot of ambiguity about why exactly they are attained, and such events give much less exploitable information about the secret keys than in DC for DES [2].

Summary. The best advanced multiple differential attack proposed in [18] allows to break between 12 and 17 rounds of GOST depending on the key, some keys being weaker. In this paper we greatly improve on the state of the art and develop the first differential attack on full 32 rounds.

4   From GOST to New Differential Attacks on GOST

GOST is a block cipher with a simple Feistel structure, 64-bit block size, 256-bit keys and 32 rounds. Each round contains a key addition modulo 2^{32}, a set of 8 bijective S-boxes on 4 bits, and a simple rotation by 11 positions.

Differential characteristics in GOST, need to take into account not only the S-boxes, like in DES, but also the key addition modulo 2^{32}, which makes that their probabilities depend on the key. In this paper we summarize the state of the art and report some very important new results. The (very technical) explanation on how to obtain this type of results through extended computer simulations is outside the scope of this paper and will appear elsewhere.

5   Vocabulary: Aggregated Differentials

We define *an aggregated differential* A, B as the transition where any non-zero difference $a \in A$ will produce an arbitrary non-zero difference $b \in B$ with a certain probability.

In the previous work on GOST exactly the same sorts of differentials are exploited for GOST, see [18]. The are called "sets of differential characteristics" however this would suggest that any set of characteristics is possible, for example $a \Rightarrow b$ and $a' \Rightarrow b'$ could be permitted but not $a \Rightarrow b'$. This is an unnecessarily general notion. Our notion of Aggregated Differentials only allows "sets of differential characteristics" which are in a Cartezian direct product of two sets $A \times B$.

Similar sets of differentials are also called "almost iterative differentials" in [1], however the word "almost" can be seen as misleading, because here and elsewhere [1,5] we will have "perfectly" iterative differentials, which are perfectly periodic, and can propagate for an arbitrary number of rounds, from set A, to exactly the same set A.

6   Multiple Differential Attacks on GOST

This attack on GOST was introduced in 2000 [18]. For example the difference of type 0x70707070,0x07070707, where each 7 means an arbitrary difference on 3 bits, plus extra rules to exclude all-zero differentials, propagates for one round with a probability of about $2^{-5.3}$. Here what we report will already start to differ from the combination of theoretical probabilities given in [18]. This is because it is very hard to predict what really happens with complex sets of differentials by theory. In fact it is rather impossible for complex differentials which could propagate over many rounds, to enumerate all possible differential paths which could at the end produce one of the differentials in our set. Moreover they strongly depend on the key. Therefore the more rounds we have, the more the actual (experimental) results will differ from predictions. Moreover the difference is in our experience almost always beneficial to the attacker: as we will see below, better attacks than expected are almost always obtained.

6.1   New Results

Many very good characteristics exist for GOST. Here we give one example. This example has been constructed by hand by the authors from differential characteristics of various S-boxes and already reported in one paper [5]. Consider the following differential set:

$$\Delta = 0x80700700$$

by which we mean all differences with between 1 and 7 active bits (but not 0) and where the active bits are contained within the mask 0x80700700. Similarly, an aggregated differential (Δ, Δ) means that we have 14 active bits, and that any non-zero difference is allowed. There are $2^{14} - 1$ differences in this set of ours. The following fact can be verified experimentally:

Fact 6.2. *The aggregated differential (Δ, Δ) with uniform sampling of all differences it allows, produces an element of the same aggregated differential set (Δ, Δ) after 4 rounds of GOST with probability about $2^{-13.6}$ on average over all possible keys.*

Importantly, for 8 rounds the result is better than the square of $2^{-13.6}$ which would be $2^{-27.2}$. It is:

Fact 6.3. *The aggregated differential (Δ, Δ) (again with uniform sampling) produces the same aggregated differential (Δ, Δ) after 8 rounds of GOST with probability about $2^{-25.0}$ on average over all possible keys.*

6.4   Propagation for 16 Rounds

Fact 6.5. *The aggregated differential (Δ, Δ) produces the same aggregated differential (Δ, Δ) after 16 rounds of GOST with probability about 2^{-48} on average over all possible keys.*

Justification: A more precise result need to be obtained by computer simulations.

This needs to be compared to the probability that the output difference set (Δ, Δ) will also occur naturally. In this set there are exactly 50 inactive bits where the difference must always be 0. Therefore:

Fact 6.6. *The 64-bit output difference being a member of our set (Δ, Δ) occurs naturally with probability about 2^{-50}.*

6.7   Detailed Comparison New vs. Previous Results

We need to compare our result with the Japanese paper [18] from 2000. If we apply the probabilities found in [18], in theory, we expect that the difference of type 0x70707070,0x07070707 will propagate for 8 rounds with a probability of about $2^{-42.7}$. Our simulations show it is **much** higher. It is about $2^{-28.4}$ in practice.

Our aggregated differential (Δ, Δ) with $\Delta = 0x80700700$ propagates with a better probability of about 2^{-48}, while the output difference in this set occurs naturally with probability of about 2^{-50}. Clearly with the new method we are able to distinguish 16 rounds of GOST from a random permutation. Some of these results were already reported in [5]. Further values have less precision and are extrapolations.

Input Aggregated Differential	0x70707070,0x07070707	0x80700700,0x80700700
Output Aggregated Differential	0x70707070,0x07070707	0x80700700,0x80700700
Reference	Seki-Kaneko [18]	this paper and [5]
Propagation 2 R	$2^{-8.6}$	$2^{-7.5}$
Propagation 4 R	$2^{-16.7}$	$2^{-13.6}$
Propagation 6 R	$2^{-24.1}$	$2^{-18.7}$
Propagation 8 R	$2^{-28.4}$	$2^{-25.0}$
Propagation 10 R	2^{-35}	$2^{-31.1}$
Propagation 12 R	2^{-43}	2^{-36}
Propagation 14 R	2^{-50}	2^{-42}
Propagation 16 R	2^{-56}	2^{-48}
Propagation 18 R	2^{-62}	2^{-54}
Propagation 20 R	2^{-70}	2^{-60}
Propagation 22 R	2^{-77}	2^{-66}
Output Δ Occurs Naturally	$2^{-40.0}$	$2^{-50.0}$

Fig. 1. Our results and further extrapolations vs. previous results

6.8 An Initial Extension

It appears that the best single differential suitable for the initial extension for (Δ, Δ) is one which does not modify anything in the first round, and one which will only affect the highest bit in the modular addition in the second round which does not generate any carries. This differential is $(0x80000000, 0x00000000)$.

In the following table we report some results which are computed as follows: for smaller number of rounds X they are computed experimentally. For a larger X and for all possible decompositions $X = Y + Z$ we consider that for the first Y rounds we have achieved the iterative set from the initial set, and for the remaining Z rounds we apply one of the exact results from Table 1 above. Due to the method these results are rather conservative estimations. We compare these results to those obtained assuming that one used the initial extension from [18] which again are exact results for up to 8 rounds, and beyond we again give lower bounds and based on a decomposition of $X = Y + Z$ rounds with Y rounds being as in Table 2 and Z being the main iterative piece as in Table 1, where we report the best lower bound obtain by such decomposition which again is a conservative estimation.

7   A Final Extension

In this section we propose a final extension with less active bits which seems to work well for various numbers of rounds.

Input Aggregated Differential	0x00000700,0x00000000	0x80000000,0x00000000
Output Aggregated Differential	0x70707070,0x07070707	0x80700700,0x80700700
Reference	Seki-Kaneko [18]	this paper
Propagation 2 R	$2^{-1.4}$	$2^{-0.4}$
Propagation 4 R	$2^{-5.6}$	$2^{-6.2}$
Propagation 6 R	$2^{-11.5}$	$2^{-12.2}$
Propagation 8 R	$2^{-20.1}$	$2^{-20.5}$
Propagation 10 R	2^{-28}	$2^{-24.6}$
Propagation 12 R	2^{-34}	$2^{-30.3}$
Propagation 14 R	2^{-41}	2^{-36}
Propagation 16 R	2^{-46}	2^{-42}
Propagation 18 R	2^{-55}	2^{-47}
Propagation 20 R	2^{-61}	2^{-53}
Propagation 22 R	2^{-66}	2^{-59}
Output Δ Occurs Naturally	$2^{-40.0}$	$2^{-50.0}$

Fig. 2. Some results with our initial extension

Fact 7.1. *The ordinary differential* $(0x80000000, 0x00000000)$ *produces a nonzero differential in the set* $(0x00000100, 0x80600200)$ *after 20 rounds of GOST with probability roughly at least about* 2^{-58} *on average over all possible keys.*

Justification: Currently we have no good method to estimate this probability. We consider an affine model. Our best aggregated differential which is $(0x80000000, 0x00000000) \Rightarrow (0x00000100, 0x80600200)$ Experimental results obtained for 8, 10 and 12 rounds are respectively $2^{23.6}$, $2^{28.4}$, and $2^{33.2}$. If we extrapolate from the last two values we get that maybe for 20 rounds the result could be $2^{-28.4-4.8\cdot(20-10)/2} \approx 2^{-52}$. Being conservative we postulate it is at least 2^{-58} due to the propagation (cases with many intermediate differentials of small Hamming weight) and another 2^{-59} which occur by accident because we have 59 inactive bits in $(0x00000100, 0x80600200)$. We do not have enough computing power to confirm this result. **This result is inexact.** A better method to estimate this probability needs to be developed in the future.

7.2   Our Distinguisher For 20 Rounds

We can note that the aggregated differential $(0x00000100, 0x80600200)$ has 5 active bits and occurs naturally with probability 2^{-59}. In contrast the propagation we predict is expected to occur with probability of about 2^{-58} (with many intermediate differentials of small Hamming weight).

We are finally able to distinguish 20 rounds from a random permutation. We study this distinguisher in more details.

For a random permutation, if we consider 2^{63} possible pairs with an input difference $(0x80000000, 0x00000000)$, about $2^4 = 2^{63-59}$ pairs will have an output difference in the desired form in $(0x00000100, 0x80600200)$ purely by accident (a collision on 59 bits in the last round, arbitrary differentials in the middle of the computation).

In the case of the actual 20 rounds of GOST we expect that there will be another and additional number of about $2^5 = 2^{63-58}$ "good" pairs and with output difference in $(0x80700700, 0x80700700)$ and with many intermediate differentials of small Hamming weight. It is essential to understand that the overlap between these sets of 2^4 and 2^5 pairs should be most of the time negligible, because we are well below the birthday paradox bound for two sets to overlap.

Therefore in our attacks on 20 rounds we expect to get about 2^4 pairs when the key guessed is incorrect, and about $2^4 + 2^5$ when it is correct. Can we distinguish between these two cases?

The standard deviation for the number of cases (collisions on 59 bits which occur by accident) can be computed as a sum of 2^{63} independent random variables equal to 1 with probability 2^{-59} and the result is 2^2. Our additional 2^5 cases amounts to 8 standard deviations. By applying the central limit theorem and assuming that our sum of 2^{63} independent random variables is Gaussian, and by applying the Gauss error function we obtain that the probability that by accident the number reaches a threshold of $2^4 + 2^5$ when it is correct, which is outside 8 standard deviations, is about 2^{-50}. In contrast if the permutation has these additional pairs which come from the propagation of our differential, we expect to be above the threshold of $2^4 + 2^5$ with probability 2^{-1}.

This is the basis of our attack and this distinguisher will be used to filter out a large proportion of wrong assumptions on GOST keys.

Future Work: Our aggregated output differential is in fact a collection of $2^5 - 1$ ordinary differentials, and the frequency of these differentials is not uniform. Thus better distinguishers can probably be developed. However this is **not** very easy because the distribution strongly depends on the key.

8 Key Recovery Attacks on Full 32-Round GOST

The key property which makes that we can substantially reduce the number of rounds in full 32-round GOST is that the order of 32-bit words in the key schedule is inversed in the last 8 rounds. In the fist 8 rounds we have:

$$k_0, k_1, k_2, k_3, k_4, k_5, k_6, k_7, \ldots$$

In the last 8 rounds we have:

$$\ldots, k_7, k_6, k_5, k_4, k_3, k_2, k_1, k_0$$

Thus for example if we guess $k_0, k_1, k_2, k_3, k_4, k_5$ we are left with only 20 rounds inside GOST. Then the simplest attack one can think of based on Fact 7.1 would work as follows:

8.1 First Differential Attack on GOST Faster Than Brute Force

For each 192-bit guess $k_0, k_1, k_2, k_3, k_4, k_5$ and for each of 2^{64} P/C pairs for 32 rounds, we compute the first 6 rounds forwards, and the last 6 rounds backwards.

Thus we get 2^{64} P/C pairs for 20 rounds. This would require a total time spent in this step of about $2^{192} \cdot 2^{64} \cdot 12/32$ GOST encryptions which is $2^{254.6}$ GOST encryptions, slightly less than brute force but not much less. Then we can discard a proportion about 2^{-50} of keys on 192 bits. Remaining key bits are found by brute force.

Summary. This attack requires 2^{64} KP and allows to break full 32-round GOST in time of about $2^{254.6}$ GOST encryptions for a success probability of 50 %. This is faster than brute force.

9   Conclusion

In 2000 Russian researchers claimed that as few as 7 rounds out of 32 would protect GOST against differential cryptanalysis, see [9]. In the same year two Japanese researchers [18], show that approximatively 13 rounds can be broken by joining several differential characteristics together [18]. More recently it was shown that the characteristics from [18] propagate better than expected, for example they allows to easily distinguish 12 rounds from a random permutation, see Fig. 2 and [5]. Ne and better sets of differentials able to distinguish 16 rounds of GOST were proposed in [5]. In this paper we extend previous results with suitable initial and final extensions and show how to distinguish 20 rounds of GOST from a random permutation, cf. Fact 7.1. From here, given the weakness in ordering of round keys in GOST, we develop a first differential attack on full 32-round GOST which is (only slightly) faster than brute force.

GOST is a standardized block cipher intended to provide a military level of security and to protect the communications for the government, the military, large banks and other organisations. Designed in the Soviet times, it remains today the official encryption standard of the Russian Federation. While in the United States DES could be used ONLY for unclassified documents, GOST "does not place any limitations on the secrecy level of the protected information", see [11]. GOST is a very economical cipher in hardware implementation, cf. [15]. In 2010 GOST was submitted to ISO to become an international standard and it is still in the process of being standardized at the time of writing. It is extremely rare to see such a cipher being broken by a mathematical attack faster than brute force.

The attack presented in this paper is just a sketch and a proof of concept. There is no systematic method known to find good aggregated differential characteristics. We have been conservative in estimations of probabilities and these probabilities alone require more work or/and more simulations to be computed exactly. We have also estimated that it is possible to lower the time complexity of this attack to about 2^{226} by a more progressive guessing of key bits, and filtering out pairs which cannot occur. Due to the lack of space, and the necessity to do more work on exact probabilities, these more complex attacks need more space and attention and will be developed in future publications. Some further but still early results are reported in [4].

References

1. Biham, E., Furman, V., Misztal, M., Rijmen, V.: Differential Cryptanalysis of Q. In: Matsui, M. (ed.) FSE 2001. LNCS, vol. 2355, pp. 174–186. Springer, Heidelberg (2002)
2. Biham, E., Shamir, A.: Differential Cryptanalysis of the Full 16-Round DES. In: Brickell, E.F. (ed.) CRYPTO 1992. LNCS, vol. 740, pp. 487–496. Springer, Heidelberg (1993)
3. Courtois, N.T.: Security Evaluation of GOST 28147-8. View Of International Standardisation, document officially submitted to ISO in May 2011. In: Cryptology ePrint Archive, Report 2011/211, May 1 (2011),
   http://eprint.iacr.org/2011/211/
4. Courtois, N.T., Misztal, M.: Differential Cryptanalysis of GOST. In: Cryptology ePrint Archive, Report 2011/312, June 14 (2011),
   http://eprint.iacr.org/2011/312
5. Courtois, N.T., Misztal, M.: Aggregated Differentials and Cryptanalysis of PP-1 and GOST. In: 11th Central European Conference on Cryptology, Post-proceedings Expected to Appear in Periodica Mathematica Hungarica
6. Courtois, N.T.: General Principles of Algebraic Attacks and New Design Criteria for Cipher Components. In: Dobbertin, H., Rijmen, V., Sowa, A. (eds.) AES 2005. LNCS, vol. 3373, pp. 67–83. Springer, Heidelberg (2005)
7. Courtois, N.T.: Algebraic Complexity Reduction and Cryptanalysis of GOST. Preprint, submitted to Crypto 2011, later split in several papers, a short and basic version exactly as submitted to Asiacrypt (2011),
   http://www.nicolascourtois.com/papers/gostac11.pdf
8. Furuya, S.: Slide Attacks with a Known-Plaintext Cryptanalysis. In: Kim, K.-c. (ed.) ICICS 2001. LNCS, vol. 2288, pp. 214–225. Springer, Heidelberg (2002)
9. Shorin, V.V., Jelezniakov, V.V., Gabidulin, E.M.: Linear and Differential Cryptanalysis of Russian GOST. Preprint submitted to Elsevier Preprint, April 4 (2001)
10. Zabotin, I.A., Glazkov, G.P., Isaeva, V.B.: Cryptographic Protection for Information Processing Systems, Government Standard of the USSR, GOST 28147-89, Government Committee of the USSR for Standards (1989) (in Russian, Translated to English in [11])
11. An English translation of [10] by Aleksandr Malchik with an English Preface co-written with Whitfield Diffie, can be found at,
    http://www.autochthonous.org/crypto/gosthash.tar.gz
12. Dolmatov, V. (ed.): RFC 5830: GOST 28147-89 encryption, decryption and MAC algorithms, IETF (March 2010) ISSN: 2070-1721,
    http://tools.ietf.org/html/rfc5830
13. A Russian reference implementation of GOST implementing Russian algorithms as an extension of TLS v1.0. is available as a part of OpenSSL library. The file gost89.c contains eight different sets of S-boxes and is found in OpenSSL 0.9.8 and later, http://www.openssl.org/source/
14. Isobe, T.: A Single-Key Attack on the Full GOST Block Cipher. In: Joux, A. (ed.) FSE 2011. LNCS, vol. 6733, pp. 290–305. Springer, Heidelberg (2011)
15. Poschmann, A., Ling, S., Wang, H.: 256 Bit Standardized Crypto for 650 GE – GOST Revisited. In: Mangard, S., Standaert, F.-X. (eds.) CHES 2010. LNCS, vol. 6225, pp. 219–233. Springer, Heidelberg (2010)
16. Charnes, C., O'Connor, L., Pieprzyk, J., Safavi-Naini, R., Zheng, Y.: Comments on Soviet Encryption Algorithm. In: De Santis, A. (ed.) EUROCRYPT 1994. LNCS, vol. 950, pp. 433–438. Springer, Heidelberg (1995)

17. Saarinen, M.-J.: A chosen key attack against the secret S-boxes of GOST (1998) (unpublished manuscript)
18. Seki, H., Kaneko, T.: Differential Cryptanalysis of Reduced Rounds of GOST. In: Stinson, D.R., Tavares, S. (eds.) SAC 2000. LNCS, vol. 2012, pp. 315–323. Springer, Heidelberg (2001)
19. Schneier, B.: Section 14.1 GOST. In: Applied Cryptography, 2nd edn. John Wiley and Sons (1996) ISBN 0-471-11709-9
20. Dai, W.: Crypto++, a public domain library containing a reference C++ implementation of GOST and test vectors, http://www.cryptopp.com

Collision Attack for the Hash Function Extended MD4[*]

Gaoli Wang[1,2]

[1] School of Computer Science and Technology, Donghua University,
Shanghai 201620, China
wanggaoli@dhu.edu.cn
[2] State Key Laboratory of Information Security, Institute of Software,
Chinese Academy of Sciences, Beijing 100049, China

Abstract. Extended MD4 is a hash function proposed by Rivest in 1990 with a 256-bit hash value. The compression function consists of two different and independent parallel lines called Left Line and Right Line, and each line has 48 steps. The initial values of Left Line and Right Line are denoted by IV_0 and IV_1 respectively. Dobbertin proposed a collision attack for the compression function of Extended MD4 with a complexity of about 2^{40} under the condition that the value for $IV_0 = IV_1$ is prescribed. In this paper, we gave a collision attack on the full Extended MD4 with a complexity of about 2^{37}. Firstly, we propose a collision differential path for both lines by choosing a proper message difference, and deduce a set of sufficient conditions that ensure the differential path hold. Then by using some precise message modification techniques to improve the success probability of the attack, we find two-block collisions of Extended MD4 with less than 2^{37} computations. This work provides a new reference to the collision analysis of other hash functions such as RIPEMD-160 etc. which consist of two lines.

Keywords: Cryptanalysis, Collision, Differential path, Hash functions, Extended MD4.

1 Introduction

Cryptographic hash functions remain one of the most used cryptographic primitives, and they can be used to guarantee the security of many cryptosystems and protocols such as digital signature, message authentication code and so on. In 1990, Rivest introduced the first dedicated hash function MD4 [20, 21]. After the publication of MD4, several dedicated hash functions were proposed, and these functions are called MD4-family. Depend on the method of the message expansion and the number of parallel of computations, the MD4-family are divided into three subfamilies. The first is MD-family, which consists of MD4 [20, 21], MD5 [23] and HAVAL [33]. The characteristics of MD-family is using roundwise permutations for the message expansion

[*] This work is supported by "Chen Guang" project (supported by Shanghai Municipal Education Commission and Shanghai Education Development Foundation), the National Natural Science Foundation of China (No. 61103238), the Fundamental Research Funds for the Central Universities, and the open research fund of State Key Laboratory of Information Security.

and only one line of computation. The second is RIPEMD-family, which consists of RIPEMD [19], RIPEMD-{128,160,256,320} [10] and Extended MD4 [20, 21]. The crucial difference between MD-family and RIPEMD-family is that RIPEMD-family uses two parallel lines of computations. The third is SHA-family, which consists of SHA-{0,1,224,256,384,512} [13–15]. These functions use only one line of computation, but the message expansion is achieved by some recursively defined function. Several important breakthroughs have been made in the cryptanalysis against hash functions and they imply that most of the currently used standard hash functions are vulnerable against these attacks. In this circumstance, National Institute of Standards and Technology (NIST) launches the NIST Hash Competition, a public competition to develop a new hash standard, which will be called SHA-3 [18] and announced by 2012.

The first analysis of MD4 and MD5 were made by Vaudenay [24] and by den Boer and Bosselaers [7]. Along with the development of the hash functions, there are several analysis on them [4, 8, 9, 11, 12, 22]. The continuous works on analysis of hash functions reveal that most of them are not as secure as claimed [2, 3, 17, 25]. Wang et al. presented a series collision attacks on the most prevailing hash functions including MD4, RIPEMD, RIPEMD-128, MD5, SHA-0, SHA-1 and HAVAL [16, 26–30, 32] using an attack technique which is based on differential cryptanalysis [1]. Wang's method was also used in searching the second-preimage of MD4 [31], and was further developed and used in the analysis of SHA-1 [5, 6].

There are four steps in attacking a hash function by using Wang's method. The first step is to select an appropriate message difference, which determines the success probability of the attack. The second step is to select a feasible differential path according to the selected message difference. The third step is to derive a set of sufficient conditions on the chaining variables to ensure the differential path hold, and a correct differential path implies that all the chaining variable conditions don't contradict each other. The last step is to use message modification techniques to force the modified messages to satisfy most of the sufficient conditions, so to greatly improve the success probability of the attack.

Every step is important for the attack. Many studies have been conducted on the security of MD-family and SHA-family hash functions using Wang's method, such as MD4, MD5, SHA-0, SHA-1 and HAVAL [26–30, 32]. However, owing to the two parallel lines of RIPEMD-family, it is hard for the attacker to deduce the correct differential path and to use message modification technique to improve the success probability for RIPEMD-family. The security of RIPEMD-family hash functions against collision attack has been strengthened greatly. [26] reported that among 30 selected collision differential paths, only one can produce the real collision, and in other paths, the conditions of both lines in some step cannot hold simultaneously. Extended MD4 is such a representative hash function of RIPEMD-family. It is difficult to deduce a correct differential path for both lines and to modify the message to greatly improve the success probability of the attack, so to find a practical collision.

Extended MD4 was proposed in the original article [20] by Rivest in 1990 with 256-bit result. Its compression function consists of two parallel lines called Left Line and Right Line, and each line has 48 steps. It is difficult to deduce a correct collision differential path because the sufficient conditions for the path in both lines are more likely to contradict each other. Dobbertin proposed a collision attack for the compression function of Extended MD4 with the same prescribed initial values in both lines with the complexity of about 2^{40}. However, no collision of the full Extended MD4 was found yet. In this paper, we propose a practical collision attack on the full Extended MD4 using Wang's method. By choosing a proper message difference, we can find a differential path of both Left Line and Right Line, and deduce the corresponding sufficient conditions that ensure the differential path hold. We use the message modification techniques to modify the message so that almost all sufficient conditions hold. Our attack requires less than 2^{37} computations to get a collision of the full Extended MD4. To the best of our knowledge, this is the first work that a practical collision attack on the full Extended MD4 has been proposed.

The rest of the paper is organized as follows. Section 2 introduces some notations and describes the Extended MD4 algorithm. Section 3 introduces some useful properties of the nonlinear functions in Extended MD4. Section 4 proposes the detailed description of the collision attack on Extended MD4. Finally, Section 5 concludes the paper.

2   Background and Definitions

2.1   Notation

In order to describe our analysis conveniently, we introduce some notation, where $0 \leq j \leq 31$.

1. $M = (m_0, m_1, \ldots, m_{15})$: 512-bit block M, where m_i $(0 \leq i \leq 15)$ is a 32-bit word
2. $\neg, \wedge, \oplus, \vee$: bitwise complement, AND, XOR and OR
3. $\lll s$: circular shift s-bit positions to the left
4. $x \| y$: concatenation of the two bitstrings x and y
5. $+, -$: addition and subtraction modulo 2^{32}
6. $x_{i,j}$: the j-th bit of 32-bit word x_i, where the most significant bit is the 31-st bit
7. $\Delta x_i = x_i' - x_i$: the modular subtraction difference of two words x_i' and x_i
8. $x_i' = x_i[j]$: the value obtained by modifying the j-th bit of x_i from 0 to 1, i.e. $x_{i,j} = 0$, $x_{i,j}' = 1$, and the other bits of x_i and x_i' are all equal. Similarly, $x_i[-j]$ is the value obtained by modifying the j-th bit of x_i from 1 to 0
9. $x_i[\pm j_1, \pm j_2, \ldots, \pm j_k]$: the value obtained by modifying the bits in positions $j_1, \ldots, j_k$ of x_i according to the $\pm$ signs
10. (a_i, b_i, c_i, d_i), (aa_i, bb_i, cc_i, dd_i) $(0 \leq i \leq 12)$: the chaining variables corresponding to the message block M_1 of Left Line and Right Line respectively
11. (a_i', b_i', c_i', d_i'), $(aa_i', bb_i', cc_i', dd_i')$ $(0 \leq i \leq 12)$: the chaining variables corresponding to the message block M_1' of Left Line and Right Line respectively

Note that the differential definition in Wang's method is a kind of precise differential which uses the difference in terms of integer modular subtraction and the difference in terms of XOR. The combination of both kinds of differences gives attackers more information. For example, the output difference in Step 1 of Table 5 is $\Delta a_1 = a_1' - a_1 = 2^{19}$, for the specific differential path, we need to expand the one-bit difference in bit 19 into a three-bit differences in bits 19, 20, 21. That is, we expand $a_1[19]$ to $a_1[-19, -20, 21]$, which means the 19-th and 20-th bits of a_1 are 1, and the 21-st bit of a_1 is 0, while the 19-th and 20-th bits of a_1' are 0, and the 21-st bit of a_1' is 1.

2.2   Description of Extended MD4

The hash function Extended MD4 compresses a message of length less than 2^{64} bits into a 256-bit hash value. Firstly, the algorithm pads any given message into a message with the length of 512-bit multiple. We don't describe the padding process here because it has little relation with our attack, and the details of the message padding can refer to [20, 21]. Each 512-bit message block invokes a compression function of Extended MD4. The compression function takes a 256-bit chaining value and a 512-bit message block as inputs and outputs another 256-bit chaining value. The initial chaining value is a set of fixed constants. The compression function consists of two parallel operations called Left Line and Right Line, which have the same structure. Each line has three rounds, and the nonlinear functions in each round are as follows:

$$F(X,Y,Z) = (X \wedge Y) \vee (\neg X \wedge Z),$$
$$G(X,Y,Z) = (X \wedge Y) \vee (X \wedge Z) \vee (Y \wedge Z),$$
$$H(X,Y,Z) = X \oplus Y \oplus Z.$$

Here X, Y, Z are 32-bit words. The operations of the three functions are all bitwise. Each round of the compression function in each line consists of sixteen similarly steps, and in each step one of the four chaining variables a, b, c, d is updated.

$$\phi_0(a,b,c,d,m_k,s) = (a + F(b,c,d) + m_k) \lll s$$
$$\phi_1(a,b,c,d,m_k,s) = (a + G(b,c,d) + m_k + 0x5a827999) \lll s$$
$$\phi_2(a,b,c,d,m_k,s) = (a + H(b,c,d) + m_k + 0x6ed9eba1) \lll s$$
$$\psi_0(a,b,c,d,m_k,s) = (a + F(b,c,d) + m_k) \lll s$$
$$\psi_1(a,b,c,d,m_k,s) = (a + G(b,c,d) + m_k + 0x50a28be6) \lll s$$
$$\psi_2(a,b,c,d,m_k,s) = (a + H(b,c,d) + m_k + 0x5c4dd124) \lll s$$

The initial value of Left Line is (a_0, b_0, c_0, d_0) = $(67452301, efcdab89, 98badcfe, 10325476)$. The initial value of Right Line is $(aa_0, bb_0, cc_0, dd_0) = (33221100, 77665544, bbaa9988, ffeeddcc)$.

Compression Function of Extended MD4. For a 512-bit message block M = $(m_0, m_1, \ldots, m_{15})$ of the padded message $\overline{M}$, the compression function consists of Left Line and Right Line.

Left Line. For the 512-bit block M, Left Line is as follows:

1. Let (a_0, b_0, c_0, d_0) be the input of Left Line for M. If M is the first message block to be hashed, then (a_0, b_0, c_0, d_0) are set to be the initial value. Otherwise they are the output from compressing the previous message block by Left Line.
2. Perform the following 48 steps (three rounds):
   For $j = 0, 1, 2$,
   For $i = 0, 1, 2, 3$,
   $a = \phi_j(a,b,c,d,m_{ord(j,16j+4i+1)}, s_{j,16j+4i+1})$,
   $d = \phi_j(d,a,b,c,m_{ord(j,16j+4i+2)}, s_{j,16j+4i+2})$,
   $c = \phi_j(c,d,a,b,m_{ord(j,16j+4i+3)}, s_{j,16j+4i+3})$,
   $b = \phi_j(b,c,d,a,m_{ord(j,16j+4i+4)}, s_{j,16j+4i+4})$.

The compressing result of Left Line is $(A, B, C, D) = (a_0 + a, b_0 + b, c_0 + c, d_0 + d)$.

Right Line. For the 512-bit block M, Right Line is as follows:

1. Let (aa_0, bb_0, cc_0, dd_0) be the input of Right Line process for M. If M is the first block to be hashed, (aa_0, bb_0, cc_0, dd_0) are the initial value. Otherwise they are the output from compressing the previous message block by Right Line.
2. Perform the following 48 steps (three rounds):

For $j = 0, 1, 2$,
For $i = 0, 1, 2, 3$,

$$aa = \psi_j(aa, bb, cc, dd, m_{ord(j,16j+4i+1)}, s_{j,16j+4i+1}),$$
$$dd = \psi_j(dd, aa, bb, cc, m_{ord(j,16j+4i+2)}, s_{j,16j+4i+2}),$$
$$cc = \psi_j(cc, dd, aa, bb, m_{ord(j,16j+4i+3)}, s_{j,16j+4i+3}),$$
$$bb = \psi_j(bb, cc, dd, aa, m_{ord(j,16j+4i+4)}, s_{j,16j+4i+4}).$$

The compressing result of Right Line is $(AA, BB, CC, DD) = (aa_0 + aa, bb_0 + bb, cc_0 + cc, dd_0 + dd)$.

Note that after every 16-word block is processed, the values of the a register in Left Line and the aa register in Right Line are exchanged. The ordering of message words and the details of the shift positions can be seen in Table 1.

If M is the last block of $\overline{M}$, $(A\|B\|C\|D\|AA\|BB\|CC\|DD)$ is the hash value of the message $\overline{M}$. Otherwise, repeat the above process with the next 512-bit message block and (A, B, C, D) as the input chaining variables of Left Line, (AA, BB, CC, DD) as the input chaining variables of Right Line.

Table 1. Order of the message words and Shift positions in Extended MD4

Step i	1	2	3	4	5	6	7	8	9	10	11	12	13	14	15	16
$ord(0,i)$	0	1	2	3	4	5	6	7	8	9	10	11	12	13	14	15
$s_{0,i}$	3	7	11	19	3	7	11	19	3	7	11	19	3	7	11	19
Step i	17	18	19	20	21	22	23	24	25	26	27	28	29	30	31	32
$ord(1,i)$	0	4	8	12	1	5	9	13	2	6	10	14	3	7	11	15
$s_{1,i}$	3	5	9	13	3	5	9	13	3	5	9	13	3	5	9	13
Step i	33	34	35	36	37	38	39	40	41	42	43	44	45	46	47	48
$ord(2,i)$	0	8	4	12	2	10	6	14	1	9	5	13	3	11	7	15
$s_{2,i}$	3	9	11	15	3	9	11	15	3	9	11	15	3	9	11	15

3   Some Basic Conclusions of the Three Nonlinear Functions

We will recall some well-known properties of the three nonlinear Boolean functions in the following because they are very helpful for determining the collision differential path and the corresponding sufficient conditions.

Proposition 1. For the nonlinear function $F(x, y, z) = (x \wedge y) \vee (\neg x \wedge z)$, here and in the follows, $x \in \{0, 1\}$, $y \in \{0, 1\}$ and $z \in \{0, 1\}$, there are the following properties:

1. (a) $F(x, y, z) = F(\neg x, y, z)$ if and only if $y = z$.

   (b) $F(x, y, z) = x$ and $F(\neg x, y, z) = \neg x$ if and only if $y = 1$ and $z = 0$.

   (c) $F(x, y, z) = \neg x$ and $F(\neg x, y, z) = x$ if and only if $y = 0$ and $z = 1$.
2. (a) $F(x, y, z) = F(x, \neg y, z)$ if and only if $x = 0$.

   (b) $F(x, y, z) = y$ and $F(x, \neg y, z) = \neg y$ if and only if $x = 1$.
3. (a) $F(x, y, z) = F(x, y, \neg z)$ if and only if $x = 1$.

   (b) $F(x, y, z) = z$ and $F(x, y, \neg z) = \neg z$ if and only if $x = 0$.

Proposition 2. For the nonlinear function $G(x, y, z) = (x \wedge y) \vee (x \wedge z) \vee (y \wedge z)$, there are the following properties:

1. $G(x, y, z) = G(\neg x, y, z)$ if and only if $y = z$.
   $G(x, y, z) = x$ and $G(\neg x, y, z) = \neg x$ if and only if $y \neq z$.
2. $G(x, y, z) = G(x, \neg y, z)$ if and only if $x = z$.
   $G(x, y, z) = y$ and $G(x, \neg y, z) = \neg y$ if and only if $x \neq z$.
3. $G(x, y, z) = G(x, y, \neg z)$ if and only if $x = y$.
   $G(x, y, z) = z$ and $G(x, y, \neg z) = \neg z$ if and only if $x \neq y$.

Proposition 3. For the nonlinear function $H(x, y, z) = x \oplus y \oplus z$, there are the following properties:

1. $H(x, y, z) = \neg H(\neg x, y, z) = \neg H(x, \neg y, z) = \neg H(x, y, \neg z)$.
2. $H(x, y, z) = H(\neg x, \neg y, z) = H(x, \neg y, \neg z) = H(\neg x, y, \neg z)$.

4   The Practical Collision Attack against Extended MD4

In this section, we present a practical collision attack on Extended MD4. Each message in the collision includes two 512-bit message blocks. We search the collision pair $(M_0\|M_1, M_0\|M_1')$ in the following four parts:

1. Denote Extended MD4 by h and the hash value $h(M_0)$ by $(a\|b\|c\|d\|aa\|bb\|cc\|dd)$. (a, b, c, d) and (aa, bb, cc, dd) are also the input chaining variables of Left Line and Right Line respectively of the next compression function. Find a message block M_0 such that $h(M_0)$ satisfy some conditions which are part of the sufficient conditions that ensure the differential path hold, and the conditions of $h(M_0)$ are $b_i = c_i(i = 19, 21)$, $b_i = 0(i = 20, 27, 28)$, $c_{20} = 1$, $bb_i = cc_i(i = 19, 21)$, $bb_i = 0(i = 20, 27, 28)$ and $cc_{20} = 1$.
2. Choose an appropriate message difference $\Delta M_1 = M_1' - M_1$ and deduce the differential path according to the specified message difference.
3. Derive a set of sufficient conditions which ensures the differential path hold. This means that if $h(M_1)$ satisfies all the conditions in Table 6, then $(M_0\|M_1, M_0\|M_1')$ consist of a collision.
4. Modify the message M_1 to fulfill most of the sufficient conditions.

Obviously the first part is easy to be carried out. We will describe the last three parts in details.

4.1   Collision Differential Path for Extended MD4

Constructing the differential path and deriving the sufficient conditions go on simultaneously. On one hand, we derive the sufficient conditions according to the differential path. On the other hand, we can adjust the differential path to avoid the contradictory conditions. If the sufficient conditions contradict each other, the corresponding differential path is error and a collision cannot be found. The sufficient conditions in Left Line and Right Line of Extended MD4 in some step cannot hold simultaneously, so we must search other differential paths from scratch.

Almost all the conditions in the first round and some conditions in the second round can be modified to be hold by the message modification technique, the other conditions in the last rounds are difficult to be modified to hold. Therefore, we will ensure the sufficient conditions in the last rounds to be as less as possible. In order to find such a differential path, we select a difference between two messages as follows: $\Delta M_1 = M_1' - M_1 = (\Delta m_0, \Delta m_1, \ldots, \Delta m_{15})$, where $\Delta m_0 = 2^{16}$, $\Delta m_i = 0, 0 < i \le 15$.

The whole differential path are shown in Table 5. The first column denotes the step, the second is the chaining variable in each step for M_1, the third is the message word of M_1 in each step, the fourth is the shift rotation, the fifth is the message difference between M_1 and M_1', the sixth is the chaining variable difference for M_1 and M_1', and the seventh is the chaining variable for M_1'. The empty items both in the fifth and the sixth columns denote zero differences, and steps those aren't listed in the table have zero differences for message words and chaining variables.

4.2   Deriving the Sufficient Conditions for Differential Path

In light of the propositions of the nonlinear Boolean functions given in Section 3, we can derive the conditions that guarantee the differential path in Table 5 hold. A set of sufficient conditions is shown in Table 6.

We give an example to describe how to derive a set of sufficient conditions that guarantees the differential path in Step 9 of Table 5 hold. Other conditions can be derived similarly. The differential path in Step 9 of Table 5 is

$$(a_2[-10, 22, -30], d_2[-2, -3, 4], c_2[17], b_2[21, -22])$$

$$\longrightarrow (d_2[-2, -3, 4], c_2[17], b_2[21, -22], a_3[1, -2, -13]).$$

1. According to $a_3 = (a_2 + F(b_2, c_2, d_2) + m_8) \lll 3$ and 1(b) of Proposition 1, the conditions $c_{2,22} = 1$ and $d_{2,22} = 0$ ensure that the change of $b_{2,22}$ results in $F(b_2[-22], c_2, d_2) - F(b_2, c_2, d_2) = -2^{22}$, combined with $\Delta a_2 = 2^{22}$, which will lead to no change in a_3.
2. According to 1(a) of Proposition 1, the condition $c_{2,21} = d_{2,21}$ ensures that the change of $b_{2,21}$ results in no change in a_3.
3. According to 2(a) of Proposition 1, the condition $b_{2,17} = 0$ ensures that the change of $c_{2,17}$ results in no change in a_3.
4. According to 3(a) of Proposition 1, the conditions $b_{2,2} = 1$, $b_{2,3} = 1$ and $b_{2,4} = 1$ ensure that the changes in the 2-nd, 3-rd and 4-th bits of d_2 result in no change in a_3.

5. Because the shift is 3 in Step 9, $\Delta a_2 = -2^{10}$ must lead to $\Delta a_3 = -2^{13}$, and the condition $a_{3,13} = 1$ results in $a'_{13} = a_{13}[-13]$.

6. Similarly, $\Delta a_2 = -2^{30}$ must lead to $\Delta a_3 = -2$, and the condition $a_{3,1} = 0$ and $a_{3,2} = 1$ result in $a'_3 = a_3[1, -2]$.

This means the above 10 conditions consist of a set of sufficient conditions for the differential path in Step 9.

4.3 Message Modification

In order to improve the collision probability, we modify M_1 so that most of the sufficient conditions in Table 6 hold. The modification includes the basic and advanced techniques. Because Extended MD4 has two lines, the modification is much more complicated than that of MD4, MD5, HAVAL etc. which only have one line operation.

1. We modify M_1 word by word so that both lines with the modified M_1 satisfy almost all the conditions in the first round.
   (a) By using the basic modification technique, we modify m_{i-1} such that the i-th step conditions in the first round of Left Line hold. For example, to ensure the 8 conditions of d_1 in Table 6 hold, we modify m_1 as follows:
   $$d_1 \longleftarrow d_1 \oplus (d_{1,19} \lll 19) \oplus (d_{1,20} \lll 20) \oplus (d_{1,21} \lll 21) \oplus (d_{1,28} \lll 28) \oplus ((d_{1,27} \oplus 1) \lll 27) \oplus ((d_{1,6} \oplus a_{1,6}) \lll 6) \oplus ((d_{1,7} \oplus a_{1,7}) \lll 7) \oplus ((d_{1,8} \oplus a_{1,8}) \lll 8),$$

   $$m_1 \longleftarrow (d_1 \ggg 7) - d_0 - F(a_1, b_0, c_0).$$

   (b) By using the advanced modification technique, we modify the message word from low bit to high bit to correct the corresponding conditions in the first round of Right Line.
      i. Firstly, we can correct the conditions by bit carry. For example, because there is no constraint conditions in $a_{1,18}$ in Table 6, we can correct $aa_{1,19} = 0$ to $aa_{1,19} = 1$ as follows. If $a_{1,18} = 0$ and $aa_{1,18} = 1$, let $m_0 \longleftarrow m_0 + 2^{15}$, then there is a bit carry in Right Line and no bit carry in Left Line, so the condition in $aa_{1,19}$ can be corrected, and the corrected $a_{1,19}$ will not be changed. Similarly, if $a_{1,18} = 1$ and $aa_{1,18} = 0$, let $m_0 \longleftarrow m_0 - 2^{15}$, then $aa_{1,19}$ can be corrected and $a_{1,19}$ will not be changed. If $a_{1,18} = aa_{1,18}$, we can use the lower bit carry to change $a_{1,18}$ or $aa_{1,18}$ such that $a_{1,18} \neq aa_{1,18}$, and then use the bit carry. The details for correcting $aa_{1,19}$ are given in Table 2.
      ii. Secondly, we can correct the condition on $a_{i,j}$ by changing the corresponding variables in the previous steps. For example, we can correct $dd_{1,20} = 1$ to $dd_{1,20} = 0$ as follows. If $b_{0,13} \oplus c_{0,13} \neq bb_{0,13} \oplus cc_{0,13}$ (which means when $b_{0,13} = c_{0,13}$, then $bb_{0,13} \neq cc_{0,13}$; when $b_{0,13} \neq c_{0,13}$, then $bb_{0,13} = cc_{0,13}$), let $m_0 \longleftarrow m_0 \pm 2^{10}$, then $a_{1,13}$ and $aa_{1,13}$ will be changed, and the changed $a_{1,13}, aa_{1,13}$ only cause one of $d_{1,20}$ and $dd_{1,20}$ change according to 1 of Proposition 1. Then if $d_{1,20} = dd_{1,20} = 1$, let $m_1 \longleftarrow m_1 - 2^{13}$, if $d_{1,20} = dd_{1,20} = 0$, modify the next bit of dd_1. Note that there is no condition in $a_{1,13}$ and $aa_{1,13}$ in Table 6, so the changes in $a_{1,13}$ and $aa_{1,13}$ don't invalidate the differential path. The details for correcting $dd_{1,20}$ are given in Table 3.

2. There are $18 \times 2 = 36$ conditions in total in the second round in both lines. We can utilize some more precise modification techniques to correct some conditions in the second round. Sometimes, it needs to add some extra conditions in the first round in advance such that the change of any condition doesn't affect all the corrected conditions.

Table 2. The message modification for correcting $aa_{1,19} = 0$ to $aa_{1,19} = 1$

Known Conditions	The Modified m_0	New Chaining Variables
$a_{1,18} = 0$	$m_0 \longleftarrow m_0 + 2^{15}$	$aa_{1,19} = 1$
$aa_{1,18} = 1$		$a_{1,19}$ unchanged
$a_{1,18} = 1$	$m_0 \longleftarrow m_0 - 2^{15}$	$aa_{1,19} = 1$
$aa_{1,18} = 0$		$a_{1,19}$ unchanged
$a_{1,18} = aa_{1,18} = 1$	$m_0 \longleftarrow m_0 + 2^{14}$	$aa_{1,19} = 1$
$a_{1,17} = 0$		$a_{1,19}$ unchanged
$aa_{1,17} = 1$		
$a_{1,18} = aa_{1,18} = 1$	$m_0 \longleftarrow m_0 - 2^{14} - 2^{15}$	$aa_{1,19} = 1$
$a_{1,17} = 1$		$a_{1,19}$ unchanged
$aa_{1,17} = 0$		
$a_{1,18} = aa_{1,18} = 0$	$m_0 \longleftarrow m_0 + 2^{14} + 2^{15}$	$aa_{1,19} = 1$
$a_{1,17} = 0$		$a_{1,19}$ unchanged
$aa_{1,17} = 1$		
$a_{1,18} = aa_{1,18} = 0$	$m_0 \longleftarrow m_0 - 2^{14}$	$aa_{1,19} = 1$
$a_{1,17} = 1$		$a_{1,19}$ unchanged
$aa_{1,17} = 0$		

4.4   Overview of the Collision Attack Algorithm

From the above description, an overview of the collision attack algorithm on Extended MD4 can be expressed as follows.

1. Find a message block M_0 such that $h(M_0) = (a\|b\|c\|d\|aa\|bb\|cc\|dd)$ satisfy $b_i = c_i(i = 19, 21)$, $b_i = 0(i = 20, 27, 28)$, $c_{20} = 1$, $bb_i = cc_i(i = 19, 21)$, $bb_i = 0(i = 20, 27, 28)$ and $cc_{20} = 1$.
2. Repeat the following steps until we can find a message block M_1 which satisfies all the sufficient conditions in the first round of Left Line and Right Line in Table 6.
   (a) Select a random message block M_1.
   (b) Modify M_1 by Step 1 of message modification described above.
   (c) Test if the hash value of M_1 satisfy all the sufficient conditions in the first round in both lines in Table 6.
3. Repeat the following steps until a collision $(M_0\|M_1, M_0\|M_1')$ is found.
   (a) Select random message words m_{14} and m_{15} of M_1.
   (b) Modify M_1 by Step 1 of message modification described above such that all the conditions in c_4, b_4, cc_4 and bb_4 satisfied.

Table 3. The message modification for correcting $dd_{1,20} = 1$ to $dd_{1,20} = 0$

Case	Step	m_i	Shift	Modified m_i	Chaining Variables	Conditions
	1	m_0	3	$m_0 \leftarrow$ $m_0 \pm 2^{10}$	$a_{1,13}, aa_{1,13}$ changed	
Case 1	2	m_1	7		$d_{1,20}$ changed i.e. $d_{1,20} = 1$	$b_{0,13} \neq c_{0,13}$
					$dd_{1,20}$ unchanged i.e. $dd_{1,20} = 1$	$bb_{0,13} = cc_{0,13}$
				$m_1 \leftarrow$ $m_1 - 2^{13}$	$d_{1,20} = 0$ $dd_{1,20} = 0$	
Case 2	2	m_2	7		$d_{1,20}$ unchanged i.e. $d_{1,20} = 0$	$b_{0,13} = c_{0,13}$
					$dd_{1,20}$ changed i.e. $dd_{1,20} = 0$	$bb_{0,13} \neq cc_{0,13}$

(c) Modify M_1 by Step 2 of message modification described above such that some conditions in the second round satisfied.

(d) Then M_1 and $M_1' = M_1 + \Delta M_1$ satisfy all the sufficient conditions in both lines in Table 6 with the probability higher than 2^{-36}.

(e) Test if the hash value of M_1 is equal to the hash value of M_1'.

It is easy to find proper M_0 in Step 1 and to find M_1 which satisfy all the sufficient conditions in the first round in both lines in Table 6, and the complexity can be neglected. There are 36 conditions in total in the second round in both lines, so M_1 and M_1' lead to a collision with probability higher than 2^{-36}, and the complexity to find a collision $(M_0\|M_1, M_0\|M_1')$ is less than 2^{37} Extended MD4 computations. A collision for Extended MD4 can be seen in Table 4.

Table 4. A collision of Extended MD4. H_0 is the hash value for the message block M_0 with little-endian and no message padding. H is the common hash value for the message $M_0 \| M_1$ and $M_0 \| M_1'$ with little-endian and no message padding.

M_0	a4eff7cd 87afe33e b96f8657 1054fe49 8397de8d 23bc04b8 b683a020 3b2a5d9f c69d71b3 f9e99198 d79f805e a63bb2e8 45dd8e31 97e31fe5 2794bf08 b9e8c3e9
H_0	b5aac7e7 c1664fe2 01705583 ac3cc062 65c931e6 452829ae 527e12c7 30fafffb
M_1	54b7b7e1 65336f98 7621fe73 ffa42822 13dda7e1 1c28a008 bf20c341 3e8e28f2 578bdb87 afd42be4 b9ecab2e 0aaa9293 02e7070b eab6f4cf 2e96aaf7 5ab41efd
M_1'	54b8b7e1 65336f98 7621fe73 ffa42822 13dda7e1 1c28a008 bf20c341 3e8e28f2 578bdb87 afd42be4 b9ecab2e 0aaa9293 02e7070b eab6f4cf 2e96aaf7 5ab41efd
H	3055a689 7fe0b4a6 88d59251 af8afd0f 3826bda2 942f0939 c2673493 a6c56bac

Table 5. Collision Differential Path of Extended MD4

Step	Chaining Value for M	m_i	Shift	Δm_i	The step difference	Chaining Value for M'
1	a_1	m_0	3	2^{16}	2^{19}	$a_1[-19, -20, 21]$
2	d_1	m_1	7		2^{27}	$d_1[-27, 28]$
3	c_1	m_2	11		2^6	$c_1[-6, -7, 8]$
4	b_1	m_3	19			b_1
5	a_2	m_4	3		$-2^{10} + 2^{22} - 2^{30}$	$a_2[-10, 22, -30]$
6	d_2	m_5	7		2^2	$d_2[-2, -3, 4]$
7	c_2	m_6	11		2^{17}	$c_2[17]$
8	b_2	m_7	19		-2^{21}	$b_2[21, -22]$
9	a_3	m_8	3		$-2 - 2^{13}$	$a_3[1, -2, -13]$
10	d_3	m_9	7		2^9	$d_3[-9, 10]$
11	c_3	m_{10}	11		2^{28}	$c_3[28]$
12	b_3	m_{11}	19		-2^8	$b_3[8, -9]$
13	a_4	m_{12}	3		$-2^4 - 2^{16}$	$a_4[-4, -16]$
14	d_4	m_{13}	7			d_4
15	c_4	m_{14}	11		2^7	$c_4[-7, 8]$
16	b_4	m_{15}	19			b_4
17	a_5	m_0	3	2^{16}	-2^7	$a_5[7, -8]$
18	d_5	m_4	5			d_5
19	c_5	m_8	9			c_5
20	b_5	m_{12}	13			b_5
21	a_6	m_1	3		-2^{10}	$a_6[-10]$
22	d_6	m_5	5			d_6
23	c_6	m_9	9			c_6
24	b_6	m_{13}	13			b_6
25	a_7	m_2	3		-2^{13}	$a_7[-13]$
26	d_7	m_6	5			d_7
27	c_7	m_{10}	9			c_7
28	b_7	m_{14}	13			b_7
29	a_8	m_3	3		-2^{16}	$a_8[-16]$
30	d_8	m_7	5			d_8
31	c_8	m_{11}	9			c_8
32	b_8	m_{15}	13			b_8
33	a_9	m_0	3	2^{16}		a_9
...	...	...	...	...	...	...
48	b_{12}	m_{15}	15			b_{12}

Table 6. A Set of Sufficient Conditions for the Differential Path given in Table 5

c_0	$c_{0,20} = 1$
b_0	$b_{0,19} = c_{0,19}, b_{0,20} = 0, b_{0,21} = c_{0,21}, b_{0,27} = 0, b_{0,28} = 0$
a_1	$a_{1,19} = 1, a_{1,20} = 1, a_{1,21} = 0, a_{1,27} = 1, a_{1,28} = 1$
d_1	$d_{1,6} = a_{1,6}, d_{1,7} = a_{1,7}, d_{1,8} = a_{1,8}, d_{1,19} = 0, d_{1,20} = 0, d_{1,21} = 0, d_{1,27} = 1, d_{1,28} = 0$
c_1	$c_{1,6} = 1, c_{1,7} = 1, c_{1,8} = 0, c_{1,19} = 1, c_{1,20} = 1, c_{1,21} = 1, c_{1,27} = 0, c_{1,28} = 0$
b_1	$b_{1,6} = 0, b_{1,7} = 1, b_{1,8} = 0, b_{1,10} = c_{1,10}, b_{1,22} = c_{1,22}, b_{1,27} = 0, b_{1,28} = 1, b_{1,30} = c_{1,30}$
a_2	$a_{2,2} = b_{1,2}, a_{2,3} = b_{1,3}, a_{2,4} = b_{1,4}, a_{2,6} = 1, a_{2,7} = 1,$
	$\quad a_{2,8} = 1, a_{2,10} = 1, a_{2,22} = 0, a_{2,30} = 1$
d_2	$d_{2,2} = 1, d_{2,3} = 1, d_{2,4} = 0, d_{2,10} = 0, d_{2,17} = a_{2,17}, d_{2,22} = 0, d_{2,30} = 0$
c_2	$c_{2,2} = 1, c_{2,3} = 0, c_{2,4} = 0, c_{2,10} = 1, c_{2,17} = 0, c_{2,21} = d_{2,21}, c_{2,22} = 1, c_{2,30} = 1$
b_2	$b_{2,1} = c_{2,1}, b_{2,2} = 1, b_{2,3} = 1, b_{2,4} = 1, b_{2,13} = c_{2,13}, b_{2,17} = 0, b_{2,21} = 0, b_{2,22} = 1$
a_3	$a_{3,1} = 0, a_{3,2} = 1, a_{3,9} = b_{2,9}, a_{3,10} = b_{2,10}, a_{3,13} = 1, a_{3,17} = 1, a_{3,21} = 0, a_{3,22} = 0$
d_3	$d_{3,1} = 0, d_{3,2} = 0, d_{3,9} = 1, d_{3,10} = 0, d_{3,13} = 0, d_{3,21} = 1, d_{3,22} = 1, d_{3,28} = a_{3,28}$
c_3	$c_{3,1} = 1, c_{3,2} = 1, c_{3,8} = d_{3,8}, c_{3,9} = 0, c_{3,10} = 0, c_{3,13} = 1, c_{3,28} = 0$
b_3	$b_{3,4} = c_{3,4}, b_{3,8} = 0, b_{3,9} = 1, b_{3,10} = 1, b_{3,16} = c_{3,16}, b_{3,28} = 0$
a_4	$a_{4,4} = 1, a_{4,8} = 0, a_{4,9} = 1, a_{4,16} = 1, a_{4,28} = 1$
d_4	$d_{4,4} = 0, d_{4,7} = a_{4,7}, d_{4,8} = 1, d_{4,9} = 1, d_{4,16} = 0$
c_4	$c_{4,4} = 1, c_{4,7} = 1, c_{4,8} = 0, c_{4,16} = 1$
b_4	$b_{4,7} = d_{4,7}, b_{4,8} = d_{4,8}$
a_5	$a_{5,7} = 0, a_{5,8} = 1$
d_5	$d_{5,7} \neq b_{4,7}, d_{5,8} \neq b_{4,8}$
c_5	$c_{5,7} = d_{5,7}, c_{5,8} = d_{5,8}$
b_5	$b_{5,10} = c_{5,10}$
a_6	$a_{6,10} = 1$
d_6	$d_{6,10} = b_{5,10}$
c_6	$c_{6,10} = d_{6,10}$
b_6	$b_{6,13} = c_{6,13}$
a_7	$a_{7,13} = 1$
d_7	$d_{7,13} = b_{6,13}$
c_7	$c_{7,13} = d_{7,13}$
b_7	$b_{7,16} = c_{7,16}$
a_8	$a_{8,16} = 1$
d_8	$d_{8,16} = b_{7,16}$
c_8	$c_{8,16} = d_{8,16}$

5   Conclusions

In this study, the security of the hash function Extended MD4 which consists of two parallel lines against collision analysis is examined. A practical attack on Extended MD4 for finding 2-block collision is proposed. A true collision instance of Extended MD4 can be found with less than 2^{37} computations. Future analysis should be able to explore the security of other hash functions which consist of two parallel lines against the collision analysis.

References

1. Biham, B., Shamir, A.: Differential cryptanalysis of DES-like cryptosystems. Journal of Cryptology 4(1), 3–72 (1991)
2. Biham, E., Chen, R.: Near-Collisions of SHA-0. In: Franklin, M. (ed.) CRYPTO 2004. LNCS, vol. 3152, pp. 290–305. Springer, Heidelberg (2004)
3. Biham, E., Chen, R., Joux, A., Carribault, P., Lemuet, C., Jalby, W.: Collisions of SHA-0 and Reduced SHA-1. In: Cramer, R. (ed.) EUROCRYPT 2005. LNCS, vol. 3494, pp. 36–57. Springer, Heidelberg (2005)
4. Chabaud, F., Joux, A.: Differential Collisions in SHA-0. In: Krawczyk, H. (ed.) CRYPTO 1998. LNCS, vol. 1462, pp. 56–71. Springer, Heidelberg (1998)
5. De Cannière, C., Rechberger, C.: Finding SHA-1 Characteristics: General Results and Applications. In: Lai, X., Chen, K. (eds.) ASIACRYPT 2006. LNCS, vol. 4284, pp. 1–20. Springer, Heidelberg (2006)
6. De Cannière, C., Mendel, F., Rechberger, C.: Collisions for 70-Step SHA-1: On the Full Cost of Collision Search. In: Adams, C., Miri, A., Wiener, M. (eds.) SAC 2007. LNCS, vol. 4876, pp. 56–73. Springer, Heidelberg (2007)
7. den Boer, B., Bosselaers, A.: Collisions for the Compression Function of MD-5. In: Helleseth, T. (ed.) EUROCRYPT 1993. LNCS, vol. 765, pp. 293–304. Springer, Heidelberg (1994)
8. Dobbertin, H.: Cryptanalysis of MD4. In: Gollmann, D. (ed.) FSE 1996. LNCS, vol. 1039, pp. 53–69. Springer, Heidelberg (1996)
9. Dobbertin, H.: Cryptanalysis of MD5 Compress. In: The Rump Session of EUROCRYPT 1996 (1996)
10. Dobbertin, H., Bosselaers, A., Preneel, B.: RIPEMD-160: A Strengthened Version of RIPEMD. In: Gollmann, D. (ed.) FSE 1996. LNCS, vol. 1039, pp. 71–82. Springer, Heidelberg (1996)
11. Dobbertin, H.: RIPEMD with Two Round Compress Function Is Not Collision-Free. Journal of Cryptology 10(1), 51–70 (1997)
12. Dobbertin, H.: The First Two Rounds of MD4 are Not One-Way. In: Vaudenay, S. (ed.) FSE 1998. LNCS, vol. 1372, pp. 284–292. Springer, Heidelberg (1998)
13. FIPS 180: Secure Hash Standard, Federal Information Processing Standards Publication£NIST£ (May 1993)
14. FIPS 180-1: Secure Hash Standard, Federal Information Processing Standards Publication, NIST, US Department of Commerce, Washington D.C. (1996)
15. FIPS 180-2: Secure Hash Standard, Federal Information Processing Standards Publication, NIST (2002),
http://csrc.nist.gov/publications/fips/fips180-2/fips180-2.pdf
16. Wang, G., Wang, M.: Cryptanalysis of reduced RIPEMD-128. Journal of Software 19(9), 2442–2448 (2008)

17. Joux, A.: Collisions for SHA-0. In: The Rump Session of CRYPTO 2004 (2004)
18. National Institute of Standards and Technology, Cryptographic hash project,
    `http://csrc.nist.gov/groups/ST/hash/index.html`
19. RIPE: Integrity Primitives for Secure Information Systems, Final Report of RACE Integrity
    Primitives Evalution (RIPE-RACE 1040). LNCS, vol. 1007. Springer, Heidelberg
20. Rivest, R.: The MD4 Message Digest Algorithm. In: Menezes, A., Vanstone, S. (eds.)
    CRYPTO 1990. LNCS, vol. 537, pp. 303–311. Springer, Heidelberg (1991)
21. Rivest, R.: The MD4 message-digest algorithm. Request for Comments (RFC) 1320, Internet
    Activities Board, Internet Privacy Task Force (1992)
22. Van Rompay, B., Biryukov, A., Preneel, B., Vandewalle, J.: Cryptanalysis of 3-pass HAVAL.
    In: Laih, C.S. (ed.) ASIACRYPT 2003. LNCS, vol. 2894, pp. 228–245. Springer, Heidelberg
    (2003)
23. The MD5 Message-digest Algorithm. In: Request for Comments (RFC) 1321, Internet Ac-
    tivities Board, Internet Privacy Task Force (1992)
24. Vaudenay, S.: On the Need for Multipermutations: Cryptanalysis of MD4 and SAFER. In:
    Preneel, B. (ed.) FSE 1994. LNCS, vol. 1008, pp. 286–297. Springer, Heidelberg (1995)
25. Wang, X., Feng, D., Lai, X., Yu, H.: Collisions for Hash Functions MD4, MD5, HAVAL-128
    and RIPEMD. In: The Rump Session of CRYPTO 2004 (2004)
26. Wang, X., Lai, X., Feng, D., Chen, H., Yu, X.: Cryptanalysis of the Hash Functions MD4 and
    RIPEMD. In: Cramer, R. (ed.) EUROCRYPT 2005. LNCS, vol. 3494, pp. 1–18. Springer,
    Heidelberg (2005)
27. Wang, X., Yu, H.: How to Break MD5 and Other Hash Functions. In: Cramer, R. (ed.) EU-
    ROCRYPT 2005. LNCS, vol. 3494, pp. 19–35. Springer, Heidelberg (2005)
28. Wang, X., Yu, H., Yin, Y.L.: Efficient Collision Search Attacks on SHA-0. In: Shoup, V. (ed.)
    CRYPTO 2005. LNCS, vol. 3621, pp. 1–16. Springer, Heidelberg (2005)
29. Wang, X., Yin, Y.L., Yu, H.: Finding Collisions in the Full SHA-1. In: Shoup, V. (ed.)
    CRYPTO 2005. LNCS, vol. 3621, pp. 17–36. Springer, Heidelberg (2005)
30. Wang, X., Feng, D., Yu, X.: An attack on HAVAL function HAVAL-128. Science in China
    Ser. F Information Sciences 48(5), 1–12 (2005)
31. Yu, H., Wang, G., Zhang, G., Wang, X.: The Second-preimage Attack on MD4. In: Desmedt,
    Y.G., Wang, H., Mu, Y., Li, Y. (eds.) CANS 2005. LNCS, vol. 3810, pp. 1–12. Springer,
    Heidelberg (2005)
32. Yu, H., Wang, X., Yun, A., Park, S.: Cryptanalysis of the Full HAVAL with 4 and 5 Passes.
    In: Robshaw, M. (ed.) FSE 2006. LNCS, vol. 4047, pp. 89–110. Springer, Heidelberg (2006)
33. Zheng, Y., Pieprzyk, J., Seberry, J.: HAVAL-A One-way Hashing Algorithm with Variable
    Length of Output. In: Zheng, Y., Seberry, J. (eds.) AUSCRYPT 1992. LNCS, vol. 718, pp.
    81–104. Springer, Heidelberg (1993)

Linear Cryptanalysis of ARIA Block Cipher

Zhiqiang Liu[1], Dawu Gu[1], Ya Liu[1], Juanru Li[1], and Wei Li[2,3]

[1] Department of Computer Science and Engineering,
Shanghai Jiao Tong University, Shanghai 200240, China
{ilu_zq,dwgu,liuya0611,jarod}@sjtu.edu.cn
[2] School of Computer Science and Technology,
Donghua University, Shanghai 201620, China
liwei.cs.cn@gmail.com
[3] Shanghai Key Laboratory of Integrate Administration Technologies
for Information Security, Shanghai 200240, China

Abstract. In this paper, we firstly present an approach to derive a kind of special linear characteristics for byte-oriented SPN block ciphers. Then based on this approach, we study the security of the block cipher ARIA against linear cryptanalysis and propose an attack on 7-round ARIA with 128/192/256-bit key size, an attack on 9-round ARIA with 192/256-bit key size as well as an attack on 11-round ARIA with 256-bit key size. The designers of ARIA expect that there isn't any effective attack on 8 or more rounds of ARIA with 128/192/256-bit key size by means of linear cryptanalysis. However, our work shows that such attacks do exist. Moreover, our cryptanalytic results are the best known cryptanalytic results of ARIA so far.

Keywords: Cryptanalysis, Linear cryptanalysis, Block cipher, ARIA.

1 Introduction

The block cipher ARIA [1,2] was presented at ICISC 2003 by a group of Korean experts, and it was later selected as a data encryption standard by the Korean Ministry of Commerce, Industry and Energy. As an involutional SPN structure block cipher, ARIA supports the block size of 128 bits and a variable key size of 128/192/256 bits. The number of rounds adopted in ARIA depends on the key size and 12/14/16 rounds will be used in ARIA v1.0 (the latest version of ARIA) with 128/192/256-bit key size respectively.

Up to now, the security of ARIA has already been analyzed by many cryptographists. In [1], the designers Kwon et al evaluated the security of ARIA by using the cryptanalytic methods such as differential cryptanalysis [3], linear cryptanalysis [4], truncated differential cryptanalysis [5], impossible differential cryptanalysis [6], integral cryptanalysis [7], and so on. In [8], Wu et al firstly found some 4-round impossible differential characteristics of ARIA which could lead to effective attacks on 6-round ARIA with 128/192/256-bit key size, and the cryptanalytic result was later improved by Li et al [9] and Du et al [10] respectively. In [11], Li et al presented some 3-round integral distinguishers of

S. Qing et al. (Eds.): ICICS 2011, LNCS 7043, pp. 242–254, 2011.

ARIA which could be used to attack 4/5/6-round ARIA with 128/192/256-bit key size, then based on this work, Li et al [12] demonstrated an integral attack on 7-round ARIA with 256-bit key size. In [13], Fleischmann et al proposed some attacks on 5/6-round ARIA with 128/192/256-bit key size and 7-round ARIA with 256-bit key size by means of boomerang attack [14]. In [15], Tang et al introduced some attacks on 5/6-round ARIA with 128/192/256-bit key size, 7-round ARIA with 192/256-bit key size and 8-round ARIA with 256-bit key size via meet-in-the-middle attack [16].

In this paper, we firstly present an approach to derive a kind of special linear characteristics for byte-oriented SPN block ciphers. Then according to this approach, we investigate the security of ARIA against linear cryptanalysis and propose an attack on 7-round ARIA with 128/192/256-bit key size, an attack on 9-round ARIA with 192/256-bit key size as well as an attack on 11-round ARIA with 256-bit key size. As a matter of fact, the designers of ARIA expect that there isn't any effective attack on 8 or more rounds of ARIA with 128/192/256-bit key size by means of linear cryptanalysis. However, our work shows that such attacks do exist. Furthermore, our cryptanalytic results are the best known cryptanalytic results of ARIA so far.

The remainder of this paper is organized as follows. Section 2 introduces the notations used throughout this paper, gives a brief description of ARIA as well as the method of linear cryptanalysis. Section 3 presents a kind of special linear characteristics for byte-oriented SPN block ciphers. Section 4 proposes several special 4-round linear characteristics of ARIA and demonstrates our attacks on reduced-round ARIA based on such linear characteristics. Finally, Section 5 summarizes the paper.

2   Preliminaries

The following notations are used throughout the paper.

- $\oplus$ denotes bitwise exclusive OR (XOR).
- $\bullet$ denotes bitwise inner product.
- $|x|$ denotes absolute value of a real number x.
- $\circ$ denotes the composition operation.
- $\#S$ denotes the cardinality of a set S.
- 0x denotes the hexadecimal notation.
- $\|$ denotes the concatenation operation.
- For a real number x, $\lceil x \rceil$ denotes the integer such that $x \leq \lceil x \rceil < x + 1$.

2.1   Description of ARIA

ARIA is a 128-bit block cipher with an involutional SPN structure. It accepts keys of 128, 192 or 256 bits and the number of rounds is 12, 14 or 16 respectively. The input and output of each round of ARIA are treated as 16-byte vectors, and each byte within the vectors could be regarded as an element in $GF(2^8)$.

The round function of ARIA applies following three basic operations subsequently:

Round Key Addition (RKA): This is done by XORing the 128-bit round key. All round keys are derived from the master key by means of the key schedule.

Substitution Layer (SL): Apply 16 non-linear 8×8-bit S-boxes to the 16 bytes of the intermediate 16-byte vector respectively. ARIA adopts four distinct S-boxes, i.e., S_1, S_2 and their inverses S_1^{-1}, S_2^{-1}. In addition, ARIA has two types of substitution layers as shown in Fig. 1, where type 1 is used in the odd rounds and type 2 is used in the even rounds.

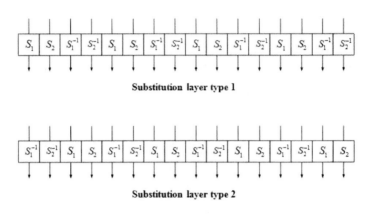

Substitution layer type 1

Substitution layer type 2

Fig. 1. The two types of substitution layers in ARIA

Diffusion Layer (DL): An involutional linear transformation $P : GF(2^8)^{16} \rightarrow GF(2^8)^{16}$ is performed on the intermediate 16-byte vector. The transformation P is defined as

$$(x_0, x_1, \ldots, x_{15}) \rightarrow (y_0, y_1, \ldots, y_{15}),$$

where

$$y_0 = x_3 \oplus x_4 \oplus x_6 \oplus x_8 \oplus x_9 \oplus x_{13} \oplus x_{14},$$
$$y_1 = x_2 \oplus x_5 \oplus x_7 \oplus x_8 \oplus x_9 \oplus x_{12} \oplus x_{15},$$
$$y_2 = x_1 \oplus x_4 \oplus x_6 \oplus x_{10} \oplus x_{11} \oplus x_{12} \oplus x_{15},$$
$$y_3 = x_0 \oplus x_5 \oplus x_7 \oplus x_{10} \oplus x_{11} \oplus x_{13} \oplus x_{14},$$
$$y_4 = x_0 \oplus x_2 \oplus x_5 \oplus x_8 \oplus x_{11} \oplus x_{14} \oplus x_{15},$$
$$y_5 = x_1 \oplus x_3 \oplus x_4 \oplus x_9 \oplus x_{10} \oplus x_{14} \oplus x_{15},$$
$$y_6 = x_0 \oplus x_2 \oplus x_7 \oplus x_9 \oplus x_{10} \oplus x_{12} \oplus x_{13},$$
$$y_7 = x_1 \oplus x_3 \oplus x_6 \oplus x_8 \oplus x_{11} \oplus x_{12} \oplus x_{13},$$
$$y_8 = x_0 \oplus x_1 \oplus x_4 \oplus x_7 \oplus x_{10} \oplus x_{13} \oplus x_{15},$$
$$y_9 = x_0 \oplus x_1 \oplus x_5 \oplus x_6 \oplus x_{11} \oplus x_{12} \oplus x_{14},$$
$$y_{10} = x_2 \oplus x_3 \oplus x_5 \oplus x_6 \oplus x_8 \oplus x_{13} \oplus x_{15},$$
$$y_{11} = x_2 \oplus x_3 \oplus x_4 \oplus x_7 \oplus x_9 \oplus x_{12} \oplus x_{14},$$
$$y_{12} = x_1 \oplus x_2 \oplus x_6 \oplus x_7 \oplus x_9 \oplus x_{11} \oplus x_{12},$$
$$y_{13} = x_0 \oplus x_3 \oplus x_6 \oplus x_7 \oplus x_8 \oplus x_{10} \oplus x_{13},$$
$$y_{14} = x_0 \oplus x_3 \oplus x_4 \oplus x_5 \oplus x_9 \oplus x_{11} \oplus x_{14},$$
$$y_{15} = x_1 \oplus x_2 \oplus x_4 \oplus x_5 \oplus x_8 \oplus x_{10} \oplus x_{15}.$$

Note that in the last round of ARIA, the DL operation is replaced by an additional RKA operation. Please refer to [2] for detailed information about the S-boxes S_1, S_2, S_1^{-1}, S_2^{-1} and the key schedule algorithm.

2.2   Linear Cryptanalysis

Linear cryptanalysis [4] analyzes a block cipher E by investigating a correlation between the inputs and outputs of E and then obtains a linear approximation (also called linear characteristic and denoted as $\Gamma_P \to \Gamma_C$) of E with following type:

$$\Gamma_P \bullet P \oplus \Gamma_C \bullet C = \Gamma_K \bullet K, \qquad (1)$$

where P, C and K denote plaintext, ciphertext and master key of E respectively, Γ_P, Γ_C and Γ_K stand for the masks of P, C and K respectively.

If equation (1) holds with probability $p \neq 1/2$, we call it an effective linear approximation of the block cipher E, and the linear approximation can be used to distinguish E from a random permutation since equation (1) holds with probability $1/2$ for a random permutation. Let $\varepsilon = p - 1/2$ be the bias of the linear approximation given in equation (1), then the greater $|\varepsilon|$ is, the more effective the linear approximation will be. Moreover, based on the above linear approximation, an adversary can mount a key recovery attack on $E' = E_1 \circ E$ by means of guessing part of round keys used in E_1, where E_1 represents the last few rounds of the cipher E'. Following the technique introduced in [4], the number of plaintext-ciphertext pairs required in the key recovery attack can be estimated as $c_N \times \frac{1}{\varepsilon^2}$, where the coefficient c_N, which is closely related to the number of guessed round key bits and the desired success rate of the attack, can be measured by using the approach given in [17].

3   A Kind of Special Linear Characteristics for Byte-Oriented SPN Block Ciphers

Let E be an n-round byte-oriented SPN block cipher with m-byte block size. Let I^i, O^i, K^i be the input, output and round key of the i-th ($1 \leq i \leq n$) round of E respectively. Let X^i, Y^i be the input and output of the substitution layer of the i-th round respectively. Then I^i, O^i, K^i, X^i and Y^i can be treated as m-byte vectors. The round function of the i-th round of E is depicted in Fig. 2, where the round key addition is done by XORing K^i, S_j^i ($1 \leq j \leq m$) is a non-linear byte permutation which operates on the j-th byte of X^i, and the diffusion layer is essentially a linear transformation $P: GF(2^8)^m \to GF(2^8)^m$ which is performed on Y^i.

Let $(a_1, a_2, \ldots, a_m)$, $(b_1, b_2, \ldots, b_m) \in GF(2^8)^m$ be the input and output of the diffusion layer respectively. We firstly find that if there is subscript set Λ such that

$$\oplus_{\lambda \in \Lambda} a_\lambda = \oplus_{\lambda \in \Lambda} b_\lambda,$$

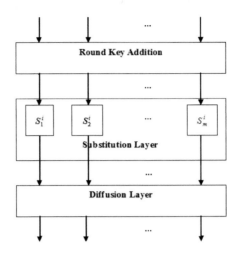

Fig. 2. The round function of the i-th round of E

special linear characteristics for t $(2 \leq t < n)$ consecutive rounds of E can be constructed as below (without loss of generality, linear characteristics for the first t rounds of E will be derived):

Step 1. For the first round of E, investigate the linear distribution tables of the S-boxes $\{S_\lambda^1\}_{\lambda \in \Lambda}$ and find all possible linear characteristics with the following form:

$$\oplus_{\lambda \in \Lambda}(\Gamma X_\lambda^1 \bullet X_\lambda^1 \oplus \Gamma Y_\lambda^1 \bullet Y_\lambda^1) = 0,$$

where X_λ^1, Y_λ^1 are the input and output of S_λ^1 respectively, ΓX_λ^1, ΓY_λ^1 are the masks of X_λ^1 and Y_λ^1 respectively, ΓY_λ^1 keeps constant for any $\lambda \in \Lambda$ and is denoted as ΓY^1. Then extend the above linear characteristics for the S-boxes $\{S_\lambda^1\}_{\lambda \in \Lambda}$ to the linear approximations of the first round described as follows:

$$\oplus_{\lambda \in \Lambda}(\Gamma X_\lambda^1 \bullet I_\lambda^1 \oplus \Gamma Y^1 \bullet O_\lambda^1) = \oplus_{\lambda \in \Lambda}(\Gamma X_\lambda^1 \bullet K_\lambda^1),$$

where I_λ^1, O_λ^1, K_λ^1 are the λ-th bytes of I^1, O^1 and K^1 respectively.

Step 2. For the i-th $(2 \leq i \leq t)$ round of E, study the the linear distribution tables of the S-boxes $\{S_\lambda^i\}_{\lambda \in \Lambda}$ and get all possible linear characteristics with the following form:

$$\oplus_{\lambda \in \Lambda}(\Gamma X_\lambda^i \bullet X_\lambda^i \oplus \Gamma Y_\lambda^i \bullet Y_\lambda^i) = 0,$$

where X_λ^i, Y_λ^i are the input and output of S_λ^i respectively, ΓX_λ^i, ΓY_λ^i are the masks of X_λ^i and Y_λ^i respectively, ΓX_λ^i is the same for any $\lambda \in \Lambda$ and is denoted as ΓX^i, ΓY_λ^i remains unchanged for any $\lambda \in \Lambda$ and is denoted as ΓY^i. Then based on the above linear characteristics for the S-boxes $\{S^i_\lambda\}_{\lambda \in \Lambda}$, generate the linear approximations of the i-th round as shown below:

$$\oplus_{\lambda \in \Lambda}(\Gamma X^i \bullet I^i_\lambda \oplus \Gamma Y^i \bullet O^i_\lambda) = \oplus_{\lambda \in \Lambda}(\Gamma X^i \bullet K^i_\lambda),$$

where I^i_λ, O^i_λ, K^i_λ are the λ-th bytes of I^i, O^i and K^i respectively.

Step 3. Denote the first t rounds of E as E_t. Obtain linear characteristics of E_t with the following form by concatenating t linear approximations on each round of E_t respectively which satisfy $\Gamma Y^{i-1} = \Gamma X^i$ $(2 \leq i \leq t)$:

$$\begin{aligned}
&\oplus_{\lambda \in \Lambda}(\Gamma X^1_\lambda \bullet I^1_\lambda \oplus \Gamma Y^t \bullet O^t_\lambda) \\
&= \oplus_{\lambda \in \Lambda}(\Gamma X^1_\lambda \bullet K^1_\lambda) \oplus^t_{i=2} \oplus_{\lambda \in \Lambda}(\Gamma X^i \bullet K^i_\lambda).
\end{aligned} \tag{2}$$

Let E_s denote the first s $(t < s \leq n)$ rounds of E. With the help of the linear characteristic for E_t given in equation (2), an adversary can mount an effective key recovery attack on E_s. Note that the smaller $\#\Lambda$ is, the more effective the above linear characteristic will be. We will demonstrate the effectiveness of such kind of linear characteristics by proposing some attacks on reduced-round ARIA in Section 4.

4   Attacking Reduced-Round ARIA

In this section, we firstly present some special 4-round linear characteristics of ARIA by using the approach mentioned in Section 3. Then based on the 4-round linear characteristics, we mount an attack on 7-round ARIA with 128/192/256-bit key size, an attack on 9-round ARIA with 192/256-bit key size as well as an attack on 11-round ARIA with 256-bit key size.

Let I^i, O^i, K^i be the input, output and round key of the i-th $(1 \leq i \leq n$, where n depends on the key size) round of ARIA respectively. Let X^i, Y^i be the input and output of the substitution layer of the i-th round respectively. Let I^i_j, O^i_j, K^i_j, X^i_j, Y^i_j denote the $(j+1)$-th $(0 \leq j \leq 15)$ bytes of I^i, O^i, K^i, X^i and Y^i respectively. As a matter of fact, the diffusion layer adopted in ARIA has the following property:

$$a_0 \oplus a_3 \oplus a_{12} \oplus a_{15} = b_0 \oplus b_3 \oplus b_{12} \oplus b_{15},$$

where $(a_0, a_1, \ldots, a_{15})$, $(b_0, b_1, \ldots, b_{15}) \in GF(2^8)^{16}$ are the input and output of the diffusion layer respectively. Thus according to the method given in Section 3, we construct several linear characteristics for the first 4 rounds of ARIA described as below:

$$\begin{aligned}
&\text{0x17} \bullet (I^1_0 \oplus I^1_{12}) \oplus \text{0x10} \bullet (I^1_3 \oplus I^1_{15}) \\
&\oplus \text{0x4D} \bullet (O^4_0 \oplus O^4_3 \oplus O^4_{12} \oplus O^4_{15}) \\
&= \text{0x17} \bullet (K^1_0 \oplus K^1_{12}) \oplus \text{0x10} \bullet (K^1_3 \oplus K^1_{15}) \\
&\oplus \text{0x17} \bullet (K^2_0 \oplus K^2_3 \oplus K^2_{12} \oplus K^2_{15}) \\
&\oplus \text{0x4D} \bullet (K^3_0 \oplus K^3_3 \oplus K^3_{12} \oplus K^3_{15}) \\
&\oplus \text{0x17} \bullet (K^4_0 \oplus K^4_3 \oplus K^4_{12} \oplus K^4_{15}),
\end{aligned} \tag{3}$$

$$\begin{aligned}
&0x0E \bullet (I_0^1 \oplus I_{12}^1) \oplus 0x15 \bullet (I_3^1 \oplus I_{15}^1) \\
&\oplus 0xB1 \bullet (O_0^4 \oplus O_3^4 \oplus O_{12}^4 \oplus O_{15}^4) \\
&= 0x0E \bullet (K_0^1 \oplus K_{12}^1) \oplus 0x15 \bullet (K_3^1 \oplus K_{15}^1) \\
&\oplus 0x09 \bullet (K_0^2 \oplus K_3^2 \oplus K_{12}^2 \oplus K_{15}^2) \\
&\oplus 0xB1 \bullet (K_0^3 \oplus K_3^3 \oplus K_{12}^3 \oplus K_{15}^3) \\
&\oplus 0x09 \bullet (K_0^4 \oplus K_3^4 \oplus K_{12}^4 \oplus K_{15}^4),
\end{aligned} \tag{4}$$

$$\begin{aligned}
&0x40 \bullet (I_0^1 \oplus I_{12}^1) \oplus 0x1B \bullet (I_3^1 \oplus I_{15}^1) \\
&\oplus 0xED \bullet (O_0^4 \oplus O_3^4 \oplus O_{12}^4 \oplus O_{15}^4) \\
&= 0x40 \bullet (K_0^1 \oplus K_{12}^1) \oplus 0x1B \bullet (K_3^1 \oplus K_{15}^1) \\
&\oplus 0x08 \bullet (K_0^2 \oplus K_3^2 \oplus K_{12}^2 \oplus K_{15}^2) \\
&\oplus 0xED \bullet (K_0^3 \oplus K_3^3 \oplus K_{12}^3 \oplus K_{15}^3) \\
&\oplus 0x08 \bullet (K_0^4 \oplus K_3^4 \oplus K_{12}^4 \oplus K_{15}^4),
\end{aligned} \tag{5}$$

and

$$\begin{aligned}
&0xB4 \bullet (I_0^1 \oplus I_{12}^1) \oplus 0xD9 \bullet (I_3^1 \oplus I_{15}^1) \\
&\oplus 0x4A \bullet (O_0^4 \oplus O_3^4 \oplus O_{12}^4 \oplus O_{15}^4) \\
&= 0xB4 \bullet (K_0^1 \oplus K_{12}^1) \oplus 0xD9 \bullet (K_3^1 \oplus K_{15}^1) \\
&\oplus 0x03 \bullet (K_0^2 \oplus K_3^2 \oplus K_{12}^2 \oplus K_{15}^2) \\
&\oplus 0x4A \bullet (K_0^3 \oplus K_3^3 \oplus K_{12}^3 \oplus K_{15}^3) \\
&\oplus 0x03 \bullet (K_0^4 \oplus K_3^4 \oplus K_{12}^4 \oplus K_{15}^4),
\end{aligned} \tag{6}$$

where each of the above 4-round linear characteristics holds with probability $1/2 - 2^{-50.15}$ approximately. Next, we will demonstrate some effective key recovery attacks on reduced-round ARIA in terms of the linear characteristic given in equation (3).

4.1 Key Recovery Attacks on 7-Round ARIA, 9-Round ARIA and 11-Round ARIA

Let E denote the first s rounds of ARIA and $s = 7$. We now propose our key recovery attack on E. First of all, the linear characteristic described in equation (3) can be rewritten as follows:

$$\begin{aligned}
&0x17 \bullet (I_0^1 \oplus I_{12}^1) \oplus 0x10 \bullet (I_3^1 \oplus I_{15}^1) \\
&\oplus 0x4D \bullet (X_0^5 \oplus X_3^5 \oplus X_{12}^5 \oplus X_{15}^5) \\
&= 0x17 \bullet (K_0^1 \oplus K_{12}^1) \oplus 0x10 \bullet (K_3^1 \oplus K_{15}^1) \\
&\oplus 0x17 \bullet (K_0^2 \oplus K_3^2 \oplus K_{12}^2 \oplus K_{15}^2) \\
&\oplus 0x4D \bullet (K_0^3 \oplus K_3^3 \oplus K_{12}^3 \oplus K_{15}^3) \\
&\oplus 0x17 \bullet (K_0^4 \oplus K_3^4 \oplus K_{12}^4 \oplus K_{15}^4) \\
&\oplus 0x4D \bullet (K_0^5 \oplus K_3^5 \oplus K_{12}^5 \oplus K_{15}^5).
\end{aligned} \tag{7}$$

Then we mount an attack on E based on the linear characteristic depicted in equation (7). The detailed description of our attack is given as below:

Step 1. Collect N pairs (P_μ, C_μ) $(1 \le \mu \le N)$, where P_μ, C_μ are the plaintext and ciphertext of E respectively. Let X_μ^i, Y_μ^i $(1 \le i \le s)$ denote the intermediate

16-byte vectors X^i and Y^i respectively which are relevant to the pair (P_μ, C_μ). Let $P_{\mu,j}$, $C_{\mu,j}$, $X_{\mu,j}^i$, $Y_{\mu,j}^i$ denote the $(j+1)$-th $(0 \leq j \leq 15)$ bytes of P_μ, C_μ, X_μ^i and Y_μ^i respectively. Derive $Y_{\mu,0}^s$, $Y_{\mu,3}^s$, $Y_{\mu,12}^s$ and $Y_{\mu,15}^s$ from the following expressions:

$$Y_{\mu,0}^s = C_{\mu,3} \oplus C_{\mu,4} \oplus C_{\mu,6} \oplus C_{\mu,8} \oplus C_{\mu,9} \oplus C_{\mu,13} \oplus C_{\mu,14},$$
$$Y_{\mu,3}^s = C_{\mu,0} \oplus C_{\mu,5} \oplus C_{\mu,7} \oplus C_{\mu,10} \oplus C_{\mu,11} \oplus C_{\mu,13} \oplus C_{\mu,14},$$
$$Y_{\mu,12}^s = C_{\mu,1} \oplus C_{\mu,2} \oplus C_{\mu,6} \oplus C_{\mu,7} \oplus C_{\mu,9} \oplus C_{\mu,11} \oplus C_{\mu,12},$$
$$Y_{\mu,15}^s = C_{\mu,1} \oplus C_{\mu,2} \oplus C_{\mu,4} \oplus C_{\mu,5} \oplus C_{\mu,8} \oplus C_{\mu,10} \oplus C_{\mu,15}.$$

Initialize 2^{32} counters $\{T_l\}_{0 \leq l \leq 2^{32}-1}$ (the size of each counter could be set to $\lceil \log_2^N \rceil$ bits), where T_l corresponds to l which represents the possible value of $Y_{\mu,0}^s \| Y_{\mu,3}^s \| Y_{\mu,12}^s \| Y_{\mu,15}^s$. For each pair (P_μ, C_μ), increase (or decrease) the counter T_l by 1 if the parity of

$$\text{0x17} \bullet (P_{\mu,0} \oplus P_{\mu,12}) \oplus \text{0x10} \bullet (P_{\mu,3} \oplus P_{\mu,15})$$

is 0 (or 1) as well as the value of $Y_{\mu,0}^s \| Y_{\mu,3}^s \| Y_{\mu,12}^s \| Y_{\mu,15}^s$ is equal to l.

Step 2. Let K_g^{s-1}, K_g^s denote $K_0^{s-1} \oplus K_3^{s-1} \oplus K_{12}^{s-1} \oplus K_{15}^{s-1}$ and $K_0^s \oplus K_3^s \oplus K_{12}^s \oplus K_{15}^s$ respectively. Let θ_1, θ_2, ξ denote $Y_{\mu,0}^{s-1} \| Y_{\mu,3}^{s-1} \| Y_{\mu,12}^{s-1} \| Y_{\mu,15}^{s-1}$, $Y_{\mu,0}^{s-2} \| Y_{\mu,3}^{s-2} \| Y_{\mu,12}^{s-2} \| Y_{\mu,15}^{s-2}$ and $K_g^{s-1} \| K_g^s \| \theta_1 \| \theta_2$ respectively. Initialize 2^{80} counters $\{T_\xi'\}_{0 \leq \xi \leq 2^{80}-1}$ (the size of each counter could be set to $\lceil \log_2^N \rceil$ bits), where T_ξ' corresponds to ξ. For each possible value of $K_g^{s-1} \| K_g^s$, do the following:
(I). For each possible vaule of l, calculate $X_{\mu,0}^s$, $X_{\mu,3}^s$, $X_{\mu,12}^s$ and $X_{\mu,15}^s$ according to the corresponding S-boxes. Then compute the value of $Y_{\mu,0}^{s-1} \oplus Y_{\mu,3}^{s-1} \oplus Y_{\mu,12}^{s-1} \oplus Y_{\mu,15}^{s-1}$ and denote the value as v^{s-1}. Go to (II).

(II). For any of the 2^{24} possible values of θ_1 satisfying $Y_{\mu,0}^{s-1} \oplus Y_{\mu,3}^{s-1} \oplus Y_{\mu,12}^{s-1} \oplus Y_{\mu,15}^{s-1} = v^{s-1}$, derive $X_{\mu,0}^{s-1}$, $X_{\mu,3}^{s-1}$, $X_{\mu,12}^{s-1}$ and $X_{\mu,15}^{s-1}$ according to the corresponding S-boxes. Then get the value of $Y_{\mu,0}^{s-2} \oplus Y_{\mu,3}^{s-2} \oplus Y_{\mu,12}^{s-2} \oplus Y_{\mu,15}^{s-2}$ and denote the value as v^{s-2}. Go to (III).

(III). For any of the 2^{24} possible values of θ_2 satisfying $Y_{\mu,0}^{s-2} \oplus Y_{\mu,3}^{s-2} \oplus Y_{\mu,12}^{s-2} \oplus Y_{\mu,15}^{s-2} = v^{s-2}$, obtain $X_{\mu,0}^{s-2}$, $X_{\mu,3}^{s-2}$, $X_{\mu,12}^{s-2}$ and $X_{\mu,15}^{s-2}$ according to the corresponding S-boxes. Then calculate the parity of

$$\text{0x4D} \bullet (X_{\mu,0}^{s-2} \oplus X_{\mu,3}^{s-2} \oplus X_{\mu,12}^{s-2} \oplus X_{\mu,15}^{s-2}).$$

If the parity is 0, increase the relevant counter T_ξ' by the value of T_l, and decrease by the value of T_l otherwise.

Step 3. For the ξ such that the value of $|T_\xi'|$ is maximal, take the value of the corresponding $K_g^{s-1} \| K_g^s$ as the correct key information.

Actually, we need to guess about 80 bits in the above attack. Thus following the Theorem 2 proposed in [17], the number of plaintext-ciphertext pairs required in the attack can be estimated as $2^{5.5} \times \frac{1}{(2^{-50.15})^2} = 2^{105.8}$ in order to achieve a high success probability of 88% approximately (i.e., $N = 2^{105.8}$). The time complexity of the attack is dominated mainly by the calculations of $Y^s_{\mu,0}$, $Y^s_{\mu,3}$, $Y^s_{\mu,12}$ and $Y^s_{\mu,15}$ in the step 1 and the decryptions of the S-boxes in the step 2(III). Consequently, the time complexity of the attack is around $2^{105.8} \times \frac{4}{16 \times 7} + 2^{16} \times 2^{32} \times 2^{24} \times 2^{24} \times \frac{4}{16 \times 7} \approx 2^{100.99}$ 7-round ARIA encryptions. Regarding the memory complexity of the attack, it is primarily owing to keeping the counters $\{T'_\xi\}_{0 \le \xi \le 2^{80}-1}$ (the size of each counter is set to 106 bits) in the step 2. Accordingly, the memory complexity of the attack is about $2^{80} \times 106/8 \approx 2^{83.73}$ bytes.

For the cases of $s = 9$ and $s = 11$, the procedures of the attacks on the first 9 rounds and the first 11 rounds of ARIA are the same as that in the case of $s = 7$ except the step 2 and step 3 which are described as below.

Case 1: $s = 9$.

Step 2. Let K^{s-3}_g, K^{s-2}_g, K^{s-1}_g, K^s_g denote $K^{s-3}_0 \oplus K^{s-3}_3 \oplus K^{s-3}_{12} \oplus K^{s-3}_{15}$, $K^{s-2}_0 \oplus K^{s-2}_3 \oplus K^{s-2}_{12} \oplus K^{s-2}_{15}$, $K^{s-1}_0 \oplus K^{s-1}_3 \oplus K^{s-1}_{12} \oplus K^{s-1}_{15}$ and $K^s_0 \oplus K^s_3 \oplus K^s_{12} \oplus K^s_{15}$ respectively. Let θ_1, θ_2, θ_3, θ_4, ξ denote $Y^{s-1}_{\mu,0}\|Y^{s-1}_{\mu,3}\|Y^{s-1}_{\mu,12}\|Y^{s-1}_{\mu,15}$, $Y^{s-2}_{\mu,0}\|Y^{s-2}_{\mu,3}\|Y^{s-2}_{\mu,12}\|Y^{s-2}_{\mu,15}$, $Y^{s-3}_{\mu,0}\|Y^{s-3}_{\mu,3}\|Y^{s-3}_{\mu,12}\|Y^{s-3}_{\mu,15}$, $Y^{s-4}_{\mu,0}\|Y^{s-4}_{\mu,3}\|Y^{s-4}_{\mu,12}\|Y^{s-4}_{\mu,15}$ and $K^{s-3}_g\|K^{s-2}_g\|K^{s-1}_g\|K^s_g\|\theta_1\|\theta_2\|\theta_3\|\theta_4$ respectively. Initialize 2^{160} counters $\{T'_\xi\}_{0 \le \xi \le 2^{160}-1}$ (the size of each counter could be set to $\lceil \log^N_2 \rceil$ bits), where T'_ξ corresponds to ξ. For each possible value of $K^{s-3}_g\|K^{s-2}_g\|K^{s-1}_g\|K^s_g$, do the following:

(I). For each possible vaule of l, calculate $X^s_{\mu,0}$, $X^s_{\mu,3}$, $X^s_{\mu,12}$ and $X^s_{\mu,15}$ according to the corresponding S-boxes. Then compute the value of $Y^{s-1}_{\mu,0} \oplus Y^{s-1}_{\mu,3} \oplus Y^{s-1}_{\mu,12} \oplus Y^{s-1}_{\mu,15}$ and denote the value as v^{s-1}. Go to (II).

(II). For any of the 2^{24} possible values of θ_1 satisfying $Y^{s-1}_{\mu,0} \oplus Y^{s-1}_{\mu,3} \oplus Y^{s-1}_{\mu,12} \oplus Y^{s-1}_{\mu,15} = v^{s-1}$, derive $X^{s-1}_{\mu,0}$, $X^{s-1}_{\mu,3}$, $X^{s-1}_{\mu,12}$ and $X^{s-1}_{\mu,15}$ according to the corresponding S-boxes. Then get the value of $Y^{s-2}_{\mu,0} \oplus Y^{s-2}_{\mu,3} \oplus Y^{s-2}_{\mu,12} \oplus Y^{s-2}_{\mu,15}$ and denote the value as v^{s-2}. Go to (III).

(III). For any of the 2^{24} possible values of θ_2 satisfying $Y^{s-2}_{\mu,0} \oplus Y^{s-2}_{\mu,3} \oplus Y^{s-2}_{\mu,12} \oplus Y^{s-2}_{\mu,15} = v^{s-2}$, obtain $X^{s-2}_{\mu,0}$, $X^{s-2}_{\mu,3}$, $X^{s-2}_{\mu,12}$ and $X^{s-2}_{\mu,15}$ according to the corresponding S-boxes. Then compute the value of $Y^{s-3}_{\mu,0} \oplus Y^{s-3}_{\mu,3} \oplus Y^{s-3}_{\mu,12} \oplus Y^{s-3}_{\mu,15}$ and denote the value as v^{s-3}. Go to (IV).

(IV). For any of the 2^{24} possible values of θ_3 satisfying $Y^{s-3}_{\mu,0} \oplus Y^{s-3}_{\mu,3} \oplus Y^{s-3}_{\mu,12} \oplus Y^{s-3}_{\mu,15} = v^{s-3}$, derive $X^{s-3}_{\mu,0}$, $X^{s-3}_{\mu,3}$, $X^{s-3}_{\mu,12}$ and $X^{s-3}_{\mu,15}$ according to the corresponding S-boxes. Then get the value of $Y_{\mu,0}^{s-4} \oplus Y_{\mu,3}^{s-4} \oplus Y_{\mu,12}^{s-4} \oplus Y_{\mu,15}^{s-4}$ and denote the value as v^{s-4}. Go to (V).

(V). For any of the 2^{24} possible values of θ_4 satisfying $Y_{\mu,0}^{s-4} \oplus Y_{\mu,3}^{s-4} \oplus Y_{\mu,12}^{s-4} \oplus Y_{\mu,15}^{s-4} = v^{s-4}$, obtain $X_{\mu,0}^{s-4}$, $X_{\mu,3}^{s-4}$, $X_{\mu,12}^{s-4}$ and $X_{\mu,15}^{s-4}$ according to the corresponding S-boxes. Then calculate the parity of

$$0x4D \bullet (X_{\mu,0}^{s-4} \oplus X_{\mu,3}^{s-4} \oplus X_{\mu,12}^{s-4} \oplus X_{\mu,15}^{s-4}).$$

If the parity is 0, increase the relevant counter T_ξ' by the value of T_l, and decrease by the value of T_l otherwise.

Step 3. For the ξ such that the value of $|T_\xi'|$ is maximal, take the value of the corresponding $K_g^{s-3}\|K_g^{s-2}\|K_g^{s-1}\|K_g^s$ as the correct key information.

Case 2: $s = 11$.

Step 2. Let K_g^{s-5}, K_g^{s-4}, K_g^{s-3}, K_g^{s-2}, K_g^{s-1}, K_g^s denote $K_0^{s-5} \oplus K_3^{s-5} \oplus K_{12}^{s-5} \oplus K_{15}^{s-5}$, $K_0^{s-4} \oplus K_3^{s-4} \oplus K_{12}^{s-4} \oplus K_{15}^{s-4}$, $K_0^{s-3} \oplus K_3^{s-3} \oplus K_{12}^{s-3} \oplus K_{15}^{s-3}$, $K_0^{s-2} \oplus K_3^{s-2} \oplus K_{12}^{s-2} \oplus K_{15}^{s-2}$, $K_0^{s-1} \oplus K_3^{s-1} \oplus K_{12}^{s-1} \oplus K_{15}^{s-1}$ and $K_0^s \oplus K_3^s \oplus K_{12}^s \oplus K_{15}^s$ respectively. Let θ_1, θ_2, θ_3, θ_4, θ_5, θ_6, ξ denote $Y_{\mu,0}^{s-1}\|Y_{\mu,3}^{s-1}\|Y_{\mu,12}^{s-1}\|Y_{\mu,15}^{s-1}$, $Y_{\mu,0}^{s-2}\|Y_{\mu,3}^{s-2}\|Y_{\mu,12}^{s-2}\|Y_{\mu,15}^{s-2}$, $Y_{\mu,0}^{s-3}\|Y_{\mu,3}^{s-3}\|Y_{\mu,12}^{s-3}\|Y_{\mu,15}^{s-3}$, $Y_{\mu,0}^{s-4}\|Y_{\mu,3}^{s-4}\|Y_{\mu,12}^{s-4}\|Y_{\mu,15}^{s-4}$, $Y_{\mu,0}^{s-5}\|Y_{\mu,3}^{s-5}\|Y_{\mu,12}^{s-5}\|Y_{\mu,15}^{s-5}$, $Y_{\mu,0}^{s-6}\|Y_{\mu,3}^{s-6}\|Y_{\mu,12}^{s-6}\|Y_{\mu,15}^{s-6}$ and $K_g^{s-5}\|K_g^{s-4}\|K_g^{s-3}\|K_g^{s-2}\|K_g^{s-1}\|K_g^s\|\theta_1\|\theta_2\|\theta_3\|\theta_4\|\theta_5\|\theta_6$ respectively. Initialize 2^{240} counters $\{T_\xi'\}_{0 \le \xi \le 2^{240}-1}$ (the size of each counter could be set to $\lceil \log_2^N \rceil$ bits), where T_ξ' corresponds to ξ. For each possible value of $K_g^{s-5}\|K_g^{s-4}\|K_g^{s-3}\|K_g^{s-2}\|K_g^{s-1}\|K_g^s$, do the following:

(I). For each possible vaule of l, calculate $X_{\mu,0}^s$, $X_{\mu,3}^s$, $X_{\mu,12}^s$ and $X_{\mu,15}^s$ according to the corresponding S-boxes. Then compute the value of $Y_{\mu,0}^{s-1} \oplus Y_{\mu,3}^{s-1} \oplus Y_{\mu,12}^{s-1} \oplus Y_{\mu,15}^{s-1}$ and denote the value as v^{s-1}. Go to (II).

(II). For any of the 2^{24} possible values of θ_1 satisfying $Y_{\mu,0}^{s-1} \oplus Y_{\mu,3}^{s-1} \oplus Y_{\mu,12}^{s-1} \oplus Y_{\mu,15}^{s-1} = v^{s-1}$, derive $X_{\mu,0}^{s-1}$, $X_{\mu,3}^{s-1}$, $X_{\mu,12}^{s-1}$ and $X_{\mu,15}^{s-1}$ according to the corresponding S-boxes. Then get the value of $Y_{\mu,0}^{s-2} \oplus Y_{\mu,3}^{s-2} \oplus Y_{\mu,12}^{s-2} \oplus Y_{\mu,15}^{s-2}$ and denote the value as v^{s-2}. Go to (III).

(III). For any of the 2^{24} possible values of θ_2 satisfying $Y_{\mu,0}^{s-2} \oplus Y_{\mu,3}^{s-2} \oplus Y_{\mu,12}^{s-2} \oplus Y_{\mu,15}^{s-2} = v^{s-2}$, obtain $X_{\mu,0}^{s-2}$, $X_{\mu,3}^{s-2}$, $X_{\mu,12}^{s-2}$ and $X_{\mu,15}^{s-2}$ according to the corresponding S-boxes. Then compute the value of $Y_{\mu,0}^{s-3} \oplus Y_{\mu,3}^{s-3} \oplus Y_{\mu,12}^{s-3} \oplus Y_{\mu,15}^{s-3}$ and denote the value as v^{s-3}. Go to (IV).

(IV). For any of the 2^{24} possible values of θ_3 satisfying $Y_{\mu,0}^{s-3} \oplus Y_{\mu,3}^{s-3} \oplus Y_{\mu,12}^{s-3} \oplus Y_{\mu,15}^{s-3} = v^{s-3}$, derive $X_{\mu,0}^{s-3}$, $X_{\mu,3}^{s-3}$, $X_{\mu,12}^{s-3}$ and $X_{\mu,15}^{s-3}$ according to the corresponding S-boxes. Then get the value of $Y_{\mu,0}^{s-4} \oplus Y_{\mu,3}^{s-4} \oplus Y_{\mu,12}^{s-4} \oplus Y_{\mu,15}^{s-4}$ and denote the value as v^{s-4}. Go to (V).

Table 1. Summary of Attacks on Reduced-round ARIA

Type of Attack	Key Size	Rounds	Data	Time	Memory
ID [9]	all	5	$2^{71.3}$ CP	$2^{71.6}$ Enc	2^{76} B *
MIMA [15]	all	5	2^{25} CP	$2^{65.4}$ Enc	$2^{126.5}$ B *
BA [13]	all	5	2^{109} ACPC	2^{110} Enc	2^{61} B *
IA [11]	all	5	$2^{27.5}$ CP	$2^{76.7}$ Enc	$2^{31.5}$ B *
ID [8]	all	6	2^{121} CP	2^{112} Enc	2^{125} B *
ID [9]	all	6	$2^{120.5}$ CP	$2^{104.5}$ Enc	2^{125} B *
ID [9]	all	6	2^{113} CP	$2^{121.6}$ Enc	2^{117} B *
IA [11]	192/256	6	$2^{124.4}$ CP	$2^{172.4}$ Enc	$2^{128.4}$ B *
MIMA [15]	all	6	2^{56} CP	$2^{121.5}$ Enc	$2^{126.5}$ B *
BA [13]	all	6	2^{128} KP	2^{108} Enc	2^{60} B *
IA [12]	all	6	$2^{99.2}$ CP	$2^{71.4}$ Enc	−
MIMA [15]	192/256	7	2^{120} CP	$2^{185.3}$ Enc	2^{191} B *
BA [13]	256	7	2^{128} KP	2^{236} Enc	2^{188} B *
ID [10]	256	7	2^{125} CP	2^{238} Enc	−
IA [12]	256	7	$2^{100.6}$ CP	$2^{225.8}$ Enc	−
LC (This paper)	all	7	$2^{105.8}$ KP	$2^{100.99}$ Enc	$2^{83.73}$ B
MIMA [15]	256	8	2^{56} CP	$2^{251.6}$ Enc	2^{256} B *
LC (This paper)	192/256	9	$2^{108.3}$ KP	$2^{154.83}$ Enc	$2^{163.77}$ B
LC (This paper)	256	11	$2^{110.3}$ KP	$2^{218.54}$ Enc	$2^{243.8}$ B

ID: Impossible Differential, MIMA: Meet-in-the-Middle Attack,
BA: Boomerang Attack, IA: Integral Attack, LC: Linear Cryptanalysis,
CP: Chosen plaintexts, KP: Known plaintexts,
ACPC: Adaptive chosen plaintexts and ciphertexts,
Enc: Encryptions, B: Bytes,
-: Not given in the related paper, *: Estimated in [13].

(V). For any of the 2^{24} possible values of θ_4 satisfying $Y_{\mu,0}^{s-4} \oplus Y_{\mu,3}^{s-4} \oplus Y_{\mu,12}^{s-4} \oplus Y_{\mu,15}^{s-4} = v^{s-4}$, obtain $X_{\mu,0}^{s-4}$, $X_{\mu,3}^{s-4}$, $X_{\mu,12}^{s-4}$ and $X_{\mu,15}^{s-4}$ according to the corresponding S-boxes. Then compute the value of $Y_{\mu,0}^{s-5} \oplus Y_{\mu,3}^{s-5} \oplus Y_{\mu,12}^{s-5} \oplus Y_{\mu,15}^{s-5}$ and denote the value as v^{s-5}. Go to (VI).

(VI). For any of the 2^{24} possible values of θ_5 satisfying $Y_{\mu,0}^{s-5} \oplus Y_{\mu,3}^{s-5} \oplus Y_{\mu,12}^{s-5} \oplus Y_{\mu,15}^{s-5} = v^{s-5}$, derive $X_{\mu,0}^{s-5}$, $X_{\mu,3}^{s-5}$, $X_{\mu,12}^{s-5}$ and $X_{\mu,15}^{s-5}$ according to the corresponding S-boxes. Then get the value of $Y_{\mu,0}^{s-6} \oplus Y_{\mu,3}^{s-6} \oplus Y_{\mu,12}^{s-6} \oplus Y_{\mu,15}^{s-6}$ and denote the value as v^{s-6}. Go to (VII).

(VII). For any of the 2^{24} possible values of θ_6 satisfying $Y_{\mu,0}^{s-6} \oplus Y_{\mu,3}^{s-6} \oplus Y_{\mu,12}^{s-6} \oplus Y_{\mu,15}^{s-6} = v^{s-6}$, obtain $X_{\mu,0}^{s-6}$, $X_{\mu,3}^{s-6}$, $X_{\mu,12}^{s-6}$ and $X_{\mu,15}^{s-6}$ according to the corresponding S-boxes. Then calculate the parity of

$$\text{0x4D} \bullet (X_{\mu,0}^{s-6} \oplus X_{\mu,3}^{s-6} \oplus X_{\mu,12}^{s-6} \oplus X_{\mu,15}^{s-6}).$$

If the parity is 0, increase the relevant counter T_{ξ}' by the value of T_l, and decrease by the value of T_l otherwise.

Step 3. For the ξ such that the value of $|T'_\xi|$ is maximal, take the value of the corresponding $K_g^{s-5}\|K_g^{s-4}\|K_g^{s-3}\|K_g^{s-2}\|K_g^{s-1}\|K_g^s$ as the correct key information.

Since we need to guess about 160 bits and 240 bits in case 1 and case 2 respectively, according to the Theorem 2 proposed in [17], the number of plaintext-ciphertext pairs required in these cases can be estimated as $2^8 \times \frac{1}{(2^{-50.15})^2} = 2^{108.3}$ and $2^{10} \times \frac{1}{(2^{-50.15})^2} = 2^{110.3}$ respectively in order to achieve a high success probability of 88% approximately (i.e., $N = 2^{108.3}$ in case 1 and $N = 2^{110.3}$ in case 2). The time complexities and memory complexities in these cases can be measured similarly to those in the case of $s = 7$. Thus the time complexities in these cases are around $2^{32} \times 2^{32} \times 2^{24} \times 2^{24} \times 2^{24} \times 2^{24} \times \frac{4}{16 \times 9} \approx 2^{154.83}$ 9-round ARIA encryptions and $2^{48} \times 2^{32} \times 2^{24} \times 2^{24} \times 2^{24} \times 2^{24} \times 2^{24} \times 2^{24} \times \frac{4}{16 \times 11} \approx 2^{218.54}$ 11-round ARIA encryptions respectively, and the memory complexities in these cases are about $2^{160} \times 109/8 \approx 2^{163.77}$ bytes and $2^{240} \times 111/8 \approx 2^{243.8}$ bytes respectively.

5 Conclusion

In this paper, we introduce a new idea of deriving a kind of special linear characteristics for byte-oriented SPN block ciphers. Following this idea, we present several special 4-round linear characteristics of ARIA. Then based on such linear characteristics, we mount a key recovery attack on 7-round ARIA with 128/192/256-bit key size, a key recovery attack on 9-round ARIA with 192/256-bit key size as well as a key recovery attack on 11-round ARIA with 256-bit key size. In fact, the designers of ARIA expect that there isn't any effective attack on 8 or more rounds of ARIA with 128/192/256-bit key size by means of linear cryptanalysis. However, our work shows that such attacks do exist. Furthermore, the results of our attacks are better than the previously known cryptanalytic results of ARIA. The complexities of our attacks together with the formerly existing attacks on ARIA are summarized in Table 1.

Acknowledgements. This work has been supported by the National Natural Science Foundation of China (No. 61073150 and No. 61003278), the Opening Project of Shanghai Key Laboratory of Integrate Administration Technologies for Information Security, and the Fundamental Research Funds for the Central Universities. Moreover, we are very grateful to the anonymous referees for their comments and editorial suggestions.

References

1. Kwon, D., Kim, J., Park, S., Sung, S.H., et al.: New Block Cipher: ARIA. In: Lim, J.-I., Lee, D.-H. (eds.) ICISC 2003. LNCS, vol. 2971, pp. 432–445. Springer, Heidelberg (2004)

2. National Security Research Institute, Korea. Specification of ARIA. Version 1.0 (2005)
3. Biham, E., Shamir, A.: Differential Cryptanalysis of DES-like Cryptosystems. In: Menezes, A., Vanstone, S.A. (eds.) CRYPTO 1990. LNCS, vol. 537, pp. 2–21. Springer, Heidelberg (1991)
4. Matsui, M.: Linear Cryptanalysis Method for DES Cipher. In: Helleseth, T. (ed.) EUROCRYPT 1993. LNCS, vol. 765, pp. 386–397. Springer, Heidelberg (1994)
5. Knudsen, L.R.: Truncated and Higher Order Differentials. In: Preneel, B. (ed.) FSE 1994. LNCS, vol. 1008, pp. 196–211. Springer, Heidelberg (1995)
6. Biham, E., Biryukov, A., Shamir, A.: Cryptanalysis of Skipjack Reduced to 31 Rounds Using Impossible Differentials. Journal of Cryptology 18(4), 291–311 (2005)
7. Knudsen, L.R., Wagner, D.: Integral Cryptanalysis. In: Daemen, J., Rijmen, V. (eds.) FSE 2002. LNCS, vol. 2365, pp. 112–127. Springer, Heidelberg (2002)
8. Wu, W., Zhang, W., Feng, D.: Impossible Differential Cryptanalysis of Reduced-Round ARIA and Camellia. Journal of Computer Science and Technology 22(3), 449–456 (2007)
9. Li, R., Sun, B., Zhang, P., Li, C.: New Impossible Differentials of ARIA. Cryptology ePrint Archive, Report 2008/227 (2008), http://eprint.iacr.org/
10. Du, C., Chen, J.: Impossible Differential Cryptanalysis of ARIA Reduced to 7 Rounds. In: Heng, S.-H., Wright, R.N., Goi, B.-M. (eds.) CANS 2010. LNCS, vol. 6467, pp. 20–30. Springer, Heidelberg (2010)
11. Li, P., Sun, B., Li, C.: Integral Cryptanalysis of ARIA. In: Bao, F., Yung, M., Lin, D., Jing, J. (eds.) Inscrypt 2009. LNCS, vol. 6151, pp. 1–14. Springer, Heidelberg (2010)
12. Li, Y., Wu, W., Zhang, L.: Integral Attacks on Reduced-Round ARIA Block Cipher. In: Kwak, J., Deng, R.H., Won, Y., Wang, G. (eds.) ISPEC 2010. LNCS, vol. 6047, pp. 19–29. Springer, Heidelberg (2010)
13. Fleischmann, E., Forler, C., Gorski, M., Lucks, S.: New Boomerang Attacks on ARIA. In: Gong, G., Gupta, K.C. (eds.) INDOCRYPT 2010. LNCS, vol. 6498, pp. 163–175. Springer, Heidelberg (2010)
14. Wagner, D.: The Boomerang Attack. In: Knudsen, L.R. (ed.) FSE 1999. LNCS, vol. 1636, pp. 156–170. Springer, Heidelberg (1999)
15. Tang, X., Sun, B., Li, R., Li, C.: A Meet-in-the-middle Attack on ARIA. Cryptology ePrint Archive, Report 2010/168 (2010), http://eprint.iacr.org/
16. Demirci, H., Selçuk, A.A.: A Meet-in-the-Middle Attack on 8-Round AES. In: Nyberg, K. (ed.) FSE 2008. LNCS, vol. 5086, pp. 116–126. Springer, Heidelberg (2008)
17. Selçuk, A.A.: On Probability of Success in Linear and Differential Cryptanalysis. Journal of Cryptology 21(1), 131–147 (2008)

Latin Dances Revisited: New Analytic Results of Salsa20 and ChaCha

Tsukasa Ishiguro, Shinsaku Kiyomoto, and Yutaka Miyake

KDDI R&D Laboratories Inc.,
2-1-15 Ohara, Fujimino, Saitama 356-8502, Japan
{tsukasa,kiyomoto,miyake}@kddilabs.jp

Abstract. In this paper, we propose new attacks on 9-round Salsa20 and 8-round ChaCha. We constructed a distinguisher of double-bit differentials to improve Aumasson's single-bit differential cryptanalysis. We searched for correlations using a PC, and found strong correlations in 9-round Salsa20 and 8-round ChaCha. The complexities of the introduced attacks are 2^{16} in 9-round Salsa20 and 2 in 8-round ChaCha, which are much less than the complexities of an exhaustive key search and existing attacks on those ciphers. The results show that an adversary can distinguish keystream bits from random bits using a few input and output pairs of an initial keys and initial vectors. This method has potential to apply to a wide range of stream ciphers; a double-bit correlation would be found in case that no single-bit correlation is found.

Keywords: Stream cipher, Salsa20, ChaCha, eSTREAM.

1 Introduction

Efficient implementations of stream ciphers are useful in any application which requires high-speed encryption, such as SSL[13] and WEP[14]. The stream cipher project of ECRYPT(eSTREAM)[11] was launched to identify new stream ciphers that realizes secure and high-speed encryption. This project ended with a proposal of a list of new eight algorithms in 2008, and one was removed from the list in 2009[2] due to a new vulnerability of the cipher. Four algorithms are assumed to apply to software implementations, and remaining three are for lightweight hardware implementations.

Salsa20, one of algorithms for software implementations, was proposed by Bernstein[5] in 2005, and the cipher is the finalist of the eSTREAM. Salsa20 offers a simple, clean, and scalable design and is suitable for software implementations. Bernstein advocated use of 8, 12 and 20 round versions of Salsa20. However, in eSTREAM, the 12-round version was adopted due to the balance, combining a very nice performance profile with what appears to be a comfortable margin for security.

More recently, he has proposed the ChaCha[3], a new variant of the Salsa20 family. ChaCha follows the same design principles as Salsa20, and a difference between Salsa20 family and ChaCha is the core function; the core function of ChaCha realizes faster diffusion than that of Salsa20 family. ChaCha achieves faster software speed than Salsa20 in some platforms.

S. Qing et al. (Eds.): ICICS 2011, LNCS 7043, pp. 255–266, 2011.
© Springer-Verlag Berlin Heidelberg 2011

Related work. There are many ciphers proposed in eSTREAM, and some have been broken by distinguishing attacks. NLS proposed by Hawkes et al[15], is an extended version of SOBER[16]. NLS is a software-oriented cipher based on simple 32-bit operations (such as 32-bit XOR and addition modulo 2^{32}), and is related to small fixed arrays. This stream cipher was broken by a distinguishing attack[8] and a Crossword Puzzle Attack[7] which is a variant of the distinguishing attack. LEX[6] has a simple design and based on AES. A variant of the distinguishing attack[10] was found on LEX. Yamb[17] is a synchronous encryption algorithm that allows keys of any length in the range 80-256 bits and allows initial vectors IV of any length in the range 32-128 bits. Yamb was broken by a distinguishing attack proposed by Wu et al.[18]. Some other stream ciphers have been broken by distinguishing attacks[19,20].

Some independent cryptanalyses on Salsa20 have been published, to report key-recovery attacks for its reduced versions with up to 8 rounds, while Salsa20 has a total of 20 rounds. Previous attacks on Salsa20 used a distinguishing attack exploiting a truncated differential over 3 or 4 rounds. The first attack was presented by Crowley[9], and it was claimed that an adversary could break the 5-round version of Salsa20 within 3^{165} trials using a 256-bit key. Later, a four round differential was exploited by Fischer et al.[12] to break 6 rounds in 2^{177} trials and by Tsnunoo et al.[21] to break 7 rounds in about 2^{190} trials.

The best attack is proposed by Aumasson et al.[22] so far, and it covers the 8-round version of Salsa20 with an estimated complexity of 2^{251}. Regarding the 128-bit key, Aumasson proposed key-recovery attacks for reduced versions with up to 7 rounds[22]. Priemuth-Schmid proposed a distinguishing attack using slid pairs[23], but Bernstein showed that time complexity of the attack is higher than brute force attack[4].

For ChaCha, Aumasson attacked the 6-round version with an estimated complexity of 2^{139} and the 7-round version with an estimated complexity of 2^{248} using a 256-bit key. Regarding the 128-bit key, Aumasson proposed key-recovery attacks for reduced versions with up to 7 rounds with an estimated complexity of 2^{107}[22].

These attacks are single-bit differential attacks, a type of correlation attacks. In this method, an adversary chooses the input pair X, X' and observes the output pair Z, Z', where there is a differential in one bit between X and X'. Then, the adversary collects many output pairs by changing input pair and observes the one bit differential from the output pair. If the position of the input differential correlates strongly with the position of output differential, the adversary could distinguish real keystream from a random bit stream. Additionally, it was indicated a strong correlation from his experimental results.

Contribution. In this paper, we propose a new attack on 9-round Salsa20 and 8-round ChaCha. We construct a distinguisher using double-bit differentials to improve Aumasson's method, called single-bit differential cryptanalysis[1]. In our attack, the adversary chooses the input pair X, X' with a one-bit differential in the same way for a single-bit differential. Then, the adversary collects many output pairs by changing the input pair and observing the double-bit difference from the output pair. Finally, the adversary observes a correlation of the double-bit of the output pair and distinguishes keystream from the random bits. We searched correlations to compute 2-3 days using a PC, and found strong correlations in 9-round Salsa20 and 8-round ChaCha. This results suggest that the double-bit differential cryptanalysis is more powerful attack than the single-bit differential cryptanalysis and it reduces total cost of attacks on Salsa20 and ChaCha. The double-bit differential cryptanalysis has potential to apply a wide range of stream ciphers; a double-bit correlation may be found in case that even if no single-bit correlation is found.

The rest of the paper is organized as follows; in section 2, we describe specifications of Salsa20 and ChaCha. Next, we define the scenario of a distinguishing attack and explain details of the distinguishing attack in section 3. Then, we demonstrate that the attack achieves a reasonable level of efficacy from the experimental results in section 4. Finally, we conclude this paper in section 5.

2   Latin Dances

In this section, we describe the specifications of Salsa20[5] and ChaCha[3].

2.1   Salsa20

Algorithm 1 shows Salsa20 algorithm. The stream cipher Salsa20 operates on 32-bit words, takes as input a 256-bit key $k = (k_0, k_1, ..., k_7)$ or 128-bit key $k = (k_0, k_1, ..., k_3)$ and a 64-bit nonce $v = (v_0, v_1)$, and produces a sequence of 512-bit keystream blocks. The i-th block is the output of the Salsa20 function that takes as input the key, the nonce, and a 64-bit counter $t = (t_0, t_1)$ corresponding to the integer i. This function acts on the 4×4 matrix of 32-bit words written as:

$$X = \begin{pmatrix} x_0 & x_1 & x_2 & x_3 \\ x_4 & x_5 & x_6 & x_7 \\ x_8 & x_9 & x_{10} & x_{11} \\ x_{12} & x_{13} & x_{14} & x_{15} \end{pmatrix} = \begin{pmatrix} \tau_0 & k_0 & k_1 & k_2 \\ k_3 & \tau_1 & v_0 & v_1 \\ i_0 & i_1 & \tau_2 & k_4 \\ k_5 & k_6 & k_7 & \tau_3 \end{pmatrix} \text{ or,}$$

$$X = \begin{pmatrix} x_0 & x_1 & x_2 & x_3 \\ x_4 & x_5 & x_6 & x_7 \\ x_8 & x_9 & x_{10} & x_{11} \\ x_{12} & x_{13} & x_{14} & x_{15} \end{pmatrix} = \begin{pmatrix} \sigma_0 & k_0' & k_1' & k_2' \\ k_3' & \sigma_1 & v_0 & v_1 \\ i_0 & i_1 & \sigma_2 & k_0' \\ k_1' & k_2' & k_3' & \sigma_3 \end{pmatrix},$$

where σ and τ are constants dependent on the key length.

Then a keystream block Z is defined as:

$$Z = X + X^{20},$$

where $X^r = Round^r(X)$ with the round function of Salsa20 and $+$ is word-wise addition modulo 2^{32}. If $Z = X + X^r$, it is called "r-round Salsa20". A round function is called a doubleround function, and it consists of a columnround function followed by a rowround function. The doubleround function of Salsa20 is repeated 10 times. A vector (x_0, x_1, x_2, x_3) of four words is transformed into (z_0, z_1, z_2, z_3) by calculating as:

Algorithm 1. Algorithm of Salsa20

INPUT: Initial matrix X, $r \in \mathbb{N}$
OUTPUT: $Z = X + X^r$
 1: $X' \leftarrow X$
 2: **for** $l = 0$ up to $\frac{r}{2}$ **do**
 3:     $(x'_0, x'_1, x'_2, x'_3) \leftarrow quarterround(x'_0, x'_1, x'_2, x'_3)$ /* 3-6:Colmnround */
 4:     $(x'_5, x'_6, x'_7, x'_4) \leftarrow quarterround(x'_5, x'_6, x'_7, x'_4)$
 5:     $(x'_{10}, x'_{11}, x'_8, x'_9) \leftarrow quarterround(x'_{10}, x'_{11}, x'_8, x'_9)$
 6:     $(x'_{15}, x'_{12}, x'_{13}, x'_{14}) \leftarrow quarterround(x'_{15}, x'_{12}, x'_{13}, x'_{14})$
 7:     $(x'_0, x'_4, x'_8, x'_{12}) \leftarrow quarterround(x'_0, x'_4, x'_8, x'_{12})$ /* 7-10:Rowround */
 8:     $(x'_5, x'_9, x'_{13}, x'_1) \leftarrow quarterround(x'_5, x'_9, x'_{13}, x'_1)$
 9:     $(x'_{10}, x'_{14}, x'_2, x'_6) \leftarrow quarterround(x'_{10}, x'_{14}, x'_2, x'_6)$
10:     $(x'_{15}, x'_{[3}, x'_7, x'_{11}) \leftarrow quarterround(x'_{15}, x'_{[3}, x'_7, x'_{11})$
11: **end for**
12: **return** $X + X'$

$$z_1 = x_1 \oplus ((x_0 + x_3) \lll 7)$$
$$z_2 = x_2 \oplus ((z_1 + x_0) \lll 9)$$
$$z_3 = x_3 \oplus ((z_2 + z_1) \lll 13)$$
$$z_0 = x_0 \oplus ((z_3 + z_2) \lll 18)$$

This nonlinear operation is called a quarterround function and it is a basic part of the columnround function where it is applied to columns (x_0, x_4, x_8, x_{12}), (x_5, x_9, x_{13}, x_1), $(x_{10}, y_{14}, y_2, y_6)$ and $(y_{15}, y_3, y_7, y_{11})$, and then rowround function transforms rows (x_0, x_1, x_2, x_3), (x_4, x_5, x_6, x_7), $(x_8, x_9, x_{10}, x_{11})$, and $(x_{12}, x_{13}, x_{14}, x_{15})$.

2.2   ChaCha

Algorithm 2 shows ChaCha algorithm. ChaCha is similar to Salsa20 except the following two points. First, the composition of the quarterround function is defined as below.

$$z_0 = z_0 + z_1, \quad z_3 = z_3 \oplus z_0, \quad z_3 = z_3 \lll 16,$$
$$z_2 = z_2 + z_3, \quad z_1 = z_1 \oplus z_2, \quad z_1 = z_1 \lll 12,$$
$$z_0 = z_0 + z_1, \quad z_3 = z_3 \oplus z_0, \quad z_3 = z_3 \lll 8,$$
$$z_2 = z_2 + z_3, \quad z_1 = z_1 \oplus z_2, \quad z_1 = z_1 \lll 7$$

Second, the composition of the initial matrix defined as below.

$$X = \begin{pmatrix} \sigma_0 & \sigma_1 & \sigma_2 & \sigma_3 \\ k'_0 & k'_1 & k'_2 & k'_3 \\ k'_0 & k'_1 & k'_2 & k'_3 \\ v_0 & v_1 & i_0 & i_1 \end{pmatrix}, \text{ or } \begin{pmatrix} \tau_0 & \tau_1 & \tau_2 & \tau_3 \\ k_0 & k_1 & k_2 & k_3 \\ k_4 & k_5 & k_6 & k_7 \\ v_0 & v_1 & i_0 & i_1 \end{pmatrix}$$

Algorithm 2. Algorithm of ChaCha

INPUT: Initial matrix X, $r \in \mathbb{N}$
OUTPUT: $Z = X + X^r$
 1: $X' \leftarrow X$
 2: **for** $l = 0$ up to $\frac{r}{2}$ **do**
 3:    $(x'_0, x'_4, x'_8, x'_{12}) \leftarrow quarterround(x'_0, x'_4, x'_8, x'_{12})$ /* 3-6:Colmnround */
 4:    $(x'_1, x'_5, x'_9, x'_{13}) \leftarrow quarterround(x'_1, x'_5, x'_9, x'_{13})$
 5:    $(x'_2, x'_6, x'_{10}, x'_{14}) \leftarrow quarterround(x'_2, x'_6, x'_{10}, x'_{14})$
 6:    $(x'_3, x'_7, x'_{11}, x'_{15}) \leftarrow quarterround(x'_3, x'_7, x'_{11}, x'_{15})$
 7:    $(x'_0, x'_5, x'_{10}, x'_{15}) \leftarrow quarterround(x'_0, x'_5, x'_{10}, x'_{15})$ /* 7-10:Rowround */
 8:    $(x'_1, x'_6, x'_{11}, x'_{12}) \leftarrow quarterround(x'_1, x'_6, x'_{11}, x'_{12})$
 9:    $(x'_2, x'_7, x'_8, x'_{13}) \leftarrow quarterround(x'_2, x'_7, x'_8, x'_{13})$
10:    $(x'_3, x'_4, x'_9, x'_{14}) \leftarrow quarterround(x'_3, x'_4, x'_9, x'_{14})$
11: **end for**
12: **return** $X + X'$

---

3 Attack on Latin Dances

In this section, we discuss a distinguishing attack on Salsa20 and ChaCha. First, we define the *semi-regular distinguisher* and explain construction of the distinguisher. Next, we propose a distinguishing attack using double-bit differentials. Finally, we analyze the attack based on experimental results using a PC and estimate the number of keystream bits required for the attack and time complexity of the attack.

3.1 Types of Distinguisher

Three types of a distinguisher are known[24] as below.

1. *Regular Distinguisher.*
   The adversary selects a single key/IV randomly and produces keystream bits, seeded by the chosen key/IV, which is long enough to distinguish it from a random bit stream with a high probability.

2. *Prefix Distinguisher.*
   The adversary uses many randomly chosen key/IV's rather than a single key and a few specified bytes from each of the keystream bits generated by those key/IV's.

3. *Hybrid Distinguisher.*
   The adversary uses many key/IV's and for each key/IV the adversary collects long keystream bits.

In this paper, we define the *Semi-regular Distinguisher* as follows;

Semi-regular Distinguisher. An adversary uses a single random key and enough randomly chosen IVs to distinguish keystream from random bits with a high probability. The adversary's ability is intermediate between a regular distinguisher and prefix distinguisher.

3.2 Construction of Distinguisher

The adversary chooses a key at random. Then the adversary randomly generates IV and inputs matrix X, X' that has a difference of i-th bit. The number of inputs is m. Output sequences are $\{z_0, \cdots, z_{m-1}\}, \{z'_0, \cdots, z'_{m-1}\}$, where $z_i, z'_i \in \{0, 1\}$. After that, the adversary observes $t_i = z_i \oplus z'_i, (0 \leq i < m)$, where $\oplus$ is exclusive-or.

If $\{z_0, \cdots, z_{m-1}\}, \{z'_0, \cdots, z'_{m-1}\}$ were random bit sequences, the probabilities:

$$\Pr[t_i = 1] = \Pr[t_i = 0]$$
$$= \frac{1}{2}, (0 \leq i < m)$$

are hold.

If $\{z_0, \cdots, z_{m-1}\}$ and $\{z'_0, \cdots, z'_{m-1}\}$ were keystream bits from a stream cipher, we obtain the following equations:

$$\Pr[t_i = 1] = \frac{1}{2}(1 + \varepsilon_d)$$
$$\Pr[t_i = 0] = \frac{1}{2}(1 - \varepsilon_d), (0 \leq i < m)$$

In this instance, the number of keystream bits required for a distinguishing attack is $O(\varepsilon_d^{-2})$, where ε_d is the differential bias explained in Section 3.3. If ε_d is large enough, an adversary can distinguish keystream bits from random bit sequences. For example ε_d is sufficiently large for 7-round Salsa20 to distinguish keystream bits[22]. We propose a double-bit distinguisher for 9-round Salsa20 and 8-round ChaCha in the later section.

3.3 Distinguishing Attack Using Double-Bit Differentials

In this section, we propose a distinguishing attack using double-bit differentials, which extends the single-bit distinguishing attack in[22]. Let x_i, x'_i be the i-th word of the initial matrix X, X', and j-th bit of x_i is denoted $[x_i]_j$. Then, let $[\Delta^r_i]_j$ be a differential of j-th bit of i-th word after r rounds, where $[\Delta^r_i]_j = [x_i]_j \oplus [x'_i]_j$. In[22], the differential of r rounds output under $[\Delta^0_i]_j = 1$ is denoted $([\Delta^r_p]_q|[\Delta^0_i]_j)$ [1], and a single-bit differential is defined by

$$\Pr([\Delta^r_p]_q|[\Delta^0_i]_j) = \frac{1}{2}(1 + |\varepsilon_s|).$$

The bias ε_s represents the strength of the correlations between one bit in input and one bit in output. If a keystream bit is pseudorandom, ε_s must come close to 0. Aumasson indicated significant differentials between keystream bits and random bit sequences in 8 rounds of Salsa20 and 7 rounds of ChaCha. However, he could not find a significant differential, where there were more than 9 rounds and 7 rounds.

---

[1] This notation is different from [22] in a precise sense. We defined the reduced version as $X + X^r$ where r is the number of rounds.

In a distinguishing attack using double-bit differentials, the bias ε_d of the output differential is defined by

$$\Pr(([\Delta_p^r]_q \oplus [\Delta_s^r]_t = 1)|[\Delta_i^0]_j) = \frac{1}{2}(1 + |\varepsilon_d|).$$

When ε_s is zero, pairs of $(p, q), (s, t)$ have no significant single-bit differentials. That means zero and one appear with a probability of $\frac{1}{2}$. In other words, a single-bit differential only indicates a frequency of $[\Delta_p^r]_q = 1$. There is a possibility that a correlation exists between cases of $[\Delta_p^r]_q = 1$ and $[\Delta_s^r]_t = 1$. If the bias $\varepsilon_d \neq 0$, a double-bit differential indicates such correlations.

In concrete terms, an adversary chooses $[\Delta_i^0]_j$ from a nonce v or a counter i; therefore, i and j for Salsa20 are chosen within the ranges $7 \leq i < 11, 0 \leq j < 32$. In ChaCha, i and j are chosen within the ranges $12 \leq i < 16, 0 \leq j < 32$. The bias ε_d is dependent on keys k, and it is difficult to calculate all values of ε_d due to huge time complexity. The value ε_d can be guessed as a median value $\varepsilon_d^\star$ as follows;

$$\Pr_k(([\Delta_p^r]_q \oplus [\Delta_s^r]_t = 1)|[\Delta_i^0]_j) = \frac{1}{2}(1 + |\varepsilon_d^\star|).$$

4   Experimental Results

In this section, we discuss the experimental results for distinguishing attacks using double-bit differentials. In Section 4.1, we present an algorithm searching for the maximum double-bit differential. Then, we demonstrate efficacy of our method using experimental results.

4.1   Algorithm

In a distinguishing attack using double-bit differentials, the adversary previously has obtained the positions of the maximum double-bit differential in order to distinguish keystream bits from random bits. First, the adversary chooses a key K at random and fixes it. Then, the adversary generates many input pairs which have a one-bit differential each other. After the calculation of the output pair corresponding to each input, the adversary searches all combinations of output positions for double-bit differentials, and calculate the median value to collect these differentials. Finally, the adversary calculates the averages of each median value with randomly changing keys.

Algorithm 3 shows details of the search algorithm. This algorithm requires r, α and $\beta \in \mathbb{N}$, where r is a number of round, α is the number of trials required to calculate the average, and β is the number of trials required to calculate the median. The balance between the precision of outputs and the time complexity depends on these parameters. We discuss the balance and our adoptions in section 4.2. After the choice of K at step 3, the chosen key is used for the next loop (from step 4 to step 15). In the loop, we calculate the median values of the double-bit differential for fixed key K are calculated. Values

---

Algorithm 3. Search for double-bit differentials

INPUT: $r, \alpha, \beta \in \mathbb{N}$
OUTPUT: Average of double-bit differential of r round
 1: Initialize all *count* by zero
 2: **for** $l = 0$ up to α **do**
 3:    Choose key K at random
 4:    **for** $k = 0$ up to β **do**
 5:       **for all** $[\Delta_i^0]_j$ such that i, j in *controllable value* **do**
 6:          Choose X, X' at random where $X \oplus X' = [\Delta_i^0]_j = 1$
 7:          $Z \leftarrow X + X^r$
 8:          $Z' \leftarrow X' + X'^r$
 9:          **for all** $[\Delta_p^r]_q$ such that $0 \le p < 16, 0 \le q < 32$ **do**
10:             **for all** $[\Delta_s^r]_t$ such that $0 \le s < 16, 0 \le t < 32$ **do**
11:                $count_{p,q,r,s}[j] \leftarrow ([\Delta_s^r]_t \oplus [\Delta_p^r]_q)$
12:             **end for**
13:          **end for**
14:       **end for**
15:    **end for**
16:    $median_{p,q,r,s}[i] \leftarrow$ median value of $count_{p,q,r,s}$ for all (p, q, r, s)
17: **end for**
18: $average_{p,q,r,s} \leftarrow$ average of $median_{p,q,r,s}[i]$ for all $i, (p, q, r, s)$
19: **return** $average_{p,q,r,s}$

$[\Delta_i^0]_j$ for all i, j of *controllable value* have to be chosen at step 5, where *controllable values* are *nonce* or *counter* in the initial matrix (see Section 2, Section 3.2). Hence, in the case of Salsa20, we choose i and j within the ranges $7 \le i < 11, 0 \le j < 32$, or in ChaCha, we choose them within the ranges $12 \le i < 16, 0 \le j < 32$. From step 6 to step 13, we calculate the double-bit differential using XOR operation; the computational cost of these steps is dominant in the whole algorithm. The time complexity of the step is $(2^9)^2/2 = 2^{17}$. Remaining computational costs of the algorithm is calculated as follows; the number of iterations of the loop from step 5 is 2^7, and the number of iterations of the loop from step 2 and 4 is $\alpha\beta$. Thus, the total cost of the algorithm is $\alpha\beta \cdot 2^{24}$.

4.2   Results

In the distinguishing attack using double-bit differentials, we need to find the maximum values of ε_d. Accordingly, we conducted an experiment shown in **Algorithm 3** to find the maximum values for Salsa20 and ChaCha. We input $\alpha = 2^{12}$ and $\beta = 2^{12}$. The total time complexity of the experiment is 2^{48}: the space of IV is 128 bits($=2^7$), the combination of output is $2^{18}/2 = 2^{17}$, and the number of trials is 2^{24}. A Intel Core i7 3.3GHz PC requires 2 days computation for the experiment.

We sampled 2^{24} output pairs for each per one input pair. Let σ be the variance of samples, N be the average and N' is the population mean of $[\Delta_s^r]_t \oplus [\Delta_p^r]_q$, where $\sigma \approx \sqrt{N}$. The confidence interval is $[N' - \theta, N' + \theta]$ and $\theta \approx 2^{-12}$, where the confidence

Table 1. Salsa20 Distinguisher

Round	key length	$[\Delta^0_i]_j$	$[\Delta^r_p]_q$	$[\Delta^r_s]_t$	$\varepsilon^\star_d$
9	256	$[\Delta^0_6]_{17}$	$[\Delta^9_1]_{15}$	$[\Delta^9_{11}]_{22}$	0.003112
9	256	$[\Delta^0_6]_{17}$	$[\Delta^9_{11}]_{22}$	$[\Delta^9_1]_{15}$	0.003112
9	256	$[\Delta^0_8]_{11}$	$[\Delta^9_2]_{16}$	$[\Delta^9_7]_{25}$	0.002292
9	256	$[\Delta^0_8]_{11}$	$[\Delta^9_7]_{25}$	$[\Delta^9_2]_{16}$	0.002292
9	256	$[\Delta^0_7]_{19}$	$[\Delta^9_1]_{26}$	$[\Delta^9_{10}]_{18}$	0.001832
9	256	$[\Delta^0_7]_{19}$	$[\Delta^9_{10}]_{18}$	$[\Delta^9_1]_{26}$	0.001832
9	256	$[\Delta^0_7]_{13}$	$[\Delta^9_1]_{16}$	$[\Delta^9_3]_{24}$	0.001216
9	256	$[\Delta^0_7]_{13}$	$[\Delta^9_3]_{24}$	$[\Delta^9_1]_{16}$	0.001216
9	256	$[\Delta^0_6]_{14}$	$[\Delta^9_3]_{19}$	$[\Delta^9_4]_{25}$	0.000619
9	256	$[\Delta^0_6]_{14}$	$[\Delta^9_4]_{25}$	$[\Delta^9_3]_{19}$	0.000619
9	128	$[\Delta^0_6]_{10}$	$[\Delta^9_{13}]_{18}$	$[\Delta^9_1]_{12}$	0.003657
9	128	$[\Delta^0_6]_{10}$	$[\Delta^9_1]_{12}$	$[\Delta^9_{13}]_{18}$	0.003657
9	128	$[\Delta^0_8]_9$	$[\Delta^9_{12}]_{19}$	$[\Delta^9_{13}]_{11}$	0.002112
9	128	$[\Delta^0_8]_9$	$[\Delta^9_{13}]_{11}$	$[\Delta^9_{12}]_{19}$	0.002112
9	128	$[\Delta^0_7]_{28}$	$[\Delta^9_{11}]_{26}$	$[\Delta^9_4]_{18}$	0.001287
9	128	$[\Delta^0_7]_{28}$	$[\Delta^9_4]_{18}$	$[\Delta^9_{11}]_{26}$	0.001287
9	128	$[\Delta^0_6]_7$	$[\Delta^9_1]_{16}$	$[\Delta^9_{13}]_{28}$	0.000756
9	128	$[\Delta^0_6]_7$	$[\Delta^9_{13}]_{28}$	$[\Delta^9_1]_{16}$	0.000756
9	128	$[\Delta^0_6]_{14}$	$[\Delta^9_{51}]_{11}$	$[\Delta^9_{14}]_{25}$	0.000251
9	128	$[\Delta^0_6]_{14}$	$[\Delta^9_{14}]_{25}$	$[\Delta^9_{15}]_{11}$	0.000251

coefficient is 95%. In our experiment, $\varepsilon^\star_d$ is larger than 2^{-12}; thus, the results obtained from the experiment are reliable.

The results for the maximum values of $\varepsilon^\star_d$ are shown in table 1, and table 2. In Salsa20, the maximum value of $\varepsilon^\star_d$ is 0.003112. In[24], the number of streams for the distinguisher was estimated as $N = 0.4624 \cdot M^2$, where $\frac{1}{M} = P[z_j \oplus z_{j'}] - \frac{1}{2}$. Therefore, if the adversary obtains 2^{16} keystreams bits in Salsa20, the keystream bits can be distinguished keystream from random bit sequences. The adversary can also distinguish keystream bits from random bit sequences using only two bits of keystream in case of ChaCha.

We compare our results with existing results in Table 3. The best attack was proposed by Aumasson et al.[22] and it covers the 8-round version of Salsa20 using a 256-bit key with an estimated complexity of 2^{251}. Regarding the 128-bit key, Aumasson proposed key-recovery attacks for the reduced versions with up to 7 rounds[22] with an estimated complexity of 2^{111}. For ChaCha, Aumasson attacked the 6-round version with an estimated complexity of 2^{139} and the 7-round version with an estimated complexity of 2^{248} using a 256-bit key. Regarding the 128-bit key, Aumasson proposed key-recovery attacks for the reduced versions with up to 7 rounds with an estimated complexity of 2^{107}[22]. Our results show that our distinguishing attacks are lower cost (i.e. time and memory complexity) than the above results of existing researches. In both Salsa20 and ChaCha, an adversary could attack more rounds version with lower cost. Especially, for ChaCha, we estimated that an adversary only required 2 input pairs for a distinguisher.

Table 2. ChaCha Distinguisher

Round	key length	$[\Delta_i^0]_j$	$[\Delta_p^r]_q$	$[\Delta_s^r]_t$	$\varepsilon_d^\star$
8	256	$[\Delta_{13}^0]_{13}$	$[\Delta_3^8]_{16}$	$[\Delta_{14}^8]_{24}$	0.890259
8	256	$[\Delta_{13}^0]_{13}$	$[\Delta_{14}^8]_{24}$	$[\Delta_3^8]_{16}$	0.890259
8	256	$[\Delta_{14}^0]_{14}$	$[\Delta_0^8]_{17}$	$[\Delta_{15}^8]_{25}$	0.878544
8	256	$[\Delta_{14}^0]_{14}$	$[\Delta_{15}^8]_{25}$	$[\Delta_0^8]_{17}$	0.878544
8	256	$[\Delta_{13}^0]_{15}$	$[\Delta_3^8]_{18}$	$[\Delta_{14}^8]_{26}$	0.878052
8	256	$[\Delta_{13}^0]_{15}$	$[\Delta_{14}^8]_{26}$	$[\Delta_3^8]_{18}$	0.878052
8	256	$[\Delta_{12}^0]_{13}$	$[\Delta_2^8]_{16}$	$[\Delta_{13}^8]_{24}$	0.871461
8	256	$[\Delta_{12}^0]_{13}$	$[\Delta_{13}^8]_{24}$	$[\Delta_2^8]_{16}$	0.871461
8	256	$[\Delta_{13}^0]_{14}$	$[\Delta_3^8]_{17}$	$[\Delta_{14}^8]_{25}$	0.871338
8	128	$[\Delta_{12}^0]_{13}$	$[\Delta_{12}^8]_{19}$	$[\Delta_{14}^8]_1$	0.781044
8	128	$[\Delta_{12}^0]_{13}$	$[\Delta_{14}^8]_1$	$[\Delta_{12}^8]_{19}$	0.781044
8	128	$[\Delta_{13}^0]_{14}$	$[\Delta_{20}^8]_{18}$	$[\Delta_{15}^8]_{12}$	0.761928
8	128	$[\Delta_{13}^0]_{14}$	$[\Delta_{15}^8]_{12}$	$[\Delta_{20}^8]_{18}$	0.761928
8	128	$[\Delta_{14}^0]_{11}$	$[\Delta_{14}^8]_1$	$[\Delta_{11}^8]_{13}$	0.741681
8	128	$[\Delta_{14}^0]_{11}$	$[\Delta_{11}^8]_{13}$	$[\Delta_{14}^8]_1$	0.741681
8	128	$[\Delta_{13}^0]_9$	$[\Delta_{14}^8]_8$	$[\Delta_{13}^8]_{24}$	0.739875
8	128	$[\Delta_{13}^0]_9$	$[\Delta_{13}^8]_{24}$	$[\Delta_{14}^8]_8$	0.739875
8	128	$[\Delta_{13}^0]_{11}$	$[\Delta_{19}^8]_{21}$	$[\Delta_7^8]_1$	0.720158
8	128	$[\Delta_{13}^0]_{11}$	$[\Delta_7^8]_1$	$[\Delta_{19}^8]_{21}$	0.720158

Table 3. Time complexity

Type	Round/Key length	time complexity	Reference
Salsa20	5/256	2^{248}	[9]
Salsa20	6/256	2^{139}	[22]
Salsa20	7/256	2^{151}	[22]
Salsa20	8/256	2^{251}	[22]
Salsa20	9/256	2^{16}	**This work**
Salsa20	8/128	2^{111}	[22]
Salsa20	9/128	2^{16}	**This work**
ChaCha	6/256	2^{139}	[22]
ChaCha	7/256	2^{248}	[22]
ChaCha	8/256	2	**This work**
ChaCha	6/128	2^{107}	[22]
ChaCha	8/128	2	**This work**

5   Concluding Remarks

We proposed new distinguishing attacks on 9-round Salsa20 and 8-round ChaCha, which uses double-bit differentials. The complexities of the introduced attacks are 2^{16} in 9-round Salsa20 and 2 in 8-round ChaCha, which are much less than the complexities of an exhaustive key search and existing attacks. Our attacks could not be directly applied to the full-round Salsa20 and the full-round ChaCha due to computational complexities for finding double-bit differentials; thus, these ciphers are not presently under threat. Obviously, the distinguishing attack using double-bit differentials can be extended to distinguishing attacks using a triple-bit differential or more-bit differentials. We will improve the applicability of our method to extend the number of bits for differentials in our future research.

References

1. Aumasson, J.P., Fischer, S., Khazaei, S., Meier, W., Rechberger, C.: New Features of Latin Dances: Analysis of Salsa, ChaCha, and Rumba. In: Nyberg, K. (ed.) FSE 2008. LNCS, vol. 5086, pp. 470–488. Springer, Heidelberg (2008)
2. Babbage, S., Cannière, C.D., Canteaut, A., Cid, C., Gilbert, H., Johansson, T., Parker, M., Preneel, B., Rijmen, V., Robshaw, M.: The estream portfolio (rev. 1). eSTREAM, ECRYPT Stream Cipher project (2008),
   http://www.ecrypt.eu.org/stream/portfolio_revision1.pdf
3. Bernstein, D.J.: ChaCha, a variant of Salsa20. In: The State of the Art of Stream Ciphers SASC 2008 (2008), http://cr.yp.to/ChaCha.html
4. Bernstein, D.J.: Response to "Slid pairs in Salsa20 and Trivium" (2008),
   http://cr.yp.to/snuffle/reslid-20080925.pdf
5. Bernstein, D.J.: The Salsa20 Family of Stream Ciphers. In: Buell, D. (ed.) New Stream Cipher Designs. LNCS, vol. 4986, pp. 84–97. Springer, Heidelberg (2008),
   http://cr.yp.to/salsa20.html
6. Biryukov, A.: A new 128-bit key stream cipher LEX. eSTREAM, ECRYPT Stream Cipher project (2005), http://www.ecrypt.eu.org/stream/nls.html
7. Cho, J.Y., Pieprzyk, J.: Crossword puzzle attack on NLS. Cryptology ePrint Archive, Report 2006/049 (2006), http://eprint.iacr.org/
8. Cho, J.Y., Pieprzyk, J.: Linear distinguishing attack on NLS. In: eSTREAM The ECRYPT Stream Cipher Project, No. 2006/044, pp. 285–295 (2006)
9. Crowley, P.: Truncated differemtial cryptanalysis of five round Salsa20. In: The State of the Art of Stream Ciphers SASC 2006, pp. 198–202 (2006)
10. Englund, H., Hell, M., Johansson, T.: A note on distinguishing attacks. IEEE Trans. on Info. Theory, 1–4 (2007)
11. eSTREAM. Ecrypt stream cipher project, http://www.ecrypt.eu.org/stream
12. Fischer, S., Meier, W., Berbain, C., Biasse, J.-F., Robshaw, M.J.B.: Non-randomness in eS-TREAM Candidates Salsa20 and TSC-4. In: Barua, R., Lange, T. (eds.) INDOCRYPT 2006. LNCS, vol. 4329, pp. 2–16. Springer, Heidelberg (2006)
13. Freier, A.O., Kocher, P., Kaltorn, P.C.: The SSL protocol version 3.0 draft,
    http://home.netscape.com/eng/ssl3/draft302.txt
14. Hawkes, P., Paddon, M., Rose, G., Wiggers de Vries, M.: Primitive specification for NLS. eSTREAM, ECRYPT Stream Cipher project (2005),
    http://www.ecrypt.eu.org/stream/nls.html
15. Khazaei, S.: Neutrality-Based Symmetric Cryptanalysis. PhD thesis, Lausanne EPFL (2010)
16. Kunzli, S., Meier, W.: Distinguishing attack onMAG. eSTREMA report, Report 2005/053 (2005), http://www.ecrypt.eu.org/stream/papersdir/053.pdf
17. Lebedev, A.N., Ivanov, A., Starodubtzev, S., Kolchkov, A.: Yamb LAN crypto submission to the ecrypt stream cipher project. In: eSTREAM The ECRYPT Stream Cipher Project, No. 2005/034 (2005)
18. Paul, S., Preneel, B., Sekar, G.: Distinguishing Attacks on the Stream Cipher Py. In: Robshaw, M.J.B. (ed.) FSE 2006. LNCS, vol. 4047, pp. 405–421. Springer, Heidelberg (2006)

19. Priemuth-Schmid, D., Biryukov, A.: Slid Pairs in Salsa20 and Trivium. In: Chowdhury, D.R., Rijmen, V., Das, A. (eds.) INDOCRYPT 2008. LNCS, vol. 5365, pp. 1–14. Springer, Heidelberg (2008)
20. Rose, G.G.: A Stream Cipher Based on Linear Feedback Over $GF(2^8)$. In: Boyd, C., Dawson, E. (eds.) ACISP 1998. LNCS, vol. 1438, pp. 135–146. Springer, Heidelberg (1998)
21. IEEE Computer Society. Wireless lan medium access control (MAC) and physical layer (PHY) speciffications. IEEE Std802.11 (1999)
22. Tsunoo, Y., Saito, T., Kubo, H., Shigeri, M.: Cryptanalysis of Mir-1, a T-function based stream cipher (2006)
23. Tsunoo, Y., Saito, T., Kubo, H., Suzaki, T., Nakashima, H.: Differential cryptanalysis of Salsa20/8. In: The State of the Art of Stream Ciphers SASC 2007 (2007)
24. Wu, H., Preneel, B.: Distinguishing attack on stream cipher Yamb. In: eSTREAM The ECRYPT Stream Cipher Project, No. 2005/043 (2005)

Behavior Analysis-Based Dynamic Trust Measurement Model

Dan Wang, Xiaodong Zhou, and Wenbing Zhao

College of Computer, Beijing University of Technology, Beijing 100124, China
wangdan@bjut.edu.cn

Abstract. The trust of an entity is based on its behavior's trust in trusted computing technology, and software's trust can be measured dynamically by its behavior when it is executing. However, conducting dynamic measurement is a big challenge. Defining and building software's behavior is the basic work of measuring software trust. A behavior-based dynamic measurement model for an execution program is provided, which applies the method of describing program behavior by control flow graph to dynamic trust measurement. The model first measures the program before it is loaded, then generates the expected behavior model of the program according to static analysis. Then, the model monitors the program's execution in real time by verifying the flow branches of the program with the expected behavior model. Finally, the paper analyzes the security of this model and indicates that this model is able to protect against some code-injection attacks which can't be handled by the traditional static measurement method.

Keywords: Program, dynamic, trust measurement, behavior analysis.

1   Introduction

Trusted computing technology has become a research hotspot in the computer security area. If a software's behavior and running result can meet its user's expectation and can provide continuous service when interfered, it can be regarded as a kind of trusted software[1]. Defining and building software's behavior is the basic work of measuring software trustworthiness

At present, the trust measurement technology is based on the integrity measurement. There are two mechanisms that use integrity measurement technology in the system boot process. One is the secure boot[2][3] mechanism which is designed to verify the integrity of the booting process and stop the boot process when the integrity measurement fails. The other mechanism is called trusted boot[4]. Unlike secure boot, this mechanism only takes measurements and leaves it up to the remote party to determine the system's trust.

However, during the period of the operating system kernel loading and the users' applications executing, there are many problems such as the users' uncertain operation to the system, and the huge variety of user applications. There are also some security problems during the program's execution period such as follows:

S. Qing et al. (Eds.): ICICS 2011, LNCS 7043, pp. 267–281, 2011.
© Springer-Verlag Berlin Heidelberg 2011

- The intruders may get the root privilege of the system illegally and then modify the program without the user's notification, and then the modified programs are executed by the user.
- System users download and install untrusted software.
- Many applications have code injection (such as buffer overflow) vulnerabilities. In these cases, intruders can alter the behavior and the execution flow of the program when they find that such program has this kind of vulnerability.
- The intruders get the root privilege of the system illegally and then modify the kernel of the system. In Linux, the root user can modify the kernel data by loading and unloading kernel modules.

1.1   Integrity Measurement

The integrity measurement technology before the program loading is able to resolve the first problem well. Before the program to execute, the integrity measurement component generates the hash digest with certain algorithm, and compares it with original digest. Then the integrity measurement component can make sure the information of the software is not tampered just before it is loaded. The software must acquire certain authorization and execute under these authorization only it is measured to be trust. Therefore, integrity measurement can find whether the software is tampered or not (but still can't prevent the intruder to get the root privilege), and the tampered program can't execute. However, this kind of integrity measurement process is not a dynamic one which can take trust measurement during the program's execution period, such as the code injection attack as problem 3 mentioned above.

1.2   Related Works

The research literature indicates the presence of many efforts in the area of software integrity measurement. The Linux Integrity Measurement Architecture (IMA)[5] can measure code loaded and static date files such as configurations used, such that a remote party can verify that a Linux system contains no low integrity components. PRIMA[6] is based on IMA and can minimize the performance impact on the system. With PRIMA the number of measurement targets can be reduced to those that have information flows to trusted objects. The BIND[7] system measure discrete computation steps by their inputs and code. But the integrity measurement technology still can't well resolve the time-of-measurement and time-of-used problem and their measurements granularity are in file level. The integrity measurement only reflects the memory state right after the program is loaded but the software may be compromised at run time. Reference [8-10] proposed a model combined static analysis and dynamic binding, which had a more powerful capability of detection and lower rates of false alarm. Some research used system calls came out from software runtime to construct behavior models.Systrace[11] is a computer security utility which limits an application's access to the system by enforcing access policies for system calls. It was developed by Niels Provos and runs on various Unix-like operating systems.Systrace is particularly useful when running untrusted or binary-only applications and provides facilities for privilege elevation on a system call basis, helping to eliminate the need for potentially dangerous setuid programs. Promon's

Integrated Application Protection (IAP)[12] makes applications tamper proof and ensures the privacy of all associated application data. It is offered to all software application providers that have a need to protect sensitive information and ensure application integrity. Promon IAP is integrated into the applications as a separate compiled module which interacts with the core application through an API. This raises the security level of a single application without influencing the main system.

1.3   Contributions

In this paper, we focus on the behavior of the software when it is executing and we propose a model that can measure the program's trust by determining if the program follows its expect behavior during their execution. We treat the control flow graph of the executable as its expected behavior. We first generate the program's expected behavior by static analyze the binary code of the executable program, and then we monitor the program's execution within the control flow graph.

Our behavior-based dynamic trust measurement model for an executable program focuses on the problem 3 mentioned above. Our model is a dynamic measurement model based on the integrity measurement. But our architecture does not guarantee that an attacker cannot obtain root privileges, which is beyond the scope of this paper.

The rest of this paper is organized as follows. Section 2 contains a description of the expected behavior. In Section 3, we describe our model architecture and its main parts. Section 4 describes our system's implementation by using the NFA model. In Section 5 we apply our approach to some executable program and verify its performance by Pin tool. We summarize our plan for future works in Section 6.

2   Expected Behavior Description

To date, there have been many related researches focusing on how to describe the software's behavior. And the most representative approach to describe the software's behavior is the system-call sequences generated during the program's execution. In the Linux operating system, system call is the only method for the kernel to provide services to the user applications. The user applications use all kinds of system resources by trapping into kernel mode from user mode, and system calls are the only mechanism for this interface. Many important operations such as read or write of files, creating processes and so on are all implemented by system calls. So the system call sequences generated during the program's execution can be used to describe the behavior of the program to a certain extent.

Currently there are two major methods for modeling the behavior of a program through the tracking of system call sequences. One is the dynamic learning method[13], and the other is the static analysis method[14][15][16]. The dynamic learning method can capture the run-time data on system call sequences and timing over many program executions within a safe and controlled system environment. The behavioral model for the program is based on the statistical data for the captured sequences. However, regardless of the number of times the program runs under these conditions, the model cannot reflect all possible paths the program traces during execution. Consequently, we believe that the method of dynamic learning to capture the system call sequences produces an insufficiently complete model of the software, and is therefore unsuitable for dynamic trust measurement.

In contrast, the static analysis modeling method which statically analyzes the source or the binary code of the program is capable of capturing the whole flow graph of the execution. Thus, it can well reflect the expected behavior of the software. More specifically, an analysis of the binary program code is more efficient than an analysis of the source code for two reasons. First, the source code for most software is difficult to obtain, and second the binary provides a better representation of the program's behavior on the specific hardware platform. So the static analysis of the binary software code is more general.

We statically analyze the binary code of a program to generate the flow graph. Then we use this graph-based model to describe the dynamic behavior of the program.

3   Our Model

Before we describe our model, we first make some assumptions about the system: (1) all programs are obtained from trust sources. The digital signature of the software is also obtained, accompanied by the software itself. (2) The system is implemented based on secure boot, so the boot processes are not tampered with. The first assumption means the content(code files) of the program must not be tampered with before the issue of dynamically trust of a running program to be discussed. The second assumption means that the trust of the program on application level is based on the trust of the lower level program. These two assumptions are the basis of the application's trust.

At first, we present a simple stack overflow attack example and analyze the software is how to change its behavior from the control flow perspective.The example is shown in Fig.1.

```
Int single_source(char *frame)
{
Char buf[256];
FILE *src;
Src=fopen(fname,"rt");
While(fgets(bug,1044,src)){
......
}
Return 0;
```

Fig. 1. An example of a Stack overflow attack

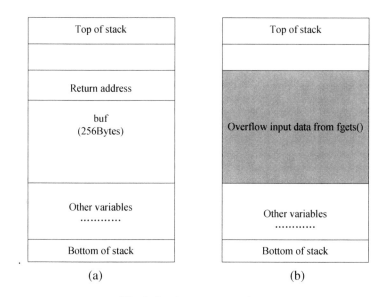

Fig. 2. Stack states comparison

The program above reads data from files line by line and stores them into buffer buf. The initial stack state of the program is shown in Fig.2(a). The stack state is shown in Fig.2(b) after execution. So attackers can overlay the return address of buffer with any data in order to change the control flow of the program.

When a program is running, the instructions which can change its control flow include CALL, JMP, JXX (JNZ, JE, etc.), RET. The changes of the control flow during program running can be seen as the behavior of the running program. A program always runs from a fixed code segment. Our model sets a corresponding initial state. When a program is running, it is considered that a new state is transferred into every time the program's control flow changes. Therefore, it is feasible to acquire a program's expected behavior before starting it by analyzing its control flow from the instruction code. Then, when the program is running, whether its behavior corresponds with the expected one can be judged.

3.1 Model structure

The structure of our model is shown in Fig.3. The model is based on the integrity measurement. First the software would be verified its integrity according to the integrity check process, then the binary code of the software is verified to make the expected behavior model. At last, when the software is being executed, the execution trace of the software is verified whether it followed the model or not. It is a dynamic process.

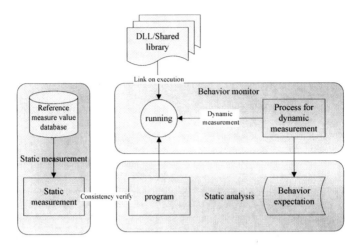

Fig. 3. Behavior-based dynamic measurement model

3.2   Main Components

Our model is constituted with a static measurement component, a static analysis component, and an expected behavior monitor.

(1) Static measurement component: Before the program's execution, this component applies integrity measurement to the executable and other relevant files. A program which passes the integrity measurement can be loaded to execute. The static measurement component guarantees the integrity of the program. A program not only executes the code itself, in most cases, the program needs the support of many other files (such as the library, configuration files and so on). So the static measurement component can't measure the integrity of the executable only, but also needs to measure the integrity of these support files. For the lib files needed by the program, under the static link situation, all the lib code is linked into the executable, so the integrity of the executable itself can be directly measured. But under the dynamic link situation, all the dynamic link libraries used by the program should also be measured for their integrity. For example, in the Linux system, the identification information for all the shared objects accessed by the program can obtained from the head section of the ELF format executable. So it is feasible to measure the integrity of the shared objects.

(2) Static analysis component: The static analysis component statically analyzes the executable library code in the system to form the expected behavior model. The dynamic library code can be analyzed early and the result saved to disk. When the program accesses one of these shared objects, the object's model can be merged with the model of the executable program to form an integrated model. Because the expected behavior model is saved to files, the integrity of these data files should also be guaranteed.

(3) Expected behavior monitor. The program which passes the integrity measurement will execute under the expected behavior monitor. The monitor will get the current state of the execution, and determine if the state is in the expected

behavior model generated by the static analysis component. If the program enters an unexpected state according to the behavior model, the monitor will decide that the program does not follow the expected behavior and terminate the execution.

3.3   Data Structure Design

As described above, the dynamic measurement is executed in the process of program running. Therefore, our experiment is correspondingly divided into two steps: static analysis and dynamic measurement.

The analyzed object is the executable instructions during the static analysis. Due to a number of potential different execution paths of a binary, we use a static link to refer to the actual executable file of our experiments.

Since our model regards the jump among the control flow during the program execution as the state transfer, the corresponding data structure to represent the program's state is designed and shown in Fig.4. The whole state graph is a graph structure, each node represents a state, which contains start address, next state pointer while existing sate transfer and next state pointer without sate transfer.

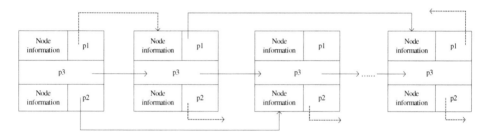

Fig. 4. State graph data structure

In Fig.4, pointer p1 will point to the next right state when sate transfer happens. When Call or Jump instruction executes, pointer p1 will point to the state which represents the target address. Pointer p2 will point to the next state when there isn't sate transfer. For example, when the condition jump instruction executes, the next sate should be the state which p1 points to if the condition is true. On the other hand, if the condition is false, the next sate should be the state which p2 points to. All states will be linked together by pointer p3. The states among the linked stated by p3 don't have jump relation. Pointer p3 is assigned a value after the first scan. The node information field of the state node saves the start address of the instruction segment and other information.

After making static analysis to the executable file, each point field of the node in sate graph is assigned a value. The first node in state graph is the program's first sate. Program executes from the first state. As we know, program always executes from a fixed starting address which is called the entrance function, but it isn't the main() function. This entrance function has different name and it depends on the platform. After the OS creates a process, the control is passed on to the entrance function, which is always to run certain function in its lib. This entrance function initializes the runtime lib and runtime environment including heap, I/O, thread, global variant, etc.

As soon as this initialization process is completed by the entrance function, the main() function can be invoked. Since the entrance function of the lib glibc is _start on Linux platform, this _start function later invokes __lib_start_main, therefore in state graph, the first sate node represent _start function. After main() function executes, it will return to the entrance function and do some clear work such as to destruct the global variants, to destroy heap, close I/O, etc. Later, it terminates the process by executing certain system call. Consequently, the last node in state graph represents the last function of entrance function to do clear work.

4   Implementations

The technology of statically analyzing the binary code of the program has been used in some intrusion detection researches. For modeling the executable and library code, there are two main methods. One is the context-insensitive non-Deterministic Finite State Automaton (NFA) which neglects the return information of functions. The other is the context-sensitive pushdown automaton (PDA) which records all the return addresses of functions with a stack. When a function returns, the return state is determinate according to the top of the stack. Both of these two models are merged by local function automaton. The NFA model will add a transition directly from the call state to the target state. When the function returns, another transition will be added from the return state to the call state's next state. Because a function may be called more than one time from different addresses, there will be several transitions from the return state. The PDA model uses a stack structure to remember the exactly return address of one function call. When the function call returns, the top of the stack is the return state for that call and the transition is definite.

Because the NFA model is much more efficient, our implementation is based on the NFA model. First we statically analyze every function's binary code and generate the local function control flow graph (CFG). The CFG of the program consists of many basic blocks and the transition among these basic blocks. The branch is based on the JMP instruction and the CALL instruction. The state of the program in our model is based on these basic blocks. For the CALL or the conditional JMP instruction (such as JNE, JE and so on), two new states will be created if they aren't in the states set. One is the state reflecting the target address, the other is the state reflecting the next instruction just below the current instruction. For the JMP instruction, only the target state will be created. Fig.5 shows the states in the control flow graph according to the branch or call instructions. These branches or call instructions make the control flow of the execution change. We treat a set of instructions of the executable which has no control flow transfer in it as a basic block. And we also treat the one basic block as one state of the execution.

One of the most important attributes of a state is the address of the first instruction of the state's related basic blocks. When the monitor component observes a transfer, the state of the execution will be changed. The static analysis is taken by two steps. In the first step, we statically analyze the whole binary code and find out all possible states into which an execution may transfer. In the second step, we analyze the executable again and for every possible state, find out all its possible next state. As a result, a control flow graph with numbers of states (basic blocks) and transitions is created.

When we monitor the program's execution, we dynamically capture every instruction in the trace of that execution. At the beginning, the state of the program is in an init state of the execution. Every executable begins its execution from an init routine instead of main function. When an instruction is executed, the monitor makes a decision based on the state of that instruction. If the address of that instruction is a target address of a call or jump instruction, the instruction must be in a new state. If this situation happens, the current state of this execution will transfer to the new state.

Because all the possible states and all the possible transitions have been obtained by the two-step static analysis, if the current state of one time execution doesn't transfer into the approved state, the program's behavior is not following the expected one.

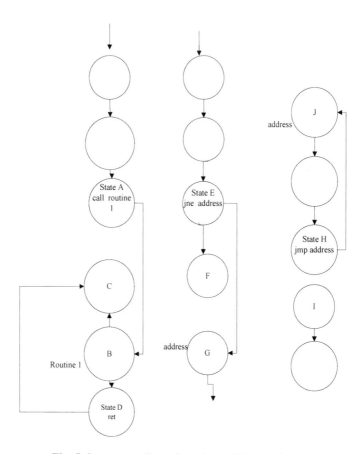

Fig. 5. States according to branch or call instructions

Then we use a kind of common technique used to construct a system control flow graph, the call site replacement, as shown in Fig.6. We replace every edge representing a function call with the related local call graph. At this point, the whole control flow graph of the program based on the NFA model is complete. If the $G =<V,E>$ is the control flow graph of the program, V is the set of basic block, E is the set of the edges among V ,according to the control flow graph, every basic block is a state, and every edge can be treated as an input symbol table. Then the NFA model can be described as follows:

$P = (Q,\Sigma,\delta,q_0,F)$, Q is the states set, Σ is the input alphabet, $\Sigma = (call + address \cup jump + address)$, $call$ is the function call instruction and $jump$ is the branch instruction including JMP or JE and so on. $address$ is the related instruction address ; q_0 is first state of the automaton, and is the only entry of the CFG ; F is the set of accepting states, that is, the exit basic blocks of the program. δ is the transition relation and $\delta(q_1,a) = q_2$, $a \in \Sigma$ means state q_1 transport to state q_2 according a .

Clearly, the JMP and the CALL instructions will cause a state transition of the program. But there is another situation where one state can transfer control to another without a CALL or JUMP instruction. When the instructions are executed fall through, the next instruction that will be executed may be a target of some CALL or JUMP instruction. This instruction is a beginning of a new state. In this situation, states transfer also happens.

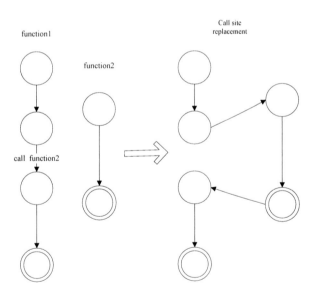

Fig. 6. The merger of the function automaton

After getting the expect behavior model of the program, the expected behavior monitor will do the dynamic measurement to the program when it is executing. The measurement arithmetic is shown in Fig.7.

```
InputStateGraph(stateGraph);     //Input the state graph
State currentState = stateGraph.firstState();
 //set the current state as the first state
for every instruction ins that is executed
 do
    State state = stateGraph.getState(ins);
    if(state exists)     // a new state is trasferred to
        if(currentState.nextState()==state)
 // transtition exists between the two states
            currentState=state;
            continue;
        else                //or the program is untrusted
            untrusted;
        end if
    else continue;              // in the same state
    end if
  end do;
end for;
```

Fig. 7. Dynamic measurement process description

5   Test and Evaluation

Because we use the whole control flow graph as the program's expected behavior model, a tool that can analyze the binary code of executable will help significantly. There are a large number of related works in the areas of instrumentation of executables with the instrumentation consisting of both static and dynamic approaches. Most of the static analysis based intrusion detection systems are implemented by EEL[17], the Executable Editing Library which provides an abstract interface to parse and rewrite SPARC binary executables. But one of the limitations of EEL is that it is a tool within the SPARC platform and it is not supported by other platforms.

We use Pin [18][19], a tool for the dynamic instrumentation of programs to implement our model. Pin supports Linux binary executables; Windows executables; and MacOS executables on different platforms. With Pin's help, arbitrary code (written in C or C++) can be injected at arbitrary places in the executable. Pin adds the code dynamically while the executable is running. But at the same time, it is also possible to use pin to examine binaries such as images without running them. This is useful when we need to know static properties of an image. So Pin has the combined benefit of both static and dynamic analysis of the executables.

In our static analysis component, we use the Pin's static ability to examine the binaries in the image granularity, and the measurement monitor component is implemented with the help of Pin's dynamic instrument ability. Pin provides a number of API calls in different granularity. Pin can instrument executables at instruction level, the basic block level, the routine level and the image level. So Pin can help the users to inject their own code when an image is loaded. We use Pin's API to make up our own pin tools. The IMG_AddInstrumentFunction API call can examine every image loaded by the program. We add our own static analysis arithmetic into the API and make up our own static analysis pin tool. Every time when an image is loaded, the code in the IMG_AddInstrumentFunction API function will be executed. The INS_AddInstrumentFunction API call can inject arbitrary code before the instruction is executed. And every time when an instruction is executed, the code in the IMG_AddInstrumentFunction API function will be executed. We add our own monitor code into this API call and make up our own dynamic monitor Pin tool. In addition, Pin provides a rich API that operates the executables. More details of other Pin API functions can be found in the Pin user's manual.

5.1   Test and Analysis

A code segment which overflow vulnerability exists is shown in Fig.8. Function pass () applies for 4 bytes of stack space to store the password that the user entered. If the password the user entered is identical with that the program sets, the function will print a welcome message. However, overflow vulnerability exists in this code segment. If the length of the password which is entered is 4 bytes, the program will run correctly. However, if the length is more than 4 bytes, the return address of the function will be overwritten. As a result, the function can't return normally. If the password which is entered is carefully designed, the program will jump to any location specified by the user.

```
/* overflow.c*/
#include <stdio.h>
int pass()
{
    char password[4];
    scanf("%s",password);
    if(strcmp(password,"1234")==0)
        printf("Welcome!\n");
            return 0;
}
int main()
{
    pass();
    printf("go ahead!\n");
            return 0;
}
```

Fig. 8. Return address overflow example

Our experiment of the behavioral-based dynamic measurement model is implemented using the open-source binary instrument tool PIN. The implementation includes three stages :firstly, static analyze the executable using a two-step scanning algorithm ,secondly , generate the expected behavior according the result of the first stage, and finally do the trust measurement to the program by checking whether the actual behavior of the running program corresponding with the expected behavior. The measurement process of the test code above is shown in Fig.9.

The first scan to the executable will generate all possible states the program may reach when it is running. For the test code segment above, a total of 23045 states may reach. After the second scan the pointer field *p1* and *p2* of every state node will be assigned a value. For the program's last state, its instruction's first address is 809f948. As this is the address of the last function, which indicates it is the last state, the analysis results show that the next state's address can't be found. During the dynamic measurement stage, a password is entered with more than 4 bytes. Then the returned address of the function pass() is overwritten, so measurement results shows that there has error in the return address 8048200 and the program is terminated.

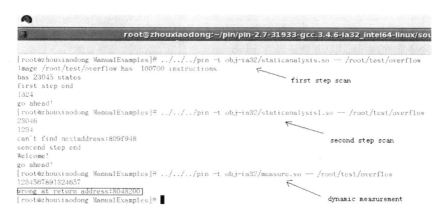

Fig. 9. Some test examples

5.2   Security Analysis

Measurement model presented in this paper integrates the static measurement of an executable program before it is loaded and dynamic measurement in the process of running, which increases security and reflects dynamic feature.

As for the malicious attacks which will modify the code(such as rootkits), because the integrity of the program files is destroyed , the program isn't allowed to run before passing the static measurement, which is the same as the traditional static measurement method, and it makes the program can't get the opportunities to execute. At the same time, this model can prevent some code injection attacks dynamically.

Buffer overflow attack is a typical code injection attack. If an intruder finds out a buffer overflow vulnerability of the program, the executing program may deviates from the expected way by inputting malicious parameters without modifying the program file, and turns to execute other codes (usually the codes appointed by intruders). If intruders successfully attack the program, the control flow of the program will change dynamically. Here, the monitor will find that the actual control flow does not match the expected one, and the application will be terminated. Therefore, this model can prevent this kind of buffer overflow attack. Meanwhile, the model monitors the behavior of running program, which means that the model is dynamic compared with traditional static measurement method.

Because Pin runs in the user space, it may be possibly bypassed. However, when run as root, Pin is no more vulnerable than the kernel. And if all user programs in the system will under the protection of our model, the act of attempting to bypass Pin will also be observed. So in our opinion, it is feasible to implement the prototype with Pin.

6   Conclusions and Future Works

In this paper, we propose a dynamic measurement model to measure the executable's trust. If each program execution state is followed by its expected states based on the control flow analysis, that program can be said to be trusted. So the key problem is how to describe the expected behavior of one program. In our model, we take the control flow as the program's expected behavior. The control flow graph is analyzed in advance. And the result is the expected behavior of the program. If an executable is suffered from some code injection attacks, its control flow will be unexpected and that the program will be untrusted dynamically when it is running.

In our future works, we will further enhance the practicality of the expected behavior model. So far, our experiments are all based the static linked executables. Next, we will improve the analysis ability of dynamically linked executables by taking advantage of the Pin's dynamic instrument capability. At the same time, we will add the integrity measurement component to the implementation of the model to make the model more complete.

Acknowledgment. This work was supported by a grant from the Major State Basic Research Development Program of China (973 Program) (No.2007CB311106), the funding project for academic human resources development in institutions of higher learning under the jurisdiction of Beijing municipality.

References

1. Shen, C., Zhang, H., Wang, H., et al.: Survey of information security. Sci. China Ser. F-Inf. Sci. 50, 139–166 (2010) (in Chinese)
2. Arbaugh, W.A., Farber, D.J., Smith, J.M.: A Secure and Reliable Bootstrap Architecture. In: IEEE Computer Society Conference on Security and Privacy (1997)
3. Arbaugh, W.A., Keromytis, A.D., Farber, D.J., Smith, J.M.: Automated recovery in a secure bootstrap process. In: Proceedings of Symposium on Network and Distributed Systems Security (NDSS), pp. 65–71 (1997)
4. Maruyama, H., Munetoh, S., Yoshihama, S., Ebringer, T.: Trusted platform on demand. IPSJ SIG. Notes Computer Security Abstract No.024-032

5. Sailer, R., Zhang, X., Jaeger, T., van Doorn, L.: Design and implementation of a TCG-based integrity measurement architecture. In: Proceedings of the 13th USENIX Security Symposium, pp. 9–13 (2004)
6. Jaeger, T., Sailer, R., Shankar, U.: PRIMA: Policy-reduced integrity measurement architecture. In: SACMAT 2006: Proceedings of the Eleventh ACM Symposium on Access Control Models and Technologies (2006)
7. Shi, E., Perrig, A., van Doorn, L.: Bind: A Fine-grained Attestation Service for Secure Distributed Systems. In: Proceedings for the IEEE Symposium on Security and Privacy (2005)
8. Forrest, S., Hofmeyr, S.A., Somayaji, A., Longstaff, T.A.: A sense of self for Unix processes. In: IEEE Symposium on Security and Privacy, California, pp. 120–128 (1996)
9. Hofmeyr, S., Somayaji, A., Forrest, S.: Intrusion detection system using sequences of system calls. Journal of Computer Security 6(3), 151–180 (1998)
10. Chinchani, R., van den Berg, E.: A Fast Static Analysis Approach to Detect Exploit Code Inside Network Flows. In: Valdes, A., Zamboni, D. (eds.) RAID 2005. LNCS, vol. 3858, pp. 284–308. Springer, Heidelberg (2006)
11. Systrace (2011), http://en.wikipedia.org/wiki/Systrace
12. Intergrated Application Protection approaches such as Promon's Shield (2011), http://www.promon.no/integrated.html
13. Wespi, A., Dacier, M., Debar, H.: Intrusion Detection Using Variable-length Audit Trail Patterns. In: Debar, H., Mé, L., Wu, S.F. (eds.) RAID 2000. LNCS, vol. 1907, pp. 110–129. Springer, Heidelberg (2000)
14. Wagner, D., Dean, D.: Intrusion Detection via Static Analysis. In: IEEE Symposium on Security and Privacy, Oakland, California (2001)
15. Giffin, J., Jha, S., Miller, B.: Detecting manipulated remote call streams. In: 11th USENIX Security Symposium, San Francisco, California (2002)
16. Feng, H.H., Giffin, J.T., Huang, Y., Jha, S., Lee, W., Miller, B.P.: Formalizing sensitivity in static analysis for intrusion detection. In: IEEE Symposium on Security and Privacy, pp. 194–208. IEEE Press (2004)
17. Larus, J.R., Schnarr, E.: EEL: Machine Independent Executable Editing. In: SIGPLAN 1995 Conference on Programming Language Design and Implementation (1995)
18. Luk, C.-K., Cohn, R., Muth, R., et al.: Pin: building customized program analysis tools with dynamic instrumentation. In: Proceedings of the 2005 ACM SIGPLAN Conference on Programming Language Design and Implementation, June 12-15 (2005)
19. (2011), http://www.pintool.org/

Improvement and Analysis of VDP Method in Time/Memory Tradeoff Applications

Wenhao Wang[1,2], Dongdai Lin[1], Zhenqi Li[1,2], and Tianze Wang[1,2]

[1] SKLOIS, Institute of Software, Chinese Academy of Sciences, Beijing, China
[2] Graduate University of Chinese Academy of Sciences, Beijing, China
{wangwenhao,ddlin,lizhenqi,wangtz83}@is.iscas.ac.cn

Abstract. In many cases, cryptanalysis of a cryptographic system can be interpreted as the process of inverting a one-way function. TMTO is designed to be a generic approach that can be used on any one-way function independent of the structure of the specific target system. It was first introduced to attack block ciphers by Hellman in 1980. The distinguished point (DP) method is a technique that reduces the number of table look-ups performed by Hellman's algorithm. A variant of the DP (VDP) method is introduced to reduce the amount of memory required to store the pre-computed tables while maintaining the same success rate and online time. Both the DP method and VDP method can be applied to Hellman tradeoff or rainbow tradeoff.

We carefully examine the technical details of the VDP method and find that it is possible to construct functions for which the original method fails. Based on the analysis, we propose a modification of the VDP method. Furthermore, we present an accurate version of the tradeoff curve that does not ignore the effect of false alarms and takes storage reduction techniques into consideration. We find optimal parameter sets of this new method by minimizing the tradeoff coefficient. A more exact and fair comparison between tradeoff algorithms is also given, which shows that our method applied to the Hellman tradeoff performs best among them.

1   Introduction

The objective of a time memory tradeoff (TMTO) algorithm is to do some one-time work so that each time the algorithm is executed it is more efficient. TMTO method can be applied to numerous cryptosystems. In 1980, Hellman described a chosen plaintext attack against the Data Encryption Standard, which is the first time memory tradeoff attack for block ciphers [3]. Let $E_k()$ be the encryption function of the block cipher. A fixed message msg is chosen and a one-way function f is defined from keys to ciphertexts by $f(k) = E_k(msg)$. The task of the cryptanalyst is to obtain k given msg and the corresponding ciphertext. This can be seen as inverting a one-way function f and later work has viewed TMTO as a general one-way function inverter.

Hellman's TMTO attack achieves a middle ground between the exhaustive key search and the massive pre-computation of all possible ciphertexts for a given

S. Qing et al. (Eds.): ICICS 2011, LNCS 7043, pp. 282–296, 2011.

plaintext. In an off-line phase, a set of tables are constructed. The tables store keys and an encryption of *msg* under an unknown key. In the online phase, the goal is to find the unknown key by making use of these pre-computed tables. The main idea of Hellman tradeoff is to store only part of the tables. This incurs a cost in the online phase and leads to a tradeoff between the memory and online time requirements.

After the inspiring work of Hellman, several articles have dealt with time memory tradeoff. In 1982, Rivest suggested an optimization based on distinguished points (DP) which greatly reduces the amount of look-up operations needed to detect a matching end point. Simply put, a DP is a point in the one-way chain that satisfies a preset condition. Chains are not generated with a given length but they stop at the first occurrence of a distinguished point. During the online phase, a look-up is carried out only when a distinguished point appears. Because merging chains significantly degrade the efficiency of the tradeoff, Borst, Preneel, and Vandewalle suggested in 1998 to clean the tables by discarding the merging and cycling chains [1]. This new kind of tables, called perfect table, substantially decreases the required memory. Later, Standarert dealt with a more realistic analysis of distinguished points in [9].

In 2003, Oechslin introduced the tradeoff based on rainbow tables, which reduces the TMTO attack complexity by a factor of 2 [8]. A rainbow table uses a different reduction function for each column of the table. Thus two different chains can merge only if they have the same key at the same position of the chain. This makes it possible to generate much larger tables. Up until now, tradeoff techniques on rainbow tables are the most efficient ones. In 2008, J. Hong proposed a variant of the DP technique, named variable DP (VDP) [4]. It completely removes the need to store the start points, as the chain end contains information about the chain beginning.

We carefully examine the details of J. Hong's method and find that it is possible to construct functions for which the original method fails. In fact, Fiat and Naor showed that there exists functions which are polynomial time indistinguishable from a random function and for which Hellman's attack fails [2]. We show that a Fiat-Naor type counterexample works for the VDP method. This leads us to the question of figuring out a method to obtain uniformly distributed start points. We propose a modification of the VDP method by suggesting the use of a generic diffusion function for generating start points. Furthermore, we present an accurate version of the tradeoff curve that does not ignore the effect of false alarms and takes storage reduction techniques into consideration. We find optimal parameter sets of this new method by minimizing the tradeoff coefficient. A more exact and fair comparison between tradeoff algorithms is also given, which shows our method applied to the Hellman tradeoff performs best among them.

The rest of the paper is organized as follows. We start by briefly reviewing some of the previous TMTO works. We provide in Section 3 our improvement over VDP method. In Section 4 we apply this new VDP method to both Hellman tradeoff and rainbow tradeoff. A brief comparison of previous TMTO algorithms is given in Section 5. We end the paper with a short conclusion in Section 6.

2   Previous Works

Let $f : \mathcal{N} \to \mathcal{N}$ be the one-way function to be inverted and we always suppose that $\mathcal{N} = \{0,1\}^n$ and $N = 2^n$. As a rule, the time memory tradeoff methodology tries to invert an arbitrary one-way function and we will follow this approach.

All tradeoff algorithms consist of a pre-computation phase and an online phase. In the off-line phase, the attacker constructs tables that contain possible keys; this process is approximately equivalent to the exhaustive search however only a part of the tables are stored. If the attack is only to be executed once then an exhaustive key search would be more efficient. But if the attack is to be conducted many times, the pre-computation work can be amortized. During the online phase, the attacker expects to recover the key from the pre-computed tables. This leads to a tradeoff between the memory required in the off-line stage and time required in the online phase.

2.1   Hellman Tradeoff

During the pre-compute phase we build m Hellman chains with the form($1 \le j \le m$): $SP_j = X_{j,1} \xrightarrow{f} Y_{j,1} \xrightarrow{r} X_{j,2} \xrightarrow{f} Y_{j,2} \xrightarrow{r} \cdots \xrightarrow{f} Y_{j,t} \xrightarrow{r} EP_j$. Then we discard all intermediate points of the Hellman chains and just pairs of start points and ending points $\{(SP_j, EP_j)\}_{j=1}^m$ are stored in one table. The stored pairs are sorted with respect to the ending points. In practice we suppose l tables are built. A different reduction function r_i is used in each table, and we denote $r_i(f(x))$ by $f_i(x)$.

In the online phase, given y_0, it is required to find x_0 satisfying $y_0 = f(x_0)$. We demonstrate the search for x_0 in the i-th table as follows.

Recursively we compute $Y_0 = r_i(f(x_0)) = f_i(x_0)$ and $Y_k = f_i(Y_{k-1})$, where $k = 1, 2, \cdots, t-1$. After each Y_k is obtained, check if it appears as an ending point in the table. Whenever a match $Y_k = EP_j$ is found, we compute $x = X_{j,t-k-1} = f_i^{t-k-1}(SP_j)$. There is a large chance that $f_i(x) = Y_0$, which is equivalent to $f(x) = f(x_0)$, due to r_i being injective. In such a case, the algorithm returns the correct x. But, as f_i^k is not injective, there could be a merge between the Hellman chains and online chains, and it is possible to have $f(x) \ne f(x_0)$. This is referred to as a false alarm.

2.2   Rainbow Tradeoff

Rainbow tradeoff is proposed by Oechslin to reduce the online time cost and the probability that a merge appears in a table. Instead of using the same reduction function f_i for each table, t different reduction functions are used to generate different columns in a single table.

A rainbow chain is build with the form: $SP_j = X_{j,1} \xrightarrow{f} Y_{j,1} \xrightarrow{r_1} X_{j,2} \xrightarrow{f}$ $Y_{j,2} \xrightarrow{r_2} \cdots \xrightarrow{f} Y_{j,t} \xrightarrow{r_t} EP_j$. In the online phase, we apply r_t to the ciphertext and look up the result in the endpoints of a table. If a match is found, we can rebuild the chain from the corresponding start point. Otherwise, we continue to apply r_{t-1}, f to the ciphertext. The total calculations of the rainbow method is half that of the Hellman method.

2.3 Distinguished Points Method

Distinguished points are keys that satisfy a given criterion, e.g., the last k bits are all zero. The crucial insight is that we don't use fixed-length chains, and instead, we simply construct a chain until some easily distinguished point is found. In practice, we would want to set a limit on the maximum length of a chain as $\hat{t}$ and reject any chain that exceeds the limit. Instead of looking up in the table each time a key is generated, a look-up is carried out in the table only when the online chain reaches a distinguished point.

2.4 Variable Distinguished Points Method

The main objective of the VDP method is to eliminate the need to store the start points. Just as the original DP method, generation of a Hellman chain is continued until a point satisfying a certain condition is found. We allow this condition to depend on the start point of the chain and the ending point contains information about the corresponding start point. We are able to recover the start point from the ending point.

First, we restrict to the typical parameters $m = t = N^{\frac{1}{3}}$ and set $d = \frac{1}{3}log_2 N$. When generating the j-th chain of the i-th table. Set the start point $SP_j^i = (0 \parallel i \parallel j)$, where each of the three concatenated components are of d bits. Iteratively we generate a Hellman chain by $X_{j,k} = f_i(X_{j,k-1})$. It is terminated only when the most significant d bits of some $X_{j,k}$ is found to be j. Chains longer than a preset $\hat{t}$ are discarded. Just the last $2d$ bits of the ending point in the j-th chain is stored in the j-th position of the i-th table and no table sorting is involved. Storing chain length information would reduce online time spent dealing with false alarms, but this is not mandatory. The online phase of the VDP method is same as the DP method. When a match is found, we can recover the corresponding start point using the table number and the position index.

3 Improvement of VDP Method

In this section, we first present a counter-example for which the VDP method fails. This is similar to the example given by Fiat and Naor for the Hellman tradeoff. Then we give the description of our improvement over VDP method.

3.1   Construction of a Counter-Example to VDP Method

For both Hellman and rainbow method to work, the functions f_i's need to be pairwise unrelated. This requirement for the Hellman method was carefully examined by Fiat and Naor [2]. Sourav Mukhopadhyay examined the requirements for rainbow method and showed that the counter based method to generate the iterate functions makes it possible to construct one-way functions for which both the Hellman tradeoff and rainbow tradeoff fail [7].

Start points of the i-th table in the original VDP method are chosen with the form $(0 \parallel i \parallel j)$. They are not uniformly distributed and the original VDP method suffers from a problem similar to the one described by Fiat and Naor for the Hellman method. Denote $\frac{n}{3}$ by d for convenience. Now we can construct a function f as follows: $f : \{0,1\}^n \rightarrow \{0,1\}^n$ with the property that for any $x = (x_1, x_2, \cdots, x_n) \in \{0,1\}^n$, if $x_1 = x_2 = \cdots x_d = 0$ and $x_{2d+d_0} = x_{2d+d_0+1} = \cdots x_{3d} = 0$, then $f(x) = 0$. Map of the rest x's induces a permutation. We may construct a cryptographic scheme considering such a function f by choosing d_0 properly to make f perform like a random function. For a VDP table, huge number of start points map into zeroes, leaving a large number of merges inside a table. This will lead to the failure of the method.

3.2   Main Idea of Our Improvemet

Based on the analysis, we present a modification of the VDP method and try to invert any one-way function. We would prefer to treat the start points as a univariant function of j over $\mathcal{N}$, denoted by $sp(j)$, where j is the chain index. Before the description of our improvement, we first provide the requirements of the function sp.

1. Given the chain index j, we obtain the corresponding start point by an invocation of the function sp. The invocation is called each time we intend to generate a new chain during the pre-computation phase or we find a match of the ending point during the online phase. It is strongly recommended that the function can be efficiently computed to reduce both the pre-computation time and the online time.

2. As mentioned above, output of sp needs to distribute uniformly over $\mathcal{N}$. This ensures that it is not possible to construct a Fiat-Naor type example prior for the new VDP method.

3. Obviously, start points should be chosen pairwise not equal. It precludes the possibility that chains merge from the very beginning. This can be easily ensured by choosing injective functions as sp.

4. Referring to flexibility, the discussion is focused on the generation of a series of function sp's. Parameters of the new VDP method are being thoroughly analysed in the following section. Selection of sp will put restriction on the choice of parameters in our method. Enough flexibility leaves us room to optimize the new VDP method.

5. As we need to generate nearly up to $2^{\frac{n}{3}}$ chains in each table, that means we need at least $2^{\frac{n}{3}}$ different start points. In terms of the cases that different start points map into same images, image set of sp is required to cover most of the range.

A univariant function filling the above requirements will hereinafter to be referred as a generic diffusion function. As the computation of power of an integer can be time-consuming, we suggest using linear functions with the form $sp(j) = x_i + k \cdot j$, $1 \leq i \leq r$ and $0 \leq j \leq s-1$ as start point while generating the j-th chain in a VDP table. When we create a new table in the off-line phase, we fix r and s and choose r different x_i's. Each x_i can generate up to s different start points. We will show that linear functions is sufficient. Uniform distribution and good coverage are easy to reach. The flexibility lies in the fact that we choose x_i and j freely only if the following equations hold (injection): $\gcd(k, 2^n) = 1$, $x_{i_1} + k \cdot j_1 \neq x_{i_2} + k \cdot j_2 \pmod{2^n}$ for different i_1, i_2 and j_1, j_2.

Let k be an integer not less than r and k has no common factor with N. x_i's belong to different congruence classes modulo k. We obtain an improvement over VDP method. If we choose 1 as k, the table index multiplies $2^{\frac{n}{3}}$ as x_1 and $2^{\frac{n}{3}}$ as s, we obtain the original VDP method. If we choose $2^n - 1$ as k, $2^{\frac{n}{3}}$ as r and 1 as s, we obtain the original DP method. We emphasize again that this flexibility makes it possible to optimize the new method and seek better performance.

4   Applying the New Method to Hellman Tradeoff and Rainbow Tradeoff

4.1   Applying the New VDP Method to Hellman Tradeoff

When creating a new table, we choose r different x_i's belonging to different congruence classes modulo k. For each x_i, we generate s start points with the form

$$sp(i, j) = x_i + k \cdot j, \ 0 \leq j \leq s - 1.$$

The new VDP chains applied to Hellman tradeoff are of the form:

$$sp(1,0) = X_{1,1} \xrightarrow{f} Y_{1,1} \xrightarrow{r} X_{1,2} \xrightarrow{f} Y_{1,2} \xrightarrow{r} \cdots \xrightarrow{f} Y_{1,t} \xrightarrow{r} EP_1$$

$$\vdots$$

$$sp(1, s-1) = X_{s,1} \xrightarrow{f} Y_{s,1} \xrightarrow{r} X_{s,2} \xrightarrow{f} Y_{s,2} \xrightarrow{r} \cdots \xrightarrow{f} Y_{s,t} \xrightarrow{r} EP_s$$
$$sp(2,0) = X_{s+1,1} \xrightarrow{f} Y_{s+1,1} \xrightarrow{r} X_{s+1,2} \xrightarrow{f} Y_{s+1,2} \xrightarrow{r} \cdots \xrightarrow{f} Y_{s+1,t} \xrightarrow{r} EP_{s+1}$$

$$\vdots$$

$$sp(2, s-1) = X_{2s,1} \xrightarrow{f} Y_{2s,1} \xrightarrow{r} X_{2s,2} \xrightarrow{f} Y_{2s,2} \xrightarrow{r} \cdots \xrightarrow{f} Y_{2s,t} \xrightarrow{r} EP_{2s}$$

$$\vdots$$

The $((i-1)s + j + 1)$-th chain ends with EP only when the most significant bits of EP is found to be $(i \parallel j)$. The ending points we have reached are stored sequentially. We have to store x_i's but neither the start points nor the first $\lceil log_2(s) \rceil + \lceil log_2(r) \rceil$ bits of the ending points need to be stored. In the online phase when we want to check whether a point from the online chain is an ending point, we determine i and j from the first $\lceil log_2(s) \rceil + \lceil log_2(r) \rceil$ bits of the point and compute the corresponding index of the off-line table by $index = j + (i-1) \cdot s$. No searching is involved. If a match is found, the corresponding start point can be recovered by $sp(i, j) = x_i + k \cdot j$.

There remains a question of choosing proper r and s to optimize the new VDP method. We first present the result of optimal parameters in DP tradeoff. We do not store chain length information. As is expected, it increases the effort in resolving false alarms. But it turns out that the increase in total computation is minimal in comparison to the reduction in storage. We denote t, m, $\hat{t}$ and l the parameters of the tradeoff, which are respectively the average length of the chains constituting the tables, the number of chains per table, the maximum chain length in the table and the number of tables.

Proposition 1. *Let* $0 < D_{ps} < 1$ *be any fixed value. The DP tradeoff, under any set of parameters* $m, t, l,$ *and* $\hat{t},$ *that are subject to the relations*

$$mt^2 = 1.47N, \ l = 1.25ln(\frac{1}{1 - D_{ps}})t, \ and \ \hat{t} = 1.97t$$

attains the given value D_{ps} *as its probability of success, and exhibits tradeoff performance corresponding to*

$$D_{tc} = 6.5452 D_{ps} \{ln(1 - D_{ps})\}^2$$

as the four parameters are varied. The time memory tradeoff curve for the DP tradeoff is $TM^2 = D_{tc}N^2$.

Under any such choice of parameters, the number of one-way function invocations required for the pre-computation phase is

$$D_{pc} = 1.8349ln(\frac{1}{1 - D_{ps}})$$

in multiples of N.

The three relations restricting the parameter choices give optimal parameters in the sense that no choice of m, t, l, and $\hat{t}$ can lead to a tradeoff coefficient smaller than the above while achieving D_{ps} as its probability of success. The storage size M appearing in the above tradeoff curve is the total number of start point and ending point pairs that need to be stored in the tradeoff tables. Proof of Proposition 1 is similar to that of Proposition 35 in [5]. We exhibit it in Appendix A.

Noting that performance of the new VDP method and DP method differs only in storage if we disregard the time spent on table look-ups, we find optimal parameters of our method by applying Proposition 1.

Proposition 2. *Given N and D_{ps}, the optimal parameters of the new VDP tradeoff are subjected to the following relations*

$$rs = 1.20N^{\frac{1}{3}}, \ l = 1.49ln(\frac{1}{1 - D_{pc}}) \cdot N^{\frac{1}{3}}, \ \hat{t} = 2.35N^{\frac{1}{3}}, \ and \ k = N^{\frac{1}{3}} + 1.$$

The tradeoff coefficient for the new VDP method under the above optimal parameters is

$$D_{tc} = 0.7384D_{ps}\{ln(1 - D_{ps})\}^2.$$

The number of one-way function invocations required for the pre-computation phase is

$$D_{pc} = 1.8349ln(\frac{1}{1 - D_{ps}})$$

in multiples of N.

Proof. To apply Proposition 1 to our new VDP method, we first update the tradeoff parameters. If a chain is generated with a random function, with the chain length bound set to $\hat{t}$, the probability of not obtaining a DP chain will be $(1 - \frac{1}{t})^{\hat{t}} \approx e^{-\frac{\hat{t}}{t}}$. During the pre-computation phase we generate rs distinct start points, so after discarding chains not reaching a distinguished point, the expected number of chains is $rs(1 - e^{-\frac{\hat{t}}{t}})$. Chains end only when some point with its most significant bits being $(i \parallel j)$ is found. Thus the average length of the chains is $2^{\lceil log_2(s) \rceil + \lceil log_2(r) \rceil}$. Approximately we replace it by rs. So we get $t = rs$.

Now referring to Proposition 1, the relations may equivalently be stated as

$$rs(1 - e^{-\frac{\hat{t}}{t}}) \cdot (rs)^2 = 1.47N, \ l = 1.25ln(\frac{1}{1 - D_{ps}})rs, \ and \ \hat{t} = 1.97t.$$

Then

$$rs = 1.20N^{\frac{1}{3}}, \ l = 1.49ln(\frac{1}{1 - D_{pc}}) \cdot N^{\frac{1}{3}}, \ \hat{t} = 2.35N^{\frac{1}{3}}.$$

As only the last $\frac{2}{3}n$ bits of the ending points are stored, the new VDP method saves the memory cost by a factor of $\frac{1}{3}$. We replace M in the tradeoff curve of Proposition 1 by $\frac{M}{3}$ and obtain tradeoff curve of the new VDP method. The time-memory tradeoff curve of the new VDP method is $TM^2 = D_{tc}N^2$, where

$$D_{tc} = 0.7384D_{ps}\{ln(1 - D_{ps})\}^2.$$

Recall that k is greater than r and coprime with N. We simply assign k a value of $N^{\frac{1}{3}} + 1$. □

Before continuing, note that we always suppose $m = t$ in the VDP method. In such a case we reach the best tradeoff performance in theory. When we want parameters m and t to differ by a large factor or when m and t are not powers of 2, we may need to convert Proposition 2 to other forms through applying Proposition 1.

4.2   Extending the New VDP Method to Rainbow Tradeoff

As mentioned above, the rainbow method applies a different f_i to every column. During the online phase, given a target $f(x_0)$, it is necessary to know the chain length to decide which f_i to use. Results for DP method applied to rainbow tradeoff are listed below, and they are easy to be extended to the new VDP method. In this section, we denote by t the inverse of the probability to find a distinguished point and set $\hat{t} = ct$.

During the pre-computation phase, we first choose $\tilde{m}_0$ start points and use different iteration f_i's for different columns. We denote the number of different keys in column i by $\tilde{m}_i$. When $0 \le i < \hat{t}$, as about $\tilde{m}_i \cdot \frac{1}{t}$ points reach distinguished points, we can easily find out a recurrence relation on $\tilde{m}_i$: $\tilde{m}_{i+1} = N(1 - (1 - \frac{1}{N})^{\tilde{m}_i(1-\frac{1}{t})})$, which can be approximated by $\tilde{m}_{i+1} = \tilde{m}_i(1 - \frac{1}{t})$. So we get $\tilde{m}_i = \tilde{m}_0(1 - \frac{1}{t})^i$.

Then we discard all chains not reaching a DP in length $\hat{t}$. The number of different keys in column i after this process is denoted by m_i. Thus

$$m_i = \tilde{m}_i - \tilde{m}_{\hat{t}}(1 - \frac{1}{t}) = \tilde{m}_0(1 - \frac{1}{t})^i - \tilde{m}_0(1 - \frac{1}{t})^{\hat{t}+1}. \tag{1}$$

Following this, the rainbow table is sorted first with respect to chain lengths and then with respect to the ending points within those chains of same length. The start point, the ending point and the chain length are stored. The total number of chains that need to be stored is $m_0 = \tilde{m}_0(1 - e^{-c})$.

During the online phase, we assume that the l tables are processed with the simultaneous approach, which means the chains of same length in different tables are searched before moving to the next column.

Probability of success. The number of distinct nodes expected in each column is given by the stated m_i. So the probability for the first k iterations of the online phase to fail, denoted by P_k, is

$$\prod_{i=1}^{k-1}(1 - \frac{m_{\hat{t}-i}}{N})^l.$$

We have ignored the interdependence between columns and approximate it by

$$P_k = \prod_{i=1}^{k-1}(1 - \frac{m_{\hat{t}-i}}{N})^l \approx \prod_{i=1}^{k-1} e^{-\frac{m_{\hat{t}-i}l}{N}} = e^{-\frac{l\sum_{i=1}^{k-1}m_{\hat{t}-i}}{N}}$$
$$= e^{-\frac{l}{N}\sum_{i=1}^{k-1}[(\tilde{m}_0(1-\frac{1}{t})^{\hat{t}-i}-\tilde{m}_0(1-\frac{1}{t})^{\hat{t}})]} = e^{-\frac{l\tilde{m}_0 t}{N}(e^{\frac{k-1}{t}-c}-e^{-c}-\frac{k}{t}\cdot e^{-c})}.$$

We already know that the pre-computation requirement of DP method is $m_0 tl$ regardless of the chain length bound and we set $RN = m_0 tl$, where R means the pre-computation coefficient. We finally yield

$$P_k = e^{-\frac{lt}{e^c-1}(e^{\frac{k-1}{t}}-1-\frac{k}{t})}. \tag{2}$$

So, the success rate of DP method applied to rainbow tradeoff is

$$P = 1 - P_{\hat{t}} = 1 - e^{-\frac{lt}{e^c-1}(e^c-1-c)}. \tag{3}$$

Tradeoff curve. We first provide the result of expected numbers of false alarms associated with a single rainbow matrix at the i-th iteration, denoted by $E_{fa}(i)$. A collision happens with probability of $\frac{1}{N}$ under an invocation of f. During the i-th iteration, for a chain of length $\hat{t}$, f is computed $\hat{t}-(\hat{t}-i)$ times. The probability that a false alarm occurs is $1 - (1 - \frac{1}{N})^{\hat{t}-(\hat{t}-i)}$, which can be approximated by $\frac{\hat{t}-(\hat{t}-i)}{N}$. Thus, taking false alarms associated with all rows into consideration,

$$E_{fa}(i) = \sum_{j=\hat{t}-i+1}^{\hat{t}}(m_j - m_{j+1}) \cdot \frac{j-(\hat{t}-i)}{N} = \frac{1}{N}\sum_{j=\hat{t}-i+1}^{\hat{t}}\widetilde{m}_0(1 - \frac{1}{t})^j \cdot \frac{1}{t} \cdot (j - \hat{t} + i)$$
$$= \frac{\widetilde{m}_0 t}{N}[(1 - \frac{1}{t})^{\hat{t}-i+2} \cdot (1 - (1 - \frac{1}{t})^{i-1}) - \frac{i}{t}(1 - \frac{1}{t})^{\hat{t}+1})].$$

Hence, the expected total running time can be written as

$$T = \sum_{i=1}^{\hat{t}} l[(i-1) + (\hat{t} - i + 1) \cdot E_{fa}(i)] \cdot P_i$$
$$= t^2 l \sum_{i=1}^{\hat{t}} [\frac{i-1}{t} + \frac{\hat{t}-i+1}{t} \cdot E_{fa}(i)]e^{-\frac{R}{e^c-1}(e^{\frac{i-1}{t}}-1-\frac{i}{t})} \cdot \frac{1}{t}.$$

This may be approximated by the definite integral

$$T = t^2 \int_0^c [lu + (c - u) \cdot \frac{R}{e^c - 1}(e^u - 1 - u)]e^{-\frac{R}{e^c-1}(e^u-1-u)}du. \qquad (4)$$

It now suffices to combine this with the storage size $M = m_0 l$ and obtain the tradeoff curve $TM^2 = DN^2$, where the tradeoff coefficient is

$$D = R^2 \int_0^c [lu + (c - u) \cdot \frac{R}{e^c-1}(e^u - 1 - u)]e^{-\frac{R}{e^c-1}(e^u-1-u)}du. \qquad (5)$$

Optimal parameters. Recalling that a smaller tradeoff coefficient implies better tradeoff performance, we show next how to choose optimal parameters l, P and c to minimize the tradeoff coefficient. As a much smaller parameter l is used in rainbow tradeoff, we treat it as discrete numbers $1, 2, 3, 4$ and so on. For a fixed l and R, we plot the tradeoff coefficient D to display the relationship between D and P. Results are shown in Figure 1.

Using numerical method, we find out that the tradeoff coefficient increases strictly with the increasing of l, c or P. It is obvious to choose 1 as l and a smallest c to obtain the best tradeoff performance. However, the tradeoff curve does not take pre-computation time into account. As a matter of fact the above optimal tradeoff is achieved at the cost of high pre-computation time. According to Equation 3,

$$R = -\frac{ln(1-P) \cdot (e^c - 1)}{e^c - 1 - c}. \qquad (6)$$

In practice, the pre-computation coefficient R is not too large. We numerically solve Equation 5 and results are shown in Table 1. We explain the content of the table with examples. Suppose one aims to achieve the success probability of 0.85, and the pre-computation time is upper bounded by $3N$. It is optimal to build one DP-Rainbow table and set $\hat{t}$ equals $1.75t$. The tradeoff coefficient is expected to be around 8.7968.

As chain length information is stored in our new VDP method when applied to rainbow tradeoff, it saves the memory cost by a factor of $\frac{3}{4}$. It follows that:

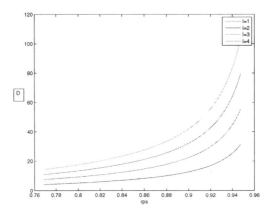

Fig. 1. Tradeoff coefficient D with different P and l, R $= 3.5$

Proposition 3. *Let $0 < P < 1$ be any given fixed value. The pre-computation time is upper bounded by RN. Locate c in the above table. Then the new VDP method applied to rainbow tradeoff with optimal parameters satisfying*

$$l = 1, \ rs = \sqrt{\frac{RN}{1 - e^{-c}}}, \ \hat{t} = c\sqrt{\frac{RN}{1 - e^{-c}}}, \ k = \sqrt{N} + 1$$

attains the given value P as its success probability. The tradeoff coefficient is

$$D = \frac{9R^2}{16} \int_0^c [lu + (c - u) \cdot \frac{R}{e^c - 1}(e^u - 1 - u)]e^{-\frac{R}{e^c - 1}(e^u - 1 - u)} du.$$

5   Comparison

In this section, we compare our new VDP method with previous tradeoff algorithms using tradeoff curves. It should first be noticed that a better tradeoff coefficient should always be achievable, if one decides to sacrifice the success probability for finding the correct password. A fair comparison of the algorithms should compare them at the same success rate. We summarize the relevant facts in Table 2.

The presented time complexity T of the first half of the table disregards false alarms and uses general parameters satisfying matrix stopping rule. The second half of the table deals with real world cracking, which takes false alarms into consideration. The optimal parameters are obtained at the given success rate. From the table, we can clearly figure out that our new method applied to Hellman table achieves a better performance. As to the method applied to rainbow tradeoff, chains are sorted with respect to the chain lengths and we have to store chain length information. It doesn't bring us a significantly better result.

Table 1. Optimal parameters and corresponding tradeoff coefficient for a given P

l	P	R	c	tradeoff coefficient	l	P	R	c	tradeoff coefficient
1	0.7	2.8802	1.00	2.9915	1	0.75	3.3163	1.00	3.8091
1	0.8	3.8501	1.00	4.8997	1	0.85	4.5383	1.00	6.4366
1	0.9	5.5083	1.00	8.8241	1	0.95	7.1664	1.00	13.4272
1	0.7	2.5	1.2	3.2549	1	0.7	3	1.0	2.9915
1	0.75	2.5	1.45	4.5906	1	0.75	3	1.13	3.9939
1	0.8	2.5	1.8	6.8245	1	0.8	3	1.38	5.7169
1	0.85	2.5	2.39	11.6141	1	0.85	3	1.75	8.7968
1	0.9	2.5	3.92	31.0272	1	0.9	3	2.44	16.3704
1	0.95	2.5	-	-	1	0.95	3	8.49	180.7163
1	0.7	3.5	1.0	2.9915	1	0.7	4	1.0	2.9915
1	0.75	3.5	1.0	3.8091	1	0.75	4	1.0	3.8091
1	0.8	3.5	1.13	5.1822	1	0.8	4	1.0	4.8997
1	0.85	3.5	1.4	7.5863	1	0.85	4	1.17	6.8800
1	0.9	3.5	1.86	12.6852	1	0.9	4	1.52	10.9405
1	0.95	3.5	3.12	34.1475	1	0.95	4	2.33	24.0022

Table 2. Comparison of tradeoff algorithms, denote success rate by P

	parameter selection	Pre-computation time:$\times$ N	tradeoff curve
Hellman	$mt^2 = N$	1	$TM^2 = N^2$
Rainbow	$mt^2 = N$	1	$TM^2 = \frac{1}{2}N^2$
Hellman+DP	$mt^2 = N$	-	$TM^2 = N^2$
Hellman+VDP	$mt^2 = N, \hat{t} = ct$	-	$TM^2 = cN^2$
Rainbow+DP	$mt^2 = N, \hat{t} = ct$	-	$TM^2 = \frac{c^2}{2}N^2$
Rainbow+VDP	$mt^2 = N, \hat{t} = ct$	-	$TM^2 = \frac{c^2}{2}N^2$
Hellman	Optimal, $P = 80\%$	2.1733	$TM^2 = 3.11N^2$
Rainbow	Optimal, $P = 80\%$	1.9814	$TM^2 = 2.20N^2$
Hellman+DP	Optimal, $P = 80\%$	2.9532	$TM^2 = 13.77N^2$
Rainbow+DP	Optimal, $P = 80\%$	3	$TM^2 = 5.72N^2$
Hellman+new VDP	Optimal, $P = 80\%$	2.9532	$TM^2 = 1.53N^2$
Rainbow+new VDP	Optimal, $P = 80\%$	3	$TM^2 = 3.22N^2$
Hellman	Optimal, $P = 90\%$	3.1093	$TM^2 = 7.17N^2$
Rainbow	Optimal, $P = 90\%$	2.8068	$TM^2 = 4.68N^2$
Hellman+DP	Optimal, $P = 90\%$	4.2250	$TM^2 = 31.68N^2$
Rainbow+DP	Optimal, $P = 90\%$	3.5	$TM^2 = 12.69N^2$
Hellman+new VDP	Optimal, $P = 90\%$	4.2250	$TM^2 = 3.52N^2$
Rainbow+new VDP	Optimal, $P = 90\%$	3.5	$TM^2 = 7.14N^2$

6   Conclusion

In this paper, we present a rigorous analysis of the VDP method and suggest using a generic diffusion function to generate start points. Optimal parameters of the new VDP method are also given. Furthermore, we give a careful analysis on how to apply this method to rainbow tradeoff. We present an accurate version of the tradeoff curve that does not ignore the effect of false alarms and takes storage reduction techniques into consideration. A fair comparison of all previous tradeoff algorithms are presented, which shows that our method applied to Hellman tradeoff performs best among them.

The optimal parameters are determined by just minimizing the tradeoff coefficient. However, parameters achieving better tradeoff performance may require more pre-computation, and with large scale implementations of the tradeoff technique, lowering the pre-computation cost may be significantly more valuable than achieving better tradeoff performance. Our analysis may seem interesting in view of optimal usage of tradeoff algorithms, but can be of limited value in practice. One should consider our work as a guide and use it to arrive at their final judgements.

References

1. Borst, J., Preneel, B., Vandewalle, J.: On the time-memory tradeoff between exhaustive key search and table precomputation. In: Symposium on Information Theory in the Benelux, pp. 111–118. Citeseer (1998)
2. Fiat, A., Naor, M.: Rigorous time/space tradeoffs for inverting functions. In: Proceedings of the Twenty-third Annual ACM Symposium on Theory of Computing, pp. 534–541. ACM (1991)
3. Hellman, M.: A cryptanalytic time-memory trade-off. IEEE Transactions on Information Theory 26(4), 401–406 (1980)
4. Hong, J., Jeong, K.C., Kwon, E.Y., Lee, I.-S., Ma, D.: Variants of the Distinguished Point Method for Cryptanalytic Time Memory Trade-offs. In: Chen, L., Mu, Y., Susilo, W. (eds.) ISPEC 2008. LNCS, vol. 4991, pp. 131–145. Springer, Heidelberg (2008)
5. Hong, J., Moon, S.: A comparison of cryptanalytic tradeoff algorithms. Technical report, Cryptology ePrint Archive, Report 2010/176 (2010)
6. Kim, I.J., Matsumoto, T.: Achieving higher success probability in time-memory trade-off cryptanalysis without increasing memory size. IEICE Transactions on Fundamentals of Electronics, Communications and Computer Sciences 82(1), 123–129 (1999)
7. Mukhopadhyay, S., Sarkar, P.: Application of lFSRs in Time/Memory Trade-off Cryptanalysis. In: Song, J.-S., Kwon, T., Yung, M. (eds.) WISA 2005. LNCS, vol. 3786, pp. 25–37. Springer, Heidelberg (2006)
8. Oechslin, P.: Making a Faster Cryptanalytic Time-memory Trade-off. In: Boneh, D. (ed.) CRYPTO 2003. LNCS, vol. 2729, pp. 617–630. Springer, Heidelberg (2003)
9. Standaert, F.X., Rouvroy, G., Quisquater, J.J., Legat, J.D.: A Time-memory Tradeoff Using Distinguished Points: New Analysis & FPGA Results. In: Kaliski Jr., B.S., Koç, Ç.K., Paar, C. (eds.) CHES 2002. LNCS, vol. 2523, pp. 13–30. Springer, Heidelberg (2003)
10. Thing, V.L.L., Ying, H.M.: A novel time-memory trade-off method for password recovery. Digital Investigation 6, S114–S120 (2009)

A   Proof of Proposition 1

We first fix notation that is used in our analysis of DP tradeoff.

m: number of chains in a single DP table
t: the DP property is satisfied with a probability of $\frac{1}{t}$
D_{msc}: the matrix stopping constant, $mt^2 = D_{msc}N$, $D_{msc} = \Theta(1)$
l: number of DP tables, $l = \Theta(t)$
$\hat{t}$: chain length bound, $\hat{t} = ct$, $c = \Theta(1)$

Proposition 4. *[5] The pre-computation phase of the DP tradeoff is expected to require mtl one-way function invocations. Denote the pre-computation coefficient by $D_{pc} = \frac{mtl}{N}$. The success probability of the DP tradeoff is*

$$D_{ps} = 1 - \left(1 - \frac{D_{cr}mt}{N}\right)^l \approx 1 - exp\left(-D_{cr}\frac{mtl}{N}\right) = 1 - e^{-D_{cr}D_{pc}}.$$

D_{cr} is the coverage rate of a DP table, and

$$D_{cr} = \frac{2}{e^{\hat{t}/t} - 1} \int_0^{\hat{t}/t} \frac{exp(\Xi u) - 1}{(\Xi + 1)exp(\Xi u) + (\Xi - 1)} exp(u)du$$

where $\Xi = \sqrt{1 + \frac{2D_{msc}}{1 - e^{-\hat{t}/t}}}$.

Proposition 5. *[5] Fix a random function $f : N \to N$ and suppose that we are given a pre-computed DP chain of length $j < \hat{t}$, generated with f from a random non-DP start point. If a second chain is generated with f from a random start point, the probability for it to become a DP chain of length i and merge with the given pre-computed chain is*

$$\frac{t}{N}\{exp(\frac{min\{i, j\}}{t} - 1)exp(-\frac{i}{t})\}.$$

Lemma 1. *The number of extra one-way function invocations induced by alarms is expected to be*

$$t\frac{D_{msc}}{1 - e^{-c}}(-2 + c + 2ce^{-c} + e^{-c} + e^{-2c} - \frac{c^2}{2}e^{-c})$$

for each DP table.

Proof. Proof is same as that in [5] except that we do not store the chain length information, which causes extra effort in dealing with false alarms.

Recall the probability for a random chain to become a DP chain within the chain length bound $\hat{t}$ is $1 - e^{-\hat{t}/t}$. Rather than requiring each table to contain exactly m entries, we assume that each pre-computation DP table is always generated from $m_0 = \frac{m}{1 - e^{-\hat{t}/t}}$ distinct start points. Then we can expect to collect approximately m chains that terminate at DPs.

When the chains are generated from m_0 non-DP start points, one can expect to collect

$$\frac{m}{1-e^{-\hat{t}/t}}(1-\frac{1}{t})^{j-1}\frac{1}{t} \approx \frac{\frac{m}{t}}{1-e^{-\hat{t}/t}}exp(-\frac{j}{t})$$

DP chains of length j.

As we do not store the chain length information, the number of iterations required when a collision happens is $\hat{t} - i + 1$. The only exception is when a pre-image is found, which is rare enough to be ignored.

Now referring to Proposition 5, the number of extra one-way function invocations induced by alarms can be expressed as

$$\sum_{i=1}^{\hat{t}}\sum_{j=1}^{\hat{t}}\frac{\frac{m}{t}}{1-e^{-\hat{t}/t}}exp(-\frac{j}{t})\cdot\frac{t}{N}\{exp(\frac{min\{i,j\}}{t})-1)exp(-\frac{i}{t})\}\cdot(\hat{t}-i+1).$$

This can be approximated by the integration

$$\frac{\frac{mt^2}{N}t}{1-e^{-\hat{t}/t}}\int_0^{\hat{t}/t}\int_0^{\hat{t}/t}exp(-u)exp(-v)\{exp(min\{u,v\}-1)(\frac{\hat{t}}{t}-u)\}dvdu.$$

We reach the claimed value by replacing $\hat{t}/t$ by c and computing this definite integral. □

The following time memory tradeoff curve of DP tradeoff is obtained using the same approach as in [5].

Proposition 6. *The time memory tradeoff curve is* $TM^2 = D_{tc}N^2$, *where the tradeoff coefficient is*

$$D_{tc} = \{(-2+c+2ce^{-c}+e^{-c}+e^{-2c}-\frac{c^2}{2}e^{-c})\cdot D_{msc}+(1-e^{-c})^2\}\frac{D_{ps}\{ln(1-D_{ps})\}^2}{(1-e^{-c})D_{cr}^3 D_{msc}}. \tag{7}$$

Now we can find optimal parameter sets by minimizing the tradeoff coefficient and obtain Proposition 1. We drop from Equation 7 any part that depends only on D_{ps} and consider

$$D_{tmp}[D_{msc},c] = \frac{(-2+c+2ce^{-c}+e^{-c}+e^{-2c}-\frac{c^2}{2}e^{-c})\cdot D_{msc}+(1-e^{-c})^2}{(1-e^{-c})D_{cr}^3 D_{msc}}. \tag{8}$$

We substitute D_{cr} given by Proposition 4 into Equation 8. $D_{tmp}[D_{msc},c]$ can be viewed as a function of variables D_{msr} and c. We plot D_{tmp} and using numerical methods we find that the minimum value of $D_{tmp} = 6.5452$ is obtained at $D_{msc} = 1.47$ and $c = 1.97$. Referring to Proposition 4 again, we get the rest optimal parameters and this leads us to the claim of Proposition 1.

Analyzing the Performance of Dither Modulation in Presence of Composite Attacks

Xinshan Zhu

Information Engineering College of Yangzhou University,
Yangzhou 225007, China
{xszhu_hm}@hotmail.com

Abstract. In this paper, we analyze the performance of dither modulation (DM) against the composite attacks including valumetric scaling, additive noise and constant change. The analyses are developed under the assumptions that the host vector and noise vector are mutually independent and both of them have independently and identically distributed components. We derive the general expressions of the probability density functions of several concerned signals and the decoding error probability. The specific analytical results are presented for the case of generalized Gaussian host signal. Numerical simulations confirm the validity of the given theoretical analyses.

1 Introduction

Due to cancelling the host inference completely, quantization index modulation (QIM) becomes a popular class of digital watermarking schemes. Chen et al. [1] presented the basic QIM algorithm called dither modulation (DM) and several variants of it, i.e., distortion compensated dither modulation (DC-DM) and spread transform dither modulation (STDM) [1]. The theoretical performance of QIM methods is a key issue and has received considerable attention.

In [1], Chen et al. considered the simple case where the watermark is transmitted in an additive white Gaussian noise (AWGN) channel. They gave a relatively crude approximation to the error probability of the minimal distance detector. Eggers et al. [2] proposed the scalar Costa scheme (SCS), approximately equivalent to DC-QIM, and analyzed the decoding performance of it under the AWGN attack. The careful performance analyses were done by Gonzàlez et al. [3] for a large class of QIM methods. They assumed that the watermark is impaired by an additive attacker and considered the following two cases: the channel noise follows a uniform and Gaussian distributions. Bartolini et al. [4] concentrated on analyzing the performance of the STDM algorithm at a practical level. By assuming the host signal is normally distributed, they derived the theoretical error probabilities in closed form for the gain attack plus noise addition, and the quantization attack. Boyer et al. [5] theoretically evaluated the performance of scalar DC-QIM against AWGN from the detection viewpoint. In [6], the authors proposed an improved DM scheme to resist linear-time-invariant filtering and provided a thorough analysis of it, resulting in both accurate predictions and

S. Qing et al. (Eds.): ICICS 2011, LNCS 7043, pp. 297–305, 2011.
© Springer-Verlag Berlin Heidelberg 2011

bounds on the error probability. Recently, a new logarithmic QIM (LQIM) was presented in [7] and its analytical performance was obtained in the presence of AWGN.

The objective of this paper is to analyze the performance of DM against composite attacks including valumetric scaling, additive noise and constant change. The paper is organized as follows. Section 2 reviews the original DM and describes the problem to be solved. Next, Section 3 accurately derives the general PDF models concerned with our analysis. In Section 4, the performance of DM under the composite attacks is mathematically analyzed by the derived PDFs. Then, in Section 5, the theoretical results are confirmed by numerical simulations. Finally, Section 6 concludes.

Notation: We use boldface lower-case letters to denote column vectors, e.g. $\boldsymbol{x}$, and scalar variables are denoted by italicized lower-case letters, e.g. x. The probability distribution function (PDF) of a random variable (r.v.) x is denoted by $p_X(x)$, whereas if x is discrete its probability mass function (PMF) is designated by $P_X(x)$. We write $x \sim p_X(x)$ to indicate that a r.v. x is distributed as $p_X(x)$. $p_{X|Y}(x|y)$ means the conditional probability of x given y. And the subscripts of the distribution functions will be dropped wherever it is clear the random variable they refer to. Finally, the mathematical expectation and standard deviation are respectively represented by μ_x and σ_x for a r.v. x.

2   Review of DM and Problem

The uncoded binary DM can be summarized as follows. Let $\boldsymbol{x} \in \mathbb{R}^N$ be a host signal vector in which we wish to embed the watermark message m. First, the message m is represented by a vector $\boldsymbol{b}$ with NR_m binary antipodal components, i.e., $b_j = \pm 1, j = 1, \cdots, NR_m$, where R_m denotes the bit rate. The host signal $\boldsymbol{x}$ is then decomposed into NR_m subvectors of length $L = \lfloor 1/R_m \rfloor$, denoted by $\boldsymbol{x}_1, \cdots, \boldsymbol{x}_{NR_m}$. In the binary DM, two L-dimensional uniform quantizers $Q_{-1}(\cdot)$ and $Q_{+1}(\cdot)$ are constructed, whose centroids are given by the lattices $\Lambda_{-1} = 2\Delta\mathbb{Z}^L + \boldsymbol{d}$ and $\Lambda_{+1} = 2\Delta\mathbb{Z}^L + \boldsymbol{d} + \Delta\boldsymbol{a}$ with $\boldsymbol{d} \in \mathbb{R}^L$ a key-dependent dithering vector and $\boldsymbol{a} = (1, \cdots, 1)^T$. Each message bit b_j is hidden by using $Q_{b_j}(\cdot)$ on $\boldsymbol{x}_j$, resulting in the watermarked signal $\boldsymbol{y} \in \mathbb{R}^N$ as

$$\boldsymbol{y}_j = Q_{b_j}(\boldsymbol{x}_j), \quad j = 1, \cdots, NR_m \tag{1}$$

The watermark detector receives a distorted, watermarked signal, $\boldsymbol{z}$, and decodes a message $\widehat{m}$ using the decoder

$$\widehat{b}_j = \arg\min_{-1,1} \|Q_{b_j}(\boldsymbol{z}_j) - \boldsymbol{z}_j\|, \quad j = 1, \cdots, NR_m \tag{2}$$

where $\| \cdot \|$ stands for Euclidean (i.e., ℓ_2) norm.

In practical watermarking applications, the watermarked signal might undergo composite attacks. It is well known that quantization-based watermarking is vulnerable to valumetric scaling and constant change, i.e., $\boldsymbol{z}_j = \rho_j \boldsymbol{y}_j$ and

$z_j = y_j + c_j a$. In this work, the two attacks are considered together with additive noise ν_j, yielding the attacked signal as

$$z_j = \rho_j y_j + \nu_j + c_j a. \tag{3}$$

We will analyze the performance of DM in the case. In the analysis, x, y, z and ν are all regarded as random vectors. And we assume that both x and ν have independently and identically distributed (i.i.d.) components and ν is independent from y. Since the mean value of ν can be counted by the third term in (3), it is reasonable to assumed that $\mu_\nu = 0$.

3   PDF Models

Define the extracted vector r, $r \stackrel{\triangle}{=} Q_b(z) - z$. Obviously, a crucial aspect when performing a rigorous analysis lies in computing the PDF of r. Let us begin with the issue.

We use a lower-case letter to indicate any element of the vector denoted by the boldface one. The previously used index j is dropped for no specific values (or subverctors) are concerned. Given $x \sim p_X(x)$, from the relation (1), we get

$$p_Y(y|b) = \sum_{k=-\infty}^{\infty} \delta(y - y_k) \int_{y_k - \Delta}^{y_k + \Delta} p_X(x)dx, \tag{4}$$

where $y_k = 2k\Delta + (b+1)\Delta/2 + d$ and $\delta(\cdot)$ denotes the delta function. By (3) and using the independence of y and ν, the PDF of z is obtained by convolution

$$p_Z(z|b) = \sum_{k=-\infty}^{\infty} P_Y(y_k|b)p_\nu(z - \rho y_k - c), \tag{5}$$

In (5), if the effect of d on $P_Y(y)$ is ignored (this generally holds when the embedding distortion is acceptable), $p_Z(z|b, d \neq 0)$ can be approximately viewed as the translate of $p_Z(z|b, d = 0)$, i.e., $p_Z(z + \rho d|b, d \neq 0) \approx p_Z(z|b, d = 0)$.

With the given definition of r previously, we can write

$$p_R(r|b) = \begin{cases} \sum\limits_{j=-\infty}^{\infty} p_Z(z_j - r|b, d), & r \in [-\Delta, \Delta) \\ 0, & \text{else} \end{cases} \tag{6}$$

where $z_j = (4j + b + 1)\Delta/2 + d$. Inserting (5) into (6) yields

$$p_R(r|b) = \sum_j \sum_k P(y_k|b)p_\nu(\mu_{jk} - r), \tag{7}$$

with $\mu_{jk} = z_j - \rho y_k - c$ and $r \in [-\Delta, \Delta)$. If ignoring the effect of d on $P_Y(y)$, from (7), we derive $p_R(r - \epsilon d|b, d \neq 0) \approx p_R(r|b, d = 0)$ with $\epsilon = \rho - 1$. This shows that $p_R(r|b)$ can be approximately obtained by translating $p_R(r|b, d = 0)$ for the

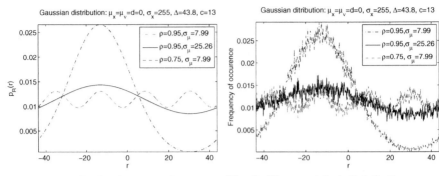

Fig. 1. The PDF curves of r

Fig. 2. The empirical distribution curves of r

case $d \neq 0$. Further, while $|\epsilon|$ is small enough, $p_R(r|b, d \neq 0) \approx p_R(r|b, d = 0)$ holds. Thus, despite the choice of d, $p_R(r)$ approximately remains unchanged for small $|\epsilon|$.

Fig. 1 and Fig. 2 respectively plot the analytical and empirical probability density curves of r with Gaussian host and noise in use. It is shown that the values of r are distributed around zero with higher probability for weak attacks, and the density curve of r becomes smooth as attacks become stronger, resulting in the increase of bit error rate (BER). By the scale factor ρ, the distribution curve of r is either dilated or compressed. Simultaneously, it is approximately translated by $\epsilon d + c$. Comparison of Fig. 1 and Fig. 2 reveals the analytical PDF of r fits perfectly with its empirical distribution.

4　Performance Analysis

As the previous literatures, the decoding bit error probability P_e is used as the final performance measurement. Applying the definition of r, it is straightforward to write P_e as

$$P_e = P(\|r\| > \|\Delta \mathbf{a} - |r|\| \, |b).\tag{8}$$

where $|r|$ denotes the vector of absolute values of components of r. Defining $s \triangleq |r|^T \mathbf{a}$, the expression (8) is equivalent to

$$P_e = \int_{L\Delta/2}^{L\Delta} p_S(s|b)ds.\tag{9}$$

To compute P_e, we need know the PDF $p_S(s)$ of s. The exact solution for $p_S(s)$ may be achieved by performing multifold integral operation. However, it becomes impractical as L increases. To solve the problem, it is nature to use mathematically tractable approximations. Let us assume that all components of d are equal, so that the vector r has i.i.d components. By the well known central limit theorem (CLT), s thus can be approximated by a Gaussian r.v. with mean $L\mu_{|r|}$ and variance $L\sigma_{|r|}^2$. Using (7), $\mu_{|r|}$ and $\sigma_{|r|}^2$ are represented as

$$\mu_{|r|} = \sum_j \sum_k P(y_k|b) \int_{-\Delta}^{\Delta} |r| p_\nu(\mu_{jk} - r) dr \qquad (10)$$

$$\sigma_{|r|}^2 = \sum_j \sum_k P(y_k|b) \int_{-\Delta}^{\Delta} r^2 p_\nu(\mu_{jk} - r) dr - \mu_{|r|}^2. \qquad (11)$$

Then, the probability P_e is computed as

$$P_e \approx \Phi\left(\frac{\sqrt{L}(\Delta - \mu_{|r|})}{\sigma_{|r|}}\right) - \Phi\left(\frac{\sqrt{L}(\Delta/2 - \mu_{|r|})}{\sigma_{|r|}}\right), \qquad (12)$$

where $\Phi(\cdot)$ stands for the cumulative distribution function (CDF) of the standard Gaussian distribution. It should be pointed out the CLT approximation to P_e is only valid for very large L. In reality, the condition is generally met in order to improve the watermarking robustness.

For the following analysis we consider a specific case where the host signal is statistically modeled by the generalized Gaussian distribution (GGD). The GGD model is used because it includes a family of distributions and suitable for many practical applications. The PDF $p(t)$ of the GGD is

$$p(t) = \frac{\kappa\beta}{2\Gamma(\beta^{-1})} e^{-|\kappa(t-\mu)|^\beta}, \qquad (13)$$

where $\kappa = \frac{1}{\sigma}\sqrt{\Gamma(3\beta^{-1})/\Gamma(\beta^{-1})}$, and $\Gamma(u) = \int_0^\infty t^{u-1}e^{-t}dt$ is the Gamma function. Thus, the distribution is completely specified by the mean μ, the standard deviation σ and the shape parameter β, and is denoted as $GGD(\beta; \mu, \sigma)$.

First, the PMF $P_Y(y)$ is calculated according to the distribution model of x. Given $p_X(x) \sim GGD(\beta_x; \mu_x, \sigma_x)$, in view of (4), we immediately write

$$P_Y(y_k|b) = \Psi_x(y_k + \Delta) - \Psi_x(y_k - \Delta), \qquad (14)$$

where the CDF $\Psi_x(t)$ is defined as

$$\Psi_x(t) = \frac{1}{2} + sgn(t - \mu_x)\frac{\gamma(\beta_x^{-1}, |\kappa_x(t - \mu_x)|^{\beta_x})}{2\Gamma(\beta_x^{-1})}$$

[8], $\gamma(s, u) = \int_0^u t^{s-1}e^{-t}dt$ is the lower incomplete gamma function, and $sgn(t)$ denotes the sign function. Then, the integration terms in (10) and (11) are derived by the PDF $p_\nu(\nu)$. As an example, the additive Gaussian noise is considered, i.e., $p_\nu(\nu) \sim \mathcal{N}(0, \sigma_\nu^2)$. This leads to

$$\int_{-\Delta}^{\Delta} |r| p_\nu(t - r) dr = f_1(t) + f_2(t) + f_3(t) \qquad (15)$$

and

$$\int_{-\Delta}^{\Delta} r^2 p_\nu(t-r)dr = f_4(t) + f_5(t) + f_6(t), \tag{16}$$

where

$$f_1(t) = \frac{\sigma_\nu}{\sqrt{2\pi}} (e^{-\frac{t^2}{2\sigma_\nu^2}} - e^{-\frac{(t+\Delta)^2}{2\sigma_\nu^2}}) \quad f_2(t) = f_1(-t)$$

$$f_3(t) = t(2\Phi(\frac{t}{\sigma_\nu}) - \Phi(\frac{t-\Delta}{\sigma_\nu}) - \Phi(\frac{t+\Delta}{\sigma_\nu}))$$

$$f_4(t) = t^2(\Phi(\frac{t+\Delta}{\sigma_\nu}) - \Phi(\frac{t-\Delta}{\sigma_\nu}))$$

$$f_5(t) = 2t(f_1(-t) - f_1(t))$$

$$f_6(t) = \frac{\sigma_\nu(t-\Delta)}{\sqrt{2\pi}} e^{-\frac{(t-\Delta)^2}{2\sigma_\nu^2}} - \frac{\sigma_\nu(t+\Delta)}{\sqrt{2\pi}} e^{-\frac{(t+\Delta)^2}{2\sigma_\nu^2}}$$
$$+ \sigma_\nu^2(\Phi(\frac{t+\Delta}{\sigma_\nu}) - \Phi(\frac{t-\Delta}{\sigma_\nu}))$$

Using the above results, the mean and variance of $|r|$ become

$$\mu_{|r|} = \sum_{j=-\infty}^{\infty} \sum_{k=-\infty}^{\infty} \sum_{i=1}^{3} P(y_k|b) f_i(\mu_{jk}) \tag{17}$$

$$\sigma_{|r|}^2 = \sum_{j=-\infty}^{\infty} \sum_{k=-\infty}^{\infty} \sum_{i=4}^{6} P(y_k|b) f_i(\mu_{jk}) - \mu_{|r|}^2. \tag{18}$$

Therefore, the approximated P_e is obtained for large L by computing (14), (17), and (18), then putting them into (12). In particular, the theoretical results can be easily extended by modeling the host and noise signals with other distributions. In the complex case, $p_Y(y)$, $\mu_{|r|}$, and $\sigma_{|r|}^2$ are computed using (4), (10) and (11) by means of numerical integration,

5   Experimental Results

We conduct experiments on real images (see Fig. 3) to verify the obtained theoretical results. The watermark embedding is performed in the spatial domain, which allows us to measure the performance of DM without the impact of transform operations. Specifically, all pixels of one image are pseudorandomized and arranged in a vector as the host signal. Each 32 pixels conceal one bit information. Under the composite attacks, we obtain the empirical BER. And the theoretical values of P_e are calculated in the same cases. In the plots, Lines and symbols stand for theoretical values and empirical data, respectively.

Fig. 3. Three standard test images: Lenna (left), Mandrill(middle) and Crowd(right)

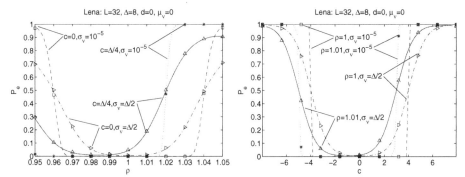

Fig. 4. Bit error probability versus ρ while fixing σ_ν and c

Fig. 5. Bit error probability vs. c while fixing ρ and σ_ν

The experimental results on the Lena image are shown in Fig. 4-6. Fig.4 depicts the plots of the P_e's versus the scaling factor ρ for several values of σ_ν and c. It is shown that DM is definitely very sensitive to the scaling attack. While $c \neq 0$, P_e is not symmetrical around $\rho = 1$ yet. The additive noise attack increases BER for small scaling distortions, but reduces BER as the scaling distortions become serious enough. Fig. 5 illustrates the sensitivity of DM to the addition/subtraction of a constant luminance value while fixing ρ and σ_ν. As can be seen, without scaling and noise attacks, P_e jumps from 0 to 1 at $|c| = \Delta/2$. After the noise is added, P_e degrades more smoothly as $|c|$ increases. Valumetric scaling distortions transmit the performance curves of DM. The performance of DM against Gaussian noise attack is exhibited in Fig. 6 while fixing ρ and c. Clearly, the probability of error becomes larger as σ_ν and ρ increases, and the effect of constant change on P_e becomes relatively distinct for strong noise. All the tests show that the analytical prediction and empirical results for DM are sufficiently close, which verifies the validity of the given theoretical results.

Since the performance of DM depends on the distribution of host signal, different test results will be obtained on different images. We tested the performance of DM on 'Crowd' and 'Mandrill' images for comparison purpose. The estimated distribution parameters of each image are displayed in Table. 1. The robustness to amplitude scaling is shown in Fig. 7. We observe that DM achieves the best performance on Crowd. That is, DM is more robust to valumetric scaling if the host signal has smaller distribution parameters. We also note that the analytical

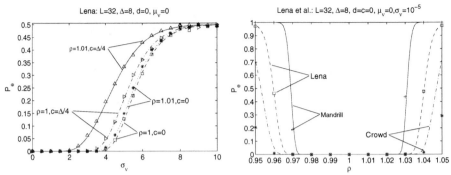

Fig. 6. Bit error probability vs. σ_ν while fixing ρ and c

Fig. 7. Bit error probability vs. ρ for different images

Table 1. Distribution parameters

Image	μ_x	σ_x	β_x
Crowd	85.2	50.9	1.5
Mandrill	129.1	42.4	3.3
Lena	99.1	47.9	10.6

P_e departs from the empirical data too much on Crowd. That is mainly due to the fact that GGD is a poor model for the Crowd image. With respect to other two attacks, DM is insensitive to the statistical properties of host signal. We may get similar results on other images as shown in Fig. 5 and Fig. 6. Thus, they are not provided here.

6   Conclusion

Throughout this paper, we have theoretically evaluated the performance of DM facing the combination of valumetric scaling, additive noise and constant change. By assuming that both the host vector and noise vector have i.i.d components and the two vectors are independent, we derived the PDFs of several concerned signals and the decoding error probability in closed form. Simulations on images show us the analytical error probability agrees with the empirical one very well. Meanwhile, it is discovered that the performance of DM against valumetric scaling depends on the statistical properties of the host signal.

Acknowledgments. This work was supported by the National Natural Science Foundation of China (Grant No. 60803122).

References

1. Chen, B., Wornell, G.W.: Quantization index modulation: a class of provably good methods for digital watermarking and information embedding. IEEE Transactions on Information Theory 47(4), 1423–1443 (2001)

2. Eggers, J.J., Bauml, R., Tzschoppe, R., Girod, B.: Scalar costa scheme for information embedding. IEEE Transactions on Signal Processing 51(4), 1003–1019 (2003)
3. Pérez-Gonzàlez, F., Balado, F., Martin, J.R.H.: Performance analysis of existing and new methods for data hiding with known-host information in additive channels. IEEE Transactions on Signal Processing 51(4), 960–980 (2003)
4. Bartolini, F., Barni, M., Piva, A.: Performance analysis of st-dm watermarking in presence of nonadditive attacks. IEEE Transactions on Signal Processing 52(10), 2965–2974 (2004)
5. Boyer, J.P., Duhamel, P., Blanc-Talon, J.: Performance analysis of scalar dc-qim for zero-bit watermarking. IEEE Transactions on Information Forensics and Security 2(2), 283–289 (2007)
6. Pérez-Gonzàlez, F., Mosquera, C.: Quantization-based data hiding robust to linear-time-invariant filtering. IEEE Transactions on Information Forensics and Security 3(2), 137–152 (2008)
7. Kalantari, N.K., Ahadi, S.M.: A logarithmic quantization index modulation for perceptually better data hiding. IEEE Transactions on Image Processing 19(6), 1504–1517 (2010)
8. Saralees, N.: A generalized normal distribution. Journal of Applied Statistics 32(7), 685–694 (2005)

Applying Time-Bound Hierarchical Key Assignment in Wireless Sensor Networks

Wen Tao Zhu[1], Robert H. Deng[2], Jianying Zhou[3], and Feng Bao[3]

[1] State Key Lab of Information Security,
Graduate University of Chinese Academy of Sciences,
19A Yuquan Road, Beijing 100049, China
wtzhu@ieee.org
[2] School of Information Systems,
Singapore Management University,
80 Stamford Road, Singapore 178902
robertdeng@smu.edu.sg
[3] Cryptography and Security Department,
Institute for Infocomm Research,
1 Fusionopolis Way, Singapore 138632
{jyzhou,baofeng}@i2r.a-star.edu.sg

Abstract. Access privileges in distributed systems can be effectively organized as a partial-order hierarchy that consists of distinct security classes, and are often designated with certain temporal restrictions. The time-bound hierarchical key assignment problem is to assign distinct cryptographic keys to distinct security classes according to their privileges so that users from a higher class can use their class key to derive the keys of lower classes, and these keys are time-variant with respect to sequentially allocated temporal units called time slots. In this paper, we explore applications of time-bound hierarchical key assignment in a wireless sensor network environment where there are a number of resource-constrained low-cost sensor nodes. We show time-bound hierarchical key assignment is a promising technique for addressing multiple aspects of sensor network security, such as data privacy protection and impact containment under node compromise. We also present the technical challenges and indicate future research directions.

1 Introduction

1.1 Hierarchical Key Assignment for Distributed Systems

With the rapid growth and pervasive deployment of information systems, sharing resources among multiple users over an open environment has become widespread. Access control on user permissions is an important issue in any system that manages distributed resources. In this paper, we consider a multilevel security scenario, where users and data of an information system are organized into a security hierarchy composed of m disjoint classes. A *hierarchical* key assignment (KA) is to assign a distinct cryptographic key to each class so that users attached

S. Qing et al. (Eds.): ICICS 2011, LNCS 7043, pp. 306–318, 2011.

to any "base" class can also derive the keys of "lower" classes. As confidential data are classified into such security classes, they can be protected with respective encryption keys using a symmetric cipher, where the decryption operation asks a user for the same encryption key so as to recover the data.

For ease of presentation, we have the classes partially ordered according to a binary relation "$\preceq$". They form a partial-order hierarchy $(C, \preceq)$, where $C_j \prec C_i$ means the clearance or security level of class C_j is lower than that of C_i, and $C_j \preceq C_i$ allows for the additional case of $j = i$. The hierarchical KA problem is to assign a key K_ℓ to each class C_ℓ, so that a user attached to her base class C_i can use the issued K_i to derive any K_j (thus to recover the data in C_j), if and only if $C_j \preceq C_i$. The hierarchy can be mapped to a directed acyclic graph, where each class corresponds to a vertex. A class may have multiple immediate ancestors. For example in Fig. 1, vertex C_7 has two immediate ancestors C_2 and C_4. If there is a top-level class with no ancestor, and each of the rest classes has exactly one immediate ancestor, the hierarchy representation then reduces to a rooted tree [1].

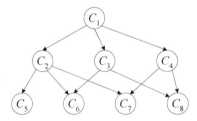

Fig. 1. A partial-order hierarchy $(C, \preceq)$ of $m = 8$ security classes. One class may have multiple immediate ancestors (e.g., $C_7 \prec C_2$ and $C_7 \prec C_4$). Although there is a top-level class C_1, this graph is not a rooted tree.

1.2 Time-Bound Hierarchical Key Assignment

In many applications such as electronic archive subscription, there is a temporal restriction so that a user is attached to her base class for only a limited period of time (typically the subscription period) consisting of a consecutive set of time units. Let the time dimension be discretized into even units (i.e., time slots or intervals) $t = 0, 1, \cdots, z$. Here the maximum index z should not be considered as a limitation of the access control policy, because the system lifetime can be arbitrarily large. For example, if each unit represents a minute, $z = 5.256 \times 10^6$ denotes 10 years. The *time-bound* hierarchical KA is to have the K_i of class C_i further mapped to a volatile key $k_{i,t}$, i.e., let the data categorized into class C_i at time t be encrypted with $k_{i,t} (1 \leq i \leq m, 0 \leq t \leq z)$. By specifying the following, we say a *class key* is instantiated with a series of *session keys*:

- The static K_i for C_i is only used for generating session keys $\{k_{i,t}\}$ as well as deriving the time-invariant class key K_j of any lower class $C_j \prec C_i$, but not used directly for data encryption.

- Only the time-variant $k_{i,t}$ is employed by the aforementioned symmetric cipher for actual data protection with respect to security class C_i, from session to session indexed by time t.

A typical application of time-bound hierarchical KA is the pay TV broadcasting, where a service provider organizes the channels into several subscription packages for users' choices. For example in Fig. 1 there are four independent TV channels C_5, C_6, C_7, and C_8, and subscription to package C_3 allows for the access to two of them (C_6 and C_8), while subscription to package C_1 allows for all. In such applications, a trusted central authority (CA) manages the key assignment. Upon registration, a user authorized to her base class C_i ($1 \leq i \leq m$) for period of time $[t_1 \cdots t_2]$ ($0 \leq t_1 \leq t_2 \leq z$) is assigned by the CA a *private primitive* denoted as $I(i, t_1, t_2)$. She should only be able to derive from $I(i, t_1, t_2)$ the session keys $\{k_{j,t}\}$ satisfying $C_j \preceq C_i$ and $t_1 \leq t \leq t_2$, thus only authorized to access the data stored in C_j at time t. The session key derivation is constrained by both the security hierarchy $(C, \preceq)$ and the time bounds (t_1 and t_2), and the derived $k_{j,t}$ should equal the instance of the class key K_j at time t. The CA is active only at user registration. After the issuance of the private primitive, no private channel exists between the CA and the user, i.e., the user should derive $k_{j,t}$ from only $I(i, t_1, t_2)$ and certain static public information, but with no interaction with the CA or any other user. Interested readers can refer to [2] for a comprehensive overview of time-bound hierarchical KA.

This work complements [2] by exploring prospect applications of time-bound hierarchical KA in wireless sensor networks (WSNs), though in the literature little work has been done to address this topic. The motivation stems from the following observation. Historically, the hierarchical KA technique was introduced to implement multilevel access control [3], which is concerned with the protection of classified data and their aggregation, dissemination, update control, etc., and thus can be connected to emerging distributed data acquisition systems like WSNs. We discuss certain application scenarios in WSNs, and show how time-bound hierarchical KA can be utilized with two case studies. The first leverages the hierarchical property for privacy protection, while the second leverages the time-bound property for enhanced security. We also present the technical challenges and indicate possible future research directions.

2   Applying Time-Bound Hierarchical Key Assignment in WSNs: General Considerations

A WSN consists of a number of sensor nodes, and is an efficient approach to delivering data from the real world to the digital world. Sensor nodes have stringent resource constraints in terms of communication, computation, storage, and energy. These limitations along with possibly harsh deployment scenarios lead to many critical security and privacy issues.

We envision time-bound hierarchical KA to be a promising technique to meet many security and privacy requirements in emerging wireless networks including

WSNs. Indeed, in some cases the clearance designated to (hence cryptographic information like $I(i, t_1, t_2)$ entitled to) a sensor node can be predetermined according to contextual information [4] after network deployment. The next section presents such a scenario. For most WSN applications, however, it is unlikely to obtain the context apriori; there may be no way to predetermine the nodes' clearances. A walkaround is to preload all sensor nodes with private primitives concerning the top-level class C_{top} (if any). After deployment, each node gathers the contextual information and decides its clearance C_i in the partial-order hierarchy $(C, \preceq)$; if $C_i \prec C_{top}$, the node "downgrades" its private primitive. This is expected for the majority of the nodes as few (sometimes only the base station) would remain in C_{top}, but to be done within a short time interval. Here we follow the assumption in [5] of introductory security at the early deployment stage: sensor nodes are manufactured to sustain possible break-in attacks at least for a short interval (say several seconds) when captured, and the time necessary for an adversary to compromise a sensor node is larger than the time needed for nodes to complete the key derivation. An example in the literature that can be accommodated by this framework is the location-based compromise-tolerant security mechanism for wireless sensor networks [6], the autonomous implementation of which preloads each node with the network master secret κ, from which the so called location-based key can be derived.

Practical time-bound hierarchical KA schemes typically adopt a decoupled structure [2] that can be formulated as $k_{i,t} = H(K_i, w_t)$, where H is a one-way hash function and w_t is the *instance secret* enabling time constraints. The above "downgrade" may then be done by deriving an appropriate base class key K_i from K_{top} and immediately erasing K_{top} for the sake of security. For example, in [7] an energy-efficient level-based hierarchical system for secure routing is proposed, where context-aware sensor nodes are self-organized into 4 levels after deployment. Although therein the self-organized hierarchy is for secure routing, a similar approach can be employed to constitute a multilevel security paradigm for hierarchical and session-oriented WSN applications like secure data aggregation, where time-bound hierarchical KA can be applied. The technique may also help with role-based and/or subscription-based applications.

Applying time-bound hierarchical KA to sensor networks is of particular interest due to the fact that, although there has been extensive research on cryptographic key management in WSNs [8–10], little work has been done to address such a particular topic. Some research efforts such as [4] took into consideration the hierarchical KA property, but the proposed scheme only considers time-invariant cryptographic keys, and thus does not represent a full fledged access control solution. Note that sensor nodes may employ ciphers with relatively short keys, and thus even simply updating the encryption keys periodically shall lead to much improved security. Other research such as [11] claimed a dynamic key derivation, but the paradigm is event-driven (by active revocation, in contrast to scheduled, spontaneous, and non-interactive key expiration), and thus is far from the perception (and benefits) of time-bound KA. Moreover, in [11] the active rekeying by the CA is based on the specious assumption that there exists a secure broadcast channel from the CA to all non-compromised sensor nodes, which actually drives the work [11] into a contradictive chicken-and-egg situation. Therefore, we envision that integrating time-bound hierarchical KA with certain WSN applications shall be an interesting and valuable research area. As a possible direction, one of the metrics that are appropriate for evaluating a security scheme for WSNs is assurance [8]; it is an ability to disseminate different information at different assurance levels to the end user. This is similar to the multilevel security paradigm, and time-bound hierarchical KA is a prospective approach.

Nevertheless, many pragmatic issues need to be considered. For example, usually sensor nodes are not made tamper-resistant due to cost concerns, but practical time-bound hierarchical KA schemes require tamper-resistance to thwart *collusion attacks* [2]. More research efforts are needed to address the problem. Of course, these KA schemes can be adopted once technical development has made it possible for massive production of tamper-resistant sensor nodes; actually, such tamper-resistance is already assumed in recent publications like [4, 12]. Even for the current generation of WSNs, it is possible that the network is heterogeneous and composed of a mix of sensor nodes with different capabilities, some of which are tamper-resistant. It would be interesting to apply time-bound hierarchical KA to such a heterogeneous WSN while minimizing the impacts by possible collusion attacks. Last, even if tamper-resistant sensor nodes are not available currently, it is still feasible to employ time-bound hierarchical KA for sensor networks. Next we present such a case study.

3   Case Study One: Protecting Data Privacy in Body Sensor Networks

Many WSN applications such as health-care and automotive ones need access control to sensed data; otherwise, attackers may easily jeopardize user privacy (e.g., in medical solutions, or in vehicular and urban sensing networks). We take the former for a case study, as medical solutions are considered as one of the two application fields where WSN security and privacy are of most importance [9] (with the other being military solutions like battlefield surveillance). In hospitals (or at home), future e-Health systems known as body sensor networks (BSNs) will consist of low-power on-body wireless sensors attached to mobile users that interact with an ubiquitous computing environment to monitor the health and well-being of patients [13]. Whilst the sensors for e-Health are a reality today, the configuration and management of the multiple sensors and software components still require considerable technical computing expertise [13]. Since physiological data collected from BSNs are legally required to be kept private, any implementation should take the trouble to protect patients' privacy [9, 14]. Traditional access control policies may be difficult to implement as sensor nodes have limited capabilities for the evaluation of complex access control rules.

A BSN is an attended network composed of on-body sensors, which are hardly subject to physical capture. Unlike a military WSN, the environment for a BSN is far from adversarial, and the major concern lies in privacy rather than security against attacks. Assume it is legally required that the sensed physiological data of each patient (referred to as a *record* hereinafter) be encrypted with a distinct cryptographic key, and a patient's record should only be accessed by his or her attending doctor and the doctor's direct or indirect superiors. The policy can be enforced by encrypting the record of any patient before it is transmitted to a central database, and this can be done by associating each patient with an identifier, and associating his or her sensors with a corresponding encryption key. If a patient once discharged from the hospital is hospitalized again, he or she should be regarded as a new case and associated with a new identifier (and thus a new key), as he or she may neither have the same illness nor be treated by the same attending doctor.

The above paradigm fits into the familiar problem of multilevel security, and at first glance may be tackled with any hierarchical KA scheme. It may seem comparable to the access control in a corporation (or government department), where data are usually classified into only a few classes, say "unclassified" $\prec$ "confidential" $\prec$ "secret" $\prec$ "top-secret". The corporation example is relatively simple, as there are merely four classes, and all the data of the same clearance are protected with the same class key. In the considered BSN, however, the record of each case should be protected with a *distinct* encryption key, and a large hospital may accommodate thousands of patients. Instead of how to guard the BSN against attacks, the real challenge stems from how to efficiently organize the encryption keys to ensure privacy concerning a large and continuously growing number of cases. Derivatives of the exponentiation-based Akl-Taylor KA scheme [3], typically involving a 1-affects-n problem, may not apply to a BSN, since there are an overwhelming and growing number of classes, and thus the exponentiations may be extremely difficult to manage. On the other hand, modern schemes based on a reference table will involve heavy cost for public storage, and the maintenance of a voluminous reference table will be error-prone, as health practitioners may have little technical computing expertise [13]. We refer readers interested in exponentiation-based and reference-table-based KA schemes to [2] for technical details. Herein, a preferable solution is expected to be self-configuring and self-managing with little or no user input. That is, an effective system that works out of the box is desired.

Without loss of generality, we assume the following partial-order hierarchy in the e-Health system. Patients monitored by the BSN are directly taken care of (i.e., treated) by attending doctors, who are mostly interns and sometimes residents. An intern is supervised by a resident, who is in turn supervised by a physician. At the top of the medical hierarchy is the senior physician who supervises the physicians. Regarding the access rights to a patient's record, the hierarchy is "intern" $\prec$ "resident" $\prec$ "physician" $\prec$ "senior physician". There may be quite a few senior physicians in the hospital, in charge of different (i.e., non-overlapping) departments respectively. As usually one patient is attended by only one doctor (an intern or a resident), and any doctor (an intern, a resident, or a physician) is only directly supervised by one superior (a resident, a physician, or a senior physician, respectively), a favorable KA solution to the medical hierarchy could be based on a tree-like structure (recall Section 1.1), where Sandhu's KA scheme [1] can be employed.

In this scenario, the physiological data collected by sensors attached to a patient are encrypted and then sent to the central database, involving the partial-order hierarchy illustrated in Fig. 2. Assume the senior physician in a medical department is assigned a key K_{sp}, and there is a pseudo-random function F for key derivation, which maps a secret key k of a specified length and a binary string x of arbitrary length to $F_k(x)$ of the same length with k. Then the senior physician can derive the key of a subordinate physician by $K_p = F_{K_{sp}}(ID_p)$, where ID_p is the identifier of the physician. Note that in the KA scheme, only K_{sp} can be chosen randomly (known as "information-theoretic"), while other keys like K_p are derived with F (known as "computational"). Similarly, a physician can derive the key of a subordinate resident by $K_r = F_{K_p}(ID_r)$, where ID_r is the identifier of the resident. Next, a resident can derive the access key of a subordinate intern by $K_i = F_{K_r}(ID_i)$ where ID_i is the identifier of the intern, and the encryption key of the sensors attached to a patient attended by the resident (if any) according to $K_{c(r)} = F_{K_r}(ID_c)$ where ID_c is the case identifier of the patient. Last, an intern can derive the encryption key of the sensors attached to an attended patient with the case identifier ID_c following $K_{c(i)} = F_{K_i}(ID_c)$.

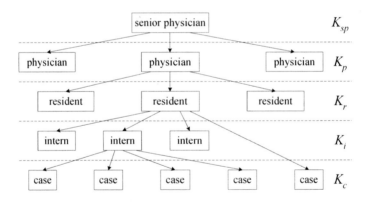

Fig. 2. The proposed key assignment for the medical hierarchy in a certain hospital department, where physiological data collected from a body sensor network (BSN) are encrypted before being sent to a central database

The above scheme is depicted in Fig. 2. Each doctor in the hierarchy is assigned a smart device, where his or her access key (typically computed from the superior's key) is embedded. The key derivation can be easily implemented with the device which only takes as input certain identifiers. Once a patient is hospitalized, he or she is attached with sensors preloaded with the corresponding encryption key K_c (either $K_{c(r)}$ or $K_{c(i)}$). Importantly, the addition of a new case, hence the addition of a new K_c (or other keys like K_i), does not affect any existent keys. This is an advantage over the Akl-Taylor style hierarchical KA [2], where adding a new class tends to be painful. When a doctor needs to access his or her patient's record, he or she inputs the patient's case identifier ID_c (e.g., via RFID) and the device derives the access key K_c; if the doctor is not the patient's attending doctor, additional identifier(s) of his or her corresponding subordinate(s) can be input manually or automatically.

This paradigm can be improved to have better privacy protection by instantiating all the class keys with time-bound session keys. It can be done by employing the afore-mentioned structure $k_{i,t} = H(K_i, w_t)$, where the time-variant instance secret w_t may be computed from dual hash chains [2]. For a doctor, the access period $t_1 \leq t \leq t_2$ for $k_{i,t}$ can be constrained according to his or her tenure (i.e., term of service in the hospital). For a sensor, irrespective of how long the attaching patient may be hospitalized, the time bounds can simply be specified according to the sensor's lifetime estimated from its battery sustainment. In a BSN, the smart device of a doctor or the sensors attached to a patient do not necessarily need to be tamper-resistant. This is due to the attended (also legally protected) nature of BSN, and health practitioners may not have the commercial incentive to tamper with the time-bound hierarchical KA system. Last, note the one-key-per-record policy already contributes significantly to security and privacy, while the adopted KA system by no means hinders healthcare workers from on-the-spot checks of an patient in case of emergency.

4   Case Study Two: Enhancing Multicast Security

Key management is an important aspect of WSN security [8–10]. It is recently understood that key management schemes offering group or multicast abilities are much more compatible with industry trends; based on the new tendency in IEEE 802.15.4b and the ZigBee Enhanced standard, it is envisioned that a purely random or pairwise key management scheme would be economically unviable [10]. Unfortunately, existent multicast key management schemes (also called rekey schemes), be they stateful (represented by [15]) or stateless (represented by [16]), are shown [17] to be seriously challenged by the threats in a WSN: an outside active adversary who compromises a single node could obtain not only the current multicast key but also some or all past keys, as well as future keys if detection and revocation are not promptly taken. Particularly, detection of node compromise is a nontrivial task. Therefore, even the compromise of a single node at an arbitrary time may jeopardize the *entire* multicast communication. This is highly counterintuitive: the impact of just a single node compromise may not be even worse, as it already reaches the worst case. In-depth analysis on rekey security is beyond the scope of this paper but is referred to [15–17].

We aim at improving multicast security based on purely time-bound KA, i.e., the security setting considered in Section I-B reduces to only one universal class comprising all sensor nodes. Hence, instead of following traditional and mainstream rekey schemes [15, 16] driven by group membership changes, we secure multicast traffic with time-dependent session keys, thus featuring scheduled, spontaneous, and non-interactive key expiration. In a dynamic WSN where new nodes are added while old nodes perish, different nodes have different life cycles. Consider a certain node entitled to the multicast session key $k(t)$ (simplified from the previous form of $k_{i,t}$, as the partial-order hierarchy is absent) for $t \in [t_1 \cdots t_2] \subset [0 \cdots z]$, where the lower and upper time bounds can be determined based on its scheduled deployment time (right before t_1) and the estimated end of battery life (t_2 at the most). The node is only preloaded with the private primitive $I(t_1, t_2)$. As a result, even if it is later captured, the attacker cannot gain more session keys beyond the pre-specified time scope $[t_1 \cdots t_2]$. Furthermore, if the adopted algorithm has the nice feature of memory deallocation to timely erase used cryptographic materials, the attacker can barely reveal secret keys between t_1 and the time she compromises the node.

Considering the implementation constraints for low-cost sensor nodes, an affordable time-bound multicast KA scheme should be as cost-efficient as possible. In existent schemes [2], an instance secret w_t based on an algebraic tool known as the Lucas sequence seems competent for a time-bound session key; it favorably impedes collusion attacks even in the absence of tamper-resistant hardware. However, the Lucas sequence computation is prohibitive for sensor nodes of low processing profile. On the other hand, utilizing the computation-efficient technique of the afore-mentioned dual hash chains to generate multicast session keys requires nodes be protected by tamper-resistant casing; otherwise, the compromise of a node with $I(t_1, t_2)$ and another node with $I(t_3, t_4)$ is equivalent to the compromise of every session key $k(t)$ for $t_1 \leq t \leq t_4$, where t_2 can be far less than t_3. The tamper-resistant prerequisite is cost-expensive or even unrealistic for the current generation of sensor nodes. (We notice, however, dual hash chains are exactly adopted in [12].) In a nutshell, a sensible solution that neither incurs heavy computational overhead nor asks for tamper-resistant protection is needed. Our scheme proposed below is a variant of Briscoe's MARKS [18].

Assume there is a one-way hash function H whose output is of size $2|k(t)|$. For example, if the standard cipher AES-128 is employed for encrypting the multicast traffic, a good choice for H is SHA-256. For brevity, assume the maximum time index is $z = 2^h - 1$, where h is an integer. Then we can build a virtual binary "tree of computational secrets" of height h employing $H(\cdot) = H_L(\cdot) \| H_R(\cdot)$, where H_L and H_R are the left and right halves of H, respectively (thus $|H_L| = |H_R| = |k(t)|$). The 2^h leaf nodes of the binary tree are associated with the $z + 1$ session keys for securing the multicast. As depicted in Fig. 3, the CA randomly selects from a key space the seed secret s_1 for the root node, and applies H for z times, to each secret s_i ($1 \leq i \leq z$) in the tree respectively. Hence every secret s_i for $2 \leq i \leq 2z + 1$ is computational. Then the CA assigns each leaf node secret to a session key according to $k(t) = s_{t+z+1}$ for $0 \leq t \leq z$.

Upon registration, a sensor node entitled to time period $[t_1 \cdots t_2]$ is preloaded with the private primitive $I(t_1, t_2)$ of size $\mathcal{O}(\log z)$. The private primitive consists of all and only the secrets closest to the root node in the tree that exactly enable computation of the authorized range of session keys. In [18], Briscoe presented a very simple but efficient algorithm for identifying such a minimum set of secrets. For example in Fig. 3, a node entitled to $k(t)$ for $1 \leq t \leq 8$ is assigned with

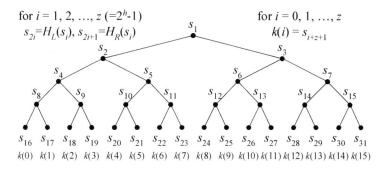

Fig. 3. A "tree of computational secrets" of height $h = 4$ generated by a one-way hash function H covering a system lifetime starting from 0 and ending at $z = 2^h - 1 = 15$. H_L and H_R are the left and right halves of H, respectively.

$I(1,8) = \{s_{17}, s_9, s_5, s_{24}\}$. The leaf node secrets s_{17} and s_{24} are directly mapped to $k(1)$ and $k(8)$, respectively. By applying H to the seed secret s_9, the sensor node can derive $k(2)$ and $k(3)$. By applying H three times, the sensor node can derive $k(4)$ to $k(7)$ from s_5. A sensor node only needs to derive a session key $k(t)$ when necessary (usually right before time t). Implementation details for the multicast client (herein the sensor node) like smart memory deallocation and storage/processing tradeoff can be found in [18].

One may be concerned with the computation load for the CA to generate the entire tree. Actually, the proposed scheme differs slightly from MARKS in the way the tree is generated. Instead of employing any one-to-one (typically the rotary) function as in [18], we choose a "size-doubling" one-way hash function $H(\cdot) = H_L(\cdot) \| H_R(\cdot)$, where no covert channel (as concerned in [18]) should arise. This facilitates the tree generation, which can be efficiently implemented with a standard programming language. For example, even if each time unit represents only one minute (hence the sensor nodes only need loose time synchronization) and the network lifetime is as long as 16 years, it is enough to specify $h = 23$. We tested the scheme with C on an ordinary Lenovo ThinkPad T61 laptop powered by the free download edition of Mandriva Linux 2009.1 i586. In our experiment, assuming each $k(t), 0 \leq t \leq z$ is 128-bit, generation of the full binary tree invoked $z = 2^h - 1 = 8,388,607$ times of the one-way hash function SHA-256, but the overall running time turned out to be only 10.1 seconds.

Compared with mainstream multicast key management schemes [15, 16], adopting a time-bound approach has the distinct benefit of no interaction between a user and the CA (recall Section 1.2), completely avoiding rekey communication overhead. This also implies no dependence on a reliable multicast channel for rekeying, as well as intrinsic immunity to eavesdropping. In the context of a WSN, the proposed scheme involving only efficient processing but no tamper-resistant requirement lends itself to improved multicast security, as the capture at time t_c of a node preloaded with $I(t_1, t_2)$ may not affect multicast communications either before t_c or after t_2. Besides memory deallocation for timely erasing used secrets, if upon detection of low power the sensor nodes have the intelligence to erase unused secrets, additional security against key exposure can be achieved. In a nutshell, even if compromise of low-cost sensor nodes may be unavoidable, time-bound multicast KA translates into impact containment. The philosophy is not to eliminate attacks (which is unrealistic), but to minimize the breakage.

Finally, the above scheme can be extended to a more general case, where a sensor node is authorized to an *arbitrary* set of time slots. Let T be a random combination of any t non-overlapping periods of time: $\mathsf{T} = \cup_{i=1}^{t}[t_{i_1} \cdots t_{i_2}]$, where $t_{i_1} \leq t_{i_2}$ for $1 \leq i \leq \mathsf{t}$, and $t_{i_2} < t_{(i+1)_1}$ for $1 \leq i \leq \mathsf{t} - 1$. (The afore-discussed $I(t_1, t_2)$ is just a special case where $\mathsf{t} = 1$, i.e., T is consecutive.) Although as a whole T appears intermittent, a sensor node still only needs to be preloaded with the private primitive $I(\mathsf{T})$ in order to access exactly any $k(t)$ for $t \in \mathsf{T} \subseteq [0 \cdots z]$. Such a scenario regarding an arbitrarily specified set of time slots caters to certain WSN applications. For example, sensor nodes may be deployed for monitoring the tourism traffic and/or ecological environment at a local scenery spot, but not in off-season. That is, to reduce the maintenance expense, the nodes are scheduled for hibernation in off-season, and the monitoring is only in operation during peak season. Another example is school campus monitoring, which is unnecessary in summer and winter vacations. These applications necessitate time-based KA concerning an arbitrary (i.e., intermittent) set of time slots.

The data structure in Fig. 3 can still accommodate the generation of session keys even with respect to an arbitrary set of time slots T. For example, assume $\mathsf{t} = 3$ and $\mathsf{T} = \{2, 3, 8 \cdots 11, 14\}$. A sensor node only needs to be preloaded with $I(\mathsf{T}) = \{s_9, s_6, s_{30}\}$ in Fig. 3 to derive $k(2)$, $k(3)$, $k(8)$ to $k(11)$, and $k(14)$. This bears much similarity to the broadcast encryption problem following the Subset-Cover framework, particularly, the Complete Subtree Method [16], though both the scenario (revocation of stateless receivers for digital content protection) and the meaning of the employed data structure (a tree of information-theoretic keys shared by a large number of potential receivers) there are completely different. Following the results in [16], the size of the private primitive $I(\mathsf{T})$ assigned to a sensor node is increased from $\mathcal{O}(\log z)$ to $\mathcal{O}(r \log \frac{z}{r})$, where $r = |[0 \cdots z] \setminus \mathsf{T}| = z + 1 - |\mathsf{T}|$. In case t in T is small, $|I(\mathsf{T})|$ simply reduces to $\mathcal{O}(\mathsf{t} \log z)$. Therefore, adopting the tree depicted in Fig. 3 is promising for multicast KA in sensor networks, even if the upper application has an unusual demand for intermittent monitoring.

5   Conclusion

In this paper we addressed the problem of time-bound hierarchical key assignment, and explored possible applications of the technique in the context of wireless sensor network security. Due to cost considerations, some existent time-bound hierarchical KA schemes may not be readily applicable to the current generation of sensor nodes, which may neither afford heavy computations nor have tamper-resistant casing. More research efforts are needed to develop efficient and practical KA solutions. Nevertheless, the technique is still feasible and preferable in a few typical applications. For example, time-bound hierarchical KA is valuable for application scenarios where the contextual information is available for sensor nodes. The technique can be adopted in future e-Health systems for protecting patients' privacy. A related topic, post-deployment clearance evaluation based on context acquisition, may be a prospective direction for future research. For another example, sensor network key management schemes that offer multicast abilities are more compatible with industry trends, and time-bound KA is an approach to improving multicast security with breakage alleviation. Even if the group oriented upper application requires intermittent monitoring, the technique is still promising for impact containment under node compromise.

Acknowledgement. This work was supported by the Singapore A∗STAR project SEDS-0721330047 and by the National Natural Science Foundation of China under Grant 60970138.

References

1. Sandhu, R.S.: Cryptographic implementation of a tree hierarchy for access control. Information Processing Letters 27, 95–98 (1988)
2. Zhu, W.T., Deng, R.H., Zhou, J., Bao, F.: Time-bound hierarchical key assignment: An overview. IEICE Transactions on Information and Systems E93-D, 1044–1052 (2010)
3. Akl, S.G., Taylor, P.D.: Cryptographic solution to a problem of access control in a hierarchy. ACM Transactions on Computer Systems 1, 239–248 (1983)
4. Shehab, M., Bertino, E., Ghafoor, A.: Efficient hierarchical key generation and key diffusion for sensor networks. In: Proc. 2nd Annual IEEE Communications Society Conference on Sensor and Ad Hoc Communications and Networks (SECON 2005), pp. 76–84 (2005)
5. Zhu, S., Setia, S., Jajodia, S.: LEAP+: Efficient security mechanisms for large-scale distributed sensor networks. ACM Transactions on Sensor Networks 2, 500–528 (2006)
6. Zhang, Y., Liu, W., Lou, W., Fang, Y.: Location-based compromise-tolerant security mechanisms for wireless sensor networks. IEEE Journal on Selected Areas in Communications 24, 247–260 (2006)
7. Tubaishat, M., Yin, J., Panja, B., Madria, S.: A secure hierarchical model for sensor network. ACM SIGMOD Record 33, 7–13 (2004)
8. Chen, X., Makki, K., Yen, K., Pissinou, N.: Sensor network security: A survey. IEEE Communications Surveys & Tutorials 11, 52–73 (2009)
9. Li, Z., Gong, G.: A survey on security in wireless sensor networks. Technical Report, University of Waterloo, CACR 2008-20 (October 2008)
10. Lee, J.C., Leung, V., Wong, K.H., Cao, J., Chan, H.: Key management issues in wireless sensor networks: Current proposals and future developments. IEEE Wireless Communications 14, 76–84 (2007)
11. Sorniotti, A., Molva, R., Gomez, L.: Efficient access control for wireless sensor data. In: Proc. 19th IEEE International Symposium on Personal, Indoor and Mobile Radio Communications (PIMRC 2008), pp. 1–5 (2008)

12. Jiang, Y., Lin, C., Shi, M., Shen, X.: Self-healing group key distribution with time-limited node revocation for wireless sensor networks. Ad Hoc Networks 5, 14–23 (2007)

13. Lupu, E., Dulay, N., Sloman, M., Sventek, J., Heeps, S., Strowes, S., Twidle, K., Keoh, S.-L., Schaeffer-Filho, A.: AMUSE: autonomic management of ubiquitous e-Health systems. Concurrency and Computation: Practice and Experience 20, 277–295 (2008)

14. Leavitt, N.: Researchers fight to keep implanted medical devices safe from hackers. Computer 43, 11–14 (2010)

15. Wong, C.K., Gouda, M., Lam, S.S.: Secure group communications using key graphs. IEEE/ACM Transactions on Networking 8, 16–30 (2000)

16. Naor, D., Naor, M., Lotspiech, J.: Revocation and Tracing Schemes for Stateless Receivers. In: Kilian, J. (ed.) CRYPTO 2001. LNCS, vol. 2139, pp. 41–62. Springer, Heidelberg (2001)

17. Xu, S.: On the security of group communication schemes. Journal of Computer Security 15, 129–169 (2007)

18. Briscoe, B.: MARKS: Zero Side Effect Multicast Key Management Using Arbitrarily Revealed Key Sequences. In: Rizzo, L., Fdida, S. (eds.) NGC 1999. LNCS, vol. 1736, pp. 301–320. Springer, Heidelberg (1999)

A Unified Security Framework for Multi-domain Wireless Mesh Networks

Ze Wang[1, *], Maode Ma[2], Wenju Liu[1], and Xixi Wei[1]

[1] School of Comp. Science & Software,
Tianjin Polytechnic University, Tianjin, China
{wangze,liuwj,weixx}@tjpu.edu.cn
[2] School of EEE., Nanyang Technological University, Singapore
emdma@ntu.edu.sg

Abstract. The research issues of large scale wireless mesh networks (WMNs) have attracted increasing attention due to the excellent properties of WMNs. Although some proposals for WMN security framework with different security aspects have been put forward recently, it is a challenging issue of employing uniform public key cryptography to maintain trust relationships flexibly among domains and to achieve key-escrow-free anonymous access control. In this paper, a unified security framework (USF) for multi-domain wireless mesh networks is proposed, which unifies id-based encryption and certificateless signature in a single public key cryptography context. Trust relationship between different domains and anonymous access control of wireless clients can be realized by employing of cryptography operations on bilinear groups. To achieve perfect forward secrecy and attack-resilience, trust domain construction methods and authentication protocols are devised within the security framework without key escrow.

Keywords: Wireless mesh networks, security, identity-based cryptography, certificateless signature.

1   Introduction

Security issues inherent in Wireless mesh network (WMN) need be considered because of the intrinsically open and distributed nature. Be aware of the embarrassing situation of WMN security, state-of-the-art schemes [1-4] addressing different WMN security issues have been devised sophisticatedly. Special signature methods have been utilized in [1,2] to achieve security objectives, wherein conventional public key signature has been employed to build trust relationships. To mitigate complex conventional public key certificates management, authors in [3,4] have proposed WMN security architectures based on id-based cryptography (IBC) [5].

The proposal in [3] has attempted to apply IBC into the WMN security scheme while it has adopted a credit-card-based model for the inter-domain authentication. Focusing on anonymity, IBC and blind signature mechanism have been combined in

---

* Corrresponding author.

S. Qing et al. (Eds.): ICICS 2011, LNCS 7043, pp. 319–329, 2011.
© Springer-Verlag Berlin Heidelberg 2011

one security architecture to achieve anonymity and traceability in [4]. Although IBC is promising with an attractive feature of public key self authenticity, it suffers from private key escrow problem. As a result, it is still a challenging issue of employing uniform public key cryptography without key escrow problem for flexible maintenance of domain trust relationships and anonymous access control.

To overcome the shortcomings of the existing solutions, in this paper, we propose to build a security framework in a unified cryptography context without key escrow while possessing anonymous and attack-resilient features. To obviate all the private keys of clients escrowing in a centralized private key generator (PKG), we adopt certificateless public key cryptography (CL-PKC) [6] to avoid possible keys leakage. We propose a unified security framework (USF) for multi-domain wireless mesh networks, which unifies IBC and CL-PKC in a single cryptography context where both IBC and CL-PKC master keys are generated with the same public cryptology parameters. Trust domain construction methods and anonymous authentication protocols with perfect forward secrecy are devised within the key-escrow-free framework to achieve attack-resilience.

The remainder of this paper is organized as follows. In Section 2, the system models are described. In Section 3, the details of the security framework are presented. In Section 4, the security analysis of our scheme is performed. Performance comparison is shown in Section 5. The paper is concluded with a summary in Section 6.

2   System Models

2.1   Network Model

Large scale WMNs are composed of a great number of WMN domains with different scales. As the fundamental components in a WMN, mesh routers have much more powerful computation and communication capacities than those of mesh clients. Mesh clients, which can choose a mesh router to access the Internet, are mobile nodes served by the networks. The traffics from mesh clients are mainly forwarded through mesh routers in WMN, which yields a natural design to control clients' access directly by a mesh router. In the WMN under the study, to show compatibility of the proposed solution, routing scheme is not specified and the clients may communicate with mesh routers through either a single hop or a multi-hop link.

2.2   Trust Model

A trust domain of a WMN covers the same area as a physical domain and includes all the member nodes in it. The domain operator (DO) is responsible for the management of the wireless clients and routers in the domain. In the deployment of the trust domain, a mesh router has to register with the domain operator and build secure associations with it and other neighbor mesh routers. Each mesh client has to first register with the domain operator which, in turn, issues a user access ticket (UAT) to the client. The entire WMN is composed of numerous such trust domains, among which the trust relationships may exist or not exist between each of two peers. An interdomain authentication is a necessary authentication process for a mesh client to obtain access to the mesh router belonging to a foreign domain of the client. Trust relationships among domains should be built to approve interdomain access requests.

A trusted third party (TTP) used to sponsor different trust domains registration should be built in the security framework, so as to establish trust relationships among trust domains. TTP generates global public parameters in the form of global access token (GAT), which should be easily obtained by any nodes in the network. Each domain operator has to first deliver the domain public parameters to the TTP which, in turn, issues a domain access token (DAT) to the operator. A trust domain list is used, which is a list of DATs stored by a DO, to record the domains, which the DO should trust. Considering domain A and domain B in a WMN, a domain operator DO_A can claim to trust domain B by insertion of DAT of DO_B into its local trust domain list. Vice versa, DO_B inserts DAT of DO_A into its local trust domain list to trust domain A. The easy yet flexible way of trust construction allows unidirectional or bidirectional trust relationship between peer domains.

The above trust model fits in well with the deployment structure of Wireless Internet Service Providers (WISPs) providing Internet access via WMNs.

2.3   Cryptographic Background

Let q be a large prime. Let G_1 and G_2 be an additive group and a multiplicative group, respectively, of the same prime order q. Bilinear map is denoted by $e: G_1 \times G_1 \rightarrow G_2$. Let $H_1 : \{0,1\}^* \rightarrow G_1^*, H_2 : \{0,1\}^* \rightarrow Z_q^*$ and $H_3 : G_1^* \rightarrow \{0,1\}^n$ be three secure cryptographic hash functions. A trust authority chooses a random number $s \in Z_q^*$ and a generator P of G_1. It sets the system master public key $P_{pub} = sP$, master secret key as s and publishes $\{q, G_1, G_2, e, P, P_{pub} H_1, H_2, H_3\}$. The user ID chooses a random number $x_{ID} \in Z_q^*$ and sets x_{ID} as his secret value. Let $f(ID)$ denote a function that maps ID and other corresponding important information into an element in G_1^*. We can get certificateless public key as $x_{ID}P, f(ID)$ and private key as $x_{ID}, sf(ID)$ for certificatleless signature. Meanwhile, we can extract id-based public key $f(ID)$ and private key $sf(ID)$ for id-based encryption defined as in [7].

The second certifcateless signature and verification method in [8] is modified to fit in our security scheme, which is shown as follows.

Certificateless-Sign: For a message m, the user ID computes the signature $\sigma = (u,v,W)$ where:

$u = H_2(m \| f(ID) \| x_{ID}P \| r_1 P \| e(P,P)^{r_2})$ for random numbers $r_1, r_2 \in Z_q^*$ which are chosen by user ID. $v = r_1 - ux_{ID} \pmod q$, $W = r_2 P - usf(ID)$.

Certificateless-Verify: Given a message and signature pair $(m, \sigma = (u, v, W))$ and user ID's public key $x_{ID}P, f(ID)$, anyone can check whether $u = H_2(m \| f(ID) \| x_{ID}P \| vP + ux_{ID}P \| e(W,P)e(f(ID), P_{pub})^u)$. If the equation holds, results *true*. Otherwise, results *false*.

The common notation in our scheme are listed as follows.

- **IDD_i, ID_j, IDR_k:** The unique identity of a trusted domain i, a wireless client j, and a mesh router k, respectively.
- **$\|$:** concatenation symbol.
- **PK_x, SK_x:** The certificateless public key and private key for entity x.
- **$Sig_x(m)$:** The certificateless signature on a message m using the signer x's certificateless private key.
- **$Ver_x(\sigma)$:** The verification process of the above signature using the signer x's certificateless public key, which returns *true* or *false*.
- **$Enc_x(m)$:** The id-based encryption to a message m using the entity x's id-based public key.
- **$Dec_x(c)$:** The id-based decryption to a cipher text c using the entity x's id-based private key.
- **$H_{MIC}(m)$:** A hash function such as SHA-1.
- **$H_{KD}(m)$:** A hash function for symmetric key generation, usually implemented by one to several rounds of hash operations on a message m.

3   Proposed Security Framework

The essential components of the proposed framework are intradomain authentication and interdomain authentication protocols based on trust among domains. The prerequisite to execution of the authentication protocols is the initialization of the TTP and DOs at the very beginning followed by the construction of trust relationships and registration of intradomain wireless nodes. In the following, we will describe the initialization, registration and authentication protocols in detail, together with the master key generation, session key agreement, and confidential communications that may take place during the execution of these protocols.

3.1   Trust Domain Initialization

The trust domains should be initialized before wireless clients gain the opportunities of access by registration on the operator of certain domain. At the very beginning, a trusted third party *TTP* should be constructed to build authenticity of trust domain parameters. *TTP* generates global parameters and the global public access token *GAT* as follows:

$$GAT = global - params \,\|\, \Gamma \tilde{H}_1(global - params)$$
$$global - params = \{\tilde{q}, \tilde{G}_1, \tilde{G}_2, \tilde{e}, \tilde{P}, \tilde{P}_{pub}, \tilde{H}_1, \tilde{H}_2, \tilde{H}_3\}$$

The global secret $\Gamma \in Z_{\tilde{q}}^*$ is random selected by TTP. The *GAT*, which contains global public parameters, should be distributed freely to each node in the WMNs. However, *GAT* is not an essential element if a wireless client is expected to keep inside the master domain.

TTP generates the public domain cryptography parameters $(q,G_1,G_2,e,P,H_1,H_2,H_3)$ and domain operator DO_i picks a random $s_i \in Z_q^*$ as the domain secret whereby to compute a domain public key as $P_{pub} = s_i P$.

Next DO_i registers its domain public parameters *domain-params* to *TTP*, whereby *GAT* and domain access token *DAT* are returned. The domain access token *DAT* is defined as follows:

$$DAT = domain - params \parallel \Gamma \tilde{H}_1 (domain - params)$$
$$domain - params = \{IDD_i, Exp_i, q, G_1, G_2, e, P, P_{pub}, H_1, H_2, H_3\}$$

IDD_i is the global unique identity of domain i provided by the TTP. Exp_i is the expiration time of DAT for domain i. If $e(\Gamma \tilde{H}_1 (domain - params), \tilde{P}) = e(domain - params, \tilde{P}_{pub})$ holds, it is the authenticity evidence of *domain-params*. *DAT* is the unique representation of a domain. *DO* should determine whether to insert *DAT* of another domain B into its local trust domain list in order to approve the access requests from the clients belonging to domain B. Thus, registered domains will build their trust relationships to enable interdomain access.

3.2   Intradomain Registration

After the domain is initialized, DO takes the responsibility of domain security management. A wireless client must register to DO through a secure link for future network access. Registration steps are as follows.

1. $CL \rightarrow DO$: *SSN, credentials*, etc.
2. $DO \rightarrow CL$: *GAT, DAT*, ID_j, exp_j, c_j
3. $CL \rightarrow DO$: $x_j P$, $f(ID_j)$
4. $DO \rightarrow CL$: $s_i f(ID_j)$, *UAT*

A wireless client CL_j supplies personal information such as social security number (SSN), date of birth, telephone number and other identity credentials in message 1 to a domain operator DO_i. After examining the credentials, DO_i generates a unique identity ID_j, expiration time exp_j and a service contract c_j and sends them together with *GAT* in message 2 to CL_j. After approving the service contract and validating *DAT* through *GAT*, CL_j chooses a random number $x_j \in Z_q^*$, calculates $x_j P$ and $f(ID_j) = H_1(IDD_i \parallel H_1(ID_j) \parallel x_j P \parallel exp_j \parallel c_j)$. CL_j sends $PK_j = (x_j P, f(ID_j))$ in message 3 to DO_i. In turn, DO_i issues an user access ticket *UAT* and parital secret $s_i f(ID_j)$ in message 4 to CL_j where $UAT = \{IDD_i, H_1(ID_j), exp_j, c_j, PK_j\}$.

CL_j checks whether $e(f(ID_j), P_{pub}) = e(s_i f(ID_j), P)$ and stores ID_j, certificateless private key $SK_j = (x_j, s_i f(ID_j))$ and *UAT*. DO_i will save ID_j, *UAT* and identity credentials as a user record. As a proof of CL_j's legality, *UAT* contains the certificateless public key and the master domain identity IDD_i. To implement anonymous access control, CL_j's identity ID_j is not included in *UAT*. Validity of *UAT* is restricted by the field exp_j so that CL_j must renew registration for a new valid *UAT* when the old one expired. Through registration, CL_j gets the certificateless public key $(x_j P, f(ID_j))$ and private key $(x_j, s_i f(ID_j))$, from which the id-based public key $f(ID_j)$ and private key $s_i f(ID_j)$ can be naturally extracted. CL_j must keep x_j secret to ensure the confidentiality of certificateless private key to DO_i.

For mesh routers, similar registration steps are as follows.

1. $MR \rightarrow DO$: *MAC, SN, credentials*, etc.
2. $DO \rightarrow MR$: *GAT, DAT, IDR_k, exp_j*
3. $MR \rightarrow DO$: $x_k P$, $g(IDR_k)$
4. $DO \rightarrow MR$: $s_i g(IDR_k)$, *RAT*

Different from a mesh client, a mesh router should supply the MAC address, the sequence number (SN), and other corresponding credentials. At the end of the registration, a mesh router obtains certificateless private key $(x_k, s_i g(IDR_k))$ and router access ticket (RAT) as follows:

$$RAT = \{ IDD_i \parallel IDR_k, exp_k, PK_k \}$$
$$PK_k = (x_k P, g(IDR_k))$$
$$g(IDR_k) = H_1(IDD_i \parallel IDR_k \parallel x_k P \parallel exp_k)$$

DO allocates a unique identity IDR_k for the mesh router and sets expiration time in exp_k. The length of IDR_k must be different from that of $H_1(ID_i)$ to distinguish UAT and RAT. Certifcateless public key PK_k and id-based public key $g(IDR_k)$ are generated in a similar way but with a different function $g(ID)$. The identity of a mesh router is explicitly given in *RAT* since a client would be reluctant to access via an anonymous mesh router.

3.3   Intradomain Authentication Protocols

A registered client may access the network after authentication with a mesh router belonging to the same master domain. When a wireless client moves into the coverage of a mesh router, the intradomain authentication could be carried out to complete bidirectional authentication and session key agreement between them.

The intradomain authentication protocol between a CL and a MR is described as follows.

1. $MR \rightarrow *$:   *RAT*
2. $CL \rightarrow MR$: $UAT, aP, N_1, Sig_{CL}(UAT \parallel aP \parallel N_1)$
3. $MR \rightarrow CL$: $RAT, bP, N_2, Sig_{MR}(RAT \parallel aP \parallel bP \parallel N_1 \parallel N_2), H_{MIC}(abP \parallel N_1 \parallel N_2 \parallel bP)$
4. $CL \rightarrow MR$: $H_{MIC}(abP \parallel N_2 \parallel N_1 \parallel aP)$

The MR periodically broadcasts a beacon in message 1 to announce its presence. The beacon should include *RAT*. Upon receiving message 1, a client *CL* may first check the IDD_i field in the *RAT* to confirm he is within the scope of a master domain router and then justify the legality of the *RAT* by computing $g(IDR_k)$ and examining its exp_k field. If tests passed, *CL* selects random numbers $a, N_1 \in Z_q^*$, computes key negotiation factor aP and sends *UAT, aP, N_1* and certificateless signature via message 2. Upon receipt of message 2, *MR* first justifies the legality of *UAT* and then verifies the signature. In case of passed, *MR* selects random numbers $b, N_2 \in Z_q^*$, computes bP, *abP* and calculates signature and message integration code (MIC) $H_{MIC}(abP\|N_1\|N_2\|bP)$ to form and send message 3. When the message 3 arrives, *CL* computes *abP* with obtained *bP* and secret number *a* after the verification to the signature succeeded. *CL* confirms the session key by checking $MIC = H_{MIC}(abP \| N_1 \| N_2 \| bP)$, then calculates session key $K_s = H_{KD}(abP \| N_1 \| N_2)$ and stores it for future secure communication. Finally, *CL* calculates and sends $MIC = H_{MIC}(abP \| N_2 \| N_1 \| aP)$ to *MR*. Upon receipt of message 4, *MR* confirms the session key through *MIC* and computes session key K_s with the knowledge of *aP* and secret number *b*.

After the above process of authentication protocol, both sides have completed the bidirectional authentication and session key agreement. Compared to ARSA [3], in our scheme a wireless client needs not to launch an interdomain protocol before intra-domain access. The localized intradomain authentication process is carried out without participation of a trust authority e. g. *DO* or authentication server (AS) in comparison to EAP-TLS protocol of 802.11i [9].

For registered mesh clients in a certain domain, owning *DAT*, *UAT* and corresponding keys enables authentication between any neighbor peers. Suppose CL_1 and CL_2 are two adjacent wireless clients. They can share a common session key $K = e(f(ID_{CL_2}), s_i f(ID_{CL_1})) = e(f(ID_{CL_1}), s_i f(ID_{CL_2}))$ with solely the knowledge of each other's public key just as [3]. However, we prefer to carry out session key negotiation process to mitigate possible leakage problem of master private keys. The authentication protocol between adjacent clients is as followed:

1. $CL_1 \rightarrow CL_2$: $UAT_1, aP, N_1, Sig_{CL_1}(UAT_1 \| aP \| N_1)$
2. $CL_2 \rightarrow CL_1$: $UAT_2, bP, N_2, Sig_{CL_2}(UAT_2 \| aP \| bP \| N_1 \| N_2), H_{MIC}(abP \| N_1 \| N_2 \| bP)$
3. $CL_1 \rightarrow CL_2$: $H_{MIC}(abP \| N_2 \| N_1 \| aP)$

During the authentication process, the adjacent clients verify the certificateless signatures and build the session key $K_s = H_{KD}(abP \| N_1 \| N_2)$ just like the process between *CL* and *MR*. It should be noted that the authentication initiator needs to launch an interdomain authentication at first when the target client doesn't belong to the same domain.

3.4   Interdomain Authentication Protocol

Wireless clients may access a foreign domain which trusts their master domain by finishing an interdomain authentication process. When a wireless client sends an access request to a mesh router in a foreign domain, the mesh router will forward the request to *DO* of that domain for verification. The verification includes to retrieve the client's DAT_h in the trust domain list and to verify UAT_h through DAT_h. In case the verification passed, *DO* would issue a temporal user access ticket UAT_f including the hash value $H_1(ID_f)$ for a unique temporal idenity ID_f to the client. The field c_j in UAT_f should indicate temporality of the ticket. Holding a valid temporal ticket, mesh client may access through other mesh routers in that domain by only finishing an intrado-main authentication process.

Let IDD_h denotes the master domain identity and IDD_f denotes the foreign one. UAT_h represents the access ticket in the master domain and UAT_f represents the temporal access ticket in the foreign domain. Suppose MR and DO trust each other and build a secure link between them. The interdomain authentication protocol among CL, MR and DO is showed as follows:

1. $MR \rightarrow *$: RAT
2. $CL \rightarrow MR$: $UAT_h, aP, x_fP, N_1, AUTH_{CL}$
3. $MR \rightarrow DO$: $UAT_h, aP, x_fP, N_1, AUTH_{CL}$
4. $DO \rightarrow MR$: $UAT_f, Enc_{CL}(s_ff(ID_f))$
5. $MR \rightarrow CL$: $DAT_f, UAT_f, Enc_{CL}(s_ff(ID_f)), bP, N_2, AUTH_{MR}, H_{MIC}(abP\|N_1\|N_2\|bP)$
6. $CL \rightarrow MR$: $H_{MIC}(abP\|N_2\|N_1\|aP)$

Therein, $AUTH_{CL} = Sig_{CL}(UAT_h \| aP \| x_f P \| N_1)$ and $AUTH_{MR} = Sig_{MR}(DAT_f \| UAT_f \|$ $ENC_{CL}(s_f f(ID_f)) \| aP \| bP \| N_1 \| N_2)$. The MR periodically broadcasts a beacon frame including RAT to announce its presence. Upon receipt of message 1, a client CL may first check the IDD_i field in the RAT to confirm that he is in the scope of a foreign domain router and then justify the legality of RAT through examination of $g(IDR_k)$ and exp_k. If the verification successful, CL selects random numbers a, N_1, $x_f \in Z_q^*$, computes aP, x_fP and sends UAT_h, aP, x_fP, N_1 and certificateless signature via message 2. Upon receipt of message 2, MR first checks the IDD field of UAT_h to confirm that the request is from a foreign domain client and then justify the legality of UAT_h. In case of success, MR forwards UAT_h, aP, x_fP, N_1 and the signature to DO. After retrieving DAT_h in the local trust domain list by IDD_h, DO justifies the legality of UAT_h and verifies the signature. If all success, DO generates a unique temporal indentity ID_f, calculates partial secret $s_ff(ID_f)$ and encrypts it with CL's id-based public key in the master domain before generating a temporal access ticket UAT_f including $H_1(ID_f)$. DO sends back UAT_f and the encrypted partial secret encapsulated in message 4. Upon receiving message 4, MR collects UAT_f as the proof of approval of the access request and then generates session key negotiation element bP, nonce N_2, signature to the message and MIC for session key confirmation, then sends all of them together with DAT_f in message 5. CL gets UAT_f and corresponding partial secret $s_ff(ID_f)$ by decrypting with id-based private key in the master domain h after verifing DAT_f through GAT and the certificateless signature, then checks authenticity of the partial secret by examining $e(f(ID_f), P_{pub}) = e(s_ff(ID_f), P)$. If the equation holds, CL stores DAT_f, UAT_f and corresponding private key and sends MIC in message 6. After the final session key confirmation message 6 is approved, a shared session key will be built between the peers. Holding UAT_f and corresponding certificateless private keys, the client will access any mesh router in foreign domain f after carrying out a more simplified intradomain authentication whenever necessary.

4   Security Analysis

In the proposed framework, DO plays an important role to safeguard the domain security through administration to all the wireless nodes inside the master domain and authentication to foreign domain clients. The costs for the intradomain authentication will be distributed to mesh routers to remove the bottleneck caused by a centralized authentication scheme. Another advantage for the localized authentication is that suppose DO fails in an accident, the survival parts of the domain may still work in a local area. Free of key escrow, our scheme renders survivability even when the master key of DO is exposed, which will guarantee the confidentiality of certificateless private keys and the session keys by the authentication protocols. This is a security improvement over those pure IBC based schemes. Further more, the embedded session key agreement in our authentication protocol yields the attribute of perfect forward secrecy (PFS) [10]. When all the master private keys of communication participants are exposed, the previous session keys will not be affected. In contrast to existing IBC based schemes [3,4], if the master private key of a wireless client is leaked or the master key of the trust authority is disclosed, the confidentiality of exchanged data encrypted with the session key will still be kept by our scheme.

Different from the schemes combining special signature mechanism and conventional public key signature mechanism [1,2], IBC and CL-PKC have been integrated into a single cryptography context to exempt complex management of public key certificates by our proposed scheme. Furthermore, the clients or mesh routers can have id-based encryption/decryption or certifcateless signature/verification with consistent keying material, bilinear groups and hash functions, which renders the uniformity of cryptography operations. Besides its fundamental security functionality, other security aspects of our scheme can be deduced as follows.

Identity and Location Privacy Protection: Identity and location privacy is a growing concern to wireless network users. To keep anonymity of a client, since only hash value of the identity is used to generate part of the public key in the *UAT*, from it the real identity cannot be inferred. When a wireless client accesses a foreign domain, identity will not be disclosed due to the anonymous design of *UAT* which is shown as interdomain access admission. Moreover, a wireless client cannot link any meaningful identity with a neighbor client's location. Furthermore, it is difficult to link a master domain *UAT* to a temporal *UAT* of a foreign client except for the *DO* and the mesh router firstly accessed in the corresponding domain. It should be noted that absolute anonymity and location privacy is impossible to achieve because the administrators of wireless networks would prefer to reserve the rights of tracing malicious nodes, which could be realized by retrieving the original credentials from DO's user records.

Impersonation Attack Protection: A legal wireless client cannot impersonate another legal client because a legal *UAT* is bound to a unique identity by partial private key generated by *DO*. A legal wireless client cannot impersonate a legal mesh router to phish other clients because the partial public key generation function $g(ID)$ of the *RAT* is different from the function $f(ID)$ of the *UAT*. By our scheme, the identity of a mesh router is explicitly given in the *RAT* while the identity of a client is disguised in the *UAT*. Due to its authoritative status, DO is capable of generating a legal *UAT* with the same identity as an existing legal client, but it cannot forge a legal certificatelss signature related to the existing *UAT* without the knowledge of the secret value x_j selected by the client j.

Bogus data injection attacks can be easily thwarted by the access control based on the essential authentication and session key negotiation. To deal with DoS attacks,

mesh routers can limit the frequency of authentication requests from the clients belonging to foreign domains to reduce the possibility of DoS attacks to a centralized
domain operator. From above, we claim that security functionality of our scheme is
strong even when the trust authority has been compromised. Due to the space limit, a
formal verification on our protocols are not shown in this paper.

In the Table 1, we present the security comparison of intradomain authentication
protocols among different security schemes. Other two IBC based schemes, ARSA
and SAT, don't possess key-escrow-free and perfect forward secrecy for the authentication protocol as our scheme. By consolation from a compromised operator, wireless
nodes can still perform confidential communication in a local area by both PEACE
and USF schemes. However, different from other three IBC based schemes, PEACE
must support both conventional signature cryptography operations and special signature cryptography operations based on bilinear groups.

Table 1. Security attributes comparison for intradomain authentication

Attributes	ARSA	PEACE	SAT	USF
Key-escrow-free				√
Perfect forward secrecy		√		√
Independent from PKI	√		√	√
Anonymity		√	√	√
Attack resilience	√	√	√	√

Table 2. Performance comparison for intradomain authentication

Attributes	ARSA	PEACE	SAT	USF
Message counts	2	3	4	4
Signing/verifying counts (client side)	1V	1S+2V	1S+1V	1S+1V
Signing/verifying counts (network side)	1S	1S+1V	1S+1V	1S+1V

5   Performance Analysis

In the Table 2, we present the performance comparison among different security
schemes. Among the four schemes, ARSA needs the least authentication messages
and the least computation overhead at the cost of ignoring key escrow problem. For
the scheme PEACE, the message counts are the second least. However, a client has to
perform one more verification process for validating the public key certificate of the
mesh router. As a result, the computation and communication overhead of intradomain protocols in PEACE, SAT and USF are nearly in the same level.

6 Conclusion

In this paper, we have proposed a unified security framework for multi-domain wireless mesh networks by integration of id-based encryption and certificateless signature in a unified cryptography context. Trust relationships among WMN domains can be constructed in a simple yet flexible way. The certificateless key generation scheme can be free of key escrow while anonymity of wireless clients is guaranteed.

Acknowledgements. This work was supported in part by the National Natural Science Foundation of China under grant 60970016 and Natural Science Foundation of Tianjin under grant 11JCYBJC00800.

References

1. Zhu, H., Lin, X., Lu, R., Ho, P., Shen, X.: SLAB: A Secure Localized Authentication and Billing Scheme for Wireless Mesh Networks. IEEE Trans. Wireless Communications 7(10), 3858–3868 (2008)
2. Ren, K., Yu, S., Lou, W., Zhang, Y.: PEACE: A Novel Privacy-Enhanced Yet Accountable Security Framework for Metropolitan Wireless Mesh Networks. IEEE Trans. Parallel and Distributed Systems 21(2), 203–215 (2010)
3. Zhang, Y., Fang, Y.: ARSA: An Attack-Resilient Security Architecture for Multihop Wireless Mesh Networks. IEEE J. Selected Areas Comm. 24(10), 1916–1928 (2006)
4. Sun, J., Zhang, C., Zhang, Y., Fang, Y.: SAT: A Security Architecture Achieving Anonymity and Traceability in Wireless Mesh Networks. IEEE Trans. Dependable and Secure Computing 8(2), 295–307 (2011)
5. Shamir, A.: Identity-based Cryptosystems and Signature Schemes. In: Blakely, G.R., Chaum, D. (eds.) CRYPTO 1984. LNCS, vol. 196, pp. 47–53. Springer, Heidelberg (1985)
6. Al-Riyami, S.S., Paterson, K.G.: Certificateless Public Key Cryptography. In: Laih, C.-S. (ed.) ASIACRYPT 2003. LNCS, vol. 2894, pp. 452–473. Springer, Heidelberg (2003)
7. Dutta, R., Barua, R., Sarkar, P.: Pairing-based Cryptography: A Survey. Cryptology ePrint Archive Rep. 2004/064 (2004)
8. Huang, X., Mu, Y., Susilo, W., Wong, D., Wu, W.: Certificateless Signature Revisited. In: Pieprzyk, J., Ghodosi, H., Dawson, E. (eds.) ACISP 2007. LNCS, vol. 4586, pp. 308–322. Springer, Heidelberg (2007)
9. IEEE Standard Supplement to Standard for Telecommunications and Information Exchange between Systems—LAN/MAN Specific Requirements—Part 11: Wireless LAN Medium Access Control (MAC) and Physical Layer (PHY) Specifications: Specification for Enhanced Security: IEEE 802.11i. IEEE, Piscataway (2004)
10. Canetti, R., Krawczyk, H.: Analysis of Key-exchange Protocols and Their Use for Building Secure Channels. In: Pfitzmann, B. (ed.) EUROCRYPT 2001. LNCS, vol. 2045, pp. 453–474. Springer, Heidelberg (2001)

Ontology Model-Based Static Analysis of Security Vulnerabilities

Lian Yu[1], Shi-Zhong Wu[2], Tao Guo[2], Guo-Wei Dong[2],
Cheng-Cheng Wan[1], and Yin-Hang Jing[1]

[1] School of Software and Microelectronics,
Peking University, Beijing 102600, China
[2] China Information Technology Security Evaluation Center,
Beijing 100085, China
lianyu@ss.pku.edu.cn,
{tiger,guotao,donggw}@itsec.gov.cn,
sitang@pku.edu.cn

Abstract. Static analysis technologies and tools have been widely adopted in detecting software bugs and vulnerabilities. However, traditional approaches have their limitations on extensibility and reusability due to their methodologies, and are unsuitable to describe subtle vulnerabilities under complex and unaccountable contexts. This paper proposes an approach of static analysis based on ontology model enhanced by program slicing technology for detecting software vulnerabilities. We use Ontology Web Language (OWL) to model the source code and Semantic Web Rule Language (SWRL) to describe the bug and vulnerability patterns. Program slicing criteria can be automatically extracted from the SWRL rules and adopted to slice the source code. A prototype of security vulnerability detection (SVD) tool is developed to show the validity of the proposed approach.

Keywords: Static analysis, Program slicing, Vulnerability ontology model, Reasoning.

1 Introduction

Software security has become a matter of paramount concerns in many kinds of modern organizations today. This trend has motivated considerable researches in software security assurance. At present, there are many possible techniques that can be applied to detect software vulnerabilities and to improve software security, such as code reviews, inspections, testing technology, runtime verification, and static analysis. Among these, static analysis is particularly well suitable to security because many security problems occur in corner cases and hard-to-reach states that can be difficult to exercise by actually running the code. Good static analysis tools provide a fast way to get a consistent and detailed evaluation of a body of code.

In recent years, many static analysis tools have been developed to find bugs in software. For example, the ESC/Java (http://kind.ucd.ie/products/opensource/ESCJava2/), FindBugs (http://findbugs.sourceforge.net/), JLint (http://artho.com/jlint)

S. Qing et al. (Eds.): ICICS 2011, LNCS 7043, pp. 330–344, 2011.

and PMD (http://pmd.sourceforge.net) are all bug finding tools. The general process of static analysis performed by these tools can usually be divided into three steps:

1. Build the models of the source code by parsing the source code file.
2. Collect bug & vulnerability patterns and develop models for them. Different static analysis tools have different representation of bug pattern models, for example, PMD directly writes the bug patterns as rules in the form of Java classes and checks the rules while traversing the AST of the source code to find bugs.
3. Check the defects in the program models derived in the first step against the rules developed in the second step, and then produce the bug and vulnerabilities reports.

There are a number of limitations in these traditional static analysis approaches.

- Most of the bug patterns are for general classes of software defects rather than software security vulnerabilities. Moreover, bug pattern models are tightly coupled with the tools' implementation, thus extending new bug patterns applicable with a specific context will be difficult to perform, since people need to get involved in the great details of the programmatic implementation. Although some tools, such as ESC/Java2, provide means to write custom detectors, the extensibility is still limited by the design and capability of the analysis tools.
- There is a lack of formal and expressive mathematical language to define and describe the security vulnerabilities and bug patterns. Informal definition of software vulnerabilities and bugs involuntarily leads to ambiguous understanding about software defects and will potentially bring up false positives which can be time-consuming to address. Moreover, traditional bug categorization is not sufficient to describe the complex concepts in a specific context and the relationships that hold between those concepts, thus potentially it brings up false negatives which hide deeply within the system but may cause big problems under specific environments.
- The detecting approaches based on certain programming language models differ as the language changes. The models and analysis modules are hard to reuse, so it will be costly if the static analysis tools want to support various kinds of programming languages. Implementation of similar security rules in different languages may differ greatly, thus the whole system is unable to reusable.

To address these problems, we propose an ontology-model based static analysis approach to detect software vulnerabilities. We have put forward a preliminary idea of using a similar approach to automatically detect bugs in the source code of Java programs in the paper [1] and have developed a tool to verify its effectiveness. However, the greatest challenge at the moment adopting the approach is the enormous scale of program models the approach may generate when dealing with large software systems. The large scale problem could reduce the performance of the whole reasoning system to a large extent. This paper goes a step further to discuss the possibility of combining the ontology-based approach with traditional static analysis technologies such as program slicing, which we will describe later in this paper, to address the problem and improve the practical utility of the methodology. This paper uses Ontology Web Language (OWL) to model the source codes and Semantic Web Rule Language (SWRL) to describe the bug and vulnerability patterns. Program slicing criterion can be automatically extracted from the SWRL rules and adopted to slice the source code. Program elements that are irrelevant to those criteria will be sliced off and will not be considered in the following phases. The adoption of program slicing can greatly improve the performance of the security vulnerability detection tool.

The rest of the paper will be organized as follows. We first present and discuss the improved overall process of the analysis approach in Section 2. We describe the details of modeling programming language and vulnerability rules in Section 3, and the program slicing solution in Section 4. We carry out experiments in Section 5 and review related work in Section 6, and finally we conclude the paper and scratch the future work in Section 7.

2   Overall Process

In this section we discuss the overall process of the program slicing-enhanced ontology model-based static analysis approach.

The approach follows the three steps which are similar to the general approach of static analysis but in different ways: modeling Java specification and bug patterns using ontology techniques; modeling source code into an abstract syntax tree (AST) and then converting to ontology individuals, where we use program slicing technology in this step to reduce the number of individuals and so as to improve the efficiency of the following reasoning task; and reasoning and generating bug reports. A more detailed process consisting of three phases is shown in Figure 1.

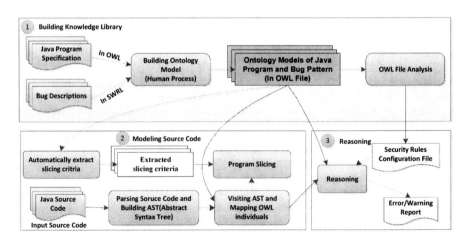

Fig. 1. Process of Ontology Model-Based Static Analysis

1. The first phase, called "Building Knowledge Library", consists of the following two steps.

    a. Modeling Java programming language specifications into ontology models in OWL. Most traditional approaches won't have this modeling step, they usually directly implements language models in specific data structures and program modules. We will illustrate this phase in details in Section 3.

    b. Describing bug patterns and vulnerabilities with SWRL (Semantic Web Rule Language). The purpose of this step is to convert the bug and vulnerability patterns to internal representations that are suitable for a particular analysis. There are many vulnerability listings and publications such as the Common Vulnerabilities and Exposures (CVE) list(http://cve.mitre.org/), CWE(http://cwe.mitre.org/), CERT (http://www.cert.org/nav/index_red.html/), SANS(http://www.sans. org/), and the Open Web Application Security Project (OWASP), all of which can be the sources of the bug and vulnerability patterns.

2. The second phase, called "Modeling Source Code", can be divided into four steps.

    a. Parsing the source code and converting to an AST.

    b. Constructing the Procedure Dependence Graphs (PDGs) for the procedures (methods) and the System Dependence Graph (SDG) of the entire system.

    c. Slicing over the dependence graphs using the criteria automatically extracted from the SWRL rules. The adoption of program slicing technique is to reduce the scale of the program to be detected.

    d. Mapping the sliced nodes to OWL individuals. Based on the AST, a module that can traverse the AST will then map the nodes to OWL individuals, which are the target outputs of the entire second phase and thus the "internal representations" of the source code.

3. The third phase is reasoning. The purpose of this step is to analyze the internal representations of the source code so as to detect vulnerabilities and generate reports. In our approach this task is performed by a reasoning engine. We will discuss this step in Section 4.4.

3 Modeling Language Specification and Bug Patterns Using Ontology Techniques

This section discusses how to model programming language specification and vulnerability patterns with ontology techniques. We will take the Java language as a case study.

3.1 Modeling Java Specification

In computer science and information science, ontology is a formal representation of knowledge as a set of concepts within a domain, and the relationships between those concepts.

OWL is a famous ontology language for making ontology statements and it's a W3C standard. OWL is developed based on RDF (Resource Description Framework) and RDFS (RDF Schema). All of its elements (classes, properties and individuals) are defined as RDF resources, and are identified by URIs. In our approach we choose OWL to model the Java specification.

Thing in OWL domain is similar to the java.lang.Object in Java, as all OWL classes are Thing's descendants, while all Java classes are descendants of the java.lang.Object class. Both Java and OWL use the term Class to describe concepts in a domain. Class instances represent individuals in OWL and objects in Java. OWL defines some built-ins (properties) to describe relationships of concepts. These properties can also be used to describe the relationships of Java elements. For example, the "owl:subclass-of" property can be used to describe the inheritance relationship of Java classes.

As a formal language representation, BNF (Backus-Naur Form) production is the most widely used form of language lexical and syntax definition. Many tools such as JavaCC (Jhttp://javacc.java.net/) and ANTLR (http://www.antlr.org/) use BNF to describe the Java grammars. We also use the Java BNF in our modeling phase. We use OWL Class to describe all elements of Java language, and use OWL properties to describe the relationships between these elements.

Totally, we define 98 OWL classes to cover all the Java elements. We give part of the OWL classes and properties together with their corresponding Java explanations in Table 1 and Table 2. For more detailed information, see our previous work in paper [1].

Table 1. Relationship between Classes in OWL and Java Elements

OWL Classes	Elements in Java Specification
ClassDesc	Class in Java
InterfaceDesc	Interface in Java
MethodDesc	user defined methods
AttributeDesc	The fields in class or interface file
ObjectDesc	The object variable used in Java source code
ModifierDesc	Modifier of class, interface method attribute, such as: public, private, protected

Table 2. OWL properties and corresponding relationships in Java

OWL Properties	Relationships Between Java Elements
ClassDesc_hasExtends	Inheritance relationship between Java classes
ClassDesc_hasMehtod	Each class may have a few methods
ClassDesc_hasAttribute	Each class may have a few attributes
ClassDesc_hasModifier	Each class must have a modifier, most common it's
ObjectDesc_hasType	Each object must belong to some type(class)
AttributeDesc_hasType	Attribute also has types

3.2   Modeling Bug and Vulnerability Patterns

We collect more than 200 Java bug patterns from OWASP, CWE, and Jtest and convert them into SWRL rules. In this section, we will illustrate how to construct SWRL rules from bug patterns.

Take the TRS.CSTART-3 rule from Jtest which indicates that "Do not call the start method of threads from inside a constructor" as an example. We write the following SWRL rule (see Figure 2) which describes "A class with any constructor within which a thread object's start method is invoked will infer an error report".

```
SWRL Rule

ClassDesc(?className) ∧ ClassDesc_hasMethod(?className, ?methodName) ∧ MethodDesc(?methodName) ∧
name(?className, ?classLableName) ∧name(?methodName, ?methodLableName) ∧swrlb:equal(?classLableName, ?methodLableName) ∧
MethodDesc_hasClause(?methodName, ?c) ∧InvokeClause(?c) ∧InvokeClause_invokedObject(?c, ?o) ∧Object_hasType(?o, ?n) ∧
name(?n, "Thread") ∧InvokeClause_invokedMethod(?c, ?m) ∧
name(?m, "start") ∧NotCallStartInConstructMethodWarning(?w)
  → errorReport(?c, ?w)
```

Fig. 2. The detection rule definition in SWRL

SWRL rules are critical for the reasoning process because it directly influences the results. If we adopt the rule in Figure 2 to detect the following codes as shown in Figure 3, it will generate an error report since the codes violate the rule. However, this is a typical false positive caused by the ambiguous understanding about the software defect.

```
package basicbugs;
import java.util.List;

public class CallStartInConstructMethod {
    private List<Thread> workingList;
    public CallStartInConstructMethod(){
        if(workingList != null){
            for(Thread e:workingList){
                e.start();
            }
        }
    }
}
```

Fig. 3. False positives caused by the imprecise rule

The precise definition of this rule, which should be "Code where 'start()' is invoked inside the constructors of classes that extend java.lang.Thread will be considered as an error", is shown in Figure 4. Note the added conditions in the antecedent in the rule are marked with red box.

```
SWRL Rule

ClassDesc(?className) ∧ClassDesc_hasMethod(?className, ?methodName) ∧MethodDesc(?methodName) ∧
ClassDesc_hasExtend(?className,?extend_c) ∧ name(?extend_c, "Thread") ∧
name(?className, ?classLableName) ∧name(?methodName, ?methodLableName) ∧ swrlb:equal(?classLableName, ?methodLableName) ∧
MethodDesc_hasClause(?methodName, ?c) ∧InvokeClause(?c) ∧InvokeClause_invokedObject(?c, ?o) ∧Object_hasType(?o, ?n) ∧
name(?n, "Thread") ∧InvokeClause_invokedMethod(?c, ?m) ∧
name(?m, "start") ∧NotCallStartInConstructMethodWarning(?w)
  → errorReport(?c, ?w)
```

Fig. 4. The precise rule definition in SWRL

4   Modeling Source Code and Vulnerability Reasoning

After the Java specification and bug patterns are modeled, Java source code should be modeled to detect bugs. Taking the execution times and memory consumption into account, we will not map all the Java elements to OWL individuals. Instead, we only model those elements within our domain of interests. To reduce the number of individuals, program slicing technique is used. The process is described in the Figure 5.

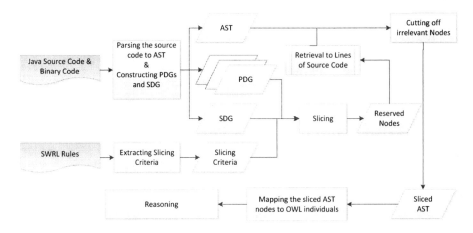

Fig. 5. The process of modeling source code and slicing

The five steps of this phase are described as bellow, and we will discuss them in details in the following sections.

1.   Extracting slicing criteria automatically from the SWRL rules.
2.   Constructing PDGs for the procedures (methods) and the SDG for the entire system.
3.   Once the dependence graphs have been constructed, slicing task is performed over the dependence graphs using the criteria automatically extracted from the SWRL rules.
4.   Adopting the slicing results to AST and removing irrelevant nodes, and mapping the rest of AST nodes to OWL individuals.
5.   Performing vulnerability reasoning based on the extracted SWRL rules and created OWL individuals from the sliced nodes.

4.1   Slicing over Method and Variable

Program Slicing [2] is a program analysis technique that reduces programs to those statements that are relevant for a particular computation.

This paper uses program slicing algorithms to slice Java source at two levels: method level and variable level. At the method level, it creates call graph based on control flow analysis, the slicing criterion is a list of method name. The slicing result only contains the methods in the criterion list and the methods that call them. At the variable level, it analyzes control flow and data flow information of each method, and constructs dependence graphs, for example, the procedure dependence graphs (PDGs) and the system dependence graph (SDG) [3]. The slicing criterion at variable level is a list of variables in a method, and the slicing result is all statements which can influence the variable values or can be influenced by the variables.

Figure 6 shows an example of how to slice a class with slicing criteria at the method level. Figure 6(a) is the source code and Figure 6(b) is the slicing result when the slicing criterion is "callMethod" method. Because of the "callMethod" invokes "call" method, the "call" method is reserved, while "notCall" method is cut off.

```
1public class CallMehtod(              1public class CallMehtod(
2    public void callMethod() {        2    public void callMethod() {
3        try (                         3        try (
4            call("");                 4            call("");
5            // ...                     5            // ...
6        ) finally (                   6        ) finally (
7            // ...                     7            // ...
8            System.gc(); // VIOLATION  8            System.gc(); // VIOLATION
9        )                             9        )
10   )                                 10   )
11                                     11
12   public void call(String op)(      12   public void call(String op)(
13       //Do Something                13       //Do Something
14   )                                 14   )
15                                     15
16   public void notCall(String op)(   16
17       //Do Something                17
18   )                                 18
19)                                    19)
```

(a)   (b)

Fig. 6. Static program slicing example, slicing criterion = "callMethod"

The source code in Figure 7(a) is used to calculate $\sum_{i=1}^{n} i$ and $\prod_{i=1}^{n} i$, if the slicing criterion is <12, product> and the strategy is at the variable level, the slicing result will look like the one shown in Figure 7(b). All the statements that influence the variable *product* are reserved. Statements (4), (7), and (10) are not related with variable *product*, so they will be cut off.

```
2  public void calculate(int n)(      2  public void calculate(int n)(
3      int i = 1;                      3      int i = 1;
4      int sum = 0;                    4
5      int product = 1;                5      int product = 1;
6      while(i <= n){                  6      while(i <= n){
7          sum = sum + i;              7
8          product = product * i;      8          product = product * i;
9          i = i + 1;                  9          i = i + 1;
10     )                               10     )
11     System.out.println(sum);        11
12     System.out.println(product);    12     System.out.println(product);
13 )                                   13 )|
```

(a)   (b)

Fig. 7. Static program slicing example, slice criterion = <12, product>

Both the examples in Figure 6 and Figure 7 achieve to reduce the number of Java elements. The Java elements sliced will not be mapped to OWL individuals, thus it reduces the reasoning complexity.

For practical use, both slicing levels need inter-procedural analysis, and slicing over variable is fine-grained and obviously much more complex. We will discuss the variable level slicing in more details in the following sections.

4.2   Extracting Program Slicing Criterion

Each bug or vulnerability pattern can detect specific types of bugs. A vulnerability SWRL rule can be used to identify Java elements. In program slicing terminology, we call these Java elements as a slicing criterion.

Program slice criterion can be automatically extracted from the SWRL rules. One example of the program slice criterion is shown in Figure 4. From the SWRL rule statements name(?n, "Thread") and name(?o, "Start"), we can infer that this slicing criterion has two concerns related to "Thread" and "start". If we are using method level slicing strategy, methods that contains the keyword "Thread" or "start" will be reserved first, and other methods that do not contain the keywords and have no effect on global variables used in reserved methods will be cut off.

Take the typical SQL injection vulnerability as a more detailed example. The primary means of preventing SQL injection are sanitizing and validating untrusted input and parameterizing the query. The code example shown in Figure 8 permits an SQL injection attack because the SQL statement sqlString accepts un-sanitized input arguments.

```
class Login {
  public Connection getConnection() throws SQLException {
    DriverManager.registerDriver(new com.microsoft.sqlserver.jdbc.SQLServerDriver());
    String dbConnection = PropertyManager.getProperty("db.connection");
    // can hold some value like "jdbc:microsoft:sqlserver://<HOST>:1433,<UID>,<PWD>"
    return DriverManager.getConnection(dbConnection);
  }

  String hashPassword(char[] password) {
    // create hash of password
  }

  public void doPrivilegedAction(String username, char[] password) throws SQLException {
    Connection connection = getConnection();
    if (connection == null) {
      // handle error
    }
    String pwd = hashPassword(password);

    String sqlString = "SELECT * FROM db_user WHERE username = '" + username +
                       "' AND password = '" + pwd + "'";
    Statement stmt = connection.createStatement();
    ResultSet rs = stmt.executeQuery(sqlString);

    if (!rs.next()) {
        throw new SecurityException("User name or password incorrect");
    }

    // Authenticated; proceed
  }
}
```

Fig. 8. SQL injection vulnerability example

The SWRL rule for SQL injection is shown in Figure 9. There are 11 variables defined in this rule (*?c, ?s, ?str, ?m, ?p, ?clause, ?executeQuery, ?sql_p, ?asc, ?plus, ?w*), the "*name*" property is directly related to the source code and can be used to extract slicing criterion. From the rule statement *name(?executeQuery, "executeQuery")* and *InvokeClause_invokedMethodParameter(?executeQuery,? sql_p)* we can infer the pattern statement *stmt.executeQuery(sql_string)*. Taking this pattern to the source code in Figure 8, the Java elements to construct slicing criterion can be identified as the statement "*ResultSet rs = stmt.executeQuery(sqlString)*".

Thus if we are taking backward slicing form, the statements that have some effect on the slicing criterion (the *stmt* and *sqlString* variable) will be reserved.

SWRL Rule

ClassDesc(?c) ∧ ClassDesc(?s) ∧ name(?s, "java.sql.Statement") ∧ ClassDesc(?str) ∧ name(?str, "String") ∧ ClassDesc_hasMethod(?c, ?m) ∧ MethodDesc_hasParameter(?m, ?p) ∧ MethodDesc_hasClause(?m, ?clause) ∧ InvokeClause_invokedMethod(?clause, ?executeQuery) ∧ name(?executeQuery, "executeQuery") ∧ InvokeClause_invokedObject(?clause, ?stmt) ∧ Object_hasType(?stmt, ?s) ∧ InvokeClause_invokedMethodParameter(?executeQuery, ?sql_p) ∧ Object_hasType(?sql_p, ?str) ∧ AssignClause(?asc) ∧ MethodDesc_hasClause(?m, ?asc) ∧ AssignClause_hasLeftExpression(?asc, ?sql_p) ∧ ExpressionClause(?exp) ∧ AssignClause_hasRightExpression(?asc, ?exp) ∧ Plus(?plus) ∧ ExpressionClause_hasOperator(?exp, ?plus) ∧ ExpressionClause_hasRight(?exp, ?p) ∧ SQL_Injection_Warning(?w) → errorReport(?c, ?w)

Fig. 9. A SWRL rule for SQL injection detection

4.3   Slicing over the Dependence Graphs

Now we have got the criterion, the next step is to construct the procedure dependence graphs (PDGs) and the system dependence graph (SDG) of the program. This work is done by a slicing module. For now, the PDGs and SDG are constructed based on the work described in paper [4] which is based on the ASM [5] library. ASM is a Java byte-code engineering library. We have started to build our own library to construct dependence graphs from AST which can be built from source code.

For the purpose of reducing memory usage, we use a two-dimensional array matrix to store the procedure dependence graphs. The matrix is N * N size where N is the number of the nodes of the program. Let $Matrix_{i,j}$ be the element in row i and column j in PDG matrix. $Matrix_{i,j} = 0$ means $node_i$ has no dependence relationships with $node_j$. $Matrix_{i,j} = 1$ means $node_i$ is data dependent on $node_j$. $Matrix_{i,j} = 2$ means $node_i$ is control dependent on $node_j$.

SDG is designed as a map data structure in the slicing module. The keys of the SDG map are the call nodes of the entire system, while the values of the SDG map are the PDGs corresponding with the key.

After PDG and SDG have been constructed, the criteria are transformed to the nodes in the dependence graphs, and then the slicing module performs cross-functional slicing task. Only the nodes that are relevant with the criterion node will be reserved. Relevant nodes mean the nodes that are directly or indirectly data dependent or control dependent on the given node together with those nodes that can have effect on the given node.

Take the SQL injection vulnerability in Figure 8 as an example. We have the criterion *"ResultSet rs = stmt.executeQuery(sqlString);"* be automatically extracted based on the SWRL rules. When the slicing module traverses the dependence graphs, the assignment node of *"String sqlString ="* and *"Statement stmt ="* will be detected and reserved because they have effect on the criterion statement. To be more precise, the criterion nodes of *"sqlString"* and *"stmt"* are data dependent on the assignment nodes. Nodes like *"if (!rs.next())"* and *"new SecurityException"* will also be reserved because they are directly or indirectly dependent on the criterion node. Each node in dependence graph has a "line" attribute which indicates the node's line number in source code. Using this attribute we can retrieve the slicing results back to source code and AST. Irrelevant statements such as *"if (connection == null){}"* will be removed from the AST. The sliced AST will be then mapped to OWL individuals.

4.4   Generating OWL Individuals and Vulnerability Reasoning

Once the AST has been sliced, the reserved nodes will be mapped to OWL individuals. We build a parser based on JavaCC to translate the source code into an AST and an OWL generator to visit AST nodes and map them to OWL individuals. JavaCC provides some basic support for the visitor design pattern. For object-oriented programming, the visitor pattern enables the definition of a new operation on an object structure without changing the classes of the objects. In our approach, the "new operation" is to map the nodes to OWL individuals. We defined many visitor classes to visit different nodes and create corresponding OWL individuals.

Since all Java classes begin with a class or interface declaration, a *"JavaTreePars erForJessVisitor"* which implements the *visit(ClassOrInterfaceDeclaration, Object)* method of the *Vistor* interface is constructed as the entrance visitor.

Once the *JavaTreeParserForJessVisitor* object is passed to the accept method of the *CompilationUnit*, which represents the AST of the source code, the visitor will begin to traverse the nodes of AST and create corresponding OWL individuals.

The *JavaElementToJessMapping* class is the key class we have built to help create OWL individuals for source code. It holds a member of *JenaOWLModel* which contains all the Java elements that are defined in the "modeling the Java specification" phase. It also contains a set of create methods to create all the individuals.

For example, there is an OWL class defined as *"ClassDesc"*. The *ClassDesc* class is used to represent the concept of *"Class"* in Java program language (Interface is a special kind of class). Once the *JavaTreeParserForJessVisitor* is accepted, the *visit(ClassOrInterfaceDeclaration, Object)* that it implements will be called to create an *OWLIndividual* of the *ClassDesc* class. Now we have created an individual which represents the class that is being analyzed. As the creation process continues, more individuals that represent the methods, statements and variables will be created.

So far, the OWL model for Java specification, SWRL rules for vulnerabilities, such as the rule in Figure 9 Section 4.2, and OWL individuals for Java elements are ready. The remaining task is to load these OWL classes, individuals and SWRL rules into the rule engine and let the rule engine perform the reasoning task. If some of the individuals violate the rules, the reasoning engine will assert an "errorReport" property which is considered as a bug or vulnerability.

5   Experiments and Analyses

In order to facilitate ontology model-based static analysis approach, a prototype is developed named SVD, we have carried out some experiments to validate the approach.

In general, if mapping all Java elements to ontology individuals, there will be a lot of individuals that actually will not be used in the reasoning step. What's more, the unused individuals may result in false positives. Program slicing is a mature traditional static analysis method. It can ensure that code within our domain of interest will be reserved while others cut off. We mark the system which is not combined with program slicing module as SVD1, and the current system combined with program slicing module as SVD2.

Table 3 shows the experimental results about running time of SVD1 and SVD2. Within column of SVD1 (or SVD2), Total Time indicates the time (in HH:MM:SS format) that consumes to detect each target, and Total Bugs are the bug number that the systems find.

Table 3. Comparing bug detecting capabilities between SVD1 and SVD2

Name	Number of Class Files	SVD1		SVD2	
		Total Time	Total Bugs	Total Time	Total Bugs
Soot-2.4.0	1134	21:29	187	12:46	184
Struts-2.1.6	753	11:34	164	08:04	162
DOM4j-1.6.1	179	16:08	98	08:43	96
MySQL Connector 3.2.0	122	10:53	58	6:29	57

In Table 3, system SVD2 uses only half of time that SVD1 does to detect the bugs, although the total bug number is slight less than SVD1. In order to figure out how the program slicing module improves the system performance. We take the DOM4j as the target, and carry out another experiment.

Table 4 shows experimental results about time of every part in SVD1 and SVD2. The system without program slicing module shows that reasoning time is accounting about 68 percent of the total time, loading time is accounting about 21 percent of the total time, and they take almost 90 percent of the total time. But after combined with program slicing, they only take 67 percent of the total time. What's more, the total run time of the system reduces 45.9 percent, and the program slicing only takes 13 percent of the total time. From analyzing the Table 4, it can be seen that combing with program slicing can greatly improve the performance.

Table 4. Comparing performance of SVD1 and SVD2

Time/System	Slicing	Parsing	Loading	Reasoning	Total Time
SVD1	0	1:47	3:23	10:58	16:08
SVD2	01:08	01:38	01:56	04:01	08:43

6   Related Work

Algorithms and techniques for source-code analysis have been changed, sometimes dramatically, for more than thirty years. But the anatomy of source-code analysis has always been the same. David Binkley [6] summed up the three components of source-code analysis as parser, internal representation and the analysis of this representation.

Parsers convert source code, the concrete syntax, into internal representations which are in abstract syntax and are better suited to a particular analysis. Most parsers are compiler-based and process the entire language [8]. There are lighter-weight techniques that handle only part of the language. For example, an island grammar [9] allows portions (islands) of the concrete syntax to be parsed while ignoring the remainder. Our approach also provides a means to control the scale of the language syntax by constructing the ontology models of language specification, although we consider it unnecessary in most cases.

The internal representation abstracts a particular aspect of the program into a form more suitable for automated analysis. Common examples of internal representation include the control flow graph, the abstract syntax tree (AST) and the call graph. Static single-assignment (SSA) form [10] is another popular internal representation. SSA form simplifies and improves the precision of a variety of data-flow analyses [6].

Graph is the most common internal representation. For example, the value dependence graph (VDG) represents control flow as data flow and thus simplifies analysis [11]. Dynamic call graphs [12] [13] and XTA graphs built in support of dynamic reachability-based inter-procedural analysis [12]. Trace Flow Graph (TFG) consists of a collection of CFGs with additional vertices and edges to represent inter-task control flow, and is used to represent concurrent programs [14].

In event-driven systems or distributed programs, finite state automata (FSA) is usually used to represent the analysis, FSA provides an excellent abstraction of program models [15].

For the consideration of interoperability, there are some internal representations that are "external" to the individual tools. For example, srcML (http:// www. sdml.info/index.html), which is a combination of source code (text) and selective AST information (tags) in a single XML document. SrcML is taken to support understanding, analysis, and transformation of large software systems undergoing evolution. In our ontology model-based analysis approach, program models are represented as first AST and then ontology models, ontology models have the advantage same as srcML or XML, since OWL is a W3C standard, program models built in form of ontology models can be understood by all the tools implementing the standard.

The third part of the component in source-code analysis is the actual analysis itself. Analyses can be classified along six dimensions [6]: static versus dynamic, sound versus unsound, safe versus unsafe, flow sensitive versus flow insensitive, context sensitive versus context insensitive, and complexity. A slightly different classification that focuses on object-oriented analysis is discussed by Ryder [16]. There are almost as many analyses as there are internal representations. Most analysis problems have a spectrum of solutions that represent precision-effort trade-offs. For example, imprecise points-to sets can be computed in near linear time, while the computation of flow- and context- sensitive points-to sets is NP-hard [17]. To discuss the details of each analysis methodology is beyond this paper's topic. In our ontology model-based analysis approach, the analysis task, or more accurately the reasoning task, is delegated to reasoning engines that implement OWL and SWRL standards. This brings up the versatility to apply this approach to different languages.

7   Conclusion and Future Work

This paper proposes program slicing-enhanced ontology model-based static analysis for security vulnerability detection. Programming language specification is modeled as OWL classes and properties, and vulnerability patterns are modeling in rules in SWRL. Java source code is parsed into AST and then mapped into OWL individuals. The huge number of OWL individuals impacts significantly the performance the vulnerability reasoning. To reduce the number of OWL individuals, program slicing technique is introduced to remove the irrelevant OWL individuals regarding to a specific type of vulnerability, thus reducing the reasoning complexity.   We developed a prototype tool named SVD to show the validity of the proposed static security vulnerability analysis approach.

Detection capability to a large extent depends on the number of OWL individuals and SWRL rules. To realize a full-fledged SVD tool, we will keep on implementing SWRL rules and OWL classes for more bug patterns, and writing AST visitors to generate the corresponding individuals. We are planning to adopt more other traditional static analysis technologies such as symbolic execution, type inference, and interval analysis, together with the ontology model based approach.

Acknowledgments. The research is partially supported by the National Science Foundation of China (No. 60973001, No. 61100047).

References

[1] Yu, L., Zhou, J., Yi, Y., Li, P., Wang, Q.: Ontology Model-Based Static Analysis on Java Programs. In: Proceedings of the 2008 32nd Annual IEEE International Computer Software and Applications Conference, July 28-August 01, pp. 92–99 (2008)

[2] Weiser, M.: Program slices: formal, psychological, and practical investigations of an automatic program abstraction method. PhD thesis, University of Michigan, Ann Arbor (1979)

[3] Ferrante, J., Ottenstein, K., Warren, J.: The program dependence graph and its use in optimization. ACM Transactions on Programming Languages and Systems 9(3), 319–349 (1987)

[4] Java System Dependence Graph API,
http://www4.comp.polyu.edu.hk/~cscllo/teaching/SDGAPI/

[5] ASM, http://asm.ow2.org/

[6] Binkley, D.: Source Code Analysis: A Road Map. In: 2007 Future of Software Engineering (FOSE 2007), pp. 104–119. IEEE Computer Society, Washington, DC, USA (2007), doi:10.1109/FOSE.2007.27

[7] Cordy, J., Dean, T., Malton, A., Schneider, K.: Source transformation in software engineering using the TXL transformation system. Information and Software Technology 44(13) (2002)

[8] Edison Design Group. Compiler front ends (2006)

[9] Moonen, L.: Generating robust parsers using island grammars. In: Working Conference on Reverse Engineering (2001)

[10] Cytron, R., Ferrante, J., Rosen, B., Wegman, M., Zadeck, K.: Efficiently computing static single assignment form and the control dependence graph. ACM Trans. Prog. Lang. Syst. 13(4) (1991)

[11] Weise, D., Crew, R.F., Ernst, M., Steensgaard, B.: Valuedependence graphs: Representation without taxation. In: Conference Record of POPL 1994: 21st ACM SIGPLAN-SIGACT Symposium on Principles of Programming Languages. ACM SIGACT and SIGPLAN, ACM Press (1994)

[12] Qian, F., Hendren, L.: Towards dynamic interprocedural analysis in jvms. In: Proc. of the 3rd Virtual Machine Research and Technology Symposium, San Jose, USA. Usenix (May 2004)

[13] Pheng, S., Verbrugge, C.: Dynamic data structure analysis for Java programs. In: ICPC 2006: Proc. of the 14th IEEE International Conference on Program Comprehension. IEEE Computer Society (2006)

[14] Cobleigh, J., Clarke, L., Osterweil, L.: Flavers: A finite state verification technique for software systems. IBM Systems Journal – Software Testing and Verification 41(1) (2002)

[15] Schmidt, D.: Structure-preserving Binary Relations for Program Abstraction. In: Mogensen, T.Æ., Schmidt, D.A., Sudborough, I.H. (eds.) The Essence of Computation. LNCS, vol. 2566, pp. 245–265. Springer, Heidelberg (2002)

[16] Ryder, B.: Dimensions of Precision in Reference Analysis of Object-oriented Programming Languages. In: Hedin, G. (ed.) CC 2003. LNCS, vol. 2622, pp. 126–137. Springer, Heidelberg (2003)

[17] Landi, W., Ryder, B.G.: Pointer-induced aliasing: A problem classification. In: Conference Record of the Eighteenth Annual ACM Symposium on Principles of Programming Languages, Orlando, FL. ACM Press (January 1991)

A Multi-compositional Enforcement on Information Flow Security

Cong Sun[1,2,3], Ennan Zhai[4], Zhong Chen[2,3], and Jianfeng Ma[1]

[1] Key Lab. of Computer Networks and Information Security,
Xidian Univ., MoE, China
[2] Key Lab. of High Confidence Software Technologies, Peking Univ., MoE, China
[3] Key Lab. of Network and Software Security Assurance, Peking Univ., MoE, China
[4] Institute of Software, Chinese Academy of Sciences
suncong@xidian.edu.cn

Abstract. Interactive/Reactive computational model is known to be proper abstraction of many pervasively used systems, such as client-side web-based applications. The critical task of information flow control mechanisms aims to determine whether the interactive program can guarantee the confidentiality of secret data. We propose an efficient and flow-sensitive static analysis to enforce information flow policy on program with interactive I/Os. A reachability analysis is performed on the abstract model after a form of transformation, called multi-composition, to check the conformance with the policy. In the multi-composition we develop a store-match pattern to avoid duplicating the I/O channels in the model, and use the principle of secure multi-execution to generalize the security lattice model which is supported by other approaches based on automated verification. We also extend our approach to support a stronger version of termination-insensitive noninterference. The results of preliminary experiments show that our approach is more precise than existing flow-sensitive analysis and the cost of verification is reduced through the store-match pattern.

Keywords: Information flow security, pushdown system, interactive model, security policy, program analysis.

1 Introduction

Security-sensitive resources in computing system need to be protected from untrusted applications. Enforcing the information flow policies focuses on protecting confidentiality of these resources and ensures that attackers cannot learn any secret by observing the public behavior of multiple runs of program. Language-based techniques have been widely used for a long time in the studies on information flow security, surveyed in [16]. Goguen and Meseguer [9] introduce *noninterference* as the baseline confidential requirement to formalize the condition which enables secret system input to avoid being inferred by untrusted users of that system. Intuitively speaking, noninterference requires that the system behaviors should be indistinguishable from a perspective of attacker regardless of the confidential inputs to the system.

S. Qing et al. (Eds.): ICICS 2011, LNCS 7043, pp. 345–359, 2011.

There has been great progress on tracking information flow in languages with increasing complexity. Recently the community has paid increasing attention to the information flow security problem for languages with interactive I/Os, esp. through some forms of input/output channels [10,18,8,3,15,5,7]. In contrast to batch-job model which takes input before execution and generates output at termination, the computational model with interactive I/Os involves ongoing communications with external environment. It is a proper abstraction of various client-side web-based applications. Generally speaking, the interactivity can be characterized differently. In some existing efforts [15,5], the intermediate inputs can be decided by the previous outputs and this dependency is formally defined, e.g., through the user strategy [15], while in other models [18,8,7], the intermediate inputs can be considered simply as indefinite or abstracted as security levels. It means that compared with the first type of interactivity, the second type of interactivity can be preestablished and even totally indefinite throughout the execution. We mainly focus on programs with the second type of interactivity.

From a perspective of enforcement mechanisms, the approaches involving program with interactive I/Os can be either dynamic [10,7] or static based on type system [18,15,5] or abstract interpretation [8]. Automated verification has been used to check conformance with noninterference property on batch-job models [4,23,14]. This category of approach is flow-sensitive and commonly considered more precise than type system [4]. Because noninterference is not a safety property [23], it relies on program transformation, more specifically, some form of *self-composition* [4], to reduce noninterference on original model to a safety property on the model after transformation. With a requirement on duplicating the inputs and outputs, this approach will largely increase the state space of model and the cost of verification when it is adopted on interactive models. Automated verification is also restricted to support the simple security level lattice $L \preceq H$. Although in [23] the authors suggested to partition the memory stores multiple times to adopt more general lattices, there is no specific approach and it is still not clear how I/O channels leverage this category of partitioning approach.

In this work, we propose a novel approach using algorithmic verification technique to analyze information flow security on language with interactive I/Os. We utilize our previous idea to incorporate self-composition with reachability analysis [20] to check the conformance with noninterference property, and adopt our store-match pattern [21] to avoid duplicating I/O channels. Moreover, we adopt the idea of *secure multi-execution* proposed by Devriese et al. [7] to deal with complex lattice models. With secure multi-execution, the program is executed once on each security level. The outputs to channels with different security levels are handled respectively by each execution on the level. The high inputs of low execution are replaced by default value, while the low inputs of high execution are dependent on whether they have been obtained in the low execution. The secure multi-execution of noninterferent/secure program preserves the semantic soundness w.r.t. the normal execution. For interferent/insecure program, the multi-execution changes the semantics of original program by replacing interferent behaviors with noninterferent behaviors. This variation makes

P	L_1	L_2	H
input$(x,\mathcal{I}_1)$;	$x := \mathcal{I}_1[p_1]$,sig$(\underline{p_1})$,	if $r_1 \leq \underline{p_1}$ wait;	if $r_1 \leq \underline{p_1}$ wait;
	$r_1 := ++p_1$;	else $x := \mathcal{I}_1[\underline{p_1}]$;	else $x := \mathcal{I}_1[\underline{p_1}]$;
while$(x > 0)\{$	while$(x > 0)\{$	while$(x > 0)\{$	while$(x > 0)\{$
output$(1,\mathcal{O}_2)$;	skip;	$\mathcal{O}_2[q_2] := 1; q_2++$;	skip;
input$(x,\mathcal{I}_H)$;	$x := v_{default}$;	$x := v_{default}$;	$x := \mathcal{I}_H[p_H]$,sig$(\underline{p_H})$,
			$r_H := ++p_H$;
$\}$	$\}$	$\}$	$\}$

Fig. 1. Multi-Execution of Motivating Example

$\ldots$	reset(p,q);	reset(p);
$x := \mathcal{I}_1[p_1], p_1++$;	$x := \mathcal{I}_1[p_1], p_1++$;	$x := \mathcal{I}_1[p_1], p_1++$;
while$(x > 0)\{$	while$(x > 0)\{$	while$(x > 0)\{$
$\mathcal{O}_2[q_2] := 1, q_2++$;	skip;	$\overline{\mathcal{O}_2[q_2]} := 1, q_2++$; $(*)$
$x := \bot$;	$x := \bot$;	$x := \bot$;
$\}$	$\}$	$\} \ldots$

Fig. 2. Result of Composition

the normal execution and the multi-execution different from a perspective of observer on public output channels. That means when the normal execution and multi-execution behave diversely on public output channels, we can infer that the program violates noninterference. Our transformation composes the model w.r.t. normal execution with the model w.r.t. a serialized multi-execution using schedular select$_{lowprio}$ [7, Sec.II.D], which stipulates that lowest security execution runs first.

1.1   Motivating Example

When we use reachability analysis instead of deduction on partial correctness judgements to check noninterference of program, e.g. $l := h$, the program can be transformed to

$$l' := l; l := h; l' := h'; \textbf{if } l' \neq l \textbf{ then} \text{ goto } error;$$

Here the self-composition is evolved into three phases: basic self-composition, auxiliary interleaving assignments between initial low variables, and illegal-flow state construction. Consider program P in Fig.1 with a security lattice $L_1 \preceq L_2 \preceq H$, the outputs to channel $\mathcal{O}_2$ are dependent on the inputs from $\mathcal{I}_1$ and $\mathcal{I}_H$. This program is interferent because the inputs from $\mathcal{I}_H$ flow implicitly to $\mathcal{O}_2$ when the first input from $\mathcal{I}_1$ is greater than zero. In the multi-execution given in Fig.1, the outputs to $\mathcal{O}_2$ have turned to depend on default value, which we models as indefinite value. $sig(p_1)$ allows the thread L_2 and H to proceed after waiting for thread L_1 to obtain input from $\mathcal{I}_1$. Because thread H becomes noninterferent to the low outputs, from a perspective of low observer, we only need to serially model the low threads and compose the result with the model of normal execution. With a lowest-first scheduler, the input side-effect mentioned in [7] can be achieved by resetting the index of low channels and reusing the inputs each time a higher level execution starts, instead of using the $sig/wait$ signal. The result of composition is given in Fig.2. The low inputs are used

$$e ::= v \mid x \mid e \oplus e'$$

$$c ::= \mathbf{skip} \mid x := e \mid c; c' \mid \mathbf{if}\ e\ \mathbf{then}\ c\ \mathbf{else}\ c' \mid \mathbf{while}\ e\ \mathbf{do}\ c \mid input(x, \mathcal{I}_i) \mid output(e, \mathcal{O}_i)$$

Fig. 3. Program Syntax

$$\frac{}{(\mu, \mathcal{I}, \mathcal{O}, p, q, \mathbf{skip}; c) \to (\mu, \mathcal{I}, \mathcal{O}, p, q, c)} \qquad \frac{\mu(e) = v}{(\mu, \mathcal{I}, \mathcal{O}, p, q, x := e; c) \to (\mu[x \mapsto v], \mathcal{I}, \mathcal{O}, p, q, c)}$$

$$\frac{\mu(e) = b}{(\mu, \mathcal{I}, \mathcal{O}, p, q, \mathbf{if}\ e\ \mathbf{then}\ c_{\mathbf{true}}\ \mathbf{else}\ c_{\mathbf{false}}) \to (\mu, \mathcal{I}, \mathcal{O}, p, q, c_b)}$$

$$\frac{\mu(e) = \mathbf{true}}{(\mu, \mathcal{I}, \mathcal{O}, p, q, \mathbf{while}\ e\ \mathbf{do}\ c) \to (\mu, \mathcal{I}, \mathcal{O}, p, q, c; \mathbf{while}\ e\ \mathbf{do}\ c)}$$

$$\frac{\mu(e) = \mathbf{false}}{(\mu, \mathcal{I}, \mathcal{O}, p, q, \mathbf{while}\ e\ \mathbf{do}\ c) \to (\mu, \mathcal{I}, \mathcal{O}, p, q, \mathbf{skip})}$$

$$\frac{\mathcal{I}_i[p_i] = v \qquad p'_i = p_i + 1}{(\mu, \mathcal{I}, \mathcal{O}, p, q, input(x, \mathcal{I}_i); c) \to (\mu[x \mapsto v], \mathcal{I}, \mathcal{O}, p', q, c)}$$

$$\frac{\mu(e) = \mathcal{O}'_i[q_i] \qquad q'_i = q_i + 1}{(\mu, \mathcal{I}, \mathcal{O}, p, q, output(e, \mathcal{O}_i); c) \to (\mu, \mathcal{I}, \mathcal{O}', p, q', c)} \qquad \frac{(\mu, \mathcal{I}, \mathcal{O}, p, q, c_1) \to (\mu', \mathcal{I}', \mathcal{O}', p', q', c'_1)}{(\mu, \mathcal{I}, \mathcal{O}, p, q, c_1; c_2) \to (\mu', \mathcal{I}', \mathcal{O}', p', q', c'_1; c_2)}$$

Fig. 4. Operational Semantics

multiple times to avoid the initial interleaving assignment, while the low output channels need to be duplicated, e.g. $\overline{\mathcal{O}}$ in Fig.2, to construct the illegal-flow state later. In order to avoid this duplication on low output channels, we match the low outputs generated in the serialized multi-execution with what generated and stored in the normal execution. For example we can substitute the command (∗) in Fig.2 with

$$\mathbf{if}\ \mathcal{O}_2[q_2] \neq 1\ \mathbf{then}\ \text{goto}\ error;\ \mathbf{else}\ q_2{+}{+};$$

The state *error* is the target state of reachability analysis. This variation reduces the state space of model. If the program is secure, e.g. substituting $input(x, \mathcal{I}_H)$ with $input(x, \mathcal{I}_2)$ in program P, the state *error* will be unreachable. The approach also captures the flow from channel on L_2 to channel on L_1 within the same model, therefore it is different from a memory-partitioning approach.

The structure of the paper is as follows. Section 2 presents the program model and the information flow security property for program with interactive I/Os. In Section 3 we describe the reachability analysis based on the multi-composition and extend the approach to a stronger termination-insensitive noninterference. Section 4 shows the experimental studies for evaluating precision and performance improvement. We conclude in Section 5.

2   Program Model and Security Property

The presentation language is deterministic and the syntax is given in Fig.3. $\mathcal{I}$ and $\mathcal{O}$ are respectively the set of input and output channels. $\mathcal{I}$ maps each channel identifier i to a linear list, denoted by $\mathcal{I}_i$, and $\mathcal{O}$ is defined similarly.

The command $input(x, \mathcal{I}_i)$ indicates the sink of input from $\mathcal{I}_i$ is x, and $output(e, \mathcal{O}_i)$ stores the value of expression e in the correct position of $\mathcal{O}_i$. The small-step operational semantics of the presentation language are given in Fig.4. Here we assume the evaluation of expression is atomic and unambiguous. A *configuration* is a tuple $(\mu, \mathcal{I}, \mathcal{O}, p, q, c)$, where $\mu : Var \mapsto \mathbb{N}$ is a memory store mapping variables to values and c is the command to be executed. p and q are set of indices. p_i denotes the index of next element to be input from $\mathcal{I}_i$, and q_i is the index of location of $\mathcal{O}_i$ where the next value is stored. The elements of p and q are explicitly increased by the computation of inputs and outputs.

Although the confidential data of high inputs may be related to previous low outputs according to the specification of environment, it cannot be exposed in any form during the execution of program, especially through the subsequent low outputs. In order to define the security condition for noninterference property, we assume $\sigma : \mathcal{I} \cup \mathcal{O} \mapsto \mathcal{D}$ maps the I/O channels to security levels of the lattice $\mathcal{D}$. We suppose initial values of variables in μ are irrelevant to the definition of noninterference and initialized to indefinite. This is different from batch-job model which attaches security level on each variable and uses equivalence relation on low part of memory stores to semantically specify noninterference. We can specify certain variable with input from a special channel to obtain the flexibility of security level of variables. The indistinguishability relation on $\mathcal{I}$ and $\mathcal{O}$ w.r.t. certain security level ℓ is given as below.

Definition 1 (ℓ-indistinguishability). *For security level $\ell(\ell \in \mathcal{D})$, The ℓ-indistinguishability relation, denoted by $\sim_\ell$, is defined respectively on input and output channels of a program:*

1. $\mathcal{I} \sim_\ell \mathcal{I}'$, iff $\forall i : \sigma(\mathcal{I}_i) \preceq \ell \Rightarrow \mathcal{I}_i \sim_\ell \mathcal{I}'_i$
2. $\mathcal{O} \sim_\ell \mathcal{O}'$, iff $\forall i : \sigma(\mathcal{O}_i) \preceq \ell \Rightarrow \mathcal{O}_i \sim_\ell \mathcal{O}'_i$
where $\mathcal{I}_i \sim_\ell \mathcal{I}_j$ iff $(\sigma(\mathcal{I}_i) = \sigma(\mathcal{I}_j) \preceq \ell) \wedge (p_i = p_j \wedge \forall 0 \le k < p_i : \mathcal{I}_i[k] = \mathcal{I}_j[k])$, and $\mathcal{O}_i \sim_\ell \mathcal{O}_j$ iff $(\sigma(\mathcal{O}_i) = \sigma(\mathcal{O}_j) \preceq \ell) \wedge (q_i = q_j \wedge \forall 0 \le k < q_i : \mathcal{O}_i[k] = \mathcal{O}_j[k])$.

For the two channels with same security level, the linear lists should have the same length and identical content. The content of channels with $\ell'(\ell' \succ \ell)$ is unobservable and irrelevant to the ℓ-indistinguishability as well as noninterference specification.

Then we specify the multi-execution of program with the simple lowest-first scheduler $\mathsf{select}_{\mathrm{lowprio}}$. This deterministic scheduler depends on a total order of the security lattice $\mathcal{D}$. If $\mathcal{D}$ is not a totally ordered lattice, because $\mathcal{D}$ is finite (the number of I/O channels is finite), a totally ordered extension $\hat{\mathcal{D}}$ of $\mathcal{D}$ always exists (see *linear extension*, 1.29,[6]). The extension can bring in additional legitimate channel for information leakage, e.g., if the example P in Sec.1.1 has a lattice $\{L_1 \preceq L_2, L_1 \preceq H, L_2 \preceq \top, H \preceq \top\}$ (H and L_2 are incomparable), P is judged secure under the extension $L_1 \preceq H \preceq L_2 \preceq \top$. To close this kind of channel from H to L_2, we require that each time we extend the lattice with $\ell_i \preceq \ell_j$, there should be $\exists \mathcal{I}_x \in \mathcal{I}.\sigma(\mathcal{I}_x) = \ell_j \vee \forall \mathcal{I}_x \in \mathcal{I}.\sigma(\mathcal{I}_x) \neq \ell_i$. That means ℓ_j should be attached to an input channel otherwise there are only outputs on ℓ_i. With the lowest-first scheduler, the secure multi-execution will be serialized

$$\frac{}{(\hat{\mathcal{D}},\mu,\mathcal{I},\mathcal{O},p,q,\mathbf{skip};c)\twoheadrightarrow(\hat{\mathcal{D}},\mu,\mathcal{I},\mathcal{O},p,q,c)}\qquad\frac{\mu(e)=v}{(\hat{\mathcal{D}},\mu,\mathcal{I},\mathcal{O},p,q,x:=e;c)\twoheadrightarrow(\hat{\mathcal{D}},\mu[x\mapsto v],\mathcal{I},\mathcal{O},p,q,c)}$$

$$\frac{\mu(e)=b}{(\hat{\mathcal{D}},\mu,\mathcal{I},\mathcal{O},p,q,\mathbf{if}\ e\ \mathbf{then}\ c_{\mathbf{true}}\ \mathbf{else}\ c_{\mathbf{false}})\twoheadrightarrow(\hat{\mathcal{D}},\mu,\mathcal{I},\mathcal{O},p,q,c_b)}$$

$$\frac{\mu(e)=\mathbf{true}}{(\hat{\mathcal{D}},\mu,\mathcal{I},\mathcal{O},p,q,\mathbf{while}\ e\ \mathbf{do}\ c)\twoheadrightarrow(\hat{\mathcal{D}},\mu,\mathcal{I},\mathcal{O},p,q,c;\mathbf{while}\ e\ \mathbf{do}\ c)}$$

$$\frac{\mu(e)=\mathbf{false}}{(\hat{\mathcal{D}},\mu,\mathcal{I},\mathcal{O},p,q,\mathbf{while}\ e\ \mathbf{do}\ c)\twoheadrightarrow(\hat{\mathcal{D}},\mu,\mathcal{I},\mathcal{O},p,q,\mathbf{skip})}$$

$$\frac{(\hat{\mathcal{D}},\mu,\mathcal{I},\mathcal{O},p,q,c_1)\twoheadrightarrow(\hat{\mathcal{D}}',\mu',\mathcal{I}',\mathcal{O}',p',q',c_1')}{(\hat{\mathcal{D}},\mu,\mathcal{I},\mathcal{O},p,q,c_1;c_2)\twoheadrightarrow(\hat{\mathcal{D}}',\mu',\mathcal{I}',\mathcal{O}',p',q',c_1';c_2)}$$

$$\frac{\sigma(\mathcal{O}_i)\neq\hat{\mathcal{D}}_\perp}{(\hat{\mathcal{D}},\mu,\mathcal{I},\mathcal{O},p,q,output(e,\mathcal{O}_i);c)\twoheadrightarrow(\hat{\mathcal{D}},\mu,\mathcal{I},\mathcal{O},p,q,c)}$$

$$\frac{\sigma(\mathcal{O}_i)=\hat{\mathcal{D}}_\perp\qquad\mu(e)=\mathcal{O}_i'[q_i]\qquad q_i'=q_i+1}{(\hat{\mathcal{D}},\mu,\mathcal{I},\mathcal{O},p,q,output(e,\mathcal{O}_i);c)\twoheadrightarrow(\hat{\mathcal{D}},\mu,\mathcal{I},\mathcal{O}',p,q',c)}$$

$$\frac{\hat{\mathcal{D}}_\perp\prec\sigma(\mathcal{I}_i)}{(\hat{\mathcal{D}},\mu,\mathcal{I},\mathcal{O},p,q,input(x,\mathcal{I}_i);c)\twoheadrightarrow(\hat{\mathcal{D}},\mu[x\mapsto\perp],\mathcal{I},\mathcal{O},p,q,c)}$$

$$\frac{\sigma(\mathcal{I}_i)\preceq\hat{\mathcal{D}}_\perp\qquad\mathcal{I}_i[p_i]=v\qquad p_i'=p_i+1}{(\hat{\mathcal{D}},\mu,\mathcal{I},\mathcal{O},p,q,input(x,\mathcal{I}_i);c)\twoheadrightarrow(\hat{\mathcal{D}},\mu[x\mapsto v],\mathcal{I},\mathcal{O},p',q,c)}$$

$$\frac{\hat{\mathcal{D}}\neq\{\hat{\mathcal{D}}_\perp\}\qquad\hat{\mathcal{D}}'=\hat{\mathcal{D}}\setminus\{\hat{\mathcal{D}}_\perp\}\qquad\forall i:p_i'=0}{(\hat{\mathcal{D}},\mu,\mathcal{I},\mathcal{O},p,q,\mathbf{skip})\twoheadrightarrow(\hat{\mathcal{D}}',\mu,\mathcal{I},\mathcal{O},p',q,P)}\qquad\frac{}{(\{\hat{\mathcal{D}}_\perp\},\mu,\mathcal{I},\mathcal{O},p,q,\mathbf{skip})\twoheadrightarrow(\emptyset,\mu,\mathcal{I},\mathcal{O},p,q,\mathbf{skip})}$$

Fig. 5. Semantics of Serialized SME with select$_{\mathrm{lowprio}}$

in that an execution on higher level should start after the executions on lower levels finished. For this special case we do not need to emit any signal between executions as a general scheduler does in [7], because the value should have been read by the execution on $\sigma(\mathcal{I}_i)$ when the execution on ℓ wants to read a value from $\mathcal{I}_i$ where $\sigma(\mathcal{I}_i)\preceq\ell$, otherwise the execution will be stuck and we do not need to weak up the waiting queue since it is always empty.

The formal semantics of the serialized secure multi-execution is given in Fig.5. Here $\twoheadrightarrow$ represents the secure multi-execution relation. Each configuration is extended with the total order lattice $\hat{\mathcal{D}}$. $\hat{\mathcal{D}}_\perp$ is the lower bound of $\hat{\mathcal{D}}$. $\hat{\mathcal{D}}$ shrinks during the execution. Each time an execution on $\hat{\mathcal{D}}_\perp$ is finished and $\hat{\mathcal{D}}_\perp$ is not the upper bound of the current $\hat{\mathcal{D}}$, $\hat{\mathcal{D}}_\perp$ is excluded from $\hat{\mathcal{D}}$ and an execution on a higher level is launched, otherwise $\hat{\mathcal{D}}$ reduces to $\emptyset$ and the execution terminates, see the last two rules of Fig.5 for details. The most obvious difference with common secure multi-execution [7] is the absence of global input pointer r. This will influence the manner of inputs from channel $\mathcal{I}_i$ on security level ℓ where $\sigma(\mathcal{I}_i)\prec\ell$. For the common secure multi-execution, when the input from a lower-level channel is allowed, the local input pointer does not need to be increased because the boundary of current input is held by $r(i)$ and this input is modeled as shared use. But in our semantics the reuse of these inputs is achieved by resetting the index of next element for each input channel. Another difference is the termination behavior of execution. The common secure multi-execution permits some execution to be divergent (then the final L_f won't be $\emptyset$) while our serialized version requires that each execution terminates to launch the execution on a higher level. Based on this requirement, the noninterference property we enforce is termination-insensitive. Let $\hat{\mathcal{D}}^\ell$ be the sublattice of $\hat{\mathcal{D}}$ consisting of all security levels lower or equal to ℓ. Noninterference is defined as follows.

Definition 2 (Noninterference). *Let* $(\mu, \mathcal{I}, \mathcal{O}, p, q, P) \rightarrow^* (\mu_f, \mathcal{I}, \mathcal{O}_f, p_f, q_f, $ **skip**$)$ *be any normal execution on inputs* $\mathcal{I}$, *and* $(\hat{\mathcal{D}}^\ell, \mu', \mathcal{I}', \mathcal{O}', p', q', P) \rightarrow^*$ $(\emptyset, \mu'_f, \mathcal{I}', \mathcal{O}'_f, p'_f, q'_f, $ **skip**$)$ *be any multi-execution on inputs* $\mathcal{I}'$. *Program* P *is noninterferent w.r.t. security level* ℓ, *if for any* $\mathcal{I}$ *and* $\mathcal{I}'$, *we have* $\forall \ell' \preceq \ell.\mathcal{I} \sim_{\ell'} \mathcal{I}'$ *implies* $\mathcal{O}_f \sim_{\ell'} \mathcal{O}'_f$.

This definition is more specific than the normal noninterference in [7] since we specify that the two correlative executions are taken firstly as normal execution and secondly as multi-execution. Because for terminating runs of noninterferent program, the secure multi-execution produces the same low observable outputs with normal execution, when the low inputs are indistinguishable, we can identify the interferent program by observing whether the outputs are different. We do not concentrate on whether the outputs generated by multi-execution of interferent program are meaningful, but just use the technique as a judgement on the conformance of program with security property. The enforcement is static, based on reachability analysis of pushdown model derived by a multi-compositional transformation, which is introduced in detail below.

3   Multi-compositional Enforcement

Self-composition is a model transformation technique composing program and its variable-renamed copy in order to reduce noninterference to a safety property on finite computations of program after composition. The multi-compositional approach does not compose program with a variable-renamed copy, but composes it with a sequential program serially modeling the multi-execution on the low security levels. We adapt the store-match pattern [21] to the multi-compositional approach. With this technique, only low channels need to be modeled and no channel needs to be duplicated in the model after multi-composition.

3.1   Model Construction

The abstract model we use is symbolic pushdown system. A pushdown system is a stack-based state transition system whose stack contained in each state can be of unbounded length. It is a natural model for sequential program with procedures. Symbolic pushdown system is a compact representation of pushdown system encoding the variables and computations symbolically.

Definition 3 (Symbolic Pushdown System). *Symbolic Pushdown System is a triple* $\mathcal{P} = (\mathcal{G}, \Gamma \times \mathcal{L}, \Delta)$. $\mathcal{G}$ *and* $\mathcal{L}$ *are respectively the domain of global variables and local variables.* Γ *is the stack alphabet.* Δ *is the set of symbolic pushdown rules* $\{\langle \gamma \rangle \hookrightarrow \langle \gamma_1 \cdots \gamma_n \rangle (\mathcal{R}) \mid \gamma, \gamma_1, \cdots, \gamma_n \in \Gamma \wedge \mathcal{R} \subseteq (\mathcal{G} \times \mathcal{L}) \times (\mathcal{G} \times \mathcal{L}^n) \wedge n \leq 2\}$.

The relation $\mathcal{R}$ specifies the variation of abstract variables before and after a single step of symbolic execution directed by the pushdown rule. The stack symbols denote the flow graph nodes of program.

Table 1. Normal Model Construction

c	$\Phi(c, \gamma_j, \gamma_k)$
skip	$\{\langle\gamma_j\rangle \hookrightarrow \langle\gamma_k\rangle\ rt(\mu, \cdots)\}$
$x := e$	$\{\langle\gamma_j\rangle \hookrightarrow \langle\gamma_k\rangle\ (x' = e) \wedge rt(\mu \setminus \{x\}, \cdots)\}$
IF	$\{\langle\gamma_j\rangle \hookrightarrow \langle\gamma_t\rangle\ rt(\mu, \cdots) \wedge e\} \cup \Phi(c_{\text{true}}, \gamma_t, \gamma_k) \cup$
	$\{\langle\gamma_j\rangle \hookrightarrow \langle\gamma_f\rangle\ rt(\mu, \cdots) \wedge \neg e\} \cup \Phi(c_{\text{false}}, \gamma_f, \gamma_k)$
WHILE	$\{\langle\gamma_j\rangle \hookrightarrow \langle\gamma_t\rangle\ rt(\mu, \cdots) \wedge e\} \cup \Phi(c_{\text{body}}, \gamma_t, \gamma_j) \cup$
	$\{\langle\gamma_j\rangle \hookrightarrow \langle\gamma_k\rangle\ rt(\mu, \cdots) \wedge \neg e\}$
$c_1; c_2$	$\Phi(c_1, \gamma_j, \gamma_{\text{mid}}) \cup \Phi(c_2, \gamma_{\text{mid}}, \gamma_k)$

The model construction of the commands other than I/O operations in Fig.3 is similar to the one in our previous work [19]. The abstract variable context with respect to certain stack symbol maps the abstract global and local variables to the value in $\mathcal{G}$ and $\mathcal{L}$. The model construction adds constraints to regulate each $\mathcal{R}$ of pushdown rule. The constraint is expressed with logical operation on abstract variables. The construction function Φ is presented in Table 1. Here rt means retainment on value of global variables and on value of local variables of the procedure locating the pushdown rule.

Then we explain how to construct the model for I/O operations. In our approach all channels are global. Because no variable can rely on an element of input channel except through an *input* command, we can simply omit the confidential channel $\mathcal{I}_i$ $(\sigma(\mathcal{I}_i) \succ \ell)$ and model $input(x, \mathcal{I}_i)$ as

$$\langle\gamma_j\rangle \hookrightarrow \langle\gamma_k\rangle\ (x' = \perp) \wedge rt(\mathcal{I}^\ell, \mathcal{O}^\ell, p^\ell, q^\ell, \cdots)$$

where $\mathcal{I}^\ell, \mathcal{O}^\ell, p^\ell, q^\ell$ are set of channels or indices with security level $\ell'(\ell' \preceq \ell)$. For $input(x, \mathcal{I}_i)$ where $\sigma(\mathcal{I}_i) \preceq \ell$, we need to model $\mathcal{I}_i$ explicitly and repeatedly use it in the model of multi-execution at level ℓ' where $\sigma(\mathcal{I}_i) \preceq \ell' \preceq \ell$:

$$\langle\gamma_j\rangle \overset{i}{\hookrightarrow} \langle\gamma_k\rangle\ (x' = \mathcal{I}_i[p_i]) \wedge (p'_i = p_i + 1) \wedge rt(\mathcal{I}^\ell, \mathcal{O}^\ell, p^\ell \setminus \{p_i\}, q^\ell)$$

Because there may be a certain thread in multi-execution with level $\ell'' \prec \sigma(\mathcal{I}_i)$ and we also want to identify the leakage to this lower level, we record the channel identifier i to distinguish different low threads in the multi-composition.

The output to confidential channel $\mathcal{O}_i$ with $\sigma(\mathcal{O}_i) \succ \ell$ can be substitute with a rule for **skip** since the confidential outputs do neither interfere with low part of subsequent states in normal execution nor interfere with the low threads in multi-execution. But for the public outputs on channel $\mathcal{O}_i$ with $\sigma(\mathcal{O}_i) \preceq \ell$, the command $output(e, \mathcal{O}_i)$ is modeled by the following pushdown rules

$$\langle\gamma_j\rangle \overset{i}{\hookrightarrow} \langle\text{out}_e\gamma_k\rangle\ (tmp' = e) \wedge rt(\mathcal{I}^\ell, \mathcal{O}^\ell, p^\ell, q^\ell) \wedge rt_2(\cdots)$$
$$\langle\text{out}_x\rangle \hookrightarrow \langle\epsilon\rangle\ \ \ \ \ \ \ \ \ \ rt(\mathcal{I}^\ell, \mathcal{O}^\ell, p^\ell, q^\ell)$$

Here tmp is a global variable. out_e and out_x are respectively the entry and exit node of flow graph of procedure *output*. rt_2 denotes retainment on value of local variables of the caller of procedure f in $\langle \gamma_j \rangle \hookrightarrow \langle f_{entry} \gamma_k \rangle$. The channel identifier is also explicitly recorded when entering procedure *output*. The body of model of procedure *output* is vacuous and will be constructed with pushdown rules acting a store-match pattern by the following model transformation.

3.2   Model Transformation

We perform the model transformation, i.e. multi-composition, on pushdown system constructed in the last section. The result has two parts. The first part is the pushdown rules w.r.t. the normal execution, which are actually the result of model construction except for the body of procedure *output*. The second part is the pushdown rules w.r.t. the multi-execution on low security levels. According to Definition 2, the input sequences used on certain low channel by normal execution and multi-execution should be identical as the precondition of proposition. Moreover, according to the semantics of serialized secure multi-execution (see Fig.5), the indices of input channels should be reset at the beginning of each thread. Therefore on each level of multi-execution, we reset the indices of input channels to reuse the elements on these channels. The output sequences are treated in a store-match pattern. When an output to $\mathcal{O}_i$ with $\sigma(\mathcal{O}_i) \preceq \ell$ has been computed in the multi-execution, we compare it with the corresponding output in the normal execution instead of storing it. If they are not equal, we direct the symbolic execution to the illegal-flow state, which has only itself as the next state. The pushdown rule for the body of procedure *output* in the normal execution is given as Out_s in Table 2. In the thread of multi-execution with security level $\ell' = \sigma(\mathcal{O}_i)$, the Out_m rules in Table 2 are used as the model of the body of *output*. Note that Out_s and Out_m are parameterized by the identifier i of output channel. Out_m is also parameterized by the security level of thread, i.e. ℓ'. ξ is a rename function on the stack symbols for generating new flow graph nodes for each low thread of multi-execution. When the illegal-flow state is reached, the postcondition of noninterference is violated. The precondition is satisfied by reusing the public input channels therefore from the reachability of state *error* we can ensure the violation of noninterference without considering the relation on the subsequent outputs.

The multi-composition algorithm is given in Algorithm 1. It derives the final set of symbolic pushdown rules Δ' from Δ of the result of model construction. *LastTrans* returns the pushdown rule corresponding to the last return command of program. The pushdown rules modeling the multi-execution are in fact parameterized by the security level ℓ_0 of each thread. ℓ_1 is recorded to construct the entry to the next thread. In particular, the pushdown rules w.r.t. the inputs and outputs in each thread are related to both the identifier of channel and the security level of thread.

Theorem 1 (Correctness). *Suppose $\mathcal{D}$ is a finite security lattice. For a security level ℓ ($\ell \in \mathcal{D}$), $\mathcal{P} \triangleright ME(\mathcal{P})$ is the pushdown system generated by the Multi-Composition on the model of program P, if the state* error *of $\mathcal{P} \triangleright ME(\mathcal{P})$ is not reachable from any possible initial state, P is noninterferent w.r.t. ℓ.*

(The proof is sketched in our technical report [22].)

Table 2. Stuffer Rules for Multi-Compositions

Abbr.	Pushdown Rules
$Out_s(i)$	$\langle out_c \rangle \hookrightarrow \langle out_x \rangle \ (\mathcal{O}'_i[q_i] = tmp) \wedge (q'_i = q_i + 1) \wedge rt(\mathcal{I}^\ell, \mathcal{O}^\ell \setminus \{\mathcal{O}_i[q_i]\}, p^\ell, q^\ell \setminus \{q_i\})$
$Out_m(i, \ell')$	$\langle \xi(\ell', out_c) \rangle \hookrightarrow \langle error \rangle \ (\mathcal{O}_i[q_i] \neq tmp) \wedge rt(\mathcal{I}^\ell, \mathcal{O}^\ell, p^\ell, q^\ell)$
	$\langle \xi(\ell', out_c) \rangle \hookrightarrow \langle \xi(\ell', out_x) \rangle \ (\mathcal{O}_i[q_i] = tmp) \wedge (q'_i = q_i + 1) \wedge rt(\mathcal{I}^\ell, \mathcal{O}^\ell, p^\ell, q^\ell \setminus \{q_i\})$
$Out'_s(i)$	$\langle out_c \rangle \hookrightarrow \langle out_m \rangle \ (\mathcal{O}'_i[q_i] = tmp) \wedge (q'_i = q_i + 1) \wedge rt(\mathcal{I}^\ell, \mathcal{O}^\ell \setminus \{\mathcal{O}_i[q_i]\}, p^\ell, q^\ell \setminus \{q_i\})$
	$\langle out_m \rangle \hookrightarrow \langle end \rangle \ (q_i = len) \wedge rt(\mathcal{I}^\ell, \mathcal{O}^\ell, p^\ell, q^\ell)$
	$\langle out_m \rangle \hookrightarrow \langle out_x \rangle \ (q_i \neq len) \wedge rt(\mathcal{I}^\ell, \mathcal{O}^\ell, p^\ell, q^\ell)$
$Out'_m(i, \ell')$	$\langle \xi(\ell', out_c) \rangle \hookrightarrow \langle error \rangle \ (\mathcal{O}_i[q_i] \neq tmp) \wedge rt(\mathcal{I}^\ell, \mathcal{O}^\ell, p^\ell, q^\ell)$
	$\langle \xi(\ell', out_c) \rangle \hookrightarrow \langle \xi(\ell', out_m) \rangle \ (\mathcal{O}_i[q_i] = tmp) \wedge (q'_i = q_i + 1) \wedge rt(\mathcal{I}^\ell, \mathcal{O}^\ell, p^\ell, q^\ell \setminus \{q_i\})$
	$\langle \xi(\ell', out_m) \rangle \hookrightarrow \langle \xi(\ell', succ) \rangle \ (q_i = len) \wedge rt(\mathcal{I}^\ell, \mathcal{O}^\ell, p^\ell, q^\ell)$
	$\langle \xi(\ell', out_m) \rangle \hookrightarrow \langle \xi(\ell', out_x) \rangle \ (q_i \neq len) \wedge rt(\mathcal{I}^\ell, \mathcal{O}^\ell, p^\ell, q^\ell)$

3.3   Security Enforcement for Divergent Program

As illustrated in [23], the automated safety analysis based on the self-composition actually enforces a *termination-insensitive noninterference* [24] (TINI), which is weaker than *termination-sensitive noninterference* [25] (TSNI). TSNI requires when an execution terminates on some input, any correlative execution on the low indistinguishable inputs should also terminate, and both executions generate low indistinguishable outputs. In another word, the executions from two indistinguishable inputs should both terminate or both diverge to satisfy TSNI. On the contrary, TINI allows the termination behavior to leak information. When an execution terminates on some input, there may be some divergent execution on low indistinguishable input. It only validates the indistinguishability on low outputs when both executions terminate. As mentioned in Section 2, the serialized secure multi-execution requires each thread terminates to launch the thread on a higher security level. Therefore the noninterference specified in Definition 2 and enforced in the last section is termination insensitive.

Askarov el al. [3] have demonstrated that for language with I/Os a divergent run can possibly leak all secret. Nonterminating program, which does not violate batch-job termination-insensitive noninterference, should be judged insecure. In order to adapt this requirement on termination-insensitive noninterference, we have to explicitly terminate the normal execution of program and ensure the terminated execution has the same semantic effect as the original divergent execution. Suppose the length of I/Os is finite. The key is to find the upper bound UB of the length of outputs. The algorithm to check conformance with this stronger termination-insensitive noninterference is given in Algorithm 2. The model $\mathcal{P}_{len}$ is parameterized by the length of channel len. We find the upper bound of the length of output sequence through a stepwise exponential reduction and linear extension. When the normal execution generates the len-th output, we explicitly direct to state end to terminate the execution. $Out_s(i)$ has to be extended to $Out'_s(i)$ in Table 2. If the upper bound is smaller than len, the divergent run will not get to end. For terminated program, we direct the last transition of normal execution to an idle state $noend$ in order to capture the upper bound of length of outputs. $\mathcal{P}_{len} \triangleright ME(\mathcal{P}_{len})$ is the model with pushdown rules generated by Algorithm 1. In the model the $Out_m(i, \ell')$ rules w.r.t. different security levels

Algorithm 1. Multi-Composition

1. $\Delta' \leftarrow \Delta \setminus LastTrans(\mathcal{P})$
2. **for all** $r \in \Delta$ **do** /*add connection from normal execution to multi-execution*/
3.   **if** $r.expr = \langle\gamma_j\rangle \hookrightarrow \langle\epsilon\rangle \wedge r = LastTrans(\mathcal{P})$ **then**
4. $\Delta' \leftarrow \Delta' \cup \{\langle\gamma_j\rangle \hookrightarrow \langle\xi(Lowest(\hat{\mathcal{D}}^\ell), startConf(\mathcal{P}))\rangle \; Reset(p^\ell, q^\ell)\}$
5.   **end if**
6. **end for**
7. **while** $(\ell_0, \ell_1) \leftarrow LowestTwo(\hat{\mathcal{D}}^\ell) \wedge \ell_0 \preceq \ell$ **do** /*deal with model on security level ℓ_0*/
8. $\hat{\mathcal{D}}^\ell \leftarrow \hat{\mathcal{D}}^\ell \setminus \{\ell_0\}$
9.   **for all** $r \in \Delta$ **do**
10.   **if** $r.expr = \langle\gamma_j\rangle \xrightarrow{i} \langle\text{out}_c\gamma_k\rangle$ **then** /*meet an output on channel $\mathcal{O}_i$*/
11. $\Delta' \leftarrow \Delta' \cup Out_s(i)$
12.   **if** $\sigma(\mathcal{O}_i) = \ell_0$ **then** /*the channel is on current security level*/
13. $\Delta' \leftarrow \Delta' \cup \{\langle\xi(\ell_0, \gamma_j)\rangle \hookrightarrow \langle\xi(\ell_0, \text{out}_c)\xi(\ell_0, \gamma_k)\rangle \; r.\mathcal{R}\} \cup Out_m(i, \ell_0)$
14.   **else**
15. $\Delta' \leftarrow \Delta' \cup \{\langle\xi(\ell_0, \gamma_j)\rangle \hookrightarrow \langle\xi(\ell_0, \gamma_k) \; rt(\mathcal{I}^\ell, \mathcal{O}^\ell, p^\ell, q^\ell, \cdots)\rangle\}$
16.   **end if**
17.   **else if** $r.expr = \langle\gamma_j\rangle \hookrightarrow \langle\gamma_s\gamma_k\rangle$ **then** /*normal inter-procedural calls other than outputs*/
18. $\Delta' \leftarrow \Delta' \cup \{\langle\xi(\ell_0, \gamma_j)\rangle \hookrightarrow \langle\xi(\ell_0, \gamma_s)\xi(\ell_0, \gamma_k)\rangle \; r.\mathcal{R}\}$

19.   **else if** $r.expr = \langle\gamma_j\rangle \xrightarrow{i} \langle\gamma_k\rangle$ **then** /*meet an input on channel $\mathcal{I}_i$*/
20.   **if** $\sigma(\mathcal{I}_i) \succ \ell_0$ **then** /*public input but confidential to the current security level*/
21. $\Delta' \leftarrow \Delta' \cup \{\langle\xi(\ell_0, \gamma_j)\rangle \hookrightarrow \langle\xi(\ell_0, \gamma_k)\rangle \; (x' = \bot) \wedge rt(\mathcal{I}^\ell, \mathcal{O}^\ell, p^\ell, q^\ell, \cdots)\}$
22.   **else**
23. $\Delta' \leftarrow \Delta' \cup \{\langle\xi(\ell_0, \gamma_j)\rangle \hookrightarrow \langle\xi(\ell_0, \gamma_k)\rangle \; r.\mathcal{R}\}$
24.   **end if**
25.   **else if** $r.expr = \langle\gamma_j\rangle \hookrightarrow \langle\gamma_k\rangle$ **then** /*normal intra-procedural transitions*/
26. $\Delta' \leftarrow \Delta' \cup \{\langle\xi(\ell_0, \gamma_j)\rangle \hookrightarrow \langle\xi(\ell_0, \gamma_k)\rangle \; r.\mathcal{R}\}$
27.   **else if** $r \neq LastTrans(\mathcal{P})$ **then** /*normal return*/
28. $\Delta' \leftarrow \Delta' \cup \{\langle\xi(\ell_0, \gamma_j)\rangle \hookrightarrow \langle\epsilon\rangle \; r.\mathcal{R}\}$
29.   **else** /*the last return, add connection to the next thread*/
30. $\Delta' \leftarrow \Delta' \cup \{\langle\xi(\ell_0, \gamma_j)\rangle \hookrightarrow \langle\xi(\ell_1, startConf(\mathcal{P}))\rangle \; Reset(p^\ell)\}$
31.   **end if**
32.   **end for**
33. **end while**

Algorithm 2. TINI for divergent program

1. $len \leftarrow 2^{MAX}$;
2. **while** $\neg Reachable(\mathcal{P}_{len}, end) \wedge len \neq 0$ **do** /*exponential reduction for region of upper bound*/
3. $len \leftarrow len/2$;
4. **end while**
5. $UB \leftarrow len$; $N \leftarrow len + 1$;
6. **while** $Reachable(\mathcal{P}_N, end) \wedge N < 2 \cdot len$ **do** /*linear extension to find the upper bound*/
7. $UB \leftarrow N$; $N \leftarrow N + 1$;
8. **end while**
9. **return** $\neg\bigvee_{len=1}^{UB} Reachable(\mathcal{P}_{len} \rhd ME(\mathcal{P}_{len}), error)$;

---

are extended to $Out'_m(i, \ell')$ in Table 2, where $\xi(\ell', succ)$ labels the last transition of thread on level ℓ' in the model of multi-execution. We can observe that the complexity is largely increased to $O((MAX + UB/2) \cdot C(\mathcal{P}) + UB \cdot C(\mathcal{P} \rhd ME(\mathcal{P})))$ where $C(\mathcal{P})$ is the complexity of reachability problem introduced in [17].

4 Evaluation

We embed our implementation in the parser of Remopla [11] and use the model checker Moped [12] as the back-end black-box engine for reachability analysis. The experimental environment is 1.66GHz×2 Intel CPU/1GB RAM/Linux ker-nal 2.6.27-14-generic. We investigated the following research questions: (1) Is the new approach as precise as other flow-sensitive static analysis, e.g. based on abstract interpretation [8]? (2) Does the store-match pattern really improve the performance of analysis compared with the common self-composition? (3) What is the real cost when we adapt the new approach to analyze termination-insensitive noninterference of divergent program? There are several factors that contribute to the experimental results to answer these questions. First is the length of channels. Because the low channels are semantically modeled in our approach, the increase on length of channels will also increase the size of BDDs as well as the state space of model. When we evaluate the efficiency of the new approach, we time the experimental results correlated with different lengths of channels. The second factor is the number of bits for each element of channels. The regions and operations on regions expressed with BDDs may require overall larger number of bits and state space to capture the behavior of concrete model.

To answer the questions, we first choose the test cases from related work. P1~P8 are from Fig.4 of [8] and `tax` is from Section 7 of [8]. 3_7, 3_8 and 3_11 are respectively the example 3.7, 3.8 and 3.11 from [5]. P0 is the motivating example in Section 1. A comparison of precision is given in Table 3. *NI* means the security of program w.r.t. the definition of noninterference. ✓ means the program is noninterferent and × means interferent. 3_7, 3_8 and 3_11 are judged by the definition of ID-security in [5]. *AI* means the analysis result using Iflow [13] and *SM* means the analysis result using our approach with store-match pattern. *LEN* is the length of channels used in our approach. Here we suppose all of the elements in channel are binary.

Table 3. Precision

Case	From	NI	AI	SM(LEN)	
				=1	≥2
P0	Sec.1	×	×	✓	×
P1	Fig.4,[8]	×	×	×	×
P2	Fig.4,[8]	×	×	×	×
P3	Fig.4,[8]	×	×	×	×
P4	Fig.4,[8]	×	×	×	×
P5	Fig.4,[8]	×	×	✓	×
P6	Fig.4,[8]	✓	✓	✓	✓
P7	Fig.4,[8]	✓	✓	✓	✓
P8	Fig.4,[8]	×	×	×	×
tax	Sec.7,[8]	×	×	✓	×
3_7	Ex3.7,[5]	×	×	×	×
3_8	Ex3.8,[5]	×	×	✓	×
3_11	Ex3.11,[5]	✓	×	✓	✓

We use static structure in P8 and `tax` to model dynamical object allocation. P1 and P2 show respectively typical explicit and implicit flow. P3 is verified insecure when we allow the boundary of input channel to be stored explicitly as output. At the end of the model of multi-execution we compare the boundary with the stored one and direct the state to *error* when they are not equal. P4 shows the leakage caused by the length of public output sequence. This leakage is captured by our approach since we can reach a case when the outputs of multi-execution is longer than that of normal execution and some newly output 1 is unequal to an indefinite value not covered by the output of normal execution. 3_8 is similar to P4. Our approach cannot close the terminating channel therefore 3_11 is treated as noninterferent program. On the other hand, the approach based on abstract interpretation is termination-sensitive. It captures the leakage of 3_11 though the ID-security is termination-insensitive. Because in P0,P5,`tax` and 3_8 the

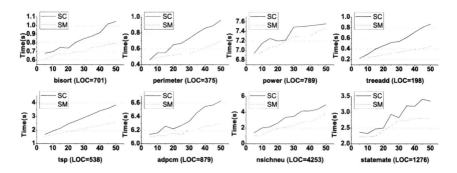

Fig. 6. Performance Improvement by Store-Match Pattern

leakages of confidential input are reflected by the second output, we can verify the program insecure only when $LEN \geq 2$. But with a sufficiently large boundary, our approach will not lose precision in these cases.

There are two limits on the precision of approach based on abstract interpretation. First, when the security lattice is more complex than $L \preceq H$, it has to partition the security lattice and the corresponding memory multiple times to capture all the leakages. For example, Iflow can capture the leakage of P0 from H to L_2 when partitioning the lattice by L_2 (that means P0 is the same as P5). But it cannot capture the leakage from L_2 to L_1 meanwhile with the same partitioning. Instead we need an individual model to capture this leakage. Second, although the both approaches are flow-sensitive, our approach can capture the value-dependent behavior of program while the approach based on abstract interpretation cannot. For example, although Iflow can judge P7 as secure program, it will mistakenly treat the program inH?x;y:=x-x;outL!y; to be insecure. Another example can be found in [23, Fig.1]: When we use Iflow to analyze the program, x is abstracted to H and y is abstracted to L in the final state. The security level of the output channel is raised from L to H if l is the output and the program is conservatively rejected. On the other hand, our approach recording the value of computation can verify it secure. The program in [23, Fig.9] is a similar case. The results indicate that our approach is more precise than the analysis based on abstract interpretation to enforce termination-insensitive noninterference.

Then we evaluate the performance improvement achieved by the store-match pattern. With multi-execution, the common self-composition duplicates the low output channels and constructs the illegal-flow state following the model of multi-execution. Here we choose 8 C-programs: the first five are from the Olden benchmarks [1], while adpcm, nsichneu and statemate are from the WCET benchmarks [2]. We model these programs with Remopla. The system calls and library calls are treated as stubs. The standard I/Os are considered as the I/Os to the channels. The external values and random values are modeled to be indefinite. The confidential input channels are randomly selected. Fig.6 shows the experimental results. SC denotes the results of common self-composition.

The length of channels ranges from 5 to 50. The number of bits of each integer variable and element in channels is set to 2. The results indicate the store-match pattern, which avoids duplication of channels, can improve the performance of reachability analysis.

We choose P0, P6, tax, 3_8 and 3_11 to evaluate the reduction on efficiency caused by adapting our approach to analyze termination-insensitive noninterference of divergent program. We suppose the initial MAX is 5 in Algorithm 2. The experimental results are presented in Fig.7. T_UB is the time to derive the upper bound of length of outputs (corresponding to the

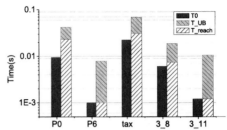

Fig. 7. Efficiency Reduction by divergence

cost of line 1~8 of Algorithm 2), while T_reach is the time of conjunction of reachability analysis (corresponding to the cost of line 9 of Algorithm 2). T0 is the time of reachability analysis proposed in Section 3.2. In P6 and 3_11 the length of output is 1 therefore T0 equals to T_reach in these cases. For terminating programs, the precision will not be lost when using Algorithm 2. The results also show that the cost to derive the upper bound UB becomes a major cost when UB is small. Another factor is MAX. It is clear that greater MAX will increase the cost to derive UB.

5   Conclusion

We present an approach based on automated verification to analyze two different versions of termination-insensitive noninterference of program with interactive I/Os on more complex security lattice. A store-match pattern is used to reduce the state space of model. The precision of the approach and the effect of store-match pattern are evaluated.

Acknowledgments. This work is supported by the Major National S&T Program (2011ZX03005-002), the National Natural Science Foundation of China under grant Nos. 60821003,60872041,60970135, the Fundamental Research Funds for the Central Universities (JY10000903001), and GAD Advanced Research Foundation (9140A15040210HK6101).

References

1. The olden benchmark suite v1.0, http://www.martincarlisle.com/olden.html
2. The worst-case execution time (wcet) analysis project/benchmarks (2006), http://www.mrtc.mdh.se/projects/wcet/benchmarks.html

3. Askarov, A., Hunt, S., Sabelfeld, A., Sands, D.: Termination-insensitive Noninterference Leaks More Than Just a Bit. In: Jajodia, S., Lopez, J. (eds.) ESORICS 2008. LNCS, vol. 5283, pp. 333–348. Springer, Heidelberg (2008)
4. Barthe, G., D'Argenio, P.R., Rezk, T.: Secure information flow by self-composition. In: CSFW, pp. 100–114. IEEE (2004)
5. Bohannon, A., Pierce, B.C., Sjöberg, V., Weirich, S., Zdancewic, S.: Reactive noninterference. In: CCS, pp. 79–90. ACM (2009)
6. Davey, B.A., Priestley, H.A.: Introduction to Lattices and Order. Cambridge University Press (2002)
7. Devriese, D., Piessens, F.: Noninterference through secure multi-execution. In: IEEE Symposium on Security and Privacy, pp. 109–124 (2010)
8. Francesco, N.D., Martini, L.: Instruction-level security typing by abstract interpretation. Int. J. Inf. Sec. 6(2-3), 85–106 (2007)
9. Goguen, J.A., Meseguer, J.: Security policies and security models. In: IEEE Symposium on Security and Privacy, pp. 11–20 (1982)
10. Le Guernic, G., Banerjee, A., Jensen, T.P., Schmidt, D.A.: Automata-based Confidentiality Monitoring. In: Okada, M., Satoh, I. (eds.) ASIAN 2006. LNCS, vol. 4435, pp. 75–89. Springer, Heidelberg (2008)
11. Holeček, J., Suwimonteerabuth, D., Schwoon, S., Esparza, J.: Introduction to remopla, http://www.fmi.uni-stuttgart.de/szs/tools/moped/remopla-intro.pdf
12. Kiefer, S., Schwoon, S., Suwimonteerabuth, D.: Moped: A model-checker for pushdown systems (2002), http://www.fmi.uni-stuttgart.de/szs/tools/moped/
13. Martini, L.: Iflow: a tool for information flow checking (2005), http://www.iet.unipi.it/l.martini/iflow.html
14. Naumann, D.A.: From Coupling Relations to Mated Invariants for Checking Information Flow. In: Gollmann, D., Meier, J., Sabelfeld, A. (eds.) ESORICS 2006. LNCS, vol. 4189, pp. 279–296. Springer, Heidelberg (2006)
15. O'Neill, K.R., Clarkson, M.R., Chong, S.: Information-flow security for interactive programs. In: CSFW, pp. 190–201. IEEE (2006)
16. Sabelfeld, A., Myers, A.C.: Language-based information-flow security. IEEE Journal on Selected Areas in Communications 21(1), 5–19 (2003)
17. Schwoon, S.: Model Checking Pushdown Systems. Ph.D. thesis, Technical University of Munich, Munich, Germany (2002)
18. Smith, S.F., Thober, M.: Improving usability of information flow security in java. In: PLAS, pp. 11–20. ACM (2007)
19. Sun, C., Tang, L., Chen, Z.: Secure information flow by model checking pushdown system. In: UIC-ATC, pp. 586–591. IEEE (2009)
20. Sun, C., Tang, L., Chen, Z.: Secure information flow in java via reachability analysis of pushdown system. In: QSIC, pp. 142–150. IEEE (2010)
21. Sun, C., Tang, L., Chen, Z.: A new enforcement on declassification with reachability analysis. In: INFOCOM Workshops, pp. 1024–1029. IEEE (2011)
22. Sun, C., Zhai, E., Chen, Z., Ma, J.: A multi-compositional enforcement on information flow security. Tech. rep., Institute of Software, School of EECS, Peking University (2011), http://infosec.pku.edu.cn/~suncong/sun2011a-tr.pdf
23. Terauchi, T., Aiken, A.: Secure Information Flow as a Safety Problem. In: Hankin, C., Siveroni, I. (eds.) SAS 2005. LNCS, vol. 3672, pp. 352–367. Springer, Heidelberg (2005)
24. Volpano, D.M., Irvine, C.E., Smith, G.: A sound type system for secure flow analysis. Journal of Computer Security 4(2/3), 167–188 (1996)
25. Volpano, D.M., Smith, G.: Eliminating covert flows with minimum typings. In: CSFW, pp. 156–169. IEEE (1997)

HyperCrop: A Hypervisor-Based Countermeasure for Return Oriented Programming*

Jun Jiang[1], Xiaoqi Jia[1], Dengguo Feng[1], Shengzhi Zhang[2], and Peng Liu[2]

[1] State Key Laboratory of Information Security,
Institute of Software, Chinese Academy of Sciences,
Beijing 100190, China
{jiangjun,xjia,feng}@is.iscas.ac.cn
[2] Pennsylvania State University,
University Park, PA 16802, USA
suz116@psu.edu, pliu@ist.psu.edu

Abstract. Return oriented programming (ROP) has recently caught great attention of both academia and industry. It reuses existing binary code instead of injecting its own code and is able to perform arbitrary computation due to its Turing-completeness. Hence, It can successfully bypass state-of-the-art code integrity mechanisms such as NICKLE and SecVisor. In this paper, we present HyperCrop, a hypervisor-based approach to counter such attacks. Since ROP attackers extract short instruction sequences ending in `ret` called "gadgets" and craft stack content to "chain" these gadgets together, our method recognizes that the key characteristics of ROP is to fill the stack with plenty of addresses that are within the range of libraries (e.g. libc). Accordingly, we inspect the content of the stack to see if a potential ROP attack exists. We have implemented a proof-of-concept system based on the open source Xen hypervisor. The evaluation results exhibit that our solution is effective and efficient.

Keywords: Return oriented programming, Hypervisor-based security, Hardware assisted virtualization.

1 Introduction

Recently, return oriented programming (ROP) has drawn a lot of researchers' attention [18]. ROP attacks stem from previous return-to-libc (RTL) attacks [20]. Generally, RTL attacks construct a stack via techniques, such as buffer overflow, to transfer the control flow of a program to a function of libc (e.g., system) with provided parameters (e.g., "/home/user/evil") to perform function

---

* This work was supported by National Natural Science Foundation of China (NSFC) under Grant No. 61100228 and 61073179. Peng Liu was supported by AFOSR FA9550-07-1-0527 (MURI), ARO W911NF-09-1-0525 (MURI), and NSF CNS-0905131.

S. Qing et al. (Eds.): ICICS 2011, LNCS 7043, pp. 360–373, 2011.

calls from the victim program. ROP attacks refine this idea and use a stack to redirect the control flow to a specific location inside a library, rather than the entry of a function. The location is carefully chosen so that the attacker can retain the control of the execution flow. Specifically, the attacker firstly identifies instruction sequences that end in `ret` instruction, which are called "gadgets". Due to the large code base provided by libraries installed on a common computer, theses gadgets can constitute a Turing-complete gadget set. The attacker can select several useful gadgets to perform desired computations. Since each gadget ends in `ret`, the attacker can exploit the buffer overflow vulnerability of the victim program and fill the stack with corresponding addresses. We will illustrate the ROP attacks by an example in Section 2.1.

The key point of ROP attacks is that no code injection is needed. Instead, the existing legitimate library code is misused intentionally to perform malicious behavior. Hence, many code integrity mechanisms such as NICKLE [15] and SecVisor [17] are not designed to protect the system against such attacks. Besides, libraries leveraged by ROP attacks are also essential to benign programs, so it's not feasible to counter such attacks by removing these libraries. Moreover, though the ROP attack was first introduced on the x86 architecture, now it has been extended to various architectures such as ARM [9] and SPARC [4]. Featuring these characteristics, ROP has become a new threat to computer security.

Several solutions for ROP have been proposed by researchers and can be categorized in instrumentation-based solutions [5,6] and compiler-based solutions [10,14]. However, these existing countermeasures suffer from various disadvantages and practical deficiencies. We will discuss the details in Section 7.

In this paper, we present HyperCrop, a hypervisor-based approach for ROP detection and prevention. We summarize the key characteristic of ROP attacks, and perform the stack content inspection method to calculate library addresses within the stacks and to protect the target system from the attacks. We also leverage the contemporary hardware virtualization technique, i.e., Intel VT, to facilitate our design.

In summary, we make the following contributions:

- We propose a hypervisor-based approach to defend ROP attacks. To the best of our knowledge, we are the first to use hardware-assisted virtualization as the underlying technology for ROP defense. Our approach is transparent to the protected system and does not rely on its correctness.
- We present a novel algorithm to detect ROP attacks by inspecting the content of current thread stack. By adjusting the parameters, this algorithm can effectively detect ROP attacks and has low false alarm rate.
- We have implemented a proof-of-concept system called HyperCrop based on the open source Xen hypervisor [2]. Our evaluation shows that this system is effective and efficient.

The rest of this paper is organized as follows. In section 2, we discuss the attack scenario and threat model of ROP attacks. Our system design and implementation are presented in Section 3 and Section 4, respectively. Then we give the evaluation results in Section 5. After that, possible limitations and future work are discussed in Section 6. Finally, we discuss related work in Section 7 and conclude our paper in Section 8.

2   Attack Scenario and Threat Model

In this section, we first give a typical example to show how ROP attacks are constructed and applied. Then we identify the key feature of ROP attacks and take advantage of it for defense. Finally, we generalize a threat model of ROP and make some assumptions in our countermeasure.

2.1   ROP Attack Scenario

We demonstrate how a ROP attack is constructed. First, we can consider how one instruction is written in a return-oriented way. Take `inc eax` as an example, the attacker first obtains that its machine code is `0x40`, and appends it with a `ret` whose machine code is `0xc3`. Then he searches the byte sequence `0x40c3` in a library, and obtains the location of the sequence. This location is translated into a runtime memory address, which is finally put on top of the stack. Since complicated functionality is composed by multiple instructions, the attacker can use the above method to process instructions one by one to accomplish a real attack. Note this can be done totally in an automatic way [7]. When the payload is generated, the attacker feeds it to a program with buffer overflow vulnerability. On top of the stack resides the address of the first instruction to be executed, and a simple `ret` will trigger the attack.

Several observations are presented below. Firstly, some buffer overflow vulnerabilities are caused by `strcpy`, so null byte should be avoided in the payload. Secondly, it is difficult to find a gadget corresponding to a complicated instruction whose machine code is really long, so such instruction should be decomposed into several smaller ones. Finally, immediate data can also be put on the stack. Specific details can be found in [16].

From above we summarize that the key characteristic of the ROP attack is filling the stack with a payload containing plenty of addresses that are within libraries and a few immediate data. Normally, the stack is used for local variables, function parameters and return addresses. We believe that these two kinds of stack usage can be distinguished with reasonable effort, which is the key of our countermeasure.

2.2   Threat Model and Assumption

Inspired by the above scenario, we generalize the threat model of ROP attacks. We assume that there are programs in the protected system that are vulnerable to stack overflow attack. We consider those programs to be our protection targets. The attacker tries to exploit such overflow vulnerability to perform ROP attacks.

Since our method involves virtualization technology, we also make the assumption that the VMM is always trusted. This is usually a fundamental assumption for hypervisor-based security researches and is consolidated (though not guaranteed) by existing hypervisor protection mechanisms [12,1,19]. In our threat model, we assume that the VMM is secure and the attacks to the VMM are out of the scope of this paper.

3   System Design

In this work, we design a hypervisor-based approach to defend ROP attacks. Specifically, we utilize the higher privilege of the VMM to intercept write operations to the stack and to inspect the content of the stack for the detection of ROP attacks. Moreover, our system should work effectively and introduce as low performance overhead as possible.

Our system is built upon the existing VMM and contains four parts: an event handling component, a stack marking component, a breakpoint locating component and a stack inspecting component. The system architecture is shown in Fig. 1.

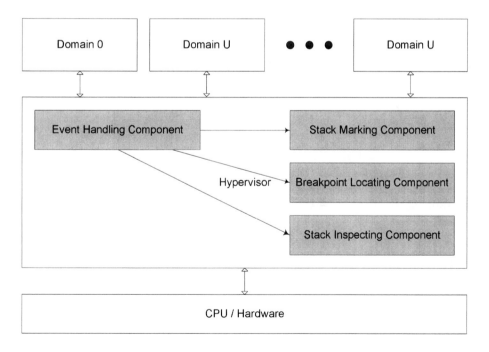

Fig. 1. Architecture of HyperCrop

3.1   Event Handling Component

Since we use hypervisor based approach to defend ROP attacks, in order to intercept stack write and perform stack content inspection correctly, we need to modify the following three event handlers of the VMM.

Context Switch Handler. Because our protection target is a single program, we limit our scope to a specific process. We modify the context switch handler of the VMM to identify if the next-to-be-scheduled process is our protection target. If so, the stack marking component is called to mark the stack of the process read-only in the shadow page table. Detailed explanations are given in Section 3.2.

Page Fault Handler. The page fault handler of the VMM needs to be modified in order to intercept write operations to the stack and call our breakpoint locating component. Since the stack is marked as read-only, a write to the stack will cause a page fault and will be trapped by the VMM. The default page fault handler will notice that this page fault is caused by intentionally marking a writable memory region as read-only, so it will mark the corresponding stack area writable again. Our additional handler will then call the breakpoint locating component to find a specific position as a hardware breakpoint. The selection method of the breakpoint is discussed in Section 3.3.

Debug Exception Handler. The hardware breakpoint will trigger a debug exception, which is also trapped by the VMM. We modify the handler to perform two operations: a) mark the stack area read-only again; b) call the stack inspecting component to detect whether a ROP attack is present.

3.2   Stack Marking Component

This component will be used under two circumstances: a) when a context switch happens and the next-to-be-scheduled process is our protection target; b) when a stack inspection is performed. The purpose of marking stack as read-only is to arouse page fault so that write operations to the stack can be intercepted and processed.

Under x86 architecture, the top of a stack is designated by the general purpose register esp. However, as the program executes, its value changes frequently. Since modern operating systems usually allocate fixed memory space for the stack, stack range can be obtained from the OS data structures and the corresponding memory pages can be marked as read-only. Under virtualization environment, shadow paging is a common software solution for memory virtualization. When shadow paging is utilized in virtualization environment, a shadow page table is used for address translation, so its entries should be set as non-writable.

3.3   Breakpoint Locating Component

A breakpoint is a checkpoint where inspection of the stack content should be performed. This component is called by the page fault handler, and the value provided by this component will be used to set as the breakpoint.

Since a ROP attack is initiated by a `ret` instruction, this component will find the next `ret` in the instruction stream from current `eip`. Instructions between current `eip` and the breakpoint will run natively and will not be disturbed. This is an important performance guarantee of our system since the stack is used very frequently. Inspecting the content of the stack every time when it is written would introduce significant performance overhead.

3.4   Stack Inspecting Component

When a breakpoint is met, HyperCrop performs stack content inspection in order to identify whether a ROP attack is present.

According to the feature summarized in Section 2.1, we devise the following algorithm to inspect the content of the stack.

Definition 1. *Potential Gadget Address Set (PGAS) is a set of addresses that are within the address space of the libraries (e.g., libc) which attackers could potentially exploit. We use Φ to represent PGAS.*

Definition 2. *Top N Stack Element Array (TNSEA) is an array of elements that is located on top of the stack. Each element is 4-byte long for alignment, and the stack grows down. So the TNSEA occupies the virtual address space ranging from [esp] to [esp] - 4 * N. We use $\mathcal{A}$ to represent TNSEA, and $\mathcal{A}[i]$ to represent the i-th element of TNSEA, which is located at [esp] - 4 * (i - 1).*

Definition 3. *Suspected Gadget Address Ratio (SGAR) is a value indicating the number of elements in TNSEA which belong to PGAS. We use R(N) to represent SGAR, where N is the size of TNSEA. So we have $R(N) = \frac{\sum_{i=1}^{N}(\mathcal{A}[i]\in\Phi)?1:0}{N}$. Obviously, the range of R(N) is from 0 to 1.*

Since attackers fill the stack with plenty of return addresses, the values returned from function R will be much larger (e.g., > 0.8) if a ROP attack is present. We may set up a threshold and compare it with the calculated value R to identify such attacks. The threshold must be carefully chosen in order to balance the false positive rate and the false negative rate.

4   Implementation

We have developed a proof-of-concept system based on Xen 4.0.1, running fully-virtualized Windows XP SP3 (x86-32) on top of a 64-bit VMM. Our development machine has an Intel Core i5 processor with the latest hardware virtualization technology support. In the following, we present some implementation details for the key techniques in our approach.

4.1 Modifications to Xen's Handlers

In hardware-assisted virtualization environment, if a guest OS tries to perform some privileged or sensitive operations, an event called VMEXIT will occur. The processor switches its privilege level from VMX non-root mode to VMX root mode, and calls a previously registered VMEXIT handler to deal with this event. Xen handles these events appropriately for correct virtualization, and we make several modifications to fulfill our needs.

Modifications to the Context Switch Handler. The context switch mechanism provided by the x86 architecture called TSS (Task State Segment) is not used by modern operating systems. Instead, we find that a context switch involves the change of the page table base address register (i.e., CR3), because modern operating systems utilize the paging mechanism to achieve process space isolation. Therefore, our modification target is CR_ACCESS instead of TASK_SWITCH. Moreover, the stack area of a certain thread is fixed. We locate the range of the stack through the kernel data structure information every time when a context switch occurs and save it for future use.

Modifications to the Page Fault Handler. The page fault handler is one of the most complicated parts of the VMEXIT handler under shadow paging mode. We write our own page fault handler to wrap the original one. The return value of the page fault handler is either "1" or "0". The former indicates that the page fault is caused by the "out of sync" shadow page table, while the latter indicates that this is a real guest page fault and the operating system should handle it. So we define a page fault is caused by stack write if the following three conditions are satisfied: a) the original page fault handler returns "1"; b) the page fault linear address is within the stack range; c) the page fault error code indicates a write access. For stack writes, an appropriate hardware breakpoint is set via x86 debugging mechanism. The DR0 register is used to save this breakpoint and relevant bits in DR7 are set to enable this breakpoint.

Modifications to the Debug Exception Handler. The original debug exception handler is a part of Xen's debugging facility. We modify the handler to implement our functionality. First of all, the original handler crashes a domain if a debugger is not attached or the monitor flag is not set. We remove this restriction to prevent the domain crashing. Moreover, we clear the content of the DR0 register to disable the current breakpoint. Finally, we trigger the stack inspecting component to identify potential ROP attacks and stack marking component to mark the stack as read-only again so a later stack write will cause a new inspection loop.

4.2 Marking the Stack

To mark the stack as read-only, we utilize several shadow page table related functionalities provided by Xen hypervisor. Firstly we walk through the shadow page table for the specific linear address. We obtain the corresponding page table entry from the walk-through results and reset the RW bit. Then the new page table entry is written to the shadow page table. Finally a TLB flush is performed since the access privilege is lowered.

4.3   Locating Breakpoints

In order to locate a breakpoint where stack content inspection needs to be performed, we disassemble the instructions from current `eip` to find the next `ret` instruction to be executed. Furthermore, we are only concerned about the length of the instructions instead of exact disassembling results. Thus, we only need to identify the opcode, which determines the addressing mode and ultimately the instruction length. Since the implementation is inside Xen kernel without any method to resort to third party libraries, we have to write the disassembling code by our own.

The instruction complexity of x86 (a kind of CISC architecture) imposes several challenges to our implementation. Moreover, besides `ret`, there are other control transfer related instructions whose execution may diverge the control flow:

- Conditional jumps. Since Xen does not emulate the execution of the instructions, we cannot calculate whether the instructions before conditional jumps have effects on the EFLAGS register.
- Jumps and calls whose targets are given by registers or memory locations. Similarly, we do not calculate whether the instructions before them change the value of the specific register or memory location. Hence, we do not determine these jumps/calls' targets. Instead, we only handle conditional jumps and calls whose target is specified in the form of immediate number.
- Instructions that cause privilege level change. These instructions cause control flow transfer as well as privilege level change. Since we currently do not trace into kernel, we ignore these instructions.
- Some complicated instructions. These instructions include infrequently used 2-byte-opcode instructions, e.g., all MMX, SSE, VMX instructions. Actually they are rarely used in our experimental instruction sequences. So we think not handling them will not affect the effectiveness and performance.

When we encounter the above instructions, we consider them to be the breakpoint locations as well as `ret`.

4.4   Inspecting the Stack Content

In order to inspect the content of the stack, we first read the stack elements by copying 400 bytes from `esp` (since we inspect the top 100 elements). For each element, we check if it is within the range of libraries. If so, we increase a counter α. Finally, we calculate the ration $\rho = \frac{\alpha}{100}$. In our implementation, we find that sometimes the `esp` points to the kernel stack instead of the user stack. Since the kernel stack is not of our concern, we ignore such cases.

5   Evaluation

In this section, we give the experimental evaluation of our HyperCrop prototype. Our evaluation has two goals. The first is to evaluate the effectiveness of HyperCrop for defending real ROP attacks, while the second is to measure the performance overhead introduced by the system using benchmarks.

The following experiments were all conducted on a machine with Intel Core i5-760 processor and 8GB memory. The version of Xen used in our experiment is 4.0.1 and the dom0 is 64 bit CentOS 5.5 with kernel version 2.6.34.4. The guest OS is Windows XP SP3 allocated with one processor core and 2 GB memory.

5.1   Effectiveness

In order to evaluate the effectiveness of our system, we first recall the characteristics of the ROP attack we summarized in Section 2.1. The stack contains many return addresses within the libraries, which can be easily distinguished from normal stacks. We consider this anomaly by previously defined function R(N). Specifically, we run 12 normal programs and calculate the results of the function R(N). These results are corresponding to "normal" stacks. We select the DLL memory regions which are related to the protected program such as 0x7d590000 ˜ 0x7dd84000 (shell32.dll), 0x7c800000 ˜ 0x7c91e000 (kernel32.dll), 0x7c920000 ˜ 0x7c9b3000 (ntdll.dll) and 0x77d10000 ˜ 0x77da0000 (user32.dll)[1]. These four DLLs are similar to libc since they are dynamically linked to almost every executable.

Table 1 shows that the results of function R(N) are relatively small for normal programs. The above four DLLs are selected because the attacker usually hopes that the code base is general to all programs. Some attackers may specifically analyze a certain program for exploitation, hence all the DLLs linked by the program can be available as code base. We also conducted such experiment by selecting 0x20000000 ˜ 0x7ffd0000[2] as the range. This range is big enough to contain almost all DLLs linked by a program (occupying almost 3/4 of the user space). The corresponding Max R(100) and Average R(100) are 56% and 19%, respectively. In contrast, a typical ROP attack payload usually contains tens or hundreds of return addresses and a few immediate data. There does exist a manifest boundary between normal stacks and attacked stacks. Hence, we believe that our system provides an effective countermeasure for ROP attacks. However, several elaborate attacks may affect our inspection algorithm as discussed in Section 6.

---

[1] We parse the PE structure manually to obtain these memory ranges. Windows XP does not support ASLR (address space layout randomization) so these addresses are fixed. On operating systems that support ASLR, these addresses can be obtained by traversing the VAD (virtual address descriptor).

[2] 0x7ffd0000U to 0x7fffffffU are used for PEB and TEB, so we don't include this area to avoid false alarms.

Table 1. Result of function R(N) for normal stacks

Program	Inspection Count	Max R(100)	Average R(100)
Notepad	3679	24%	5.5%
MS Paint	3730	33%	8.4%
Calculator	2507	27%	5.1%
Mine Sweeper	953	24%	10.0%
RegEdit	616	22%	8.1%
7-Zip	307	27%	8.2%
WinRAR	960	21%	5.8%
Internet Explorer	8140	27%	5.1%
Mozilla Firefox	6899	30%	3.6%
Microsoft Word	9302	31%	4.6%
Microsoft Excel	15605	32%	5.7%
Microsoft PowerPoint	6983	29%	6.5%

5.2 Performance

In order to evaluate the performance of our system, we use DAMN Hash Calculator and Everest to perform several benchmark tests. We show the normalized performance overhead in Fig. 2. The evaluation results demonstrate that our system incurs acceptable performance overhead and provides a practical countermeasure for ROP attacks.

6 Discussion

The above evaluation exhibits that our current prototype can successfully and practically defend ROP attacks. In this section, we discuss several limitations of HyperCrop prototype.

Firstly, several researchers have put forward other relevant attacks. Instead of `ret` instructions, attackers can use other control flow transfer instructions like `jmp` to initiate similar attacks and compromise the control flow [3]. Since these attacks do not rely on the stack for control flow retention, our countermeasure cannot defeat such attacks. Moreover, ROP attacks can also be mounted on the operating system kernel [7], while our system currently protects user applications only. We leave defense measures for these new attacks as our future work.

Secondly, the hardware-assisted virtualization is currently only available for x86 architecture, limiting its application for other architectures. Software-based virtualization is able to solve this problem though it may introduce more overhead. We believe hardware-assisted virtualization for other platforms will be available as the VM techniques develop, then our approach can be extended to those platforms.

Finally, our algorithm may be subverted by some tricks, e.g., replacing `ret` instruction with `retn` instruction. The `retn` instruction has an immediate parameter. It not only pops the top of stack to `eip` but also changes the value of `esp`.

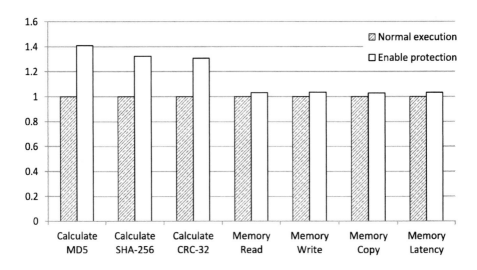

Fig. 2. Normalized performance overhead

Hence, the return addresses in the stack can be separated by junk data, which makes the stack resemble normal. However, we don't think such attack is a big threat to our system. First, `retn` instruction is not frequently used in libraries making it difficult to generate a Turing-complete gadget set with `retn`. Second, to subvert our approach, the return addresses must be distributed sparsely enough within the stack. However, the stack size of the system is limited, and performing a task in a return-oriented way needs more instructions (return addresses) than normal. These constraints make it difficult for the attackers to use `retn` in their attacks. Finally, we can enhance our inspection algorithm. For example, we can use approaches similar to program shepherding [8] for fine grained ROP detection or integrating existing ROP defending techniques in our framework [5,6].

7   Related Work

W^X Mechanism. W^X mechanism [21] is an effective countermeasure to code injection attacks, but not for ROP attacks. An attacker utilizes vulnerabilities like stack overflow to inject his or her own code to the stack of the victim program. A key feature of code injection is that the code is written to memory as data but executed as code. The W^X mechanism ensures that the writable memory region must not be executable, hence naturally defeats code injection attacks. However, the data written by ROP attacks to the stack are return addresses and immediate data, which are never executed as code. Hence, ROP attacks can succeed without violation of W^X policy.

ROP Defense. There are several existing solutions for ROP attacks, relying on different characteristics of such attacks. On one hand, since ROP attacks rely on the `ret` instructions of the library files, an intuitive idea is to remove all `ret` instructions, both intentional and unintentional, and to use return indices to replace return addresses in the stack to avoid pop-jmp scheme which is also exploitable to attackers [10]. The approach proposed in [14] is more deliberate and eliminates almost all possibilities that a benign library could be misused. These compiler-based solutions require the availability of the library source code, hence are not able to protect commercial operating systems (e.g. Microsoft Windows) against such attacks. On the other hand, a key feature of ROP attacks is frequent appearance of `ret` in the instruction sequence [5]. Furthermore, these `ret` instructions are deliberately crafted and have no corresponding `calls`, so the stack's First-In-Last-Out property is violated [6]. Hence several researchers use dynamic binary instrumentation frameworks like Pin [11] or Valgrind [13] to instrument program code to identify such attacks. These instrumentation-based solutions incur high overhead (e.g., > 400%). Compared to those kinds of methods, HyperCrop does not require source code and has low performance penalty.

8   Conclusion

In this paper, we present HyperCrop, a hypervisor-based system for defending ROP attacks. We leverage the contemporary hardware assisted virtualization technology as well as novel algorithm design to achieve high detection rate and low performance overhead. Our experiments exhibit that HyperCrop can effectively and efficiently detect ROP attacks before their initiation. We believe that our system provides a practical defense again ROP attacks.

References

1. Azab, A.M., Ning, P., Wang, Z., Jiang, X., Zhang, X., Skalsky, N.C.: HyperSentry: enabling stealthy in-context measurement of hypervisor integrity. In: Proceedings of the 17th ACM Conference on Computer and Communications Security, CCS 2010, pp. 38–49. ACM, New York (2010)
2. Barham, P., Dragovic, B., Fraser, K., Hand, S., Harris, T., Ho, A., Neugebauer, R., Pratt, I., Warfield, A.: Xen and the art of virtualization. In: Proceedings of the Nineteenth ACM Symposium on Operating Systems Principles, SOSP 2003, pp. 164–177. ACM, New York (2003)
3. Bletsch, T., Jiang, X., Freeh, V.W., Liang, Z.: Jump-oriented programming: a new class of code-reuse attack. In: Proceedings of the 6th ACM Symposium on Information, Computer and Communications Security, ASIACCS 2011, pp. 30–40. ACM, New York (2011)
4. Buchanan, E., Roemer, R., Shacham, H., Savage, S.: When good instructions go bad: generalizing return-oriented programming to RISC. In: Proceedings of the 15th ACM Conference on Computer and Communications Security, CCS 2008, pp. 27–38. ACM, New York (2008)

5. Chen, P., Xiao, H., Shen, X., Yin, X., Mao, B., Xie, L.: DROP: Detecting Return-Oriented Programming Malicious Code. In: Prakash, A., Sen Gupta, I. (eds.) ICISS 2009. LNCS, vol. 5905, pp. 163–177. Springer, Heidelberg (2009)

6. Davi, L., Sadeghi, A.-R., Winandy, M.: ROPdefender: a detection tool to defend against return-oriented programming attacks. In: Proceedings of the 6th ACM Symposium on Information, Computer and Communications Security, ASIACCS 2011, pp. 40–51. ACM, New York (2011)

7. Hund, R., Holz, T., Freiling, F.C.: Return-oriented rootkits: bypassing kernel code integrity protection mechanisms. In: Proceedings of the 18th Conference on USENIX Security Symposium, SSYM 2009, pp. 383–398. USENIX Association, Berkeley (2009)

8. Kiriansky, V., Bruening, D., Amarasinghe, S.P.: Secure execution via program shepherding. In: Proceedings of the 11th USENIX Security Symposium, pp. 191–206. USENIX Association, Berkeley (2002)

9. Kornau, T.: Return oriented programming for the ARM architecture. Master's thesis, Ruhr-Universitat Bochum (2010)

10. Li, J., Wang, Z., Jiang, X., Grace, M., Bahram, S.: Defeating return-oriented rootkits with "return-less" kernels. In: Proceedings of the 5th European Conference on Computer Systems, EuroSys 2010, pp. 195–208. ACM, New York (2010)

11. Luk, C.-K., Cohn, R., Muth, R., Patil, H., Klauser, A., Lowney, G., Wallace, S., Reddi, V.J., Hazelwood, K.: Pin: building customized program analysis tools with dynamic instrumentation. In: Proceedings of the 2005 ACM SIGPLAN Conference on Programming Language Design and Implementation, PLDI 2005, pp. 190–200. ACM, New York (2005)

12. Murray, D.G., Milos, G., Hand, S.: Improving Xen security through disaggregation. In: Proceedings of the Fourth ACM SIGPLAN/SIGOPS International Conference on Virtual Execution Environments, VEE 2008, pp. 151–160. ACM, New York (2008)

13. Nethercote, N., Seward, J.: Valgrind: a framework for heavyweight dynamic binary instrumentation. In: Proceedings of the 2007 ACM SIGPLAN Conference on Programming Language Design and Implementation, PLDI 2007, pp. 89–100. ACM, New York (2007)

14. Onarlioglu, K., Bilge, L., Lanzi, A., Balzarotti, D., Kirda, E.: G-Free: defeating return-oriented programming through gadget-less binaries. In: Proceedings of the 26th Annual Computer Security Applications Conference, ACSAC 2010, pp. 49–58. ACM, New York (2010)

15. Riley, R., Jiang, X., Xu, D.: Guest-transparent Prevention of Kernel Rootkits with VMM-based Memory Shadowing. In: Lippmann, R., Kirda, E., Trachtenberg, A. (eds.) RAID 2008. LNCS, vol. 5230, pp. 1–20. Springer, Heidelberg (2008)

16. Roemer, R., Buchanan, E., Shacham, H., Savage, S.: Return-oriented programming: systems, languages, and applications. ACM Trans. Inf. Syst. Secur. (to appear, 2011)

17. Seshadri, A., Luk, M., Qu, N., Perrig, A.: SecVisor: a tiny hypervisor to provide lifetime kernel code integrity for commodity OSes. In: Proceedings of Twenty-first ACM SIGOPS Symposium on Operating Systems Principles, SOSP 2007, pp. 335–350. ACM, New York (2007)

18. Shacham, H.: The geometry of innocent flesh on the bone: return-into-libc without function calls (on the x86). In: Proceedings of the 14th ACM Conference on Computer and Communications Security, CCS 2007, pp. 552–561. ACM, New York (2007)

19. Wang, Z., Jiang, X.: HyperSafe: a lightweight approach to provide lifetime hypervisor control-flow integrity. In: Proceedings of the 2010 IEEE Symposium on Security and Privacy, SP 2010, pp. 380–395. IEEE Computer Society, Washington, DC, USA (2010)
20. Wikipedia. Return-to-libc attack (2010),
    http://en.wikipedia.org/wiki/Return-to-libc_attack
21. Wikipedia. WˆX (2010), http://en.wikipedia.org/wiki/W%5EX

An Efficient Finger-Knuckle-Print Based Recognition System Fusing SIFT and SURF Matching Scores

G.S. Badrinath, Aditya Nigam, and Phalguni Gupta

Department of Computer Science and Engineering,
Indian Institute of Technology,
Kanpur, 208016, India
{badri,naditya,pg}@cse.iitk.ac.in

Abstract. This paper presents a novel combination of local-local information for an efficient finger-knuckle-print (FKP) based recognition system which is robust to scale and rotation. The non-uniform brightness of the FKP due to relatively curvature surface is corrected and texture is enhanced. The local features of the enhanced FKP are extracted using the scale invariant feature transform (SIFT) and the speeded up robust features (SURF). Corresponding features of the enrolled and the query FKPs are matched using nearest-neighbour-ratio method and then the derived SIFT and SURF matching scores are fused using weighted sum rule. The proposed system is evaluated using PolyU FKP database of 7920 images for both identification mode and verification mode. It is observed that the system performs with CRR of 100% and EER of 0.215%. Further, it is evaluated against various scales and rotations of the query image and is found to be robust for query images downscaled upto 60% and for any orientation of query image.

1 Introduction

Biometric based authentication system has been used widely in commercial and law enforcement applications. The use of various biometric traits such as fingerprint, face, iris, ear, palmprint, hand geometry and voice has been well studied [4]. It is reported that the skin pattern on the finger-knuckle is highly rich in texture due to skin folds and creases, and hence, can be considered as a biometric identifier [11]. Further, advantages of using FKP include rich in texture features [3], easily accessible, contact-less image acquisition, invariant to emotions and other behavioral aspects such as tiredness, stable features [16] and acceptability in the society [7].

Despite of these characteristics and advantages of using FKP as biometric identifier, limited work has been reported in the literature [5]. Like any other recognition system, a FKP based recognition system also consists of four stages i.e., image acquisition, extraction of region of interest, feature extraction and matching. Systems reported in literature have used global features, local features and their combinations [16] to represent FKP images. Efforts have been made to build a FKP system based on global features. In [6], FKP features are extracted using principle component analysis (PCA), independent component analysis (ICA) and linear discriminant analysis (LDA).

S. Qing et al. (Eds.): ICICS 2011, LNCS 7043, pp. 374–387, 2011.

These subspace analysis methods may be effective for face recognition but they are not found to be effective to represent the FKP [14]. In [13], FKP is transformed using the Fourier transform and the band-limited phase only correlation (BLPOC) is employed to match the FKP images.

Global feature gives the general appearance (holistic characteristics) of the FKP which is suitable for coarse level representation, while local feature provides more detailed information from specific local region and is appropriate for finer representation [16]. There exist systems where local features of FKP are extracted using the Gabor filter based competitive code (CompCode) [12] and combined orientation and magnitude information (ImCompCode&MagCode)[14]. Further, in [7], orientation of random knuckle lines and crease points (KnuckleCodes) of FKP which are determined using radon transform are used as features. In [11], FKP is represented by curvature based shape index. Morales et. al., [10] have proposed an FKP based authentication system (OE-SIFT) using scale invariant feature transform (SIFT) from orientation enhanced FKP. In [3], an hierarchical based verification system using probabilistic hough transform (PHT) for coarse level classification and the speeded up robust features (SURF) for finer classification has been proposed. SIFT and SURF features of FKP are matched using similarity threshold [10]. In [15], features are extracted using Hilbert transform (MonogenicCode). Further, Zhang *et.al* [16] have proposed a verification system which is designed by fusing the global information extracted by BLPOC [13] and the local information obtained by Compcode [12]. However, there does not exist any system which is robust to scale and rotation.

This paper uses local-local information extracted from SIFT and SURF for a FKP recognition. An approach to correct the non-uniform brightness and to improve the texture of the FKP is proposed. The nearest-neighbour-ratio method [9] which is better than similarity-threshold based matching for SIFT and SURF based matching has been used to obtain the SIFT and SURF matching scores between the enrolled and the query FKPs. These matching scores are fused using weighted sum rule to obtain final matching score. The proposed system has been evaluated on publicly available PolyU [1] database of 7920 FKP images of 4 fingers of 165 users. Further, it is also tested for its performance against changes due to scales and orientations of the query image and has been observed that the proposed system is robust to scale and rotation.

Rest of the paper is organized as follows. Section 2 describes SIFT and SURF which are used to extract the local features of FKP. Next section presents the proposed system. Performance of the system has been analyzed in Section 4. Conclusions are presented in the last Section.

2   Local Information

This section describes SIFT [8] and SURF [2] which are used to extract the local features from a FKP image. Both of them determine scale invariant key-points and then describe these key-points by means of local patterns around key-points.

2.1   Scale Invariant Feature Transform

Feature vectors through SIFT are formed by means of local patterns around key-points from scale space decomposed image [8]. Following are the major steps to generate SIFT features of a given image.

1. *Scale-space extrema detection*: The first step of computation searches over all scales and image locations. It is implemented efficiently by using a Difference-of-Gaussian function to identify potential interest points that are invariant to scale.
2. *Key-point localization*: At each candidate location, a detailed model is fitted to determine location and scale. Key-points are selected based on measures of their stability.
3. *Orientation assignment*: Consistent orientation is assigned to the key-point following local image properties to make the key-point descriptor rotation invariant.
4. *Key-point descriptor*: Feature vector of 128 values is computed from the local image region around the key-point.

2.2   Speeded up Robust Features

Feature vectors through SURF are formed by means of local patterns around key-points which are detected using scaled up filter [2]. Following are the major steps to determine the SURF feature vectors of a given image.

1. *Key-point detector*: At this step, SURF key-points are detected using Hessian-matrix approximation. The second order Gaussian derivatives for Hessian matrix are approximated using box filters. Key-points are localized in scale and image space by applying a non-maximum suppression in a $3 \times 3 \times 3$ neighbourhood.
2. *Key-point descriptor*: This stage describes the key-points. It fixes a reproducible dominant orientation based on information from a circular region around the interest point. Feature vector of 64 values is computed from the oriented square local image region around key-point.

Fig. 1. Sample of finger-knuckle-print images from PolyU database [1]

3   Proposed System

This section presents a robust FKP based recognition system which is designed by fusing SIFT and SURF features at matching score level. Sample of FKP images of PolyU database [1] are shown in Fig. 1. The FKP image is subjected for non-uniform brightness correction and contrast enhancement. SIFT and SURF features are extracted

Finger-Knuckle-Print

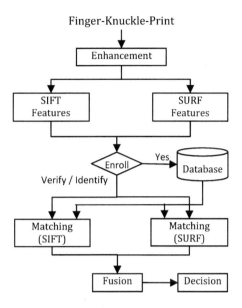

Fig. 2. Block diagram of the proposed recognition system

from the enhanced FKP images. During recognition, corresponding feature vectors of query and enrolled FKPs are matched using nearest-neighbourhood-ratio method [9] to obtain the respective matching scores and these SIFT and SURF matching scores are fused using weighted sum rule. The block diagram of the proposed FKP based system for recognition is shown in Fig. 2.

3.1   Enhancement

The finger-knuckle surface represents a relatively curvature surface and results in non-uniform reflections. FKP has low contrast and non-uniform brightness (as shown in Fig. 3(a)). To obtain the well distributed texture image following operations are applied on FKP.

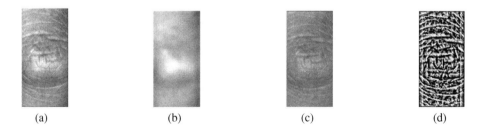

(a)   (b)   (c)   (d)

Fig. 3. (a) Finger-knuckle-print (b) Estimated coarse reflection (c) Uniform brightness knuckle-print image (d) Enhanced Knuckle-print image

Each FKP image is divided into sub-blocks of 11×11 pixels. Mean of each block is calculated which estimates the reflection of the block. The estimated coarse reflection is expanded to the original size of the FKP image using bi-cubic interpolation. For the coarse estimate of reflection, if the block size is very small, the estimate is almost same as the extracted FKP and if the block size is high, the estimate becomes improper. Based on the experiments, block size of 11×11 pixels has been chosen for computing the coarse estimate of reflection. Estimated coarse reflection is shown in Fig. 3(b). The estimated reflection is subtracted from the original image to obtain an uniform brightness of the image which is shown in Fig. 3(c). Histogram equalization is performed on blocks of 11×11 pixels to improve the contrast in the texture of FKP and then is subjected to perform filtering to smooth the boundaries between blocks. Enhanced image is shown in Fig. 3(d).

3.2   Feature Extraction

Features are extracted from all FKP images. SIFT and SURF are used to extract the local features of FKP. Both SIFT [8] and SURF [2] have been designed for extracting highly distinctive invariant features from images. Further, extracted feature vectors are found to be distinct, robust to scale, robust to rotation and partially invariant to illumination. Thus features can be matched correctly with high probability against features from a large database of FKPs. SIFT and SURF key-points extracted from the FKP images are shown in Fig. 4.

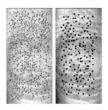

(a) SIFT (b) SURF

Fig. 4. Key-points

3.3   Matching and Fusion

In this paper, feature template of the FKP is represented by two local feature vectors extracted using SIFT and SURF. During recognition, SIFT and SURF features of the query FKP are matched with the corresponding features of all the knuckle-prints in the database. The matching scores between corresponding feature vectors are computed using nearest-neighbour-ratio method [9] as follows.

Let Q and E be vector arrays of key-points of the query and the enrolled FKP respectively obtained using either SIFT or SURF

$$Q = \{q_1, q_2, q_3, \cdots q_m\} \tag{1}$$

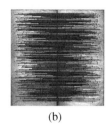
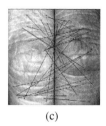

(a)   (b)   (c)

Fig. 5. (a) SIFT key-points detected (b) Genuine matching of SIFT key-points (c) Imposter matching of SIFT key-points

$$E = \{e_1, e_2, e_3, \cdots e_n\} \tag{2}$$

where q_i and e_j are the feature vectors of key-point i in Q and that of key-point j in E respectively. If $\|q_i - e_j\|$ and $\|q_i - e_k\|$ are the Euclidean distance between q_i and its first nearest-neighbour e_j and that between q_i and its second nearest-neighbour of e_k respectively, then

$$q_i = \begin{cases} \text{Matched with } e_j & \text{if } \frac{\|q_i - e_j\|}{\|q_i - e_k\|} < T \\ \text{Unmatched} & \text{Otherwise} \end{cases} \tag{3}$$

where T is a predefined threshold.

The matched key-points q_i and e_j are removed from Q and E respectively. The matching process is continued until there are no more matching points either in Q or E. Total number of matching pairs M is considered as the matching score. More the number of matching pairs between two images, greater is the similarity between them. Matching between FKP images of same user is called genuine matching while that of different users is known as imposter matching. An example of genuine matching and imposter matching using SIFT is shown in Fig. 5. Similarly, Fig. 6 shows an example of genuine matching and imposter matching using SURF.

Let M_T and M_S be SIFT and SURF matching scores respectively between the query and an enrolled FKP. These SIFT and SURF matching scores are fused by weighted sum rule to obtain the final matching score S as

$$S = W_T * M_T + W_S * M_S \tag{4}$$

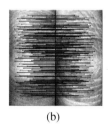
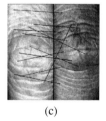

(a)   (b)   (c)

Fig. 6. (a) SURF key-points detected (b) Genuine matching of SURF key-points (c) Imposter matching of SURF key-points

where W_T and W_S are weights assigned to SIFT matching score M_T and SURF matching score M_S respectively, with $W_T + W_S = 1$. In this paper, $W_T = C_T/(C_T + C_S)$
and $W_S = C_S/(C_T + C_S)$ are considered where C_T and C_S are the correct recognition
rate (CRR) of the system using SIFT alone and SURF alone respectively.

4   Experimental Results

This section analyses the performance of the proposed system on a publicly available
PolyU FKP database [1]. This database contains 7920 FKP images of 4 different fingers
obtained from 165 users [12]. The users comprise of 125 males and 40 females. Out of
165 users, 143 users are of age lying between 20 years and 30 years while remaining
are between 30 years and 50 years. Images of each user are collected in two separate
sessions. For each user, six images of 4 fingers, *viz.* index and middle finger of each hand
have been acquired in each session. Images collected in first session are considered for
training while remaining are used for testing.

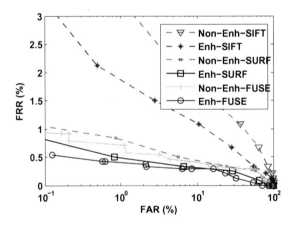

Fig. 7. ROC curves of the proposed system

Metrics like correct recognition rate (CRR) for identification and the receiver operating characteristic (ROC) curve and equal error rate (EER) for recognition are used
to measure the performance of the system. CRR of the system is defined as

$$CRR = \frac{N_1}{N_2} \times 100 \tag{5}$$

where N_1 denotes the number of correct (Non-False) recognitions of FKP images and
N_2 is the total number of FKP images in the testing set.

At a given threshold, the probability of accepting the imposter, known as false acceptance rate (FAR) and probability of rejecting the genuine user, known as false rejection
rate (FRR) are obtained. Equal error rate (EER) is the error rate where $FAR = FRR$.
Again, the receiver operating characteristics (ROC) curve which is another measure

Table 1. Performance of the proposed system and [10, 12–16]

Systems	CRR (%)	EER (%)
CompCode [12]	-	1.658
BLPOC [13]	-	1.676
ImCompCode&MagCode [14]	-	1.475
MonogenicCode [15]	-	1.720
OE-SIFT [10]	-	0.850
LGIC [16]	-	0.402
Proposed Non-Enh-SIFT	98.667	2.691
Proposed Enh-SIFT	99.125	1.900
Proposed Non-Enh-SURF	99.902	0.833
Proposed Enh-SURF	99.916	0.317
Proposed Non-Enh-FUSE	100.00	0.508
Proposed Enh-FUSE	**100.00**	**0.215**

used for measuring performance of a verification system is generated by plotting FAR against FRR at different thresholds. Besides, the testing of the proposed system using the fusion of SIFT and SURF matching scores of FKP images, we have studied the performance of the system using only SIFT matching scores or SURF matching scores on FKP images with or without enhancement. In Fig. 7, there are six ROC curves. Non-Enh-SIFT, Enh-SIFT, Non-Enh-SURF, Enh-SURF, Non-Enh-FUSE and Enh-FUSE are ROC curves of the proposed systems using SIFT matching scores on FKP images without enhancement, using SIFT matching score on enhanced FKP images, using SURF matching scores on FKP images without enhancement, using SURF matching score on enhanced FKP images, using fusion on FKP images without any enhancement and using fusion on enhanced FKP images respectively.

It is observed that the proposed system based on fusion of SIFT and SURF matching scores on enhanced FKP images is found to perform better than that on FKP images without enhancement. Further, it is observed that at low FAR, the proposed system with the fusion has low FRR compared to system using either SIFT or SURF scores on enhanced or non enhanced FKP images. Hence the proposed system with the fusion of the SIFT matching scores and SURF matching scores improves the performance. The proposed system has been compared with existing systems presented in [10, 12–16]. All these systems have used PolyU database for testing. Table 1 shows the claimed EER of these systems along with EER of the proposed system under different constraints. It has been observed that EER of the proposed system with fusion of SIFT matching scores and SURF matching scores on enhanced FKP images which is 0.215% is lowest. Further, the existing systems are not evaluated for identification mode; hence CRR are not known. The performance of the proposed system could not be compared with the existing systems. However, the proposed system using fusion of SIFT matching scores and SURF matching scores on enhanced FKP images has achieved 100% CRR.

4.1 Performance of the System against Scale

The proposed system with the fusion of SIFT matching scores and SURF matching scores have used the local features of FKP images extracted with the help of SIFT and SURF which describe an image using local regions around the key-points. The extracted key-point features using SIFT and SURF are invariant to scale of the image; so the proposed system is robust to scale (spatial resolution).

In order to investigate the performance of the proposed system against scale, each FKP image in the query set are down scaled to 90%, 80%, 70%, 60% and 50% size of original image using bi-cubic interpolation. Matching points between the enrolled image and the scaled query FKP images of the same user using SIFT and SURF are shown in Fig. 10 and Fig. 11 respectively.

ROC curves for matching with different scales of query images are shown in Fig. 8. CRR and EER obtained for the different scales of query images are given in Table 2. It can be observed that when the query images are downscaled upto 60%, the proposed system performs with CRR more than 98.625% and EER less than 5.25%. Hence, it can be inferred that the proposed system is robust to downscaled query FKP images of size upto 60%.

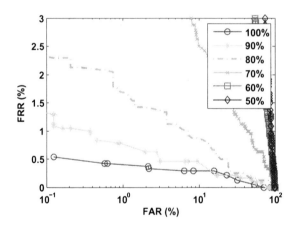

Fig. 8. ROC curves of the proposed system for various scales of query image

Table 2. Performance of the proposed system for various scales of query image

Scale (%)	CRR (%)	EER (%)
100	100.00	0.215
90	100.00	0.458
80	99.917	1.458
70	99.792	3.708
60	98.625	5.25
50	95.000	12.75

4.2   Performance of the System against Rotation

Further, feature vector of a key-point described by SIFT and SURF are relative to the dominant orientation of the key-point. Hence the key-point features remain the same irrespective of the orientation of the FKP image. Thus, the proposed system is robust to the rotation of FKP image.

In order to investigate the performance of the system against rotation, FKP images in the query set are synthetically rotated using bi-cubic interpolation by $2°$, $5°$, $10°$, $45°$, $70°$, $90°$ and $180°$. Matching points between the enrolled and the query FKP images of a user for various rotations using SIFT and SURF are shown in Fig. 12 and Fig. 13 respectively. ROC curves obtained for different rotations of query image are shown in Fig. 9. CRR and EER of the system for different rotations of the query image are given

Table 3. Performance of the proposed system for various angles of query image

Angle	CRR (%)	EER (%)
$0°$	100.00	0.215
$5°$	99.875	0.833
$10°$	99.833	0.416
$45°$	99.792	0.925
$70°$	99.917	0.750
$90°$	99.958	0.358
$180°$	99.917	0.441

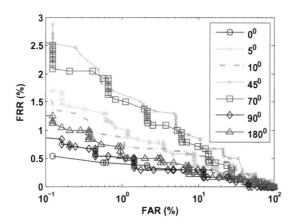

Fig. 9. ROC curves of the proposed system for various orientation of query image

Table 4. Speed of the Proposed System

	SIFT	SURF	Total
Feature Extraction (ms)	58.091	17.970	76.061
Matching (ms)	4.782	0.083	**4.865**
Total (ms)	62.873	18.053	**80.926**

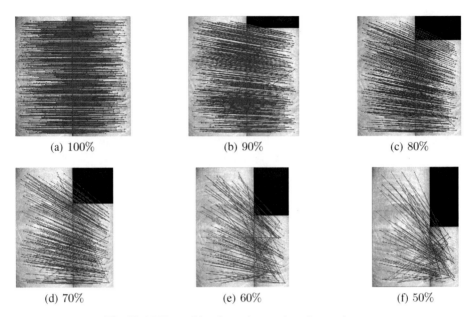

Fig. 10. SIFT matching for various scales of query image

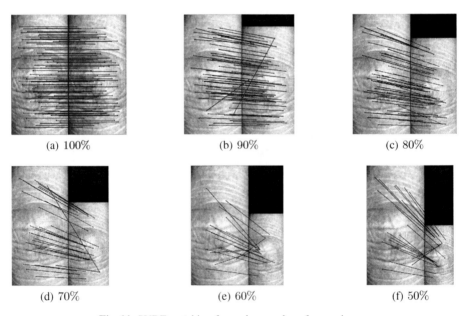

Fig. 11. SURF matching for various scales of query image

in Table 3. It is observed that the system performs with CRR minimum of 99.79% and maximum EER of 0.92% for any orientation of query images. Hence, it can be said that the system is robust to rotation.

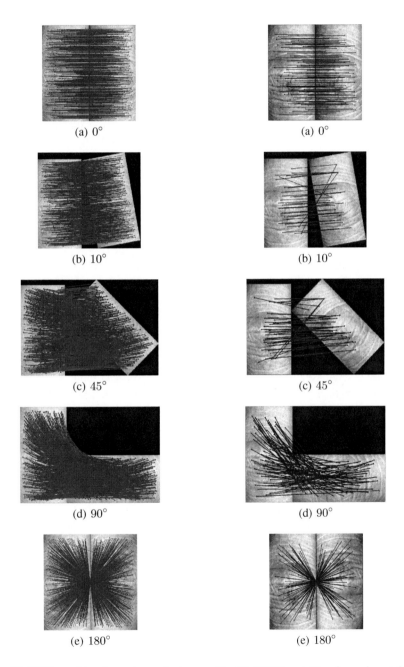

(a) 0°   (a) 0°

(b) 10°   (b) 10°

(c) 45°   (c) 45°

(d) 90°   (d) 90°

(e) 180°   (e) 180°

Fig. 12. SIFT matching for various orientations of query image

Fig. 13. SURF matching for various orientations of query image

4.3 Speed

This sub-section discusses the time taken by the proposed system for feature extraction and matching. The system has been implemented on a Oct-Core ($8 \times 2.5GHz$) workstation with 8 GB RAM. Time taken by the system for feature extraction and matching are given in Table 4. The feature extraction time is the time taken to extract SIFT and SURF features on entire database and dividing by the total number of images. It is found that the system takes $58.091ms$ and $17.970ms$ for extracting SIFT and SURF features respectively. For average matching time, all possible matches that include both genuine and imposter cases are considered. It is observed that the system takes $4.782ms$ and $0.083ms$ for matching SIFT and SURF feature vectors respectively. Total time taken by the system is $80.926ms$, out of which matching takes $4.865ms$ only and is significantly fast.

5   Conclusions

This paper has proposed an FKP based recognition system which is robust to scale and rotation. Local information of the FKP are extracted using SIFT and SURF and they are fused at matching score level. An approach to correct the non-uniform brightness and to improve the contrast is proposed. During recognition, the corresponding features of enrolled and query FKPs are matched using nearest-neighbourhood-ratio method and the derived SIFT and SURF matching scores are fused using weighted sum rule to obtain fused matching score. The proposed system has been evaluated using publicly available PolyU database [1] of 7920 images. It is observed that the proposed system performs with CRR of 100.00% and EER of 0.215%, and is found to be better than best known systems [10, 12–16]. Further, the system is evaluated for various scales and rotations of the query image. It is observed that the system performs with CRR of atleast 98.62% and EER of atmost 5.25% for query image downscaled upto 60% and performs with CRR of 99.75% and EER of 0.925% for any orientation of query image.

Acknowledgments. This work has been supported by the Department of Information Technology, Government of India, New Delhi, INDIA.

References

1. PolyU Finger-Knuckle-Print Database,
   http://www.comp.polyu.edu.hk/biometrics/FKP.htm
2. Bay, H., Ess, A., Tuytelaars, T., Van Gool, L.: Speeded-up robust features. Computer Vision and Image Understanding 110, 346–359 (2008)
3. Choras, M., Kozik, R.: Knuckle biometrics based on texture features. In: International Workshop on Emerging Techniques and Challenges for Hand-Based Biometrics, pp. 1–5 (2010)
4. Jain, A.K., Flynn, P., Ross, A.A.: Handbook of Biometrics. Springer, USA (2007)

5. Jungbluth, W.O.: Knuckle print identification. Journal of Forensic Identification 39, 375–380 (1989)
6. Kumar, A., Ravikanth, C.: Personal authentication using finger knuckle surface. IEEE Transactions on Information Forensics and Security 4(1), 98–110 (2009)
7. Kumar, A., Zhou, Y.: Personal identification using finger knuckle orientation features. Electronics Letters 45(20), 1023–1025 (2009)
8. Lowe, D.G.: Distinctive image features from scale-invariant keypoints. International Journal of Computer Vision 60, 91–110 (2004)
9. Mikolajczyk, K., Schmid, C.: A performance evaluation of local descriptors. IEEE Transaction Pattern Analysis Machine Intelligence 27, 1615–1630 (2005)
10. Morales, A., Travieso, C.M., Ferrer, M.A., Alonso, J.B.: Improved finger-knuckle-print authentication based on orientation enhancement. Electronics Letters 47(6), 380–381 (2011)
11. Woodard, D.L., Flynn, P.J.: Finger surface as a biometric identifier. Computer Vision and Image Understanding 100, 357–384 (2005)
12. Zhang, L., Zhang, L., Zhang, D.: Finger-knuckle-print: A new biometric identifier. In: International Conference Image Processing, pp. 1981–1984 (2009)
13. Zhang, L., Zhang, L., Zhang, D.: Finger-knuckle-print Verification Based on Band-limited Phase-only Correlation. In: Jiang, X., Petkov, N. (eds.) CAIP 2009. LNCS, vol. 5702, pp. 141–148. Springer, Heidelberg (2009)
14. Zhang, L., Zhang, L., Zhang, D., Zhu, H.L.: Online finger-knuckle-print verification for personal authentication. Pattern Recognition 43(7), 2560–2571 (2010)
15. Zhang, L., Zhang, L., Zhang, D.: Monogeniccode: A novel fast feature coding algorithm with applications to finger-knuckle-print recognition. In: International Workshop on Emerging Techniques and Challenges for Hand-Based Biometrics, pp. 1–4 (2010)
16. Zhang, L., Zhang, L., Zhang, D., Zhu, H.: Ensemble of local and global information for finger-knuckle-print recognition. Pattern Recognition 44(9), 1990–1998 (2011)

Multivariate Correlation Analysis Technique Based on Euclidean Distance Map for Network Traffic Characterization

Zhiyuan Tan[1,2], Aruna Jamdagni[1,2], Xiangjian He[1],
Priyadarsi Nanda[1], and Ren Ping Liu[2]

[1] Research Centre for Innovation in IT Services and Applications (iNEXT),
University of Technology, Sydney, Broadway 2007, Australia
[2] CSIRO Marsfield, Australia
{Zhiyuan.Tan,Aruna.Jamdagni}@student.uts.edu.au,
{Xiangjian.He,Priyadarsi.Nanda}@uts.edu.au,
ren.liu@csiro.au

Abstract. The quality of feature has significant impact on the performance of detection techniques used for Denial-of-Service (DoS) attack. The features that fail to provide accurate characterization for network traffic records make the techniques suffer from low accuracy in detection. Although researches have been conducted and attempted to overcome this problem, there are some constraints in these works. In this paper, we propose a technique based on Euclidean Distance Map (EDM) for optimal feature extraction. The proposed technique runs analysis on original feature space (first-order statistics) and extracts the multivariate correlations between the first-order statistics. The extracted multivariate correlations, namely second-order statistics, preserve significant discriminative information for accurate characterizations of network traffic records, and these multivariate correlations can be the high-quality potential features for DoS attack detection. The effectiveness of the proposed technique is evaluated using KDD CUP 99 dataset and experimental analysis shows encouraging results.

Keywords: Euclidean Distance Map, Multivariate Correlations, Second-order Statistics, Characterization, Denial-of-Service Attack.

1 Introduction

The growing number of network intrusive activities poses a serious threat to the reliability of network services. Businesses and individuals are suffering from these malicious interceptions. Billions of dollars loss has been recorded over the past few years [1].

As one of the major network intrusive activities, Denial-of-Service (DoS) attack receives much attention due to its continuous growth and serious impact on the Internet. A victim, such as host, router or entire network, can be overwhelmed by a DoS attack using imposed computationally intensive tasks, using

S. Qing et al. (Eds.): ICICS 2011, LNCS 7043, pp. 388–398, 2011.

exploitation of system vulnerability or using floods with a huge amount of useless packets. The victim is then temporarily unavailable for the outside networks from a few minutes to even several days. The availability of network services is severely degraded by this type of network intrusive activities, thus effective detection mechanisms for DoS attack are highly required.

However, the work that has been done so far is still far away from being perfect. Currently, the commercially used DoS attack detection systems are mainly dominated by signature-based detection techniques [2][3]. In spite of having high detection rates to the known attacks and low false positive rates, signature-based techniques are easily evaded by new attacks and even variants of the existing attacks.

Therefore, research community has started to explore a way to achieve novelty-tolerant detection systems and developed the concept of anomaly-based detection [4][5]. The idea of anomaly-based detection is that network intrusions exhibit significantly different behaviors than the normal network activities [6], and any significant deviation from the normal network behaviors is identified as an intrusion. To implement this idea, various techniques, such as clustering [7][8], neural network [9][10], pattern recognition [11][12], support vector machine [13], nearest neighbor [14] and statistical detection techniques [15][16][17] have been used to establish anomaly-based detection systems. However, some of the techniques [7][10][14] suffer from relatively low accuracy in the task of attack detection, though they show encouraging results in other tasks.

The aforementioned discussed problem is partly raised by the low quality features which fail to provide sufficient discriminative power for correct traffic discrimination. To address the problem, this paper presents the Euclidean Distance Map (EDM) to analyze the original feature space (first-order statistics) and extracts the multivariate correlations between the first-order statistics. These multivariate correlations contain significant discriminative information and play key roles in detection accuracy. The occurrence of network intrusions cause changes to these multivariate correlations so that the changes can be used as metrics for identifying intrusive activities. Moreover, various types of traffic namely normal traffic and attack traffic can be easily and accurately characterized by using the proposed EDM-based analysis technique. By looking into the patterns, i.e. EDMs, the intrusive activities can be clearly identified and differentiated from each other.

The rest of this paper is organized as follows. Section 2 provides current work related to our research. Section 3 details the EMD-based multivariate correlation analysis technique. Section 4 evaluates the performance of the proposed approach in pattern extraction of DoS attack and makes some discussions. Finally, conclusions are drawn and future work is given in Section 5.

2   Related Work

Multivariate correlations are second-order statistics generated to reveal the relations between or among the original features, i.e. first-order statistics.

This correlative information provides important discriminative power and is proven to be more effective for object clustering and classification.

Recently, researchers have investigated to explore extracting effective multivariate correlations for DoS attack detection, and different techniques have been proposed. A team of researchers from the Hong Kong Polytechnic University [17] proposed a covariance matrix based approach to mine the multivariate correlations for sequential samples and reveal characteristics of different classes of traffic records. This idea is later adopted by Travallaee et al. [18], who further used the Principal Component Analysis (PCA) to reduce the redundant information contained in the original feature space from statistical point of view. Such performance of the covariance matrix based approach can be refined by using the appropriately selected features.

Apart from the above discussed statistical-based approaches, new solutions proposed lately tend to consider the geometrical structure of the features. Jamdagni et al. [11] developed a distance measure based correlation extraction approach, in which the Mahalanobis Distance (MD) is used to measure the weighted distance between each pair of features extracted from network traffic packet payload. In addition, Tsai and Lin [19] estimated the sizes of triangle areas constructed by any signal observed data object and any two centroids of distinct clusters. New data formed by the areas of these triangles is used as a new feature space.

Although these approaches introduce some interesting concepts for multivariate correlation extraction and show their abilities in extracting discriminative power, they have some weaknesses and drawbacks. On one hand, techniques [17] [18], such as the covariance matrix, will not work under the situation where an attack linearly changes all monitored features and is vulnerable to mix-traffic containing both normal and attack traffic. On the other hand, the distance measure based techniques either suffer from high computation complexity [11] or are dependent on prior knowledge of both normal and attack traffic that causes wrong characterization of any novelty [19].

Different from the above discussed techniques, our EDM-based analysis technique is independent on prior knowledge of the features of different classes and withstands the issue of linearly changes all monitored features. It is robust to mix-traffic and does not rely on the volume of network traffic. More importantly, it is computationally efficient.

3   EDM Based Multivariate Correlation Analysis

The behavior of network traffic is reflected by its statistical properties. DoS attempts to exhaust a victims resources, and its traffic behaves differently from the normal network traffic. Therefore, the statistical properties can be used to reveal the difference. To present the statistical properties, we propose a multivariate correlation analysis approach which employs Euclidean distance for extracting correlative information (named inner correlation) from the original feature space of an observed data object. This approach shares similar proporties with the one developed in [21]. The detail of the proposed approach is given in the following section.

3.1   Multivariate Correlation Extraction

Given an arbitrary dataset $X^T = [x_1^T \, x_2^T \, \cdots \, x_n^T]$, where $x_i^T = [f_1^i \, f_2^i \, \cdots \, f_m^i] \, (1 \leq i \leq n)$ represents the ith m-dimensional traffic record. The dataset can be represented in detail as

$$X = \begin{bmatrix} f_1^1 & f_2^1 & \cdots & f_m^1 \\ f_1^2 & f_2^2 & \cdots & f_m^2 \\ \vdots & \vdots & \ddots & \vdots \\ f_1^n & f_2^n & \cdots & f_m^n \end{bmatrix}, \tag{1}$$

where f_l^i is the value of the lth feature in the ith traffic record, l and i are varying from 1 to m and from 1 to n respectively.

In order to further explore the inner correlations of the ith traffic record on a multi-dimensional space, the record x_i^T is first transformed into a new m-by-m feature matrix $x_i^{'}$ by simply multiplying an m-by-m identity matrix I as shown in Equation (2).

$$x_i^T I = x_i^{'} = \begin{bmatrix} f_1^i & 0 & \cdots & 0 \\ 0 & f_2^i & \cdots & 0 \\ \vdots & \vdots & \ddots & \vdots \\ 0 & 0 & \cdots & f_m^i \end{bmatrix}_{m \times m}. \tag{2}$$

The elements on the diagonal of the matrix $x_i^{'}$ are the features of the record x_i^T. Each column of the matrix $x_i^{'}$ is a new m-dimensional feature vector denoted by

$$F_j^{iT} = [F_{j,1}^{'i} \, F_{j,2}^{'i} \, \cdots \, F_{j,m}^{'i}], \tag{3}$$

where $F_{j,p}^{'i} = 0$ if $j \neq p$ and $F_{j,p}^{'i} = f_j^i$ if $j = p$. The parameters satisfy the conditions of $1 \leq i \leq n$, $1 \leq j \leq m$ and $1 \leq p \leq m$. Thus, the m-by-m feature matrix can be rewritten as

$$x_i^{'} = [F_1^i \, F_2^i \, \cdots \, F_m^i]. \tag{4}$$

Once the transformation is finished, we can apply the Euclidean distance to extract the correlation between the feature vectors j and k in the matrix $x_i^{'}$, which can be defined as

$$ED_{j,k}^i = \sqrt{(F_j^i - F_k^i)^T (F_j^i - F_k^i)}. \tag{5}$$

where $1 \leq i \leq n$, $1 \leq j \leq m$ and $1 \leq k \leq m$. Therefore, the correlations between features in the traffic record x_i^T defined by a Euclidean Distance Map (EDM) are given below.

$$EDM^i = \begin{bmatrix} ED_{1,1}^i & ED_{1,2}^i & \cdots & ED_{1,m}^i \\ ED_{2,1}^i & ED_{2,2}^i & \cdots & ED_{2,m}^i \\ \vdots & \vdots & \ddots & \vdots \\ ED_{m,1}^i & ED_{m,2}^i & \cdots & ED_{m,m}^i \end{bmatrix}. \tag{6}$$

For the dataset, its inner correlations can be represented by Equation (7).

$$EDM_X = (EDM^1 \, EDM^2 \, \cdots \, EDM^i \, \cdots \, EDM^n) \tag{7}$$

In comparison with [21], which considers only the lower triangle of the Euclidean distance map, the multivariate correlation analysis approach proposed in this paper takes the entire map into account. The EDM is then employed as a means of network traffic characterization and a visualization tool to reveal the patterns of various traffic.

3.2   Discussions

By making use of the multivariate correlations, various types of network traffic can be clearly characterized. Additionally, the distance measure facilitates our analysis to withstand the issue of linear change for all features.

The two primary advantages of the proposed EDM-based analysis technique are supported by two underlying mathematical structures. They are the transformed traffic record matrix and the Euclidean distance. These two mathematical tools help solve the dilemmas caused by the occurrence of two distinct pairs of features having the same distance on one-dimensional space and the linear change of all features.

Assume that there are three pairs of features $A(1, 2)$, $B(4, 8)$ and $C(9, 10)$ shown in Fig. 1. In this case, the ratio between the two features of A and that between the two features of B have the same value which is equal to $1/2 = 4/8 = 0.5$, and the one-dimensional linear distance between the two features of A and the distance between the two features of C have the same value which is equal to $|1 - 2| = |9 - 10| = 1$. For the conventional techniques, using ratio or one-dimensional linear distance cannot differentiate the points which coincidentally have the same value.

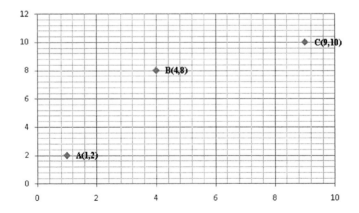

Fig. 1. Three pairs of features

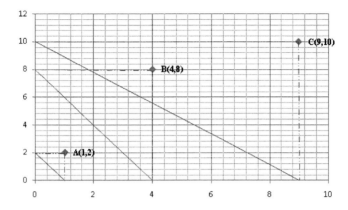

Fig. 2. Distances between the features with three pairs

However, the proposed EDM-based analysis technique can successfully withstand these difficulties. By applying the technique, the distances between the features in the A, B and C are $\sqrt{(1-0)^2 + (0-2)^2} = \sqrt{5}$, $\sqrt{(4-0)^2 + (0-8)^2} = \sqrt{80}$ and $\sqrt{(9-0)^2 + (0-10)^2} = \sqrt{181}$ respectively. Therefore, the proposed technique can properly characterize network traffic records and is not affected by the linear change of all features.

4   Experimental Results and Analysis

The performance of our proposed EMD-based analysis technique for characterizing normal and DoS attack traffic records is evaluated using KDD CUP 99 dataset [1]. Although the dataset is not without criticism [20], it is the only public dataset with labeled attack samples. Moreover, many research works have been evaluated using this dataset as well.

4.1   Experimental Data

The 10 percent labeled dataset of the KDD CUP 99 dataset is involved in our experimentation. Six different types of DoS attacks (including Teardrop, Smurf, Pod, Neptune, Land and Back attacks) and normal network traffic from the labeled dataset are used for evaluation. The DoS attacks launch their malicious activities by exploiting three widely used network protocols respectively. Neptune, Land and Back attacks make use of TCP protocol. Teardrop sends its attack payload over UDP. The payloads of Smurf and Pod attack are carried by ICMP packets.

Fig. 3. EDM of normal TCP traffic record

4.2 Results and Analysis

According to the working mechanisms discussed in Section 1, DoS attacks are expected to present different behaviors to that of the normal traffic. Thus, the EDMs of DoS attacks should be different from the EDM of normal traffic. If significant differences can be found from these maps, the performance of the proposed technique can be proven to be good in extracting discriminative power from the first-order features of the different types of network traffic.

To demonstrate how EDM presents the correlations between the first-order features, the EDMs of normal and attack traffic records generated using 32 numerical features are given in this subsection. As shown in Fig. 3, the EDM of normal TCP traffic record is a symmetric matrix and the values of the elements along its diagonal from top left hand side to bottom right hand side are all equal to zeros. This is because the Euclidean distance measure is insensitive to the orientation of a straight line formed by any two objects in the Cartesian coordinate system, and the distance from a feature vector to itself is always zero. In other words, the distance from object D to object E is equivalent to the distance from object E to object D, and if object D and object E are the same object, then their distance is zero.

Although we can directly compare the raw EDMs to confirm the differences, it is a time-consuming task. In order to offer friendly visualization for the raw

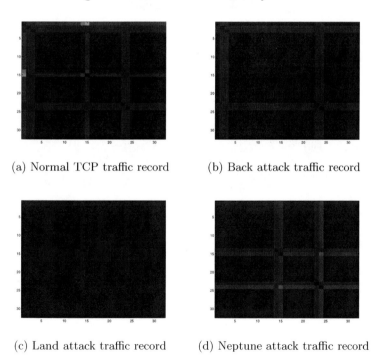

(a) Normal TCP traffic record   (b) Back attack traffic record

(c) Land attack traffic record   (d) Neptune attack traffic record

Fig. 4. Images of the EDMs of normal TCP traffic record and Back, Land and Neptune attack records

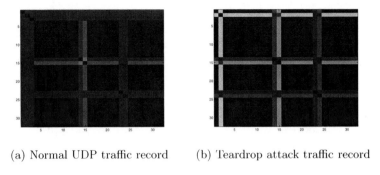

(a) Normal UDP traffic record   (b) Teardrop attack traffic record

Fig. 5. Images of EDMs of UDP traffic record and Teardrop attack record

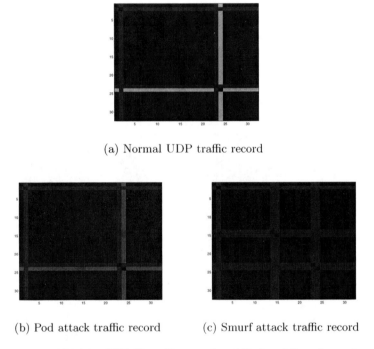

(a) Normal UDP traffic record

(b) Pod attack traffic record   (c) Smurf attack traffic record

Fig. 6. Images of EDMs of ICMP traffic record and Pod and Smurf attack records

EDMs, we convert them into color images. The images of normal TCP traffic record and Neptune, Land and Back attack records are given in Fig. 4, and the images of normal UDP traffic record and Teardrop attack record are shown in Fig. 5. Finally, Fig. 6 presents the images of normal ICMP traffic record and Smurf and Pod attack records.

As can be seen from Fig. 4(a), the image represents the visualized pattern of the EDM of normal TCP traffic record. The color of an image point stands for the value of an element on the EDM. The lighter and warmer the color is, the greater value the element has. In other words, the darkest cold blue color areas on the image are the lowest value areas on the EDM, and conversely the lightest warm red color areas on the image are the highest value areas on the EDM. Figs. 4(b), (c) and (d) visualize the EDMs of Back, Land and Neptune attack records in the same manner respectively. The images of the attack EDMs show clear differences from the EDM of the normal TCP traffic record.

Similarly, the images of the EDMs of UDP traffic record and Teardrop attack record are exhibited in Fig. 5. The image of Teardrop shows apparent dissimilarity to the image of normal UDP traffic. In addition, the images in Fig. 6 reveal that the behaviors of ICMP-based attacks, namely Pod and Smurf attacks, are away from the normal ICMP traffic as well.

The above experimental results demonstrate that our proposed EDM-based technique achieves promising performance in characterizing various network traffic records. Our experimental results also suggest that, by taking advantage of the retained significant discriminative power, utilization of the generated multivariate correlations can improve the performance of DoS attack detection system. Moreover, by looking into the images, we can easily identify the patterns of the different traffic records. Therefore, the proposed EDM-based technique can be further applied to creating the statistical signatures of network intrusions. For detailed comparisons of effectiveness in intrusion detection wtih some other existing approaches, please refer to [21].

5 Conclusions and Future Work

This paper has proposed a multivariate correlation analysis approach based on Euclidean distance to extract the multivariate correlations (second-order statistics) of network traffic records. This proposed approach can better exhibit the network traffic behaviors. We have evaluated the analysis approach on the records of normal and DoS attack traffic from the KDD CUP 99 dataset. The results illustrate that these second-order statistics can clearly reveal the correlations between the first-order statistics and accurately characterize the various types of traffic records. In future, we will further evaluate the proposed technique on the task of DoS attack detection using Support Vector Data Description (SVDD) technique, which is believed to be more promising in one-class classification than SVM and NN techniques. We may also extend our research to the characterization of temporal information.

References

1. Cheng, J., Hatzis, C., Hayashi, H., Krogel, M.A., Morishita, S., Page, D., Sese, J.: KDD Cup 2001 Report. ACM SIGKDD Explorations Newsletter 3, 47–64 (2002)
2. Paxson, V.: Bro: A System for Detecting Network Intruders in Real-time. Computer Networks 31, 2435–2463 (1999)
3. Roesch, M.: Snort-lightweight Intrusion Detection for Networks. In: Proceedings of the 13th USENIX Conference on System Administration, pp. 229–238. USENIX, Seattle (1999)

4. Patcha, A., Park, J.M.: An Overview of Anomaly Detection Techniques: Existing Solutions and Latest Technological Trends. Computer Networks 51, 3448–3470 (2007)
5. Garcia-Teodoro, P., Diaz-Verdejo, J., Macia-Fernandez, G., Vazquez, E.: Anomaly-Based Network Intrusion Detection: Techniques, Systems and Challenges. Computers & Security 28, 18–28 (2009)
6. Denning, D.E.: An Intrusion-detection Model. IEEE Transactions on Software Engineering, 222–232 (1987)
7. Jin, C., Wang, H., Shin, K.G.: Hop-count Filtering: An Effective Defense Against Spoofed DDoS Traffic. In: The 10th ACM Conference on Computer and Communications Security, pp. 30–41. ACM (2003)
8. Lee, K., Kim, J., Kwon, K.H., Han, Y., Kim, S.: DDoS Attack Detection Method Using Cluster Analysis. Expert Systems with Applications 34, 1659–1665 (2008)
9. Amini, M., Jalili, R., Shahriari, H.R.: RT-UNNID: A Practical Solution to Real-time Network-based Intrusion Detection Using Unsupervised Neural Networks. Computers & Security 25, 459–468 (2006)
10. Wang, G., Hao, J., Ma, J., Huang, L.: A new approach to intrusion detection using Artificial Neural Networks and fuzzy clustering. Expert Systems with Applications 37, 6225–6232 (2010)
11. Jamdagni, A., Tan, Z., Nanda, P., He, X., Liu, R.P.: Intrusion Detection Using GSAD Model for HTTP Traffic on Web Services. In: The 6th International Wireless Communications and Mobile Computing Conference, pp. 1193–1197. ACM (2010)
12. Tan, Z., Jamdagni, A., He, X., Nanda, P., Liu, R., Jia, W., Yeh, W.: A Two-tier System for Web Attack Detection Using Linear Discriminant Method. In: Soriano, M., Qing, S., López, J. (eds.) ICICS 2010. LNCS, vol. 6476, pp. 459–471. Springer, Heidelberg (2010)
13. Fugate, M., Gattiker, J.R.: Computer Intrusion Detection with Classification and Anomaly Detection Using SVMs. International Journal of Pattern Recognition and Artificial Intelligence 17, 441–458 (2003)
14. Lane, T., Brodley, C.E.: Temporal Sequence Learning and Data Reduction for Anomaly Detection. ACM Transactions on Information and System Security (TISSEC) 2, 295–331 (1999)
15. Ye, N., Emran, S.M., Chen, Q., Vilbert, S.: Multivariate Statistical Analysis of Audit Trails for Host-based Intrusion Detection. IEEE Transactions on Computers, 810–820 (2002)
16. Manikopoulos, C., Papavassiliou, S.: Network Intrusion and Fault Detection: A Statistical Anomaly Approach. IEEE Communications Magazine 40, 76–82 (2002)
17. Jin, S., Yeung, D.S., Wang, X.: Network Intrusion Detection in Covariance Feature Space. Pattern Recognition 40, 2185–2197 (2007)
18. Tavallaee, M., Lu, W., Iqbal, S.A., Ghorbani, A.A.: A Novel Covariance Matrix Based Approach for Detecting Network Anomalies. In: The Communication Networks and Services Research Conference, pp. 75–81. IEEE (2008)
19. Tsai, C.F., Lin, C.Y.: A Triangle Area Based Nearest Neighbors Approach to Intrusion Detection. Pattern Recognition 43, 222–229 (2010)
20. Tavallaee, M., Bagheri, E., Lu, W., Ghorbani, A.A.: A Detailed Analysis of the KDD Cup 99 Data Set (2009)
21. Tan, Z., Jamdagni, A., He, X., Nanda, P., Liu, R.: Denial-of-Service Attack Detection Based on Multivariate Correlation Analysis. In: The 18th International Conference on Neural Information Processing (accpeted for publication, 2011)

Situational Assessment of Intrusion Alerts: A Multi Attack Scenario Evaluation

Hadi Shiravi*, Ali Shiravi*, and Ali A. Ghorbani

Information Security Centre of Excellence,
University of New Brunswick, Canada
{hadi.shiravi,ali.shiravi,ghorbani}@unb.ca

Abstract. In this research study, we focus on intrusion alerts and the burden of analyzing numerous security events by network administrators. We present Avisa$_2$, a network security visualization system that can assist in the comprehension of IDS alerts and detection of abnormal pattern activities. The quantity of security events triggered by modern day intrusion systems, accompanied by the level of complexity and lack of correlation between events, limits the human cognitive process in identifying anomalous behavior. This shortcoming induces the need for an automated process that would project critical situations and prioritize network hosts encountering peculiar behaviors. At the heart of Avisa$_2$ lies a collection of heuristic functions that are utilized to score, rank, and prioritize internal hosts of the monitored network. We believe this contribution elevates the practicality of Avisa$_2$ in identifying critical situations and renders it to be far superior to traditional security systems that solely focus on visualization. The effectiveness of Avisa$_2$ is evaluated on two multi-stage attack scenarios; each intentionally focused on a particular attack type, network service, and network range. Avisa$_2$ proved effective and accurate in prioritizing hosts under attack or hosts in which attacks were performed from.

Keywords: Visualization, IDS Alerts, Situational Awareness, Heuristic Function, Exponential smoothing.

1   Introduction

Intrusion signatures are continuously updated to generalize the behavior of a known exploit rather than to be targeted towards a specific malware. As a consequence of this behavior, a higher volume of legitimate traffic is flagged as malicious, generating a higher number of intrusion alerts leading to the phenomenon of false positives. A major issue that false positives create is that they can easily distort legitimate alerts from being seen by an administrator. Network security visualization is an emerging field that has been developed with these shortcomings in mind. Security visualization accentuates fundamental matters

---

* Hadi Shiravi and Ali Shiravi contributed equally to this work.

S. Qing et al. (Eds.): ICICS 2011, LNCS 7043, pp. 399–413, 2011.

of information visualization and synthesizes it with security audit traces, demanding novel techniques for the purpose of exploratory analysis [1]. The main goal of security visualization is to give insight with which the ability to identify, process, and comprehend malicious behavior is achieved. However, the human visual system has rules of its own. We can only perceive patterns, trends, and exceptions if they are displayed in certain ways, or in better words, if they obey the rules of the human visual system [2]. In order to design visualizations that exploit this fast and powerful processor we need to find features that can be perceived rapidly, properties that are good discriminators, and characteristics that abide by the laws of our visual system. This in return allows for a more effective analysis of complex data while enhancing the situational awareness of the security analyst.

Situational awareness is viewed in [3] as a "state of knowledge that results from a process" and must be distinguished from the process used to acquire that state. Subsequently, situation assessment is "the process" used to achieve that knowledge and is considered an aid in the cognitive process of situation awareness. A situation assessment process must automatically identify and evaluate the impact of underlying events and relate them to assets of the monitored network.

In this paper, we utilize a collection of time based, parameterized heuristic functions as the basis of our situation assessment component to collectively identify and prioritize hosts of peculiar behavior. The output of the situation assessment component- a collection of hosts within the monitored network with a higher abnormality score- is then visualized through a novel security visualization system. The situation assessment component is evaluated on two multi-step attack scenarios executed on our Centre's benchmark dataset, each carefully crafted and aimed towards recent trends in security threats.

In this paper, we make the following contributions;

- Formalization of parameterized heuristic functions as the basis of a situation assessment component to combat constraints imposed on conventional security visualization systems.
- Design and implementation of a novel security visualization system for displaying a selective number of hosts and their corresponding alerts in an interactive and exploratory manner.

The remainder of this paper is organized as follows. Section 2 looks deep into security visualization as issues and concerns regarding modern network security visualization systems are elaborated on. Section 3 articulates the philosophy of incorporating heuristic functions as an automated process of estimating and projecting critical situations. Section 4 introduces seven distinct features utilized in identifying hosts with malicious behavior. In Section 5 the host selection algorithm is proposed and its functionality is described in length. In Section 6, we express the proposed visualization system, Avisa$_2$, with details regarding its design. The visualization system and its underlying heuristic functions are evaluated in Section 7. The paper is summarized in Section 8 with suggestions for future work and further extensions.

2   Limitations of Security Visualization Systems

A class of visualization systems, namely [4,5], have focused greatly on not only visualizing the state of one or a limited number of hosts as seen in [6], but on depicting the interaction of a large number of internal hosts with respect to external sources. This class solely focuses on visualization techniques to combat large quantities of network related data, often resulting in occlusion as most systems are largely faced with scalability issues. This fact reiterates the need for a process that can identify hosts with anomalous behavior and to project the processed results on a visualization system. In this manner, the load on the visualization system is reduced considerably; allowing for a near real time analysis of events and thereby a more responsive system is accessible.

As apposed to the aforementioned systems, where the emphasis is mainly on higher level activity of hosts, a collection of visualization systems are geared towards visualizing the port activity of a single or a collection of hosts within a monitored network [7]. Developers of these system assert that various malware programs often manifest themselves in abnormal port activity which can be detected through visualization systems. This argument may have been correct in the past, but as applications tend to evolve over time and adjust how they communicate over the Internet, they become increasingly evasive. Almost two thirds of all enterprise traffic is currently routed through ports 80 (HTTP) and 443 (HTTPS) [8]. This change in behavior greatly influences the objectives of port activity visualization systems as their focus should shift towards in-depth analysis of only a predominant number of ports rather than depicting the activity of the full port range.

The fascinating ability of visualization in providing insight into the attack detection process should be considered as the main contribution of a security visualization system. Current visualization systems devised for the process of detecting attack patterns [9], are in most cases used independent of other security products in a network. Visualization systems should be thought as systems that provide insight into areas that other security systems fail to enlighten. Any malicious behavior detected should then be analyzed and automated, if possible, so that an automated application can handle the task in future; conserving human time and attention.

3   Enhancing Situation Awareness via Automated Heuristic Functions

In this study we have taken an approach to decrease the amount of visual clutter by decreasing the number of hosts and consequently reducing the number of alerts displayed at each interval through a situation assessment process comprised of multiple heuristic functions. These functions are further elaborated below.

3.1   Exponential Smoothing

In an exponential moving average the effect of recent values is expected to decline exponentially over time to mitigate the effects of extreme observations. Let $\{y_t\} = \{\cdots y_{t-1}, y_t, y_{t+1} \cdots\}$ denote a sequence of non-negative real numbers indexed by some time subscript t. Call such a sequence of variables a time series. An n-period exponential smoothing of a time series y_t is defined as

$$\tilde{Z}_t(n) = \sum_{j=0}^{n-1} w_j \cdot y_{t-j}, \quad w_j = \frac{\alpha^{j-1}}{\sum_{j=0}^{n-1} \alpha^{j-1}} \tag{1}$$

where $0 \le \alpha < 1$ is the smoothing constant. As $n \to \infty, \alpha^n \to 0, w_n \to 0$, Equation 1 can be defined independently of the window width n. The geometric decline in Equation 1 can be calculated efficiently using recursion

$$\tilde{Z}_t(\alpha) = (1-\alpha)\, y_t + \alpha \tilde{Z}_{t-1}(\alpha) \tag{2}$$

where y_t is the observation at time t, $\tilde{Z}_{t-1}$ is the value of the exponential smoothing in the previous period, and $\tilde{Z}_t$ is the value of exponential smoothing at time t. The smoothing constant, α, controls the memory of the process such that the smaller the smoothing constant, the more weight is given to recent observations.

3.2   Exponential Smoothing Difference

In this category of heuristic function, emphasis is put toward the changing behavior of a feature's value rather than the absolute value itself. Running an exponential moving average over the difference of the current and previous values of a feature provides a means to filter constant activity and to reward increasing values. An n-period exponential smoothing difference of a time series y_t is defined recursively as

$$\tilde{D}_t(\alpha) = (1-\alpha)(y_t - y_{t-1}) + \alpha \tilde{D}_{t-1}(\alpha) \tag{3}$$

where $0 \le \alpha < 1$ is the smoothing constant, y_t is the observation at time t, y_{t-1} is the observation at time $t-1$, $\tilde{D}_{t-1}$ is the value of the exponential smoothing difference in the previous period, and $\tilde{D}_t$ is the value of the exponential smoothing difference at time t.

3.3   Dispersion

A measure of dispersion can give a numerical indication of how scattered, or concentrated, a collection of events are over a certain period of time. The most commonly used measure of dispersion is the sample standard deviation, s, the square root of the sample variance given by

$$s = \sqrt{\frac{1}{n-1} \sum_{i=1}^{n} (x_i - \bar{x})^2} \tag{4}$$

where $x_1, x_2, \cdots, x_n$ are the n samples observations and $\bar{x}$ is the sample mean.

4   Distinctive Set of Features

Let $r(R)$ denote a relation on the relation schema $R(A_1, A_2, \cdots, A_n)$, where $\{A_1, A_2, \cdots, A_n\}$ is a set of attributes. Also, let D_i denote the domain of permitted values of attribute A_i. A relation r is a set of n-tuples $(a_1, a_2, \cdots, a_n)$ where each $a_i \in D_i$. This paper models alerts as relation Λ, where Λ is a subset of the Cartesian product of the domains of its attributes. Based on this definition and for the attribute set $\{ID, Category, SrcIP, Time, \cdots\}$, current time window $\tau_1 = t_a \leq Time < t_b$, and prior time window $\tau_0 = t_0 \leq Time < t_a$ the following seven features have been defined:

(1) $\mathcal{A}^i_{\tau_1} := F_{count(ID)} \left(\sigma_{Time=\tau_1} (\Lambda_i) \right)$

(2) $\mathcal{AC}^i_{\tau_1} :=_{Category} F_{count(*)} \left(\sigma_{Time=\tau_1} (\Lambda_i) \right)$

(3) $\mathcal{S}^i_{\tau_1} := F_{count(SrcIP)} \left(\pi_{SrcIP} \left(\sigma_{Time=\tau_1} (\Lambda_i) \right) \right)$

(4) $\mathcal{PS}^i_{\tau_1, \tau_0} := \dfrac{F_{count(SrcIP)}(\pi_{SrcIP}(W^i_{\tau_1} - W^i_{\tau_0}))}{F_{count(SrcIP)}(\pi_{SrcIP}(W^i_{\tau_1}))}, \; W^i_\tau := \pi_{SrcIP} \left(\sigma_{Time=\tau} (\Lambda_i) \right)$

(5) $\mathcal{C}^i_{\tau_1} := F_{count(AlertType)} \left(\pi_{AlertType} \left(\sigma_{Time=\tau_1} (\Lambda_i) \right) \right)$

(6) $\mathcal{PC}^i_{\tau_1, \tau_0} := \dfrac{F_{count(Type)}(\pi_{Category}(V^i_{\tau_1} - V^i_{\tau_0}))}{F_{count(Category)}(\pi_{Category}(V^i_{\tau_1}))}, \; V^i_\tau := \pi_{Category} \left(\sigma_{Time=\tau} (\Lambda_i) \right)$

(7) $\mathcal{AT}^i_{\tau_1} := \pi_{Time} \left(\sigma_{Time=\tau_1} (\Lambda_i) \right),$

5   Heuristic Host Selection Algorithm

Algorithm 1 describes the heuristic host selection procedure. The algorithm takes as arguments a set of IDS generated alerts Λ from the current time window $t_a \leq \tau_1 < t_b$ and a set of features $\mathcal{F}$ accompanied with their respective user defined weights $\mathcal{W}$. The procedure outputs the top n hosts with the highest abnormality scores. The host selection procedure is performed in two major steps: **(1)** For each host $i \in \mathcal{H}$ within the IDS alert stream input in the current time window (τ_1), three heuristic functions as defined in Section 3 are calculated on the set of features $\mathcal{F} = \{\mathcal{A}, \mathcal{AC}, \mathcal{S}, \mathcal{PS}, \mathcal{C}, \mathcal{PC}, \mathcal{AT}\}$ (Lines 3-14). The exponential smoothing is calculated on the first six features ($\tilde{Z}^{ij}_{\tau_1}$) (Lines 4-6), the exponential smoothing difference on the first two features ($D^{ij}_{\tau_1}$) (Lines 7-9), and the dispersion heuristic on the last feature ($s^{ij}_{\tau_1}$) (Lines 10-14). **(2)** The final score of each host is composed of the sum of three components: sum of exponential smoothings ($S^{\tau_1}_{\tilde{Z}_i}$), sum of exponential smoothing differences ($S^{\tau_1}_{D_i}$), and sum of dispersion ($S^{\tau_1}_{s_i}$) (Lines 15-25). The value of each component is calculated by multiplying the normalized value of a feature ($\overline{Z^{ij}_{\tau_1}}, \overline{D^{ij}_{\tau_1}}, \overline{s^{ij}_{\tau_1}}$) by its respective user defined weight($\mathcal{W}_j$) and subsequently summing them for all features of a heuristic category (Line 24).

In the final step the algorithm outputs the top n hosts with the highest scores.

Algorithm 1. Heuristic Host Selection Algorithm

Input: Set of Alerts Λ, Set of Features $\mathcal{F} = \{\mathcal{A}, \mathcal{AC}, \mathcal{S}, \mathcal{PS}, \mathcal{C}, \mathcal{PC}, \mathcal{AT}\}$, Set of user defined weights $\mathcal{W} = \{w_{\mathcal{A}}^{Z}, w_{\mathcal{AC}}^{Z}, w_{\mathcal{S}}^{Z}, w_{\mathcal{PS}}^{Z}, w_{\mathcal{C}}^{Z}, w_{\mathcal{PC}}^{Z}, w_{\mathcal{A}}^{D}, w_{\mathcal{AC}}^{D}, w_{\mathcal{AT}}^{s}\}$, $t_0 \leq \tau_0 < t_a, t_a \leq \tau_1 < t_b, n$.

Output: Top n hosts with highest scores.

1 **begin**

2 $\quad$ $\mathcal{H} \longleftarrow \pi_{DIP}(\sigma_{Time=\tau_1}(\Lambda))$

$\quad$ // Calculate heuristic function for each host

3 $\quad$ **foreach** $i \in \mathcal{H}$ **do**

$\quad\quad$ // Exponential smoothing of first six features

4 $\quad\quad$ **for** $j \longleftarrow 1\,to\,6$ **do**

5 $\quad\quad\quad$ $\tilde{Z}_{\tau_1}^{ij} \longleftarrow (1 - \alpha)\,\mathcal{F}_{\tau_1}^{ij} + \tilde{Z}_{\tau_0}^{ij}$

6 $\quad\quad$ **end**

$\quad\quad$ // Exponential smoothing difference of first two features

7 $\quad\quad$ **for** $j \longleftarrow 1\,to\,2$ **do**

8 $\quad\quad\quad$ $\tilde{D}_{\tau_1}^{ij} \longleftarrow (1 - \alpha)\,(\mathcal{F}_{\tau_1}^{ij} - \mathcal{F}_{\tau_0}^{ij}) + \tilde{D}_{\tau_0}^{ij}$

9 $\quad\quad$ **end**

$\quad\quad$ // Dispersion of last feature

10 $\quad\quad$ $j \longleftarrow 7$

11 $\quad\quad$ $k \longleftarrow \left|\mathcal{F}_{\tau_1}^{ij}\right|$

12 $\quad\quad$ $\bar{x} \longleftarrow \dfrac{\sum_{x \in \mathcal{F}_{\tau_1}^{ij}} x}{k}$

13 $\quad\quad$ $s_{\tau_1}^{ij} \longleftarrow \sqrt{\frac{1}{k-1}\sum_{x \in \mathcal{F}_{\tau_1}^{ij}}(x - \bar{x})^2}$

14 $\quad$ **end**

$\quad$ // Calculate score for each host

15 $\quad$ **foreach** $i \in \mathcal{H}$ **do**

$\quad\quad$ // Sum score for normalized value of exponential smoothings

16 $\quad\quad$ **for** $j \longleftarrow 1\,to\,6$ **do**

17 $\quad\quad\quad$ $S_{\tilde{Z}_i}^{\tau_1} \longleftarrow S_{\tilde{Z}_i}^{\tau_1} + (\mathcal{W}_j \cdot \overline{\tilde{Z}_{\tau_1}^{ij}})$

18 $\quad\quad$ **end**

$\quad\quad$ // Sum score for normalized value of exponential smoothing differences

19 $\quad\quad$ **for** $j \longleftarrow 7\,to\,8$ **do**

20 $\quad\quad\quad$ $S_{\tilde{D}_i}^{\tau_1} \longleftarrow S_{\tilde{D}_i}^{\tau_1} + (\mathcal{W}_j \cdot \overline{\tilde{D}_{\tau_1}^{ij}})$

21 $\quad\quad$ **end**

$\quad\quad$ // Sum score for normalized value of standard deviation

22 $\quad\quad$ $j \longleftarrow 9$

23 $\quad\quad$ $S_{s_i}^{\tau_1} \longleftarrow S_{s_i}^{\tau_1} + (\mathcal{W}_j \cdot \overline{s_{\tau_1}^{ij}})$

$\quad\quad$ // Sum final score of host

24 $\quad\quad$ $Score_{\tau_1}^{i} \longleftarrow S_{\tilde{Z}_i}^{\tau_1} + S_{\tilde{D}_i}^{\tau_1} + S_{s_i}^{\tau_1}$

25 $\quad$ **end**

$\quad$ // Return top n hosts with highest scores

26 $\quad$ **return** $top(Score_{\tau_1}, n)$

27 **end**

6 Avisa₂: A Network Security Visualization System

A screen shot of Avisa₂ in action is illustrated Fig. 1. The system is composed of two main components, the *radial visualization* on the left and the *information stack* on the right. Both components work in collaboration with each other to maintain effective security situational awareness. This enables a rapid assessment and investigation of relevant security events through direct user interaction and analysis. Avisa₂ presents an up-to-date display of network state by providing an interactive visualization of real-time security events. This, combined with the automatic situational assessment powers of the heuristic functions presents an ideal visualization system that is capable of displaying prioritized situations to security analysts for a better situation awareness.

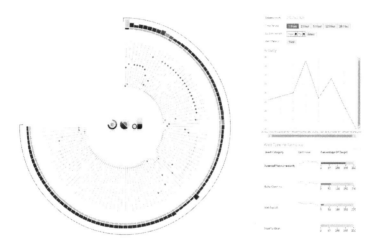

Fig. 1. A screen shot of Avisa₂ in action. The radial visualization on the left is the focal point of the display, while the information stack on the right illustrates detail.

6.1 Radial Visualization

The radial visualization component of Avisa₂ constitutes the focal point of the display. As the output of the heuristic functions are calculated in 5 minute intervals, the top n hosts of the monitored network are selected and are piped as input to the visual component. The radial visualization creates an interactive environment for analysts to perceive patterns, trends, and exceptions within the already prioritized data. Primitive attributes are the unique properties that allow a visual element to be seen from an image. Primitive attributes such as hue, motion, size, length, intensity, and spatial grouping are used extensively to establish visual prominence. The radial visualization itself is composed of two subcomponents, namely the *network host radial panel* and the *alert category dot panel*.

Network Host Radial Panel. The *network host radial panel* is designed to represent the output of the heuristic functions along with several attributes in a perceivable fashion. The prioritized network hosts are arranged along a radial panel while the final quarter of the panel is reserved for displaying additional information. As hosts are added or removed from the panel, they are animated in place to assist in highlighting system transitions from one state to another. The primitive attributes *length* and *color* are utilized to visually differentiate hosts with higher and lower scores. At each time interval the height, color, and position of each host is animated from its previous value to its current value. This is a feature that is rarely seen in security visualization systems due to the selected development framework and complicated implementation issues surrounding animation.

Alert Category Dot Panel. The *alert category dot panel* is designed to encode the alert activity of a host. For each alert category a circle shaped element is displayed along a vertical line. Currently the panel is capable of displaying twenty alert categories with room for further extensions. In order to encode the number of alerts in each category as a color, the number of alerts in each alert category is normalized over all hosts. Accordingly, the values are arranged into equal length intervals while each interval is assigned a color. In this manner, it is very clear for an analyst to see the different types of alerts a host or a collection of hosts are experiencing in one glance. Consequently, based on the assigned colors an analyst can also grasp an idea on the number of alerts and if further detailed information is required, she can use the *information stack* on the right side of the system for further analysis.

6.2 Information Stack

The *information stack* works in collaboration with the radial visualization component to provide a greater insight into the underlying data. When a user selects a host on the radial panel, the information stack queries for the required data and displays it in an informative and interactive manner. The stack is composed of three main components: the *date time selector*, the *activity graph*, and the *alert type performance table*. The *date time selector* displays a panel of predefined or custom time periods for an analyst to select. The toggle buttons are data bound to the underlying data and when pressed, the stack is updated dynamically. The *activity graph* displays a zoomable line chart and is used to display alert activity in greater detail. The *alert type performance table* displays an overview of the alert categories experienced by the selected host by incorporating sparklines and bullet graphs. Sparklines provide a bare-bones and space efficient time-series graph. Selecting an alert category from the performance table displays its respective sparkline graph in greater detail on the *activity graph*. A simplified version of the bullet graph is also used to provide a comparison mechanism for the number of alerts in each category. Avisa$_2$ also provides low level details of the actual IDS alerts through the *Alert Detail* button of the stack.

7   Experimental Results and Evaluation

7.1   Scenario 1: Network Infiltration from the Inside

It is very common for computers on a network to access the Internet through a NAT server. This attack scenario is designed to show how a network with all workstations located behind a NAT can be infiltrated. In this case, while the target computers will be able to make connections to the Internet, it will not be possible to establish a connection from outside to the target network. Thereby, client-side techniques such as executable encoding, host pivoting, social engineering, and shell migration are utilized to exploit vulnerabilities on internal hosts and servers. Figure 2 provides a detailed illustration of the attack scenario. Each stage of the attack scenario accompanied with the analysis of Avisa$_2$'s results is articulated below and depicted in Fig. 3. The output score of each host within the time window of Scenario 1 is also detailed in Appendix A.

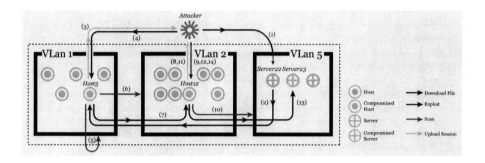

Fig. 2. An infographic detailing the multiple stages of attack scenario 1

(1) 15:30→15:35: A corrupt PDF file, containing a TCP connection binary, is sent as an email attachment to all testbed users.

(2,3) 16:10→16:15: Host 192.168.1.105 opens the corrupted PDF file, an Adobe PDF vulnerability is exploited and a Meterpreter session is generated back to the attacker. Avisa$_2$ detects this and as shown in Fig. 3(a) and Table 1(a), host5 is ranked first and has received the highest score.

(4) 16:25→16:30: Nmap directory is download on host 192.168.1.105.

(5) 16:35→16:40: Nmap is run to scan subnet 192.168.1.0/24 of testbed from host 192.168.1.105. Port scans often trigger numerous alerts and as illustrated in Fig. 3(b) and Table 1(b), Avisa$_2$ has prioritized users of subnet 1.

(6) 16:40→16:45: Nmap is run to scan subnet 192.168.2.0/24 of testbed from host 192.168.1.105. Avisa$_2$ picks up on this behavior and as illustrated in Fig. 3(c) and Table 1(c), users of subnet 2 have received the highest scores.

(7,8) 16:45→16:50: SMB vulnerability on host 192.168.2.112 is exploited and a Meterpreter session is generated back to the attacker. Avisa$_2$ detects this peculiar behavior and as illustrated in Fig. 3(*d*) and Table 1(*d*), host12 has received the highest score and is ranked first.

(9,10) 16:55→17:00: Nmap directory is downloaded on host 192.168.1.112; Nmap is run to scan subnet 192.168.5.0/24 of testbed from host 192.168.2.112. Although snort correctly alerted on the exploit and the port scans, it failed to detect the Nmap directory being downloaded on host12 and only a number of false positives were generated. But as illustrated in Figures 3(*e*),(*f*) and Tables 1(*e*), Avisa$_2$ ranks host12 the highest in two consecutive time periods due to its peculiar behavior. Due to the port scans performed on subnet 5, servers 23 and 24 are ranked in the top 5 in Table 1(*f*) even though they have received no alerts in previous intervals.

(13) 17:10→18:30: Browser on host 192.168.1.112 connects to the internal web application running on 192.168.5.123 and starts performing SQL injection attacks. The attacker iterates through database tables and creates a new user account with administrator privileges. The *user* table of the database is subsequently deleted to disallow further logins. The SQL injection attacks were not detected by snort, but due to the remote desktop connection accessing server23, Avisa$_2$ was able to rank server23 as the first or second host in this period. This is seen in detail in Tables 1(*j*) and (*k*).

(14) 20:45→21:00: Attacker downloads a backdoor on host 192.168.2.112 and disconnects all established sessions and finishes the attack scenario.

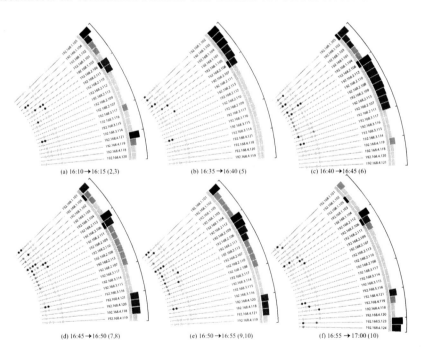

Fig. 3. Screen shots of Avisa$_2$ displaying the stages of attack scenario 1

7.2   Scenario 2: HTTP Denial of Service

The second attack scenario is designed towards performing a stealthy, low bandwidth denial of service attack without the need to flood the network. We will be utilizing `Slowloris` as the main tool in this scenario as it has proven to make Web servers completely inaccessible using a single machine. Slowloris starts by making a full TCP connection to the remote server. The tool holds the connection open by sending valid, incomplete HTTP requests to the server at regular intervals to keep the sockets from closing. Since any Web server has a finite ability to serve connections, it will only be a matter of time before all sockets are used up and no other connection can be made. This scenario picks up where scenario 1 left off by connecting to the backdoor created in the final stage. A detailed description on each stage of the attack scenario accompanied with the analysis of Avisa$_2$'s results and subsequent screen shots are given below. The output score of each host within the time window of Scenario 2 is also illustrated in Appendix B.

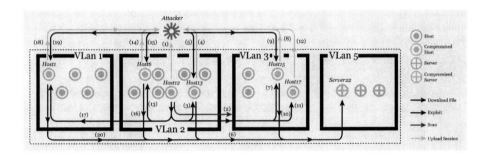

Fig. 4. An infographic detailing the multiple stages of attack scenario 2

(1) 16:55→17:00: Host 192.168.2.112 makes an outbound connection to the attacker through a backdoor. Snort detects host12 connecting to the attacker's machine and subsequently, and as illustrated in Table 2(a), Avisa$_2$ ranks host12 the top host.

(2) 17:15→17:20: Nmap is run to scan subnet 192.168.3.0/24 of testbed from host 192.168.2.112. Due to the scan on subnet 3, hosts 14,15,16, and 17 have received higher scores and as shown in Fig. 5(a) and Table 2(b), they are ranked amongst the top 5 hosts.

(3,4) 17:20→17:25: SMB vulnerability is exploited on host 192.168.2.113 and a remote desktop connection is returned to the attacker. This exploit is partially detected by snort, but since the number of alerts generated in the previous period is substantial, hosts 17,12, and 14 remain top hosts while host13 is ranked 4th. Figure 5(b) depicts this behavior.

(5) 17:25→17:30: Host 192.168.2.113 downloads malicious files from remote server.

(6) 17:30→17:35: Slowloris is run from host 192.168.2.113 against server 192.168.5.122. Even though the required signatures for detecting `Slowloris` attacks are turned on, Snort is unable to detect this attack. As a result of shutting the server down, hosts are unable to access the site and Snort triggers a collection of alerts. $Avisa_2$ is able to pick up on this behavior and as illustrated in Fig. 5(c) and Table 2(d), server22 is ranked second in the period under attack.

(7,8) 17:35→17:40: SMB vulnerability is exploited on host 192.168.3.115 and a remote desktop connection is returned to the attacker. $Avisa_2$ detects this behavior and as illustrated in Table 2(e), host15 is ranked second.

(9) 17:40→17:45: Host 192.168.2.115 downloads malicious files from remote server.

(10) 17:45→17:50: Slowloris is run from host 192.168.3.115 against server 192.168.5.122. $Avisa_2$ is able to pick up on this behavior and as illustrated in Table 2(f), host15 and server22 are amongst the top 3 hosts in the period under attack.

(11,12) 17:50→17:55: SMB vulnerability is exploited on host 192.168.3.117 and a remote desktop connection is returned to the attacker-Conncetion Lost. $Avisa_2$ detects this behavior and as illustrated in Table 2(g) host17 is ranked first.

(13,14) 18:00→18:05: SMB vulnerability is exploited on host 192.168.2.106 and a remote desktop connection is returned to the attacker. $Avisa_2$ detects this behavior and as illustrated in Table 2(h) host6 is ranked second.

(15,16) 18:05→18:10: Slowloris is run from host 192.168.2.106 against server 192.168.5.122. $Avisa_2$ is able to pick up on this behavior and as illustrated in Table 2(i), host6 and server22 are amongst the top 3 hosts in the period under attack.

(17,18) 18:10→18:15: SMB vulnerability is exploited on host 192.168.1.101 and a remote desktop connection is returned to the attacker. $Avisa_2$ detects this behavior and as illustrated in Table 2(j) host1 is ranked second.

(19)18:15→18:20: Host 192.168.1.101 downloads malicious files from remote server.

(20) 18:20→18:25: Slowloris is run from host 192.168.1.101 against server 192.168.5.122. $Avisa_2$ is able to pick up on this behavior and as illustrated in Table 2(k), host1 and server22 are amongst the top 3 hosts in the period under attack.

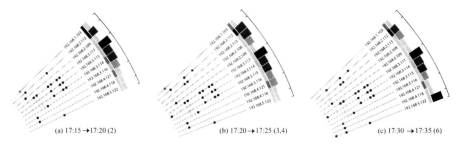

(a) 17:15 →17:20 (2)   (b) 17:20 → 17:25 (3,4)   (c) 17:30 → 17:35 (6)

Fig. 5. Screen shots of $Avisa_2$ displaying the stages of attack scenario 2

8   Conclusion

In this research we presented Avisa$_2$, a network security visualization system that can assist in comprehending IDS alerts and detecting abnormal pattern activities within a network. Visual constraints, complexity of relations between intrusion alerts, and limitations on perceiving situational awareness in high volume environments were the driving force behind the development of the heuristic functions. Three categories of heuristic functions along with seven heuristic features were introduced and formalized. The effectiveness of Avisa$_2$ in detecting malicious and abnormal behavior was evaluated on two multi-step attack scenarios, each intentionally focused on a particular attack type, network service, and network range. Avisa$_2$ was capable of prioritizing hosts that were the subject of attacks or hosts on which the attacks were executed. The effectiveness of Avisa$_2$ is reliant primarily on the detection of the underlying IDS, or in formal terms, its true positive rate. However, this does not mean that the false positive rate of the IDS must also be low, as the heuristic functions of Avisa$_2$ are capable of filtering and eliminating recurring events and prioritizing hosts receiving alerts from multiple sources and types.

Acknowledgment. This work was supported in part by the Natural Sciences and Engineering Research Council of Canada (NSERC) through a grant STPGP-381091 to Dr. Ghorbani.

References

1. Shiravi, H., Shiravi, A., Ghorbani, A.A.: A survey of visualization systems for network security. IEEE Transactions on Visualization and Computer Graphics 99(PrePrints) (2011)
2. Few, S.: Now You See It: Simple Visualization Techniques for Quantitative Analysis, 1st edn. Analytics Press (2009)
3. Endsley, M.: Toward a theory of situation awareness in dynamic systems: Situation awareness. Human Factors 37(1), 32–64 (1995)
4. Ball, R., Fink, G.A., North, C.: Home-centric visualization of network traffic for security administration. In: Proceedings of the ACM Workshop on Visualization and Data Mining for Computer Security, pp. 55–64 (2004)
5. Goodall, J.R., Lutters, W.G., Rheingans, P., Komlodi, A.: Preserving the big picture: visual network traffic analysis with tnv. In: IEEE Workshop on Visualization for Computer Security (VizSEC 2005), pp. 47–54 (2005)
6. Erbacher, R., Walker, K., Frincke, D.: Intrusion and misuse detection in large-scale systems. IEEE Computer Graphics and Applications, 38–48 (2002)
7. McPherson, J., Ma, K., Krystosk, P., Bartoletti, T., Christensen, M.: PortVis: a tool for port-based detection of security events. In: Proceedings of the ACM Workshop on Visualization and Data Mining for Computer Security, pp. 73–81 (2004)
8. PaloAltoNetworks: Re-Inventing Network Security (2010), http://www.paloaltonetworks.com/literature/whitepapers/Re-inventing-Network-Security.pdf (online; accessed July 12, 2011)

9. Shiravi, H., Shiravi, A., Ghorbani, A.: Ids Alert Visualization and Monitoring through Heuristic Host Selection. In: Soriano, M., Qing, S., López, J. (eds.) ICICS 2010. LNCS, vol. 6476, pp. 445–458. Springer, Heidelberg (2010)

Appendix A: Output scores of Avisa₂ in attack scenario 1

Table 1. Output scores of Avisa₂ in attack scenario 1

(a) TIME: 16:10 → 16:15

HOST	SCORE
192.168.1.105	3.62
192.168.4.121	3.35
192.168.2.106	2.53
192.168.2.111	2.32
192.168.1.104	2.19
192.168.4.119	1.99
192.168.1.102	1.94
192.168.1.101	1.74
192.168.3.117	1.73
192.168.2.110	1.48
192.168.3.116	1.48
192.168.2.112	1.48
192.168.1.103	1.48
192.168.4.118	1.48
192.168.3.115	1.48

(b) TIME: 16:35 → 16:40

HOST	SCORE
192.168.1.102	3.37
192.168.1.103	3.10
192.168.1.104	2.95
192.168.1.101	2.60
192.168.1.105	2.48
192.168.2.106	2.27
192.168.2.107	1.00
192.168.3.117	0.92
192.168.2.111	0.92
192.168.4.121	0.87
192.168.2.113	0.86
192.168.3.116	0.76
192.168.2.112	0.76
192.168.2.110	0.76
192.168.4.118	0.76

(c) TIME: 16:40 → 16:45

HOST	SCORE
192.168.2.106	3.27
192.168.2.112	2.63
192.168.2.110	2.63
192.168.2.108	2.63
192.168.2.109	2.63
192.168.1.105	2.52
192.168.2.113	2.27
192.168.2.107	2.13
192.168.1.102	2.11
192.168.2.111	1.82
192.168.1.103	1.70
192.168.1.101	1.02
192.168.1.104	1.02
192.168.4.119	1.60
192.168.3.117	0.75

(d) TIME: 16:45 → 16:50

HOST	SCORE
192.168.2.112	3.07
192.168.1.101	2.35
192.168.2.106	2.34
192.168.4.118	2.05
192.168.4.120	2.04
192.168.4.121	2.03
192.168.1.105	1.27
192.168.1.102	1.21
192.168.2.110	1.20
192.168.2.108	1.20
192.168.2.109	1.20
192.168.2.111	1.20
192.168.2.113	1.18
192.168.2.107	1.09
192.168.1.103	0.93

(e) TIME: 16:50 → 16:55

HOST	SCORE
192.168.2.112	2.60
192.168.2.109	2.53
192.168.1.101	2.39
192.168.2.106	2.12
192.168.4.120	1.60
192.168.4.118	1.45
192.168.4.121	1.45
192.168.1.102	1.26
192.168.2.111	1.23
192.168.2.110	1.00
192.168.2.108	1.00
192.168.1.105	0.97
192.168.2.107	0.97
192.168.1.103	0.94
192.168.2.113	0.92

(f) TIME: 16:55 → 17:00

HOST	SCORE
192.168.5.123	3.06
192.168.2.112	2.66
192.168.5.124	2.48
192.168.2.106	1.96
192.168.1.101	1.77
192.168.4.121	1.69
192.168.2.111	1.15
192.168.2.109	0.99
192.168.4.119	0.93
192.168.1.102	0.92
192.168.1.103	0.66
192.168.1.104	0.62
192.168.2.113	0.58
192.168.4.118	0.57
192.168.2.110	0.56

(g) TIME: 17:00 → 17:05

HOST	SCORE
192.168.2.112	2.29
192.168.1.101	2.28
192.168.5.123	2.20
192.168.2.106	2.19
192.168.5.124	2.01
192.168.2.111	1.38
192.168.1.102	1.04
192.168.2.109	1.03
192.168.1.103	0.78
192.168.1.104	0.73
192.168.1.105	0.71
192.168.2.113	0.70
192.168.2.110	0.67
192.168.4.118	0.67

(h) TIME: 17:05 → 17:10

HOST	SCORE
192.168.2.112	2.74
192.168.1.101	2.35
192.168.4.119	2.27
192.168.2.106	2.10
192.168.4.121	1.68
192.168.5.123	1.67
192.168.2.111	1.60
192.168.5.124	1.44
192.168.2.109	1.24
192.168.1.102	1.10
192.168.2.113	1.05
192.168.1.105	1.02
192.168.2.110	1.01
192.168.2.108	1.01
192.168.4.118	0.88

(i) TIME: 17:10 → 17:15

HOST	SCORE
192.168.5.123	3.16
192.168.2.106	2.05
192.168.1.104	1.97
192.168.2.112	1.66
192.168.1.101	1.57
192.168.1.105	1.30
192.168.4.121	1.11
192.168.2.111	1.02
192.168.5.124	0.94
192.168.1.102	0.87
192.168.2.109	0.74
192.168.4.118	0.63
192.168.2.113	0.62
192.168.1.103	0.60
192.168.2.110	0.57

(j) TIME: 17:15 → 17:20

HOST	SCORE
192.168.5.123	3.20
192.168.1.104	2.33
192.168.2.106	2.23
192.168.2.112	1.94
192.168.1.101	1.85
192.168.1.105	1.70
192.168.2.111	1.55
192.168.4.119	1.51
192.168.5.124	1.40
192.168.2.109	1.31
192.168.4.121	1.29
192.168.1.102	1.28
192.168.2.113	1.20
192.168.2.110	1.15
192.168.2.108	1.15

(k) TIME: 17:20 → 17:25

HOST	SCORE
192.168.4.121	2.84
192.168.5.123	2.74
192.168.1.101	1.90
192.168.2.106	1.82
192.168.2.112	1.60
192.168.2.111	1.23
192.168.1.102	1.22
192.168.1.104	1.22
192.168.5.124	1.13
192.168.1.103	1.02
192.168.4.119	0.97
192.168.4.118	0.92
192.168.2.109	0.82
192.168.2.107	0.81
192.168.4.118	0.76

Appendix B: Output scores of Avisa$_2$ in attack scenario 2

Table 2. Output scores of Avisa$_2$ in attack scenario 2

(a) TIME: 16:55 → 17:00

HOST	SCORE
192.168.2.112	3.96
192.168.4.121	3.27
192.168.5.122	2.58
192.168.1.103	2.23
192.168.3.114	1.26
192.168.2.109	1.23
192.168.4.118	1.22

(b) TIME: 17:15 → 17:20

HOST	SCORE
192.168.3.117	6.34
192.168.3.115	3.76
192.168.3.114	3.74
192.168.2.112	3.02
192.168.3.116	2.59
192.168.4.121	1.02
192.168.1.103	0.86
192.168.5.122	0.12
192.168.4.118	0.10
192.168.2.109	0.10

(c) TIME: 17:20 → 17:25

HOST	SCORE
192.168.3.117	5.43
192.168.2.112	3.50
192.168.3.114	2.93
192.168.2.113	2.87
192.168.3.115	2.84
192.168.2.108	2.72
192.168.3.116	1.67
192.168.4.121	1.32
192.168.1.103	0.54
192.168.2.109	0.10
192.168.4.118	0.10
192.168.5.122	0.10

(d) TIME: 17:30 → 17:35

HOST	SCORE
192.168.3.117	4.53
192.168.5.122	3.56
192.168.3.114	2.64
192.168.3.115	2.46
192.168.2.112	2.00
192.168.2.113	1.70
192.168.3.116	1.26
192.168.4.121	0.65
192.168.2.108	0.59
192.168.1.103	0.50
192.168.2.109	0.22
192.168.4.118	0.22

(e) TIME: 17:35 → 17:40

HOST	SCORE
192.168.3.117	4.68
192.168.3.115	4.59
192.168.5.122	3.65
192.168.3.114	2.49
192.168.2.112	2.32
192.168.3.116	1.43
192.168.4.121	1.39
192.168.2.113	1.17
192.168.2.108	0.76
192.168.2.109	0.40
192.168.4.118	0.40
192.168.1.103	0.35

(f) TIME: 17:45 → 17:50

HOST	SCORE
192.168.3.115	4.97
192.168.3.117	4.63
192.168.5.122	4.40
192.168.3.114	3.12
192.168.2.112	2.12
192.168.2.113	1.81
192.168.3.116	1.66
192.168.2.108	1.43
192.168.4.121	1.19
192.168.2.109	1.14
192.168.4.118	1.14
192.168.1.103	1.02

(g) TIME: 17:50 → 17:55

HOST	SCORE
192.168.3.117	6.68
192.168.5.122	3.85
192.168.3.115	3.73
192.168.3.114	3.36
192.168.2.112	2.64
192.168.2.113	1.61
192.168.2.109	1.53
192.168.4.118	1.53
192.168.3.116	1.51
192.168.1.103	1.47
192.168.2.108	1.42
192.168.4.121	1.34

(h) TIME: 18:00 → 18:05

HOST	SCORE
192.168.3.117	4.84
192.168.2.106	4.00
192.168.2.112	2.65
192.168.3.116	2.53
192.168.5.122	2.35
192.168.2.109	2.26
192.168.4.121	2.24
192.168.3.115	2.17
192.168.3.114	1.95
192.168.4.118	1.49
192.168.1.103	1.48
192.168.2.108	1.48
192.168.2.113	1.42

(i) TIME: 18:05 → 18:10

HOST	SCORE
192.168.3.117	4.98
192.168.5.122	4.25
192.168.2.106	4.08
192.168.2.112	2.70
192.168.2.109	2.43
192.168.3.116	2.34
192.168.4.121	2.02
192.168.4.118	1.74
192.168.1.103	1.74
192.168.2.108	1.73
192.168.3.115	1.72
192.168.2.113	1.71
192.168.3.114	1.45

(j) TIME: 18:10 → 18:15

HOST	SCORE
192.168.3.117	4.42
192.168.1.101	3.37
192.168.5.122	3.36
192.168.2.112	2.30
192.168.2.106	1.62
192.168.2.109	1.35
192.168.3.116	1.32
192.168.4.121	1.29
192.168.3.115	1.22
192.168.4.118	1.13
192.168.1.103	1.13
192.168.2.108	1.13
192.168.2.113	1.13
192.168.3.114	1.11

(k) TIME: 18:20 → 18:25

HOST	SCORE
192.168.3.117	4.32
192.168.5.122	4.13
192.168.1.101	2.77
192.168.2.112	2.04
192.168.2.106	1.48
192.168.2.109	1.22
192.168.4.121	1.20
192.168.3.116	1.16
192.168.2.108	1.06
192.168.4.118	1.06
192.168.1.103	1.06
192.168.2.113	1.06
192.168.3.114	1.06
192.168.3.115	1.05

Minimising Anonymity Loss in Anonymity Networks under DoS Attacks

Mu Yang and Vladimiro Sassone

ECS, University of Southampton

Abstract. Anonymity is a security property of paramount importance as it helps to protect users' privacy by ensuring that their identity remains unknown. Anonymity protocols generally suffer from denial of service (DoS) attack, as repeated message retransmission affords more opportunities for attackers to analyse traffic and lower the protocols' privacy. In this paper, we analyse how users can minimise their anonymity loss under DoS attacks by choosing to remove or keep 'failed' nodes from router lists. We also investigate the strategy effectiveness in those cases where users cannot decide whether the 'failed' node are the targets of DoS attacks.

1 Introduction

Protecting online privacy is an essential part of today's society and its importance is increasingly recognised as crucial in many fields of computer-aided human activity, such as eVoting, eAuctions, bill payments, online betting and electronic communication. One of the most common mechanisms for privacy is *anonymity*, which generally refers to the condition of being unidentifiable within a given set of subjects, known as the *anonymity set*.

Several mechanisms have been proposed to enforce privacy through the use of anonymity networks (e.g. [5,15,19,11,18]). Yet, the open nature of such networks and the unaccountability which results from the very idea of anonymity, make the existing systems prone to various attacks (e.g. [14,16,17,9]). The evaluation of such attacks on anonymity systems has largely focused exclusively on security – that is, how likely anonymity is to be compromised – with all other possible metrics considered tangential. Recent work, however, has started to address parameters such as performance and reliability [8,13,20], which are factors are self-evident importance: an unreliable system, or anyway a scarcely unusable system, will cause users to take their communications to other channels, possibly non-anonymous, and defeat the system's purpose altogether. An adversary may selectively affect the reliability of the system in those states which are hardest to compromise, in their attempt to make the system prefer less secure states. Faced with poor reliability, many users (and a lot of software too) will naturally attempt to repeat communication (resend messages), offering more opportunities for traffic analysis and attacks. Consequently, a considerable amount of research has recently been focussing on DoS attacks to anonymity networks [27,2,3,21].

In a DoS attack, the attacker is able to deanonymise users by affecting system reliability. More specifically, the attacker will choose users who are hardest to compromise,

S. Qing et al. (Eds.): ICICS 2011, LNCS 7043, pp. 414–429, 2011.

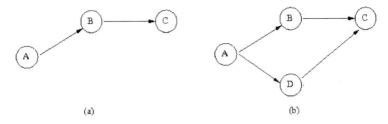

Fig. 1. Partial anonymity networks

and will attempt to make them appear as 'failed' to other users. That is, the attacker will actively make the targeted nodes very busy, so as to make them become unresponsive to their peers who seek cooperation to forward messages according to the selected anonymity protocol. Effectively, the target nodes remain cut off very soon indeed (cf. e.g. [24]). Throughout the paper, we refer to such slow/unresponsive/compromised nodes simply as *failed* (or apparently failed) nodes. While nodes under attack become unresponsive, malicious users on the network make sure to keep relative idle, thereby inducing honest users (and software alike) to attempt to communicate (viz., reroute their communication path) through them. In this way, malicious users obtain a double advantage: they decrease the ratio of cooperating users in the system, and make themselves look as very efficient communication peers, to be preferred over the others. Consider for instance the partial anonymity networks of Figure 1. In (a) user A sends a message to C via B. Assume now that B is targeted by a DoS attacker, then B appears failed to A. So A has to rebuild a path for forwarding messages to C. User A now sends the message to C via D in Figure 1(b). Therefore, if D is a malicious user, then the probability of identifying A increases because of D's own guess or both B and D's collaboration or other eavesdroppers.

Papers [2,3,21] showed that the DoS attacks in anonymous systems reduce anonymity considerably, so that in recent years, a considerable amount of research has been focusing on refining such systems. In particular, trust-and-reputation-based metrics have become quite popular in this domain [1,6,7,10,25,26]. Yet, introducing trust into the picture opens the flank to new security attacks, exploiting trust mechanisms explicitly, as proved in [24]. In such work, the authors evaluated the anonymity loss in trust-based CROWDS protocol when DoS attacks take place. At the moment, there are no perfect solutions to address the DoS attacks. So, it becomes of great practical relevance to study what a user can do to minimise her anonymity loss when exposed to such attack scenarios.

In this paper, we investigate the two strategies a user can adopt when confronted with a failed node, viz., whether to remove or keep the 'failed' node from their router list, and try to determine which one is the best approach under different scenarios.

The CROWDS protocol allows Internet users to perform anonymous web transactions by sending their messages through a random chain of users participating in the protocol. Each user in the '*crowd*' must establish a path between her and a set of servers by selecting randomly some users to act as routers (or forwarders). Such routing paths are formed so as to guarantee that users do not know whether their predecessors are message originators or just forwarders. Each user only has access to messages routed through her. It is well known that CROWDS cannot ensure strong anonymity in presence of corrupt participants [23,4], yet when the number of corrupt users is sufficiently small, it provides a weaker notion of anonymity known as *probable innocence*: informally, a sender is probably innocent if to an attacker she is no more likely to be the message originator than not to be.

In this paper we use the metric of probable innocence to measure anonymity loss. In other words, we consider DoS attacks as well as the classical insider attack to anonymity networks, which is when the malicious users in the systems collaborate to report (to some unspecified authority) the most likely initiator of each message they intercept. The list of participants (or users, or members) in CROWDS is kept by a server called *blender*, which provides it to all registered users. When new node starts running the system to join the crowd, and is willing to act as a message-forwarder, the blender adds it to its list of routers. Each user maintains their own local list of routers, which is updated when the user receives notices of new or deleted members from the blender. Yet, the user can also drop routers from her list by her own decision, if she detects failed nodes.

Structure of the paper. The paper is organised as follows: we recall the fundamental ideas behind the CROWDS protocol and its properties, including the most popular anonymity metrics, in §2 below. Then in §3 we present our first contribution: a model of the interactions between users and DoS attackers and, by using the game theoretic notion of *Nash Equilibrium*, an analysis of the strategies chosen by the users. Then, §4 repeats the analysis for a refined model in which we take into account the users' uncertainty about the nature the 'failed' node, viz., whether it is malicious or a honest user under a DoS attack. In such analysis, we introduce and discuss a key parameter, the probability that the 'failed' node is malicious, and presents some preliminary results of its analysis.

2   Related Work

Using conditional probabilities to measure anonymity level was proposed by Reiter and Rubin [23]. They proposed a hierarchy of anonymity notions in the context of CROWDS. These range from '*absolute privacy*,' where the attacker cannot perceive the presence of an actual communication, to '*provably exposed*,' where the attacker can prove a sender-and-receiver relationship. The most important level is '*probable innocence*' which was originally defined as "A sender is probably innocent if, from the attacker's point of view, she appears no more likely to be the originator than to not be the originator."

Let n be the number of users participating in the protocol and let c and $n - c$ be the number of the corrupt and honest members, respectively. Since anonymity makes only sense for honest users, we define the set of anonymous events as $\mathcal{A} = \{a_1, a_2, \ldots, a_{n-c}\}$, where a_i indicates that user i is the initiator of the message.

As it is usually the case in the analysis of CROWDS, we assume that attackers will always deliver a request to forward immediately to the end server, since forwarding it any further cannot help them learn anything more about the identity of the originator. Thus in any given path, there is at most one detected user: the first honest member to forward the message to a corrupt member. Therefore we define the set of observable events as $O = \{o_1, o_2, \ldots, o_{n-c}\}$, where o_j indicates that user j forwarded a message to a corrupted user. In this case, we also say that user j *is detected* by the attacker. The corresponding notion of probable innocence is formalised by Reiter and Rubin [23] via the conditional probability that user i is detected given that she is the initiator, in symbols $P(o_i \mid a_i)$. Probable innocence holds if

$$\forall i.\, P(o_i \mid a_i) \leq \frac{1}{2} \tag{1}$$

In [23] it is also proved that the following holds in CROWDS:

$$P(o_j \mid a_i) = \begin{cases} 1 - \dfrac{n - c - 1}{n} p_f & i = j \\ \dfrac{1}{n} p_f & i \neq j \end{cases} \tag{2}$$

Therefore, probable innocence (1) holds if and only if

$$n \geq \frac{p_f}{p_f - 1/2}(c + 1) \quad and \quad p_f \geq \frac{1}{2}.$$

The formulae above show that the number n of participating users influences substantially the anonymity level that the system can provide to its users. If honest users are lost to the network, either because compromised or voluntarily withdrawn or removed from a router list following a DoS attack, then the remaining honest users will indirecltly suffer a loss of anonymity. This happens of course as a side-effect of being part of a network which can only provide a lower anonymity guarantee, due to a less favourable ratio of honest and malicious users.

Numerous denial of service (DoS) attacks have been reported in the literature. In particular, the *'packet spinning'* attack of [21] tries to lure users into selecting malicious relays by targeting honest users by DoS attacks. The attacker creates long circular paths involving honest users and sends large amount of data through the paths, forcing the users to employ all their bandwidth and then timing out. These attacks motivate the demand for mechanisms to enhance the reliability of anonymity networks. In particular, paper [3] investigates the effects of DoS attacks on some anonymity systems, such as Tor, Hydra-Onion, Cashmere, and Salsa, and shows greater opportunities to compromise anonymity under DoS attack, and the systems cannot tolerate a majority of nodes being malicious.

To address the DoS attack, several mechanisms were proposed to enhance anonymity against DoS attacks. Trust-and-reputation-based metrics are quite popular in this domain [1,6,7,10,25,26]. Enhancing the reliability by trust and reputation, not only does improve the system's usability, but may also increase its anonymity guarantee. Indeed, a trust-based selection of relays improves both the reliability and the anonymity of the network, by delivering messages through 'trusted' routers. Moreover, the more reliable the system, the more it may attract users and hence improve the anonymity guarantee by growing the anonymity set. Introducing trust in anonymity networks does however open the flank to novel security attacks, as proved in [24].

Importantly, a users' own response to a DoS attack may effectively decrease their anonymity loss. In particular, in the design of Crowds, users can choose removing or keeping routers if they detect those routers (or nodes) failed, and each response will lead to different anonymity payoffs. In this paper, we investigate this and find out which response yields the best strategy for users under different scenarios.

3   Minimizing Users' Anonymity Loss

3.1   Preliminaries and Notations

As discussed in the previous section, the Crowds protocol and the related metrics to measure its anonymity have been enhanced against DoS attacks. Among these, the notion of trust has been considered. However, introducing trust in anonymity networks paves the way novel attack opportunities. In this section, we focus on how to minimize the anonymity loss without introducing new mechanisms. We first describe our approach based on *game theory*, then model users and DoS attackers as players in our game, and devise formulae for these players' payoffs. Finally, we investigate the strategy users should choose and its effect compared with other response actions under DoS attack.

We adopt two working assumptions: users want to forward messages to others, and they value their anonymity. Thus in our analysis of the paper, we take anonymity as part of evaluation of users' payoffs. The anonymity systems generally consist of two groups of components under the DoS attacks: users compete against DoS attackers for good anonymity services (e.g., good privacy level guaranteed by the systems) and, at the same time, the DoS attackers try their best to de-anonymize the systems. Here, users' strategic objective, their 'utility', is to minimize their anonymity loss, while the attackers endeavour to gain maximum benefits from the attacks.

As discussed in §2, the DoS attack is deployed to make the target (honest) user, say k unavailable or unresponsive. This causes the message forwarder, say i, to reroute her (anonymity) path to her messages' destinations, say D, and thus suffer anonymity loss implied by the rerouting activity and, at the same time, run an increased risk to pick the malicious users on her new paths which illustrated in Figure 2.

As such, the interaction between user i and the attackers A in the anonymity systems is best modeled as a *non-cooperative* game among the rational and strategic players. Players are rational because they wish to maximize their own gain, and they are

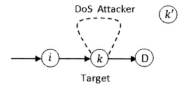

Fig. 2. The attacker targets node k making it unavailable to user i. User i chooses her strategy –whether removing k from her router list– by predicting the attacker's strategy.

strategic because they can choose their actions (e.g., remove failed node from router list) that influence both their payoffs. Another force tending to affect users' anonymity payoffs is the so-called 'churn problem' [22], which is caused by frequent 'arrivals' and 'departures' of users. In order to coordinate such membership events, the standard implementation of Crowds makes use of a dedicated process, the so-called 'blender.' Among its functions, the blender provides updates to the users' lists of crowd members at regular intervals, In this paper we use T to to represent such interval, and model a user's behaviour during the time interval between two list updating events.

With respect to the target node k, the attackers have the following two strategies:

- *Strategy S'_1*: keep targeting k;
- *Strategy S'_2*: target a user other than k, say k'.

The user i also has two strategies:

- *Strategy S_1*: remove k from router list;
- *Strategy S_2*: keep k on the router list.

With these strategies above, the payoffs of these two players are expressed in the form of 2×2 matrices, $U_i(\_)$ and $U_A(\_)$, which denote user i's and the attackers' payoff, respectively. A game is called a *zero-sum* game, if the sum of the utilities is constant in every outcome, so that whatever is gained by one player must be lost by the other players, that is, in our case, if the sum of $U_i(\_)$ and $U_A(\_)$ is constant, then our game is a zero-sum game.

Interesting economic behaviour occurs when the utility of a player depends not only on her own strategy, but on the other's strategy as well. The most popular way of characterising this dynamics is in terms of *Nash equilibrium*. Since a player's utility depends on her strategy, she might unilaterally switch her strategy to improve her utility. This switch in strategy will affect the other player, so that she might decide to switch her strategy as well. One game reaches a Nash equilibrium if no player can improve her utility by unilaterally switching strategy. In Section 3.2, we will model the scenario illustrated in Figure 2 and study the equilibrium of our game. We present here for the reader's convenience a table summarizing those variables that will appear in the modeling.

3.2   Users' Protection Model

We first discuss the notations which are used in the evaluation of i's utility function:

- $U_i(t)$: it reflects i's anonymity level guaranteed by the system. At time $t \in T$, user i suffers the DoS attack and then she chooses her strategy, thus her payoff at time $t + 1 \in T$ is defined as $U_i(t + 1)$. For time t, the payoff $U_i(t)$ can be evaluated by the anonymity measure metrics as

$$U_i(t) = 1 - P(o_j \mid a_i)_t$$

where $P(o_j \mid a_i)_t$ represents the anonymity level measuring of user i at time t. Thus, the value of $U_i(t)$ is not greater than one. The smaller the value of $P(o_j \mid a_i)_t$, the higher anonymity level of user i guaranteed, that is, the greater i's payoff $U_i(t)$;

– L_i: when user i mistakenly removes an normal honest user from her router list, she will suffer some anonymity loss which is measured by L_i. The loss here can be evaluated by the probable innocence anonymity metrics, which we described in §2. In particular, in systems like CROWDS protocol, the loss will be

$$\left[1 - \left(1 - \frac{n - c - 1}{n} p_f \right) \right] - \left[1 - \left(1 - \frac{n - 1 - c - 1}{n - 1} p_f \right) \right]$$

$$= \frac{n - c - 1}{n} p_f - \frac{n - 1 - c - 1}{n - 1} p_f$$

$$= \frac{c + 1}{n(n - 1)} p_f.$$

– L_{ik}: if the attacker successfully perpetrates a DoS attack by targeting k, then i will suffer anonymity loss related to re-routing. Here L_{ik} measures two kinds of anonymity loss: one is the information leak because of this another forwarding path, the other one is that due to the failed target node cannot response to i, the probability of choosing malicious users as forwarders on the path increases.

We define i's payoff matrix as follows:

$$U_i(t + 1) = [u_{qp}]_{2 \times 2} = \begin{bmatrix} U_i(t) & U_i(t) - L_{ik} \\ U_i(t) - L_{ik'} - L_i & U_i(t) - L_{ik'} \end{bmatrix}$$

where $[u_{pq}]_{2 \times 2}$ denotes the player's payoff when she chooses strategy p and the other player chooses strategy q. Here u_{11} represents the payoff if the players follow the strategy pair (S_1, S_1'), which is when the attacker chooses to target k and the user chooses to remove the same user k. Thus, for i, the utility is her original utility value of $U_i(t)$. The term u_{21} represents the payoff corresponding to the strategy pair (S_1, S_2'), which is when the attacker targets a new node k', but i still removes k. In this case we subtract from the original utility the loss due to the attack to k', as well as the loss of removing the honest node k. The term u_{12} represents the payoff of strategy pair (S_2, S_1'), that is the attacker still targets k and i chooses to keep k, respectively. The term u_{22} represents the payoff of strategy tuple (S_2, S_2'), which is when the attacker targets k' other than k

Table 1. Variables used in the modeling

$U_i(t)$:	user i's payoff at time t
$U_A(\text{-})$:	the DoS attacker's payoff at time t
L_i:	i's anonymity loss following the removal of an honest user from router list
L_{ik}:	i's anonymity loss because of DoS target k
n:	the number of users in the system
c:	the number of malicious users in the system
θ:	the percentage of target nodes among honest users
p_f:	the forwarding policy of the system
C_k:	the cost of targeting node k for the DoS attackers
B_k:	the benefit of de-anonymization for the DoS attackers because of successfully targeting k
B':	the benefit of de-anonymizing for the DoS attackers when one honest user is removed from router list by i
$P(o_j \mid a_i)_t$:	the anonymity level measuring of user i at time t

and i keeps k. In this case we subtract from the original utility the loss of the attack for successfully targeting k'.

We define the attacker's payoff matrix as follows:

$$U_A(\_) = \begin{bmatrix} -C_k & B_k - C_k \\ B_{k'} - C_{k'} + B' & B_{k'} - C_{k'} \end{bmatrix}$$

Here for B_k, since user i's anonymity loss measured by L_{ik} and $L_{ik'}$ are actually the attacker's aim, the benefit B_k, $B_{k'}$ are equal to L_{ik} and $L_{ik'}$, respectively. Similarly to B_k above, the benefit B' is equal to L_i. Thus, we have,

$$U_A(\_) = \begin{bmatrix} -C_k & L_{ik} - C_k \\ L_{ik'} + L_i - C_{k'} & L_{ik'} - C_{k'} \end{bmatrix}.$$

Note that when the cost C_k of targeting node k is the same as $C_{k'}$, the game is a *zero-sum* game, that is, the total payoff of these two players' at each strategy pair is always

$$U_i(t + 1) + U_A(\_) = U_i(t) - C_k.$$

User i's loss is exactly balanced by the gains of the DoS attacker.

In order to find an equilibrium of our model, we turn our attention to Nash's theorem [12], which proved that such games always have at least one equilibrium in mixed strategies, we have:

Proposition 1.

$$X = \left(\frac{(L_{ik} - L_{ik'}) - (C_k - C_{k'})}{L_i + L_{ik}}, \frac{(L_i + L_{ik'}) + (C_k - C_{k'})}{L_i + L_{ik}} \right), \qquad Y = \begin{pmatrix} \frac{L_i}{L_i + L_{ik}} \\ \frac{L_{ik}}{L_i + L_{ik}} \end{pmatrix}.$$

Proof. Typically, in a given game represented by a payoff matrix $A_{p \times q}$, vectors x_j and y_j below form a pair of mixed strategies if $\{x_j \in \mathbb{X}^p, x_j \geq 0, \sum_{j=1}^p x_j = 1\}$, and $\{y_j \in \mathbb{Y}^q, y_j \geq 0, \sum_{j=1}^q y_j = 1\}$ hold. For our game, let us suppose that user i can play:

$$X = \begin{bmatrix} x_1 & x_2 \end{bmatrix}$$

where $x_1 + x_2 = 1$. An attacker can also play:

$$Y = \begin{bmatrix} y_1 \\ y_2 \end{bmatrix}$$

where $y_1 + y_2 = 1$. Then, according to [12], the best-response correspondence function is given by: $P(x, y) = \sum_{i=1}^p \sum_{j=1}^q A_{ij} x_i y_j$. Thus, replacing A with respectively $U_i(t + 1)$ and $U_A(\_)$, we obtain the correspondence functions for user i and the attacker, respectively.

$$P_i(x, y) = U_i(t)x_1y_1 + (U_i(t) - L_{ik})x_2y_1 + (U_i(t) - L_{ik'} - L_i)x_1y_2 + (U_i(t) - L_{ik'})x_2y_2$$

$$P_A(x, y) = -C_k x_1 y_1 + (L_{ik} - C_k)x_2 y_1 + (L_{ik'} + L_i - C_{k'})x_1 y_2 + (L_{ik'} - C_{k'})x_2 y_2.$$

By solving the payoffs matrix above, we get the Nash Equilibrium of the game in mixed strategies.   □

The intuition behind the above equilibrium is that X is of the form $[\gamma, 1 - \gamma]$, that is in order to gain maximum payoff, user i should remove k with probability γ (or at γ times). If the anonymity system is symmetric (i.e., the users have the same equilibrium point) or each user updates the router list from the blender of the system, instead of managing it herself, then the two players of our game become: the DoS attackers and the group of all the users. In this case if β nodes are reported failed to the blender, then the optimal strategy for the blender in our equilibrium analysis is to remove $\beta \times \gamma$ nodes from router list.

The game can reach a pure Nash equilibrium when some conditions are satisfied.

Corollary 1. *Strategy 'Keeping k' is the best strategy, that is $X = [0, 1]$ if the following holds.*
1. $L_{ik} = L_{ik'}$;
2. $C_k = C_{k'}$.

Observe that in CROWDS protocol, users are typically indistinguishable from each other from the attacker's point of view. The formulae of Corollary 1 are therefore often satisfied in CROWDS-based systems. It follows from the above proposition that in those systems the best response strategy for user i is to keep k.

3.3 Evaluating the Anonymity Loss of the Strategies

We now focus on the impact of the choice of a strategy on the anonymity of i. Let i's utilities at $t + 1$ when i chooses strategy S be noted as $U_i(t + 1)_S$, and the mixed strategy respectively at $U_i(t + 1)_{Mixed}$.

If user i always chooses to strategy S_1 (, that is removing node k), the attacker will always answer by choosing the strategy to target a different node k', and the utility at time $t + 1$ is evaluated as

$$U_i(t + 1)_{S_1} = U_i(t) - L_{ik'} - L_i .$$

Similarly, the utilities of user i if she keeps k(, that is strategy S_2), or selects the mixed Nash equilibrium strategy can be computed respectively as follows.

$$U_i(t + 1)_{S_2} = \begin{cases} U_i(t) - L_{ik'} & L_{ik'} \geq L_{ik} \\ U_i(t) - L_{ik} & L_{ik'} \leq L_{ik} \end{cases} , \qquad U_i(t + 1)_{Mixed} = U_i(t) - \frac{L_{ik'} + L_i}{L_{ik} + L_i} L_{ik}$$

All these three utilities decrease as time increases. We are of course interested in minimizing the anonymity loss.

Proposition 2.

$$U_i(t + 1)_{S_1} < U_i(t + 1)_{Mixed} , \qquad U_i(t + 1)_{S_2} \leq U_i(t + 1)_{Mixed} .$$

Proof. Because $U_i(t + 1)_{S_1} - U_i(t + 1)_{Mixed} = -\frac{L_{ik'} + L_i^2}{L_{ik} + L_i} < 0$ holds, thus we obtain $U_i(t + 1)_{S_1} < U_i(t + 1)_{Mixed}$. If $L_{ik} \geq L_{ik'}$, then $U_i(t + 1)_{S_2} - U_i(t + 1)_{Mixed} = L_{ik}\frac{L_{ik'} - L_{ik}}{L_i + L_{ik}} \leq 0$; If $L_{ik} \geq L_{ik'}$, then $U_i(t + 1)_{S_2} - U_i(t + 1)_{Mixed} = L_{ik}\frac{L_{ik} - L_{ik'}}{L_i + L_{ik}} \leq 0$. Thus, $U_i(t + 1)_{S_2} \leq U_i(t + 1)_{Mixed}$. □

The proposition shows that by selecting the equilibrium strategy, user i will gain the maximum utility $U_i(t + 1)_{Mixed}$. And as time increases, the distance between the mixed strategy and other two will increase. Our simulations were written in Java, executed on Sun's JVM and based on CROWDS protocol with indistinguishable users. The parameters are: $c = 4$, $p_f = 0.8$; the DoS attackers always target two honest users at one time; we vary the number n of users and increase time t until T. Because the users are indistinguishable, the mixed strategy is actually the pure strategy –keeping node k– according to Corollary 1.

Figure 3(a) shows that by adopting the mixed strategy (keeping k), user i will gain better utility as time increases. Figure 3(b) depicts the utilities of user i at time $t+1$ when adopting the mixed strategy versus removing node k, compared with $U_i(t)$. The diagram shows that although these two utilities are smaller than $U_i(t)$, selecting the 'keep k' strategy will always minimise i's anonymity loss. As the number of users increases (that is, the ratio of malicious users among the users decreases), the utilities increase and the mixed strategy has more strength on decreasing the anonymity loss.

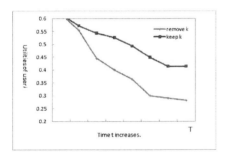

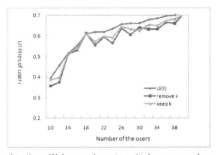

(a) i's utilities decrease as time t increases. $n = 20, c = 4, p_f = 0.8$.

(b) i's utilities at time $(t + 1)$ increase when the number n of users increases, compared with $U_i(t)$. $c = 4, p_f = 0.8$.

Fig. 3. i's utilities

4   Refined Protection Model

We have worked so far under the assumption that users know that the failed node k is the DoS target. Now we proceed to relax such an assumption and generalise our results, by taking the view that users cannot be sure about the type of k. Arguably, this is a rather realistic hypothesis in open and dynamic systems, where honest users can also be unavailable just because they suffer power cuts or network downtime or congestion and overloading. Another possibility is that the failed nodes are malicious users which are carrying out attacks, such as reporting their predecessors as the most likely initiators, which will slow them down. Because of that, their predecessors may also classify them as unavailable/unresponsive nodes. In this section we therefore assume that k may be a normal honest user or a malicious user, and repeat our analysis of DoS attack protection model under such an assumption.

This new scenario differs from those we considered so far in the paper in that when a node k is detected as a failed node, rather than just considering it as a DoS target, user i has to decide whether it is a malicious user or simply a normal honest user who is just temporarily slowed down by e.g. network congestion. We define the uncertainty about the type of a failed node as $P_{ik}(\alpha \mid F)$, where α is the type to which the failed node belongs. More specifically, the term $P_{ik}(t \mid F)$ represents the probability that k encountered by user i is one DoS target and $P_{ik}(m \mid F)$, $P_{ik}(h \mid F)$ are the probabilities of k being respectively a malicious user and normal user type. For these three probabilities, we obviously have $P_{ik}(t \mid F) + P_{ik}(h \mid F) + P_{ik}(m \mid F) = 1$.

In the rest of this section we work out again the best response strategy for user i and analyze the impact of the different strategies on i's anonymity under this refined scenario.

4.1   Re-modeling and the New Equilibrium

Our technical development proceeds *mutatis mutandis* as in the previous section. In particular, as before we first model the interactions between users and attackers building on our previous model, then we study the equilibrium from which find the best response for the users, and finally, we analyze the results.

Now, let L_i' denote the anonymity loss which user i suffers if she is attacked by a malicious user. When i encounters a failed node, she may think it as a malicious node (user) and then remove it. Thus she suffers the anonymity loss if the node is actually honest user. We use L_i (which is described in our model design section) to denote this anonymity loss incurred by i when she removes a normal honest user from router list. Then the utility function of user i becomes as follows.

Proposition 3. *The utilities of user i under different strategy pairs are evaluated as follows.*

$$
U_i(t+1) = U_i(t) -
\begin{cases}
P_{ik}(h \mid F)L_i & (S_1, S_1') \\
\left(P_{ik}(h \mid F)L_i + P_{ik}(t \mid F)(L_{ik'} + L_i) \right) & (S_1, S_2') \\
\left(P_{ik}(m \mid F)L_i' + P_{ik}(t \mid F)L_{ik} \right) & (S_2, S_1') \\
\left(P_{ik}(m \mid F)L_i' + P_{ik}(t \mid F)L_{ik'} \right) & (S_2, S_2')
\end{cases}
$$

Proof. When strategy pair (S_1, S_1') is adopted, that is user i chooses to remove k from router list and the attacker still targets k, we subtract the anonymity loss of removing an honest user with probability $P_{ik}(h \mid F)$. When i still chooses to remove k but the attacker targets a different node k', then we first subtract the loss L_i that k is a normal honest user with probability $P_{ik}(h\,|\,F)$ from the original utility $U_i(t)$. Then, with probability $P_{ik}(t\,|\,F)$ we subtract the loss exerted by a successfully DoS attack $(L_{ik'})$ and that of removing k (L_i). Here we omit the proof of the utilities under the last two strategy pairs because they are similar to the first two.   □

We then start studying the equilibrium of the refined game model.

Proposition 4. *For the DoS attacker, if all the targets look alike, that is $L_{ik} = L_{ik'}$ and $C_k = C_{k'}$, then the following two Pure Nash equilibriums hold.*

$$(S_1, S_2'), \quad if\ P_{ik}(m\,|\,F) > \frac{L_i}{L_i + L_i'};$$

$$(S_2, S_2'), \quad if\ P_{ik}(m\,|\,F) < \frac{L_i}{L_i + L_i'}.$$

Proof. Since $L_{ik} - C_k = L_{ik'} - C_{k'}$ and $L_{ik'} + L_i - C_{k'} > C_k$, the attacker will always choose strategy S_2'. Under this situation, user i will compare the two utilities of her two strategies S_1, S_2, and choose the one which brings her greater payoff. Thus we have that if

$$P_{ik}(m\,|\,F)L_i' + P_{ik}(t\,|\,F)L_{ik'} > P_{ik}(h\,|\,F)L_i + P_{ik}(t\,|\,F)(L_{ik'} + L_i),$$

then i should choose S_1, which consist of removing k from the router list. Otherwise, strategy S_2 should be chosen. From the formulae above and because $P_{ik}(t\,|\,F) + P_{ik}(m\,|\,F) + P_{ik}(h\,|\,F) = 1$, we obtain

$$P_{ik}(m\,|\,F) > \frac{L_i}{L_i + L_i'}.$$

     □

The value $\frac{L_i}{L_i+L_i'}$ depends on the certain system. The greater the value of $\frac{L_i}{L_i+L_i'}$, the better the strategy S_2. Figure 4 shows that user i's best response strategy is influenced by the probability $P_{ik}(m\,|\,F)$ that k is malicious. Note that the value of $P_{ik}(m\,|\,F)$ is in the range

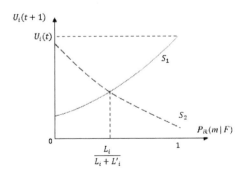

Fig. 4. Utilities $U_i(t + 1)$ of user i choosing strategy S_1 and S_2 are influenced by the probability $P_{ik}(m\,|\,F)$ that k is a malicious user

[0, 1]. The two utilities intersect at the point $P_{ik}(m \mid F) = \frac{L_i}{L_i + L_i'}$, which brings i the same utility whatever strategy she chooses. When $P_{ik}(m \mid F) = 0$, i.e., failed node k cannot be malicious but either is the DoS target or a normal honest user, i should keep k in that $U_i(t+1)_{S_2}$ is greater than $U_i(t+1)_{S_1}$. However, when $P_{ik}(m \mid F)$ increases to 1, the utility of S_1 remains at $U_i(t)$ as before, while the utility of S_1 becomes $U_i(t) - L_i'$. Therefore, user i should remove k when k is more likely to be a malicious user, more precisely in the range $[\frac{L_i}{L_i + L_i'}, 1]$.

4.2 Predictions of $P_{ik}(m \mid F)$

Our model shows that $P_{ik}(m \mid F)$ is an important parameter which determines what strategy user i should choose. However, the exact value of $P_{ik}(m \mid F)$ is difficult to determine for i. User i cannot tell what type the failed node she encountered belongs to. In this section we therefore focus on $P_{ik}(m \mid F)$ so as to give i a way to approximate and predict its value.

The probability $P_{ik}(m \mid F)$ is a conditional probability representing that given i encounters a failed node, say k, then k is malicious. By Bayes Theorem, it can be computed as follows

$$P_{ik}(m \mid F) = \frac{\Pr[F \mid k = m]\Pr[k = m]}{\Pr[F]} \tag{3}$$

where $\Pr[F \mid k = m]$ is the conditional probability of encountering a failed node given the node is malicious, $\Pr[k = m]$ is the probability that node k is a malicious user, and $\Pr[F]$ is the probability of encountering a failed node.

We first study the probability $\Pr[F]$ in Eq. 3 which can be evaluated by applying the *total probability theorem*. There are three possibilities: the node is failed because (1) he is a normal honest user but suffering accidents; (2) he is an attacker; and (3) he is the DoS target. We indicate them by respectively h, m and t these possibilities. Thus we have:

$$\Pr[F] = \sum_{\alpha = h, m, t} \Pr[F \mid k = \alpha]\Pr[k = \alpha]. \tag{4}$$

For evaluation, $\Pr[k = \alpha]$ is determined by the composition of different types of users in the system. For instance, the probability that one node is malicious $\Pr[k = m]$ is evaluated by the ratio of malicious users c among all the users n:

$$\Pr[k = m] = \frac{c}{n}. \tag{5}$$

For other two types, by introducing θ–the percentage of target nodes among honest users–defined in Table 1, we have

$$\Pr[k = t] = \frac{n - c}{n} \cdot \theta,$$

$$\Pr[k = h] = \frac{n - c}{n} \cdot (1 - \theta). \tag{6}$$

As for the probabilities $\Pr[F \mid k = \alpha]$ where $\alpha = t, h, m$, since the target nodes are always failed to other users, the equation $\Pr[F \mid k = t] = 1$ always holds. Now from Eq. 3–6, we obtain

Proposition 5.

$$P_{ik}(m \mid F) = \frac{\Pr[F \mid k = m] \cdot \frac{c}{n}}{\Pr[F \mid k = m] \cdot \frac{c}{n} + 1 \cdot \frac{n-c}{n} \cdot \theta + \Pr[F \mid k = h] \cdot \frac{n-c}{n} \cdot (1 - \theta)}$$

We then study the partial derivatives of Proposition 5 to get the relationships among $P_{ik}(m \mid F)$ and its parameters.

Corollary 2. *For user i, the following hold.*

$$\frac{\partial P_{ik}(m \mid F)}{\partial \Pr[k = m]} \geq 0 , \quad \frac{\partial P_{ik}(m \mid F)}{\partial \Pr[k = h]} \leq 0 , \quad \frac{\partial P_{ik}(m \mid F)}{\partial \Pr[F \mid k = m]} \geq 0 , \quad and \quad \frac{\partial P_{ik}(m \mid F)}{\partial \Pr[k = t]} \leq 0 .$$

From the corollary above, one sees that if user i finds the system to consists of relatively more malicious users, then $P_{ik}(m \mid F)$ is more likely in the range of $[\frac{L_i}{L_i + L_i'}, 1]$, thus it is better for her to remove failed nodes. When the probability $\Pr[k = m]$ increases to one, the probability $P_{ik}(m \mid F)$ increases to one as well.

Such a prediction of $P_{ik}(m \mid F)$ can be observed by evaluating the anonymity level guaranteed by the system, in that the anonymity level $P(o_j \mid a_i)$ reflects the portion (via $\Pr[k = m]$) of malicious users among all nodes. Consider an example where 10% of malicious users are found unavailable due to being busy at deanonymizing the systems, and 1% of normal honest users are observed as failed nodes because of overloading or other accidental reasons, then we have $\Pr[F \mid k = m] = 0.1$ and $\Pr[F \mid k = h] = 0.01$. We get Figure 5(a), 5(b) depicting the changes of $P_{ik}(m \mid F)$ by varying $\Pr[k = m]$ from 5% to 100%, increasing the percentage θ of targeted users among honest users respectively. These results are proved in Corollary 2 as well.

The probabilities $\Pr[F \mid k = \alpha]$ where $\alpha = h, m, t$ depend on the attacks and the observations of the system. Since the nodes targeted by DoS attackers always appear as failed nodes, the equation $\Pr[F \mid k = t] = 1$ always holds. The value of $\Pr[F \mid k = h]$ can be learned by observing how often normal honest users appear to have 'failed'; this should normally be relative small because not many normal users will suffer overloading, or other network accidents. As for $\Pr[F \mid k = m]$, it is usually small due to that the

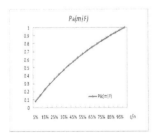 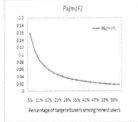 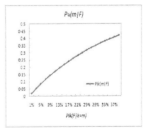

(a) The probability $P_{ik}(m \mid F)$ increases when the percentage of malicious users increases.

(b) The probability $P_{ik}(m \mid F)$ decreases when θ increases.

(c) The probability $P_{ik}(m \mid F)$ decreases when $\Pr[F \mid k = m]$ increases.

Fig. 5. The value of $P_{ik}(m \mid F)$

malicious users do not want to be noticed or detected of doing de-anonymizing things. In Figure 5(c), we have $\Pr[F \mid k = m]$ vary from 1% to 37%, $c/n = 10\%$ and $\theta = 5\%$. When $\Pr[F \mid k = m]$ is quite small, $P_{ik}(m \mid F)$ is very small and thus under this case, $P_{ik}(m \mid F)$ is more likely in the range of $[0, \frac{L_i}{L_i+L_i'}]$. Therefore, keeping k in the router list is the best strategy for i.

5   Conclusion

In this paper we have investigated the best response for users to minimise their anonymity loss when they come across 'failed' nodes under DoS attacks. We used a game-theoretic approach for our analysis.

We modelled the problem and formalised the payoffs of users and attackers according to the strategies they choose. By Nash Equilibria, we showed that in a symmetric protocol like CROWDS, keeping failed node is the strategy users should choose. We then re-modelled the problem by taking into account that the user's uncertainty about the typology of failed nodes they encounter. Our results showed that when the important parameter $P_{ik}(m \mid F)$ is in the range of $[\frac{L_i}{L_i+L_i'}, 1]$, users should remove the failed nodes and when it is smaller than $\frac{L_i}{L_i+L_i'}$, the best strategy is instead to retain them. We proposed a way to predict the value of $P_{ik}(m \mid F)$ and showed its changes when the parameters vary.

References

1. Backes, M., Lorenz, S., Maffei, M., Pecina, K.: Anonymous Webs of Trust. In: Atallah, M.J., Hopper, N.J. (eds.) PETS 2010. LNCS, vol. 6205, pp. 130–148. Springer, Heidelberg (2010)
2. Bauer, K., McCoy, D., Grunwald, D., Kohno, T., Sicker, D.: Low-resource routing attacks against tor. In: Proceedings of the 2007 ACM Workshop on Privacy in Electronic Society, WPES 2007, pp. 11–20. ACM, New York (2007)
3. Borisov, N., Danezis, G., Mittal, P., Tabriz, P.: Denial of service or denial of security? In: Proceedings of the 14th ACM Conference on Computer and Communications Security, CCS 2007, pp. 92–102. ACM, New York (2007)
4. Chatzikokolakis, K., Palamidessi, C.: Probable innocence revisited. Theor. Comput. Sci. 367(1-2), 123–138 (2006)
5. Chaum, D.: Untraceable electronic mail, return addresses, and digital pseudonyms. Commun. ACM 24(2), 84–88 (1981)
6. Damiani, E., di Vimercati, S.D.C., Paraboschi, S., Pesenti, M., Samarati, P., Zara, S.: Fuzzy logic techniques for reputation management in anonymous peer-to-peer systems. In: Wagenknecht, M., Hampel, R. (eds.) Proceedings of the 3rd Conference of the European Society for Fuzzy Logic and Technology, pp. 43–48 (2003)
7. Dingledine, R., Freedman, M.J., Hopwood, D., Molnar, D.: A Reputation System to Increase Mix-net Reliability. In: Moskowitz, I.S. (ed.) IH 2001. LNCS, vol. 2137, pp. 126–141. Springer, Heidelberg (2001)
8. Dingledine, R., Mathewson, N.: Anonymity loves company: Usability and the network effect. In: Proceedings of the Fifth Workshop on the Economics of Information Security, WEIS 2006 (2006)

9. Dingledine, R., Mathewson, N., Syverson, P.F.: Tor: The second-generation onion router. In: USENIX Security Symposium, pp. 303–320. USENIX (2004)

10. Dingledine, R., Syverson, P.F.: Reliable MIX Cascade Networks through Reputation. In: Blaze, M. (ed.) FC 2002. LNCS, vol. 2357, pp. 253–268. Springer, Heidelberg (2003)

11. Freedman, M.J., Morris, R.: Tarzan: a peer-to-peer anonymizing network layer. In: Atluri, V. (ed.) ACM Conference on Computer and Communications Security, pp. 193–206. ACM (2002)

12. Fudenberg, D., Tirole, J.: Game Theory. MIT Press (1991)

13. Golle, P., Juels, A.: Parallel mixing. In: Atluri, V., Pfitzmann, B., McDaniel, P.D. (eds.) ACM Conference on Computer and Communications Security, pp. 220–226. ACM (2004)

14. Hopper, N., Vasserman, E.Y., Chan-Tin, E.: How much anonymity does network latency leak? ACM Trans. Inf. Syst. Secur. 13(2) (2010)

15. Jakobsson, M.: Flash mixing. In: Annual ACM Symposium on Principles of Distributed Computing, PODC 1999, pp. 83–89 (1999)

16. McLachlan, J., Tran, A., Hopper, N., Kim, Y.: Scalable onion routing with Torsk. In: Al-Shaer, E., Jha, S., Keromytis, A.D. (eds.) ACM Conference on Computer and Communications Security, pp. 590–599. ACM (2009)

17. Murdoch, S.J., Danezis, G.: Low-cost traffic analysis of tor. In: IEEE Symposium on Security and Privacy, pp. 183–195. IEEE Computer Society (2005)

18. Nambiar, A., Wright, M.: Salsa: a structured approach to large-scale anonymity. In: Juels, A., Wright, R.N., di Vimercati, S.D.C. (eds.) ACM Conference on Computer and Communications Security, pp. 17–26. ACM (2006)

19. Neff, C.A.: A verifiable secret shuffle and its application to e-voting. In: ACM Conference on Computer and Communications Security, pp. 116–125 (2001)

20. Øverlier, L., Syverson, P.F.: Improving Efficiency and Simplicity of Tor Circuit Establishment and Hidden Services. In: Borisov, N., Golle, P. (eds.) PET 2007. LNCS, vol. 4776, pp. 134–152. Springer, Heidelberg (2007)

21. Pappas, V., Athanasopoulos, E., Ioannidis, S., Markatos, E.P.: Compromising Anonymity Using Packet Spinning. In: Wu, T.-C., Lei, C.-L., Rijmen, V., Lee, D.-T. (eds.) ISC 2008. LNCS, vol. 5222, pp. 161–174. Springer, Heidelberg (2008)

22. Ray, S., Slutzki, G., Zhang, Z.: Incentive-driven P2P anonymity system: A game-theoretic approach. In: ICPP, p. 63. IEEE Computer Society (2007)

23. Reiter, M.K., Rubin, A.D.: Crowds: Anonymity for web transactions. ACM Trans. Inf. Syst. Secur. 1(1), 66–92 (1998)

24. Sassone, V., Hamadou, S., Yang, M.: Trust in Anonymity Networks. In: Gastin, P., Laroussinie, F. (eds.) CONCUR 2010. LNCS, vol. 6269, pp. 48–70. Springer, Heidelberg (2010)

25. Singh, A., Liu, L.: Trustme: Anonymous management of trust relationships in decentralized P2P systems. In: Shahmehri, N., Graham, R.L., Caronni, G. (eds.) Peer-to-Peer Computing, pp. 142–149. IEEE Computer Society (2003)

26. Wang, Y., Vassileva, J.: Trust and reputation model in peer-to-peer networks. In: Shahmehri, N., Graham, R.L., Caronni, G. (eds.) Peer-to-Peer Computing. IEEE Computer Society (2003)

27. Zhuang, L., Zhou, F., Zhao, B.Y., Rowstron, A.I.T.: Cashmere: Resilient anonymous routing. In: NSDI. USENIX (2005)

Author Index